INTERMEDIATE

MACROECONOMICS

INTERMEDIATE

MACROECONOMICS

Dennis W. Jansen
Texas A&M University

Charles D. DeLorme, Jr.
University of Georgia

Robert B. Ekelund, Jr.
Auburn University

WEST PUBLISHING COMPANY
MINNEAPOLIS/ST. PAUL · NEW YORK
LOS ANGELES · SAN FRANCISCO

West's Commitment to the Environment

In 1906, West Publishing Company began recycling materials left over from the production of books. This began a tradition of efficient and responsible use of resources. Today, up to 95 percent of our legal books and 70 percent of our college and school texts are printed on recycled, acid-free stock. West also recycles nearly 22 million pounds of scrap paper annually—the equivalent of 181,717 trees. Since the 1960s, West has devised ways to capture and recycle waste inks, solvents, oils, and vapors created in the printing process. We also recycle plastics of all kinds, wood, glass, corrugated cardboard, and batteries, and have eliminated the use of Styrofoam book packaging. We at West are proud of the longevity and the scope of our commitment to the environment.

Production, Prepress, Printing and Binding by West Publishing Company.

 TEXT IS PRINTED ON 10% POST CONSUMER RECYCLED PAPER

Copyediting: Barbara Ferenstein
Composition: Carlisle Communications
Artwork: Scientific Illustrators
Interior Design: Seventeenth Street Studios
Indexing: Schroeder Indexing Services
Cover Design: Roslyn Stendahl
Cover Image: Comstock
Photo credits follow the index.

Library of Congress Cataloging-in-Publication Data

Jansen, Dennis W.
    Intermediate macroeconomics / Dennis W. Jansen, Charles D. DeLorme, Jr., Robert B. Ekelund, Jr.
      p.   cm.
    Includes index.
    ISBN 0-314-02831-5
    1. Macroeconomics. I. DeLorme, Charles D. II. Ekelund, Robert B. (Robert Burton), 1940–   . III. Title.
    HB172.5.J36   1994   93-34747
    339—dc20   CIP

To my wife Debra
and to our children,
Megan, Amy, and Mary

DJ

For Duane, Denise,
and Chuck DeLorme

CDD

For Bill Breit, who made
Economics fun for me and for
generations of students

RBE

CONTENTS IN BRIEF

CONTENTS

CHAPTER 3:
THE CLASSICAL MACROECONOMIC MODEL   76

CHAPTER 6:
AGGREGATE DEMAND AND SUPPLY   202

CHAPTER 7:
INTERNATIONAL TRADE AND THE MACROECONOMY   248

PREFACE

Important questions about our economy are neverending. Why was the decade of the 1980s one of economic growth without significant inflation? What is the role of the U.S. economy in the global marketplace and in trade blocs such as the North American Free Trade Agreement? How is the recession of 1990–91 to be explained with anemic recovery afterwards? How will deficits and deficit reduction affect you? Will Clintonomics hurt or help the economy? Could unemployment rates in the U.S. be stuck at permanently high levels? Should we expect high employment levels and inflation in the mid-to-late 1990s? What does the business cycle have in store for us as workers and consumers or as college graduates who will be entering job markets in the near future? *Intermediate Macroeconomics* provides, with a minimum of technical detail and with generous numbers of interesting applications and examples, an understanding of economic theory and policy with which to formulate answers to such questions.

Our book is designed for the business and economics student at the typical four-year state college or university. It stresses a firm knowledge of the basics, including the pervasive role of the international economy on domestic macroeconomic functioning, but with policy implications and insights woven throughout the text. *Intermediate Macroeconomics* also provides the instructor and the student with an organization that may be easily designed to fit individual needs and preferences.

It is our experience that instructors rarely have the luxury of covering an entire macroeconomics text in the all-too-short semester or quarter. Further, while all emphasize the core theoretical material, some individual instructors may wish to emphasize new contributions to Keynesian economics while others prefer to develop New Classical economics and real business cycle models. Likewise, banking and monetary matters, along with details of Federal Reserve functioning, receive diverse treatment. Our text permits maximum flexibility in these respects.

The core of modern macroeconomic theory is presented in the first 11 chapters of the book, consisting of Parts I, II, and III. Part I is an introduction to macroeconomic concepts and problems, including the recent record of U.S. output, inflation, and unemployment. Along with a thorough discussion of classical macroeconomics, Part I provides concrete meaning for the theoretical, institutional and policy discussions that follow. Part II develops the foundations of modern macroeconomic theory concerning aggregate demand and supply, including the role of international trade. This foundation includes traditional Keynesian economics, the IS-LM model, the Mundell-Fleming (and other models) of an open economy, and the basic role of money and its relation to inflation and unemployment.

Part III presents the very core of advanced modern macroeconomic theory in a set of three chapters (9, 10, and 11): New Classical economics, New Keynesian economics and the real business cycle. These topics are often developed in fairly rigorous fashion, but our presentation aims for a level that promotes better understanding and interest in difficult concepts (many of them related to labor supply). Policy issues are also emphasized throughout these chapters (and in Parts I and II), but a thorough mastery of the first three parts of this book will reward the student with a well-rounded understanding of basic macroeconomic theory.

The core of 11 chapters in Parts I, II, and III, or a somewhat abbreviated theoretical presentation using only Parts I and II, may be supplemented with chapters or sets of chapters from Parts IV, V, and VI. No general loss of continuity will result. Those instructors or readers who want to emphasize the role of monetary theory and policy in the macroeconomy may integrate Chapters 12 and 13 (Part IV) into the core presentation. Part IV uses a compact money stock model to explain the process of money creation and how the Federal Reserve System uses policy instruments to alter the money supply. The important principles underlying the demand for money are developed in Chapter 13.

The material in Part V is available to those text users who wish to emphasize consumption and investment spending—the real factors underlying private spending in the economy—in greater detail. Part VI is an exploration of important policy issues such as government budgets and budgetary processes, the interactions between politics and macroeconomic outcomes, and the principles underlying economic growth. We wish to emphasize that any of the material in Parts IV, V, or VI may be used after the core chapters (Chapters 1 through 11 or, in a less abbreviated format, Chapters 1 through 8) have been presented. This material either "stands alone" for the reader or is footed in the theory and policy of the core chapters.

PEDAGOGY AND FEATURES

The organization and features of *Intermediate Macroeconomics* are designed to provide a clear and systematic portrayal of a modern economy wherein global matters are a principal concern.

Emphasis on Policy and Institutions

In addition to the logical ordering of chapters and flexibility mentioned above, features include the reader's introduction to a large number of real-world policy and institutional issues. These occur as illustrations in the text and in boxed material. Highlighted material takes on three forms: Policy Issues, Insights, and Global Perspectives.

POLICY ISSUES

These boxes discuss alternative interpretations of contemporary issues such as Clinton-omics and the directions of macroeconomic policy in the 1990s, federal deficits and debt, the fate of "monetarism" as a theory and many more. These boxes are placed in appropriate sections and chapters of the text. Examples include:

"Reagan-Bush and the Economy: Did Republicans Toe the Classical Policy Line (1980–1992)?" (Chapter 3)
"Hurricane Andrew: An Exogenous Supply Shock" (Chapter 11)
"Is Monetarism Dead?" (Chapter 13)
"Macroeconomics, Deficits, and Urban Privatization" (Chapter 17)

INSIGHTS

These boxes, of equal number with those on policy, also deal with matters of macroeconomic and monetary policy but either utilize actual data or an analytical approach to contemporary issues or to historically oriented examples. Some of these features include the relation between deficits and economic growth, monetary panics, possible causes of the savings and loan crisis, data on trade, consumption or money demand, and issues related to macroeconomic history. Examples include:

"Economic Growth and the Federal Deficit-Debt Timebomb in the 1990s" (Chapter 1)
"Sir John R. Hicks, Alvin Hansen, and the Spread of Keynesian Economics" (Chapter 5)
"Aggregate Demand and Wartime Prosperity: Keynesian Economics or Command Economy?" (Chapter 6)
"Henry Ford and the Efficiency Wage" (Chapter 10)
"The Panic of 1907 and Its Relevance for Monetary Policy" (Chapter 12)
"Growth of Health Care Services" (Chapter 17)

GLOBAL PERSPECTIVES

These features, appearing with chapters, emphasize the interactions of domestic macroeconomics and international economic and policy relations. These items relate to issues of "free versus fair" trade, economic blocs and unions, international economic development in "transition" countries, and macroeconomic-monetary policies in other nations. Examples include:

"The North American Free Trade Agreement" (Chapter 1)
"Domestic Employment, Protection, and Trade" (Chapter 2)
"Income Growth Rates in World Economies Affected by Factors Underlying IS-LM Curves, 1988–1992" (Chapter 5)
"The Zollverein, the EC, and the NAFTA: Economic Unions, Competition, and Coordination" (Chapter 10)
"Monetary Announcements: The Bank of Japan and the Fed" (Chapter 13)

Global Emphasis

In addition to the Global Perspectives, trade issues are given special emphasis in *Intermediate Macroeconomics*. An entire chapter (Chapter 7) is devoted to the open economy and discussions of how trade issues affect the U.S. economy are fully integrated into the text.

Coverage of Real Business Cycle Theory

The study of real business cycles emphasize the supply side of the economy as initiating and perpetuating periods of growth (or decline) in income and employment. It integrates some of the characteristics of both New Classical and New Keynesian views of macroeconomic functioning. *Intermediate Economics* carries chapter-length coverage of this important theory (Chapter 11) as compared to the piecemeal treatment of other texts.

Presentation

Minimum use of mathematics and maximum use of intuitive and graphical techniques characterize the approach of this book. Where used, purely technical presentation is kept to a minimum and often relegated to footnotes or eliminated entirely. This mode of presentation helps foster introductory understanding of difficult concepts for the student.

Chapter Pedagogy

The book uses *chapter introductions* that feature student learning objectives plus summaries that tell the reader where she has been and what she has learned. *Problem sections* at the end of appropriate chapters test students' understanding of theory and concepts. One to three of these "problems" (where appropriate) test the students' ability to apply text material to some specific numerical or "thought" question. These problems are in addition to the more standard *Questions for Review and Discussion* which appear at the end of every chapter. *Recommendations for Further Reading* also conclude each chapter. *Key Terms and Concepts* are highlighted in each chapter for ease of understanding as is a text glossary at the end of the book.

Supplements

A *Study Guide for Intermediate Macroeconomics,* written by Professor John Keith Watson of the University of Southwestern Louisiana, is available. The guide is keyed to the issues and material of the text so that the student will be able to quickly review the chief issues of each chapter, to confront questions and problems relating to the text, and to "self-test" herself on the material. An *Instructor's Manual* which expands the pedagogy for each chapter is also available. It is authored by Professor Will Heath, also of the University of Southwestern Louisiana.

Interactive Software

Fully interactive software for student use has been developed especially for *Intermediate Macroeconomics* by Richard Saba of Auburn University. The student, using Windows technology, is introduced to all key concepts, theories, and issues contained in each chapter of the book. The software permits the student to explore theories by using alternative inputs in order to actually observe outcomes in alternative models of the economy. The student user is also given the opportunity to test herself or himself on the key material of each chapter with reinforced learning provided at every step.

ACKNOWLEDGMENTS

An enormous amount of help and assistance, both formal and informal, has greatly improved this text. We are deeply grateful to former reviewers of the project. They include Jack Adams, University of Arkansas–Little Rock, David C. Black, University of Toledo, Scott Bloom, North Dakota State University, Douglas W. Copeland, Pittsburg State University, Michael A. Ellis, Kent State University, James Fackler, University of Kentucky, Michael J. Ferrantino, Southern Methodist University, Andrew W. Foshee, McNeese State University, Alan G. Isaac, American University, Manfred W. Keil, Northeastern University, C. Richard Long, Georgia State University, W. Douglas McMillin, Louisiana State University, Richard McHugh, University of South Florida,

Gary Mongiovi, St. John's University, Radha Murthy, California State University-Fullerton, William J. Rieber, Butler University, Brian Taylor, California State University-Los Angeles, Douglas G. Waldo, University of Florida, Kenneth Watts, Pittsburg State University, Harland Wm. Whitmore, University of Cincinnati, and James R. Wible, University of New Hampshire.

In addition, a large number of former teachers, friends, and past and present colleagues have improved this book. Several former teachers deserve special mention: Professors Thomas R. Beard of Louisiana State University inspired deep and long-lasting interest in macroeconomics. A number of faculty, colleagues and friends at Texas A & M University, Auburn University, the University of Georgia and elsewhere read portions of the manuscript and offered criticism and advice. These include J. D. Jackson, Dan Gropper, Mark Thornton, David Robinson, Robert F. Hébert, Richard Ault, Richard Saba, Robert D. Tollison, E. O. Price, III, John Wells, Fred Bateman, Vandana Chandra, Albert Danielsen, David Kamerschen, Bill Lastrapes, John Mangel, Nadeem Naqvi, George Selgin, Art Snow, and Ron Warren. Former graduate assistants Audrey Davidson (University of Louisville) and Rand Ressler (University of South Western Louisiana) were of extremely valuable help in data collection and library research. Typists Cathy Kruse, Brenda Hickman, Tamara Ariens, and Kim Johns performed at a high standard of efficiency. We are especially grateful to our editors Rick Leyh, Esther Craig, and Brenda Owens of West for shepherding and guiding our project from beginning to end. Their encouragement got us through some potentially rough spots.

In spite of all this sage advice, we take full responsibility for the quality and usefulness of this text. We only hope that it contributes to a better understanding of problems and events that daily appear to shake and shape the foundations of our economy and that of the entire world.

DJ
CDD
RBE

PART I

INTRODUCTION AND CLASSICAL MODEL

1 AN INTRODUCTION
TO MACROECONOMICS

Economic conditions are a major and direct concern of Americans. Few matters get more consistent coverage on television, in newspapers, or in news magazines than the state of the economy as indicated by the inflation rate, the unemployment rate, and the rate of growth in GDP. (GDP—Gross Domestic product—is simply the sum of all goods and services produced within the United States over one year.) In the 1980s and 1990s, we have experienced inflation rates ranging from double-digit levels down to levels near 2 or 3 percent. We have experienced times of widespread unemployment, and times of economic growth and declining unemployment. Economic growth has varied from highs of 8 or 9 percent per year to near zero, and has even been negative during recessions. Finally, these economic conditions have led to wide variations in optimism and pessimism about the future. At times, such as in the 1981–82 and the 1990–92 periods, the good news of falling inflation was combined with the bad news of rising unemployment.

How are these economic events important to you? As a college or university student, you or your parents probably care a great deal about how inflation rates affect the cost of a college education. In the late 1980s and the early 1990s, the price of a college education rose dramatically. Moreover, as a prospective graduate of an institution of higher learning, your expectations about the availability of a well-paying job will be generally related to the employment situation and to the condition of expansion (or contraction) in the economy when you graduate. Your chances for a good job would have been somewhat better in 1984 and 1985 than in 1991 and 1992. Economic growth over your life span will, literally, determine the material conditions of your life and the lives of your family and friends.

The study of macroeconomics will give you a new perspective on important economic developments such as inflation, unemployment and recessions, trade deficits, budget deficits, and the strength or weakness of the dollar. All these and more are the province of macroeconomics. When you finish with this chapter you should have

- an understanding of what macroeconomics is, and how it is different from microeconomics
- an understanding of the basic concepts and goals of macroeconomic policy, including the distinction between fiscal and monetary policy
- an introductory understanding of aggregate demand and aggregate supply and of policy goals such as price stability, full employment, and economic growth in an open economy
- a feel for the distinctions between traditional (Classical, Keynesian, and Monetarist) and modern (New Classical, New Keynesian, and Real Business Cycle) macroeconomic models
- an idea of issues faced in macroeconomic modeling, including distinctions between real and nominal variables, stocks and flows, and endogenous and exogenous variables.

WHAT IS MACROECONOMICS?

MACROECONOMIC THEORY studies the economy as a whole.

This book explains what economists know about the critical factors that affect the economic conditions of our lives. The name given to the study of these factors is **macroeconomics,** which considers the economy as a whole and explains the causes and interrelationships of factors such as inflation, the growth in total goods and services produced, and the level of resource employment. A clear and specific understanding of the nature of macroeconomics is crucially important.

MICROECONOMICS investigates individual decision makers in an economy.

Economics is often regarded as an investigation of how individuals in society choose to allocate scarce income or resources among competing wants. Viewed in this way, economics is concerned with *micro* problems or with **microeconomics.** This of course does not mean that micro problems are small or unimportant. Rather, it means we limit the influence of outside factors in the analysis. The health care market is a case in point. A microeconomic analysis of health care services in the United States would encompass, among other matters, a study of the consumers of health care and their demand conditions as well as the supply conditions and responses of the firms providing health insurance and health care services. In a microanalysis of this issue, everything else—energy prices, demand conditions for automobiles, natural gas production in Texas—is held constant, holding these other variables constant (said to be **ceteris paribus** in the economist's language). We thus abstract from all other things so that the health care market may be considered in isolation.

CETERIS PARIBUS is economic jargon (borrowed from Latin) meaning "all other variables are held constant."

Macroeconomics starts from totally different assumptions, though the *method* for analyzing macro variables is quite the same. Here the investigator is concerned with **aggregate** (or sum total) variables such as the aggregate demand of all consumers for all goods and services produced in the United States over a year or some other period. No differentiation of markets is made. The demands for shoes, apples, movie tickets, and summer homes are all added together. Here *total* demand, and not its composition, is considered important. Government spending, private domestic investment, aggregate disposable income, employment, the price level (not just the price of Big Macs), the interest rate (not just the interest rate on auto loans), and net foreign investment are typical macroeconomic variables.

AGGREGATES are the sum of individual values of variables for the entire economy.

OUR U.S. ECONOMY: THEORY, GOALS, AND ECONOMIC POLICY

MACROECONOMIC POLICY is policy directed at achieving macroeconomic goals.

The major reason for studying macroeconomic theory should be clear: If economists know how macro variables interact and can predict the form of their interaction on output, employment, or prices, the federal government *may* wish to change or alter the variables through some form of economic policy. **Macroeconomic policy** includes a broad spectrum of related tools—

MONETARY POLICY
consists of the central
bank's actions to
manipulate the money
supply and/or interest
rates.

FISCAL POLICY is the
utilization of government
spending and/or taxing
policies to affect aggregate
economic behavior.

both monetary and fiscal—to promote the macroeconomic goals of price
stability, full employment, and high and sustained economic growth. ***Monetary policy*** is the effort exerted by the government-directed central bank (the
Federal Reserve System in the United States) to alter the course of inflation,
employment, and growth by changing the money supply.

Fiscal policy involves alterations in government spending and/or taxation in
an attempt to modify inflation, employment, growth and other macroeconomic variables. Together, fiscal policy and monetary policy constitute macroeconomic policy—changes in policy directed by government that create
improvements in economic well-being. From the outset we may view macroeconomic theory, goals, and policy implementation in familiar and simple
terms. A full understanding of the working out of this interaction of theory,
policy, and goals is what this book is about, but one of the chief results of our
study may be easily viewed in preliminary fashion. Indeed, this important
interaction has affected you directly. (See the Policy Issue: "The Importance of
Macroeconomics.")

Aggregate Demand, Aggregate Supply, Goals, and Policy

Just as the concepts of supply and demand are fundamental to understanding
the functioning of markets for computer software or French wine, concepts of
demand and supply can be applied to the performance of the *aggregate*
economy. The big difference is that the demand for French wine represents an
individual's willingness to purchase alternative quantities of wine at various
wine prices, while ***aggregate demand*** includes *everyone's*—consumers, businesses, government, and importers—willingness to spend on all goods and
services at alternative price *levels.* The aggregate demand curve, like the
demand for boots or for corn, is inversely related to the price level. At lower
price levels the aggregate amount of goods and services demanded will be
higher. Underlying aggregate demand are all kinds of factors in the economy
that affect total spending. A thorough understanding of these factors constitutes a large part of the study of macroeconomics.

AGGREGATE DEMAND
includes everyone's—
consumers, businesses,
government, and
importers—willingness and
ability to spend on all
goods and services at
alternative price *levels.*

AGGREGATE SUPPLY is the
willingness and ability of
all producers in the
economy to supply these
goods at alternative price
levels.

Like the supply of computer software or French wine, the ***aggregate supply***
of all goods and services in the economy is positively related to the price level.
Aggregate supply represents the many decisions made over some specified time
period to produce millions of goods and services consumed in the economy.
Aggregate supply is determined by the quantity and quality of human and
non-human resources in the economy. These concepts are represented in Figure
1-1. This figure combines a negatively sloped *aggregate* demand curve with a
positively sloped *aggregate* supply curve. Rather than the "price of computer
software" on the vertical axis and the "quantity of computer software bought
and sold" on the horizontal axis, Figure 1-1 displays a measure of the prices of
all output, called the price level, on the vertical axis and the output of all goods
and services on the horizontal axis. The intersection of these two curves

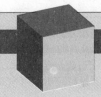

THE IMPORTANCE OF

MACROECONOMICS

Macroeconomics is the study of the behavior of the aggregate economy, and in some sense it may appear to be unrelated to your personal well-being. However, a little reflection should convince you that your personal satisfaction can be strongly affected by the state of the macroeconomy. For example, the U.S. economy experienced a recession in 1990–91 that resulted in increased unemployment. Clearly those who were unemployed saw their personal well-being adversely affected by the state of the macroeconomy. What about those who were not unemployed? Other factors affected their well-being, such as the inflation rate, which declined from double-digit levels in 1979–80 to about 3 to 4 percent per year by the early 1990s. However, reductions in inflation, if unexpected, also tend to hurt debtors—those who owe debts—at the expense of creditors—those to whom debts are owed. Finally, the variability of the inflation rate declined in the 1980s, making it easier to predict the future

path of the price level, and therefore easier to negotiate long-term nominal contracts.

The 1990s saw other changes too, such as a painfully slow recovery from the recession of 1990–91. This recovery was marked by very poor growth by the standards of past recoveries, so that employment, wages, and income rose more slowly than usual. In fact, many sectors of the economy experienced falling real wages and falling income during the early stages of the recovery. This gave the recovery the feel of an ongoing recession, and indeed the news media talked of the recovery period as if it were still the recession. This slow growth in wages and income affected almost everyone, and was a reflection of an economy in which it was difficult for established workers to receive wages or salaries that met their expectations. In many ways these events impacted on all individuals in the economy, and this impact was a large source of dissatisfaction with the state of the economy, a dissatisfaction that carried over into the political campaigns of 1992.

Other events also exerted strong influences on individuals. The low inflation rate, the recession, and perhaps the

policy actions of the Federal Reserve System all combined to give us an economy with the lowest interest rates in years. In fact, homeowners refinanced their mortgages in record numbers to take advantage of these low interest rates, and the housing industry saw an increased demand for new housing, although nothing like the record number of refinancings. Here too, the level of interest rates had an impact on individuals, whether they were refinancing mortgages, financing automobile purchases, or paying college tuition bills.

On the international front, there are also important factors that impact on both the U.S. economy and on individuals in that economy. During the 1980s and 1990s Europe contemplated full economic and monetary union as well as political union. This has implications for the U.S. trade balance, but it also has implications for U.S. policy making. Dealing with a united Europe means that the United States has to contend with an economic entity comparable to itself. Just as the United States has been able to alter market prices and world interest rates by its actions, so too a united Europe will be able to alter market prices and world interest rates. This could not be done to the same degree, by any single European nation acting alone. Moreover, this closes some channels for policy and opens others. Old rules of thumb and old knee-jerk policy responses may have to be altered to deal with the new realities.

In these ways and more, the state of the U.S. macroeconomy reflects on the individuals in the economy, and on you. A goal of this text is to increase your understanding of the macroeconomy—to better understand how it operates, how policy affects the economy, and how events from outside the economy can

cause changes in the U.S. economy. Because these changes affect you, another goal of this text is to increase your understanding of how individuals, and you personally, are affected by national and international events impinging on the U.S. economy.   ❏

FIGURE I-I:
Aggregate Demand and
Aggregate Supply Curves

The aggregate demand and aggregate supply curves for the entire economy are similar in form to the demand and supply curves for any individual good (VCRs or avocadoes). Aggregate curves, however, reflect the demand and supply for all goods and services produced in the economy over some period of time.

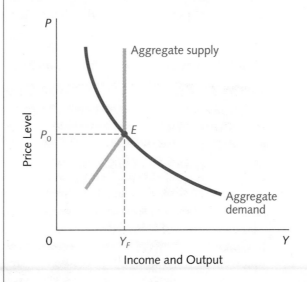

uniquely determines the price level and the aggregate output produced in the whole economy over some period of time.

Recall from basic economics that there is a cause-effect relationship between total spending (by consumers, investors, government, and importers) and aggregate demand. Increases in such spending may increase aggregate demand and heighten the level of economic activity. In this process production and employment of resources responds to changes in spending and aggregate demand. Interactions between aggregate supply and aggregate demand determine output, employment, and price levels. With continuous and changing interactions over time, trends in employment of resources, inflation, and economic growth are produced.

It is important to note that the macroeconomic analogy to basic supply and demand theory is not perfect. Consider the aggregate supply curve in Figure 1-1. The aggregate supply curve as drawn is positively sloped up to an output level that represents full employment. Full employment occurs when all workers willing and able to work at the current market wage find work. This means that labor and other resources are unavailable for output levels beyond Y_F. The aggregate supply curve becomes a vertical line at this level of output, meaning that price levels higher than P_0 cannot bring forth greater production.

Equilibrium for the economy occurs where aggregate demand equals aggregate supply. In Figure 1-1 this occurs at output level Y_F, the full employment level, and at price level P_0. Equilibrium in Figure 1-1 would not, of course, necessarily take place at full employment. The aggregate demand curve might also intersect the aggregate supply curve to the left of Y_F. In other words, aggregate demand may be insufficient to attain full employment output. But theoretical conceptions emphasizing aggregate demand and supply will recur throughout this book. For now let's take a closer look at the macroeconomic goals of full employment, price stability, and economic growth in an "open" economy that trades with other nations.

Full Employment, Price Stability, and Economic Growth

FULL EMPLOYMENT is the level of employment at which there may exist "frictional" unemployment, but at which resources are otherwise fully utilized in the production of output.

The *full employment* of resources, both human and nonhuman, is essential to the increase of our national output and income, and full employment and price stability are the goals of macroeconomic policy. But full employment does not mean that all our resources are being used at full capacity at every point in time. It is a basic economic premise that adjustments in the economy owing to shifts in the supply of and demand for individual goods require that resources be mobile and flexible. Some level of "frictional" or "transitional" unemployment of resources is considered normal, necessary, and desirable. Just what the full-employment level is at any given time in our economy is debatable. Government statisticians at various times have debated whether 4 percent, 5 percent, 6 percent, or even 7 percent unemployment is "normal." The point is that the aggregate output of goods and services is directly determined by the resources employed in production.

The shape of aggregate supply indicates how responsive resources are to increases in the price level. If resources are very responsive to increases in the price level, then an increase in aggregate demand during a period of widespread unemployment would cause increases in employment and output without large increases in the price level. Full employment might then be achieved without much inflation.

Another possibility exists. The structure and resource mix in the economy may be such that, at a point of widespread unemployment, increases in aggregate demand would not only create additions to output but would cause increases in the price level—inflation—as well. In this event, resources are not as responsive to increases in the price level. A trade-off may exist between changes in the level of output and employment and changes in the level of prices. Thus, society may have to choose between some rate of unemployment and some rate of inflation. In the extreme case, where all resources are fully employed, increases in aggregate demand will cause resource prices to rise in proportion to the demand increase, creating inflation with no change in output.

Maintaining high levels of economic growth, as measured by growth in GDP, is also a high priority that is clearly related to other macroeconomic goals. Full employment and resource development, including education and improvements in technology, are all important ingredients for economic growth. The achievement of social and economic goals—such as the provision of housing, the reduction of poverty, or income security for the elderly—would be virtually impossible without growth in the real output of goods and services. There are many impediments to growth. When the economy fails to perform at high levels of employment and production of goods and services, economic growth suffers. Many economists believe that current federal deficits and debt are a major hindrance to the achievement of economic growth. (In this regard see Insight: "Economic Growth and the Federal Deficit–Debt Timebomb in the 1990s.") We will return to these issues and problems again and again in later chapters of this book. Here, however, we note that a firm grasp of macroeconomic theory will help us gain insights into the important and interrelated economic events— such as unemployment, inflation, and economic growth—which surround us. Consider some policy tools that affect these economic events.

What are Fiscal and Monetary Tools?

Preliminary identification of the tools and their functions is easy. Fiscal policy, as we have already seen, concerns general *budget policies* such as taxation and expenditure policies. At the onset of recession, the federal government may attempt to affect aggregate demand in the economy by a combination of tax cuts and government spending programs that would increase national employment and output. *Budget deficits* with government expenditures greater than tax revenues are often the order of the day during a recession or lagging economic growth. At such times an increase in government expenditures or a reduction in taxation may fill the bill.

BUDGET POLICIES are fiscal policies dealing with the government budget, such as congressional taxation and expenditure policies.

BUDGET DEFICITS occur when government expenditures are greater than tax revenues.

INSIGHT

ECONOMIC GROWTH

AND THE FEDERAL

DEFICIT–DEBT TIMEBOMB

IN THE 1990s

Debt growth at a rate of one million dollars a minute is not a concept easily understood. For all but a precious few, the concept of a billion dollars— let alone a trillion—has virtually no tangible reference. Recent federal deficits of $250– 350 billion and a federal debt that exceeds $4 trillion seem to bear grim portents of economic disaster for the American economy of the 1990s and into the twenty-first century. Politicians have not heeded the sterling advice and the implicit warning of Thomas Jefferson who placed "economy among the first and most important virtues, and public debt as the greatest danger to be feared." As a result, Americans are flirting with an economic problem that destroyed many of the once-glorious civilizations and societies of ancient and modern history.

Deficits and debt of these magnitudes, for all their importance, seem distant and intangible. The relation between deficits (that occur when current spending exceeds current receipts) and debt, however, is simple and it is exactly the same as confronts an individual or a family. Annual deficits are simply the addition to total debt, so that if we add $350 billion in deficit spending in 1992 to a federal debt of $4.2 trillion, the debt rises to $4.55 trillion in 1993.

Such staggering numbers are also brought home when we look at the *share size* of deficits and debt for individuals and families. In 1991, each person's share of the *deficit* was $1,352 (up from $748 in 1987) and the share of the *debt* for an average family of four was about $65,000. *Changes* in the size of the debt are even more dramatic. Outstanding federal debt was 26 percent of gross domestic product in 1981, but was a full 48 percent of GDP by 1991. Not since the financing of World War II have these levels of debt been reached in the United States. Moreover, for the privilege of incurring debt, government must pay interest on the debt. The *third largest* expenditure in the federal budget, approximately $200 billion per year, is now the interest payments on the debt service. For every dollar you pay in *income* tax, more than sixty cents now goes to pay the interest on the debt. In only eight more years, if present trends continue, every dollar collected in income taxes will have to be spent simply to make the interest payment. The sky has not yet fallen, but a moment of truth is at hand for all of society.

What do deficits and debt mean to the average individual? The effects are mostly indirect, but important nonetheless. In any given year, government spending is financed by taxes, by borrowing (issuing government bonds to cover the deficit), or by printing money (printing new dollars to cover the deficit). Government spending, however financed, means that the government competes with our (private) spending in markets for goods and services. Actual tax payments reduce our private spending on homes, movies, and vacations (and some of our saving as well) up to the total amount of the tax we pay. And when our tax payments are exhausted and federal spending still exceeds revenues, the government might issue bonds. The funds that the government gets in this way come mostly from savings, reducing the amount of funds available to the private sector to finance investment.

When the federal government enters credit markets to borrow by issuing bonds, however, it tends to *crowd out* private investment. Government's fiscal policy, which relies heavily on deficits and debt, can absorb more of the economy's available private saving than will support high rates of economic growth.

It is not too much to argue that until the deficit-debt problem is resolved, long-term attempts to deal with poverty, health care, homelessness, and economic security of all kinds may be futile. The ever-growing interest payments leave little room for any additional government programs.

Perhaps this is why one of the first major efforts of President Bill Clinton's administration was to work for the passage of his deficit reduction bill, which promises to cut the deficit over the next six years by a combination of tax increases and spending cuts totalling over \$400 billion. ❏

BUDGET SURPLUSES occur when tax revenues are greater than government expenditures.

Conversely, the preferred fiscal remedy during periods of inflation is to increase taxes or tax rates in combination with reductions in government spending. A movement in the direction of a **budget surplus**, where tax revenues exceed government expenditures, would then reduce aggregate spending, thereby reducing upward pressure on prices. As a generalization, certain groups of macroeconomists, sometimes identified as fiscalists (those primarily supporting use of fiscal policy), Keynesians, or post-Keynesians support these sorts of policies in preference to, but not to the exclusion of, monetary policy.

Monetary policy, already defined, is the management of the money supply through control of the monetary reserves of the financial system. Reserves are nothing more than the "cash backing" of deposits held by commercial banks, savings and loan associations, savings banks, and so on. In controlling reserves, the Fed (short for the Federal Reserve System) attempts to direct changes in the money supply or in interest rates. The goal is management of aggregate demand, and this is accomplished by appropriate changes in the money supply or interest rates.

How do fiscal and monetary policy tools work, and what would we hope to accomplish with them? Here the theory of aggregate demand and aggregate supply is useful. Consider Figure 1-2, which reproduces the simple aggregate demand, and supply apparatus introduced earlier in this section. Assume that aggregate demand in the economy is represented by AD_0, which, when combined with the aggregate supply curve AS, produces an output and employment level Y_0, and a price level P_0. If the full-employment level of output in the economy is Y_F, then aggregate demand level AD_0 is "deficient" in that output less than Y_F implies there is an excessive amount of unemployed

PHOTO 1-1
Deficit Reduction in 1993
Meant Higher Taxes for
Many Americans, Especially
the Rich and Wealthier Social
Security Recipients.

resources. This unemployment of resources can be eliminated by increasing output to Y_F.

What can be done to cure this unemployment malady? Some economists believe that fiscal and monetary policy may be brought into play in order to increase aggregate demand and hence increase output to the full-employment level. In Figure 1-2, proper fiscal policy would be to reduce taxes or to increase government spending, thereby creating a budget deficit (if we began with a budget in balance) and increasing the governmental component of total spending. Proper monetary policy in this case would be to increase the money supply or to lower interest rates. Either of these policy actions might have the effect of shifting the aggregate demand curve rightward to its full-employment level AD_1 in Figure 1-2, thereby alleviating the unemployment associated with too little output being produced in the economy.

The International Component of U.S. Macroeconomic Policy

Of increasing importance for macroeconomic theory and policy—and for America's economic well-being—is the role of the United States in the global economy. The once-dominant position of the United States in basic industrial production for export, including the automobile and steel industries, has been severely challenged in the 1980s and 1990s. A shift to new technologies and an emphasis on service industries is part of the explanation, as are high growth and development rates in Japan and Western Europe after World War II.

FIGURE I-2:
Aggregate Demand, Aggregate
Supply, and Economic Policy

Fiscal and monetary policy are used to shift the aggregate demand
curve in order to maintain a full-employment level of income (Y_F)
with price stability. Changes in consumption, investment, government,
or net foreign spending are influenced by policy to achieve policy
goals.

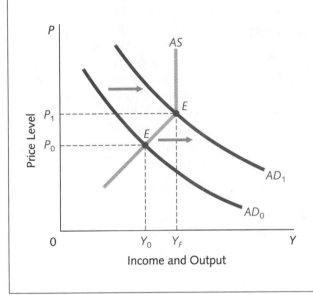

The appropriate response, in the opinion of virtually all macroeconomists, is
renewed growth and development *within* the United States and *expanded trade*
with other countries. Just how to achieve renewed growth and development
within the American economy has been and is being hotly debated. Educational reforms of various kinds, investment stimulus via various government
taxing, spending regulatory policies, and infrastructure investments are only a
few of the policies being discussed within the political process. The expansion
of international trade is yet another tactic for increasing the strength and
growth of the U.S. economy. In reality, the United States faces trading blocs
such as the European Economic Community and clever traders such as
the Japanese. In trading blocs, members of the bloc are given favored treatment
and the entire bloc sets trade relations uniformly with the rest of the world. To
expand the value of trade and the export component of aggregate demand, a
free trade association is developing in North America between Canada,
Mexico, and the United States. (See Global Perspective: "The North American
Free Trade Agreement.") As with any sort of trade—whether it be between
individuals, regions, or countries—gains of a high order may be expected based
on specialization and exchange. Matters relating the global economy to
macroeconomic theory and policy will be an integral part of our study.

GLOBAL PERSPECTIVE

THE NORTH AMERICAN

FREE TRADE AGREEMENT

In October 1992 leaders from the United States, Canada, and Mexico initialed the treaty establishing the North American Free Trade Agreement, or NAFTA. This agreement still awaits final signatures and legislative approval in the three nations, but its enactment will create the largest free trade zone in the world, eclipsing even the European Economic Community in terms of population and total gross domestic product. What is a free trade zone, and what are the benefits of NAFTA for the United States?

Fine details of free trade zones differ, but the basic idea is that certain nations agree to have free trade with each other while continuing to have trade barriers against other countries. In NAFTA, Canada, Mexico, and the United States have agreed to lower or eliminate many of the tariff and nontariff barriers to trade with each other. Tariffs are taxes on imports, so that lowering tariffs lowers the cost of imports. Thus, NAFTA will reduce the cost of Canadian and Mexican

goods that are purchased in the United States. Nontariff barriers are barriers such as quotas on imports. Quotas state absolute maximum quantities of goods that may be imported. Reducing such barriers will increase competition among producers from all the countries in NAFTA, also reducing the cost of imported goods. The net effect of NAFTA will be to increase trade among the member nations so that goods produced in these nations will be less costly and less difficult to obtain by other member nations.

Are free trade zones a good thing? Economists are strong supporters of free trade, and would almost uniformly support a *worldwide* reduction in tariff and nontariff barriers to trade. At the same time, there is some argument over the establishment of free trade zones, since these result in lowering barriers to trade only *within* the free trade zone. This has two effects. One is called "trade creation," in which the lowered trade barriers result in increased trade. Just as trade between individuals makes each party to the trade better off, trade between nations can make each party to the trade better off, and thus trade creation is a desirable feature of a free trade

zone. In fact, it is trade creation that drives the support of economists for global free trade. However, there is another effect of free trade zones, called "trade diversion." This effect occurs because the lowered barriers between members of the free trade zone may make the goods produced in a member nation less expensive than the goods produced more efficiently by a nonmember nation. In effect, the differential tariffs make the product of the member country a better buy than that of the nonmember country. The differential tariff thus diverts trade from a nonmember nation to a member nation.

Trade diversion is not a problem for the member nations, but from a global perspective trade diversion results in inefficient production, because the more efficient producer loses sales to a less efficient producer. Thus, a key feature in the debate over free trade zones is the debate over whether the free trade zone results more in trade creation or more in trade diversion.

A simple example will help illustrate this point. Consider the case of three countries: the United States, Mexico, and South Korea. U.S. consumers desire television sets. The producer of these TV sets can be either the United States, Mexico, or South Korea. The U.S. producers can make a TV for $400 and don't pay a tariff, so they sell the TV for $400 regardless of the U.S. tariff. The South Korean producers can make a TV for $350, so they sell the TV in the United States for $350 if the tariff rate is 0 percent, $385 if the tariff rate is 10 percent, and $420 if the tariff rate is 20 percent. Finally, the Mexican producers can make the TV for $380, and so they sell it in the United States for $380 if the tariff rate is 0 percent, $418 if the tariff rate is 10 percent, and $456 if the tariff rate is 20 percent. These figures are summarized in Table 1-1.

Now consider the creation of NAFTA. If U.S. tariffs are 20 percent, then before NAFTA the U.S. producers are the low-cost supplier, and there will be no trade. (We assume throughout this example that U.S. consumers will buy from the least expensive supplier.) Of course, U.S. firms are *not* the most efficient producers, because both Mexico and South Korea can produce the TV at less expense than U.S. firms. However, the existence of tariffs imposes extra costs on the foreign producers, making U.S.

TVs cheaper to U.S. consumers. The creation of NAFTA will lower tariffs between the United States and Mexico to 0 percent, so that after NAFTA the low-cost supplier will be Mexico, and the United States will import TVs from Mexico. This is trade creation, because before NAFTA there was no international trade in TVs and after NAFTA the United States imports TVs from Mexico. (The United States will, of course, sell more of other goods to Canada and Mexico as well.)

Consider, however, the case where U.S. tariffs are not 20 percent but 10 percent. In this case, before NAFTA the low cost supplier is South Korea, which can sell a TV in the United States for $385. After NAFTA, the tariff on Mexican TVs drops to 0 percent, so that Mexico producers can sell a TV in the United States for $380. The tariff on Korean TVs stays at 10 percent, so Korean TVs cost $385 in the United States. In this case, NAFTA will cause trade diversion from the low-cost producer, South Korea, to a higher-cost producer, Mexico, due to the differential tariffs imposed on these two nations. This results in inefficient production patterns, since trade is shifted to a higher-cost producer.

In addition to the benefits of trade creation, there are other benefits to the United States of a free trade zone. One is the reduction in the prices of imports to U.S. consumers because of reduced tariffs. The reduction in tariffs, even in the case of trade diversion, will lower the price of imports. This reduces the distortions in consumer spending patterns caused by tariffs. A second benefit is the increased efficiency of production and the increased competition that comes from a larger market. NAFTA in effect joins Canada, Mexico, and the United States into one large market, which allows producers to take further advantage of cost savings that can accrue to large firms facing economies of scale in production, so that increasing the scale of production lowers per unit costs. The larger market, and the increased number of firms in that large market, also means an increase in competition, with the usual effect of lowering prices to consumers. Thus, NAFTA will lower prices of internationally traded goods in the three member countries, will increase exports and hence jobs in the export-producing industries, and will improve economic efficiency to the extent that it is trade creating and not trade diverting. Indeed, some estimate that after the ten- or fifteen-year phase-in period, NAFTA could yield additional trade of $1–$2 trillion. Furthermore, the U.S. Department of Commerce estimates that every net billion dollars of new exports creates 20,000 jobs in the United States, so the increased trade could add hundreds of thousands of new jobs. Finally, consumers will benefit directly by lower costs for imported finished products, and indirectly by lower prices of imported intermediate goods, as well as by the beneficial effects of increased competition. These savings might be substantial. For instance, the quotas on Japanese auto imports are estimated to have cost over $3 billion to U.S. consumers just in 1982!

Thus, NAFTA seems like a winner. It will lower prices, create jobs for many, and increase U. S. output and economic growth. But—a big but—there will be winners and losers as free trade becomes a reality under NAFTA. Over the fifteen or so years of adjustments some U.S. business owners and employees of those businesses that cannot compete with Mexican and Canadian producers will lose. Some business owners will lose their investments and some workers will lose their jobs. Some textile firms, for example, will lose their production facilities to Mexico since labor is cheaper there.

Environmentalists, moreover, note that pollution and other environmental controls are not as stringent in Mexico as in the United States. This puts American products at an "unfair" disadvantage relative to Mexican products. The Mexican environment, already one of the most polluted in the world, would suffer further damage under NAFTA. It is likely, therefore, that separate arrangements between the United States and Mexico (and Canada) dealing with labor adjustments and the environment will become part of the total agreement. On net, most economists regard NAFTA as a positive development. Like many positive developments, however, there will be adjustment costs requiring reallocation of labor and capital from production of some goods to the production of other goods.   ❑

TABLE 1-1:
Hypothetical Example of the Possible Effects of a Free Trade Zone

CONSUMER: UNITED STATES			
Producer of TVs	*U.S. Tariff Rates on TVs*		
	0%	10%	20%
UNITED STATES	$400	$400	$400
MEXICO BEFORE NAFTA	$380	$418	$456
MEXICO AFTER NAFTA	$380	$380	$380
SOUTH KOREA	$350	$385	$420

MAP I-I

The Proposed Free Trade Agreement Between Canada, Mexico, and the United States Would Create the Largest Body of Consumers of Any Trade Association in the World.

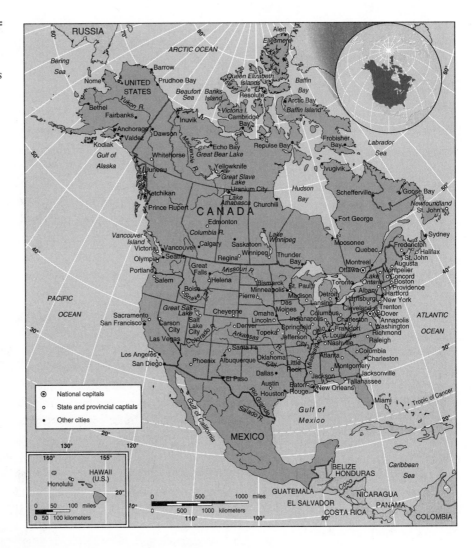

THE DEMAND SIDE OF THE ECONOMY

DISCRETIONARY POLICIES are policies that require decisions on the part of Congress, the President, or the Federal Reserve System before they can be enacted.

In simple terms, both fiscal and monetary policy may aim at the same end—control of aggregate demand and economic activity. Collectively, fiscal policy and monetary policy may be termed *discretionary policies,* that is, policies requiring decisions on the part of Congress or the President—in the case of fiscal policy—and decisions on the part of the Federal Reserve Board concerning monetary policy. Will these discretionary policies work predictably without creating more economic problems than they solve? Some economists believe that the answer is a clear "yes." But, for reasons that are discussed briefly in the next section, other economists are in serious doubt about the ability of these policies to solve national economic problems.

We must admit, at the outset, that economics is not an exact science. While economists use the *methods* of science—including observation, theory development, and testing—economic science is a social science that deals with human subjects. The development and testing of macroeconomic theories is still imperfect. Getting good data has always been a problem, of course, and efforts are constantly being made to improve the correspondence between theory and the numbers that underlie specific variables in the theory. Economists are still not in a position to make clear-cut and definitive statements concerning a *specific* theory's validity relative to another's. Therefore, we give all of the major views on macroeconomic theory and policy a hearing in this text. At this point, a brief introduction to some of the theoretical and policy alternatives and to the groups of economists sponsoring them will help you understand what is to follow in this book.

Classical Ideas

CLASSICAL macroeconomists emphasize the automatic equilibrating features of the economy, stressing that full employment will occur in a competitive system by market adjustment.

First, consider the ***Classical*** position in macro theory. This was the pre-Keynesian view that the equilibrium of the economy, if displaced, would return *automatically* to full employment. Full employment would thus be accomplished in a competitive system by market adjustments in prices, wages, and interest rates. If aggregate demand happened to be at any level other than the full-employment level, *automatic* forces in the economy would work to return the economy back to its full-employment equilibrium.

The Classical economists emphasized certain features of the economic system in support of the efficiency of automatic forces in reestablishing macroeconomic equilibrium in the economy. For example, they knew that random "shocks" such as wars, crop failures, gold discoveries, and changes in business expectations would upset the system and would create business cycles in the short run. They believed, however, that minimum government involvement, balanced budgets, and a steady predetermined money supply growth would minimize but not completely eliminate any short-term unemployment or inflation. According to the Classical theory, well-meaning policymakers employing discretion in fiscal and monetary affairs would make many mistakes, compounding problems rather than curing them. The Classicals' hallmark can be summed up in the adage, "If it ain't broke, don't fix it."

Keynesian Theory

KEYNESIAN macroeconomists emphasize institutional rigidities and the existence of nominal contracting, that prevent or slow the automatic equilibrating forces stressed by the classical economists.

In the midst of the worldwide depression of the 1930s, a British economist, John Maynard Keynes, argued otherwise. In his famous book entitled *The General Theory of Employment, Interest, and Money* (1936), Keynes said that the economy could be in a recession or depression and still be in equilibrium. Emphasizing the damage of short-run economic ills such as unemployment and sharply reduced output, Keynes pointed to union and monopoly power and, most importantly, to certain factors concerning investment demand and money demand as fatally inhibiting the automatic mechanisms assumed by the Classical theorists.

Given the failure of the automatic forces, Keynes felt that it was appropriate to resort to discretionary changes in government spending and taxation. For a number of theoretical reasons to be considered later, Keynes doubted the efficacy of the monetary means of restoring economic health and order. This means that the government (Congress or the President; Parliament or the Prime Minister) should invoke discretionary fiscal policies to alter total spending and therefore to act as a countercyclical device to oppose adverse trends in business cycles. In the face of massive unemployment and depression, an activist fiscal policy resulting in budget deficits was required of government to right matters in less time than automatic forces ever could. A period of inflation also required budget surpluses in the Keynesian policy interpretation, a sharp contrast to the laissez-faire precepts of the Classicals, who advocated minimum intervention and no discretionary tinkering. Basically, then, Keynes's position was that of an interventionist.

Keynes, of course, addressed these macro issues in a period of widespread unemployment and recession—the Great Depression of the 1930s. Keynesian theory survived the Depression. It generally became the *dominant* view held by professional economists and policy in both political parties in the United States. That view, enlarged and modified, is still a major view today. Those who do not adhere to the Keynesian school of thought point out that a vastly enlarged role for government, emphasis on discretionary policies, inflation, continuing problems of unemployment, and, especially in recent times, persistent budget deficits have all become a part of the historical scene in the post-World War II United States.

Monetarists

There have always been dissenters from the Keynesian position, but in the 1960s and 1970s there was a strong resurgence of interest in a *modified* and sophisticated version of the Classical macro theory. These economists, led by Milton Friedman of the "Chicago School," are called **Monetarists.**

Although there is some dispute over doctrinal details among the Monetarists, they would all support a version of the Classical position that you saw earlier. Balanced budgets, minimum government intervention and regulation, and steady, predictable money supply growth, along with other predictable economic policies, are the stock-in-trade of the Monetarists. In their view, discretionary policies create uncertainty and have unpredictable effects in the short run, which is the time period Keynes thought relevant for countercyclical policies. In the Monetarist view, the timing of policies has exaggerated swings in inflation rates and in the business cycle. In sum, Monetarists argue (a) that

MONETARISTS are macroeconomists who disputed some of the Keynesian positions, especially the extreme claims of the ineffectiveness of monetary policy. Monetarists tend to support Classical positions, and tend to favor policy rules instead of discretionary policies.

automatic forces will work in the economy; (b) that much governmental tinkering plus the massive growth of regulation in the economy should be sharply curtailed since these things have created artificial rigidities in the economy, making self-adjustment all the more difficult; and (c) that a balanced budget together with a monetary rule concerning growth in the money stock is called for.

Keynesians respond that the relationships Monetarists describe are unreliable and unpredictable, especially over the short run. Keynesians and Neo-Keynesians do not believe that automatic forces can be relied on to produce full employment in the economy. They also argue that the relation between interest rates and aggregate demand is not predictable. For example, the Federal Reserve lowered the rate of interest over the recession of 1990–91, but consumption and investment spending were not perceptibly stimulated. Thus Keynesians argue that a monetary rule would not make total spending predictable.

THE SUPPLY-SIDE PERSPECTIVE

There are two ways to analyze the aggregate economy. Aggregate demand analysis concerns the causes or determinants of the demand for goods and services. These are the policies we have been discussing. Both Keynesians and Monetarists have been dealing almost exclusively with demand management in modern times. As has been noted, the Keynesians favor discretionary actions, especially fiscal ones, to ensure full employment and inflationless demand. The Monetarists, on the other hand, choose demand management policies that are not discretionary—money supply rules, nonintervention in the economy, balanced budgets, and so on. In their view, these policies ensure sufficient aggregate demand.

In the not-too-distant past, however, some economists and politicians shifted the emphasis of economic policy to the *supply* of goods and services in our economy. In particular, they emphasized productivity of labor and capital. The economic events of the 1970s may be analyzed in terms of ***supply-side economics,*** which consists of tax and other policies to deal with labor and investment disincentives. For example, labor productivity—output per worker—grew slowly over the decade of the 1970s—slower than the rise in wage rates. One result of wages growing faster than output was inflation—more dollars were required to purchase fewer goods and services.

Supply-side policies of the 1980s and early 1990s were in part implemented by Presidents Ronald Reagan and George Bush. They attempted to attack the macroeconomic problems of inflation and unemployment by proposing means to enhance labor productivity and capital investment. Tax cuts, deregulation of industry, flexibility in meeting pollution standards, and movements toward budget balance are all part of the supply sider's policy kit. These policies,

SUPPLY-SIDE ECONOMICS emphasizes policies that alter aggregate supply, as opposed to the traditional emphasis on aggregate demand.

supply siders contend, would increase savings and capital formation, would reduce social welfare subsidies, and would stimulate *private* labor-training programs and work effort.

Several points about the relatively recent interest in aggregate supply should be emphasized. First, aggregate demand problems are not ignored or considered unimportant in the supply-side policy program. It is simply that the supply siders believe that productivity and capital formation have been shortchanged and discouraged in the quest to control aggregate demand. A second point is that the supply-side emphasis is not the exclusive property of Monetarists. Many Keynesians are supply-side advocates for long-run policy, but also care about short-run business cycles.

The first supply siders were the Classical economists. Adam Smith, David Ricardo, and John Stuart Mill, the collective cream of the Classical economists, all emphasized that the wealth of any nation was, first and foremost, a product of labor skill and productivity coupled with the quantity and quality of capital that labor had to work with. As such, supply-side economics is a very old idea that modern macroeconomists and politicians have exhumed to deal with contemporary problems related to inflation, unemployment, and U.S. economic growth. Modern *real business cycle theories,* discussed in Chapter 11, are a partial outgrowth of New Classical models, but are also an example of a modern model emphasizing the supply side.

NEW CLASSICAL AND NEW KEYNESIAN ECONOMICS: MODERN MACROECONOMICS

NEW CLASSICAL ECONOMISTS combine the classical ideas of the automatic adjustment of the economy with Monetarist views that policy can be destabilizing and a view that expectations are formed rationally, thereby negating the effectiveness of some predictable policy actions.

A modern theoretical view of the economy—one that has been developed within the past two decades—combines a number of the insights discussed above with particular emphasis on the self-adjusting views of the Classical economists and the Monetarists. The central tenet of the new view, called *New Classical Economics* (NCE), which is fine-tuning the economy—another term for discretionary demand management—is simply not possible since policymakers are dealing with rational human behavior. This human behavior dictates that people do not throw away useful information. Therefore, when market participants become sophisticated in the effects of macroeconomic policy, only erratic behavior or surprise actions on the part of fiscal or monetary policymakers will have any effect. Most rational expectations theorists advocate a fixed rule for setting the growth rate in the money supply, together with constant or at least predictable tax rates and well-announced fiscal policies in order to promote economic stability. Discretionary policy, such as that advocated by the Keynesians, is at best immaterial and at worst exacerbates the business cycles. In the view of the New Classical Economics, policy should be preprogrammed and predictable so that all market partici- pants will undergo less uncertainty in making economic decisions. No one can be certain whether macroeconomic thinking in the next twenty years will be dominated by the

FLOW VARIABLE is a variable that may be described as changing (growing or declining) at some rate per unit of time.

view that discretionary policy is unwise and unnecessary, but the New Classical Economics has gained in the number of its supporters.

The view that "good policy is predictable policy" has as its premise the notion that the economy both responds and reacts to policy. All market participants (consumers, savers, investors, buyers, and sellers) ultimately learn what the effects of policy are and react *rationally* to it. For example, suppose that government attempts to increase aggregate demand (see Figure 1-2) by increasing budget deficits this year. Market participants, having learned what the probable effects of big deficits will be, immediately react to the planned increase in total spending. If the anticipated effects of higher budget deficits are higher inflation or higher interest rates, investors and consumers adjust immediately to the anticipated situation, *thereby neutralizing the policy change.*

There has been a countersurge of ideas related to the Keynesian school. These **New Keynesian** economists actually *incorporate* some of the principles of the New Classical Economics, especially rational expectations, but in such a manner that discretionary fiscal and monetary policy again has meaning and usefulness to correct short-term fluctuations in business cycles. Thus, the New Keynesians utilize the assumption of rational expectations but couple it with models of various rigidities in the labor market behavior. While diverse, these models emphasize coordination failures among market participants, imperfect competition, and sticky price and wage adjustments. These features, as emphasized in Chapter 10, lead to the view that policy can actually be effective in changing output and employment.

NEW KEYNESIAN economists incorporate some of the strategies of the New Classical ideas, especially rational expectations, into the traditional Keynesian view that institutional and nominal rigidities slow or negate automatic equilibrating forces.

The Major Policy Views

REAL BUSINESS CYCLE THEORY claims output fluctuations can be explained by changes in technology and productivity.

This spectrum of views on macroeconomic theory and policy should not leave you in dismay. In this book, we provide the fundamental theoretical support that is offered for the major schools of thought, and for their policy positions. The essentials of the Classical, Keynesian, Monetarist, New Classical, New Keynesian, and Real Business Cycle arguments will be presented in logical fashion. On matters of politics, philosophy, and policy choices, you must decide for yourself. For a viewpoint on these debates, see the Policy Issue: "Macroeconomic Policy in the 1990s."

CONSTRUCTION OF MACRO MODELS

Before we turn to the important business of measuring aggregate economic activity through the national income accounts (Chapter 2), there are three basic items that are especially important in the study of macroeconomics. The first of these items concerns the difference between *real and nominal magnitudes,* which is perhaps the single greatest source of difficulty in understanding economic quantities. Basically, whenever the term *real* is used it is referring to

POLICY ISSUE

MACROECONOMIC

POLICY IN THE 1990s

Some politicians and professional and academic economists argue that discretionary macroeconomic policy is undergoing obsolescence. Macroeconomic policy, as noted in this chapter, is an activity of politicians and the Federal Reserve System. In times of recession, unemployment, or slow economic growth—according to the Keynesian prescription—politicians and the Fed should stimulate economic activity by creating budget deficits and by increasing the money supply. During periods of inflation, proper governmental policy is just the reverse—to create a budget surplus and retard growth in the money supply.

Over the past several decades this old Keynesian view has undergone serious challenge and a major refurbishing. Massive and rising deficits from ever-increasing government expenditures and the seeming inability of Congress or the government to do anything about it led to a general disenchantment with the belief that government can competently administer discretion-

ary policy. Some parts (but by no means all) of academia have become disenchanted to the point of outright rejection of discretionary policy.

The New Classical Economists reject discretionary policy as a means of solving macroeconomic problems related to unemployment, inflation, or economic growth. These economists believe that attempts by politicians and the Federal Reserve System to manipulate consumers, savers, and investors are doomed to fail, because individuals will learn (ultimately) to anticipate the effects of policy and will neutralize it. People, in other words, react not only to actual policy actions but also to their *anticipations* about the effect of those actions. For example, consider a hypothetical tax reform provision that would reintroduce tax deductions for interest payments on second-home mortgages. In anticipation of this new law, consumers may increase their demands for second homes and for loans to finance them. Consequently, even before such a law takes effect, prices of these homes may rise, and so may the demand for loanable funds. While this example illustrates how market participants could react to affect policy, the debate con-

tinues over whether individuals do indeed react in this manner. New Keynesians and other economists do not believe that the New Classicals have proved their case (see Chapter 10 for details). The issue is also much debated by politicians who do not wish to abandon pork barrel spending as a means of getting reelected.

The view that rejects discretionary policy is not new. Classical economists of the eighteenth, nineteenth, and early twentieth centuries sponsored it. Consider the view of Adam Smith, the father of economics, who in 1759 developed the central idea of the rational expectationists, which criticized the role of the central planner (whom Smith called the "man of system"):

[The man of system] seems to imagine that he can arrange the different members of a great society with as much ease as the hand arranges the different pieces upon a chess-board; he does not consider that the different pieces upon the chess-board have no other principle of motion besides that which the hand impresses upon them; but that, in the great chess-board of human society, every single piece has a principle of motion of its own, altogether different from that which the legislator might choose to impress upon it. (*The Theory of Moral Sentiments.*)

The New Classical Economists condemn policy from the same perspective—that no single individual or no group of politicians can ever know enough to second-guess market participants in a society. Discretionary macroeconomic controls, even if intentions are good, often make problems worse.

What is the role of government in a society where chess pieces will not stay put? In the rational expectationists' view, government should move to a *preprogrammed* policy. In some views, this means a constitutionally balanced budget in order to control the spending tendencies of politicians. It also means a fixed rate of growth in the money supply. In all cases, the New Classical Economists emphasize that policy should be well-announced and consistently implemented so that anticipations of the economic actors, such as consumers,

savers, and investors, will be more certain.

The ongoing debate between New Keynesians and New Classical Economists tells us that the development of macroeconomic theory and its policy component is very much alive, if unsettled. From the present vantage point it is not at all certain that the New Classical or non-activist government policies view will win the day. New Keynesians have developed theories that include a foundation in microeconomic behavior—such as the New Classicals—but which conclude that discretionary action is called for to control the business cycle. (This theory is given full treatment in Chapter 10 of this book.)

Abandonment of discretionary controls is even less clear from a policy perspective. While there was little effective call for the government to "Do Something!" in the 1981–82 recession, the 1990–91 recession (with reduced growth and high unemployment) created massive desire for "change." Part of that change came in the election and policies of President Bill Clinton. At base, in this

regard, it is wise to remember that economic theory is a theory of behavior, including *political* behavior. Contrary to the preferences of the New Classicals, and in support of New Keynesian views, discretionary action by the federal government would almost certainly follow a severe crisis. The imposition of preprogrammed rules raises other important questions, including: What would be the nature of the preprogrammed rules under which the government would operate? Who would decide what the rules would be? Would discretion play a part? Could political control of the federal purse strings be wrested from incumbent politicians? Would high inflation or depression-level unemployment rates create a wholesale dismissal of rules in a democratic society?

Discretionary policy, it would appear, is not obsolete either in theory or in practice. Perhaps economist and Nobel Laureate Franco Modigliani (1985) is right when he notes that the economy is not as stable as the New Classicals think or as unstable as the New Keynesians believe. ❏

REAL INCOME is the actual amount of goods and services that you may purchase with your money income.

NOMINAL INCOME (or MONEY INCOME) is simply the actual dollar amount of your income.

STOCK VARIABLE is the level of a variable at some point in time.

ENDOGENOUS VARIABLES in economic models are variables that are determined within a model.

EXOGENOUS VARIABLES in economic models are variables that are determined outside a model, but that have an effect on the model and in particular on the endogenous variables.

"inflation-adjusted." For example, though the fact might be obvious to most readers, there is an important difference between earning a "real" income of $500 per month and a "money" or "nominal" income of $500 per month. *Real income* is the actual amount of goods and services that you may purchase with your money income. *Money* or *nominal income* is simply the actual dollar amount of your income. If your money income remains constant over the period of a year, your total income for the year comes to $6,000. The crucial question and a far more accurate indicator of your personal economic well-being is, "What happened to prices during the year?" If the price level increased by 10 percent over the year, then on average your *real* purchasing power declined by 10 percent. Obvious as this problem may be in an era characterized by inflation, we must keep it constantly in mind when dealing with macroeconomic models, especially over periods of high inflation. Typically, though not in all cases, we express variables in *real* terms.

A second matter of importance in the construction of macro models concerns the identification of variables as stocks or flows. A *stock* is merely the level of a variable at some point in time, such as "the stock of money in January 1993." Any stock may be added to or subtracted from, and this is usually designated by a simple change in that variable, say ΔM or $-\Delta M$. Notice we use the symbol Δ for change, so that ΔM is the change in the money stock. For example, the stock of money on January 1, 1993, might be $500 billion, so $M = 500$ (in billions of dollars). During January 1993 the money supply might be reduced by $50 billion, so $\Delta M = -50$ (again in billions of dollars). On February 1, 1993, the stock of money will be 500 - 50 or 450M. The magnitude of money growth may also be described as a *flow.* That is, money may be described as growing (or declining) at some rate per unit of time. In our example, the rate of money growth is -50/500, or -10 percent per year. Symbolically, we would write this as $\Delta M/M$.

To further clarify this idea, let us consider two other important macroeconomic variables, the interest rate and the price level. The interest rate is the cost in percent of the outstanding principal that must be paid to borrow money for one year. Thus, an interest rate of 8 percent means that the cost of borrowing and using a sum of money is 8 percent of the amount borrowed per year. Thus, the interest *rate* is a variable with flow or time dimensions, since it tells the cost of borrowing per year.

A final issue about model construction concerns the endogenous or exogenous nature of the variables that appear in macroeconomic models. An *endogenous variable* is defined as one that is determined within a model. Further, an endogenous variable such as consumption is one for which some behavioral or functional characteristic is stated (e.g., consumption is a function of income). We say that the variable consumption is endogenous to our theory or model.

An *exogenous variable* is defined as a variable determined outside a model, but one that has an effect on the model. Sometimes exogenous variables are referred to as parameters—variables that are usually held constant but that can vary. When it varies or changes we say that it exerts an outside influence. Indeed, exogenous means "from without" or "outside influence." For example, if we add government spending to the model (as we will later on in the text), we would bring an outside or exogenous variable into consideration.[1] Here there is no attempt to explain why government spending is at any particular level. Government is assumed to be the product of a political system rather than an economic system and will be outside our consideration for most of the discussion.

SUMMARY

In this chapter, we have defined macroeconomics, and discussed the distinction between macroeconomics and microeconomics. We have introduced the idea of macroeconomic policy, and the distinction between fiscal and monetary policy and the tools used in conducting these policies. Aggregate demand and supply were briefly discussed, as were the concepts of full employment and price stability.

In this chapter we also introduced the alternative macroeconomic models, including the Classical, Keynesian, and Monetarist macroeconomic models, and various modern approaches. These latter included supply-side approaches, New Classical and New Keynesian models, and Real Business Cycle models. For all of these models, we point out the need to distinguish between real and nominal variables, stocks and flows, and endogenous and exogenous variables.

 As we have stressed, macroeconomics, in contrast to microeconomics, studies the formation and interrelationships between aggregate demand and aggregate supply, which determine inflation rates, employment levels, and ultimately, economic growth. Once the theory of how these interrelationships has been established, macroeconomic policy—composed of both monetary and fiscal tools—indicates how acceptable attainment of macroeconomic goals might be achieved. Fiscal and monetary policy are the two principal means of manipulating aggregate demand and aggregate supply. Fiscal policy utilizes government budget policies, and monetary policy utilizes changes in the money supply to attain desired results in the economy.

Various schools of macroeconomic theory—New Classical and New Keynesian—emphasize the necessity for some form of aggregate demand management to create economic stability, though they differ on the means required to achieve that end. Supply-side economists, who may also recognize demand management as an effective tool, emphasize that monetary and fiscal

---

[1]Though government spending and taxation are ordinarily considered exogenous to macro models, we offer a simple analysis of the *determinants* of government spending and taxation through the political process in Chapter 17 of this book. Until then, however, we treat the government as an exogenous influence on macroeconomic equilibrium.

tools may have had damaging effects on incentives to work and to invest over time; consequently, they recommend greater consideration of supply-side effects on macroeconomic policy. Rational expectationists argue that *all* discretionary macroeconomic policy has only very limited or no effect in influencing real economic problems such as unemployment and economic growth.

Finally, we have stressed that the issues with which macroeconomics is concerned are of overwhelming importance to each and every one of us, and perhaps there is more consensus among macroeconomists about how to deal with them than a mere listing of the various schools would suggest. Inflation, unemployment, recession, depression, and stifled growth are problems that all societies have faced from the dawn of civilization. Fortunately, the passage of time has also brought progress (though not perfection) in our understanding of such critical problems. Macroeconomic theory and policy aim at explaining the relationships that underlie the problems so that we may develop systems or alter institutional settings in order to deal with them effectively.

KEY TERMS

aggregate variables	Keynesian macroeconomics
aggregate demand	legal reserve requirements
aggregate supply	macroeconomic policy
budget deficits	macroeconomic theory
budget policies	microeconomics
budget surpluses	Monetarists
ceteris paribus	monetary policy
Classical macroeconomics	New Classical macroeconomics
discount rate	New Keynesian macroeconomics
discretionary policies	nominal income (money income)
endogeneous variables	real income
exogenous variables	real business cycle theory
fiscal policy	stock variable
flow variable	supply-side economics
full employment	

QUESTIONS FOR REVIEW AND DISCUSSION

1. Distinguish between microeconomics and macroeconomics. Would a study of the computer software industry or the stock market deal with micro or macro phenomena?

2. What is full employment? What is price stability? Do you believe that, politically, one of these goals is easier to achieve than the other? Discuss.

3. What is economic growth? Why do we value economic growth as a goal of macro policy?

4. Define and discuss the two primary tools of macroeconomic policy. Does the government control both monetary and fiscal policy? How? What are the aims of such policies in periods of low employment?

5. What is discretionary demand management? Do both Keynesians and Monetarists believe that the economy can be controlled by proper management of demand? What are some of their arguments?

6. What do the supply-side economists argue? Are their arguments, in your view, incompatible with discretionary demand management?

7. What are the effects of a rightward shift in aggregate demand? In aggregate supply? Which do you suppose to be better for the economy? Why?

8. What is the distinguishing feature of the New Classical Economists' (or Rational Expectationists') view of the functioning of the macroeconomy?

9. Clearly distinguish between a stock variable and a flow variable. Is the interest rate a stock or a flow?

10. How do New Keynesian views compare to Keynesian views? To New Classical views?

11. In the *Economic Report of the President*, find last year's nominal GDP and real GDP. Why do they differ?

SUGGESTIONS FOR FURTHER READING

Barro, Robert J. *Macroeconomics*. New York: John Wiley & Sons, 1993.

Council of Economic Advisors. *Economic Report of the President*. Washington, DC: U.S. Government Printing Office, available annually.

Gordon, Robert J. "What Is New Keynesian Economics?" *Journal of Economic Literature* (September 1990), pp. 1115–71.

Krugman, Paul. "The Move Toward Free Trade Zones," Federal Reserve Bank of Kansas City *Economic Review* (November/December 1991), pp. 5–26.

Mankiw, N. Gregory. "A Quick Refresher Course in Macroeconomics," *Journal of Economic Literature* (December 1990), pp. 1645–1660.

Plosser, Charles I. "Understanding Real Business Cycles," *Journal of Economic Perspectives* (Summer 1989), pp. 51–77.

Policy Implications of Trade and Currency Zones: A Symposium. Federal Reserve Bank of Kansas City, 1991.

Sowell, Thomas. *Knowledge and Decisions*. New York: Basic Books, 1980.

2

MACROECONOMIC VARIABLES:

OUTPUT, EMPLOYMENT, AND INFLATION

An attack on economic problems requires an understanding of the magnitude and direction of crucial economic variables such as output, employment, and the price level. Economists have different theories about how these quantities are determined, but certain ground rules about measurement of macroeconomic variables are generally accepted by all. This chapter provides information about key macroeconomic variables by describing the national income accounts, which include a definition of variables and a discussion of their accounting relationships. Before turning to the specific business of how quantities such as gross domestic product (GDP), unemployment, and price indices are measured, we consider in general terms the magnitude and direction of economic output in the United States over the 1980s and early 1990s. A brief look at output growth over this period prepares us for the other economic measures of how we're doing as a nation.

After you read this chapter, you will have

- an understanding of the current status of U.S. GDP in nominal, real, and real per capita terms
- an understanding of the National Income Accounts, including GDP, GNP, national income, personal income, and foreign sector transactions
- an understanding of the accounting identities that link the variables in the national income accounts, including identities linking domestic saving and investment, the government budget constraint, and the balance on certain foreign transactions

29

• an understanding of the balance of payment accounts.

• an understanding of the unemployment rate and price level indices, including how they are constructed and how they behave in the United States.

ECONOMIC GROWTH AND ECONOMIC DATA

When we look at the economy, we can ask where we stand in relation to other people, or how the economy as a whole is functioning. The first question would concern the distribution of total income among the various members of the economy. All of us would be in different positions in the income distribution, with different shares of the economy's output. These are issues of income distribution, and they are matters of obvious concern to individuals. However, macroeconomics concentrates more on the *total* output of the economy, than on the distribution of that output among individuals. Thus, we will look at measures of *overall* economic performance.

Various government and private agencies calculate the course of macroeconomic measures, such as gross domestic product, the consumer price index, and the unemployment rate. We will be looking at a number of these statistics in detail, but for the present we will consider only one of them and what it might tell us about our overall picture.

Output of Goods and Services

The aggregate output of final goods and services (GDP) is an extremely important measure of macroeconomic activity. At least in the economist's view of the world, more goods and services are preferred to less. Consider Figure 2-1, which gives us two ways of viewing gross domestic product between 1947 and 1992 as well as an illustration of the difference between real and nominal magnitudes mentioned in Chapter 1.

Since economists are often concerned with the production of the actual output of goods and services, they adjust *nominal* GDP for price-level changes and refer to it as GDP in constant or inflation-adjusted dollars, or more concisely as *real* GDP. In the graph, real GDP is in terms of 1987 prices. Putting GDP in real or constant dollar terms by way of a price index, which measures the changes in prices of all goods and services produced by the economy, is merely a means of adjusting for inflation. For instance, the *real* output of goods and services (i.e., real GDP in terms of 1987 prices) was declining in absolute terms in 1974–75, in 1981–82, and in 1990–91. In *nominal* terms, as Figure 2-1 reveals, GDP advanced fairly steadily over these periods. Given what we know about the difference between real and nominal magnitudes, we can conclude that these periods were all years of rising price levels.

Still another important measure of our recent economic record is *per capita real GDP* (i.e., real GDP divided by the population). Per capita real GDP also appears in Figure 2-1, and reveals similar behavior to real GDP. However, since population grows over time, some increase in real GDP is necessary just to keep up with population growth. Thus, very slow growth in real GDP will

These figures show the behavior of current and constant dollar GDP,
and constant dollar real GDP per capita.

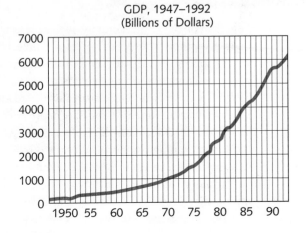

GDP, 1947–1992
(Billions of Dollars)

Real GDP, 1947–1992
(Billions of 1987 Dollars)

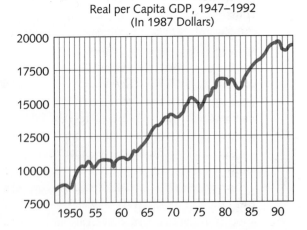

Real per Capita GDP, 1947–1992
(In 1987 Dollars)

SOURCE: U.S. Department of Commerce, Bureau of Economic Analysis and Bureau of
the Census.

manifest itself in falling per capita real GDP. For example, in late 1989 per capita real GDP started to decline (in the third quarter) while real GDP rose until the third quarter of 1990 and then started to decline. In many ways changes in per capita real GDP are an important measure of economic performance, since they measure how output per person is changing, and give at least one measure of how individual well-being might be changing. For instance, per capita real GDP was about $11,000 in 1959 (measured in 1987 dollars), and increased to about $19,000 in 1992 (also measured in 1987 dollars). That is, output per person increased by over 70 percent during this thirty-three-year period, for an average growth rate of about 1.7 percent per year.

A measure related to GDP is personal income. While GDP measures total output of final goods and services, **personal income** measures income received by households. Later in this chapter we will make the connection between these two measures more explicit. For now we just mention that *per capita real personal income* and *per capita real disposable personal income* (i.e., real personal income and real disposable personal income divided by the population) are also important indicators of economic performance. Personal income reveals the income earned by individuals, while **disposable personal income** is the after-tax income of individuals. These measures reveal similar things about U.S. economic growth and development over the period we considered earlier. Witness Figure 2-2, which shows the growth of per capita personal income and per capita disposable personal income in real terms (i.e., in terms of 1987 dollars, for the years 1959–1990). Per capita personal income rose from about $5,500 per person in 1947 (measured in terms of 1987 dollars) to about $13,500 in 1990 (again measured in 1987 dollars). Over the same period, per capita disposable personal income rose from about $4,900 in 1947 to about $11,500 in 1990, again measured in 1987 dollars. These figures indicate a number of things about the U.S. economy over these years. First, like output per person, both personal income per person and disposable personal income per person more than doubled from 1947 to 1990. Real per capita personal income grew at 2.14 percent per year over this time, and real per capita disposable income grew at 2.04 percent. Second, the ratio of personal taxes to personal income increased, from about 11 percent in 1947 to about 15 percent in 1990. Thus, disposable personal income (i.e., after-tax income) increased more slowly than personal income, and personal taxes rose more quickly than personal income. If we look over the recent decade, beginning with the end of the 1981–82 recession, we find that from 1982 fourth quarter to the end of 1990, real personal income per capita increased from $11,478 to $13,415, or at a rate of 1.97 percent per year, and real disposable personal income per capita increased from $9,749 to $11,374, a rate of 1.95 percent per year. Real personal taxes per capita increased from $1,729 in 1982 to $2,041 in 1990. Thus, the period 1982 to 1990 was a time of growth in output and income per capita, but this growth was at a somewhat slower rate than the average rate over

PERSONAL INCOME is the total amount of income people in an economy earn or are given from all sources, including earnings and transfers.

DISPOSABLE PERSONAL INCOME is what people have left to spend out of their personal income after they pay their taxes.

FIGURE 2-2
Per Capita Real Personal
Income and Per Capita Real
Disposable Personal Income,
1947–1992 (in 1987 Dollars)

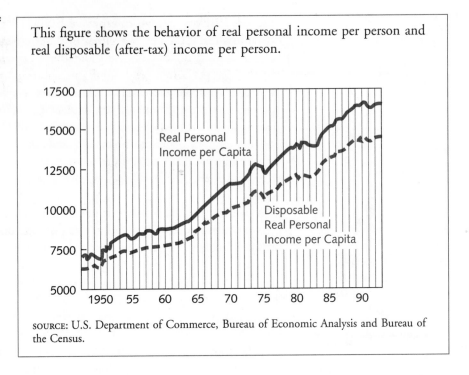

This figure shows the behavior of real personal income per person and real disposable (after-tax) income per person.

SOURCE: U.S. Department of Commerce, Bureau of Economic Analysis and Bureau of the Census.

expansions *and* contractions since 1947. The year 1990 saw this growth rate end, as a recession began that lasted into 1991. The recession of 1990–91 was characterized by falling income and an increase in the unemployment rate. Recovery between 1991 and 1993 was slow in terms of per capita income, with even slower growth in employment.

Business Cycles

The paths of real GDP and real personal income shown in Figures 2-1 and 2-2 illustrate the behavior of aggregate and per capita measures of real GDP and real personal income. We have already discussed a key feature of the economy that is revealed in these graphs, namely economic growth. Whether measured as real GDP or real personal income, and whether measured in aggregate or in per capita terms, the U.S. economy has experienced considerable growth over time. This is a very important feature of U.S. economic performance, since it allows households to enjoy an ever-improving standard of living. Indeed, over time the rate of economic growth is of paramount importance in explaining the rate of growth of consumption of goods and services in an economy. However, it is also apparent that this growth is not smooth but is instead marked by periods of growth punctuated with occasional periods of decline. This pattern of growth and decline is called the **business cycle**, because of the somewhat cyclical appearance of the periods of growth

BUSINESS CYCLES are economy-wide fluctuations in real output and employment.

and decline. The periods of growth are called expansions, while the periods of declining real GDP are called recessions. When the economy reaches the end of a decline and is poised for expansion, we say that it is at the *trough* of the business cycle. When the economy is at the end of an expansion and is poised to begin a period of decline in real GDP, we say it is at the *peak* of the business cycle. Figure 2-3 illustrates the behavior of real GDP over a hypothetical business cycle.

Business cycles are of interest to economists for a number of reasons. These cycles in real GDP are matched by cycles in unemployment. These cycles include periods of declining real GDP—recession—linked with periods of rising unemployment, and periods of rising real GDP linked with periods of falling unemployment. Because of this, recessions are regarded as a bad state of the economy, and macroeconomists have spent considerable effort investigating ways to stabilize the economy in order to smooth out the business cycle. The idea is to have the economy grow at its average growth rate all of the time, instead of experiencing periods of expansion and contraction. Policy actions that attempt to smooth the business cycle are called *stabilization policy*. While macroeconomic policies to encourage economic growth have a long-run goal of increasing the trend rate of growth in the economy, stabilization policies have a short-run goal of reducing the variability of the economy about its trend growth rate. The ability of policymakers to achieve such a goal, and the wisdom of even trying, is a topic of ongoing debate among economists. Much

FIGURE 2-3
The Business Cycle

This figure shows the major features of the business cycle, including the peak, the recession or contractionary period, the trough, and the expansion.

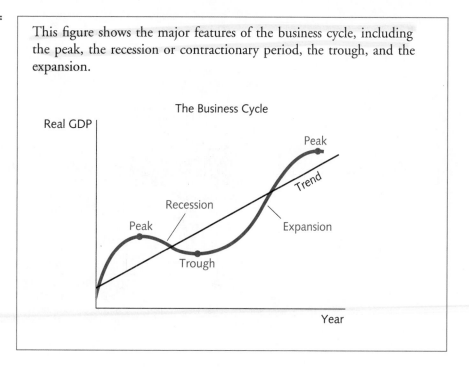

of the debate among proponents of the different models we will study in the coming chapters is a debate over these very issues.

Occasionally, the United States experiences an extended period of economic expansion, such as during the 1960s or the 1980s. During such times commentators and sometimes even policymakers and professional economists claim that the business cycle is over or that we have gained such control over the economy that we have eliminated recessions. At least to date, such pronouncements have always been shown to be incorrect by subsequent events. Figure 2-4 shows a graph of real GDP per capita and the unemployment rate from 1959 to 1992, along with a trend line showing average growth of real GDP over that time. In this graph there are clear periods during which real GDP per capita is growing above trend, and also periods in which it is declining and falling below trend. These later periods are also characterized by periods of rising unemployment rates. Consider three recent periods of recession. There was a severe recession in 1974–75 during the first OPEC oil price hike. In the figure, real GDP per capita drops sharply from a position above the trend line to end up at a position below the trend line. The

FIGURE 2-4
Real GDP Per Capita (in 1987 Dollars), Trend Real GDP Per Capita, and the Unemployment Rate (Percent)

This figure shows the business cycle behavior of real GDP per capita, and the related behavior of the unemployment rate. Notice the irregular cycles of GDP about the trend line, with clear movements above or below trend that are related to movements in the unemployment rate. In particular, when real GDP is below trend, such as in 1990–91, the unemployment rate tends to increase, and vice versa.

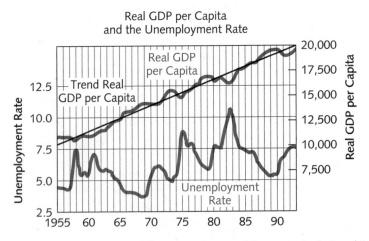

SOURCE: U.S. Department of Commerce, Bureau of Economic Analysis and Bureau of the Census; and authors' calculation of trend real GDP per capita.

unemployment rate also shows a dramatic upward spike at this time. Another severe recession occurred in 1982, on the heels of a small recession in 1980–81, and real GDP per capita showed an even longer period of decline, with unemployment spiking even higher than during 1974–75. Finally, a somewhat milder recession occurred during 1990–91, as indicated by the fall in real GDP per capita and the rise in the unemployment rate at this time.

The business cycle is very important to policymakers, and hence stabilization policy is widely studied and hotly debated. The political fortunes of local, state, and federal officials often hang in the balance.

Economists have different explanations for both economic growth and the business cycle. For example, government deficits, productivity-reducing federal taxes and regulations, and an insufficient money supply growth have all been blamed for the recession of 1990–91. However, economists generally agree on what GDP and other indicators are telling us. They differ on how to *explain* what has happened.

Alternative explanations of the kinds of simple statistics we have been viewing are what macroeconomics is really about. Only after alternative theories have been developed can various explanations for and predictions about economic performance be made. Let us first look more closely at the specific and well-recognized measurements of economic activity that are used in the United States.

THE NATIONAL INCOME ACCOUNTS

Macroeconomics is concerned with the overall economic performance of a national economy. National income accounting was developed to measure that performance over a given period of time. National income accounts had been used in earlier discussions, but when Keynes was writing *The General Theory* in the 1930s, national income accounting concepts were still in their infancy.[1] The National Bureau of Economic Research, a private research group, had started measuring national income for the United States as early as 1920. But it was not until the Great Depression of the 1930s that Congress instructed the Department of Commerce to collect and report national income statistics. National income statistics are important because they can be used to plot the previous course of the economy, to make forecasts about the future direction of the economy, to assist economists in testing various macro models, and to provide Congress and other administrative agencies with a basis for policymaking. A practical knowledge of these accounts is essential to explaining or predicting important economic phenomena.

---

[1]The generally accepted father of national income accounting was Sir William Petty, who attempted to estimate the national income of England in 1665.

Gross Domestic Product and Gross National Product

GROSS DOMESTIC PRODUCT is the total value of all the final goods and services produced by factors located in a nation during a specific period of time, usually a year.

GROSS NATIONAL PRODUCT is the total value of all the final goods and services produced by factors owned by residents of a nation during a specific period of time, usually a year.

Before proceeding directly into a national income accounting framework, let us first examine the definition of the largest national income aggregates, **gross domestic product (GDP)** and **gross national product (GNP).** It was once GNP, but now it is GDP that we hear or read about in the media. The government began emphasizing GDP in 1992 because it more closely corresponds to other indicators of economic performance, such as industrial production and employment.

Exactly what is GDP? For the United States, gross domestic product is the total market value of all final goods and services produced with factors of production *located* in the United States during a given year. The key phrase distinguishing GDP from GNP is "produced in the United States." Gross national product is the total market value of final goods and services produced by factors of production *owned* by residents of the United States. How do production and ownership differ? The key difference is that some factories in the United States are owned by foreign citizens or foreign firms, and some factories in foreign countries are owned by U.S. citizens and firms. U.S. residents receive the profits on goods produced in U.S.-owned factories located overseas, and foreign residents receive the profits on goods produced in foreign-owned factories located in the United States. GDP measures the total production of factories in the United States regardless of ownership. GNP takes GDP and adds to it net investment income from the rest of the world, which is income received by U.S. owners of overseas production facilities, minus the income received by foreign owners of U.S. production facilities. If the United States is a net recipient of investment income from the rest of the world, then GNP is greater than GDP. If the United States is a net payee of investment income to the rest of the world, then GNP is less than GDP. For many years the United States invested in building overseas factories, and these factories provide investment income to U.S. residents. Recently there has been a surge of foreign investment in the United States, but the United States remains a net recipient of foreign investment income, so U.S. GNP remains greater than U.S. GDP. For example, in 1992, GDP was $5,907.0 billion, while GNP was $5,920.3 billion. Thus, the U.S. received a net inflow of $13.3 billion in factor income from overseas production.

WHY GDP INSTEAD OF GNP?

GDP does not include profits earned from overseas production, nor does it subtract profits earned by foreigners from production in the U.S. GDP has for some time been considered the preferred measure of domestic output by most nations in the world, and in 1992 the U.S. government began emphasizing GDP over GNP as a measure of U.S. output. It actually does not make much difference for the United States which measure is used. During most of the post-World War II period, U.S. GNP has been somewhere around .5 percent higher than GDP.

GDP (or GNP) is often thought of as a measure of overall economic performance. Yet we should never make the mistake of arguing that GDP (or GNP) statistics accurately measure economic welfare. We discuss this at greater length in the Policy Issue: "Can We Measure Economic Welfare?"

GDP is reported by the Department of Commerce on a quarterly and annual basis. The word *gross* tells us that the wearing out of the existing capital stock (i.e., buildings, equipment) during the period (year) has not been subtracted out by the national income accountants. The word *domestic* refers to all of the economic agents in the domestic economy that produce output. "Total market value" in the definition means that all of the final goods and services have been valued at *market prices.*[2] We cannot sum the physical amounts of the goods and services produced in an economy over a period of time. For example, we cannot aggregate such items as the apples, pizzas, and television repairs produced in a given year. But we can total their money (market) values. Let us suppose that in the market four apples sold for 25 cents each, two pizzas for $2 each, and one television repair for $25. The total market value for all of these items is $30. Thus, as this example shows, GDP is the value of the goods and services sold in the market. It is expressed in money terms.[3]

It is also important to recognize in the definition of GDP that we are speaking of final goods. The word "final" refers to the end products of the economy. These goods have been produced during the current time period. Goods purchased for resale or included in other products are classified as intermediate goods and are not counted in GDP. If intermediate goods were included in estimating GDP, there would be double counting. For example, a number of production stages are involved in producing a pair of shoes. If we counted the value of the leather sold by the tanner to the shoemaker and in addition the value of the pair of shoes sold by the shoemaker to the retail shoe store, we would have counted the value of the leather three times. "How?" we may ask. We would have counted the value of the leather not only as a product of the tanner but also as part of the value of the finished pair of shoes sold by the shoemaker to the retail shoe store. To avoid the problem of double counting, national income accountants count only the value added at each stage of producing the final product. The **value added** is the difference between the price of the goods at that stage and the cost of the goods purchased from the previous stage.

The VALUE-ADDED approach is the dollar value of a firm's sales minus the value of intermediate goods purchased for use in production.

---

[2]Market price includes indirect taxes such as sales taxes and excise taxes and is not the same as the price the seller receives for the good or factor cost (i.e., the cost of production).

[3]Since GDP tends to understate the actual output of the final goods and services produced in the economy, the national income accountants try to partially offset this problem by imputing values to some goods and services not sold in the market. That is, they estimate a value for the good or service when no cash payment is made. For example, they impute (i.e., estimate) a value for owner-occupied housing, for food and fuel produced and consumed on a farm, and for work performed by government employees.

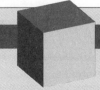

CAN WE MEASURE

ECONOMIC WELFARE?

GDP is a standard international index of output and was never intended to be an aggregate welfare index. Therefore, it should not be thought of as a measure of the economic (social) welfare or "well-being" of any particular economy. For one thing, real GDP or even real GDP per capita does not give us any information on how total output is distributed among the households in the economy. At the same time that real GDP may be growing, the distribution of income among households may be getting more uneven. In addition,

GDP does not indicate what has happened to the quality of goods over time. Nor does GDP consider nonmarket activities, such as housework by the homeowner. Thus, every time a household changes from a single-income household to a dual-income household, there is a potential for GDP to overstate the resulting increase in output. This occurs if the dual-income family hires childcare or housecleaning services. Then the move to dual-income earners leads to an increase in GDP because both husband and wife are working, and because a housecleaner or babysitter is being paid. This overstates the actual increase in output, since the housework and childcare that were done by the spouse who stayed home were not counted

in GDP. Furthermore, an important measure of welfare, namely *leisure time,* is not reflected in calculating GDP, even though until mid-1975 there had been a growth of leisure time in the U.S. economy with a reduction in the hours of work. (In recent years the trend has leveled off and even reversed itself.)

Along with an increasing GDP, there are associated social costs that are not measured in GDP. In other words, there are "bads" or external costs connected with the production of "goods" or GDP. For example, a rising GDP in the United States has at times been accompanied by both air and water pollution. Today, government and businesses, encouraged by environmental regulations, have internalized

PHOTO 2-1
The Fact that Parents are Willing to Pay For Childcare Means that Such Care Has an Economic Value. These Services, When Performed Within the Household, Are Not Counted as GDP.

some of these external (pollution) costs. Nevertheless, the growth rate of GDP in the past did not count the costs associated with pollution, and today it does not count the benefits associated with pollution reduction.

In an attempt to gauge society's welfare more closely, economists William Nordhaus and James Tobin have tried to devise a measure of social welfare.[a] Some of the changes that they suggested are (1) to include in GDP imputations for leisure and estimates for household production and consumption (i.e., meals, cleaning, and house repairs); (2) to exclude from GDP estimates of certain external (social) costs such as pollution, litter, congestion, noise, and offensive advertisements; and (3) to exclude some local and national services, such as police protection, which are judged to be real inputs to activities yielding utility. Of course, one should recognize that many problems are involved in attempting to construct a measure of social welfare, and that while these suggestions may be a step in the right direction, GDP even modified as they suggest is still a poor measure of welfare. ❏

NOTE [a]See William Nordhaus and James Tobin, "Is Growth Obsolete?" In *Economic Growth. 50th Anniversary Colloquium 5* (New York: National Bureau of Economic Research, 1972).

WHAT GDP IS NOT

Not counted in measuring GDP are some goods and services that are produced but that are not sold in the market. For example, there are those who grow and consume their own vegetables or who perform their own housework, such as cooking, sewing, or tending children. The value of these activities is not included in GDP.

Market transactions in any goods produced prior to the current production period are not counted in GDP. That is, we do not count used goods. Remember that GDP measures only newly produced final goods and services. This means goods and services produced during the current period. Thus, for example, if one sells an old car or a forty-year-old home, one is merely transferring titles of ownership. Similarly, sale of stocks or bonds do not count in GDP, since these do not involve any production. The gain or loss associated with stocks or bonds is reflected in the change in their market value, but is not directly connected to the production of new goods. It should be noted that the salaries of brokers and dealers—for example, dealers in used cars or antiques—are included in GDP since these persons perform a current service in exchanging assets or goods.

TRANSFER PAYMENTS are nominal payments made by governments and businesses to people for which no goods or services are concurrently rendered.

Certain types of business and government expenditures are excluded from GDP but added to the household's personal income. These types of expenditures are called business and government **transfer payments.** When the government pays social security benefits to households, no service is performed by the household for this income. Interest paid on the government debt (bills and bonds) is treated exactly like transfer payments.

National Income and Product

National income accounting may be viewed from two standpoints: (1) the flow of expenditures approach and (2) the flow of earnings or income approach. The *flow of expenditures approach* considers total output or national income from the standpoint of the total amount spent by all economic agents on the final output of goods and services. The *earnings* or *income approach* looks upon national income or total output as the sum of the income earned by the factors of production (land, labor, capital, entrepreneurial ability) employed in producing the final output of goods and services.

In national income accounting, the economy is broken down into four sectors: (1) household, (2) business, (3) government, and (4) foreign. Every economic agent in the economy has to be assigned to one of these sectors.

The circular flow diagram of economic activity in Figure 2-5 illustrates the two different approaches to national income accounting. The diagram shows a model of a simple economy containing only two sectors: (1) a business sector and (2) a household sector. In the upper loop of the circular flow diagram, the business sector produces and sells all of the final consumer goods and services to the household sector. There is, therefore, a flow of final goods and services to the household sector. In return, there is a matched *flow of expenditures on final goods and services* from the household sector to the business sector. From the sale of the final goods and services, the business sector receives revenue that is used to cover the cost of production. The market (dollar) value of the final output of goods and services is determined by the household sector's demand for the final product.

The lower loop of the circular flow diagram shows the business sector hiring the services of the factors of production from the household sector. The business sector combines the factor inputs to produce the final output. The factors of production are paid according to their productivity out of the business revenue generated from the sale of the final goods and services. Leftover business revenue accrues as income in the form of profit to the household (entrepreneur) that owns the business. Thus, a *flow of earnings or income* to the household sector matches the flow of factor services to the business sector.

The flow of income going to the factors of production takes the form of *wages* to labor, *rent* to land, *interest* to capital, and *profit* to entrepreneurial ability. Wages, rent, interest, and profit are the returns to the factors of production that are owned by the household sector, but they are also a cost of production to the business sector. The market (dollar) value of each factor is determined by the business sector's demand for and the household sector's supply of the factors of production.

Figure 2-5 also shows the relationship between household saving and business investment. If the household saves out of its income, we see from the diagram that savings flow into the financial market (bank deposits, bonds,

FIGURE 2-5
Circular Flow of Income

This figure shows that the sum of the flow of consumption and investment expenditures is equal to the flow of income.

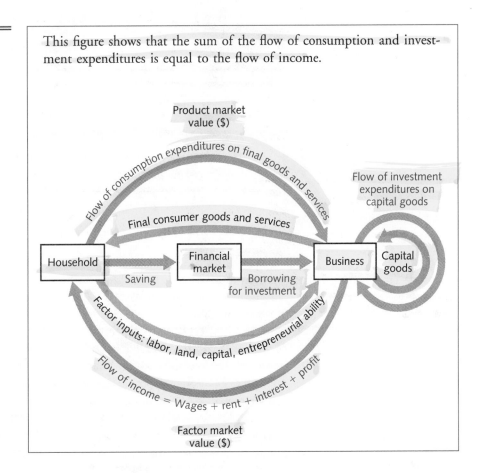

equities, etc.). The household, therefore, supplies funds (savings) to the
financial market. The business, on the other hand, has a demand for these
funds (savings) in order to purchase capital goods such as building equipment
or inventories produced by the business sector. Business investment expenditure on capital goods, then, is represented by an equivalent flow of funds but
to the business sector, as the arrow indicates in the diagram. Also, the actual
production of capital goods generates factor income in the form of wages,
rents, interest, and profit to households. This is shown by the flow line on the
bottom of the circular flow diagram. While this circular flow diagram is only
an illustration of a simple economy and does not take into consideration the
government and foreign sectors, it does show the two fundamental approaches
to national income accounting.

  In the following sections, we will examine in more detail each of these
fundamental approaches to national income accounting. We give special
attention to developing the conceptual accounting framework underlying five
income aggregates: (1) gross domestic product, (2) net national product,

(3) national income, (4) personal income, and (5) disposable personal income. We will discover that there is a close relationship between these five income aggregates. Economists, in general discussion, often use the term *national income* to refer to all five income aggregates.

The Flow of Expenditures Approach to Gross Domestic Product

In the flow of expenditures approach, GDP is determined by adding up the total amount spent on final goods and services by each of the four sectors—household, business, government, and foreign. Table 2-1 shows the breakdown of expenditures by the four sectors.

HOUSEHOLD SECTOR

CONSUMPTION is the goods and services purchased by consumers.

Expenditures by the household sector are called *personal consumption expenditures* or consumption. These include expenditures by individuals and nonprofit institutions. Table 2-1 shows personal consumption expenditures as the largest component of GDP. Such expenditures were $4,062.9 billion in 1992 and can be broken down into durable goods, nondurable goods, and services. Durable goods include tangible items such as automobiles, radios, TV sets, and appliances. Durable goods are expected to last more than one year. The purchase of a new house, however, is not considered to be a durable good item. Instead, this expenditure is placed in the investment category. Nondurable goods are tangible items such as food and clothing. They are expected to last less than one year. Services are intangible items such as recreation, entertainment, education, and medical care.

TABLE 2-1
Gross Domestic Product, 1992, Expenditure Approach (Billions of Dollars).

This table shows the expenditure approach to GDP. GDP is personal consumption expenditures, gross private domestic investment, government expenditures, and net exports of goods and services.

1. PERSONAL CONSUMPTION EXPENDITURES	$4,062.9
2. GROSS PRIVATE DOMESTIC INVESTMENT	759.1
3. GOVERNMENT EXPENDITURES	1,112.1
4. NET EXPORTS OF GOODS AND SERVICES	−27.1
Total expenditures on GDP	$5,907.0*

NOTE: GDP is in current dollars.
*Estimated by the authors.
SOURCE: Council of Economic Advisors, *Economic Report of the President* (Washington, DC: U.S. Government Printing Office, 1993), pp. 348–49.

BUSINESS SECTOR

Gross private domestic investment is the expenditure on final output by the private, profit-oriented business sector, including both unincorporated enterprises and corporations. This amount was $759.1 billion in 1992 and can be divided into fixed **investment** and change in business inventories. Under the fixed-investment category we find nonresidential and residential. Nonresidential investment consists of expenditures on the construction of buildings such as plants and stores and on producers' durable equipment such as machinery and tools. Residential investment includes expenditures on the construction of new homes by the household sector. Expenditures on fixed investment are taken as a gross value since they include expenditures on *new* plant and equipment and on the *replacement* of worn-out or destroyed capital goods. Changes in business inventories are changes in holdings of finished goods, semi-finished goods, and raw materials by all business concerns. Note that such changes can be positive or negative value. A reduction in inventory stocks is especially likely when GDP growth is accelerating, such as at the beginning of an expansion. Likewise, an increase in inventory stocks is especially likely when GDP growth slows, such as at the beginning of a recession.

INVESTMENT is business spending for capital assets such as plant, equipment, and inventory.

GOVERNMENT SECTOR

The expenditures on final goods and services by the government sector (federal, state, and local) are the third component of GDP. Such expenditures amounted to $1,112.1 billion in 1992. The federal government made purchases of $448.3 billion, and state and local governments made purchases of $663.8 billion. Note that these government purchases of final goods and services were purchased from the household, private business, or foreign sector. Government expenditures such as government transfer payments (i.e., welfare benefits, social security payments, interest on the public debt, and veterans' benefits) and grants-in-aid to state and local governments are not counted as part of GDP. The reason is that no service or production was rendered for the payments received during the given (current) time period.

GOVERNMENT PURCHASES are purchases of goods and services by the government.

FOREIGN SECTOR

Expenditures on final goods and services by the foreign sector, which includes households, businesses, and the governments outside the United States, are the final component of GDP. These expenditures are the **net export** of goods and services, which we add to or subtract from the other three components of GDP to obtain the total expenditures on GDP. The *net* export of goods and services is found by subtracting imports from exports. Net exports may be either a positive or negative value. If positive, then exports exceed imports, and vice versa. For 1992, net exports were negative.

NET EXPORTS are exports minus imports.

Why, exactly, are *net* exports a component of GDP? If we did not import any goods or services from other countries, GDP expenditures could be obtained by simply adding exports to the other three components of GDP. Purchases by the four sectors would indicate their respective demand for U.S. output. But we do import, and imports include purchases of foreign goods and services by the consumer, investment, and government sectors. The national income accountant is unable to determine the kind and amount of imports going to each sector. If we add exports to consumption, investment, and government spending, we would be counting purchases of domestic goods plus purchases of foreign goods included in our measures of consumption, investment, and government spending. This would be GDP plus imports, which would not be a measure of domestic production of goods and services. We do not want to include imports in domestic production, because imports are purchased by U.S. citizens but are not produced in the United States, and so should not be added to GDP. For this reason, we subtract imports from exports to obtain the net exports component of GDP. Let us now turn to a second approach used in measuring national income.

The Flow of Earnings or Income Approach to Gross Domestic Product

NATIONAL INCOME is the total income earned by factors in an economy as they produce goods and services.

In the flow of income approach, **national income** is determined by adding up the income earned by the factors of production (land, labor, capital, entrepreneurial ability) that were employed in producing the final output of goods and services during a given time period. National income for 1992 is shown in Table 2-2 as the summation of items 1 through 5. Let us take a closer look.

- *Compensation of employees* (item 1) is the largest component of national income. It is the sum of the wages and salaries earned by employees and the fringe benefits of employees, such as contributions made by employers to social insurance and to private pension and welfare funds on the behalf of employees.

- *Proprietors' income* (item 2) is income of sole proprietorships and partnerships. This category includes the income of self-employed professionals (doctors, lawyers, etc.) and producers' cooperatives.

- *Rental income of persons* (item 3) includes the income of persons from the rental of real property. The income earned by people in the real estate business, however, is not listed in this category. It is counted as business income and included under either proprietors' income (item 2) or corporate profits (item 4). The rental income of persons also includes royalties received from patents, copyrights, and rights to natural resources. An imputation (estimation) for rental income of self-owned (nonfarm) houses is made to provide similar treatment between rented and self-owned houses.

TABLE 2-2
Gross Domestic Product, 1992, Income Approach (Billions of Dollars)

This table shows the income approach to GDP. National income is the sum of wages, rent, interest, and profit. If we add indirect business taxes and other items to national income, we have net national product. If we add depreciation to net national product, we have GNP. If we add *net* payments of factor income to the rest of the world, we have GDP.

1. COMPENSATION OF EMPLOYEES	$ 3,505.6
2. PROPRIETORS' INCOME	396.5
3. RENTAL INCOME OF PERSONS	1.7
4. CORPORATE PROFITS	382.2
5. NET INTEREST	419.1
National Income (NI)	4,705.1
6. INDIRECT BUSINESS TAXES	499.3
7. OTHER	60.2
Net National Product (NNP)	5,264.6
8. CAPITAL CONSUMPTION ALLOWANCES	655.8
Total Gross National Product (GNP)	5,920.3
9. PLUS: PAYMENT OF FACTOR INCOME TO THE REST OF THE WORLD	117.6
10. MINUS: RECEIPT OF FACTOR INCOME FROM THE REST OF THE WORLD	131.0
Total Gross Domestic Product (GDP)	$5,907.0*

NOTE: These figures are all in current dollars. Subcategories may not total due to rounding.
*Estimated by the authors.
SOURCE: Council of Economic Advisors, *Economic Report of the President* (Washington, DC: U.S. Government Printing Office, 1993), pp. 370–73.

- *Corporate profits* (item 4) include the pretax income of all private corporations, exclusive of intercorporate dividends and capital gains and losses. Also included in corporate profits are net receipts of dividends and branch profits from foreign operations. Profits in this category are defined with respect to federal income tax regulation. In 1992 corporate profits were 8 percent of national income.

- *Net interest* (item 5) is the interest received by U.S. households and governments minus the interest paid by U.S. households and governments. That is, interest *payments* by households and governments (federal, state, and local) are not counted as part of national income, even though interest *received* by households and governments is counted. Why? Interest payments are not considered payment to resources used in current production. Remember that national income accounting is measuring the final output of goods and services over a given (current) period of time. When households or governments buy capital goods, capital goods are not treated as an investment expenditure in the national income accounts.

When businesses buy capital goods (i.e., engage in investment), the capital goods are used to produce goods that can be sold in the market. The profit to businesses and the interest payments of businesses are determined by the market and therefore provide a measure of the return on business investment that can be included in national income. But when governments and households buy capital goods such as roads, schools, and automobiles, they do not sell the services from these goods in the market. Therefore, there is no market-determined measure of investment by government or households. Because interest payments made by governments and households are received by households, however, these interest payments are counted as part of personal income just like transfer payments (i.e., social security and welfare).

The Relationship among GNP, NNP, and National Income

So far, we have found that national income (NI) is the sum of the payments earned by the factors of production. We now want to determine net national product (NNP). GNP does not make an allowance for that part of a year's output which is needed to replace the capital goods used up in production. Net national product (NNP) is the total (net) market value of final goods and services produced in an economy over a given period of time.

Table 2-2 shows that NNP is larger than national income. NNP is determined by adding items 6 and 7 to national income. Let us briefly examine each of these items to determine net domestic product.

- *Indirect business taxes* (item 6) are by far the largest single amount that must be considered in arriving at an estimate of NNP. Indirect taxes are sales and excise taxes. Corporate taxes are not included in this category since these taxes cannot be calculated until the profits have been estimated by the corporation. Because indirect business taxes are costs to the business, the national income accountants assume that the business passes on all of these costs to the buyer in the form of higher prices. But, while the business may cover the costs of its indirect taxes and nontax liabilities, it cannot distribute these costs as part of national income to the factors of production. Why? Indirect taxes and nontax liabilities are collected by the business and transferred to the various government agencies.

In addition to indirect business taxes, other minor items (item 7) such as business transfer payments have to be added to national income to obtain net national product. Business transfer payments include corporate gifts to charitable institutions, cash prizes, and theft or bad debts owed to the business by households. Business transfer payments such as gifts or bad debts are not included in national income since no services were rendered in producing the final output during the current period. Bad debts by households are looked upon by the national income accountants as a gift to the household sector by the business sector.

In Table 2-2 the net national product for 1992 was determined by adding to the national income of $4,705.1 billion, indirect business taxes of $499.3 billion, and other factors of $60.2 billion. The final figure for net national product is $5,264.6 billion.

The Difference between NNP and GNP

The only difference between GNP and NNP is capital depreciation. That is, we have:

$$\text{GNP} = \text{NNP} + \text{Capital depreciation}$$

or

$$\text{NNP} = \text{GNP} - \text{Capital depreciation}$$

Capital consumption allowances or *capital depreciation* (item 8 in Table 2-2) is an adjustment made for the wearing out of capital goods such as building and equipment during the production of output in the current period. This adjustment also includes accidental damage to the capital stock resulting from fire or flood. When capital consumption allowances of $655.8 billion are added to net national product, we have a gross national product of $5,920.3 billion.

The Relationship among National Income, Personal Income, and Disposable Personal Income

Economists are often concerned about the amount of income received by the household sector. Recall that national income is the amount of income earned by the factors of production in producing the final output. That is, national income is net output at factor prices. Personal income is the amount of income received but not necessarily earned during the current period; some households are earning income but not receiving all of it. On the other hand, other households are receiving income but not earning it through current production. For this reason national income is larger or smaller than personal income.

Table 2-3 shows two items that are earned by households but not received in the current period. The first (item 1) is *corporate profits and inventory valuation and capital consumption adjustment.* This includes the corporate profits tax liability, undistributed corporate profits, and the necessary adjustment in the inventory for inflation or deflation so that corporate profits will not be overstated or understated. Corporate profits and inventory valuation must be subtracted from national income since this amount is retained by corporations and not distributed as personal income in the form of dividends to households. The second (item 2), which is earned by households but is not received at the current time, is *contributions for social insurance,* which includes payroll deductions by the employer for social security, medicaid, unemployment compensation, and disability insurance.

Items 3 through 6 in Table 2-3, government transfer payments, interest paid by government (net) and consumers, dividends, and business transfer payments, are received by households and thus are counted as part of personal income. But since these items are not currently earned by households, they are not considered part of the national income total. *Government transfer payments* are payments made by the government sector to the household sector. These payments, which amounted to $834.4 billion in 1992, include social security

TABLE 2-3
National Income, Personal Income, and Disposable Income, 1992

This table depicts the relationship between national income, personal income, and disposable personal income.

National Income	$ 4,705.2
1. MINUS: CORPORATE PROFITS AND INVENTORY VALUATION AND CAPITAL CONSUMPTION ADJUSTMENT	− 382.2
2. MINUS: CONTRIBUTIONS FOR SOCIAL INSURANCE	− 714.3
3. PLUS: GOVERNMENT TRANSFER PAYMENTS	+834.4
4. PLUS: INTEREST PAID BY GOVERNMENT (NET) AND CONSUMERS	+419.1
5. PLUS: DIVIDENDS	+137.2
6. PLUS: BUSINESS TRANSFER PAYMENTS	+24.4
Personal Income	5,023.8
MINUS: PERSONAL TAXES	− 621.8
Disposable Personal Income	$ 4,402.0*

NOTE: Personal income is in billions of current dollars.
*Estimated by the authors.
SOURCE: Council of Economic Advisors, *Economic Report of the President* (Washington, DC: U.S. Government Printing Office, 1993), pp. 371–376.

benefits, pension payments to retired government employees, veterans' benefits, and relief payments. *Interest paid by government (net) and consumers* is subtracted from total interest payments to obtain net interest payments, which are part of national income. The interest paid by government (net) and consumers is treated exactly like transfer payments to households: It is added to national income to get personal income. *Dividends* arise from the ownership of corporate stock by households. Thus, some of corporate profits distributed to households are dividends, which become a part of personal income and are added to national income to derive personal income. *Business transfer payments* such as corporate gifts, and cash prizes, have been discussed in a previous section. Since these payments also constitute personal income to households, they are added to national income.

We note once more that national income may be larger or smaller than personal income. In periods of declining business activity, national income has tended to fall below personal income, because of a decline in corporate profits and a fall in social security contributions resulting from layoffs in manufacturing establishments. National income was below personal income in 1992.

Disposable personal income is income available to households for consumption or saving. In studying household behavior, economists most often use disposable personal income because this is the amount that households have some control over for their own use. We say some control since households already may have debt obligations they have to pay. In Table 2-3, disposable personal income is found by subtracting personal taxes from personal income.

Personal Saving

PERSONAL SAVING is the difference between a person's income and his or her consumption expenditures.

Another important economic quantity is **personal saving.** In Table 2-4, personal saving is found by subtracting personal outlays from disposable personal income. Personal outlays consist of (1) personal consumption expenditures, (2) interest paid by consumers, and (3) personal transfer payments to foreigners. It should be noted that personal saving includes the saving of unincorporated business enterprises.

ACCOUNTING IDENTITIES

AN IDENTITY is a statement that is true by definition.

So far, our discussion has been about national income accounting. Now we turn our attention to certain important accounting **identities**, which are statements that are always true. They should not be taken as statements about economic behavior. Identities are sometimes written mathematically with an ≡ sign and not with an = sign. Understanding of macroeconomic identities is important because it helps us to clarify and organize our thinking about economic activity in the macro world. Macroeconomic identities are used in

TABLE 2-4
Personal Saving, 1992

Personal saving in this table is disposable income minus personal outlays.

DISPOSABLE PERSONAL INCOME	$4,402.0
MINUS: PERSONAL OUTLAYS	
PERSONAL CONSUMPTION EXPENDITURES	4,062.9
INTEREST PAID BY CONSUMERS	112.2
PERSONAL TRANSFER PAYMENTS TO FOREIGNERS	10.2
EQUALS: PERSONAL SAVING	$ 216.7

NOTE: All data are in billions of current dollars.
*Estimated by the authors.
SOURCE: Council of Economic Advisors, *Economic Report of the President* (Washington, DC: U.S. Government Printing Office, 1993), p. 376.

building the macroeconomic models considered in this text. We first examine some national income identities for a basic three-sector economy, and then turn our attention to a four-sector economy.

A three-sector economy contains a household sector, a business sector, and a government sector. The foreign sector is excluded from the analysis. We assume that there are various types of taxes and transfer payments. Further, we assume that there is corporate activity and depreciation of capital equipment. The national income identity for the flow of expenditure approach can be written as

$$Y \equiv C + I + G \tag{2.1}$$

where Y is GDP; C is household consumption expenditures; I is business investment and G is government expenditures (federal, state, and local) on goods and services. Identity 2.1 means that real output (Y) will be consumed by the household, invested by the business in capital goods, or purchased by the government. Part of investment may be in terms of unwanted or unplanned inventories of the business, because any unsold goods that firms produce are included in inventory investment. Because of this, the identity in 2.1 always holds. If output is greater than the purchases made by consumers, government, and businesses, then we just call the excess output unplanned inventory investment.

We also have an identity for the flow of income approach,

$$Y \equiv C + S + T, \tag{2.2}$$

where Y is GDP, C is consumption expenditures, S is private saving (the sum of household and business saving), and T is net tax revenues. Net tax revenues are the difference between gross taxes paid to the government (T_g) and government payments to individuals, which include both transfer payments (TR) and net interest payments (INT). The government's net tax collections are then given by $T = T_g - TR - INT$. Identity 2.2 shows how the expenditure of income in the economy can take place. Subtracting consumption (C) from the left-hand side of identity 2.1 and identity 2.2, we have

$$Y - C \equiv I + G \equiv S + T \tag{2.3}$$

or

$$I + G \equiv S + T. \tag{2.4}$$

We see that in the three-sector economy investment plus government expenditures is identical to private saving plus net tax revenues. Identity 2.4 can be reformulated as

$$S + (T - G) \equiv I. \tag{2.5}$$

The left-hand side of identity 2.5 is total saving for the economy, where S is private saving and $(T - G)$ is public saving. If $T > G$, the government is running a budget surplus, and if $G > T$, the government is experiencing a budget deficit. From identity 2.5, we readily see that the only way saving can be identical to investment is for the government's budget to be balanced.

What if there is a government budget deficit, with $G > T$? Then private saving S must be greater than private investment I. Thus, with a government budget deficit, some of the funds from private saving have to go to finance the budget deficit, which leaves fewer funds to finance private investment.

What happens when we consider a four-sector model? Now there is a business sector, a household sector, a government sector, and a foreign sector. The national income identity for the flow of expenditure approach for this economy is

$$Y \equiv C + I + G + NX, \tag{2.1'}$$

where Y, C, I, and G are as defined above, and NX is net exports (or exports of goods and services minus imports of goods and services). Identity 2.1' says that real output (Y) will be consumed by the household, invested by the business in capital goods, purchased by the government, or purchased by foreigners net of our purchases of foreign goods.

The identity for the flow of income approach can still be written as

$$Y \equiv C + S + T, \tag{2.2}$$

where Y, C, S, and T have been defined above. Subtracting consumption from the left-hand side of identity 2.1' and identity 2.2, we have

$$Y - C \equiv I + G + NX \equiv S + T \tag{2.3'}$$

or

$$I + G + NX \equiv S + T. \tag{2.4'}$$

HOW THE U.S. ECONOMY FINANCED THE GOVERNMENT BUDGET DEFICIT IN 1991

In the text we have seen how the government budget deficit is linked to investment, saving, and net exports. In this way, the economy finances the government budget deficit by either an increase in private saving, a reduction in private investment, or a decrease in net exports. The reduction in net exports signifies additional saving by foreigners to purchase U.S. assets, including government debt. The national income accounting identity from the text can be written as

$$I + (G - T) \equiv S - NX.$$

What were the figures for saving, the government budget deficit, private investment, and net exports in 1991? In current dollars, investment was $721.1 billion, and the government budget deficit was $193.3 billion. These were the demands for funds to finance investment and government borrowing. The sources of funds to meet these demands were private saving of $901.5 billion, and *negative* net exports, or foreign saving, of −$21.8 billion. Thus, the demand for funds $I + (G - T)$ totaled $914.4 billion, and the supply of funds $S - NX$ was $901.5 billion − (−$21.8 billion) or $923.3 billion. The difference between these two figures is called a statistical discrepancy in the national income accounts, since these two totals should be equal.

What happens if the government deficit increases? Either investment must fall, or the supply of funds must increase. The supply of funds can increase if either private saving increases or net exports decreases signifying foreign supply of funds to finance investment and the deficit. ❑

In our four-sector economy we find that it is investment plus government expenditures plus net exports that is identical to private saving plus net tax revenues. Thus, identity 2.4′ can be rewritten as

$$S + (T - G) - NX \equiv I. \tag{2.1′}$$

The left-hand side of identity 2.5′ is total saving for the economy, which includes private saving S, government (or public) saving $(T - G)$, and net foreign funds $-NX$. These three sources of funds provide the savings available to fund investment. As indicated in the discussion of identity 2.5 in the three-sector case, public plus private saving or $S + (T - G)$ is national saving, while $-NX$ is net foreign funds available to fund investment in the United States. These net foreign funds are the negative of net exports. If net exports are positive, then the United States is selling more goods abroad than foreigners are purchasing from the United States, resulting in an accumulation of foreign funds in the United States. These funds will be used to purchase assets in foreign countries, since foreign currency cannot be used to purchase domestic assets in the United States. Thus, a balance of trade surplus $NX > 0$ reduces the supply of funds available to fund investment in the United States. Likewise, when net exports are negative, foreigners sell more goods in the United States than the United States sells abroad. Foreigners therefore on net accumulate U.S. funds, which they will use to purchase assets in the United States. Thus, a U.S. balance of trade deficit $NX < 0$ increases the funds available to fund investment in the United States.

Consider a case where we begin with $S = I$, $G = T$, and $NX = 0$. What happens if the government begins to run a budget deficit, so that $T - G < 0$. From identity 2.5′, we see that one of three things must happen. Private saving S must increase to cover the reduction in public saving, investment I must decrease because there are fewer funds available, or net exports NX must become negative so that foreigners can make up for the decreased public saving with an increased flow of funds to the United States. Thus, an increase in the government budget deficit must induce one or more of these changes in order to keep identity 2.5′ in force. (For an example of how the U.S. government budget deficit appears in the accounting identities for the United States, see the Insight: "How the U.S. Economy Financed the Government Budget Deficit in 1991.")

Interactions between exports and imports and the monetary flows accompanying international transactions are summarized in an economic measure called the balance of payments. An understanding of the balance of payments is essential given the important and increasing impact that international trade is having on the United States economy. This understanding will form the basis of an entire chapter (Chapter 7) on international trade and finance.

THE BALANCE OF PAYMENTS

BALANCE OF PAYMENTS is a statement of the money value of all transactions between a country and the rest of the world during a given period of time.

The **balance of payments** (BP) is a summary statement of the flow of economic transactions between the residents of one country and the rest of the world over a given period of time. This summary statement comprises such items as exports and imports of all goods and services; all capital loans abroad and all borrowing from foreign countries; all gifts to and from foreign countries, including foreign aid; and all movements of goods and international reserves into and out of the country. For the United States, the Department of Commerce is charged with the responsibility of calculating the balance of payments.

A DEBIT is any transaction that results in a money outflow or payment to a foreign country.

A CREDIT is any transaction that results in a money inflow or receipt from a foreign country.

How are debits and credits defined in international transactions? A **debit** represents the importing of an item such as a good, a service, a stock or a bond, a bank deposit, or gold. A debit item gives a nation a demand for foreign currency. It receives a negative sign (–) in the balance of payments table. A **credit** represents the exporting of an item such as a good, a service, a stock or a bond, a bank deposit, or gold. A credit item gives a nation a supply of foreign money. It receives a positive (+) in the balance of payments table.

To understand exactly how items are recorded as debits and credits in the U.S. balance of payments table, consider a few examples. Suppose a U.S. household purchases a car from Japan. The import of the car into the United States is recorded on the debit side (–). Notice also that in creating a debit the U.S. household has increased its demand for foreign currency, the Japanese yen.

In a second example, suppose a U.S. business sells a bond to a British household. The U.S. business, then, has exported a bond. This would appear on the credit side (+).

In yet another example, let us assume that a U.S. citizen travels as a tourist in West Germany. How is this vacation classified in the balance of payments? The U.S. citizen is considered to have purchased (imported) a service from a foreign country, which is a debit (–).

In a final example, suppose the U.S. government gives wheat to Egypt. The exporting of a good (wheat), even if it is a gift, is recorded as a credit (+). The giving of the gift by the United States is called a unilateral transfer to Egypt.

A simplified version of the standard method of reporting the balance of payments is shown in Table 2-5. The balance of payments table is often divided by economists into three sections: (1) current account, (2) capital account, and (3) method of financing the deficit or surplus. In Table 2-5, the word *net* is used to indicate the difference between the debit item and the credit item. The current account consists of the exporting and importing of current goods and services and unilateral transfers. In the merchandise category, we recall from our classification of debits and credits that the exporting of a current good is a credit (+) and the importing of a current good is a debit (–). In the service category, we include military expenditures, travel (tourists, etc.) and transportation (shipping services, etc.), and investment income (dividends, interest, royalties, foreign earnings). For investment income, we list the payment, such as interest, rather than the item for which the payment is made (e.g., capital services). The summation of the merchandise category (A) and the service category (B) is the balance of goods and services (A + B). This balance is often called net exports of goods and services, and as we now know, it is one of the components of national income.

The unilateral transfers classification refers to transfers of resources (money or real goods) for which no payment is expected in return. Under unilateral transfers, we find a category for government grants, which is essentially the foreign aid program, and a category for remittances and pensions, which includes such items as gifts sent to and received from foreign countries and pension payments made to households overseas. The summation of merchandise (A), services (B), and unilateral transfers (C) is known as the balance on current account (A + B + C).

The second major section of the balance of payments is the capital account. This account, which includes both long-term and short-term capital move-

This table indicates how the U.S. balance of payments is calculated. The current account consists of net exports of goods and services, and net transfers and interest payments to U.S. residents; the capital account consists of net capital flows into the United States; and the financing method indicates how the United States settles its official transactions with foreign countries.

I. Current account

   A. Merchandise

      1. Exports (+)

      2. Imports (–)

   B. Services

      1. Military (net)

      2. Travel and transportation (net)

      3. Investment income (net)

Balance of goods and services = $A + B$

   C. Unilateral transfers

      1. Government grants (excluding military)

      2. Remittances and pensions

Balance on current account = $A + B + C$

II. Capital account

   D. Long-term capital movements or flows

   E. Short-term capital movements or flows

Official reserve transactions balance = $A + B + C + D + E$

"The line"_____

III. Financing (deficit or surplus) method

   F. U.S. official reserve assets (net)

   G. U.S. liabilities to foreign official agencies

ments, records lending and borrowing by U.S. households, businesses, and financial institutions. If the United States lends to a foreign country, it imports securities (e.g., bonds) or IOUs, which are entered as debits (–). Borrowing by the United States from foreign countries is registered as a credit (+) since the United States exports securities (e.g., bonds) or IOUs. The distinction between short-term and long-term capital movements is arbitrary, and the dividing line between the two has been set at one year. Any loan contract or security that has one year or less in maturity is classified as short term. Bank demand deposits are considered short-term assets since they are payable on demand. Monetary gold is also treated as a short-term asset in the balance of payments.

Adding the current account to the capital account gives the official reserve transactions (ORT) balance. The ORT balance is important since it is what economists or politicians often refer to when they speak of a surplus or a deficit in the balance of payments. If the ORT balance is positive, then there is a surplus, and if it is negative, then there is a deficit. Notice that we have drawn what is called "the line" below the ORT balance. The question of where to draw "the line" has been a subject of controversy. Some have preferred to draw "the line" in Table 2-5 between long-term and short-term capital movements since short-term assets are temporary and can be withdrawn at a moment's notice. For our present purposes, we will accept the ORT balance as "the line" to examine for a deficit or a surplus in the U.S. balance of payments.

The final category in Table 2-5 is financing method. It shows how a deficit or a surplus is financed. An ORT surplus or an ORT deficit has to be equal to the sum of the increase or decrease in U.S. official reserve assets (F) plus the decrease or increase in liabilities to foreign central banks (G). The official reserve assets of the United States include (1) gold, (2) convertible (foreign) currencies, (3) reserve position at the International Monetary Fund (IMF)[4] and (4) Special Drawing Rights (SDRs).[5]

To understand what the expression "U.S. liabilities to foreign official agencies" (foreign central banks) means, let us use an example. Suppose our imports of goods are greater than our exports of goods. Checks (dollars) from the United States will flow to foreign businesses, which will, in turn, exchange these checks at their banks for their own foreign currencies. Foreign central banks will end up with the U.S. checks (dollars) and will therefore have a claim on demand deposits in U.S. banks. Thus, the U.S. deficit in its trade balance is made up by a credit in U.S. liabilities to foreign official agencies. In essence, the trade deficit has been financed by U.S. borrowing from those foreign central banks that hold claims on the demand deposits of U.S. banks.

OTHER IMPORTANT ECONOMIC INDICATORS

Along with "national income" and international economic measures such as the balance of payments, economists examine other indicators to determine the

---

[4]The International Monetary Fund (IMF) was established at the Bretton Woods Conference in 1944. Today, more than 130 countries are members of the IMF. Each member country subscribes to the capital of the IMF on the basis of a quota, determined by the country's importance with regard to international trade, national income, and population. A major purpose of the IMF is to lend foreign currencies to a member country that is experiencing a balance of payments deficit, in order to supplement its holdings of foreign exchange reserves.

[5]Special Drawing Rights (SDRs) were created by the IMF in 1968 because of a world shortage of international liquidity. The SDR is the official unit of account that is used between the IMF, central banks, and governments. It is composed of sixteen major currencies that are weighted according to their importance in the world.

economic performance of the U.S. economy. The most important ones are the unemployment rate and various price indices.

The Unemployment Rate

The first indicator we want to address deals with civilian unemployment. The question is, how are employment and unemployment measured in the United States? Data on employed and unemployed workers are collected by the Bureau of the Census. Since the Bureau of the Census cannot count each and every person in the United States each month to determine who has a job and who does not, it surveys a sample of households (around 60,000), called the current population survey (CPS). The survey is designed so that every civilian (that is, those persons not in the military service) sixteen years of age or over and not in an institution such as a prison or mental hospital is classified as either in the labor force or not in the labor force. Every person interviewed is placed in one of these two groups. Since January 1983, figures on the Armed Forces members stationed in the United States have been added to the CPS estimate to derive estimates of the **total labor force**.

People counted and classified in the group called the **civilian labor force** are either employed or unemployed. Persons counted and classified in the group called "not in the labor force" are persons who either have no job or are not looking for one. Among those classified as not in the labor force are (1) many students, (2) persons working only in the home, (3) persons with disabilities, and (4) retired persons.

THE TOTAL LABOR FORCE are those persons who are employed and those who are unemployed among nonmilitary persons, plus those persons employed by the military.

THE CIVILIAN LABOR FORCE is those persons who are employed and those who are unemployed among nonmilitary persons.

WHO IS COUNTED AS EMPLOYED IN THE CIVILIAN LABOR FORCE?

People are counted as employed if they did any work at all for pay or for profit during the survey week. This includes all part-time and temporary work as well as regular full-time year-round employment. Unpaid family workers are also considered employed if they worked fifteen hours or more without pay in a family-operated enterprise. If, during the survey week, a person was on vacation, was ill, was involved in an industrial dispute, was prevented from working by weather conditions, or was taking time off for personal reasons, he or she is still counted as employed.

The Bureau of the Census defines the unemployed as those persons who were available for work but did not have a job during the survey week and had actively looked for work in the past four weeks (for example, by going on job interviews or registering with employment offices). Two groups of people who do not have to look for a job to be counted as unemployed are persons waiting to start a new job within thirty days and workers waiting to be recalled from layoff. Early each month, the Bureau of Labor Statistics of the Department of Labor, using the data compiled by the Bureau of the Census, reports the total

number of employed and unemployed workers in the United States for the previous month.[6]

Figure 2-6 shows the growth in the civilian labor force in millions of persons and the fluctuations in employment and unemployment during the 1955–1992 period. The level of business activity is a major determinant of the amount of unemployment. Note the sharp rise in unemployment during recent recessions: 1974–75, 1981–82, and 1990–91.

How the Unemployment Rate is Determined

Now that we have an understanding of how civilian employment and unemployment are measured, how exactly is the unemployment rate determined? The **unemployment rate** is defined as a percentage of the civilian and military labor force and is found by dividing the number of unemployed persons by the total labor force. Thus, the unemployment rate is $UE = U/LF$, where UE is the unemployment rate, U is the number of unemployed persons, and LF is the total number of persons in the labor force.[7]

Table 2-6 shows the unemployment rate, unemployment, and the total labor force for the 1980–1992 period. The Bureau of Labor Statistics also

THE UNEMPLOYMENT RATE is the percentage of the total labor force that is unemployed.

---

[6]For further details on how unemployment is measured, see U.S. Department of Labor, Bureau of Labor Statistics, *Handbook of Methods,* BLS Bulletin 2285 (Washington, DC: U.S. Government Printing Office, 1988).

[7]Recall that the total labor force comprises the total of all civilians classified as employed or unemployed, and the resident members of the Armed Forces.

FIGURE 2-6
The Civilian Labor Force,
Total Employment, and the
Unemployment Rate,
1955–1992.

These figures illustrate the growth in the labor force and employment
over these years, as well as the behavior of the unemployment rate during this period.

The Civilian Labor Force and Total Employment,
1955–1992, (Thousands of Persons)

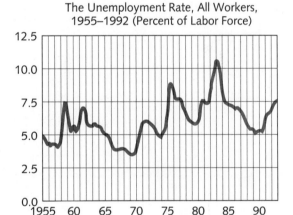

The Unemployment Rate, All Workers,
1955–1992 (Percent of Labor Force)

NOTE: The unemployment rate is measured as the percent of the labor force not employed. The civilian labor force and employment are measured as thousands of persons.
SOURCE: U.S. Department of Labor, Bureau of Labor Statistics

breaks down the total unemployment rate into various groups, which helps to
indicate the extent of unemployment within particular groups. For example,
Figure 2-7 shows the total unemployment rate for the U.S. economy and the
unemployment rate by race, sex, and age for the 1954–1992 period. Notice
that minority groups have a higher rate of unemployment than do whites.

TABLE 2-6
Estimation of the Unemployment Rate, 1980–1992

The unemployment rate is estimated in the table by dividing the number of unemployed persons by the number of persons in the total labor force.

YEAR	UNEMPLOYMENT RATE	UNEMPLOYMENT	TOTAL LABOR FORCE
1980	7.0	7,637	108,544
1981	7.5	8,273	110,315
1982	9.5	10,678	111,872
1983	9.5	10,717	113,226
1984	7.4	8,539	115,241
1985	7.1	8,312	117,167
1986	6.9	8,237	119,540
1987	6.1	7,425	121,602
1988	5.4	6,701	123,378
1989	5.2	6,528	125,557
1990	5.4	6,874	126,424
1991	6.6	8,426	126,867
1992	7.3	9,384	128,548*

NOTE: The total labor force and unemployment are in thousands of persons.
*Estimated by the authors.
SOURCE: Council of Economic Advisors. *Economic Report of the President* (Washington, DC: U.S. Government Printing Office, 1993), p. 382.

Moreover, teenagers in the sixteen-to-nineteen age group have a higher rate of unemployment than do any other age group. Further, Figure 2-7 shows that women who are twenty years of age or older had slightly lower rates of unemployment than did men of the same age classification in 1991–1992 although the difference has varied over the past. Thus, we find that while it is important to examine the total unemployment rate as an indicator of the overall health of the economy, there are also important differences in the pattern of employment and unemployment among various groups in the economy.

WHAT IS MEANT BY THE TERM FULL EMPLOYMENT?

Under the Employment Act of 1946, the federal government was charged with the responsibility of promoting "maximum employment." The act never

These figures illustrate the unemployment rates of various population groupings during this period.

Unemployment Rates for Whites, Non-whites, and All Workers, 1955–1992 (Percent)

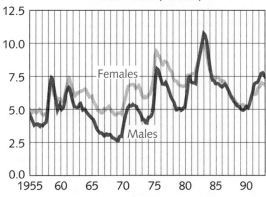

Unemployment Rates for Males and Females, 1955–1992 (Percent)

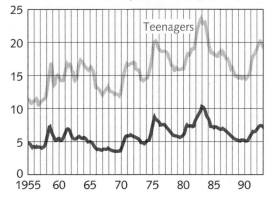

Unemployment Rate for Teenagers and for All Workers, 1955–1992 (Percent)

NOTE: The unemployment rate is measured as the percent of the labor force for each group that is not employed.
SOURCE: U.S. Department of Labor, Bureau of Labor Statistics.

specifically stated "full employment." In 1978, however, Congress committed itself to full employment by passing the Full Employment and Balanced Growth (Humphrey-Hawkins) Act. This act set forth specific objectives for both the unemployment rate and the inflation rate. An interim goal of the act was that unemployment not exceed 3 percent among individuals aged twenty and over, and 4 percent among individuals aged sixteen and over. The act also set an inflation goal of 3 percent by the early 1980s and zero by 1988, provided that achieving the inflation goal did not impede achieving the unemployment goal. According to the act, the President of the United States can modify the timetable for achievement of the interim and final goals for unemployment. Since 1973, however, the unemployment rate has not fallen below 5 percent. Many economists now consider 4 percent too low and believe that the full-employment rate should be 5–7 percent. By comparison, in early 1993 the actual unemployment rate stood at 7.1 percent.

The **NATURAL RATE OF UNEMPLOYMENT** consists of frictional and structural unemployment.

In trying to make sense of the unemployment rate, economists have developed the theoretical concept of the *natural rate of unemployment*. This idea will be analyzed in more detail later, but the basic concept will be introduced here. In brief, the natural rate of unemployment consists of what is called frictional unemployment and structural unemployment. Frictional unemployment is the unemployment that occurs because it takes time for workers departing one job to find another, even in a fully employed economy. Structural unemployment is brought about by changes in the basic characteristics of a market, such as new substitute products, a change in consumer tastes, or new technology of production. Because of these changes new job vacancies require skills or locations other than those available to the unemployed workers. The unemployment that occurs during downturns in the business cycle is called cyclical unemployment, and is *not* included in the natural rate.

The Labor Department's Bureau of Labor Statistics has developed a new definition of unemployment, implemented in January 1994. This measure (first published in February 1994) includes so-called discouraged workers in its definition. In the version adopted by the Labor Department in 1967, a person must have looked for work at some time in the previous four weeks. Otherwise, individuals in the 60,000 households interviewed were not considered members of the labor force even though the person was willing to work. Such "discouraged workers" will be captured by a new and more complex questionnaire developed by the Bureau.

The new computerized responses to the questionnaire (with 128 possible questions instead of 45 questions) will, it is argued, enable the Labor Department to pinpoint the meaning of other important data related to employment. These include "layoffs" (do individuals expect to return to their jobs?), "part-time jobs" (how many people are holding two jobs—not asked in the older questionnaire), and the male-female pay differentials (has the real 1970–1992 differential shrunk from 59 percent of what men earn to 77 percent as the current questionnaire suggests?). The difference in the rate using the new questionnaire and the traditional definition of the jobless rate is clearly significant: The rate *with* discouraged workers in 1992 was over 10 percent versus about 7 percent under the traditional definition, although the difference will vary over time. It remains to be seen how the new definition will be used and viewed in the business and political arenas.

The domestic unemployment rate is also increasingly affected by the status of United States trade relations. Clearly an increase in exports to other countries expands jobs. Tens and even hundreds of thousands of new jobs, according to some estimates, result when U.S. exports increase by a billion dollars. While free trade has been defended by economists, there is obviously a downside when domestic jobs are displaced. The ongoing economic and political debate over "free trade" versus "fair trade" has enormous implications for the future employment prospects for Americans. (See Global Perspective: "Domestic Employment, Protection, and Trade" for a discussion of some of these issues.)

PRICE INDICES: THE PROBLEM OF INFLATION MEASUREMENT

A second important issue indicating the economic performance of the economy is the construction of an "appropriate" price index with which to measure inflation. While numerous price indices are constructed and reported in the United States, there is no such thing as a perfect price index that is correct for every person because any price index will understate inflation for some households and overstate it for others. Those receiving the most attention are (1) the consumer price index, (2) the producer price index, and (3) the implicit price deflator.

The Consumer Price Index

The consumer price index is a statistical measure of a weighted average of prices for a specified set of goods and services purchased by urban consumers. The Bureau of Labor Statistics (BLS) at the Department of Labor calculates not one but two consumer price indices.[8] The BLS issues a consumer price index called CPI-W (an updated version of the unrevised CPI index), which measures price changes in a typical market basket of goods and services purchased by urban wage earners and clerical workers. The CPI market basket

---

[8]Until 1978, only one CPI was calculated by the BLS. Since this index represented only wage earners and clerical workers, the BLS felt that a more comprehensive consumer price index was needed because there had been substantial changes in what people were buying and in the way they were living. The BLS noted that the two-worker family had not only raised the income level of the family but changed family buying habits.

DOMESTIC EMPLOYMENT, PROTECTION, AND TRADE

Special interests are attached to virtually all policies, activities, and regulations of government at all levels in the United States. Nowhere does this apply more than in tariffs, quotas, and other regulations affecting international trade. Economists generally defend free and unfettered trade according to the law of comparative advantage. This involves the reduction and ultimate elimination of trade barriers in order to create maximum global specialization. Others support what they call *fair trade*. In their view, free trade should be amended in light of "unfair subsidies" by foreign governments, to cheap foreign labor, and by foreign government policies that pay too little attention to the environment. As such, the domestic employment issue has taken center stage in contemporary debates concerning trade liberalization.

Most economists argue that protection for any reason, including those reasons given for "fair" trade, reduces the welfare of all consuming Americans and future job seekers *by more* than it would benefit particular groups and special interests in the United States. A whole host of economists have argued that the cost of such protection, in terms of lower prices foregone and the misallocation of resources in the United States, could ultimately cost the United States economic leadership in the twenty-first century. This is especially so since much modern technology is available to all international players in the trade game—the United States no longer holds exclusive rights to that magic key to growth. It is equally clear that international trade is an increasingly important ingredient in the employment prospects for Americans and in economic growth.

Enter the possibilities offered by multilateral tariff reductions (GATT or the General Agreement on Tariffs and Trade) and by a new trade bloc (NAFTA or the North American Free Trade Agreement). Special interests, especially labor interests who have benefitted from tariff protection at the expense of consumers, are crying foul. Their arguments, in the case of NAFTA, are that American businesses will follow low wages to Mexico where some workers (in agricultural and raw materials production and processing) receive less than $1 per hour. U.S. interests pressuring politicians for continued protection (that is, rejecting NAFTA and GATT agreements) argue that we should not support such "slave labor" and "exploitation."

American special interests—both businesses and labor—often neglect to mention the costs to Americans of continued protection. Consider some examples. The Congressional Budget Office calculated the cost to American consumers of maintaining protection on textiles as $9,000 to $38,000 per textile worker per year *over and above* the wages of textile workers.[a] The U.S. Department of Agriculture estimates that Georgia peanuts cost $491 per metric ton to produce, but that the world market price is about $300 per ton. The USDA peanut price-support program allows U.S. farmers to sell peanuts in the U.S. market for more than $600 per ton. U.S. consumers pay more because there is a virtual ban on importation of the legumes.[b]

Americans, who must endure higher prices, are losers in both the short and long run. As noted, artificially higher prices will be paid with differences over and above the wages paid in protected industries. Wages will fall over the long term due to an increasing lack of competitiveness in the world economy. Protected industries will have little incentive to modernize or to develop new technologies. More importantly, perhaps, the killing of NAFTA by protectionist labor interests will not stem the drain of businesses to low-wage countries.

Thailand, China, and the Russian republics are all advertising for U.S. investors. Most critically, the uncertain maintenance of employment through protection will mean that hundreds of thousands of new jobs will *not* be created through enhanced *export* trade. American workers will likely have more competition from illegal immigrants from Mexico and other countries (which might fail to develop without free trade).

Protectionist arguments concerning "cheap foreign labor" carry little weight when all benefits and costs of freer trade are considered. ❏

_____

[a]Rudy Dornbusch, quoted in "Lost Labor?", *Wall Street Journal* (September 24, 1992), p. R10.
[b]David Goldberg, "Trade Pacts Inspiring Sour Taste in U.S. Peanut Belt," *Richmond Times Dispatch* (December 26, 1992), p. B10.

is developed from detailed information that families and single individuals provide on what they actually buy. About 4,800 "consumer units," or households of related or unrelated individuals who pool their funds for consumer purchases, provided information on their spending habits in a consumer expenditure survey conducted in the 1982–1984 period. The market basket of goods and services is broken down into six categories: food, housing, apparel, transportation, health and recreation, and miscellaneous services. To measure price changes in the market basket, the BLS collects data from a wide variety of retail stores and service establishments.

The BLS also publishes a consumer price index for all urban consumers, CPI-U. The new CPI reflects the buying habits of about 80 percent of the noninstitutional, civilian population of the United States. It includes self-employed, professional, managerial, and technical workers, groups whose incomes are generally higher than average; and short-term workers, the unemployed, retirees, and others not in the labor force, groups whose incomes tend to be lower than average. Both the CPI-W for wage earners and clerical workers and the CPI-U for all urban consumers have a reference base of 1982–1984 = 100. Over this base period, the price index averages 100, because this period, or **base year,** is the point of reference for comparison of prices in other years.

BASE YEAR is the year against which comparisons of relative changes are made.

Besides being used as one of the indicators of inflation, the CPI is also used as an "escalator" or an adjustment of salaries for inflation. Escalator clauses in collective bargaining contracts by unions covering millions of workers tie workers' wages to the CPI. Also, people on social security, retired military and federal civil service employees, and food stamp recipients have their pensions or other income adjusted to the CPI. In fact, it was fear by some of these groups that the new CPI-U would not reflect the same changes in prices as the older CPI-W that led these groups, especially the unions, to push for publication of both series.

WHAT THE CPI IS NOT.

The Bureau of Labor Statistics is very careful to point out that the CPI is a price index and not a cost-of-living index. The CPI does not consider any adjustment in consumer spending patterns in response to changes in relative prices. Because the CPI ignores this substitution toward goods whose prices have risen very little and away from items whose prices have risen sharply, it overstates the true change in the cost of living. For example, if the price of coffee rises rapidly relative to the price of tea, then consumers may buy more tea and less coffee. The CPI does not take into consideration the possibility of such substitutions.

The Producer Price Index

The second major index published by the Bureau of Labor Statistics is the producer price index, previously known as the wholesale price index. The producer price index is a statistical measure of prices of those commodities that businesses purchase from each other. This index covers about 3,000 commodities and measures price movements in primary markets by producers of commodities in all stages of processing. The products range from raw materials such as steel to lubricating products such as oil.

The prices reported are those of the first significant transaction in which the commodities were involved. The BLS collects about 10,000 price quotations every month from producing companies. These quotations are used to calculate various producer price indices, which are in turn aggregated into successively broader commodity groups. At each successive stage of aggregation, the indices are averaged using weights that reflect the total value of all shipments of a product class in the base year of 1982.

Usually the producer price index and the consumer price index move in similar ways. This can be seen in Table 2-7, which shows both of these indices for the years 1975–1992. The general movements in both indices are the same.

The Implicit Price Deflator

A final major index is the implicit price deflator for GDP, which pertains to the measurement of real output discussed at the beginning of this chapter. The

TABLE 2-7
The Consumer Price Index and the Producer Price Index, 1975-1992

The CPI and PPI both vary over the business cycle, but have stabilized at low rates of increase over the past few years.

YEAR	CPI	PPI
1975	53.8	58.2
1976	56.9	60.8
1977	60.6	64.7
1978	65.2	69.8
1979	72.6	77.6
1980	82.4	88.0
1981	90.9	96.1
1982	96.5	100.0
1983	99.6	101.6
1984	103.9	103.7
1985	107.6	104.7
1986	109.6	103.2
1987	113.6	105.4
1988	118.3	108.0
1989	124.0	113.6
1990	130.7	119.2
1991	136.2	121.7
1992	140.2	123.1*

NOTE: *Estimated by the authors.
SOURCE: Council of Economic Advisors, *Economic Report of the President* (Washington, DC: U.S. Government Printing Office, 1993), pp. 411, 417.

implicit price deflator is a measure of the changes in prices of all goods and services produced in the economy. The main concern of national income accountants is to measure the nation's real output of goods and services for a given time period, but the physical amounts of goods and services (e.g., apples, pizzas, and TV repairs) cannot be summed. Only the dollar amounts of goods and services produced can be added.

The use of market prices presents a problem in arriving at meaningful comparisons of gross domestic product (GDP) in different time periods. A problem exists because *both* market prices and real output change over time. An inspection of GDP for two different time periods, such as 1990 and 1991,

TABLE 2-8
Current GDP, the GDP Deflator, and Real GDP for the United States, 1972–1992

The relationship between these three variables is that the GDP deflator is equal to current GDP divided by real GDP, mutliplied by 100.

YEAR	CURRENT GDP ($ BILLIONS)	GDP DEFLATOR	CONSTANT GDP ($ BILLIONS)
1972	1,207.0	38.8	3,110.8
1973	1,349.6	41.3	3,267.7
1974	1,458.6	44.9	3,248.1
1975	1,585.9	49.2	3,223.3
1976	1,768.4	52.3	3,381.2
1977	1,974.1	55.9	3,531.4
1978	2,232.7	60.3	3,702.6
1979	2,488.3	65.5	3,798.9
1980	2,708.0	71.7	3,776.3
1981	3,030.6	78.9	3,841.0
1982	3,149.6	83.8	3,758.4
1983	3,405.0	87.2	3,904.8
1984	3,777.2	91.0	4,150.7
1985	4,038.7	94.4	4,278.2
1986	4,268.6	96.9	4,418.8
1987	4,539.9	100.0	4,539.9
1988	4,900.4	103.9	4,716.4
1989	5,250.8	108.5	4,839.4
1990	5,522.2	113.2	4,878.2
1991	5,677.5	117.8	4,819.6
1992	5,907.0	120.6	4,898.0*

NOTE: The base level for the GDP deflator is in 1987. Current GDP and real GDP are equal in 1987.
*Estimated by the authors.
SOURCE: Council of Economic Advisors, *Economic Report of the President* (Washington, DC: U.S. Government Printing Office, 1993), pp. 348, 350.

may indicate that GDP has risen. That is, it may appear to indicate that growth of goods and services has occurred. But in actuality the increase in GDP may have been due to a rise in market prices (inflation) and the real output of goods and services may have remained constant or may even have fallen. Remember that the economist is interested in measuring the economy's *real* output.

Therefore, the national income accountants along with the economists make a very careful distinction between GDP in *current* dollars and GDP in *constant* dollars.

The implicit price deflator is found by dividing current (nominal) GDP by its constant GDP value in 1987 prices. In 1985, for example, current GDP was $4,038.7 billion, and constant GDP (in 1987 prices) was $4,279.8 billion. The implicit price deflator for GDP was 4,038.7/4,279.8 = 0.94, indicating that there was a 6 percent rise in the price level over the 1985–1987 period.

To clearly see the relationship between GDP in current (nominal) dollars and constant dollars and the implicit price deflator for GDP, divide the GDP in current dollars for 1985 by its implicit price deflator for GDP for 1985. This will give GDP in constant dollars in base year prices.[9] The 1985 constant-dollar (real) GDP in terms of 1987 dollars is

$$\text{Constant GDP} = \frac{4,038.7}{94.4} \times 100 = \$4,279.8 \text{ billion.}$$

Therefore, constant-dollar (real) GDP tells us what today's real output of goods and services would be worth had it been sold in the marketplace in 1987. In other words, if there had been no inflation or rising price level from 1985 to 1987, real GDP would have been worth $4,279.8 billion in 1985. Table 2-8 shows GDP in current and constant terms and the implicit price deflator for GDP for the period 1972–1992.

It is interesting to note that in the recessions of 1974–75, 1981–82, and most recently 1990–91, GDP in current dollars was rising, but constant-dollar (real) GDP was falling, a fact also indicated in Figure 2-1. Therefore, GDP by itself is not a useful measure of the current state of the economy. To measure the real economic performance of the economy in terms of final goods and services produced, we must look at and use real, or constant-dollar, GDP.

SUMMARY

Clearly, no economic data or measurement of any kind—be it of output growth, employment, or inflation—is perfect. Standards of "absolute accuracy" are not possible but, as we have seen with employment statistics, refinements and alterations in measurements are constantly taking place. Political parties, stock markets, and international financial prospects rise and fall on the basis of such data, however imperfect they may be. The assembly and use of data, however, is most critical for the macroeconomist. Numbers correspond to theoretical categories and refer to important features of our economic lives.

The present chapter has looked at the measurement of some key macroeconomic variables in the U.S. economy. The variables on which we have focused are output, employment and unemployment, and the price level. We have

---

[9]The base period is 1987 = 100. GDP is the same in current and constant dollars for 1987.

provided a look at the current state of the economy as revealed by measures of real GDP, real personal income and disposable personal income, various unemployment rates, and statistics on the price level. In the course of this chapter we have reviewed national income accounting, balance of payments accounting, and some national accounting identities, and discussed in detail the unemployment statistics and price indices. Although this chapter has discussed only how these variables are measured in the real world and not how they are determined, variables such as these will appear in macro models developed in later chapters. Explaining how and why economic quantities such as prices, output, and employment are what they are is exactly the job of the macroeconomic theorist. We must, in other words, go behind what is happening in the economy to seek an explanation of *why* it is happening. Economists have been dealing with and dissecting the possible causes of macroeconomic events for over two hundred years. These explanations, or *macroeconomic theories,* especially as they apply to the U.S. economy, will be revealed in the remainder of this book.

KEY TERMS

balance of payments	national income
base year	natural rate of unemployment
business cycles	net exports
civilian labor force	personal income
consumption	personal saving
disposable personal income	total labor force
government purchases	transfer payments
gross domestic product	unemployment rate
gross national product	value-added
investment	

QUESTIONS FOR REVIEW AND DISCUSSION

1. Given American society's trend toward increased urbanization and industrialization, *ceteris paribus,* is the national income accountants' measure of GDP more accurate today than it was in the 1930s? If so, why?

2. What are two approaches used to estimate GDP?

3. What is the relationship between gross domestic product, gross national product, net national product, national income, personal income, and disposable personal income?

4. In the definition of GDP, the word *final* is found. Why? Are intermediate goods counted in GDP? If not, why not?

5. Why is the interest paid by the government on government debt treated like a transfer payment in the national income accounts?

6. Do the national income accountants include the value of stocks and bonds in GDP? If not, why not? What about the stockbrokers who sell stocks and bonds? Are their salaries measured in GDP? If so, why?

7. List three reasons why GDP should not be thought of as a measure of society's well-being.

8. Who is counted as unemployed in the labor force?

9. How is the unemployment rate determined?

10. What are the two major price indices published by the Bureau of Labor Statistics? How do they differ?

11. Why does the BLS not consider the consumer price index (CPI) to be a cost-of-living index?

12. Why have unions pushed to have both CPI series published?

13. What is the relationship between GDP in nominal and constant dollars and the implicit price deflator for GDP?

14. Characterize the relationship between per capita real GDP and the unemployment rate. Does the unemployment rate rise when per capita real GDP falls? Does it always fall when per capita real GDP rises?

15. Other than the magnitude of the unemployment rates, do the rates for teenagers and for nonwhites follow the general pattern of the white unemployment rate? Why do you think this is or isn't so?

PROBLEMS

1. Answer the questions below based on the following data for an imaginary country that we might call Macroville. All figures are in billions of dollars.

ITEM	AMOUNT
PERSONAL CONSUMPTION EXPENDITURES	$1291
EXPORTS	185
CORPORATE INCOME TAXES	45
DEPRECIATION (CAPITAL CONSUMPTION ALLOWANCE)	219
RECEIPTS OF FACTOR INCOME FROM THE REST OF THE WORLD	72
GOVERNMENT EXPENDITURES ON GOODS AND SERVICES	407
NET FIXED INVESTMENT	100
PAYMENT OF FACTOR INCOME TO THE REST OF THE WORLD	70

INDIRECT BUSINESS TAXES	169
IMPORTS	223
INVENTORY CHANGE	15
SOCIAL SECURITY CONTRIBUTIONS	150
PERSONAL INCOME TAXES	246
UNDISTRIBUTED CORPORATE PROFITS	37
PERSONAL INTEREST PAYMENTS	43
GOVERNMENT TRANSFERS AND INTEREST PAYMENTS BY THE GOVERNMENT	273
DIVIDENDS	15
BUSINESS TRANSFER PAYMENTS	10
PERSONAL TRANSFER PAYMENTS TO FOREIGNERS	5

(A) What is Gross National Product?

(B) What is Gross Domestic Product?

(C) What is Net National Product?

(D) What is National Income?

(E) What is Personal Income?

(F) What is Disposable Personal Income?

(G) What is Personal Saving?

2. The U.S. population is 250 million people. If 20 million people are considered unemployed and 200 million are employed, calculate the following:

A) the labor force participation rate

B) the unemployment rate.

Suppose that a wave of optimism sweeps the nation and an additional 10 million people, previously out of the labor force, begin to search for employment. Of these, 5 million find jobs. Recalculate the labor force participation rate and the unemployment rate. Is it possible for the unemployment rate and the number of employed individuals to simultaneously increase?

SUGGESTIONS FOR FURTHER READING

Clayton, Gary E. and Giesbrecht, Martin Gerhard. *A Guide to Everyday Economic Statistics.* New York: McGraw-Hill Publishing Co., 1990.

Council of Economic Advisors. *Economic Report of the President.* Washington, DC: U.S. Government Printing Office, available annually.

_____. *Economic Indicators.* Washington, DC: U.S. Government Printing Office, various issues.

Graboyes, Robert F. "International Trade and Payments Data: An Introduction." Federal Reserve Bank of Richmond *Economic Review* (September/October 1991), pp. 20–31.

Johnson, David B. *Finding and Using Economic Data: A Guide to Sources and Interpretation* Mountain View, CA: Mayfield Publishing Co., 1993.

Nordhaus, William, and James Tobin. "Is Growth Obsolete?" *Economic Growth. 50th Anniversary Colloquium* 5. New York: National Bureau of Economic Research, 1972.

Walter, John R. "Monetary Aggregates: A User's Guide." Federal Reserve Bank of Richmond *Economic Review* (January/February 1989), pp. 20–28.

Webb, Roy H. *Macroeconomic Data: A User's Guide.* Federal Reserve Bank of Richmond, 1992.

U.S. Department of Commerce. *The Statistical Tables. National Income and Product Accounts,* 1929–1982. Washington, DC: U.S. Government Printing Office, 1982.

_____. *Survey of Current Business.* Washington, DC: U.S. Department of Commerce; May issues give annual income data.

U.S. Department of Labor, Bureau of Labor Statistics. *Handbook of Methods,* BLS Bulletin 2285. Washington, DC: U.S. Government Printing Office, 1988.

_____. *Monthly Labor Review.* Washington, DC: U.S. Government Printing Office, various issues.

3

THE CLASSICAL MACROECONOMIC MODEL

n this chapter we begin a more detailed discussion of macroeconomic theory by presenting what is known as the Classical model. There are a number of good reasons for starting here. One reason is that important elements of Classical macroeconomics are deeply embedded in contemporary economic analysis. John Maynard Keynes did not start with a blank slate when he wrote his *General Theory of Employment, Interest, and Money* in 1936. Instead, he began with a slate containing Classical thinking on macroeconomics, and it is only relative to this that we can assess the contribution of Keynes and his followers to macroeconomics, and the contributions of modern schools of thought to the model presented by Keynes.

A further reason to study Classical macroeconomics is that familiarity with the Classical model contributes to understanding more contemporary models. The Monetarist school and the New Classical school (not to mention supply-side economics and real business cycle theories) draw very heavily upon Classical thought. Indeed, the work of Milton Friedman, a founder of Monetarism, may be thought of as in a direct line of descent from such "Classicals" as David Ricardo, John Stuart Mill, Alfred Marshall, Irving Fisher, and A. C. Pigou. Even models such as the Keynesian model or the New Keynesian model contain many features in common with the Classical model. For these reasons, then, we begin our formal story of macroeconomic theory with the foundations of Classical thought.

When you finish this chapter, you will understand

- Say's Law and how it applies to the Classical model
- the Classical economist's conception of the equation of exchange and the quantity theory of money
- the Classical theory of interest rate determination
- the Classical labor market , with flexible nominal wages and with equilibrium real wages determined by the interaction of labor demand and labor supply
- the role of fiscal policy in the Classical model
- the Classical economists' explanation for unemployment, and their policy prescription for dealing with this problem.

THE FOUNDATIONS OF CLASSICAL MACROECONOMICS

Classical economics was built upon certain interrelated behavioral relationships. Although these foundations cannot be found neatly listed in any one Classical reference source, four important and recurring themes emerge when we review the writings of these classical economists:

1. Say's Law.
2. The quantity theory of money.
3. A real theory of interest.
4. Wage and price flexibility.

In this chapter, each of these themes will be discussed and a Classical model will be built upon them. Let's begin with Say's Law.

SAY'S LAW

SAY'S LAW is an assumption of Classical economists that the act of supplying goods created a corresponding demand for those goods.

BARTER ECONOMY is an economy in which there is no money, so that goods are exchanged directly for other goods.

Say's Law, named after J. B. Say, a follower of Adam Smith, is a cornerstone of Classical thinking and has been stated as "supply creates its own demand." Say's Law was originally intended to apply to a **barter economy,** an economy in which there is no money, so that goods are exchanged directly for other goods. In a barter economy, a household performed work not for the sake of working, which was thought to reduce utility, but in order to produce goods that could be traded for other goods that the household desired. With no money to facilitate trade, a household would produce an output of a good, such as shoes, intending to trade these shoes for some other good that the household desired, such as bread.[1] If shoes are produced only with an eye to trading them for bread, then the very act of producing the shoes indicates a demand for some other good, such as bread. The household would then exchange its surplus of shoes for the bread it desired. In this way, the act of producing, or supplying, shoes *is* a demand for bread, so supply "creates" demand.

Each household's output (or supply) "created" a demand for some other good, because the manufacturing household wanted to trade the good it had produced. A household's demand for some other product was equal to the value of the surplus good produced by another household. Thus, surplus goods produced by a household would never go unsold. It was just a matter of determining the price of the good, and this information could easily be established through the exchange process. In this example, the price of a pair of

---

[1]We should be clear that the household may actually want to keep some of the shoes for its own use. In this case it is only the surplus of shoes over and above those reserved for own use that will be traded, and it is the production of these "surplus" shoes that creates its own demand.

shoes would be measured in terms of the number of loaves of bread offered in exchange. Therefore, the relative price of goods could be determined in the barter economy. But since there was no unit of account such as the dollar, an index of prices or an absolute price level could not be found. It is easy to see that in the barter economy Say's Law was valid since the household was producing a supply of goods that could be exchanged for other goods the household demanded. Aggregate demand had to be equal to aggregate supply.

Many Classical economists also believed that Say's Law was valid in a monetary economy whose market structure was assumed to be perfectly competitive.[2] In a monetary economy, goods are exchanged for money, which is then exchanged for other goods. When money is introduced into an economic system, problems can arise regarding the validity of Say's Law. We can gain a better understanding of Say's Law in a monetary economy through Figure 3-1.

In Figure 3-1, we see a firm producing an output (Y) of a good. To produce this output, the firm hires the factors of production from households. These factors are the familiar labor, land, capital, and entrepreneurial activity. As shown in Figure 3-1, the factors of production receive income from producing output for the firm. Income consists of wages paid to household labor, rent paid to households for use of natural resources, real interest earned by households on savings, and profit earned by households from owning businesses. Now the household receiving this current income has a choice between consumption (C) of goods and services and saving (S).

The **INTEREST RATE** is the percentage rate of return on lending and borrowing funds.

In Classical economics it was generally thought that the amount to be consumed (C) and saved (S) by the household depended on the **interest rate** (r). In order to get households to save, which meant giving up part of current income and thereby foregoing consumption of present goods and services, households had to receive interest on income saved as a reward for foregoing consumption. The question was, who borrowed the households' saving? The answer was, businesses which wanted loanable funds in order to invest in capital goods. A business's investment decision to expand a plant or add to equipment and inventories rests on the cost of borrowing capital funds, which is the interest rate. We find, then, that to the Classical economists both saving (S) and investment (I) are dependent on the interest rate (r). The determination of the equilibrium interest rate in the financial markets guarantees that saving will be equal to investment in the Classical model.

The **CAPITAL MARKET** is the market where saving or the supply of capital funds adjusts to investment or the demand for capital funds.

The market where saving or the supply of capital funds adjusts to investment or the demand for capital funds was called the ***capital market*** (which is often referred to as the financial, or loanable funds market). To ensure equilibrium in the capital market, the interest rate would fall if saving

---

[2]For a detailed discussion of Say's Law and Classical monetary theory, see Mark Blaug, *Economic Theory in Retrospect,* 2nd ed. (Cambridge: Cambridge University Press, 1978), chap. 5; and Thomas Sowell, *Say's Law: An Historical Analysis* (Princeton, NJ: Princeton University Press, 1972).

FIGURE 3-1
The Classical Circular Flow
of Income

The upper part of the figure shows the household supplying the factors of production, labor, land, capital, and entrepreneurial ability to the firm. In return, the household receives income in the form of wages (W), rent (R), interest (r), and profit (PR). The lower part of the figure shows the firm selling output (Y) to the household. Out of its income, the household consumes (C) part of it and saves (S) part of it, which flows into the capital market. The firm borrows in the capital market and invests (I) in capital goods, thereby returning funds to firms producing capital goods. The circular flow of income is unbroken.

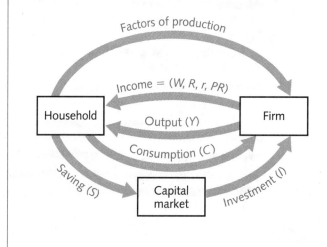

was greater than investment and would rise if investment was greater than saving. (In other words, if the quantity supplied of loanable funds—savings—exceeds the quantity demanded of loanable funds—investment—then the surplus would cause interest rates to fall.) As long as there was interest rate flexibility (a free market determining interest rates), saving would always equal investment in the capital market.

As shown in Figure 3-1, the circular flow of income would not be broken even after incorporating the capital market. Out of income earned from producing output (Y), the household would consume part (C) and would save part (S). The amount saved by the household (S) would eventually be borrowed by the firm for investment (I) in capital goods. Thus, the supplying of output (Y) generated income, which created the demand for consumer goods and services (C) and for capital goods (I), which resulted in the buying of the output (Y). Assuming that this output (Y) was sufficient to provide for full employment, then once full employment was reached there would be no excess of aggregate demand or aggregate supply of goods and services. Full employment would be guaranteed.

How the Circular Flow of Income Could Be Broken

We see, then, from our discussion so far that one essential ingredient for ensuring that the Classical economy would be at full employment was a flexible interest rate in the capital market. If the interest rate (r) were not flexible, saving (S) would not necessarily equal investment (I), the circular flow of income could not be maintained, and unemployment could result, since there could be a surplus of loanable funds, and hence a surplus of total goods in relation to total spending.

There was another way in which the circular flow of income could be broken. Suppose that a household decided not to consume part of its current money income and then, instead of saving and drawing interest on that money, put it in a box and buried the box in the ground. This act by the household of *hoarding,* defined as holding idle money balances, could break the circular flow of income. Since some goods would go unsold, household income would now be disposed of in three ways, consumption, saving, and hoarding. Consumption would be the purchase of consumer goods, saving would equal investment and hence the purchase of capital goods, but hoarding would not purchase any goods. Thus, the output of goods Y, which equals household income, would not get purchased by household spending on consumption and business spending on investment. Instead, some output would not be purchased because some household income was hoarded. This would lead to unemployment and a decline in the nation's income.

How likely were these effects? To the Classical economists, the act of holding idle money balances was irrational behavior. Why would any household want to hoard when it could save and be paid interest? Since households were "rational" in their decision making, they would save and not hoard and the circular flow of income and spending would be maintained and therefore full employment would be maintained.[3]

If full employment was to be achieved in the Classical economy, the market mechanism of flexible prices and wages had to be allowed to work in all markets. For example, in the labor market, if there was an excess supply of laborers, firms would not need to lay off workers. Instead of unemployment, competition for jobs would cause wages to fall to a level where all workers wanting to work at the prevailing wage would be employed. Likewise in the commodity market, an excess supply of goods would lead to a decline in the price of goods until equilibrium was established between supply and demand.

HOARDING is storing money that is neither saved nor spent.

---

[3]As we will see later in this chapter, price-wage flexibility in the economy also makes hoarding irrelevant as a cause of permanent unemployment in a Classical system. In the event of long-term hoarding, all prices and wages will fall, restoring equilibrium in the economy.

For the Classical economy, Say's Law was operating in a world of perfect competition—another major assumption of the Classicalists.

THE QUANTITY THEORY OF MONEY

The quantity theory of money was an important foundation of Classical macroeconomics. The versions of the quantity theory of money presented in this section appeared prior to Keynes's *General Theory* in 1936 and must be classified as naive. Since World War II, however, substantial theoretical and empirical research has been done on more sophisticated versions of the quantity theory by Milton Friedman of the University of Chicago, Maurice Allais of the University of Paris, and others. We are going to examine two formulations of the quantity theory of money. The first one emphasizes the relationship of money and the price level, the second emphasizes an interpretation of the quantity equation as a model of money demand.

The Quantity Equation

THE EQUATION OF EXCHANGE relates the stock of money and the velocity of circulation of money to the price level and the level of real output, and is written as $MV \equiv PY$.

Since the Classical economists formulated the quantity theory of money using the equation of exchange, we must be careful to distinguish between the equation of exchange and the quantity theory of money. The **equation of exchange** is written as

$$MV \equiv PY,$$

where M is the stock of money in the economy; V is income velocity, the average number of times per year the stock of money is spent for final output; P is the price level of final goods and services; and Y is physical output. The $\equiv$ makes the equation an identity. Thus, since we have measures of M, P, and Y, the equation of exchange would allow us to calculate the income velocity as PY/M.

QUANTITY THEORY OF MONEY hypothesizes that a change in the money stock causes a proportional change in the price level because velocity and physical output are unaffected by the quantity of money.

In contrast, the **quantity theory of money** is not an identity but a theory that was employed by the Classical economists to explain and predict certain behavioral relationships in the real world. The equation used in the quantity theory of money looks the same as the equation of exchange, but here there is an important difference. The Classical economists assumed that income velocity, or V, was a constant in the short run. This is a statement about economic behavior in the economy, and when combined with the equation of exchange makes the quantity theory of money a theory instead of an identity. The distinction is important, since theories can be falsified, or found to be false. In contrast, an identity or definition cannot be falsified.

What was the economic rationale for assuming that V was stable in the short run? A constant V was assumed because the methods of handling money balances by banking and financial institutions, the economic structure of the economy, and the customs and paying habits of the community changed only gradually over time. In the Classical theory, money was used simply as a medium of exchange. (Later writers included the role of money as an interest-earning asset.) If households decided to hoard money, which meant that some money would be pulled out of the income-spending stream, causing some goods or services to go unsold, V would be unstable. But since households were rational, such behavior was viewed as very unlikely.

Our theoretical assumption, then, is that V is constant. In addition, the Classical economists assumed that Y, the total output, was constant. This assumption followed from the idea that the economy would always be at full employment because of competitive labor markets. We indicate that income velocity and output are constants by the bar we place over $\bar{V}$ and $\bar{Y}$. Given these assumptions, we write our model as

$$M\bar{V} = P\bar{Y}. \tag{3.1}$$

What is the economic behavior underlying this equation? We can think of equation 3.1 as a simple model of the economy. The claim is that, with V_Y and Y constant, there is a stable relationship each year between the variables P and M. For example, suppose V was or is equal to 3. That is, suppose that the stock of money turns over three times per year in completing the circular flow of income. Also, suppose that Y was or is equal to \$300 billion of real output. With these assumptions, we can, like the Classical economists, conduct a simple experiment using the quantity theory. In this experiment, suppose that we begin with a money supply of \$100 billion and a price level of 1. The quantity theory equality holds, since $M\bar{V} = (\$100$ billion$) \times 3$ and $PY = 1 \times (\$300$ billion$)$. Suppose now that the money supply increases. One way to think of this is the helicopter drop parable told by Milton Friedman. That is, assume that helicopters fly around dropping money throughout the economy until the money supply has doubled.[4] A Classical economist could easily predict the economic outcome. Because V and Y were considered constant, the only two variables that could change in the equation were M and P. Moreover, since the government controlled the money supply M, the line of causation was assumed to run from the changes in the money stock to changes in the price level. We would say that M was an exogenous variable, under the control of the monetary authorities (such as the Federal Reserve System in the United States), and P was an endogenous variable. Thus, a doubling of M would cause a doubling of P. This result can be written as

$$(2M)\bar{V} = (2P)\bar{Y}. \tag{3.2}$$

---

[4]The purpose of the helicopter drop story is to make the increase in the money supply occur throughout the economy. Ideally, everyone's individual holding of money would double. In this way, we avoid having to deal with questions of how it matters if the initial infusion of money occurs only in one sector, or in one household. The latter problems have been labeled the Cantillon effects, after an early Classical economist who studied these issues.

GLOBAL PERSPECTIVE

IRAQ AND IRAN:

COUNTERFEITING AND

THE QUANTITY THEORY

In times ancient and modern, counterfeiting has been a critical economic problem for governments and private money issuers. The ability to counterfeit obviously takes the control over the quantity of money from the money producer. Money must possess numerous characteristics and qualities to serve as "good money" (among them portability, divisibility, durability, and so on), but another characteristic surely is "uniqueness" or the inability to reproduce whatever serves as paper currency or coins.

To increase costs to counterfeiters, governments have taken extraordinary measures to make currency and coin unique. Benjamin Franklin had several bits of advice concerning early U.S. currency: Reproduce an actual leaf on currency whose veins were unique and nonreproducible and intentionally misspell words on the currency (e.g., Pheledephia) in order to foil would-be counterfeiters! Modern producers of money

use unique papers, ink, and design to accomplish the same goal.

It does not take much imagination to understand the possibilities of the use of counterfeiting in economic warfare of one country against another. Since one of the principal advantages of using money is to help eliminate the transactions costs of barter, successful counterfeiting can quickly reduce an economy to the most primitive forms of exchange. As exchange breaks down, so do production and specialization. Goods are hoarded in anticipation of still higher prices and chaos reigns. Counterfeiting by Country 1 against Country 2 is, in effect, a *tax* on Country 2's resources and against that government's revenues from printing and issuing money.

Many examples of such economic warfare may be cited throughout history. Both sides in the U.S. Civil War made stabs at replicating the other side's currency. The United States and allied governments were reported to have made attempts to disrupt the currency system of Nazi Germany. But there are contemporary examples as well. A report from the U.S. House of Representatives alleged that, for several years prior to 1992,

the government of Iran has been printing and circulating (through Syria) U.S. $100 bills in an attempt to ease its budget deficit and to disrupt U.S. foreign exchange markets abroad. According to Representative Bill McCollum (R-Fla.), chairman of the Task Force on Terrorism and Unconventional Warfare, Iran's counterfeiting goals are to issue about $12 billion per year in $100 bills to help erase its foreign currency shortage.[a]

Iran vigorously denies the charge, but counterfeit bills of excellent quality keep appearing outside the U.S. banking system in European markets. The same bills, often composing up to 30 percent of given deposits of laundered drug money *within* the U.S. banking system, apparently slip by commercial banks and the Federal Reserve System's sorting equipment as well. The bills are so good and the source so mysterious that the counterfeiters have eluded the Secret Service (the agency charged with rooting out and destroying counterfeiters). But turnabout is fair play. The United States and other Western nations have apparently been using counterfeit currency in an ongoing economic war with Iraq. Vast

MAP 3-1
Iraq and Iran are Alleged to Be Involved in Counterfeiting Activities Against the United States.

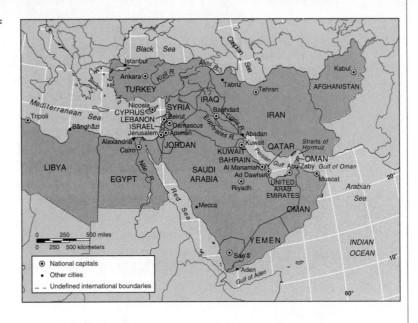

quantities of Iraqi currency have been printed and introduced into the economy in order to bring Saddam Hussein's regime to its knees.

These nonbloody techniques of warfare reveal several important features of all economies. As a cog in the wheel of trade, money has no substitute. But further, currency warfare means that virtually all governments in history and modern times have an implicit understanding, however crude, of the quantity theory of money. Counterfeiting can obviously creates runaway inflation—just as any overzealous use of the printing press does. Until control is restored, unrestrained increases in the money supply reduces an economy to primitive economic conditions and negative economic growth. ❑

NOTE a"Iran May Be Printing Dollars," *San Francisco Chronicle* (July 2, 1992), p. A3.

Thus, prices would rise in the same proportion as the rise in the stock of money.

It should be noted that while the absolute price level in our experiment would have doubled in the economy, relative prices of goods—such as the price of bread relative to shoes—were assumed to remain the same. For an illustration of this point, consider an economy that produces equal quantities of three goods—coats, shirts, and ties—with the price of these goods listed as $20, $10, and $3, respectively. The average price level based on the three goods would be ($20 + $10 + $3)/3 = $11. If the stock of money doubles, the price of the three goods would double to $40, $20, and $6, respectively, and the average price level would double to $22 because ($40 ÷ $20 + $6)/3 = $22. The relative prices of the coats, shirts, and ties have not changed. If we add the price of two shirts either before ($10 + $10) or after ($20 + $20) the experiment, we see that the price of one coat, which is $20 before and $40 after, is still the price of two shirts. The real price, then, is one coat to two shirts, and it remains the same even with a proportional increase in the money supply.

The quantity equation can also give us some perspective on recent attempts at "economic warfare." As the Global Perspective, "Iraq and Iran: Counterfeiting and the Quantity Theory," indicates, the effects of counterfeiting as economic warfare can be analyzed with the quantity theory.

Notice that we have found that Classical economists separate monetary theory from value theory (sometimes called the "Classical dichotomy"). Value theory is known today as microeconomics or price theory. From the standpoint of monetary theory, we have found that changes in the stock of money produce changes only in the absolute price level, not in relative (real) prices. As long as the economy was at full employment, money was just a "veil" that hid the true working of the economy, meaning that individual market forces of supply and demand determined the price of a good and the quantity sold. To understand what caused shifts in a good's supply and demand curves, one studied micro (value) theory. It was changes in the supply and demand curves for individual products that produced relative price changes of goods and services.

An examination of the quantity equation can also provide insights into the Classical thinking about the cause of inflation. Since an increase in the money supply could lead only to an increase in prices in a fully employed economy, inflation was caused by "too much money chasing too few goods and services." For an explanation of the economic rationale for this statement about inflation, consider the Cambridge approach to the quantity theory.

The Cambridge Cash Balance Equation

The economists of Cambridge University, England, naturally followed the approach to the quantity theory of money set forth by the famous economists of that institution—namely Alfred Marshall and A. C. Pigou. They did not write the equation in the same manner as we saw in the quantity equation.[5] However, we can use the quantity equation to obtain the Cambridge equation. From a mathematical standpoint the equations are the same, but the Cambridge equation is going to tell us a different story about economic behavior in the economy.

[5]See Edwin Dean, ed., *The Controversy Over the Quantity Theory of Money* (Lexington, MA: D. C. Heath, 1965), pp. 28–29.

Let us again write the quantity equation as

$$MV = PY.$$

If we divide both sides of the equation by V, we obtain

$$M = (1/V)PY.$$

If we let $1/V = k$, we have the Cambridge equation, which can be expressed as[6]

$$M = kPY.$$

In the Cambridge approach, this equation is an equilibrium condition relating the supply of money M and the demand for money kPY. Therefore, the above equation can be broken into two parts:

$$M_D = kPY, \text{ the demand for money,}$$

and

$$M_S = M, \text{ the supply of money.}$$

When the Cambridge economists wrote the equation with $1/V = k$, they were asking a different question about the public's behavior than were those economists who used the quantity theorem discussed above (sometimes called the Fisher equation). The Cambridge economists were focusing on the public's motive for holding money, and thereby on the demand for money. In essence, by writing $1/V$, they were asking why people want to hold money balances. If $V = 3$ in the Fisher equation, then using the Cambridge equation, one finds that the public would be keeping in its money balances 1/3 of PY, or 1/3 of nominal GDP. We note that 1/3 is the proportion of its income that the public on average keeps on hand as money balances. Therefore, if GDP were $300 billion, the demand for money by the public would be $100 billion. But we still have not explained why the public wants to hold money balances. Its only motive for holding money is to carry out day-to-day transactions. According to the Cambridge economists, this was the only reason the public demanded money. Households, for example, needed to keep a certain amount of cash on hand to pay for their goods and services. The transactions demand for money, then, depended on income, and for the economy as a whole it depended on the level of GDP. If, as in our previous example, GDP rose to $600 billion and $k = 1/3$, the public in the economy would demand cash balances of $200 billion. The Cambridge economists pointed out that while V in the Fisher equation tells us how rapidly money is being spent in a year for the purchase of goods and services, $1/V$, or k, revealed why the public is holding its money.

Using the Cambridge equation, we can gain additional insight into Classical inflation when we return to our previous experiment where the helicopter

---

[6]See A. C. Pigou, "The Value of Money," *Quarterly Journal of Economics* (November 1917), pp. 38–65.

doubles the stock of money. Since $1/V$, or k, is stable and real output Y is at full employment, a doubling of the money supply would cause the public to have a money supply of $200 billion while money demand was $100 billion. This means that the public has more money on hand than it wants in order to carry out normal day-to-day purchases or transactions. What would the public do with this excess amount of money? Spend it! People would bid with their dollars for various goods and services that are fixed in supply. This would lead to an increase in the price for these products, and the price level would increase. However, the price level does not just increase but actually doubles. When the price level doubles from 1 to 2, equilibrium is restored in the money market, with money supply of $200 billion and money demand equal to $(1/3) \times 2 \times (\$300$ billion$)$ or $200 billion.

In this example, the absolute price level has doubled, but *relative* prices (e.g., the exchange rate between shirts and ties) have not changed. Thus, just as in the quantity equation, we see that changes in the money supply affect the price level but not the relative prices of individual goods.

In summary, it is important to remember that the Cambridge equation gave additional insight into the demand for money by households and firms. The public has a transactions demand for money that depends on the level of income in the economy.

THE REAL THEORY OF INTEREST

Still another important foundation of Classical thought was the real theory of interest. To the Classical economists, the interaction of saving by households and investment by businesses determined the rate of interest. We think of saving as the supply of loanable funds and investment as the demand for loanable funds. This theory of interest was a "real" theory because the underlying forces in the economy that produced the saving and investment process at full employment were not monetary but were the real productivity of capital (plant and equipment) and the real sacrifice of consumption by households.[7]

Remember also that neither the quantity theory approach nor the Cambridge approach shed any light on the rate of interest. In these models, if households had excess cash balances, that is, more money than was needed for transactions purposes, they would spend all of these excess balances on goods and services. What happened in the money market in regard to the demand and supply of money did not affect the market for loanable funds—saving and

---

[7]A number of different definitions have been applied to the term *real interest rate*. Fisher used the term in the sense of "virtual" or "true" rate. See Irving Fisher, *Appreciation and Interest* (New York: Macmillan, 1896), pp. 8–11, 66, 67.

investment—and vice versa. Thus, increases in the stock of money did not affect the rate of interest.[8]

In the Classical model, we will think of households as choosing how much to save out of income, and businesses as choosing how much to invest (i.e., how much new capital to purchase). We admit that this distinction is a bit artificial, because households are often also businesses. For purposes of discussing saving and investment, however, we want to separate the act of saving from the act of investing. Households save by putting part of their income in a bank or other financial institution or financial market from which businesses borrow funds to buy capital goods as part of the investment process. The questions we must ask ourselves are (1) Why does the household save? and (2) Why does business invest in capital goods? When we can answer these questions, we will be providing a more specific answer to the question of what the "real factors" were that created saving and investment in the Classical world.

Recall from our discussion of Say's Law that when households received income from producing goods and services, they had a choice between consuming all of their income, or consuming part and saving part of it. It was assumed that households had a *time preference,* that is, an individual household preferred consuming present goods to consuming future goods. If households saved, they had to forego the present consumption of goods and services. For a household to make this sacrifice, it had to be paid a premium that would enable it to consume even more future goods and services. This premium would be interest income. Thus, for a household to be induced to save, it had to receive interest. The higher the interest rate, the more saving would take place in the economy; but since the economy was assumed to be at full employment, the more the saving in the economy, the less consumption there would be of goods and services. In Classical macroeconomic analysis, the important variable that determined the amount of a household's consumption and the amount of its saving was the real interest rate.

The economic behavior of all the households can be written in the form of an equation as

$$S = S(r), \tag{3.3}$$

where S is saving in the economy and r is the real interest rate. A positive relationship between the amount of saving and the various interest rates is shown as a saving schedule in Figure 3-2, with the interest rate on the vertical axis and saving on the horizontal axis.

Now turn to the demand side of the loanable funds market. First note that capital was employed by businesses because labor was generally more produc-

TIME PREFERENCE is the preference of individuals or households for consuming present goods rather than future goods. It indicates that individuals prefer current satisfaction to future satisfaction, everything else being constant.

---

[8]Don Patinkin points out that the basic Classical equations do not assign an explicit role to the rate of interest. Thus, they cannot prove the Classical proposition that the rate of interest is unaffected by a change in the stock of money. See Don Patinkin, *Money, Interest, and Prices,* 2nd edition, abridged (Cambridge, MA: The MIT Press, 1989), p. 165.

FIGURE 3-2
Determination of the Real
Interest Rate in the Classical
Capital Market

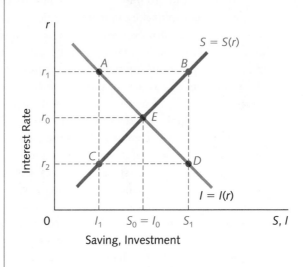

The real interest rate is determined in the Classical capital market where the investment function I intersects the saving function S at point E.

tive when used in conjunction with capital. For example, laborers could produce more cloth by using spinning wheels to spin cotton into yarn and looms to weave the cloth than by using just their hands.

Assuming that a business already had a stock of capital goods, why would it want to increase that stock? What would cause the business to invest in additional capital goods? The profit motive, that is, the desire of the business to maximize profits, would cause businesses to invest. But an important variable affecting a business investment decision was the interest rate. Underlying the investment decision was the Classical microeconomic concept of the marginal productivity of capital. Holding the labor force fixed, there would be diminishing marginal productivity of capital. Profit-maximizing businesses would borrow and add additional units of capital goods up to the point where the value of the marginal product of capital equaled the real rate of interest.

The economic behavior of businesses can be written in the form of an equation as

$$I = I(r), \tag{3.4}$$

where I is aggregate investment in the economy and r is the real interest rate. The negative or inverse relationship between the amount of investment and the various interest rates is shown as an investment schedule in Figure 3-2.

When the saving schedule is combined with the investment schedule, the intersection of the two schedules determines the equilibrium real rate of interest (r_0) and the equilibrium level of saving (S_0) and of investment (I_0) as shown in Figure 3-2.

In the Classical world, as long as there was competition on both sides of the capital market, the market rate of interest would equate saving and investment. This result is also demonstrated in Figure 3-2. If the interest rate is r_2 there is an excess demand for capital funds, as indicated by *CD,* and the interest rate would rise to r_0, again bringing investment into equilibrium with saving.

To ensure that saving was in equilibrium with investment, the interest rate had to be flexible. If, for some reason, such as government regulation of interest rates, the interest rate was "stuck" or fixed at a level above or below the equilibrium interest rate, there would be an excess supply or demand of saving. An example with excess saving is illustrated in Figure 3-2, where the distance *AB* represents excess saving at a fixed interest rate of r_1 above the equilibrium interest rate r_0. In this case, investment is less than saving. Recall that household income is made up of payments to factors, and households dispose of this income by consumption *C* or saving *S*. But this income is generated by production of goods that are sold to consumers *C* or businesses *I.* When investment *I* is below saving *S,* there is not enough demand for the goods produced. That is, some capital goods would go unsold, and unemployment in the capital goods industry would be the result. This is all caused by r_1 being fixed above r_0. Full employment could again be achieved, however, if the regulation keeping the interest rate at r_1 was removed.

If the regulation was removed, the excess of saving of amount *AB* in Figure 3-2 would produce a fall in the interest rate to r_0 and would cause additional investment. Naturally, the Classical economists recognized the possibility that resources could go unemployed, but they felt that unemployment was of short duration and due to some maladjustment in one of the markets, as was just demonstrated in the loanable funds market. Once the distortion in that market was eliminated, the economy would again be free to move to a full-employment level.

Anticipated Inflation and the Nominal Rate of Interest

In 1895, Irving Fisher began to study the effect of changes in commodity prices on market rates of interest. His work culminated in 1930 with the publication of *The Theory of Interest.*[9] In his research, Fisher pointed out the relationship between the nominal rate of interest (i.e., the market rate) and the *expected rate of change of prices* (or the anticipated rate of inflation). Economists

---

[9]See Irving Fisher, *The Theory of Interest* (New York: Macmillan, 1930).

FISHER EFFECT is the concept that shows that the market rate of interest is equal to the real rate of interest plus the anticipated rate of change of prices.

now refer to this relationship as the ***Fisher effect.*** A version of Fisher's formulation is written as

$$R = r + \pi^e,$$

where R is the nominal rate of interest, r is the "real" rate of interest, and π^e is the expected rate of inflation.

What exactly does the Fisher equation express? To understand Fisher's formulation, we must examine the economic behavior of both lenders and borrowers who anticipate inflation. This is probably best illustrated by an example. Assume that a lender and a borrower expect prices to be stable and that the lender is willing to lend $1,000 today at 5 percent to be repaid in total at the end of one year. The lender thus receives at the end of the year the original principal of $1,000 plus an interest payment of $50, or a total amount of $1,050. Since prices are expected to be stable, the lender expects her purchasing power to be 5 percent greater at the end of one year than it is today. Thus, we say that the ***real rate of interest***—the real percentage increase in purchasing power—is five percent.

REAL RATE OF INTEREST is the nominal rate of interest minus the expected rate of inflation.

Now consider what happens to the same borrower and lender when they both expect that prices will rise 10 percent over the course of the loan. What is the behavior of the lender? Just to keep the purchasing power of the principal constant, the lender would have to be repaid not $1,000 but $1,100. Moreover, this 10 percent increase in the principal only keeps the purchasing power constant. The lender also wants to earn a real increase in purchasing power, so she will also ask for a real return of 5 percent, or $50 on the initial principal. The total amount received by the lender at the end of the loan is then $1,100 in principal and $50 in interest, or $1,150. The lender, anticipating inflation of 10 percent and desiring a 5 percent real return, asks an interest rate of 15 percent. The borrower is willing to pay 15 percent since she will be returning the loan in inflated dollars (by 10 percent) and since she cannot do better than pay 5 percent in the market for funds.

The Fisher equation formalizes this idea in a formula for the nominal interest rate as the real interest rate plus the expected rate of inflation, $R = r + \pi^e$. In our example, $r = 5$ percent (.05) and $\pi^e = 10$ percent (.10), so the interest rate charged on a loan is $R = 15$ percent (.15).

DEFLATION occurs when prices decline, so that the inflation rate will be a negative number.

Note that in the Fisher equation the effect of anticipated price declines is similar but opposite to the effect of anticipated price increases. If borrowers and lenders expect that prices will be declining, so that the inflation rate will be negative, we say that there is ***deflation.*** In this case, the Fisher equation tells us that nominal interest rates will fall below the real rate of interest. To see this, consider again our above example with a real interest rate of 5 percent, but now assume that the inflation rate is –3 percent, so that we are experiencing deflation. In this case, the Fisher equation tells us that the nominal or market interest rate is 2 percent, since the real rate is 5 percent plus the expected inflation rate of –3 percent.

PHOTO 3-1
Professor Irving Fisher was an
Important Pioneer in
Monetary Theory and Policy
(1867–1947).

Does this make sense? Consider our lender, who wants to lend $1,000 at a nominal rate of 5 percent on that principal. If she lends the $1,000 principal, its equivalent purchasing power after one year of 3 percent deflation is $970, since prices have fallen by 3 percent. A five percent return on the $1,000 is $50, so the lender expects to receive back the real purchasing power she lent, $970, plus the real interest on the principal, or $50, for a total of $1,020. But that is just a 2 percent increase in the initial principal, just as the Fisher equation predicts.

Certain qualifications about the Fisher effect are in order. First, Fisher's equation does not explain the relationship between the quantity of money and interest rates, only the relationship between anticipated inflation and interest rates. However, if the quantity of money does affect prices, as the Monetarists argue, then an increase in the money supply could set a Fisher effect into motion. This is especially the case if we consider an increase in the rate of growth of the money supply, which would lead to an increase in the rate of growth of prices. Second, Fisher recognized that borrowers and lenders do not have perfect foresight about future price movements. Expectations about future changes in prices are determined by the past experiences of lenders and borrowers. Fisher hypothesized that borrowers, who are primarily business people, have a tendency to be influenced by more recent events, which affect their current profit position, while lenders (savers) are influenced by events in the more remote past and take longer to adjust to recent events.[10]

Finally, Fisher's empirical research indicated to him that the real rate of interest was not constant, as theoretically predicted, but more variable than the nominal rate of interest. This variability in the real rate was attributed by Fisher to the inability of people to perfectly foresee future price-level movements. Fisher's empirical evidence showed that there was only a partial adjustment of nominal interest rates to anticipated inflation or deflation. There is a lag, then, between the time when prices rise (or fall) and the time when interest rates rise (or fall). The length of the lag depends on the "time horizon" of people, which is the number of years it takes people to form expectations.[11] The longer the time horizon, the smaller the effect of recent price changes on nominal (i.e., market) interest rates.

The Fisher effect is an important Classical concept, which is still with us and which has been the subject of continuing empirical research to establish the exact relationship between anticipated inflation and the nominal rate of interest. In applying this concept, one must remember that nominal interest rate payments are subject to income taxes, and this modifies the Fisher equation somewhat, as discussed in the Insight: "The After-Tax Fisher Effect."

---

[10]The Fisher effect and its role in contemporary Monetarist views of inflation are discussed at length in Chapter 8.
[11]Fisher found the time horizon to be from twenty to thirty years.

THE AFTER-TAX FISHER

EFFECT

The Fisher effect (as discussed in the text) relates the nominal interest rate to the real interest rate and the expected inflation rate. This discussion has ignored questions of the effect of taxes on the Fisher effect. Nominal interest rates are subject to taxes such as the income tax in the United States or similar withholding taxes in European countries. Thus, an analysis of the effect of taxation on the Fisher effect requires us to modify our formulation that appears in the text. In addition, empirical research on the Fisher effect looks at the estimated real interest rate before taxes.

Recall that in the absence of taxes the real rate is found by rewriting the Fisher equation as

$$r = R - \pi^e,$$

where r is the real rate, i is the nominal rate and, as before, π^e is the expected rate of inflation. If nominal interest payments are taxable, we might want to modify this equation to look at the after-tax real rate of interest. The Fisher equation can be ad-

justed to reflect the after-tax real rate by writing it as

$$r^* = R(1 - t) - \pi^e,$$

where r^* is the after-tax real rate and the term $i(1-t)$ adjusts the nominal interest rate for taxes t. The tax rate t is the marginal tax rate, which is the tax rate on an additional dollar of income. To interpret this equation, consider a household with interest income. The household receives interest income of R, but the government taxes this income at rate t, so taxes are Rt. After taxes, nominal interest income is $R(1-t)$. Next we subtract the expected inflation rate π^e in order to convert the after-tax nominal interest rate to an after-tax real interest rate r^*.

Figure 3-3 shows nominal interest rates and estimates of the before- and after-tax real returns on one-year Treasury securities. The expected rate of inflation is based on the annual rate of change in the GDP deflator, and the tax rate is based on the average tax rate on personal income.

We find in Figure 3-4 that from the early 1950s to the late 1970s, nominal interest rates were on a general upward trend, with a number of smaller upward and downward movements about that trend. However, the real rate of in-

terest did not follow this trend and indeed became negative for a few quarters in 1971, and for much of 1975. By 1975 the real rate of interest had fallen below zero, and for a while was near −5 percent, while the nominal rate was at a relatively high +7 percent. In late 1979 to early 1982, short-term nominal interest rates soared to a higher level than at any time during the 1950s, 1960s, or 1970s. During this time, real interest rates were also rising. Further, it is clear that nominal interest rates began declining in 1981 and, with some deviations about this downward trend, they declined until about 1987. The before-tax real rates meanwhile had climbed to about the 5 percent level by 1981, and continued near this level through early 1985 before declining. After-tax real rates behaved in a similar fashion and were higher in the early 1980s than in the previous three decades. By 1987 both nominal rates and real rates had declined, but they remain at high levels relative to past history.[a] ❑

NOTE: [a]See Madelyn Antoncic, "High and Volatile Real Interest Rates," *Journal of Money, Credit, and Banking* 18, no. 1 (February, 1986), pp. 18–27.

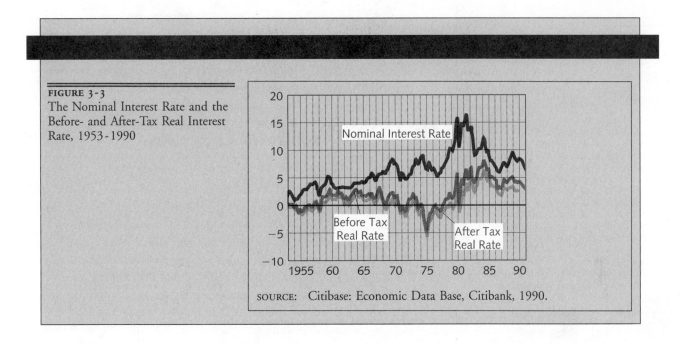

FIGURE 3-3
The Nominal Interest Rate and the Before- and After-Tax Real Interest Rate, 1953-1990

SOURCE: Citibase: Economic Data Base, Citibank, 1990.

More recent research indicates that the Fisher effect can be observed in the post-1960 data. Economists at the Federal Reserve Bank of San Francisco have found that a 1 percentage point increase in the expected inflation rate resulted in a .9 percentage point increase in the nominal interest rate on AAA corporate bonds. Their evidence suggests that the Fisher effect does operate in the post-1960 period, and they suggest that the instability in the Fisher effect prior to 1960 can be explained by shifts in the money supply growth rate.[12]

WAGE AND PRICE FLEXIBILITY

A final cornerstone of Classical macroeconomics concerns the flexibility of wages and prices in the labor market and one of the Classical policies for alleviating unemployment. The Classical position on the issue of wage and price flexibility is typified by *The Theory of Unemployment* (1933), by Cambridge economist A. C. Pigou.[13] In this section, we shall present only the essence of Classical views on wage and price flexibility.

---

[12]See Michael C. Keeley and Michael M. Hutchison, "Money and the Fisher Effect," *FRBSF Weekly Letter,* Federal Reserve Bank of San Francisco (August 7, 1987).
[13]A. C. Pigou, *The Theory of Unemployment* (London: Macmillan, 1933).

Production Function

To understand the Classicals' approach to the labor market, we first need to examine a simple ***aggregate production function.*** A production function shows the maximum amount of real output or real product that can be produced from a specified set of factor inputs, given the current state of technology. If we let Y be total product, N be units of labor (employment), and K be the fixed stock of capital, then an aggregate production function can be written as expression 3.5:

$$Y = f(N, K). \tag{3.5}$$

From expression 3.5, we see that national income Y (total product), depends on (or "is a function of") the inputs of labor N (employment), and on a fixed stock of capital K. Since the time period is the short run the capital stock is fixed at K. We find that as the units of labor N are increased, the national income Y will also increase, but at a decreasing rate because of the law of diminishing returns. The aggregate production function is depicted in Figure 3-4, with national income Y on the vertical axis and units of labor N on the horizontal axis. Figure 3-4 is drawn with diminishing returns starting from the origin, 0.

AGGREGATE PRODUCTION FUNCTION is a relationship between maximum physical output and a set of inputs, given the existing technology.

FIGURE 3-4
The Economy's Production Function

This figure indicates that as the units of labor (N) increase on the horizontal axis, national income (Y) increases on the vertical axis but it increases at a decreasing rate because of the law of diminishing marginal returns.

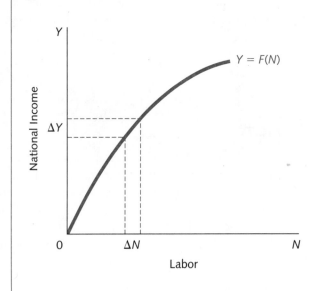

MARGINAL PRODUCT OF LABOR is the addition to total product attributable to the addition of one unit of labor to the production process, the stock of capital remaining unchanged.

The slope of the production function is called the ***marginal product of labor*** (MP_N), the additional output produced by an additional unit of labor. This can be written as $\Delta Y/\Delta N$, with the familiar Δ again simply meaning "change." The marginal product of labor, $\Delta Y/\Delta N$, is shown in Figure 3-5. Since output is assumed to be increasing at a decreasing rate, the slope of the production function declines as employment increases. In other words, the marginal product of labor, which is the slope of the production function or $\Delta Y/\Delta N$, is declining as employment increases.

Demand for Labor

To see that the marginal product of labor is the demand for labor, suppose we have only five units of labor and *each unit* of labor *added* the physical amounts shown in Table 3-1 to the national income (national product). If a graph was

FIGURE 3-5
The Demand for Labor

The demand for labor (N_D) is the marginal product of labor and is depicted with a negative slope in the figure. If the real wage was around 2 units, businesses would hire 4 units of labor because in profit maximization, price equals marginal cost.

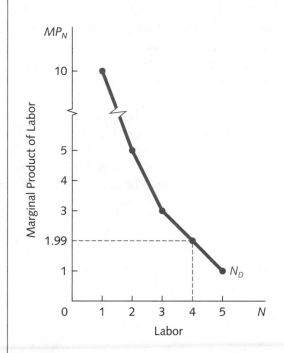

This table shows the marginal product of labor declining as units of labor are increased.

UNITS OF LABOR	$\Delta Y/\Delta N$ = MARGINAL PRODUCT
1	10
2	5
3	3
4	1.99
5	1

21 = Y = REAL NATIONAL INCOME
(TOTAL PRODUCT)

plotted for the values of the marginal products in the table, we would find that the demand for labor N_D or the marginal product of labor had a negative slope, as shown in Figure 3-5. Once the curve for the demand for labor is determined, our next question should be, how many units of labor would businesses employ? The general answer is that under competitive conditions businesses would want to maximize their returns from hiring labor.

To do this businesses would have to know the ***real wage*** of labor. We could even think of the real wage for labor as the actual physical goods that each unit of labor receives for its services. If, in Table 3-1 the real wage was determined in the market to be 1.99 units of produce (approximately 2 units), then businesses would hire up to a point on the demand curve for labor that would be equivalent to 4 units of labor. But exactly why would they want to hire 4 units instead of 3 units or 5 units?

When 4 units of labor are employed in production, they produce 20 units of total output; this total is found by adding the marginal product for the first 4 units of labor. Since the real wage paid per laborer is 1.99 units of output, the total cost for 4 units of labor is 7.96 units of output. The difference between the total product of 20 units and the total cost of 7.96 units is 12.04 units of product, which is the amount received by businesses. If 3 units of labor were hired, the total product would be 18 units of output. With the same real wage of 1.99 units of product per unit of labor, total cost would be 5.97 units for a difference of 12.03. If 5 units of labor were employed, the total product would be 21 units of output and the total cost would be 9.95 units of output. Thus, businesses would receive only 11.05 units of the product. Given the assumed real wage rate of 1.99 units of output, businesses should hire 4 units of labor for profit maximization since this would give them 12.04 units of output, which is the largest amount produced.

Since workers are normally paid ***money wages*** for the physical goods they produce rather than being paid in the goods themselves, the real wage could be

REAL WAGE is the amount of goods and services that workers can obtain with money wages.

MONEY WAGE is the money value (or face value) of what workers are paid for the use of their labor.

written as W/P, where W is the money wage and P is the price level for the economy. The real wage, then, is what the actual money wage will purchase in terms of real goods and services in the economy.

To profit maximize, firms set the marginal product of labor MP_N equal to the real wage:

$$MP_N = W/P. \tag{3.6}$$

The equation for the demand for labor (3.7) can then be written as

$$N_D = N_D(W/P, K), \tag{3.7}$$

where N_D is the demand for labor, W/P is the real wage, and K is the fixed stock of capital. The graph of this function is shown in Figure 3-6 with the real wage W/P on the vertical axis and units of labor N on the horizontal axis. Given a real wage of $(W/P)_1$, businesses would employ, for profit maximization, ON_1 units of labor, or up to point A on the N_D curve.[14]

Supply of Labor

Now that the underpinnings for the demand for labor have been determined, we need to focus our attention on the Classical supply curve for labor. Since work has disutility associated with it, businesses must offer a higher wage to attract additional workers into the labor market. But do workers think of their wages in real terms or in nominal or monetary terms? As we will see, the answer to this particular question became a very important analytical point in separating Classical economics from that of Keynes.

The Classicals believed that workers looked at their *real wage* when offering their services for hire on the market. The equation for the supply curve for labor can be written as expression 3.8:

$$N_S = N_S(W/P), \tag{3.8}$$

where N_S is the supply of labor and W/P is the real wage. To the Classicals, the supply curve for labor, like the demand curve for labor, was a function of the real wage. The supply curve for labor was generally assumed to have a positive slope because a higher real wage had to be offered in order to attract additional workers into the labor market. The positively sloped supply curve for labor is shown in Figure 3-6, with the real wage W/P on the vertical axis and units of labor (employment) N on the horizontal axis. When the two curves (demand and supply) for labor are joined together in Figure 3-6, their intersection determines the equilibrium real wage of $(W/P)_0$ and the level of full employment of N_F in the Classical economy.

---

[14]If technological progress increases labor's productivity, its occurrence can produce an upward shift in the production function. This happens because the former levels of labor and capital can now produce more real income. Since N_D is the slope of the production function, technical progress would shift it up and to the right of the original N_D curve.

FIGURE 3-6
The Labor Market

The equilibrium wage of $(W/P)_0$ and the level of full employment of N_0 are determined in the Classical labor market where the demand for labor (N_D) intersects the supply of labor (N_S) at point E in the figure.

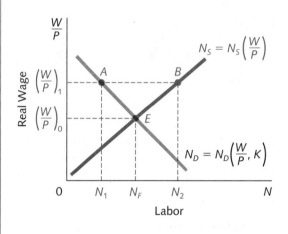

Once economic behavior in the Classical labor market is understood, the policy that Classical economists suggested to alleviate unemployment does not seem at all surprising. Suppose that in Figure 3-6 the real wage of $(W/P)_1$ in the economy was above the equilibrium real wage of $(W/P)_0$. There would be $N_2 - N_1$ units of unemployed labor. $N_F - N_1$ represents the number of workers who were employed at the original equilibrium real wage of $(W/P)_0$ but have been laid off and no longer have a job at the real wage of $(W/P)_1$. $N_2 - N_F$ is the number of workers who have been drawn into the labor force because of the higher real wage of $(W/P)_1$ but cannot find a job. For example, homemakers may find that at the real wage of $(W/P)_1$ they would prefer to take a job rather than stay in the home, and therefore they begin to search for one. However, homemakers willing and able to work at the real wage of $(W/P)_1$ but who are unable to find a job would then be counted as unemployed.

The Classicals had a simple solution to the unemployment problem. As indicated in Figure 3-6, the reason for unemployment was that the real wage of $(W/P)_1$ was "too high" for equilibrium given the supply and demand curves for labor. If the workers would take a cut in their money wage W the cost of producing goods and services would be reduced and employment and output would increase until full employment was restored. Thus, the Classicals considered unemployment the consequence of too high a nominal wage, a problem that would occur in a competitive market only if there were regulations imposing a minimum wage on the labor market. This analysis, like the analysis of the adverse consequences of interest rate regulation, explains the aversion of Classical economists to price and interest rate regulations.

THE CLASSICAL MODEL: A GRAPHICAL ANALYSIS

Our discussion of Classical macroeconomics provides us with a foundation to build a Classical model. The model can be used to analyze the various economic disturbances that could occur in the Classical economy as well as to enhance our understanding of the other models that we introduce in this text. By comparison with the Classical model, we will be able to see the similarities and differences of the various models, and to pinpoint the essential features that make these other models different from the Classical model.

The Classical Equations

Before presenting our graphical model, we need to establish the Classical model's basic equations for aggregate supply. These equations stress the important parts of the model described above.

1. $Y = Y(N,K)$ the production function
2. $N_D = N_D(W/P, K)$ the labor demand function
3. $N_S = N_S(W/P)$ the labor supply function
4. $N_D = N_S$ the condition for labor market equilibrium
5. $MV = PY$ the quantity theory of money
6. $S = S(r)$ the saving function
7. $I = I(r)$ the investment function
8. $S = I$ the equilibrium condition for the capital market.

Here we have used the following symbols:

Y = National income or national output

N = Units of labor

N_D = Demand for labor

N_S = Supply of labor

W/P = Real wage

K = Fixed stock of capital

M = Supply of money

V = Income velocity

P = Price level

S = Saving

I = Investment

r = Real interest rate.

Since the early Classical economists believed markets were competitive, it will be assumed that the interest rate is flexible and that saving and investment will adjust to the various disturbances in the economy. Thus, in presenting a graphical picture of the Classical world, a graph for the capital market need not be included.

The Aggregate Supply Side

For the aggregate supply side of the basic Classical model, the production function and the labor market are required. The production function is shown in Figure 3-7(a), with N as units of labor and Y as national income. The curved line in the graph indicates that national income is increasing at a decreasing rate because of the law of diminishing marginal returns as described earlier in the chapter. The labor market is depicted in Figure 3-7(b), with N as the units of labor and (W/P) as the real wage. The slope of the production function in Figure 3-7(a) is the demand for labor, or N_D, in Figure 3-7(b). Both N_D and N_S are functions of the real wage $(W/P)_0$. The full-employment level is N_F.

In Figure 3-7(c), a 45-degree line is drawn to make the value of national income Y_F measured on the vertical axis equal to the value of national income Y_F on the horizontal axis. In Figure 3-7(d), we construct the aggregate supply curve with the price level P on the vertical axis and national income Y on the horizontal axis.

A line drawn from the full-employment level of N_F in Figure 3-7(b) to the production function in Figure 3-7(a) indicates a full-employment level of national income of Y_F. By tracing over from the production function in Figure 3-7(a) to the 45-degree line in Figure 3-7(c), we can match the level of national income Y_F on both axes. Finally, we trace down from Y_F in Figure 3-7(c) to Figure 3-7(d) to find the level of national income Y_F. The aggregate supply curve is the vertical line AS measured at the full-employment level of national income Y_F. The Classical aggregate supply curve is vertical due to the assumptions the Classical economists made about the labor market, and the assumptions of the price and wage flexibility.[15] How does this flexibility

---

[15]Actually, even with a Classical market-clearing model of the labor market, there may not be a perfectly inelastic aggregate supply curve if labor supply is a function of other variables besides the real wage. For example, if labor supply is a function of real wealth, such as real money balances, then changes in the price level will alter real wealth and hence labor supply. In this case aggregate supply will change with the price level. See, for example, Dennis W. Jansen, "Real Balances in an Ad Hoc Keynesian Model and Policy Ineffectiveness," *Journal of Money, Credit, and Banking* (August 1985), pp. 378–86.

FIGURE 3-7
Derivation of the Classical
Aggregate Supply Curve

To derive the Classical aggregate supply curve, start with the full-employment level of N_F in the Classical labor market in (b). Trace from N_F in (b) to the production function (Y) in (a) that determines the full-employment level of national income (Y_F). Next, trace Y_F over from (a) to (c) where the 45-degree line makes Y_F equal to Y_F. Finally, trace down Y_F from (c) to (d). The vertical line AS in (d) is the Classical aggregate supply curve.

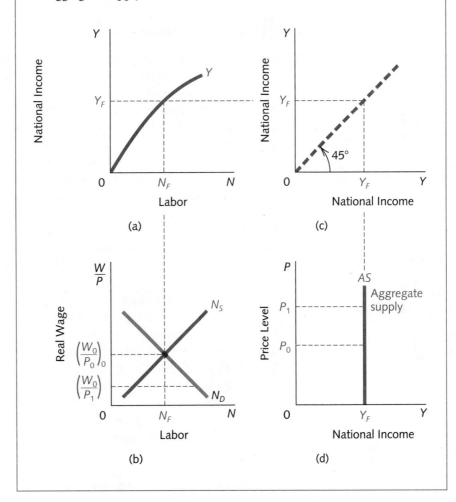

relate to Figure 3-7? Clearly if the real wage rate were, for any reason, higher or lower than $(W/P)_0$ in Figure 3-7, prices and wages would readjust to that level. Assume, for example, that the initial equilibrium real wage is W_0/P_0. National income level Y_F is then associated with price level P_0. If the price level rises to P_1, the real wage would fall, as in Figure 3-7(a), to W_0/P_1. At that lower real wage, excess demand would exist (in the amount AC) and labor demanders would bid up the nominal wage to a higher level (W_1) so that the *ratio* of the nominal price level to the nominal wage rate again becomes $(W/P)_0$. That higher nominal price level, P_1 is associated with the same level of national income Y_F. We will see in later chapters that several alternative models invoke assumptions of nominal wage rigidities to explain persistent unemployment and also to generate aggregate supply curves that are not perfectly inelastic.

The Aggregate Demand Curve

Now let's look at the aggregate demand curve of the basic Classical model. The theory of aggregate demand in Classical theory was primitive in nature and was implied by the quantity theory of money. In our earlier discussion of the quantity theory, income velocity was stable. Income velocity, then, was a known quantity. Thus, total spending on goods and services, or aggregate demand, which is MV, can be determined as soon as the money supply M is determined. Moreover, since the economy is at a full-employment level, the real output of goods and services Y is a fixed quantity. The absolute price level, however, is variable. The Classical theory of aggregate demand can be represented by a curve called a *rectangular hyperbola* since this type of curve shows the various quantities of real output that can be bought at various price levels given the same level of total spending MV in the economy. The Classical aggregate demand curve is shown in Figure 3-8 as a rectangular hyperbola convex to the origin of the graph, with the price level P on the vertical axis and real output or national income Y on the horizontal axis.

Since the aggregate demand curve is drawn as a rectangular hyperbola, any point on that curve shows the various combinations of price level P and real output Y that give the same level of money income, which is $P \cdot Y$ or aggregate demand. In Figure 3-8, for example, if P were 2 and Y were 50, the level of money income would be 100. A P of 5 and Y of 20 would give the same level of money income. Once we have the graph for the aggregate demand curve, we can complete the Classical model by combining the aggregate demand curve with the aggregate supply curve.

The Complete Classical Model: Graphics

The complete Classical model is depicted in Figure 3-9. The aggregate supply side is represented by the graphs for the aggregate production function in (a) and for the labor market in (b). The aggregate demand side is shown in (d), with the aggregate demand curve drawn as a rectangular hyperbola.

The aggregate supply side is also shown in (d), with the aggregate supply curve drawn as a vertical line at the full-employment level of national income, Y_F. The intersection of the aggregate demand curve AD and the aggregate

FIGURE 3-8
The Classical Aggregate
Demand Curve

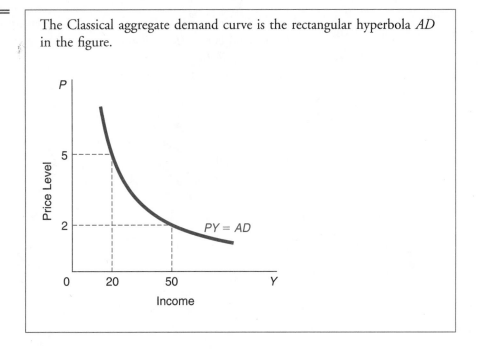

The Classical aggregate demand curve is the rectangular hyperbola AD in the figure.

supply curve AS determines the equilibrium price level P_0 and the equilibrium level of national income at full employment Y_F.

Using the Basic Classical Model

Once the real wage, employment, real income, price level, and money wage have been determined for full employment, as in Figure 3-9, the Classical model is ready to be used. We will ask how equilibrium changes in response to various changes in exogenous variables (see discussion in Chapter 1). Such exercises are called *comparative statics* because we will be comparing equilibrium before and after the change in an exogenous variable. In doing these types of exercises, you should *always start with the economy in equilibrium.* Since equilibrium in the Classical model is at a full-employment level of output and income, it follows that for the Classical model you should always start with the economy in full employment. When a particular disturbance occurs in the economy, such as a change in the supply or demand for money or in the supply or demand for labor, the Classical economist, as well as the economist of today, is concerned with what happens to the real wage rate, the level of employment, real income, and so forth. In other words, do these macro variables increase, decrease, or stay the same? While we may not be able to determine the magnitude of the change in variables, we can at least find their direction of change.

FIGURE 3-9
Equilibrium in the Classical
System

Equilibrium in the Classical system is determined where the aggregate demand curve *AD* intersects the vertical aggregate supply curve *AS* at point E in (d).

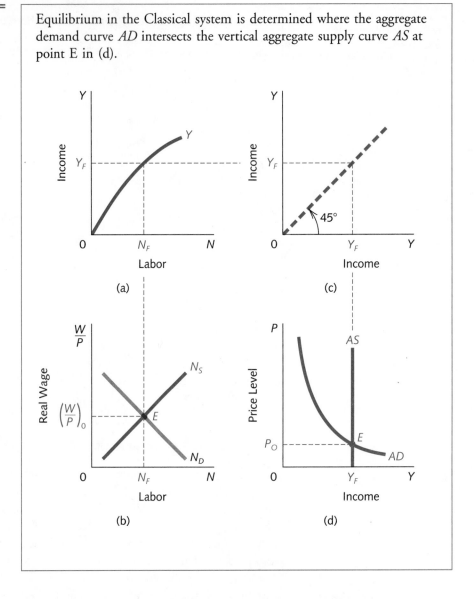

An Analysis of Monetary Disturbances in the Classical Model

Money supply and demand changes will obviously have an impact in the Classical model. The interesting question is whether or not the real variables in the system are affected. Consider three changes.

AN INCREASE IN THE MONEY SUPPLY

Let us suppose that the central bank increases the money supply. For this type of monetary disturbance in the economy, the aggregate demand curve

FIGURE 3-10
A Shift in the Classical
Aggregate Demand Curve

With an increase in the money stock, the Classical aggregate demand curve shifts from AD_0 to AD_1 in (d). The full-employment level of national income does not change, but the price level rises from P_0 to P_1 in the figure.

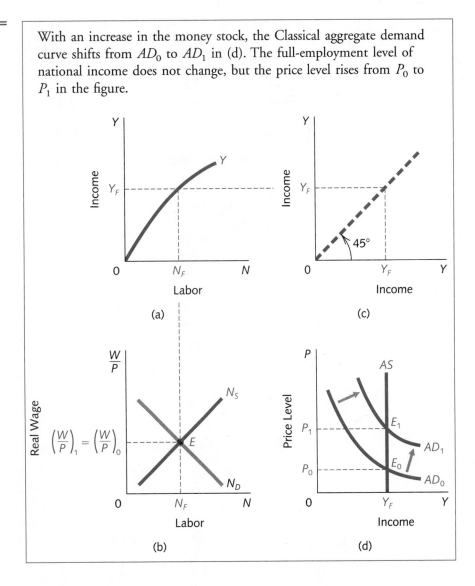

AD in Figure 3-10(d) must shift to the right, to AD_1. Why? Real output of Y_F is still at full employment, but since M has increased the level of total spending, MV has risen. Since $MV = PY$ and (V is constant), the AD curve has to shift to the right to maintain equality between MV and PY. Thus, the price level increases from P_0 to P_1. However, the real variables in the economy remain unchanged. The real wage is still $(W/P)_1 = (W/P)_0$ since a change in the money supply has not affected the demand for or supply of labor, although the money wage has increased by the same proportion as the price level increased. Real income is still Y_F and the level of employment remains at N_F.

AN INCREASE IN INCOME VELOCITY

An increase in income velocity with the money supply fixed and real income at full employment would produce the same result as an increase in the money supply. The AD curve would shift to AD_1, causing prices and money wages to increase but not changing the real wage, employment, or the level of output.

A DECREASE IN THE TRANSACTIONS DEMAND FOR MONEY

A decrease in the transactions demand for money ($k = 1/V$) would be the same as an increase in income velocity, V. The AD curve would shift right to AD_1, and prices and money wages would rise. It is interesting to see that all of these monetary disturbances—(1) an increase in the money supply, (2) an increase in income velocity, and/or (3) a fall in the transactions demand for money—have resulted in an increase in the price level and no effect on real variables such as Y and W/P.

We note that the results of a decrease in the money supply, a decrease in income velocity, and/or a rise in the transactions demand for money will be just the opposite of the results of an increase in the money supply. We leave the analysis up to the reader. We merely reiterate that none of these monetary disturbances has any effect on the "real" side of the economy, which is the aggregate supply side.

An Analysis of Real Disturbances in the Classical Model

A "real" disturbance takes place on the aggregate supply side of the Classical model and has an effect on real wages, employment, real income, prices, and money wages. These disturbances are akin to "shocks," which create business cycles in any dynamic expression of Classical theory. In such a dynamic theory (which is the subject of Chapter 11), real shocks to the demand side of the system (those that affect spending) or to the supply side (those that affect production) initiate business cycles in the economy. Naturally such shocks can produce "good" or "bad" effects for the economy. The Classicals certainly envisioned natural shocks such as floods, droughts, or wars, but modern economists extending both Classical and Keynesian macroeconomic theories find the origins of business cycles on both the demand and supply sides of the economy. A supply shock would include, for example, sudden changes in resource availability, as when the OPEC cartel suddenly formed and raised the real price of imported oil in late 1973. An example of a demand shock might be a severe decrease (or sudden increase) in the money supply—having a serious and unanticipated impact on private consumption or investment spending.

While some of the cyclical aspects of macroeconomic theory will be analyzed in Chapter 11, the impact of certain disturbances may be developed within the context of the model developed in this chapter. Recall from Figure 3-10 that the demand for labor and the supply of labor were drawn by relating to the quantity of labor demanded or the quantity of labor supplied to the real wage. While other factors affected these two curves, these variables were held constant. Therefore, a change in a variable other than the real wage will cause the labor demand or supply curve to shift. We now need to use our Classical model to predict the effect on the economy of these various shifts.

A SHIFT IN THE DEMAND FOR LABOR

Technological improvement in an economy, which enhances labor's productivity, is one of the factors that could produce an upward shift in the aggregate production function. Since the demand for labor is the slope of the production function, as we have previously demonstrated, the labor demand curve would shift to the right with an upward shift in the production function. These shifts of the production function and of the demand for labor from N_{D_0} to N_{D_1} are shown in Figure 3-11(a) and (b).

There is now a new full-employment equilibrium of E_1 in the economy with (1) a higher real wage of $(W/P)_1$, (2) a higher level of full employment of N_{F_1}, (3) a higher real income of Y_{F_1}, and (4) a lower price level of P_1. Notice that the aggregate supply curve has shifted from AS_0 to AS_1. There is a movement down the aggregate demand curve AD to the equilibrium of E_1. The reader should work out the case for a downward and leftward shift in the demand for labor. The results for the real wage, and so on, will be just the opposite from those found for an upward and rightward shift in the labor demand curve.

A SHIFT IN THE SUPPLY OF LABOR

Population growth is one factor that would lead to a rightward shift in the supply of labor. Such a shift in the labor supply curve could result in (1) a lower real wage, (2) a higher full-employment level of output, (3) a higher real income, and (4) a lower price level. Using the Classical model, the reader should verify the results for these variables and the opposite results when the supply of labor shifts upward and to the left.

EXPLAINING UNEMPLOYMENT WITH THE CLASSICAL MODEL: FIXED NOMINAL WAGES

It is interesting to see how the Classical model could be used to analyze the important problem of unemployment. Recall that the Classical explanation for unemployment was that money wages were fixed above the equilibrium level. This led Pigou to make the obvious suggestion that to solve the unemployment problem, workers should take cuts in their money wages. One "Classical"

FIGURE 3-11
A Shift in Aggregate Supply

In the figure, a rightward shift in the demand for labor from N_{D_0} to N_{D_1} in (b) causes a rightward shift in the aggregate supply curve from AS_0 to AS_1 in (d).

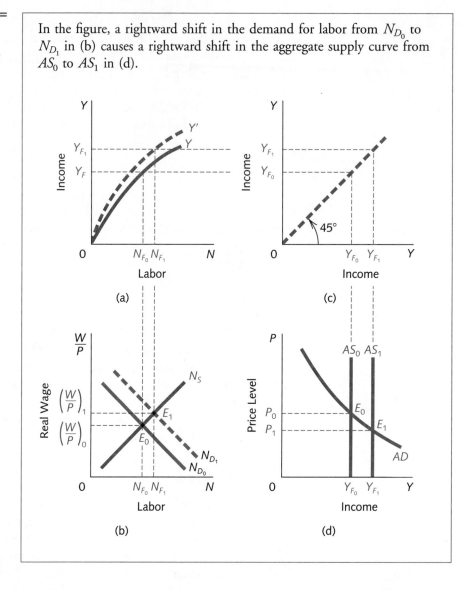

solution was to "wait out" workers and to endure temporary unemployment until workers would be willing to take cuts in their nominal wages. But suppose workers would not be willing to accept such reductions in their money wages. In other words, let us assume that money wages are inflexible in a downward direction. The Classical economists not only recognized this possibility but also offered a policy prescription to cure the unemployment malady. To analyze the unemployment case using the Classical model, we will use Figure 3-12. The variables corresponding to full employment are N_F and $(W/P)_0$, where the price level is P_0, and the money wage is W_0. Next, suppose

FIGURE 3-12
A Sticky Money Wage in the
Classical System

If the real wage $(\overline{W}_1/P_1)$ in (b) is above the equilibrium real wage (W_0/P_0) and the money wage is fixed at $\overline{W}_1$, the Classical policy solution for solving unemployment $(N_2 - N_1)$ was to increase the money stock (monetary policy). The aggregate demand curve shifts rightward from AD_0 to AD_1 in (d), raising the price level to P_2, thereby lowering the real wage to $(\overline{W}_1/P_2) = (W_0/P_0)$, which restores the economy to full employment N_F.

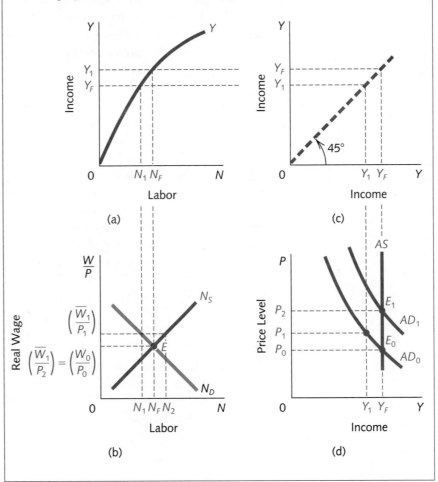

a fixed money wage of $\overline{W}_1$ greater than W_0 is imposed in Figure 3-12(b), and that the increase in the money wage will increase the real wage to $(\overline{W}_1/P_1)$ and employment will decline. This decline in employment reduces output, and moves the economy off the AS curve. In the flexible wage story, the excess supply of labor will result in the wage rate being reduced to restore equilibrium, increasing employment and output back to the full-employment level. However, with a fixed nominal wage, this adjustment cannot occur. What does happen is that the increase in the nominal wage reduces employment and output, and this moves the economy from the initial full-employment equilibrium at point E_0 on aggregate demand curve AD_0 to the point with output at the lower level Y_1. This movement along AD_0 raises the price level to P_1, in Figure 3-12(d). Notice that the increase in this price level lowers the real wage to $(\overline{W}_1/P_1)$, which is still above the full-employment level of (W_0/P_0). The unemployment equilibrium with nominal wage $\overline{W}_1$ is illustrated in Figure 3-13, with real wage $(\overline{W}_1/P_1)$, employment N_1, and output Y_1.

So far we have shown merely that the real wage is "too high" for full-employment equilibrium in the economy. When the real wage is $(\overline{W}_1/P_1)$, unemployment is in the amount of $N_2 - N_1$ in Figure 3-12(b). The level of employment is N_1 and real income is Y_1, falling below the full-employment real income of Y_F. Since the money wage is fixed at $\overline{W}_1$, the only way of lowering the real wage is to increase the price level. This would cause the real wage to fall to $(\overline{W}_1/P_2)$ and to be equal to the full-employment equilibrium real wage of (W_0/P_0).

A question pertaining to this case is, how should the price level be increased? To the Classical economists, an increase in the money supply by the central bank would increase the price level and thereby lower the real wage. The real wage would be reduced, and employment and real income would be expanded toward the full-employment level. Increases in the money supply would continue until full employment was achieved. This result is demonstrated in Figure 3-12(d) by shifting the AD_0 curve sufficiently to the right to AD_1, producing a price level of P_2, which would cause the real wage to fall to $(\overline{W}_1/P_2) = (W_0/P_0)$, or to the full-employment real wage. In the case of sticky or rigid wage rates (i.e., when wages do not easily adjust downward), the Classical economists, therefore, advocated the use of monetary policy, which was a conscious effort by the central bank to expand the money supply and thereby move the economy to full employment. Why not also use fiscal policy along with monetary policy to cure unemployment? This question is answered in the next section.

THE ROLE OF FISCAL POLICY IN CLASSICAL ECONOMICS

Fiscal policy can be defined as the federal government's change in spending on goods and services and/or taxes to achieve an economic goal such as a level of national income commensurate with full employment. Yet the Classical economists saw no role for fiscal policy. (That is the reason we did not include government and taxes in our Classical model in the previous section.) Why did the Classical economists hold this view?

In order to understand their position, first consider the policy perspective of one Classical policymaker, Britain's Chancellor of the Exchequer William Gladstone. Gladstone, who worked under the leadership of Prime Minister Robert Peel, was the conservative's conservative. Gladstone sought to eliminate as much government intervention in the private sector as possible. These policies included a reduction in import tariffs, which were a big revenue source for the British economy of the time (1840s and 1850s). The short-term effect was a budget imbalance as tax receipts fell below government expenditures. Gladstone found it necessary to impose a 10 percent income tax to cover the deficit and balance the budget. *But,* the tax was phased out over several years, and eventually eliminated altogether. Gladstone's principle was to impose taxes *only for specific projects or requirements* and, after the project was complete, to "sunset" or eliminate them. His purpose was to keep the government small relative to the private sector, but he had another reason for denying the government's access to deficits and to continuous sources of taxation—he believed fiscal policy (budget deficits in particular) would have no effect, or bad effects, on the economy.

The Classical Crowding-out Effect

Let us start with the situation where there is unemployment in the economy and the federal government attempts to increase the level of national income to solve this problem. This would be accomplished by the government's spending more on public goods (such as roads, dams, and military equipment) or on public services (such as education and data collection) than it receives in tax collections. When the federal government's expenditures G are greater than its taxes T, it is said to be running a **budget deficit.**

> **A BUDGET DEFICIT** occurs when government spending G exceeds government tax collections T. A budget surplus occurs when government spending is less than tax collections.

The federal government, faced with this deficit, has two choices in financing it: (1) it can print money through the Treasury, or (2) it can borrow, as private businesses do, by selling bonds to the general public, for example, households and private lending agencies. If the federal government printed money and used it to purchase public goods and services, then it would be increasing the money supply, and this would be considered monetary policy and not fiscal policy. Printing money would be an awkward way for the federal government to conduct monetary policy. Monetary policy could be more readily handled by the central bank through its open-market operations, which means that the central bank would buy bonds from the public to expand the money supply.

> **THE CROWDING-OUT EFFECT** is a reduction in consumption and investment spending as a result of higher interest rates brought about by budget deficits financed by federal government borrowing in the capital market.

Crowding out deals with the selling of new government bonds by the Treasury, not the central bank, to finance the federal government's deficit. The Treasury, to coax the public into buying government bonds rather than bonds issued by private businesses, has to lower the price of government bonds, which would concurrently increase the interest rate on those bonds. The Classical belief was that government spending in excess of current tax revenues crowded out private investment expenditures. The impact of a higher interest rate on

FIGURE 3-13
Crowding-Out Effect

An increase in government expenditures in the figure shifts the I line to $I + G$, which raises the interest rate from r_0 to r_1. The level of investment spending is reduced to I_1. Government spending in excess of current tax revenues crowds out private investment spending.

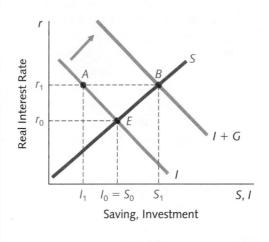

private saving and on the total demand for borrowed funds by business and government in the classical economy is illustrated in Figure 3-13.[16] The increase in government spending AB is exactly matched by a combined reduction in investment and consumption (equal to the amount by which saving is increased).

With no Treasury interference in the private capital market, private saving and private investment would be in equilibrium at an interest rate of r_0 and the budget would be balanced annually. The equilibrium level of saving and investment would be at S_0 and I_0, respectively. However, if the Treasury sold government bonds to finance the deficit in the budget, the interest rate would rise to r_1. The demand for borrowed funds would shift to the right from I to $I + G$ because of increased government spending G. Saving would rise to a level of S_1, and investment would fall to a level of I_1. Consumption would also fall by the amount $S_1 - S_0$ or $-\Delta C$. To the Classical economists, an increase in

---

[16]Note that *given the logic* of the Classical model, both investment *and* consumption are crowded out with increases in government expenditures financed by borrowing. Since saving is a positive function of interest rates, consumption is negatively related to interest rates. Clearly increases in G crowd out both investment and consumption according to the model presented in the chapter. Here we do not deal with this complication except to note that it occurs.

government spending financed by government bonds rather than tax receipts would cause a decrease in private investment spending on capital goods. By creating interest rates above the equilibrium rate, the federal government would crowd out the private business borrowing of capital funds; that is, private investment would result in no effect on national income.

The Effect of Tax Increases

Since fiscal policy deals not only with changes in government spending but also with changes in taxes, there is the question of what impact an increase in taxes would have on the level of national income in the economy. In other words, what if an increase in government spending was financed by tax revenues rather than government bonds? An increase in taxes naturally has an adverse effect on private spending. If personal income taxes were increased, then private consumption expenditures would decline, and if taxes on corporate profits were raised, then net investment spending would fall. Thus, government spending would increase and private spending would decrease, with no effect on national income and employment. The net effect of fiscal policy was that it had no effect on the level of national income! The Classical economists felt that government spending should equal tax collections $(G = T)$, that is, the government should "balance the budget" each year.

After studying the Classical view on policy, you may find it interesting to see to what extent these views have actually mattered in macroeconomic policy-making. See the Policy Issue: "Reagan-Bush and the Economy: Did Republicans Toe the Classical Policy Line (1980–1992)?"

SUMMARY

This chapter has focused on the foundations of Classical economics: Say's Law, the quantity theory of money, a real theory of interest and wages, and price flexibility. Knowledge of the pillars of Classical economics is important because it provides insight into modern thinking about the macroeconomy. Based on the Classical pillars, a Classical model was built and used to analyze the various economic disturbances that could occur in the Classical world. In addition, the chapter examined the "Fisher effect," which shows the relationship between the nominal rate of interest and the expected rate of inflation and how Fisher's equation can be adjusted to reflect the after-tax real rate of interest. The high inflation rates experienced by the U.S. economy in recent years make the concept of the Fisher effect as relevant today as in Fisher's time.

Finally, we found that fiscal policy, which is changes in federal government spending or taxing to achieve economic goals, played no role in Classical

REAGAN-BUSH AND THE ECONOMY: DID REPUBLICANS TOE THE CLASSICAL POLICY LINE (1980–1992)?

Macroeconomic theory has experienced tremendous development since the nineteenth-century writings of the Classical (and early Neoclassical) economists. The Keynesian revolution of the 1930s has been an important impetus to these modern developments. But Monetarists and New Classical economists have also presented complex extensions of Classical ideas. Along with the Classical writers themselves, modern Classicals emphasize growth through balanced budgets, minimal government interventions, and growth in the money supply to accommodate the "needs of trade."

Twelve years of the Reagan-Bush Administrations were thought to have followed these "Classical" ideas prior to the presidential administration of Democrat Bill Clinton. Ideas, however, must be separated from reality. Balanced

budgets—a mainstay of Classical macroeconomic theory—were *proposed* by Republicans through a balanced budget amendment (which, in 1991, came within three votes of passage in the House of Representatives). The reality, however, was record budget deficits between $150 and $350 billion a year (1980–1992). Growing debt amounted to $4.2 *trillion* dollars in 1991 in spite of a Classical philosophy and stopgap measures such as the Gramm-Rudman-Hollings deficit reduction bill.

Supply-side economics was also a hallmark of the Reagan-Bush Administrations, and the idea had its origins in Classical macroeconomics. Simply stated, supply-side economics means that taxes and/or restrictions on individuals and markets can be eradicated with the effect of increasing the aggregate supply of goods and services in the economy. The logic of this proposition is simple: Higher tax rates on individual work effort reduces incentives to work and produce. When investment is taxed at higher rates, capital accumulation—the mainstay of jobs and economic growth—is reduced. The Tax Reform Act of 1986 was inspired in large part by the Classical principle

that lower tax burdens on individuals mean higher work effort. The constant emphasis during the Bush administration on congressional approval (which did not materialize) of lower capital gains taxes underscored the Classical prescription that investment must be encouraged as the prime mover of economic growth.

Reduced regulation in the economy first occurred during the Carter administration (1976–1980) and continued during the Reagan years. (Bush actually increased regulations in certain types of activities such as the environment.) Carter and Reagan sponsored reductions in transportation and communications industries (e.g., airlines) in particular. Reagan's policies had a long-run flavor—much as in Classical economics. His slogan "Stay the Course," his emphasis on trickle-down economics (the idea that prosperity follows a downward course from increased industry to the poor), and his *original* emphasis on decreased spending all find their origins in Classical thought.

Despite a marginal decrease in government involvement over the Reagan-Bush years, total federal government outlays grew dramatically between

PHOTO 3-2
Presidents Bush and Reagan Attempted to Follow Some of the Classical Policy Prescriptions, but were Unsuccessful in Reducing Deficits.

1980 and 1992, due to a rapid defense buildup and to increased "entitlements" and social spending. Huge deficits began to bother the financial markets, driving long-term interest rates up. A rise in unemployment and the recession of 1990–91 was an overriding feature of the later part of the Bush administration. Reduced government spending under both Reagan and Bush proved politically infeasible. All of these factors led to the defeat of George Bush in 1992 and the election of Democrat Bill Clinton. Calls for the implementation of some classical ideas will no doubt continue. ❑

economics. The Classical economists, like a number of economists and congressmen in recent years, argued for an annually balanced federal budget.

The Classical proposal for a "balanced government budget" is a fitting concept with which to end our discussion of the Classical macroeconomic system. For all the reasons contained within the analytical sections of this chapter, the Classicals simply felt that the government was not necessary as an active policy participant or as a discretionary controller in the aggregate economy. The economy adjusted itself! (It should now be easy to see why a number of Monetarists rest easy with many Classical propositions.) But this view of the macroeconomic world met with a formidable attack in the mid-1930s. John Maynard Keynes—perhaps the most famous economist of our century—leveled a barrage of criticism upon the self-adjusting notions of Classical writers (especially A. C. Pigou) and, in doing so, changed the face of contemporary macroeconomics.

KEY TERMS

aggregate production function

barter economy

budget deficit

capital market

crowding-out effect

deflation

equation of exchange

Fisher effect

hoarding

interest rate

marginal product of labor

money wage

quantity theory of money

real rate of interest

real wage

Say's Law

time preference

QUESTIONS FOR REVIEW AND DISCUSSION

1. Is Say's Law valid for a barter economy? If so, why? Does it apply to a monetary economy? If not, why not?

2. Can Say's Law shed any light on the "new" supply-side economics? If so, explain how.

3. Explain the difference between the two versions of the quantity theory of money used by Classical economists.

4. Does the concept of time preference have any role to play in Classical economics? If so, explain how.

5. How is the interest rate determined in the Classical model? What impact does a change in the quantity of money have on the interest rate?

6. What is the relationship between anticipated inflation and the nominal rate of interest?

7. Why are economists and business people concerned with the after-tax real rate of interest?

8. On the basis of the usual assumption of perfect competition, explain clearly what effect a decrease in desired saving has on national income in the Classical model.

9. In the Classical scheme, if the money wage is held artificially above the level necessary for full employment, what method could be used to achieve full employment? Explain, and use a Classical model in your answer.

10. What policy did the Classical economists suggest to solve the problem of unemployment in the 1930s? Does this solution seem plausible for the 1990s? If not, why?

11. Why did the Classical economists argue against the use of fiscal policy to reduce unemployment?

12. Is the Classical crowding-out effect relevant to the 1990s? If so, how? (Hint: Think in terms of the large government deficit.)

13. Velocity decreased in the early 1980s. What does the Classical model predict would be the effects on the economy?

14. During the 1990s, U.S. military spending declined with the end of the cold war. What does the Classical model suggest would be the effects of this reduction in government spending?

15. The minimum wage laws in the United States have long been a bone of contention among politicians. What are the effects of increasing the minimum wage law in the Classical model? Carefully analyze the impact in the labor market. Can you suggest why workers would favor increasing the minimum wage law? Does increasing the minimum wage help all workers?

16. Suppose that, in 1993, the income of some particular economy was $800 billion. If the income velocity of money in that year was 2, what was the money supply, given the equation of exchange?

17. What is the income of Mexico in 1993 if the money supply is 270 pesos and the velocity of money (annually) is 3.0?

PROBLEM

1. If the money supply in the economy increases from $826 billion in 1992 to $900 billion in 1993, how much (in percentage terms) will the price level increase according to the quantity theory of money? What assumptions are made in the quantity theory of money that make this outcome possible? What does the quantity theory of money imply about policies that attempt to stimulate economic growth by increasing the money supply?

SUGGESTIONS FOR FURTHER READING

Breit, William, and Roger L. Ransom. *The Academic Scribblers.* Hinsdale, IL: Dryden Press, 1982, chap. 2.

Dean, Edwin, ed. *The Controversy Over the Quantity Theory of Money.* Lexington, MA. D.C. Heath, 1965.

Fisher, Irving. *Appreciation and Interest.* New York: Macmillan, 1896.

———. *The Purchasing Power of Money.* New York: Macmillan, 1922, especially chap. 4.

———. *The Theory of Interest.* New York: Macmillan, 1930.

Laidler, David E. W. *The Demand for Money.* New York: Harper-Collins, 1993, chap. 5.

Patinkin, Don. *Money, Interest, and Prices.* 2nd ed., abridged. Cambridge, MA: The MIT Press, 1989, chap. 8.

Pigou, A. C. "The Value of Money." *Quarterly Journal of Economics.* (November 1917), pp. 38–65.

———. *The Theory of Unemployment.* London: Macmillan, 1933.

Sowell, Thomas. *Say's Law: An Historical Analysis.* Princeton, NJ: Princeton University Press, 1972.

PART II

AGGREGATE DEMAND AND SUPPLY IN CLOSED AND OPEN ECONOMIES

4

AGGREGATE EXPENDITURES AND

THE GOODS MARKET

Classical macroeconomics looked at the economy in its full employment state, and made little allowance for unemployment. To be sure, there were periods of boom and bust—expansion and recession—in both the United States and Great Britain throughout the nineteenth and early twentieth centuries, but these bouts with the business cycle were looked on by Classical macroeconomists as temporary, or, more frequently, as the product of outside shocks to the economy, such as wars or droughts.

Modern macroeconomics began during the 1930s, when endemic and *persistent* unemployment plagued economies worldwide. Specifically, modern macroeconomics began with the publication in 1936 of *The General Theory of Employment, Interest, and Money* by John Maynard Keynes. Keynes challenged Classical theory (specifically, Say's Law) and focused attention on insufficient consumption spending by households and insufficient investment spending by firms. The unemployment created by "underspending" would be rectified by increases in government spending. Thus, Keynes provided a theoretical foundation for the idea of discretionary fiscal policy—the deliberate use of government spending and taxation in an attempt to change the state of the economy from one of unemployment to one of full employment. Keynes and the macroeconomists who followed him, especially in the 1930s and 1940s, devoted particular concern to unemployment and little concern to inflation, no doubt because of the experience of the Great Depression in the 1930s. As we will see in later chapters, contemporary economists have shown a greater concern with inflation and with economic growth.

In the present chapter we begin our study of modern macroeconomics with the "goods" market. The perspective is Keynesian, but it is one still widely adopted as a part of the explanation for aggregate demand. This approach models aggregate spending as consisting of four components: consumption, investment, government spending, and net exports. These four components are each modeled individually, and then total expenditures are modeled as the sum of the four components. This model of total spending will then be used to derive the equilibrium level of income, in which total spending (in real terms) equals real output or, equivalently, real income.

After reading this chapter, you will know

- how the circular flow model provides a guide to the Keynesian model of total expenditures, including equilibrium conditions for income and expenditure flows to and from households and firms
- how the consumption function explains household consumption behavior
- how we explain the investment behavior of firms
- how government fiscal variables such as government spending and net taxes are determined
- how we explain net export behavior, and how exports and imports are influenced by the exchange rate
- how this model of expenditure flows can be used to determine equilibrium income in the economy
- how the economy moves from one equilibrium level to another in the face of changes in variables that determine expenditure and income flows.

THE CIRCULAR FLOW AND MACROECONOMIC MODELING

In building a model of expenditures and income determination, we abstract from several real world issues by making certain simplifying assumptions. Although later some of these assumptions will be relaxed, for now it is easiest to focus our attention on only a few features of the model and hold other things fixed. It is important to remember what these assumptions are, because they place important qualifications on the analysis:

1. Prices and nominal wage are exogenous, or determined outside of the model.
2. The interest rate and inflation rate are exogenous.
3. Businesses pass all of their earnings over to households.
4. The exchange rate is exogenous, as are foreign income and foreign price levels.

The variables used in the model include Real national income (or real GDP), Y; Total real expenditures, TE; Real consumption expenditures, C; Real investment expenditures, I; Real government expenditures on goods and services, G; Real net exports = real exports – real import expenditures, NX. These variables, $C, I, G,$ and $NX,$ are summed to define total expenditures, TE. Equilibrium is then defined to occur when total expenditures equal real income, or when $TE = Y.$ In this chapter, we first model the four aggregate expenditure categories, $C, I, G,$ and $NX;$ then describe the determination of equilibrium income (and how income changes with changes in various spending categories via the multiplier process); and, finally, describe the economic forces leading the economy to adjust from one equilibrium to another.

Before proceeding, however, one should consider the circular flow model of the economy (Figure 4-1), which illustrates how households, firms, and government are linked by these expenditure categories. The boxes indicate economic actors or institutions, while the lines between the categories show income or expenditure flows, and the direction of these flows is indicated by arrows. Thus, the box labeled "Households" has one entering flow, labeled Y for income. Households receive income from firms, either in the form of wages for labor services, interest payments on borrowed funds, rent on natural resources owned by households, or returns to the entrepreneurial activity undertaken by households. In addition, there are three flows out of Households: The first, labeled C for consumption, represents consumer spending on the output of firms; the second, labeled T for taxes, represents household payment of taxes to the government; and the third, labeled S for saving, represents household funds that are lent in financial markets—such as banks, stock and bond markets, and so forth. The circular flow model illustrates that households receive income Y and dispose of that income by engaging in consumption $C,$ saving $S,$ and paying taxes $T.$

FIGURE 4-1
The Circular Flow of
Expenditures

This figure shows the flow of expenditures on firm output, including expenditures on consumption by households (*C*), government expenditures (*G*), investment expenditures (*I*), and net exports (*NX*). These expenditures, balanced by expenditures by business firms on factors of production, including wages, salaries, profits, and rent, make up national income (*Y*) *and are equal in value to the expenditures on the* output of business.

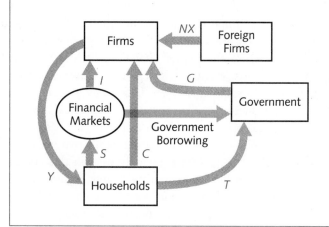

Notice the role of government and the financial market in this circular flow model. The financial market receives saving *S* from households, and lends these funds to businesses which will use them to purchase additional capital.[1] Business purchases of additional physical capital are known as investment *I* and represent a flow of spending on output by firms, since physical capital is produced by firms just as consumption goods are produced by firms. Government, too, is modeled very simply, with the government receiving taxes *T* from households and then using these tax revenues to finance government spending *G* on the output of firms. However, we do indicate with an arrow from financial markets to government that government borrowing will siphon off funds from the financial markets, so that government expenditures *G* can be greater than taxes *T*. This is a government budget deficit. Note, however, that this may reduce investment, since now household saving *S* will be divided between investment *I* and government borrowing.

---

[1]We are not allowing households to borrow in the financial markets, although clearly that is a real world possibility. Some texts would modify the circular flow model to show that some household saving is borrowed by other households, so that there would be an arrow from financial markets back to households. We would prefer to think of *S* as *net* saving of the households, after some households have lent to others. In this case *S* is the net saving of households that is available for financing investment spending by firms.

Finally, what about firms? Firms provide income Y to households, and receive revenues from the spending by households on consumer goods C as well as spending by firms themselves on physical capital I and spending by government on goods and services G. In addition, there is the possibility of trade with overseas firms, which we represent rather simply by adding a box labeled "Foreign Firms." When U.S. firms buy certain goods from abroad, the expenditure flow on those goods is to the foreign firms. Similarly, when U.S. firms sell goods abroad the expenditure flow is to the United States. The net of these expenditure flows will be called net exports NX. Net exports, or exports minus imports, will indicate whether the expenditure from the United States to foreign firms (imports) is larger or smaller than the expenditures from foreign firms to the United States (exports). When NX is positive, exports exceed imports; when NX is negative, imports exceed exports.

To summarize, then, U.S. firms generate income for households Y, which is produced by selling goods to consumers C, to firms purchasing new capital goods I, to government G, and from the net sales to foreign firms, net exports NX.

This circular flow model recalls two important national income accounting relationships that are widely used in this and future chapters. The first is the relationship of expenditure and income flows to and from a household. Households receive income Y, which they dispose of by consumption C, saving S, or paying taxes T, and we can write

$$Y = C + S + T.$$

This equation indicates that all income received by households is used in one of these three categories.

A second useful relationship can be seen by looking at firms, which receive expenditure flows from households C, from investment spending I, from government G, and net expenditures from foreign firms NX.[2] Firms also provide income to households, Y, and this income is equal to the expenditures on the firms' products. Thus, we can write that

$$Y = C + I + G + NX,$$

which indicates that firms produce income for households from spending on firm output by households themselves, by firms purchasing capital equipment, by government, and by the net purchases of foreign firms.

EXPENDITURES AND INCOME

We now turn to a discussion of the individual expenditure and income categories, beginning with the consumption and saving decisions of households.

[2]Note that net exports may be negative, in which case NX is really a net outflow from the firm. This does not alter in any way the above analysis, since a negative NX means that income paid from firms to households Y is less than $C + I + G$ by the amount of the negative NX.

Consumption Spending

In *The General Theory,* Keynes stressed that the level of consumption expenditures by households in an economy varied directly with the level of disposable income. This relationship between consumption and income, referred to as the **consumption function,** can be simply expressed as

$$C = C(Y_D); \ 1 > \Delta C/\Delta Y_D > 0. \tag{4.1}$$

The **CONSUMPTION FUNCTION** is the relationship between planned consumption expenditures of households and their current disposable income.

Here C is real consumption expenditures, and Y_D is real disposable, or after-tax, income. The term $C(Y_D)$ means that C is a function of Y_D. Here $\Delta C/\Delta Y_D$ indicates how much consumption increases when disposable income increases, and our assumption is that as disposable income rises, consumption rises by a fraction of the increase in disposable income. That is, the change in consumption due to a change in disposable income, $\Delta C/\Delta Y_D$, is between zero and one.

Disposable income itself is defined as income net of taxes, or

$$Y_D = Y - T. \tag{4.2}$$

Initially, we will assume that taxes are zero, so that disposable income and national income will be the same. That is, we can write $Y = Y_D$. That assumption will be relaxed later in this chapter.

It will be most convenient to express the consumption function in the form of an equation for a straight line, or a *linear* equation. To do this, we write the equation for the consumption function as

$$C = c_0 + c_1 Y; \ c_0 > 0, 1 > c_1 > 0. \tag{4.3}$$

Here c_0 is autonomous consumption, the amount of consumption that occurs even when disposable income is zero. This is positive because consumption of food and other necessities must occur even when income is zero. The parameter c_1 is the slope of the consumption function, and we assume that this slope is a fraction between zero and one to capture the idea that consumers increase consumption by a fraction of any increase in income. The slope c_1 is called the **marginal propensity to consume,** or MPC, and indicates the change in consumption expenditures that will occur in response to a change in disposable income.

The **MARGINAL PROPENSITY TO CONSUME** (or MPC) is the change in planned consumption expenditures divided by the change in income.

To more readily understand all of these concepts, let us explore the linear consumption function with a hypothetical example. Suppose we examined an economic report for an imaginary economy called Macroville and found the annual values—in billions of dollars—for consumption expenditures and income that are shown in Table 4-1.

The data from Table 4-1 are plotted in Figure 4-2. On the vertical axis are consumption expenditures, while on the horizontal axis is national income. Both variables are measured in real 1987 dollars, and the scale on both axes is the same. The 45-degree line drawn out of the origin is for reference. Since the scale on the vertical and horizontal axes is the same, the 45-degree line

TABLE 4-1
Consumption and Disposable Income (Billions of Dollars)

As the level of national income rises in an economy, the level of consumption expenditures also rises.

C	Y
$85	$60
$115	$100
160	160
190	200
265	300

FIGURE 4-2
The Consumption Function

If we plot the combinations of national income (Y) and planned consumption (C) from Table 4-1, we get the consumption function. The 45-degree line gives all possible points where consumption equals disposable income. For any particular consumption function, the point where the consumption function crosses the 45-degree line is the point where consumption equals disposable income. The vertical distance between the consumption line and the 45-degree line measures the amount of saving or dissaving corresponding to every level of disposable income.

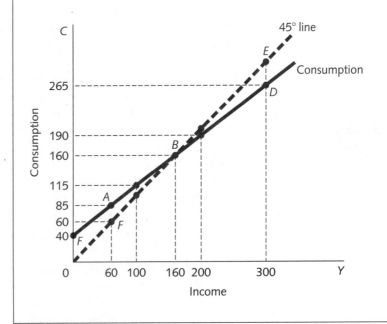

indicates the locus of points where the variable on the vertical axis has the same value as the variable on the horizontal axis. In our case, then, the 45-degree line indicates the set of points where $C = Y$. We plotted the data points from Table 4-1 on Figure 4-2, indicated by dots on the graph, and then connected the dots to draw the consumption function. Note that at only one point in Figure 4-2 does C equal Y, and that is point B, where the consumption line intersects the 45-degree line. At point B, $C = \$160$ billion $= Y$, and households spend their entire income. For income levels above \$160 billion, household consumption is less than disposable income. For instance, at point D, $Y = \$300$ billion, but $C = \$265$ billion. Income not spent is saved, so saving at point D is \$35 billion. Alternatively, at point A, $Y = \$60$ billion, but $C = \$85$ billion, so saving is a *negative* \$25 billion. At point A, we say that there is dissaving.

From Figure 4-2, we can derive the equation for the consumption function. First, we find the vertical intercept of our consumption line. When disposable income is zero, consumption is \$40 billion, so $c_0 = 40$. Next, the slope or MPC is $\Delta C / \Delta Y$. For instance, when income changes from \$100 billion to \$160 billion, consumption changes from \$115 billion to \$160 billion. Then $\Delta C / \Delta Y = (160 - 115)/(160 - 100) = 45/60 = .75$, so $c_1 = .75$. Our hypothetical consumption function is (in billions of 1982 dollars)

$$C = 40 + .75 \ Y.$$

Notice that the intercept is positive, as required, and the MPC is a fraction between zero and one.

We have briefly mentioned that consumption expenditures need not equal income, and that the difference between income and consumption is called saving. We pointed out that at one income level—\$160 billion in our example—consumption just equaled disposable income, but that for income levels higher than \$160 billion, consumption was less than income, so households would be saving. Likewise, for income levels below \$160 billion, consumption was greater than income, so households would be dissaving. How can households consume more than their income for a particular period? For consumption to exceed income, households would have to draw down savings from previous years, or they would have to borrow from financial institutions such as commercial banks or credit unions.

Is income the only determinate of consumption? Most economists think that consumer spending also depends on a number of other factors, which we will cover in more detail in Chapter 14. Keynes himself discussed other determinants of consumption as affecting the autonomous level of consumption c_0. One example might be consumer confidence about the state of the economy, and one measure of consumer confidence is the Conference Board's Consumer Confidence Index. This index is a summary of responses by individuals to five questions about current and expected future conditions. Key questions deal explicitly with the individual's job and income prospects over the next six months. When Iraq invaded Kuwait in August 1990, it took most

PHOTO 4-1
Consumption Spending is the Largest Component of Total Spending in the U.S. Economy.

Americans by surprise. The world price of oil almost doubled between July and October 1990. Because of this, and the uncertainty about the possibility of a Middle East war, there was a sharp decline in consumer confidence. In October 1990, the Conference Board's index of consumer confidence reached its lowest level since 1974. For the relationship between consumer confidence and personal consumption expenditures, see Figure 4-3.

Economic theory suggests that decreases in consumer confidence may reduce consumer spending, especially for purchases of durable goods (goods such as automobiles and household appliances). These are usually big-ticket items, which consumers are slow to purchase when they are uncertain about their future employment. Also, these are purchases that consumers can usually postpone, making do with an older car or an older appliance, perhaps by spending more on repairs and maintenance. Figure 4-3 shows the sharp decline in personal consumption spending in the latter half of 1990, which corresponds to the drop in consumer confidence associated with the soaring oil prices and the invasion of Kuwait. Although some economists debate the usefulness of consumer confidence surveys in forecasting economic performance, the surveys may be useful in exceptional circumstances such as the Gulf War. In this chapter, however, we will stress only the relationship between income and consumption, while remembering that other variables affect consumption by changing autonomous consumption c_0.

Finally, the Insight: "Let's Look at the Data on Consumption" describes actual U.S. consumption data for 1972-1992.

Driven in part by the drop in consumer confidence during the Gulf War, personal consumption expenditures fell in late 1990 before beginning to rise in early 1991.

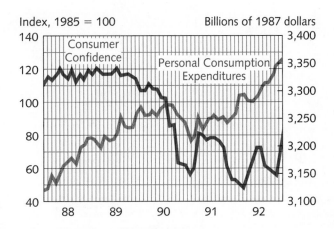

SOURCE: Council of Economic Advisors, *Economic Report of the President* (Washington, DC: U.S. Government Printing Office, 1993), p. 94.

Saving: The Counterpart of Consumption

The counterpart of the consumption function is the *saving function*. Households receive a certain amount of income Y, and they choose either to spend this on consumption C or to save it. Saving will be denoted S, and is related to consumption and income by the equation

$$Y = C + S. \tag{4.4}$$

We can rearrange this to give $S = Y - C$, and from this expression and Table 4-1, we can calculate the level of saving at each income level for our hypothetical economy. This is shown in Table 4-2.

We can also write down a linear saving function to accompany our consumption function. Since $C = c_0 + c_0Y$, and $S = Y - C$, we can write

$$S = Y - c_0 - c_1 Y, \text{ or}$$

$$S = -c_0 + (1 - c_1)Y. \tag{4.5}$$

The **MARGINAL PROPENSITY TO SAVE (OR MPS)** is the change in planned saving divided by the change in disposable income.

In the saving function, $-c_0$ is the intercept and $(1 - c_1)$ is the slope, or marginal propensity to save (MPS). The **marginal propensity to save** gives the ratio of the change in saving to the change in income, or $\Delta S/\Delta Y$. Note that, since c_1 is between zero and one, the marginal propensity to save is also

LET'S LOOK AT THE DATA

ON CONSUMPTION

In the text we present a version of Keynes's theory of consumption, in which consumption is a linear function of income. Here we will look at the data on consumption and income, to see how well the theory presented in the text works at explaining actual data.

The consumption model in the text says that consumption can be described as

$$C = c_0 + c_1 Y,$$

where C is real consumption expenditures and Y is real income. In many ways this theory is too simple to explain all of the movements in consumption. However, it is not our goal to model consumption perfectly. It is our goal to present a simple, but not overly simple, model that captures the crucial features of the macroeconomy. The theory captures the essential features of the relationship of consumption to income. As income increases, consumption increases by an amount

c_1, which is between zero and one. This is Keynes's insight.

To investigate the relationship of consumption to income, Figure 4-4 presents a graph of real consumption expenditures and real GDP for the time period 1972–1992. Consumption follows the scale on the left-hand side, while real GDP follows the scale on the right-hand side. This allows us to graph consumption and real GDP and see more clearly the relationship between the two. Notice that, while consumption is only about 60 percent of real GDP, movements in real GDP are mimicked by similar movements in consumption. For example, the downturns in real GDP in 1974, 1980, 1982, and 1990 are reflected in downturns in consumption.

Another feature of the relationship between consumption and real GDP seen in Figure 4-4 is that changes in consumption are less extreme than changes in real GDP. Consumption does not change by as large an amount as GDP. This is especially noticeable in the recession of 1982, when real GDP dropped sharply, but consumption declined very little. Similar but

less dramatic examples of this are evident in the recessions of 1974, 1980, and 1990–91.

Overall, then, consumption does behave roughly in the manner described in the theory. Consumption is a fraction of real GDP, and changes in real GDP manifest themselves as changes in consumption. Moreover, changes in GDP result in changes in consumption that are typically a fraction of the changes in real GDP.

This latter feature is often called consumption smoothing, and can be explained by the fact that consumers do not adjust their consumption spending to every change in income. In fact, consumers often save when income is atypically high, and dissave when income is atypically low. Thus, consumption doesn't increase dollar for dollar when income rises, especially when income rises above the usual level of household income, and consumption doesn't decrease dollar for dollar when income falls, especially when income falls below the usual level of household income. We'll have more to say about this in Chapter 14. ❑

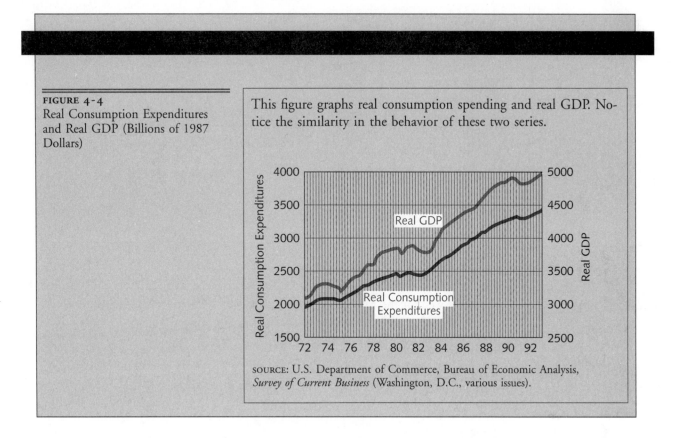

FIGURE 4-4
Real Consumption Expenditures and Real GDP (Billions of 1987 Dollars)

This figure graphs real consumption spending and real GDP. Notice the similarity in the behavior of these two series.

SOURCE: U.S. Department of Commerce, Bureau of Economic Analysis, *Survey of Current Business* (Washington, D.C., various issues).

between zero and one. Thus, any increase in disposable income is used to partly increase consumption and partly increase saving. Also, since the MPC is c_1 and the MPS is $(1 - c_1)$, it will be true that MPC + MPS = $c_1 + (1 - c_1) = 1$. That is, any increase in income is totally used up in increasing consumption and saving. These are the only two uses for an increase in income.[3]

The relationship between the saving function and the consumption function allows us to derive the saving function for our hypothetical economy from the consumption function. The consumption function was $C = 40 + .75\ Y$, so the saving function will be

$$S = Y - C$$
$$= Y - (40 + .75\ Y)$$
$$= -40 + (1 - .75)\ Y$$
$$= -40 + .25\ Y.$$

---

[3]This is actually a special feature of assuming that taxes are zero.

TABLE 4-2
Consumption, Income, and
Saving (Billions of Dollars)

This table shows planned saving in an economy. Column 3 presents saving per year, which is the difference between income and consumption.

(1)	(2)	(3)
C	Y	S = Y − C
$ 85	$ 60	$ − 25
$ 115	$ 100	$ − 15
160	160	0
190	200	10
265	300	+35

FIGURE 4-5
The Saving Function

If we plot the relationship between income (Y) and saving (S) in column 3 of Table 4-3, we arrive at the saving function shown in this figure.

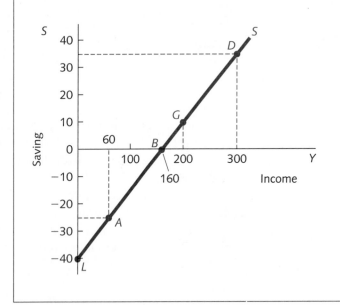

We plot the saving function in Figure 4-5. On the vertical axis is saving; on the horizontal axis is income. The vertical intercept is –$40 billion, and the slope is .25. When income is $160 billion, S = 0. As income rises above $160 billion, saving is positive; for disposable income below $160 billion saving is negative. Data points from Table 4-2 are indicated by dots. For instance, point

B is at income level $160 billion, where saving is zero. Point D, when income is $300 billion, shows saving of $35 billion. Point A, when income is $60 billion, shows saving of -$25 billion. Notice the correspondence with Figure 4-3, which shows the analogous consumption expenditures for these income levels. Thus, if we are given a saving function we can easily determine a consumption function, and vice versa.

Investment Spending

Along with consumption, a very important component of aggregate spending is investment expenditures. Businesses invest when they purchase physical capital, which includes both structures (such as factories or other buildings) and equipment (such as computers, lathes, or other fixtures placed in these structures), and they also invest when they accumulate inventories. Decisions by businesses to invest in new plants, new equipment, and even changes in inventories can depend on such factors as national income, the real interest rate, and expectations about the future. As discussed in Chapter 3, the real interest rate is the nominal interest rate (or the money interest rate) minus the expected inflation rate. We write this as

$$r = R - \pi^e, \tag{4.6}$$

where r is the real interest rate, R is the nominal rate, π is the inflation rate, and the superscript e symbolizes that we are considering the expectation of π.

To model investment expenditures, we assume that expectations about the future are constant. This assumption is made to simplify the problem, since we cannot easily model how investors' expectations of future profitability might change over time. Investment is then a function of the real interest rate and income, which we write as

$$I = I(r); \quad \Delta I/\Delta r < 0 \tag{4.7}$$

Here I is real investment spending and r is the real interest rate. Increases in the real interest rate reduce investment spending, because the opportunity cost of purchasing physical capital increases. For example, if firms are financing their investment by borrowing, the increased real interest rate increases the cost of borrowing a given sum of funds and thereby reduces investment spending. Alternatively, if firms are using retained earnings, these retained earnings have an opportunity cost—the interest income they could generate if lent out at the market interest rate. In either case, the real interest rate r measures the opportunity cost of funds used in purchasing capital.

As income increases, investment spending might also increase, because the increased income leads to an increased profitability of investment. The idea here is that an increase in income will increase spending on all goods and services, increasing the need businesses have for capital to produce and sell more goods and services. Therefore, businesses will find it more profitable to

:tion

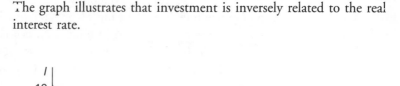

The graph illustrates that investment is inversely related to the real interest rate.

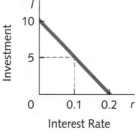

increase the capital stock via investment so as to sell more goods and services.

We will want to consider a linear version of our investment equation given in equation 4.7, which we will write as

$$I = d_0 - d_1 r \tag{4.8}$$

Here d_0 represents the constant in investment, part of which is determined by expectations about the future. The term $- d_1$ represents the reduction in I when r increases.

However, we will not explicitly model the effect of income on investment. We make the common simplifying assumption is that income does not affect investment spending directly, so $d_2 = 0$. This assumption allows a less complicated presentation of our model of the goods market.

We graph our investment function in Figure 4-6. Let our investment function be given by $I = 10 - .5r$. (Notice that income has no direct effect on investment expenditures.) We graph this investment on the vertical axis and the real interest rate on the horizontal axis as shown. The vertical intercept will give the value of investment when $r = 0\%$, which is 10, or $I = 10$, as illustrated in Figure 4-6. The investment function is downward sloping (the slope is $-.5$), indicating that every 1 percent increase in r will reduce I by $-.5$ dollars. When r rises enough, investment will be zero. In our equation, when $r = 20\%$, $I = 0$.

The actual behavior of U.S. investment data is outlined in some detail in the Insight: "Let's Look at the Data on Investment."

INSIGHT

LET'S LOOK AT THE DATA

ON INVESTMENT

In the text we present a model of investment spending in which investment is a linear function of the real interest rate. We want to look at the data on investment and the real interest rate in order to see how well this theory works at explaining movements in the data.

The investment model in the text says that investment can be described as

$$I = d_0 - d_1 r,$$

where I is real investment spending, and r is the real interest rate, defined as the nominal interest rate R minus the expected inflation rate, π^e. Notice that increases in the real interest rate are supposed to reduce investment spending. To look at this relationship, we first construct a measure of the real interest rate.

We need to choose a measure of the nominal interest rate R and a measure of the expected inflation rate π^e. For R, we use the one-year Treasury bill rate. For π^e, we use the actual inflation rate between the present date and one year in the future. Obviously this is only a proxy for the expected inflation rate, and in essence ignores the fact that individuals do not know what the inflation rate will be over the upcoming year. If individuals form expectations of inflation that are correct on average, then our measure will be correct on average, but will not be correct at any particular date.

In Figure 4-7, we graph both real private investment expenditures and our measure of the real interest rate. Real private investment expenditures are measured on the left-hand scale, while the real interest rate is measured on the right-hand scale. As is apparent in the diagram, the fit between the data and the theory is not quite as good as in the case of consumption and income, but the data do accord in large measure with the theory. In particular, during the 1974–1976 period, and during 1981–1983, the real interest rate increased, and real investment expenditures declined sharply. Thus in this preliminary investigation the data do not contradict our simple model of investment.

Other features of the investment data can be read from Figure 4-7. In particular, investment is seen to be quite volatile, with 20 percent declines occurring during the recessions beginning in 1974 and 1982, and a similar sharp drop preceding the recessions of 1980 and 1990–91. Unlike consumption, which is smoother than the real GDP data, investment responds much more sharply than real GDP to business cycle conditions. This feature led Keynes to ascribe business cycles to movements in the volatile investment series. ❑

GOVERNMENT SPENDING AND TAXES

FISCAL POLICY is a policy associated with deliberate changes on the part of the federal government with respect to taxation or spending.

Fiscal policy is the management of government expenditures on goods and services and tax collections to affect the level of aggregate demand in the economy. Fiscal policy is carried out by the federal government through the actions of the President of the United States and his administration, in conjunction with Congress. Decisions are made about the size of government

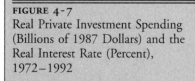

FIGURE 4-7
Real Private Investment Spending
(Billions of 1987 Dollars) and the
Real Interest Rate (Percent),
1972–1992

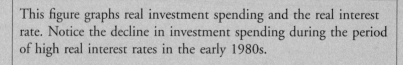

This figure graphs real investment spending and the real interest rate. Notice the decline in investment spending during the period of high real interest rates in the early 1980s.

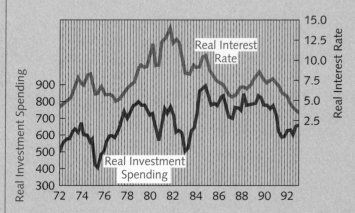

SOURCE: Investment: U.S. Department of Commerce, Bureau of Economic Analysis *Survey of Current Business* (Washington, D.C.: various issues). Real interest rate: Calculated by the authors as the difference between the one-year Treasury bill rate and a measure of the actual inflation rate calculated from the GDP deflator. Sources for underlying data are the Board of Governors of the Federal Reserve System and the U.S. Department of Commerce, Bureau of Economic Analysis.

purchases of final goods and services and about whether to reduce or increase corporate and personal taxes.

The Reagan years provide an interesting experiment on the effects of fiscal policy. Initially, the Reagan administration substantially increased defense spending, and, with the Economic Recovery and Tax Reform Act of 1981, cut tax rates for both businesses and households. One of the ideas behind cutting the tax rates on households was to stimulate personal saving, but the private saving rate either fell or at best remained fairly constant over this period, depending on the measure of saving used. The tax cut for businesses was aimed at increasing business investment in plant and equipment. The Reagan program was advanced as a plan to stimulate saving and investment, and hence aggregate supply of goods and services. But the traditional Keynesian view would analyze these policies as increasing spending and decreasing taxes, which would stimulate spending, apart from any supply-side influence.

To analyze the effect of fiscal policy on aggregate spending, we must consider the effect of both government spending and taxes. For now, we make the simplifying assumptions that 1) real government spending on goods and services G is exogenous, and 2) taxes net of transfer payments to individuals (i.e., taxes minus transfers), or T, are exogenous and lump sum. **Lump sum taxes** are taxes that are levied on households and that are unrelated to endogenous variables, most specifically income. In other words, lump sum taxes do not change with income. An example of a lump sum tax is a head tax, in which taxes are levied on people strictly on a per capita basis. If taxes are levied on the basis of income or wealth they are *not* lump sum taxes.

LUMP SUM TAXES are taxes levied on households that are unrelated to endogenous variables, most specifically income.

Based on the above assumptions, we write government spending as

$$G = G_0. \tag{4.1}$$

As for taxes net of transfers, we have

$$T = T_0; \qquad T_0 > 0. \tag{4.2}$$

Here, T_0 gives net tax collections that occur regardless of income. This is lump sum taxes. Taxes are exogenous, and therefore do not change with changes in income.

Notice that for nonzero taxes, disposable income is national income minus taxes, or

$$Y_D = Y - T. \tag{4.3}$$

Since consumption is a function of disposable income, we substitute $Y - T$ for Y_D and write the consumption function as

$$C = c_0 + c_1 Y_D, \tag{4.4}$$

or,

$$C = c_0 + c_1 (Y - T). \tag{4.5}$$

For nonzero taxes, equation 4-13 is the appropriate linear consumption function.

NET EXPORTS

Exports are goods and services that the domestic economy sells to foreign economies. In the production of goods and services for sale abroad (exports), income is created for domestic households and domestic businesses. Moreover, domestic businesses receive revenue from the sale of these goods and services. *Imports* are goods and services purchased by the domestic economy from foreign economies. Goods and services produced in foreign economies and sold in our domestic economy (imports) generate income to foreign households and businesses.

The difference between gross exports and gross imports is called *net foreign expenditures,* or *net exports.* Net exports can either be positive or negative, depending on whether the level of exports is greater than or less than the level

The EXCHANGE RATE is the number of dollars required to purchase one unit of a foreign currency.

A DEPRECIATION OF THE DOLLAR occurs when it takes more dollars to buy a single unit of a foreign currency.

An APPRECIATION OF THE DOLLAR occurs when it takes fewer dollars to buy a single unit of a foreign currency.

of imports. Gross exports are assumed to be dependent on such factors as tariff and trade policies of the domestic economy, the level of national income of foreign economies, and exchange rates. We have seen in previous chapters (see Global Perspective on NAFTA in Chapter 1, for example) that tariff barriers in trading nations—taxes on imports from other countries—reduce the level of specialization and trade. Clearly, limitations on United States exports hinder domestic job growth and industrial development. Any restrictions—tariffs or nontariffs—tend to hinder macroeconomic growth and development. The same is true of trade restrictions *within* the United States (see Global Perspective: "What About Free Trade Within the United States").

Exchange rates are also an important determinant of export growth. The factors affecting exchange rates are for the most part not determined in the domestic market, and are considered exogenous variables. We will nevertheless model the dependence of exports on the **exchange rate.** The nominal exchange rate E measures how many units of the domestic currency—how many dollars—it takes to purchase one unit of the foreign currency. As the exchange rate increases, it takes more dollars to buy a single unit of the foreign currency (a **depreciation of the dollar**). Alternatively stated, as the exchange rate rises it takes fewer units of the foreign currency to purchase a single dollar. Thus, increases in the exchange rate mean that foreigners need less of their currency to buy a dollar, or less of their currency to buy any good whose price is stated in dollar terms.

Consider an example, you might want to sell sweaters made in the United States to the English. The sweater might cost $20 to make, including a fair return for yourself. If the exchange rate is $2 per English pound, then someone in England must pay £10 [$20/($2/pound) = £10] to purchase this sweater from you. If the exchange rate increases to $4 per English pound, then someone in England must pay £5 [$20/($4/pound) = £5] to purchase this sweater from you. Thus, if the exchange rate rises, the same U.S. sweater is cheaper to English consumers, and the English will purchase more sweaters. More generally, increases in E cause exports to rise.

Decreases in E are called an **appreciation of the dollar,** and this is the opposite of depreciation of the dollar. In the above example, an appreciation of the dollar would be a decrease in the exchange rate from $2 per English pound to $1 per English pound. Now the U.S.-made sweater still costs $20 in the United States, but the English have to pay £20 to purchase the sweater, instead of £10 pounds when the exchange rate was $2 per pound. Hence the appreciation of the dollar makes the U.S. sweater more expensive in England, and the English will purchase fewer sweaters, reducing U.S. exports. A similar analysis of a product made in England and imported into the United States will reveal that an appreciation of the dollar—a decline in the number of dollars it takes to purchase an English pound—will make imports from England less expensive in the United States, and hence will encourage U.S. citizens to buy English goods. A depreciation of the dollar will make imports from England more expensive in the United States and will discourage U.S. citizens from buying English goods.

WHAT ABOUT FREE TRADE WITHIN THE UNITED STATES?

Recently economist Gerald P. O'Driscoll, Jr., has asked the question posed above. He argues that while the United States, Canada, and Mexico are busy negotiating the North America Free Trade Agreement (NAFTA) the U.S. should consider that the fifty states have yet to establish a single internal market. In other words, the U.S. itself is not a free trade area.[a]

What are the barriers to trade that exist between the fifty states? The U.S. Constitution has several clauses that pertain to trade between the states, and that generally prevent barriers to interstate trade, at least in commodities. However, these clauses have not generally been applied to services. There are also prohibitions on import duties among the states (so that Texas could not impose tariffs on goods entering from Arkansas, for example), but non-tariff barriers to trade are not prohibited.

What are these nontariff barriers? First, there are ad-ministrative restrictions, especially on agricultural goods. For example, from 1925 through 1973 California prohibited the importation of Florida avocados. This was not a direct ban on imports, which would be overthrown in court, but a requirement that avocadoes had to have more than 8 percent oil content. Florida avocadoes tend to have less oil than this, and thus were effectively banned from sale in California. The reputed reason for this ban was to protect the public health! We should note too that administrative bans such as these are what U.S. firms complain about in Japan, yet the U.S. states use these tactics against each other.

There are also restrictions on trade in services. Doctors, lawyers, teachers, and often even barbers and beauticians are required to have a license or certificate to operate within a state, and are not allowed to practice in, say, New York, just because they are licensed in New Jersey. Instead, they must either take an exam, pay a fee, or otherwise satisfy the requirements for obtaining a license or certificate in New York. This restriction on movements of services between states is a barrier to trade.

What would help free trade within the fifty states? O'Driscoll suggests adoption of the principle of mutual recognition: Each state will recognize the rules and regulations of the other states, as long as these accord with federal rules. Thus, a person, firm, or corporation chartered to operate in California must obey rules and regulations in California, but may operate in Texas and New York under rules established *in California.*

The importance of this principle of mutual recognition cannot be understated. It would allow individuals and firms to obtain a charter to operate a bank in Illinois, under Illinois law and regulations, and then to freely expand into Indiana, Kentucky, Missouri, or elsewhere, and operate banks in those states *under Illinois law.* This effectively eliminates many of the nontariff barriers to trade among the states. Indeed, this principle of mutual recognition is a key principle guiding the European move to free trade within the European Community, and is recognized already within the United States for trade in commodities. It is also recognized in establishing corporations. Commercial and industrial corporations chartered in, say,

Delaware, can operate under that charter in the other forty-nine states, subject to certain limits "in the interest of public safety and health." However, the financial service industry is not so free to charter in one state and operate in all

others. For example, commercial banks are only now getting something like this freedom to engage in interstate banking, which was nearly universally banned until the last decade. ❑

NOTE [a]See Gerald P. O'Driscoll, Jr., "What About Free Trade Within the United States?" Federal Reserve Bank of Dallas *The Southwest Economy* (January/February 1992), pp. 1–5.

The REAL EXCHANGE RATE is the exchange rate multiplied by the ratio of the foreign price level to the domestic price level; it tells us how much a unit of foreign currency can buy in the United States relative to how much a unit of foreign currency can buy in its own economy.

The nominal exchange rate measures the number of dollars it takes to buy a unit of foreign currency. Another concept, the **real exchange rate,** is a measure of the purchasing power of a dollar. The nominal exchange rate tells how many dollars it takes to buy a unit of foreign currency, such as an English pound. An increase in the exchange rate by itself, however, may be insufficient to tell us how exports or imports will respond. This is because the prices of goods in the two nations might change. Thus, in our example above a change in the exchange rate might be accompanied by a change in the price of the sweater in the United States, so that we must consider not only the nominal exchange rate but also behavior of prices in the two nations. Thus, we must consider the real exchange rate, which takes into account both the exchange rate and the price level in the two nations to tell us how much a unit of foreign currency can buy in the United States relative to how much a unit of foreign currency can buy in its own economy. For the United States and the United Kingdom, the real exchange rate can be written as $E P_{UK}/P_{US}$. This can be rewritten as $P_{UK}/(P_{US}/E)$. In the denominator is (P_{US}/E), which gives to an English consumer the average price—in pounds—of goods produced in the United States. In the numerator is P_{UK}, which is the average price to an English consumer of goods produced in the United Kingdom. Holding the price level constant in both the United States and the United Kingdom, an increase in E increases the real exchange rate and increases exports. Holding the nominal exchange rate E constant, an increase in the ratio of prices in the United Kingdom to prices in the United States, P_{UK}/P_{US}, also increases the real exchange rate and increases exports. Both effects occur because an increase in the real exchange rate makes goods produced in the United States relatively less expensive to the English than goods produced in the United Kingdom, and hence the English buy more U.S. goods.

Imports are considered to be dependent on the level of domestic income and on real exchange rates. As the level of domestic income rises, households buy more of all goods, including more goods produced in foreign countries. Likewise, when the real exchange rate increases, whether due to an increase in the nominal exchange rate or an increase in the ratio of the foreign price level to the domestic price level, imports decline. This latter effect occurs because an increase in the real exchange rate makes goods produced at home relatively less expensive than goods produced abroad.

Net exports are the difference between exports and imports. Exports respond positively to an increase in the real exchange rate, and hence cause net exports to also respond positively. Imports respond positively to increases in domestic income, which then cause net exports to fall with an increase in domestic income. Finally, imports respond negatively to an increase in the real exchange rate, which then causes net exports to increase with an increase in the real exchange rate. For now, we assume that the ratio of foreign to domestic prices remains constant, so that net exports are a function of the nominal exchange rate. Also, we assume for now that income does not directly affect net exports. These assumptions are made to simplify matters. Net exports can be written as

$$NX = n_0 + n_1 E. \tag{4.13}$$

To gain a better understanding of net exports in the United States, see the Global Perspective: "Let's Look at the Data on Net Exports."

PHOTO 4-2
Arriving Imports of Frozen Peruvian Scallops Get Extra Careful Treatment by Longshoremen at the Port of Los Angeles in San Pedro, CA.

LET'S LOOK AT THE DATA

ON NET EXPORTS

We have presented a model that writes net exports as a function of the exchange rate, given by

$$NX = n_0 + n_1 E,$$

where NX is net exports, and E is the exchange rate in dollars per unit of foreign currency. To investigate this model, we graph net exports against the exchange rate in Figure 4-8. The measure of net exports is from the national income and product accounts. The measure of the exchange rate requires some explanation.

In our theory, we write E as the exchange rate in dollars per unit of foreign currency. However, the United States does not trade with just one country, but instead trades with a whole host of nations using a whole host of currencies. This causes problems in defining the relevant exchange rate, since there is no single exchange rate to use as a measure of E. We could just use the German deutsche mark or the Japanese yen or the English pound, but the use of any one would not only ig-

nore the other two, but would also ignore many other important trading partners of the United States. The solution to this problem is to measure E as a weighted average of the exchange rates between the dollar and the currencies of the U.S. trading partners. One such index is called the trade weighted exchange rate, and adds together the exchange rates of each of the major U.S. trading partners, weighted by the extent of trade between the United States and that country.

One further issue is that trade weighted exchange rate, or TWEX, is computed as foreign currency per dollar, which is the inverse of how we defined E. That is, TWEX is actually a measure of $1/E$. Thus, increases in TWEX are *decreases* in E, and should *decrease* net exports. In sum, our theory predicts that increases in TWEX reduce net exports.

In Figure 4-8, net exports and TWEX are graphed. The scale of net exports appears on the left-hand side. It is clear that the large increase in TWEX that began in 1980 and peaked in 1984 was accompanied by a large decline in net exports. It is also clear that movements in TWEX take some time to get translated into movements in net

exports. For instance, the large decline in TWEX from 1984 to 1986 was followed by an increase in net exports beginning in 1986. As the 1990s began, the trade weighted exchange rate was declining, and net exports were rising.

Another feature apparent in Figure 4-8 is that U.S. net exports are frequently negative. That is, imports exceed exports. Beginning in 1982, net exports have been negative, with the largest shortfall in 1986.

The largest negative values for net exports together with the large government budget deficit have been labeled the *twin deficits*. Interest in the relationship between the two was stimulated in the 1980s, when there was a simultaneous increase in both the net export deficit and the government budget deficit. We will have more to say on this issue in a later chapter. For now, we merely note that while net exports moved sharply negative in the early 1980s, they reached their biggest deficit in 1986 and have since been increasing fairly steadily, although with some ups and downs, so that in the early 1990s net exports are at least approaching balance. Whether a balance or even a surplus occurs in the early to middle 1990s remains to be seen. ❏

FIGURE 4-8
Real Net Exports (Billions of 1987 Dollars) and the Trade Weighted Exchange Rate (1973 = 100), 1972–92

This graph shows the relationship between net exports and the exchange rate. Notice the large decline in net exports in the middle 1980s, corresponding to the large increase in the trade weighted exchange rate in this period. The fall in the trade weighted exchange rate in the middle part of the 1980s was followed with a lag in improvements in the U.S. net export position.

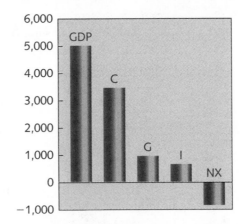

SOURCE: U.S. Department of Commerce, Bureau of Economic Analysis *Survey of Current Business* (Washington, D.C.: various issues) and *Federal Reserve Bulletin* (Washington, D.C: various issues)

EQUILIBRIUM IN THE GOODS MARKET

The basic equilibrium condition for the goods market in our model is that total real expenditures *TE* equals total income *Y*. The idea comes from consideration of the circular flow model, in which income produced by firms is *Y*, and total expenditures on the output of firms *TE* are given by adding together the four components of spending consumption (*C*) plus investment (*I*) plus government spending on goods and services (*G*) plus net exports (*NX*). In equilibrium *TE* = *Y*, or

$$C + I + G + NX = Y. \tag{4.14}$$

Each of the expenditure categories has been previously discussed. To get an idea of the relative sizes and behavior of these categories in the United States, see the Insight: "Let's Look at the Components of Total Spending."

INSIGHT

LET'S LOOK AT THE DATA

ON THE COMPONENTS OF

TOTAL SPENDING

In the text we have seen that total expenditures consist of four components: consumption, investment, govern- ment spending, and net ex- ports. These four components, and real GDP, are graphed in Figure 4-9. This figure gives an indication of the size of these four components in total spending, as well as an indica- tion of the volatility of the components series.

It is evident that consumption is the largest component of real GDP, and in fact con- sumption spending makes up about 60 percent of real GDP. Government spending and investment spending are of roughly the same size, and each makes up about 20 per- cent of real GDP. Finally, net exports are often negative, representing a subtraction from real GDP, and are less than 5 percent of real GDP in magnitude.   ❑

FIGURE 4-9
The Components of Real GDP
(Billions of 1987 Dollars)

This graph shows the components of GDP in the last quarter of 1992. Consumption is by far the largest component, with gov- ernment expenditures edging out investment spending, and net exports small and negative.

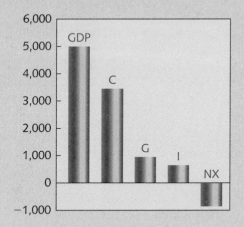

SOURCE: U.S. Department of Commerce, Bureau of Economic Analysis *Survey of Current Business* (Washington, D.C.: various issues) and *Federal Reserve Bulle- tin* (Washington, D.C.: various issues).

In order to analyze the behavior of the economy, we begin by rewriting our behavioral equations for the four expenditure categories:

$$C = c_0 + c_1\, Y_D;\; c_0 > 0,\, 1 > c_1\; 0, \tag{4.3}$$
$$\text{where } Y_D = Y - T \tag{4.12}$$
$$\text{and } T = T_0. $$
$$I = d_0 - d_1\, r, \tag{4.9}$$
$$\text{where } r = R - \pi^e. \tag{4.6}$$
$$G = G_0. \tag{4.10}$$
$$NX\!:\; NX = n_0 + n_1\, E. \tag{4.13}$$

Equilibrium occurs where income equals total spending, or $TE = Y$. We can look at this equilibrium in Figure 4-10.[4] On the vertical axis we measure real expenditures; on the horizontal axis we measure real income. The 45-degree line is the set of points where $TE = Y$, that is, the set of all possible equilibrium points.

We add together four components of aggregate expenditures to obtain the total spending line TE. Algebraically, we would calculate the total expenditure line as

$$\begin{aligned}
TE &= C + I + G + NX \\
&= [c_0 + c_1(Y - T_0)] + [d_0 - d_1\, r] + G_0 + [n_0 + n_1\, E] \\
&= \{c_0 - c_1 T_0 + d_0 - d_1\, r + G_0 + n_0 + n_1\, E\} + c_1\, Y.
\end{aligned}$$

The slope of the total expenditure line indicates how total expenditures change with income, and only consumption changes with income. Since consumption increases by the marginal propensity to consume, c_1, for each dollar that income increases, it is also the case that total expenditures increase by c_1 for each dollar that income increases. Thus, the slope of total expenditures TE is just the MPC. The rest of the terms in the total expenditure equation above determine the vertical intercept of the total expenditure function in Figure 4-10, the height of the TE curve where it intersects the vertical axis. This vertical intercept is given by $\{c_0 - c_1 T_0 + d_0 - d_1\, r + G_0 + n_0 + n_1\, E\}$.

---

[4]Algebraically, we can derive the equilibrium as follows. We add up the components of total spending and set these equal to income. That is, we can substitute the above expressions for consumption, investment, government spending, and net exports into 4.14, and also substitute the expressions for disposable income in consumption, equation 4.12. This gives us the equilibrium condition as

$$\begin{aligned}
Y &= TE \\
&= [c_0 + c_1(Y - T_0)] + [d_0 - d_1\, r] + G_0 + [n_0 + n_1\, E].
\end{aligned}$$

Rearranging, to put terms involving Y on the left-hand side, we have

$$(1 - c_1)Y = c_0 - T_0 + d_0 - d_1\, r + G_0 + n_0 + n_1\, E,$$

and dividing both sides by $(1 - c_1)$ gives equilibrium income (and equivalently equilibrium total expenditures) as

$$Y = [c_0 - c_1\, T_0 + d_0 - d_1\, r + G_0 + n_0 + n_1\, E]/(1 - c_1).$$

Notice that this is just the constant in the TE equation divided by $(1 - c_1)$.

FIGURE 4-10
Determination of Equilibrium
Income

The equilibrium level of income is determined by the intersection of the total expenditure line, *TE* and the 45-degree line. This occurs at point *E*, where equilibrium income is $600. Notice that *TE* is derived by adding up the values of consumption (*C*), investment (*I*), government spending (*G*), and net exports (*NX*). Only consumption changes with changes in national income.

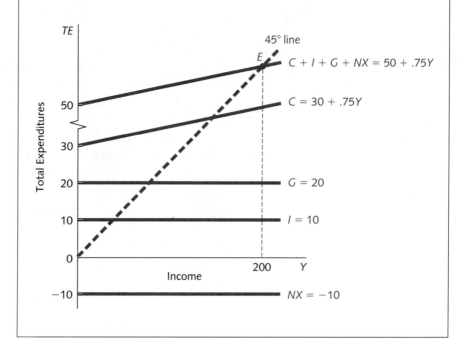

To help us understand this model, suppose we have the following values for Macroville: autonomous consumption c_0 is $45 billion; the MPC c_1 is .75; taxes T_0 are $20 billion; the constant in the investment equation d_0 is $11 billion; the parameter d_1 in the investment equation is -.1; government spending G_0 is $20 billion; the constant in net exports n_0, is -$14 billion; the parameter n_1 is .2; the real interest rate is 10 (i.e., 10 percent); and the exchange rate is 20 dollars per unit of foreign currency. What is the slope of total expenditures? It is just the MPC, or .75, because only consumption depends on income. What is the height of the total expenditure line? Substituting these numbers into the equation for the vertical intercept, we see that the total expenditure line has a vertical intercept of $50 billion. [(Alternatively, we can calculate investment as $10 billion ($11 − .1 × $10), government spending as $20 billion, net exports as −$10 (−$14 + .2 × $20) billion, and the vertical intercept of our consumption line as $30 billion ($45 − .75 × $20)]. This is graphed in Figure 4-10.

To find equilibrium, we merely look for the point where $TE = Y$. This is the level of income for which total expenditures on output of firms equal the income (or output) produced by firms. Since the 45-degree line contains all possible points where $TE = Y$, we simply find where the graph of TE crosses the 45-degree line, and, thus, find the equilibrium value of Y—and of TE. This value can be determined algebraically as the vertical intercept divided by (1 – MPC), or $50 billion divided by (1 – .75). The answer, $200 billion, is the equilibrium level of income.[5]

Changes in Equilibrium

We have seen above how equilibrium is determined in the goods market. This equilibrium is for fixed values of the model's parameters (the terms $c_0, c_1, d_0, d_1, n_0, n_1$, etc.) and for fixed values of the exogenous variables (such as G, T, r, and E). If any of these change, the equilibrium will be affected. In this section, we analyze how changes in the exogenous variables will alter the equilibrium.

We will concentrate on changes to the variables and parameters that determine the vertical intercept of the total expenditures line TE. A change in any of the variables that determine this vertical intercept (that is, that determine the level of spending when income is zero) will shift total expenditures upward or downward in parallel with its original position. This will change the equilibrium level of income, as can be seen by imagining such a shift in Figure 4-10. Such a shift will change the level of income at which the total expenditure line intersects the 45-degree line, which in turn illustrates the change in equilibrium. Changes in government spending (a change in G_0), in investment (a change in either d_0 or r), in taxes (a change in T_0), in net exports (a change in n_0 or E), or in consumption (a change in c_0) could account for the shift. In any case, the analysis of these changes is the analysis of a parallel shift in the total expenditure line.

To be concrete, let us consider Figure 4-11, where we have assumed that the initial vertical intercept of TE is $50.[6] We also assume that the slope of TE, the MPC or c_1, is .75. We can find the initial equilibrium as the vertical intercept, $50, divided by (1 – c_1), so equilibrium income is given by $50/(1 – .75) = $200.

What happens if the vertical intercept increases by $25? This can happen for a host of reasons. Investment spending might increase by $25, perhaps because businesses become more optimistic about the economy and decide to expand productive capacity. We would model this as an increase in d_0 of $25. In this

---

[5] See Footnote 4 for a derivation of this formula describing the equilibrium. One thing to keep in mind is that we wanted to simplify the analysis and so we assumed that I and NX were not functions of Y. If I and NX were functions of Y, then the slope of TE would not equal the MPC. Moreover, taxes might depend on income. These features could be added to the model at the cost of complicating the analysis.

[6] That is, we assume that $\{c_0 - c_1 T_0 + d_0 - d_1 r + G_0 + n_0 + n_1 E\} = \$50$.

The original equilibrium level of national income is $200 billion, shown where the TE_0 line crosses the 45-degree line at point E_0. When there is an increase in investment expenditures of $25 billion, the total spending line shifts upward to TE_1. The new equilibrium is where this total expenditure line crosses the 45-degree line, at point E_1. The new equilibrium level of national income is $300 billion. Thus, the $25 billion increase in investment spending has produced an increase in national income of $100 billion. This is known as the *multiplier effect*.

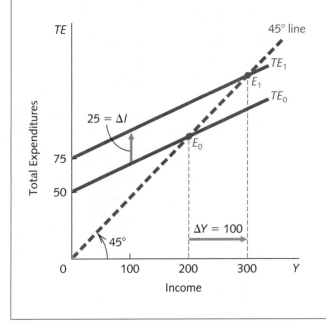

case, the *TE* line shifts upward by $25 so that the vertical intercept is now $75. With this higher vertical intercept, equilibrium income is $75/(1 − .75) = $300. This is depicted in Figure 4-11 as the shift from TE_0 (with a vertical intercept of $50) to TE_1 (with a vertical intercept of $75).

The Multiplier Process

The **MULTIPLIER** is a number by which a change in an exogenous variable is multiplied to get a change in equilibrium national income.

Notice that the *increase* in equilibrium income is $100, which can be calculated as the *change* in the vertical intercept divided by $(1 − c_1)$, or $(1 − .75)$. In this hypothetical example, the increase in investment spending of $25 results in an increase in equilibrium income of $100, or four times the increase in investment spending. Why didn't we just have a $25 increase in aggregate income? The answer is, because of the **multiplier** process.

The multiplier is a number which, when multiplied by a change in some exogenous variable, gives the resulting change in equilibrium income. We want to remember that the change in an exogenous variable—in our example, investment spending—is a change in one component of total spending. The essential question that we should ask about the multiplier is, how do we find the number from the multiplier formula, and what is the economic meaning underlying it?

Recall that our equation for TE graphed against Y has a vertical intercept and a slope. The basic multiplier formula is

$$\Delta(\text{vertical intercept of } TE)/(1 - \text{MPC}) = \Delta Y.$$

In our example above, the change in the vertical intercept of total expenditures was an increase in d_0 of \$25. Since the term $(1 - \text{MPC}) = 1 - .75 = .25$, the change in income is \$25/.25 = \$25 × 4 = \$100.

Other changes in the components of the vertical intercept are also possible, and can be analyzed in a similar way. For example, consider an increase in autonomous consumption of \$50. That is, c_0 increases by \$50. This increases the vertical intercept by \$50, and income increases by \$50/(1 - .75) = \$50 × 4 = \$200. Alternatively, consider an increase in net exports by \$50, perhaps because n_0 increases by \$50. This would also increase the vertical intercept of TE by \$50, and result in an increase in equilibrium income of \$200. An increase in government spending of \$50 (an increase in G_0 by \$50) also shifts the vertical intercept upward by \$50 and increases income by \$50/(1 - .75) = \$200.

What about an increase in taxes of \$50? Increases in taxes affect consumption, by lowering disposable income. In this case, an increase in taxes by \$50 lowers consumption by the marginal propensity to consume times \$50, or .75 × \$50 = \$37.50. That is, the vertical intercept of the consumption function and also of the total expenditure line shifts *down,* as calculated by $- \text{MPC} \times \Delta T_0$. The change in income is then the change in the vertical intercept, $-\$37.50$, divided by $(1 - \text{MPC})$, or $-\$37.50/(1 - .75) = -\$37.50 \times 4 = -\$150$. Thus, an increase in government spending of \$50 increases income by \$200, but an increase in taxes of \$50 reduces income by \$150. This means that if both government spending and taxes increase by \$50, the change in the vertical intercept is $\Delta G_0 - \text{MPC} \times \Delta T_0 = \$50 - .75(\$50) = \$12.50$, and income increases by \$12.50/(1 - .75) = \$50! This somewhat counterintuitive result is called the **balanced budget multiplier.** To understand the idea behind this result, notice that an increase in government spending directly increases total expenditures by the increase in G, while an increase in taxes works by decreasing disposable income and hence decreasing consumption by the MPC times the increase in T. Thus, an additional dollar of government spending increases autonomous total spending by one dollar, but an additional dollar of taxes decreases autonomous total spending by the MPC times one dollar. The net effect, then, is to increase autonomous spending by \$1 × (1 − MPC), and

The **BALANCED BUDGET MULTIPLIER** is a number by which an exogenous change in both government spending and taxes such that the government budget balance does not change, is multiplied to get a change in equilibrium national income. *For lump sum taxes,* the balanced budget multiplier is one.

hence to increase equilibrium Y by the multiplier times this increase in autonomous spending, or by $1 \times (1 - \text{MPC})/(1 - \text{MPC}) = \$1$.

Needless to say, this particular result is rather controversial, and a number of arguments opposing it have been made. Most of these arguments take into account the endogenous response of other variables that this multiplier analysis holds constant, such as the interest rate and the price level. Also, the taxes we consider here are lump sum taxes. We might want to consider instead income taxes or taxes that vary with income.

Other changes that might occur to alter equilibrium income are in the exchange rate E or in the real interest rate r. In these cases, we would need to know both the size of the change in E or r and the term multiplying E or r in the equations for investment and net exports. For a change in E, the change in equilibrium income would be given by $(n_1 \Delta E)/(1 - c_1) = \Delta Y$, while for a change in r the change in equilibrium income would be given by $(- d_1 \Delta r)/(1 - c_1) = \Delta Y$.

Let us return to our graphical analysis in Figure 4-11 and try to gain some intuition for the economics underlying this multiplier process. Remember, the changes in equilibrium illustrated in Figure 4-11 were initiated by an increase in investment expenditures of $25. Let us analyze what happens in the economy when investment spending increases. We'll think of this increase in investment spending as $25 million. When this new investment expenditure occurs, it accrues to households as income, since any expenditures on goods and services end up as eventual payments to the owners of resources, the households. For example, suppose Ford Motor Company spends $25 million on the construction of a new car. Construction workers and engineers would have more income to spend on televisions, clothes, and other goods and services. Real output—real GDP— would increase by the initial $25 million plus the additional spending induced by the $25 million increase in income. Thus, this new investment spending is an **injection** into the circular flow, an increase in spending on currently produced goods and services.

Part of this initial $25 million increase in income will be consumed by households, and part will be saved. The part that is consumed is determined by the marginal propensity to consume, or c_1. The remainder is saved.

To help with our explanation, let us start by designating households in the economy as Groups A, B, C, D, and so on. We assume that each group has an MPC of .75, and therefore an MPS of .25. Suppose that Group A is the construction workers and engineers on the Ford Motor Company project, the initial recipients of the $25 million of increased investment spending. They will consume $18.75 ($25 × .75) and save $6.25 ($25 × .25). This saving is referred to as a **leakage** from the income stream. A leakage is anything that reduces spending on currently produced goods and services.

The $18.75 consumed by households in Group A stays in the income stream, and becomes income for another group of households, say Group B.

AN INJECTION into the income stream is any autonomous increase in total expenditures that adds potential spending to the income-expenditure stream.

A LEAKAGE from the income stream is any autonomous decrease in total expenditures that withdraws potential spending from the income-expenditure stream.

The households in Group B then spend $14.06 ($18.75 × .75) and save $4.69 ($18.75 × .25). We note that the saving by Group B of $4.69 is also a leakage out of the income stream. The spending by Group B of $14.06 accrues as income to households in Group C, who themselves consume $10.54 ($14.06 × .75) and save $3.52 ($14.06 × .25). The leakage from the income stream here is $3.52. The $10.54 of spending by Group C becomes income for Group D, which spends $7.90 ($10.54 × .75) and saves $2.64 ($10.54 × .25), another leakage. This spending and responding continues from Group D to Group E to Groups F, G, and so on. Table 4-3 shows the result of this multiplier process for Groups A through E, and for all other groups, using MPC = .75 and MPS = .25. The change in investment ΔI is given in column 1; income groups are in column 2; income changes ΔY are in column 3; consumption changes ΔC are in column 4; and saving changes ΔS are in column 5. After an infinite number of spending rounds the summation of all the income changes, would be $100; the grand total of all the consumption changes would be $75; and the grand total of all the saving changes would be $25. Note that the grand total of all changes after the multiplier process is completed in saving equals the

TABLE 4-3   The Multiplier Process for a Single Investment Expenditure ($ Millions)

This table traces the effect of a $25 million increase in investment expenditures on the equilibrium level of national income. If we assume a marginal propensity to consume of .75, such an increase in investment expenditures will eventually bring about a $100 million increase in the equilibrium level of national income.

(1) INVESTMENT CHANGE (ΔI)	(2) HOUSEHOLD GROUP (A, B, C, etc.)	(3) INCOME CHANGES (ΔY)	(4) CONSUMPTION CHANGES (ΔC)	(5) SAVING CHANGES (ΔS)
$ 25.00				
	A	$ 25.00	$18.75	$ 6.25
	B	18.75	14.06	4.69
	C	14.06	10.54	3.52
	D	10.54	7.90	2.64
	E	7.90	5.92	1.98
	TOTAL, GROUP A-E	76.25	57.17	19.08
	TOTAL ALL OTHERS GROUPS	23.75	17.83	5.92
	GRAND TOTAL, ALL GROUPS	$100.00	$75.00	$25.00

initial change in autonomous investment, so that after the muliplier process is completed saving equals investment.[7]

Certain important qualifications related to the multiplier process, and to the equilibrium in the goods market, must be discussed. First, many—and technically an infinity of—spending rounds are required for the multiplier process to exhaust itself, and this translates into many time periods. Thus, equilibrium is not reestablished instantaneously. Second, our analysis assumed that the increase in investment is permanent, in the sense that d_0 does not change back to its original value after a short period of time. The multiplier analysis requires that the increase in investment spending is a permanent injection into the economy. Otherwise, if d_0 returns to its initial value, income would eventually return to its original level. Third, the multiplier process can work in reverse, multiplying reductions in autonomous spending into even larger reductions in equilibrium income. Finally, the multiplier process was developed under the assumption that many variables remain constant, including the price level P and the real interest rate r. In later chapters we will relax these assumptions and see that changes in P or r have the potential to greatly weaken or even eliminate or reverse the multiplier effects described in this chapter.

The Equilibrating Process

Up to now, we have been satisfied with finding the equilibrium level of income for given values of autonomous spending (such as d_0, C_0) and given values for the exogenous variables (such as G, r, or E). We have even described how the equilibrium changes with changes in these autonomous and exogenous variables. Now we want to describe what forces lead the economy to these equilibrium positions. That is, we want to answer the question, if the economy is not in equilibrium, why does it tend to move toward an equilibrium position? Alternatively, if TE is not equal to Y, what forces lead total expenditures to converge to the equilibrium, where $TE = Y$?

---

[7]The multiplier process just described, reflecting the behavior of households in Table 4-3, can be expressed in terms of a simple formula for an infinite geometric progression. This formula can be written as

$$\Delta d_0 + c_1 \Delta d_0 + c_1^2 \Delta d_0 + c_1^3 \Delta d_0 + ... + c_1^{n-1} \Delta d_0 = \Delta Y,$$

where Δd_0 is the initial change in investment, and ΔY is the change in income after n rounds of spending from household to household. We can rewrite this as

$$\Delta d_0 (1 + c_1 + c_1^2 + c_1^3 + ... + c_1^{n-1}) = \Delta Y.$$

A mathematical result is that $1 + c_1 + c_1^2 + c_1^3 + ... + c_1^{n-1}$ converges to $1/(1 - c_1)$ as n approaches infinity, so the multiplier formula becomes $\Delta d_0/(1 - c_1) = \Delta Y$, where Δd_0 is the change in autonomous total expenditures—that is, the change in the vertical intercept of the TE equation—and c_1 is the slope of the TE equation.

To answer this question, we will examine our economy when it is not in equilibrium. We will assume that the vertical intercept of our *TE* equation is $50, just as in Figure 4-11, and the slope or MPC is .75. Our discussion of Figure 4-11 led us to conclude that equilibrium income is $50/(1 − .75) = $200. We reproduce that graph here as expenditure line *TE* in Figure 4-12.

In Figure 4-12, we also include two alternative expenditure lines *TE'* and *TE"*. Expenditure line *TE'* has a vertical intercept of $75 and a slope of .75,

FIGURE 4-12
Adjustment to Equilibrium

Start with an initial situation in which the total expenditure line is *TE"*, with a vertical intercept of $25 and an equilibrium level of national income determined at point *A*, $100. If there is a $25 increase in autonomous spending, the vertical intercept of the total spending line increases to $50, and the total expenditure line shifts upward to *TE*. At the initial level of income, $100, there is now an excess of spending over income. That is, total expenditures are now $125 but income—and output—is $100. This causes an unplanned reduction in inventories, and firms will increase output (and hence income of factors of production). The increase in income will occur as long as total expenditures are above income, and this will be the case until income rises to $200, at which total spending is also $200 and the economy is in the new equilibrium. The opposite effects on income result with a decrease in total expenditures.

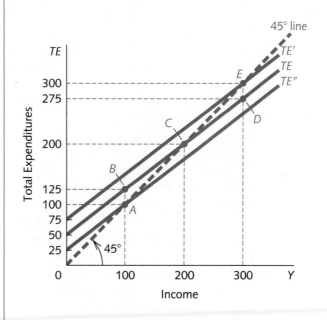

so equilibrium would be $75/(1 − .75) = $300. Expenditure line TE'' has a vertical intercept of $25 and a slope of .75, so equilibrium would be $25/(1 − .75) = $100.

To illustrate the forces that lead to equilibrium, assume we begin on expenditure line TE'' at point A, where the economy is in equilibrium with autonomous spending of $25 (i.e., a vertical intercept of $25) and equilibrium income of $100. Now assume there is an increase in autonomous spending—that is, an increase in the vertical intercept—to $50. The new expenditure line is TE, the new equilibrium income is $200. However, income initially is $100. How does an increase in income to $200 occur?

After the increase in autonomous spending, income is still $100 but the expenditure line is now TE. For an income of $100, expenditures total $125 ($50 + .75 × $100), as given by point B. What happens when expenditures exceed income? With spending of $125 and income of $100, firms must find $25 of goods and services with which to satisfy the "excess" spending. These goods and services will initially come from inventories. Firms will reduce inventories—an *unplanned reduction* in investment—in order to satisfy demand. (That is, since investment includes inventory accumulation, a reduction in inventories is a reduction in investment.) But when inventories decline, firms decide to produce more (as they can obviously sell more than the $100 they are currently producing); otherwise they would find it difficult to continue filling orders for their output. As they produce more, they hire more labor and other resources owned by households, thereby increasing income.

Perhaps income initially increases to $150. At this point, total expenditures are $162.50 ($50 + .75 × $150), which still exceeds income by $12.50. Inventories continue to decline, and firms know they can still increase output and hence income. Output increases again, and continues to increase until income equals $200. At this income and output level, income equals expenditures, and inventories are no longer drawn down to satisfy demand. Unplanned inventory investment is zero in equilibrium.

A similar equilibrating process works when income exceeds total spending. Consider a situation in which the economy initially has autonomous spending of $75 on expenditure line TE'. The initial equilibrium is at point E on TE', with equilibrium income of $300. Now consider what happens when autonomous spending declines to $50, and the expenditure line shifts to TE. Initially, income is $300 but total expenditures are $275 ($50 + .75 × $300). The excess of income—and hence output—over spending means that firms have unsold output that must be placed in inventory. (These unplanned inventory accumulations are unplanned investment in inventories.) As firms see inventories accumulate, they reduce output.

Perhaps the initial reduction in output and hence in income is to $250. When income is $250, total spending is $237.50 ($50 + .75 × $250). Again, income—and hence output—exceeds spending, so inventories are accumulating. When income finally falls to $200, income equals total expenditures, and the economy is in equilibrium. Thus, the equilibrating force when income exceeds expenditures is inventory accumulation, which causes firms to reduce output.

SUMMARY

This chapter has focused on the total spending side of the economy. The approach has been to model total spending as consisting of four components: consumption, investment, government spending, and net exports. After these four components were individually modeled, total expenditures were modeled as the sum of the four components. With this model of total spending, we derived the equilibrium level of income, in which total spending equals income. We described the multiplier process, in which changes in autonomous spending lead to a change in equilibrium income that is a multiple of the change in autonomous spending. Finally, we described the forces that lead the economy to equilibrium—unintended inventory changes.

In this chapter the discussion has taken several important macroeconomic variables as given. These include the interest rate and the exchange rate. Future chapters will consider these variables to be endogenous, or determined within the model by economic forces, and will use the model in this chapter as a building block of the Keynesian approach to aggregate demand.

KEY TERMS

appreciation of the dollar	leakage
balanced budget multiplier	lump sum taxes
consumption function	marginal propensity to consume (MPC)
depreciation of the dollar	
exchange rate	marginal propensity to save (MPS)
fiscal policy	multiplier
injection	real exchange rate

QUESTIONS FOR REVIEW AND DISCUSSION

1. List the underlying assumptions of the analysis in this chapter.

2. Consider a consumption function given by $C = 200 + .9(Y - T)$. What is autonomous consumption? What is the marginal propensity to consume? Does the MPC change with increases in income? Why or why not?

3. If the consumption function is given by $C = 200 + .9(Y - T)$, what is the saving function? What is the marginal propensity to save?

4. Consider a situation in which autonomous consumption is zero and the MPC is .7. Write down and graph this consumption function. Also, calculate and graph the corresponding saving function.

5. Consider a saving function given by $S = -250 + .15(Y - T)$. What is the marginal propensity to save? What is the corresponding consumption function?

6. Consider an investment function given by $I = 200 - .50\ r$, where r is the real interest rate. Assume r is 10 percent. Also, the saving function is given by $S = -250 + .15(Y - T)$. Graph both the saving and investment functions with S and I on the vertical axis and Y on the horizontal axis. Explain how the equilibrium between saving and investment is determined. Will an increase in autonomous saving—such as a change in the saving function to $S = -200 + .15(Y - T)$—lead to an increase in investment? Why or why not? Will an increase in investment lead to an increase in saving? Why or why not? Compare this market for saving and investment to the analysis of saving and investment in the classical model.

7. What is autonomous investment?

8. What is the relationship between the marginal propensity to consume and the marginal propensity to save?

9. What does it mean for an economy to be dissaving? What happens to investment? Looking at the data on consumption, has the United States experienced dissaving in the last two decades?

10. Assume the MPC is .6 and autonomous spending increases by $50. Explain the multiplier process.

11. Demonstrate graphically the effect on equilibrium income of an increase in the exchange rate. What is the effect on consumption? On net exports? On investment?

12. Demonstrate graphically the effect on equilibrium income of an increase in the real interest rate. What is the effect on consumption? On investment? On net exports?

PROBLEMS

1. If the marginal propensity to consume is .75, what will be the effect on equilibrium income of a $100 billion increase in government spending?

2. If the marginal propensity to save is .10, what is the effect on equilibrium income of a $200 billion increase in lump sum taxes?

3. How would you modify the multiplier if investment depended on income, so that d_2 was not zero, and if net exports depended on income, so that n_2 was not zero? Would the multiplier be larger or smaller than the multiplier when $d_2 = 0$ and $n_2 = 0$?

4. If the Clinton Administration attempts to stimulate the economy by increasing government spending by $100 million while simultaneously increasing taxes by the same amount, what net effect will such fiscal action have on equilibrium output if the MPC is 0.75? What assumptions have you made to derive your answer? In view of the size of the deficit and the discussion in the text, are these assumptions realistic? Why or why not?

SUGGESTIONS FOR FURTHER READING

Chick, Victoria. *Macroeconomics after Keynes: A Reconsideration of the General Theory.* Cambridge, MA: MIT Press, 1984.

Cullison, William E. "Is Saving Too Low in the United States?" Federal Reserve Bank of Richmond *Economic Review* (May/June 1990), pp. 20–35.

Garner, C. Alan. "Forecasting Consumer Spending: Should Economists Pay Attention to Consumer Confidence Surveys?" Federal Reserve Bank of Kansas City *Economic Review* (May/June 1991), pp. 57–71.

Hansen, A. H. *A Guide to Keynes.* New York: McGraw-Hill, 1953.

Hayashi, Fumio. "Is Japan's Saving Rate High?" Federal Reserve Bank of Minneapolis *Quarterly Review* (Spring 1989), pp. 3–9.

Jacobson, Kristina. "U.S. Foreign Exchange Operations," Federal Reserve Bank of Kansas City *Economic Review* (September/October 1990), pp. 37–50.

Keynes, John Maynard. *The General Theory of Employment, Interest, and Money.* New York: Harcourt Brace Jovanovich, 1936.

Tatom, John A. "U.S. Investment in the 1980s: The Real Story," Federal Reserve Bank of St. Louis *Review* (March/April 1989), pp. 3–15.

5

THE MONEY MARKET AND THE

IS-LM APPROACH TO TOTAL EXPENDITURES

The economy of the 1990s—and the prospects for economic leadership by the United States in the century to come—is based on present and future economic performance. Sustainable economic progress is conditioned by such factors as low inflation, high levels of employment, and high rates of growth in output of goods and services. Inflation, jobs, and the total output of goods and services in our economy are determined by aggregate demand and supply. Demanders—consumers, investors (businesses), government, and foreign buyers—purchase the nation's output and influence aggregate demand. This influence may produce growth and economic prosperity or recession and economic stagnation.

Chapter 4 concentrated on the "commodities" or "goods" market. But demand for final goods and services by consumers and other spenders is conditioned on monetary factors, including the interest rate and the supply of and the demand for money in the economy.

In analyzing the impact of spending on the determination of equilibrium income, Chapter 4 focused on the impact of *changes* in consumption, investment, government, and net foreign spending on levels of equilibrium income. That analysis made two assumptions that are particularly important to the results we obtained: that the interest rate and the price level are exogenous or "outside" the consideration of the model. Unfortunately, these assumptions are counter to the facts. This chapter and Chapter 6 will relax these assumptions. In particular, this chapter modifies the model of Chapter 4 to allow for an endogenous interest rate—an interest rate determined "inside" the model. Then in Chapter 6 we relax the assumption that the price level is exogenous and develop an aggregate demand curve that describes output as a function of the price level.

Our discussion in the present chapter is derived from the approach developed by economist and Nobel Laureate Sir John R. Hicks. It is called the *IS-LM* framework, where *IS* describes investment and saving behavior, and *LM* signifies liquidity (or money demand) and money supply. Utilizing both "goods" market (*IS*) and "money" market (*LM*) determinants of spending gives us a more complete understanding of how the equilibrium interest rate and the equilibrium level of income are produced in the economy.

After reading this chapter, you will know

- what, in simple terms, money is, why people demand it, and why the interest rate is the opportunity cost of holding money
- how equilibrium is determined in the money market by the demand for and supply of money
- the definition of the *IS* curve as the set of combinations of interest rates and income that equilibrate the goods market
- the definition of the *LM* curve as a curve showing combinations of interest rates and income that equilibrate the demand and supply of money
- how *IS* and *LM* jointly determine the *one* combination of the interest rate and income that equilibrates *both* the money market and the goods market
- how the economy adjusts when factors shift either the *IS* or the *LM* curves.

MONEY SUPPLY AND MONEY DEMAND

You may already be familiar with some of the principles of money supply and demand from basic economics. Elaborations on these concepts will be made later in this book, but a review of these principles is critical to the understanding of macroeconomics.

What is the Money Supply?

MONEY serves as a medium of exchange. It also functions as a store of wealth, a unit of account, and a standard of deferred payment.

The **MEDIUM OF EXCHANGE** is an item that is accepted in exchange for other goods.

IN BARTER, goods must be exchanged for other goods.

Everyone is familiar with *money,* but how is it defined? The economist associates the definition of money with its functions. The first and most important function of money is to serve as a **medium of exchange** when it passes from hand to hand in exchange for goods and services or in payment of debt. Money is accepted not for its own sake but for the goods and services it can buy. Regardless of whether the item used as money is paper, metal, or a demand deposit (checking account) in a bank, so long as that item is generally acceptable by society it serves as a medium of exchange.

Exchange of money for goods is preferred to **barter.** Under a barter system, goods must be exchanged for other goods, and it takes time for individuals to search out other individuals with whom to exchange goods. In a money economy, this cost of search is reduced because money is exchanged for goods. Money, then, helps to facilitate exchange in a modern industrial society. But in order to maintain the value of money in a modern economy, the supply of money must be limited. In the United States the money supply is controlled by an agency of the federal government, the Federal Reserve System (see Chapter 12 for details). In the present discussion, we abstract from practical issues of monetary control to consider a theoretical money market.

A STORE OF WEALTH is a good or financial asset that individuals hold in order to maintain a claim over present and future goods and services.

A UNIT OF ACCOUNT is an item that serves as a measuring rod for the values of all economic goods. Prices are usually stated in terms of the unit of account.

Second, money serves as a **store of wealth** to the extent that it is generally acceptable and maintains its purchasing power. By holding wealth in the form of money, the individual holds a claim over present and future goods and services. Since money is not an income-earning asset (i.e., money yields no interest), it may be an inefficient means for storing wealth. When the prices of other goods rise, the purchasing power of money is reduced in that a given amount of money will purchase a smaller amount of goods and services after the price increases.

Third, money serves as a **unit of account.** Money is the common denominator or the measuring rod in terms of which individual choices can be assessed and decided at a given point in time. The values of all economic goods are measured in terms of money. The money values of economic goods are typically called prices. One can compare goods and services with each other, once their money values have been established. For example, if the price of a pizza is $10 and the price of a loaf of bread is $5, then the money value of the pizza is twice the money value of the loaf of bread.

A STANDARD OF
DEFERRED PAYMENT is
an item that serves as a
measure of value over
time.

MI is the sum of the
following: currency,
including coins and
paper money outside
banks; demand deposits
(checking accounts) at
commercial banks and
other financial
institutions; NOW
accounts; travelers'
checks; and ATS
accounts.

Finally, money serves as a measure of value over time as a **standard of deferred payment.** When a household incurs a debt by purchasing some item on credit, it often repays the debt in terms of money. When the household receives credit measured in money terms (i.e., unit of account), there is no difficulty about the amount due in return. Thus, money is used to measure the value of repaying a debt over a given period of time.

Since there are various functions of money, money can be measured in different ways. The Federal Reserve System provides several definitions of money. These alternative definitions, along with the manner in which money is created through the banking system and the tools through which the Federal Reserve attempts to control money expansion and contraction, will be the focus of Chapter 12. For present purposes, let us accept two rather straightforward definitions of money. The first is a narrowly defined measure of money, called **M1** by the Federal Reserve: M1 is currency, including coins and paper money outside banks; demand deposits (checking accounts) at commercial banks and other financial institutions; NOW accounts, (interest-earning accounts upon which owners may write a check); travelers' checks; and ATS accounts (automatic transfer savings accounts, which are automatically transferred to an individual's checking account when the checking account falls to a minimum level). A brief definition of M1 is that it is currency and checkable deposits used for transactions purposes. Of course, M1 is only an approximation to our theoretical definition of money, but it will serve to provide us with an example of money. A broader definition, M2, adds a number of components to M1, including overnight repurchase agreements and overnight Eurodollars, money market fund balances, money market deposit accounts, and savings and small time deposits.

The Foundations of Money Demand

We do not often think of demanding money, but we all demand it in the same sense that we demand computer software, cheese, or running shoes. Of course, wealth and income limit our demand for these goods, and likewise wealth and income limit our demand for money. To explain money demand, economists identify two broad motives for demanding money: a transactions motive and a portfolio motive. We will examine these motives in turn.

THE TRANSACTIONS DEMAND FOR MONEY

The transactions motive for holding cash balances originated in the views of the Cambridge quantity theorists. In the Cambridge equation, a household held cash—for example, in a checking account—to bridge the gap between the receipt of its paycheck and its expenditure of that paycheck on goods and services. To illustrate, let us suppose that a household receives $24,000 per year in income and is paid this entire amount at the first of the year. The payment period, then, is one year. Let us also suppose that the household spends the entire $24,000 in even amounts each day over the entire year, so that by the end of the year it has spent all of the $24,000. This is illustrated in Figure 5-1(a), in which money holding is graphed on the vertical axis and the time period is graphed on the horizontal axis. Notice that the household starts with $24,000 in money on the first of the year, and spends this in a steady stream until the $24,000 is just exhausted and its money holding is zero at the end of the year. The question is, what does this household need to hold in cash

FIGURE 5-1
Transactions of the
Household

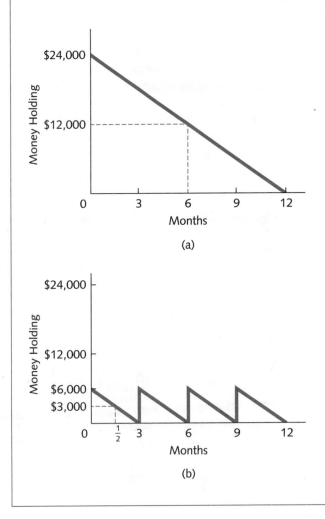

A household holds average balances of cash of $12,000 if it is paid $24,000 in income and spends in even amounts throughout the entire year. When a household is paid four times a year, the payment period is reduced and it would need to hold *on average* only $3,000.

balances *on the average* to carry out its transactions? To determine the average balances held by the household, the income for the particular payment period in question is divided by 2. By dividing, in our example, the $24,000 by 2, we find that the household holds in cash balances on the average $12,000, or an amount equal to six months of its income. Thus, a household that is paid only once a year would need to hold for transactions purposes an average money balance equal to 50 percent of its yearly income. Furthermore, if its income increased, say to $48,000, then it would hold average cash balances of $48,000 divided by 2, or $24,000. Thus, income and money demand are directly related.

Does it matter if a household is paid more often? To answer, we change the payment period for the household and assume that the business pays the household four times a year. While the household still receives $24,000 per year in income, its payment period has been reduced. This means that the household would receive $6,000 in income *every* three months and would spend all of this $6,000 in equal daily amounts in each three-month period, so that at the end of each three-month period the $6,000 would be entirely spent. This is illustrated in Figure 5-1(b). The household would need to hold *on the average* only $3,000, half of the income received each period and only 12.5 percent of its yearly income of $24,000. We may thereby conclude that when payment between the business and the household occurs more often, the household would have to hold lower cash balances out of yearly income for transactions purposes. Note, however, that if the household income doubled to $48,000 yearly, paid as $12,000 every three months, then average money holdings would be $12,000 divided by 2, or $6,000. Thus, for a given payment schedule, a doubling of income results in a doubling of money holding.

Because the Classicals believed, as we recall from Chapter 3, that both the paying and the spending habits of the community changed very little in the short run, the transactions demand for money was thought to be a constant fraction of the level of income. Money was performing its function as a medium of exchange. Moreover, as the level of nominal income increased in the economy, households desired to hold more money balances to carry out their day-to-day transactions. The reason for this can be readily seen. Since money income is composed of two variables, the price level P multiplied by the real output of goods and services Y, an increase in either variable will cause the household to hold more money for transactions purposes. When the output of goods is constant but prices are rising, the household needs more money to buy one unit of goods. If, for example, the price of a book rises from $10 to $20, the household needs more money to purchase this book. On the other hand, if the output of goods increases while their prices remain the same, households would also hold more money to buy the additional items. Therefore, any increase in money income resulting from an increase in the output of goods and services or in their prices, or both, means that households will desire to hold more money.

The transactions demand for nominal money varies directly with money income and can be written as L_{NT}:

$$L_{NT} = kPY, \tag{5.1}$$

where L_{NT} is the transactions demand for *nominal* money, k is the same as the Cambridge k and a proportion of money income, or of PY. The transactions demand for money may also be expressed in real terms—that is, in terms of the purchasing power of money holdings—by dividing the above equation by the price level P. When we divide our transactions demand for money equation by the price level P, we have real transactions demand L_T as

$$L_T = (L_{NT})/P = (kPY)/P = kY, \tag{5.2}$$

where L_T is the real money balances demanded for transactions and Y is the level of real income. This proportional relationship between the transactions demand for money and the level of real income, GDP, is depicted in Figure 5-2, with the transactions demand for real money balances L_T, located on the vertical axis and real income Y located on the horizontal axis and with $P = 1$.

To show the transactions demand for money, we must draw a straight line out of the origin of the graph. The size of k might be, for example, some value such as 1/4, 1/5, or 1/6. Let us assume, for the purpose of illustration, that $k_0 = 1/4$ and Y or real GDP = $400 billion; then, from the equation

FIGURE 5-2
The Transactions Demand for Money

The transactions demand for money is shown as directly relating to the level of income received. That is, individuals demand money for making transactions as some fraction of their income. Such factors as the payment period between receipt of income and use of money for transactions influence the fraction of income that people want to hold for transactions purposes.

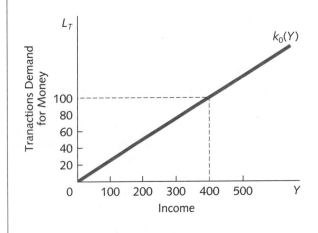

$L_T = 1/4(400)$, households would need to hold $100 billion in real transactions balances. This result is shown in Figure 5-2. Now suppose that the payment period between businesses and households becomes more frequent and, therefore, that at every level of real income Y households need to hold less money to facilitate daily transactions. Due to this change in the paying and spending habits of the community, k would change to some value that is less than 1/4. The transactions money demand line in Figure 5-2 would rotate downward toward the horizontal axis.

In the Insight: "Real Money Balances and Real Income in the United States," we examine the relationship of money demand and income for the U.S. economy. We illustrate the positive relationship between money holdings and income that is suggested by the transactions motive for holding money.

PORTFOLIO OR ASSET MOTIVES

In addition to the transactions demand for money, households have portfolio (or asset) motives for holding money.[1] The portfolio approach to money demand asks how households decide to split their wealth among money and other assets. This approach does not look at money's role in transactions, but instead looks at reasons why money might be included among the assets held in a portfolio. Why would someone choose to hold money as an asset? The answer is that money is a safe asset. Stocks and bonds can fluctuate in price, but the price of money is always the same. (Of course, inflation reduces the *real* value of money. Because inflation affects all assets valued in money terms, we will not consider it further at this point, but will consider it in more detail in Chapter 13.)

Why does the safety of money lead to money holding? The reason is that individuals like higher returns but dislike risk. Money is riskless, but it also pays a return of zero. In a portfolio, holding some money is a way of reducing the riskiness of the portfolio, since that portion held in money will not decline in (nominal) value. Bonds or stocks earn a higher return than money, on average, but they also have a probability of losing value.

When considering splitting a portfolio among alternative assets, individuals usually like higher returns and lower risk. Even though stocks and bonds pay a higher return than does money, people who want to avoid some risk may want to hold money. As the return on stocks and bonds rises, however, the opportunity cost of avoiding risk by holding money also increases. This can lead to a decrease in money holding, as people are willing to substitute into risky assets when the return increases. The increased interest rate compensates for the increased risk.

---

[1]Keynes wrote of three motives for holding money: the transactions motive, the speculative motive, and the precautionary motive. We will collapse these into the transactions motive and the portfolio motive.

INSIGHT

REAL MONEY BALANCES AND REAL INCOME IN THE UNITED STATES

In order to get a better idea of the relationship between the demand for real money balances and real income, we plot both real money balances and real income in the accompanying graph. We use real personal income as the income measure. Real money balances are the Federal Reserve Board's money stock measure, M2, divided by the consumer price index. We plot these two variables from 1959 through 1992 in Figure 5-3.

An obvious feature of these two variables is that they trend upward through time. The upward trend in real income is due to economic growth. There are a few downward movements, notably in 1974–75, and again in the early 1980s, and these correspond to recessions. The general trend is clearly up-

ward, however, and we see that real personal income has increased from under $1,500 billion to nearly $3,500 billion in the United States in just over thirty years.

Real M2 money balances also show a decided upward trend, from around $1,000 billion in 1959 to about $2,000 billion in the early 1990s. The growth in real money balances has been somewhat slower than the growth in real income, since real money balances have doubled during this thirty-year period, while real income has more than doubled during this same period. This can partly be explained by innovations in financial markets, such as the widespread use of credit cards and ATM machines, and the quantum increase in subscriptions to money market mutual funds beginning in the 1970s, all of which have led to a decrease in the holding of real money balances for given levels of real income.

It is interesting to note that real money balances show the

same downward movements as real income during recessions. In fact, the movements in real money balances seem magnified relative to the movements in real income. Notice again the severe recession of 1974–75, and of 1980–1982. During these periods, there were large declines in real M2 money balances. Finally, during the late 1980s there is a flattening or slight decline in real M2 balances that foreshadows the recession of 1990.

In general, then, we see that real money balances and real income do move together. Both grow at roughly the same rate, although financial market innovations have allowed some economizing on the holding of money balances so that real M2 has grown at a somewhat slower rate than real income. We also see that both real M2 and real income move together during recessions, and indeed that reductions in real M2 are even greater than reductions in personal income that occur during recessions. ❏

Thus, portfolio considerations also suggest that the demand for money is inversely related to the nominal interest rate. In the Insight: "Real Money Balances and the Nominal Interest Rate" we examine this hypothesis to see if increases in the nominal interest rate are related to decreases in real money balances.

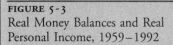

FIGURE 5-3
Real Money Balances and Real
Personal Income, 1959–1992

Both real money balances and real personal income trend upward over time. Growth in real money balances has been slower than growth in income, a fact that can be explained, in part, by innovations in financial markets.

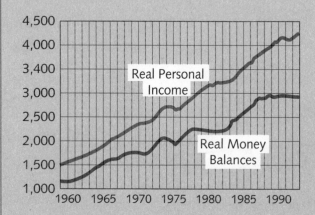

NOTE: All values in billions of 1987 dollars.

SOURCE: Department of Commerce, Bureau of Economic Analysis, and Board of Governors of the Federal Reserve System.

Putting the Pieces Together: The Demand for Money

We have seen that the demand for money responds to both income and the nominal interest rate. Assuming a given nominal interest rate, an increase in real income increases the quantity of money demanded for transactions purposes, and a decrease in real income reduces the quantity of real money people will want to hold for transactions purposes. Further, the quantity of real money that individuals wish to hold will increase as the interest rate decreases, assuming, of course, a constant level of income.

Combining these two concepts, the demand for real money balances may be viewed as follows:

$$L = L(Y,R) = L_0 + L_1 Y - L_2 R. \tag{5.3}$$

Equation 5.3 indicates that the total demand for real money balances L is related to the level of real income Y and to the nominal interest rate R. Money demand also varies with risk, and we let the constant term L_0 represent risk and other variables that affect money demand (other than the interest rate or income). For

INSIGHT

REAL MONEY BALANCES AND THE NOMINAL INTEREST RATE

Our theory of money demand predicts a relationship between real money demand and the nominal interest rate. Here we examine these variables to see if that relationship can be identified in the data. We look at real money balances M2 divided by the consumer price index, and the interest rate on six-month U.S. Treasury bills. These are short-term bonds that mature in six months and are sold by the U.S. Treasury to help finance the government debt. These two variables are plotted in Figure 5-4. Because the interest rate is measured in percentage terms and real money balances in billions of dollars, our graph has two different scales. The percentage scale for the interest rate is on the left-hand side, and ranges from 0 to 20 percent. The scale for real M2 money balances is on the right-hand side, and ranges from 0 to $3,000 billion.

Note a few things about these two variables. First, real M2 money balances show a definite upward trend, which we explain by the growth of real income and the desire to hold more real money balances for transactions purposes. In contrast, the interest rate exhibits only a slight upward trend. More apparent in the interest rate series are the occasional periods of large upward movements in the interest rate, periods that are offset after several years by large downward movements. Since we are graphing the nominal interest rate, we should remember that the nominal rate can increase either because of an increase in the real interest rate or because of an increase in the expected inflation rate. For example, inflation accelerated in the late 1970s through 1980, which led to a large upward movement in interest rates that can be observed in the graph.

Our consideration of the nominal interest rate as the opportunity cost of holding money suggests that real money balances should decline when the nominal interest rate increases. Do we see this in the data? Look at the periods of high nominal interest rates. The first is right around 1970, the second right around 1974–75, the third a massive increase in 1979–1983, and, finally, a smaller increase in the very late 1980s. During these periods, real M2 shows declines of varying intensities, with the largest decline during the 1979–1983 period, when interest rates spiked most dramatically. Thus, the data confirm the idea that increases in the nominal interest rate cause a decrease in real money demand. ❑

instance, an increase in the riskiness of nonmoney assets might increase the demand for money, and we would analyze this as an increase in L_0.

Interest Rate Determination in the Money Market

All of these concepts may be combined to show how interest rates are determined in the money market by the interaction of money supply and demand. Equilibrium may be expressed by the following set of expressions:

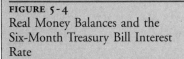

FIGURE 5-4
Real Money Balances and the
Six-Month Treasury Bill Interest
Rate

An examination of the relationship between interest rates and the
demand for money balances shows that increases in the nominal
interest rate (here measured by the six-month Treasury bill rate)
cause decreases in real money demand.

NOTE: Real money balance in billions of 1987 dollars; the six-month Treasury
bill in percent per annum.

SOURCE: Department of Commerce, Bureau of Economic Analysis, and Board of
Governors of the Federal Reserve System.

$$M = M_0 \qquad \text{(Nominal money supply)} \tag{5.4}$$

$$L = L(Y,R) \quad \text{(Real money demand)} \tag{5.5}$$

$$M/P = L \qquad \text{(Equilibrium in money market).} \tag{5.6}$$

These expressions are illustrated in Figure 5-5, which shows a vertical money
supply function (with the money supply fixed at some specific level M_0, and
the price level equal to P_0) set against a money demand curve, $L(Y_0)$. Just as
the supply and demand for cassette tapes establish a price of cassette tapes, the
interaction of money demand and supply establishes a unique interest rate. In
Figure 5-5, that unique interest rate is R_0. At any interest rate higher than
R_0, say R_1, the quantity of money supplied is greater than the quantity of
money demanded. This excess supply of money, labeled *AB* in Figure 5-5,
causes interest rates to fall back to R_0. Likewise, at all interest rates lower than
R_0, the quantity of money demanded exceeds the supply of money available. At
interest rate R_2, for instance, excess demand for money equals an amount *CD*.
Attempts by money holders to increase their stocks of cash balances by selling

FIGURE 5-5
Equilibrium in the Money
Market

The supply and demand for money determine interest rates in the money market. Demand curve $L_0(Y_0)$ in the figure is the total demand for money assuming income constant at Y_0. At interest rates higher than R_0, the equilibrium interest rate, excess supplies of money cause interest rates to fall. At any rate lower than R_0, excess demands cause interest rates to rise.

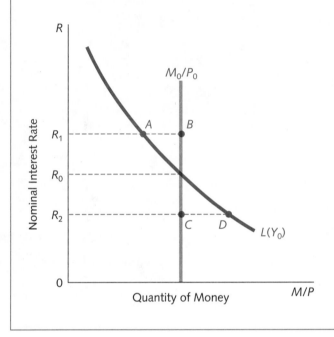

bonds cause interest rates to rise to R_0. In this sense, the supply and demand for money operate to establish interest rates just as the supply and demand for BMW automobiles establish the price of BMWs. Excess supply drives price down while excess demand drives price up.

The Effects of Changes in Money Demand and Supply

Changes in money demand or supply will have an impact in the money market just as such changes would have in any other market. Figure 5-6 conveniently summarizes these changes. Equilibrium interest rates may change with either changes in money demand or money supply. In Figure 5-6(a), for example, we assume that the level of income increases from Y_0 to Y_1. This means that, collectively, money holders will want to increase their holdings of money. Further, they will want to hold more money for these purposes *at every interest rate*. This means that the money demand function $L(Y_0)$ shifts rightward to $L(Y_1)$ in Figure 5-6(a). Given that the supply of money remains constant at

FIGURE 5-6
Interest Rate Adjustments in
the Money Market

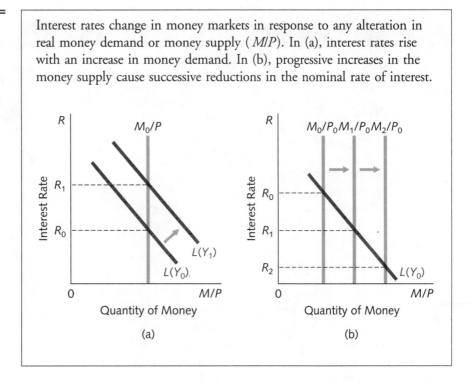

FIGURE 5-6
Interest Rate Adjustments in
the Money Market

Interest rates change in money markets in response to any alteration in real money demand or money supply (M/P). In (a), interest rates rise with an increase in money demand. In (b), progressive increases in the money supply cause successive reductions in the nominal rate of interest.

M_0/P_0, the equilibrium interest rate must rise to R_1 from R_0. No other rate is consistent with money supply and money demand. After the increase in income and the rightward shift in the demand for money, an excess demand opens up at interest rate R_0 causing demanders to bid up the equilibrium rate to R_1.

The effects of a change in money supply are shown in Figure 5-6(b). We will assume that the demand for money curve $L(Y_0)$ remains constant. As the nominal money supply is increased successively from M_0 to M_1 to M_2, the equilibrium interest rate falls from R_0 to R_1 to R_2. Reductions in the nominal supply of money would reduce the money available to money holders, and interest rates would increase.

THE *IS-LM* MODEL

As always, it is wise to keep in mind the assumptions that are made in building an economic model. In particular, it is important to remember which variables are explicitly modeled and are thus "inside" the model, or endogenous, and which variables are "outside" the model, or exogenous. The *IS-LM* model developed here is the most famous "translation" of Keynes's *General Theory*. It is the work of British economist John R. Hicks and American economist Alvin Hansen. (See the Insight: "Sir John R. Hicks, Alvin Hansen, and the

INSIGHT

SIR JOHN R. HICKS, ALVIN HANSEN, AND THE SPREAD OF KEYNESIAN ECONOMICS

John Maynard Keynes's *General Theory of Employment, Interest, and Money* was a break with then-traditional macroeconomic ideas. The idea that "unemployment equilibrium" in the private sector of the economy needed government fiscal stimulus and monetary prodding was most welcome in the depressed economies of the time. It is now clear, however, that Keynes's own conceptions of the deficiencies in Classical theory (see Chapter 3), published in 1936, evolved in his mind slowly over time. Keynes, who delighted in intellectual debates, benefitted greatly from interactions with a remarkable group of economists then at Cambridge, including Joan Robinson and D. H. Robertson, and with other economists in England. The *General Theory* was a difficult, often turgid, and poorly organized book in spite of the fact

that Keynes was one of the best literary expositors of his time. Without question, it was a difficult read for the average economist in England or America of the day.

Keynes was fortunate, however, for his book was about to alter the way in which economists viewed macroeconomic theory. Almost before the ink had dried on the *General Theory,* economists began "translating" the work, organizing it so that economists could more easily translate Keynes's ideas into policy prescriptions. Chief among these "translations" was a "general equilibrium" combination of real factors and monetary factors, which combined to produce equilibrium income and interest rates in the economy. The author was John R. Hicks, then an economist at Manchester University in England. The work was "Mr. Keynes and the Classics," published in the journal *Econometrica* in 1937. In his article on "what Keynes really meant," Hicks organized Keynesian principles of money and goods markets into the *IS-LM* curves developed in this chapter (with some elaborations). In one stroke, Hicks defined Keynesian economics

PHOTO 5-1
John Maynard Keynes
(1883-1946).

for a generation of economists around the world and the *IS-LM* diagram became "to macroeconomic textbooks what the benzene ring diagram is to textbooks of organic chemistry," in the words of one commentator.[a] Hicks, winner of the Nobel Prize in Economics in 1972, was a remarkable economist who made enormous contributions to value and capital theory as well as to macroeconomic theories of business cycles. But his characterization of Keynes "stuck" and became more influential than Keynes's own writings on the subject.

In America, where unemployment and depression were very real in 1936, Keynes was

PHOTO 5-2
John R. Hicks (1904-1989).

again lucky. In that very year Harvard University received a grant to establish the Littauer School of Public Administration, with economist Alvin H. Hansen (1887-1975) at its helm. Hansen, who arrived at Harvard in the fall of 1937, was soon convinced of the Keynesian approach—that is, of the necessity to institute discretionary fiscal and monetary policies to correct for the inability of the private sector to produce full-employment equilibrium. Hansen instituted a seminar in fiscal policy at Harvard and became the leading exponent of Keynesian economics in the United States. A generation of American economists was taught Keynesian tools in Hansen's class, including the *IS-LM* model and new applications of cycle theory and balanced budget multipliers applied to the macroeconomy of the United States. Hansen's *A Guide to Keynes* (1953) was most influential in the development of Keynesian ideas for American students of economics.

The rest, as they say, is history. The Keynesian "revolution"—for decades past the end of the Great Depression of the 1930s—was almost complete in the field of macroeconomics.[b] Governments of all major nations of the world, including that of the United States, have at least attempted to "practice" discretionary fiscal and monetary policy. While counter-revolutions containing modified "Classical" ideas have emerged (many of which will be considered in this book), Keynesian economics itself has evolved to include microeconomic foundations and other modifications (see Chapter 10). Contemporary Keynesians such as economists James Tobin and Paul Samuelson have been influential in these developments, but Hicks and Hansen were critical to the initial development of Keynesian economics. ❑

NOTE: [a]Christopher Bliss, *John Richard Hicks, The New Palgrave: A Dictionary of Economics,* edited by John Eatwell, Murray Milgate, and Peter Newman (London: The Macmillan Press Ltd., 1987), vol. 2, p. 644.
[b]The literature on Keynes and the spread of his ideas is enormous: for a guide, see Robert B. Ekelund, Jr., and Robert F. Hebert, *A History of Economic Theory and Method,* 3rd ed. (New York: McGraw-Hill, Inc., 1990), pp. 531–35.

Spread of Keynesian Economics" for details of their contribution to Keynesian economics.)

While further developments relating to aggregate demand await the introduction of endogenous prices into the *IS-LM* model, mastery of the basic model is essential to understanding macroeconomic theory.

THE *IS* CURVE

The *IS* Equation is the various combinations of the real interest rate r and output Y that are consistent with equilibrium in the goods market.

To derive the **IS** curve, we return to the model of aggregate expenditures in Chapter 4. There we modeled consumption, investment, government spending, and net exports, the four components of aggregate spending, as

$$C = c_0 + c_1 Y_D; \qquad c_0 > 0, 1 > c_1 > 0, \tag{5.7}$$

where $Y_D = Y - T.$ (5.8)

$$I = d_0 - d_1 r, \tag{5.9}$$

where $r = R - \pi^e.$ (5.10)

$$G = G_0. \tag{5.11}$$

$$NX = n_0 + n_1 E. \tag{5.12}$$

By calculating total expenditures TE as the sum of consumption, investment, government, and net export spending, we have

$$TE = C + I + G + NX,$$

or, equivalently,

$$TE = [c_0 + c_1(Y - T_0)] + [d_0 - d_1 r] + G_0 + [n_0 + n_1 E]. \tag{5.13}$$

Rewritten as an equation with an intercept and slope term, we have

$$TE = [c_0 - c_1 T_0 + d_0 + G_0 + n_0 + n_1 E - d_1 r] + c_1 Y,$$

which is the equation for the total expenditure line derived in Chapter 4.

One of the main ideas of Chapter 4, equilibrium in the goods market, suggested that income, determined by the intersection of the total expenditure line TE and the 45-degree line, was equal to the intercept of TE divided by $(1 - \text{MPC})$. Chapter 4 also introduced the idea of the multiplier effect to describe how a change in autonomous spending affects income.[2] In making use of this idea, all the variables in the vertical intercept of TE are taken as given, including the real interest rate r. It is our purpose now to modify this assumption by deriving a relationship between the real interest rate r and real output Y that holds while maintaining goods market equilibrium. This relationship is what we call the *IS* equation.

To derive the *IS* equation, we will rewrite the vertical intercept of the total expenditure equation to isolate the effect of the real interest rate on income.

---

[2]Recall that in equilibrium $Y = TE$, so that equilibrium real income is

$$Y = [c_0 + c_1(Y - T_0)] + [d_0 - d_1 r] + G_0 + [n_0 + n_1 E].$$

Solving for equilibrium Y, we have

$$Y = (c_0 - c_1 T_0 + d_0 - d_1 r + G_0 + n_0 + n_1 E)/(1 - c_1).$$

The intercept *apart from the influence of r* is given by ($c_0 - c_1 T_0 + d_0 + G_0 + n_0 + n_1 E$), and the influence of r is given by $-d_1 r$. We assume for now that the intercept is 60 *when the interest rate is zero.* For example, we assume that $c_0 = 20$, $c_1 = .75$, $T_0 = 20$, $d_0 = 10$, $G_0 = 35$, $n_0 = 9$, $n_1 = .1$, and $E = 10$, so the intercept other than the interest rate effect is 60. We also assume that $-d_1 = -2$. Income is then given by the vertical intercept of 60 divided by $1 - MPC$, so income is $60/(1 - .75) = 60 \times 4 = 240$. In Table 5-1, we record the contribution of the noninterest factors and the interest rate factor to the vertical intercept of *TE* as the interest rate varies, and we also record the implications for the level of real income.

What happens when the interest rate rises to 10 percent? With $r = 10$, the effect of the interest rate on the vertical intercept is $-2 \times 10 = -20$. Then the vertical intercept of *TE* is $60 - 20 = 40$. Income is $40/(1 - .75) = 40 \times 4 = 200$. Thus, for given values of all the terms that affect the vertical intercept of *TE* other than the interest rate, an increase in the interest rate from zero to 10 percent will decrease income from 240 to 160. The above examples give two combinations of interest rates and income that accord with equilibrium in the goods market. The first is $r = 0$, $Y = 240$, and the second is $r = 10$, $Y = 160$. We graph these two equilibria in Figure 5-7.

For given values of all the exogenous variables affecting the vertical intercept other than r, the values $r = 10$, $Y = 160$ are one set of r, Y points on the *IS* curve.

To find other sets of r, Y points on the *IS* curve, we need to ask what happens when r changes. For example, what happens if $r = 20$? In this case, the vertical intercept of *TE* is $60 - (2 \times 20) = 20$, and equilibrium income Y is $20/(1 - .75) = 80$. Thus, for given values of all the exogenous variables affecting the vertical intercept other than r, the values $r = 10$, $Y = 80$ are another set of r, Y points on the *IS* curve.

TABLE 5-1   The Effect of the Interest Rate on the Total Expenditure Line

This table shows how a change in the interest rate changes investment spending, and hence changes the vertical intercept of the total expenditure line.

INTEREST RATE	VERTICAL INTERCEPT EXCLUDING THE INTEREST RATE INFLUENCE	CONTRIBUTION OF THE INTEREST RATE TO THE INTERCEPT	VERTICAL INTERCEPT INCLUDING THE INTEREST RATE INFLUENCE	EQUILIBRIUM REAL INCOME, INTERCEPT/ $(1 - c_1)$
0	60	0	60	240
10	60	−10	40	160
20	60	−20	20	80

FIGURE 5-7
The Effect of Interest Rates
on Income

As interest rates fall, total expenditures rise, creating a new and higher
level of income. (The reduction in interest rates increases investment
spending.) Thus, lower interest rates are associated with higher levels of
income in equilibrium.

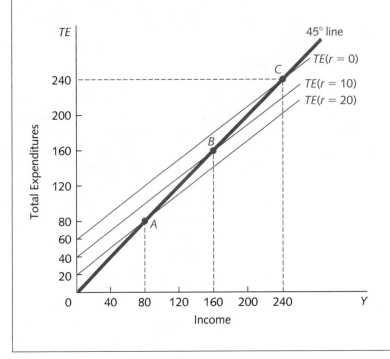

Figure 5-8 graphs the *IS* curve. The real interest rate r appears on the
vertical axis, and real income Y appears on the horizontal axis. For fixed values
of all the variables except r and Y, we graph the *IS* curve as follows. When
$r = 10$, $Y = 200$ and this is labeled B in Figure 5-8. If the interest rate
increases, what happens to the equilibrium level of income? If $r = 20$, the
equilibrium level of income is 80, the point labeled A in Figure 5-8. Points A
and B are two points on the *IS* curve. These are two sets of r,Y values that are
consistent with equilibrium in the goods market.

What if the interest rate does the unlikely, and falls to zero? If $r = 0$, income
is 240. In Figure 5-8, the corresponding point is given at point C, where
$r = 0$, $Y = 240$. For constant values of all the other variables that affect total
expenditures, point C is another combination of r and Y that is consistent with
equilibrium in the goods market.

In Figure 5-8, we connect points A, B, and C with a straight line and label
this line $IS(c_0, d_0, G_0, T_0, n_0, E)$. This signifies that the *IS* curve is drawn for
constant values of the variables c_0, d_0, G_0, T_0, n_0, and E. All points on the *IS*
curve in Figure 5-8 are possible points of equilibrium in the goods market, as
long as the values of the variables other than r and Y remained fixed.

FIGURE 5-8
The *IS* Curve

The *IS* curve, which shows all possible combinations of interest and income that will make saving equal to investment, is drawn for constant values of the variables c_0, d_0, G_0, T_0, n_0, and E. Changes in any of these variables will shift the *IS* curve.

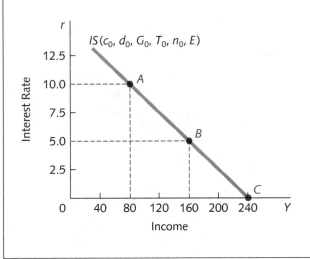

In Figure 5-8 we actually derived only three sets of r, Y points that are consistent with equilibrium in the goods market, but then we connected them with a straight line. In fact, points *A, B,* and *C* lie on a straight line because we assumed that the *TE* curve was linear in both Y and r.[3] Note that the *IS* curve is downward sloping. That is, as r decreases, Y increases, indicating an inverse relationship between the interest rate and real income. Common sense tells us that as r decreases, investment increases, so total spending *TE* rises, raising equilibrium output.

On the *IS* curve, the variables other than the interest rate that can affect the vertical intercept of the total expenditure line *TE* must remain constant. If these values change, the value of Y that corresponds to any given value of r will change. Alternatively stated, *IS* will shift to a new position, much as changes in the determinants of demand will shift the market demand curve in microeconomic analysis.

Up to now, we have held all variables constant except r and Y, and this has allowed us to derive the *IS* equation. What happens to the *IS* curve if there is a change in the variables *other than* r so that the vertical intercept of the *TE* line

---

[3]In fact, we can derive an equation for *IS* from the goods market equilibrium condition, $TE = Y$, which after some rearranging is

$$Y = (c_0 - c_1 T_0 + d_0 + G_0 + n_0 + n_1 E)/(1-c_1) - (d_1 r)/(1-c_1).$$

This is the *IS* equation.

FIGURE 5-9
The Effect of an Increase in
G on *IS*

An increase in government expenditures shifts the total expenditure function (*TE*) upward in (a). This means that one of the factors underlying *IS* has changed. In (b), *IS* will shift rightward because of the increase in *G*.

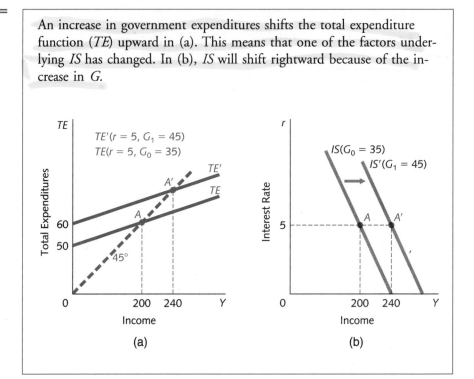

(a)   (b)

changes? For concreteness, consider congressional legislation to increase government spending G_0 from 35 to 45. This increases the vertical intercept of *TE* by 10, holding all other variables constant, *including r.* For example, consider an initial equilibrium illustrated by point *A* in Figure 5-9, in which $r = 5$, $G = 35$, the vertical intercept of *TE* is 50, and income is 200. On the *IS* curve, this is represented by point *A,* where $r = 5$ and $Y = 200$. If government spending increases to 45, the vertical intercept of *TE* becomes 60, r stays at 5, and equilibrium income rises to 240. This is illustrated by point *A'*. On the *IS* graph, point *A'* is a point where $r = 5$ but $Y = 240$. This point is on a new *IS* curve, *IS',* for which $G = G_0 + 10$ and the other variables are constant. That is, the *IS* curve has shifted to the right because of the increase in government spending. With the increase in *G,* at every interest rate (such as $r = 5$) the equilibrium level of income is higher than before.

Next, consider an increase in lump sum taxes *T* from 20 to 30. This changes the vertical intercept of *TE* by $-\Delta T_0 \times c_1 = -10 \times .75 = -7.50$, holding all other variables constant, *including r.* For example, consider an initial equilibrium illustrated by point *A* in Figure 5-10, in which $r = 5$, $T = T_0$, the vertical intercept of *TE* is 50, and $Y = 200$. Point *A* is also represented on the *IS* curve as the point where $r = 5$, $Y = 200$. If taxes increase by 10, to a value of 35, the vertical intercept of *TE* becomes $50 - 7.50 = 42.50$, r stays at 5,

FIGURE 5-10
The Effects of an Increase in
Taxes on *IS*

A rise in *T* will shift the total expenditures function downward and the *IS* function leftward.

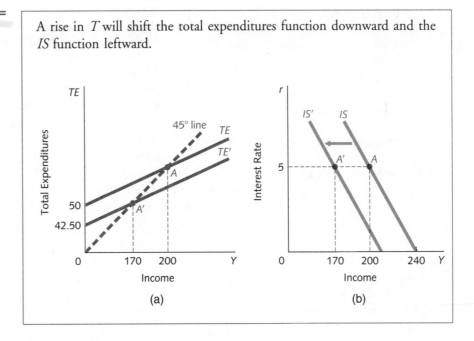

(a)   (b)

and $Y = 170$. This is illustrated by point A'. On the *IS* graph, point A' is a point where $r = 5$ but $Y = 170$. This point is on a new *IS* curve, *IS'*, for which $T = 30$ and the other variables are constant. Alternatively stated, the *IS* curve has shifted to the left because of the increase in lump sum taxes. With the increase in taxes, at every interest rate (such as $r = 5$) the level of income is lower than before.

Our discussion has been concerned with variables that shift total expenditures, including fiscal policy variables such as government purchases of goods and services and net tax collections. These fiscal policy variables are related, and together with government interest payments represent the main sources of government revenue and government spending. The Policy Issue: "Federal Government Spending and Tax Collections" provides background information on the behavior of these fiscal policy variables, as well as information on various subcomponents of these variables such as gross tax collections and transfer payments.

The above examples illustrate merely two of a large number of possible changes in exogenous variables that can lead to a shift in the *IS* curve. In fact, changes in government spending G_0, taxes T_0, autonomous consumption c_0, investment d_0, net exports n_0, and the exchange rate E will all cause the *IS* curve to shift. Anything that increases the vertical intercept of *TE, ceteris paribus,* will shift *IS* to the right (such as an increase in *G*), and anything that decreases the vertical intercept of *TE, ceteris paribus,* will shift the *IS* curve to the left (such as an increase in *T*). These effects are summarized in Table 5-2, which gives the shift in *IS* in response to changes in each of these variables.

FEDERAL GOVERNMENT SPENDING AND TAX COLLECTIONS

In the course of this chapter we have discussed fiscal policy and its role in shifting the *IS* curves. Here we examine more closely the data on government spending and tax collections in order to have a better understanding of the U.S. fiscal policy position, and, especially, of the ongoing U.S. federal deficits.

In Figure 5-11 we show total federal spending, total federal tax collections, and several main components of federal spending, all in real terms, for the period 1959–1992. Notice the continuing rise in total federal spending and total federal tax collections over this period. A federal deficit occurs when federal spending exceeds tax collections. As can be seen in the graph, spending and tax collections were fairly close until 1974, when the recession lowered tax collections substantially and the government incurred a large deficit. This deficit gradually diminished until it nearly disappeared in 1979. Then, however, tax collections again dipped substantially, in part due to the recession in the early 1980s and in part due to tax cuts implemented by President Reagan.

At the same time, the accompanying graph indicates that total federal spending continued to increase. So began the long period of budget deficits during the 1980s.

What fuels the continued increase in federal spending? An answer to this question can be found by looking at the components of government spending. One component is actual government purchases of goods and services, labeled *G* in our theoretical model. Government purchases include the purchases of goods, such as buildings, aircraft carriers, and roads, and the purchases of services, such as wages and salaries paid to government employees and the military.

PHOTO 5-3
Government Spending Includes Such Items as Defense, Infrastructure, and Space Exploration.

Federal government purchases of goods and services have fluctuated, with slight increases and decreases over time, but the general level of government purchases has remained fairly steady over the thirty or so years covered by our graph. In contrast, transfer payments, which include transfers to individuals, transfers to state and local governments, and federal subsidies to businesses and individuals, have shown a steady upward growth path. It is interesting that the growth of transfers did seem to flatten in 1974, but has grown at a relatively constant pace since then. In particular, there is no obvious decline during the Reagan presidency. Finally, the last category of spending, interest payments on the debt, has been a relatively small component of spending until the 1980s, when interest payments accelerated. This occurred for two reasons. First, the large increase in interest rates in the late 1970s and early 1980s meant that the interest rate the government paid on the outstanding debt went up as that debt was refinanced with new bond issues. Second, the large deficits incurred in the 1974–1978 period, and the even larger deficits incurred beginning in the early 1980s, caused the stock of debt to rise, so that even after interest rates fell in the middle 1980s the large stock of debt required ever larger interest payments. By 1992 interest payments on the debt made up one-sixth of all federal spending, and actually exceeded the size of the deficit.

In conclusion, we can see that the federal deficit has been persistently negative from 1974, with only a gradual move to narrow the deficit as the 1990s began. This deficit can be linked to increases in federal spending, in particular on transfers and on interest payments, that were not matched by increases in taxes. Perhaps these trends will be countered by President Clinton's deficit reduction program in the rest of the 1990s. ❑

FIGURE 5-11
Total Federal Spending, Federal Tax Collections, and Components of Spending in Real 1987 Dollars (1959–1992)

Federal tax collections have lagged behind total federal spending since the mid-1970s. Note the increase in transfer payments (federal subsidies to individuals, businesses, and transfers to local and state governments) since 1970.

NOTE: All values in billions of 1987 dollars.
SOURCE: Department of Commerce, Bureau of Economic Analysis.

TABLE 5-2
Shifts in the *IS* Curve

This table summarizes the effect of changes in the determinants of the *IS* curve on the location of *IS*.

CHANGE IN EXOGENOUS VARIABLE	DIRECTION OF SHIFT
INCREASE IN AUTONOMOUS CONSUMPTION c_0	RIGHTWARD
DECREASE IN AUTONOMOUS CONSUMPTION c_0	LEFTWARD
INCREASE IN INVESTMENT d_0	RIGHTWARD
DECREASE IN INVESTMENT d_0	LEFTWARD
INCREASE IN GOVERNMENT SPENDING G_0	RIGHTWARD
DECREASE IN GOVERNMENT SPENDING G_0	LEFTWARD
INCREASE IN TAXES T_0	LEFTWARD
DECREASE IN TAXES T_0	RIGHTWARD
INCREASE IN NET EXPORTS n_0	RIGHTWARD
DECREASE IN NET EXPORTS n_0	LEFTWARD
INCREASE IN THE EXCHANGE EQUILIBRIUM RATE E	RIGHTWARD
DECREASE IN THE EXCHANGE EQUILIBRIUM RATE E	LEFTWARD
INCREASE IN THE REAL INTEREST RATE r	NO SHIFT; MOVE ALONG *IS* CURVE
DECREASE IN THE REAL INTEREST RATE r	NO SHIFT; MOVE ALONG *IS* CURVE

THE *LM* CURVE

The *LM* Equation is the various combinations of the real interest rate r and output Y that are consistent with equilibrium in the money market.

In order to derive the **LM** model, we return to our earlier model of the money market, where we modeled money demand and money supply as

$$L(Y,R) = L_0 + L_1 Y - L_2 R \tag{5.14}$$

$$M = M_0. \tag{5.15}$$

The equilibrium condition is that the demand for real money balances $L(Y,R)$ equals the supply of real money balances M/P. Since the price level is fixed and the nominal money supply is exogenous, the supply of real money balances is exogenous. Equilibrium is given by

$$M_0/P_0 = L_0 + L_1 Y - L_2 R. \tag{5.16}$$

To derive the *LM* curve, we first graph the equilibrium between demand and supply for real money balances. Then we ask what combinations of the interest rate and income are consistent with equilibrium in the money market, and call these r,Y pairs the *LM* curve.

For concreteness, assume that initially the nominal money supply is 100 and the price level is 1, so $M_0/P_0 = 100/1 = 100$. Assume that $L_0 = 20$, $L_1 = .5$, and $L_2 = 4$, so demand for real money balances is $20 + .5Y - 4R$. Initially income is 200, so money demand is $20 + .5 \times 200 - 4R = 120 - 4R$. This is graphed as the money demand equation in Figure 5-12. When $R = 0$, the horizontal intercept is 120; when $R = 30$, money demand is zero.

For $Y = 200$, money demand equals money supply when the interest rate is 5. We label this as point A in Figure 5-12. The combination $R = 5$, $Y = 200$ is one point of equilibrium in the money market for given values of the money supply. If income increases so that $Y = 240$, money demand increases to $140 - 400R$, graphed as $L'(Y = 240)$ in Figure 5-12. When $R = 0$, the horizontal intercept is now 140. With this new money demand equation, equilibrium occurs where the interest rate is 10. We label this as point A' in Figure 5-12. The combination $R = 10$, $Y = 240$ is another point of equilibrium in the money market for given values of the money supply.

The *LM* curve is a graph of the R,Y points that are consistent with equilibrium in the money market. We have already found two such points, which we plot in Figure 5-13. In this figure, R is on the vertical axis and Y on the horizontal axis. One equilibrium point in Figure 5-12 was point A, with $R = 5$, $Y = 200$. This point is graphed and also labeled as point A in Figure 5-13. Another equilibrium point in Figure 5-12 was point A', with $R = 10$, $Y = 240$. This point is plotted and also labeled point A' in Figure 5-13. These two points, and all points on a line connecting them, are the *LM* curve. The *LM* curve is derived holding constant the values of both real money balances M_0/P_0 and the constant in money demand L_0. As long as these variables are held constant, changes in income lead to movements along the *LM* curve.

FIGURE 5-12
Equilibrium in the Money Market

A rise in income from 200 to 240 billion will increase the demand for money. Higher income is associated with a higher interest rate.

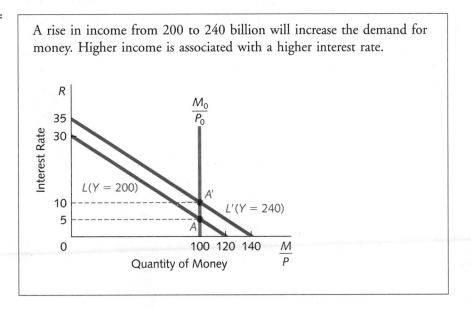

FIGURE 5-13
Deriving the *LM* Curve

The *LM* curve presents all combinations of interest rates and incomes that will equilibrate the money market. Since higher income is associated with higher interest rates in such equilibria, the *LM* curve is upward sloping.

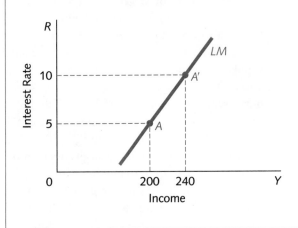

To see what is happening along the *LM* curve, remember that as income (Y) increases, money demand increases. Holding everything else constant, this causes an excess demand for money, which is eliminated by an increase in the interest rate R. Thus, there is a direct relationship between income and interest rates, reflected in the graph of *LM* by the upward slope of the *LM* curve.[4]

Before proceeding to a discussion of shifts in the *LM* equation, we need to deal with the issue of real versus nominal interest rates. The *IS* curve is graphed with the real interest rate r, on the vertical axis, while the *LM* curve in Figure 5-13 has the nominal interest rate R on the vertical axis. These two interest rates will be the same only when the expected inflation rate is zero. If the expected inflation rate is other than zero, we have to modify our discussion of the *LM* equation.

---

[4]We can derive the algebraic expression for the *LM* curve by just rearranging the money market equilibrium condition as

$$R = (L_0 + L_1 Y - M_0/P_0)/L_2.$$

For the values used in the text, the *LM* equation becomes

$$R = (20 + .5Y - 100)/400 = -20 + 125 \ Y.$$

For example, when $Y = 200$, $R = -20 + 125 \times 200 = 5$. Thus, this equation completely describes the curve plotted in Figure 5-13.

Changes in the expected inflation rate π^e will shift the *LM* curve. An increase in the expected inflation rate will shift it down and to the right.

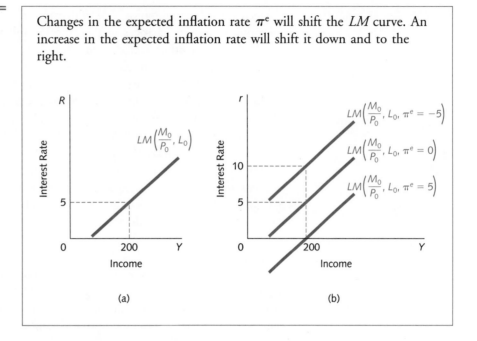

(a)   (b)

It is important to keep in mind that the expected inflation rate is exogenous. It is also important to remember that it is the *nominal* interest rate that affects money demand, and hence it is the nominal interest rate that is determined by equilibrium in the money market. Once this nominal rate is determined, the real rate can also be determined by simply subtracting the expected inflation rate from the nominal rate.[5]

We illustrate the effect of changes in expected inflation π^e in Figure 5-14. Graph (a) shows the *LM* curve with the nominal interest rate R on the vertical axis. Continuing with our ongoing example, when $Y = 200$, $R = 5$, graph (b) shows the *LM* curve with the real interest rate r on the vertical axis. Since $r = R - \pi^e$, $Y = 200$ and $\pi^e = 0$ implies that $r = 5 - 0 = 5$, while $\pi^e = 5$ implies $r = 5 - 5 = 0$. Likewise $R = 5$ when $\pi^e = -5$ implies $r = 5 - (-5) = 10$. The point is that when we graph *LM* with the real interest rate r on the vertical axis, increases in the expected inflation rate (such as π^e increasing from 0 to 5 percent) shift *LM* down or to the right, while decreases in the expected inflation rate (such as π^e falling from 0 to -5) shift *LM* up or to the left.

---

[5]Algebraically, the idea is rather straightforward. The *LM* equation is

$$R = (L_0 + L_1 Y - M_0/P_0)/L_2,$$

which determines the nominal interest rate R. Once R is determined, the real rate r is just $R - \pi^e$.

Since we will be graphing *LM* with the real rate on the vertical axis, the above illustrates that changes in the expected inflation rate will shift the *LM* curve. There are other factors that shift *LM*. One important factor is the money supply. Increases in the nominal money supply M or decreases in the price level P will increase the real money supply M/P and shift *LM* downward, as illustrated in Figure 5-15. Figure 5.15(a) shows the money market graph. The initial equilibrium occurs with $M/P = 100$, and with $R = 5$ and $Y = 200$. We assume $\pi^e = 0$, so $r = 5$. We label the initial equilibrium point A. Figure 5.15(b) shows the *LM* graph, and on the initial *LM* curve with $M/P = 100$, the equilibrium point with $r = 5$, $Y = 200$ is also labeled A. Now consider an increase in the nominal money supply to 110. Money demand is unchanged, but the increase in money supply leads to a reduction in the interest rate. The new equilibrium in the money market is where $R = 2.5$, and is labeled point A'. The point is plotted in the *LM* graph on the curve LM' on which $M/P = 110$, and is also labeled A'. Thus, an increase in real money balances shifts *LM* downward or to the right. Stated differently, an increase in money balances causes an excess supply of money at the original interest rate, so that the interest rate is bid down to restore equilibrium between money demand and money supply. Note that the money supply itself cannot adjust, since both the nominal money supply M and the price level P are exogenous. Moreover, the effect of a change in real money balances is symmetric. If real money supply declines, *LM* shifts upward or to the left.

Another factor that shifts *LM* is an exogenous shift in money demand. Remember that real money demand is given by $L(Y,R) = L_0 + L_1 Y - L_2 R$.

FIGURE 5-15
The Effect of M/P on *LM*

If the money supply rises, as shown in (a), *LM* shifts downward and to the right, as in (b).

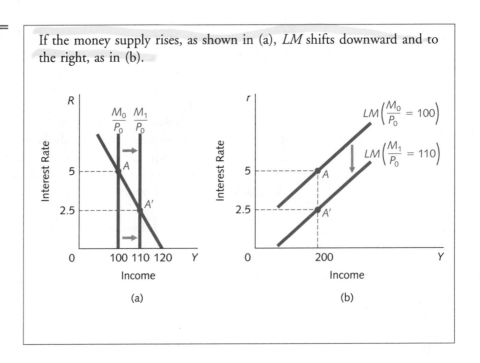

The constant term L_0 represents all those factors other than income and the nominal interest rate that can change money demand. For example, credit cards and ATMs are innovations that are thought to have reduced money demand. Credit cards make it easier to make purchases without using cash or checks, and ATMs make it easier to obtain cash when banks are normally closed, thereby allowing people to hold less money to meet unexpected needs for cash during times when banks are not open.

An exogenous increase in money demand is illustrated in Figure 5-16. Figure 5-16(a) shows a graph of the money market. The initial equilibrium occurs with $M/P = 100$, with $R = 5$ and $Y = 200$. We assume $\pi^e = 0$, so $r = 5$. We label the initial equilibrium point A. Figure 5-16(b) shows the *LM* graph, and on the initial *LM* curve, the equilibrium point with $r = 5$, $Y = 200$ is also labeled A. Now consider an exogenous increase in money demand due to an increase in L_0. With this increase in money demand, for $Y = 200$, the new equilibrium interest rate is $R = 10$, and since $\pi^e = 0$, $r = 10$. This equilibrium is labeled A'. In Figure 5-16(b), the new money market equilibrium point is plotted on the curve *LM'* which is also labeled A'. Thus, an exogenous increase in money demand shifts *LM* upward or to the left. Stated differently, an exogenous increase in money demand causes an excess demand for money at the original interest rate R, so that the interest rate is bid up to restore equilibrium between money demand and money supply. The money supply cannot itself adjust because both the nominal money supply M and the price level P are exogenous. Note too that the effect of an exogenous change in

FIGURE 5-16
The Effect of an Exogenous Money Demand Shock on LM

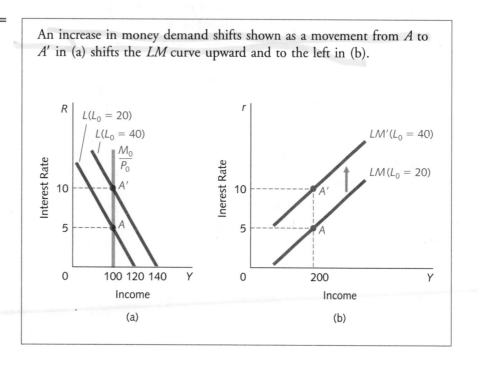

An increase in money demand shifts shown as a movement from A to A' in (a) shifts the *LM* curve upward and to the left in (b).

TABLE 5-3
Shifts in the *LM* Curve

This table summarizes the effect of changes in the determinants of the *LM* curve on the location of *LM*.

CHANGE IN EXOGENOUS VARIABLE	DIRECTION OF SHIFT
INCREASE IN EXPECTED INFLATION π^e	RIGHTWARD
DECREASE IN EXPECTED INFLATION π^e	LEFTWARD
INCREASE IN REAL MONEY BALANCES M/P	RIGHTWARD
DECREASE IN REAL MONEY BALANCES M/P	LEFTWARD
INCREASE IN NOMINAL MONEY BALANCES M	RIGHTWARD
DECREASE IN NOMINAL MONEY BALANCES M	LEFTWARD
INCREASE IN THE PRICE LEVEL P	LEFTWARD
DECREASE IN THE PRICE LEVEL P	RIGHTWARD
INCREASE IN EXOGENOUS MONEY DEMAND L_0	LEFTWARD
DECREASE IN EXOGENOUS MONEY DEMAND L_0	RIGHTWARD
INCREASE IN THE REAL INTEREST RATE r	NO SHIFT; MOVE ALONG *LM* CURVE
DECREASE IN THE REAL INTEREST RATE r	NO SHIFT; MOVE ALONG *LM* CURVE

money demand is symmetric. If money demand exogenously declines, *LM* shifts downward or to the right.

The above examples illustrate the three changes in exogenous variables that can lead to a shift in the *LM* curve: changes in expected inflation π^e, in the real money supply M/P, and in exogenous money demand L_0. We summarize the effects of these changes in Table 5-3, which gives the shift in *LM* in response to changes in each of these variables.

IS-LM EQUILIBRIUM

Now that the *IS* and *LM* curves have been derived, we can use them to determine the equilibrium real interest rate and level of real income for an economy, holding constant the price level. Remember that the *IS* curve (the set of r, Y combinations consistent with equilibrium in the goods market) is downward sloping. The *LM* curve (the set of r, Y combinations consistent with equilibrium in the money market) is upward sloping. The intersection of *IS* and *LM* gives the *one* r, Y combination that is consistent with equilibrium in both the goods market and the money market simultaneously. Such an equilibrium E is illustrated in Figure 5-17.

FIGURE 5-17
The *IS-LM* Equilibrium

Simultaneous equilibrium in both goods and money markets is shown at the intersection of *IS* and *LM*. The resulting equilibrium interest rate (5 in the figure) and income level (200) are the only combination that put both markets—goods and money—into equilibrium.

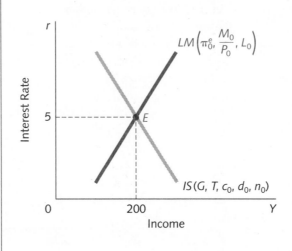

In this graph, the intersection of *IS* and *LM* occurs at $r = 5$, $Y = 200$. For the given *IS* and *LM* curves, this is the one point at which both the goods market and the money market are in equilibrium. As long as nothing occurs to change either the *IS* curve or the *LM* curve, the economy will remain at this point. Of course, this assumes that the price level is exogenous.[6]

It is important to remember that the model described in Figure 5-17 is static, and that it can give only an approximate description of the actual economy. Still, we can use this model to try and interpret the behavior of economies. For one example, see the Global Perspective: "Income Growth Rates in World Economies Affected by Factors Underlying *IS-LM* Curves, 1988–1992." This global perspective addresses the issue of differing growth rates across countries, and the possibility that at least some of these differences

---

[6]We can solve algebraically for the equilibrium r, Y combination given by the intersection of *IS* and *LM*. Recall that the *IS* equation is given by

$$Y = (c_0 - c_1 T_0 + d_0 + G_0 + n_0 + n_1 E)/(1 - c_1) - (d_1 r)/(1 - c_1).$$

Recall, too, that the *LM* equation is given by

$$r = R - \pi^e = (L_0 + L_1 Y - M_0/P_0)/L_2 - \pi^e.$$

From these, we can derive an equation for the equilibrium level of income as

$$Y = [L_2(c_0 - c_1 T_0 + d_0 + G_0 + n_0 + n_1 E) + d_1(M/P + L_2 \pi^e - L_0)]/[L_2(1 - c_1) + d_1 L_1].$$

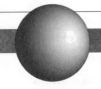

GLOBAL PERSPECTIVE

INCOME GROWTH RATES IN WORLD ECONOMIES AFFECTED BY FACTORS UNDERLYING _IS-LM_ CURVES, 1988–1992.

Clearly, the _IS-LM_ apparatus described in this chapter is a static theory—one where none of the variables affecting _IS_ (such as private consumption, investment, or taxes) or _LM_ (such as the money supply or the speculative demand for money) are "dated." This means that our model only covers shifts in either _IS, LM,_ or both. We then describe forces that return the economy to new equilibrium _levels_ of interest rates and income (price changes are not yet considered in the _IS_ apparatus, but they will be in Chapter 6).

In the real world, however, we are often interested in the dynamics of income change or in the _growth_ of income. The factors underlying _IS_ and _LM_—private and public spending, money supply and demand—can have a dramatic impact on economic growth. Consider economic growth measured by the percentage change in GDP over the pe-

MAP 5-1
Global Events Such as Economic Activity in the European Community (Shown in Map) Often Have Dramatic Effects on the U.S. Economy.

riod 1988–1992 for five major nations (the United States, Germany, Japan, the United Kingdom, and Canada) shown in Figure 5-18. Income changes varied widely among countries in given years and within countries between years over the period.

Many factors, including sudden changes in resource availability or other "shocks" to aggregate supply, affect income growth over time. Tight monetary policy (lower M) in Canada and the United Kingdom helped bring on the recession those economies experienced in 1990. Slower growth in private consumption expenditures (the C component of IS) was one major factor in explaining the slow recovery experienced by the U.S. economy in 1991 and 1992. In Japan, depressions in the real estate sector and a plummeting stock market average (a decline on the Nikkei stock market of 58.6 percent between December 1989 and August 1992) slowed Japanese spending, creating a worsening income growth in 1992.[a] Many of these kinds of changes can be analyzed within the simple confines of the *IS-LM* model of this chapter.❏

NOTE [a]See *Economic Report of the President* (Washington, DC: U.S. Government Printing Office, 1993), pp. 94–95.

FIGURE 5-18
International Real GDP Growth (in Part) Explained by Factors Affecting *IS* and *LM*

Growth rates in income varied considerably between 1988 and 1992 in the United States, Germany, Japan, the United Kingdom, and Canada. With the exception of Germany and Japan, growth slowed or turned negative by 1990 in these countries and continued into 1991 and 1992. Factors underlying *IS* and *LM* help explain these changes.

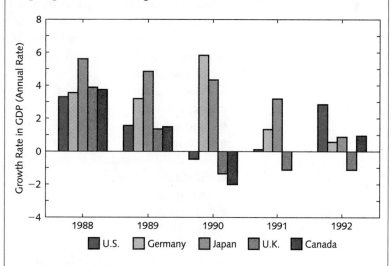

SOURCE: *Economic Report of the President* (Washington, DC: U.S. Government Printing Office, 1993).
NOTE: Data for Japan and Germany are for GNP.

might be due to factors that affect the *IS–LM* equilibrium, such as government spending, tax policies, and autonomous money demand.

Finally, what forces lead us to equilibrium in Figure 5-17? Why do the real interest rate and real income tend to the point where *IS* and *LM* intersect?

In Figure 5-19, *IS* and *LM* are graphed together, and the equilibrium is labeled point *A*. What forces drive the economy toward this equilibrium? Consider a point out of equilibrium, point *B*. Point *B* is to the left of the *IS* equation and is above the *LM* equation. Hence, it is a point of excess demand in the goods market and excess supply in the money market. In the goods market, there are unplanned inventory depletions, leading firms to increase output. Taken by itself, this would tend to move the economy toward the *IS* equation by an increase in output, but there would be no change in the interest rate. In the money market, the interest rate is above the equilibrium level, so there is an excess supply of money, which will cause the interest rate to be bid down. This will tend to move the economy toward the *LM* curve by decreasing the interest rate, but there would be no change in output. We symbolize this in the figure by having the arrows of adjustment at point *B* point down and to the right. Note that because both the money market and the goods market are out of equilibrium, there is a tendency for *both* output to increase and the real interest rate to decrease at point *B*.

Next consider point *C*. Point *C* is to the left of the *IS* equation and is below the *LM* equation. Hence it is a point of excess demand in the goods market and excess demand in the money market. In the goods market, there are unplanned inventory depletions, leading firms to increase output and therefore move the economy toward the *IS* equation. In the money market, the interest rate is below the equilibrium level, so there is an excess demand for money, which will lead the interest rate to be bid up and the economy to move toward the *LM* curve. Thus, the arrows of adjustment at point *C* point up and to the right, signifying that there is a tendency for both output and the real interest rate to increase at point *C*.

Point *D* is to the right of the *IS* equation and is below the *LM* equation. Hence, it is a point of excess supply in the goods market and excess demand in the money market. In the goods market, there are unplanned increases in inventories, leading firms to decrease output and therefore move the economy toward the *IS* equation. In the money market, the interest rate is below the equilibrium level, so there is an excess demand for money, which will lead the interest rate to be bid up and the economy to move toward the *LM* curve. Thus the arrows of adjustment at point *D* point up and to the left, because at this point there is a tendency for output to decline and the interest rate to be bid up.

Last, consider point *E*. Point *E* is to the right of the *IS* equation and is above the *LM* equation. Hence it is a point of excess supply in the goods market and excess supply in the money market. In the goods market, there are unplanned inventory accumulations, leading firms to decrease output and therefore move the economy toward the *IS* equation. In the money market, the interest rate is above the equilibrium level, so there is an excess supply of money, which will

FIGURE 5-19
Equilibrium Adjustments of
the Economy in the *IS-LM*
Framework

Market forces adjusting interest rates and income will bring the
economy to that interest rate and income level that equilibrates *both*
the goods and the money market simultaneously.

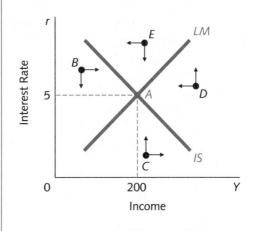

lead the interest rate to be bid down and the economy to move toward the *LM*
curve. Thus, the arrows of adjustment at point *E* point down and to the left,
showing the tendency of both interest rates and output to fall at point *E*.

We have considered points *B, C, D,* and *E* in Figure 5-19, and have shown
how an economy at these points will face forces acting simultaneously in the
goods market and in the money market to move both the interest rate and
income toward the equilibrium at point *A*. These forces do not, however, push
the economy straight toward *A*, and the actual path of adjustment may be
more nearly a spiral in toward *A*. The main point here is that in the *IS-LM*
model we can describe forces that will lead to the equilibrium *r, Y* point where
IS and *LM* intersect.

It is also worth pointing out that economists generally speak of these
adjustments as occurring fairly quickly, especially in the money market and
other financial markets. Keynes himself stressed slow adjustments in the goods
market and in the labor market, but many economists today are comfortable
with a fairly quick adjustment to equilibrium when the economy is in a state
of disequilibrium.

CHANGES IN EQUILIBRIUM

The final topic for discussion in the chapter is the response of equilibrium *r, Y*
to changes in the exogenous variables. We have already set the stage for this
analysis by tabulating the effect of the exogenous variables on the *IS* and *LM*

curves in Tables 5-2 and 5-3. Now we put that information to use to show the effect of shifts in *IS* and/or *LM* on the equilibrium interest rate and income.

Basically, there are four possible shifts that can occur, either alone or in combination with other shifts: The *IS* curve can shift left or right, and the *LM* curve can shift left or right. Given that the *IS* curve slopes downward and *LM* slopes upward, a rightward shift in *IS* results in higher equilibrium *r* and equilibrium *Y*, while a leftward shift in *IS* results in lower equilibrium *r* and equilibrium *Y*, as seen in Figure 5-20(a). A rightward shift in *LM* results in higher equilibrium *Y* but lower equilibrium *r*, and a leftward shift in *LM* results in lower equilibrium *Y* but higher equilibrium *r* as seen in Figure 5-20(b). We summarize the possible causes of the shifts in Table 5-4.

It is possible to have simultaneous shifts in *IS* and *LM*. These cause more ambiguity, just as would simultaneous shifts in demand and supply in a market. If *IS* and *LM* both shift rightward, then equilibrium *Y* will increase but equilibrium *r* may increase, decrease, or stay the same. If *IS* and *LM* both shift leftward, the equilibrium *Y* will decrease but equilibrium *r* may increase, decrease, or stay the same. If *IS* shifts to the right and *LM* shifts to the left, the equilibrium *r* will increase but equilibrium *Y* may increase, decrease, or stay the same. Finally, if *IS* shifts to the left but *LM* shifts to the right, equilibrium *r* will decrease but equilibrium *Y* may increase, decrease, or stay the same.

We will provide one example of an analysis of the behavior of equilibrium *r,Y* when *IS* and *LM* respond to exogenous variables. In Figure 5-21 the

FIGURE 5-20
Changes in *IS-LM* Equilibria

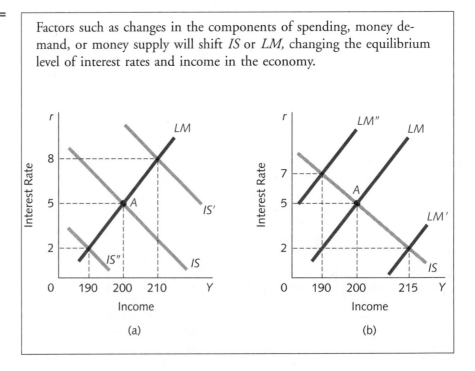

Factors such as changes in the components of spending, money demand, or money supply will shift *IS* or *LM*, changing the equilibrium level of interest rates and income in the economy.

TABLE 5-4 Shifts in IS and LM

CHANGES IN EXOGENOUS VARIABLE	EFFECT ON *IS* OR *LM*	EFFECT ON INCOME, Y	EFFECT ON REAL INTEREST RATE, r
INCREASE IN π^e	*LM* SHIFTS RIGHT	RISES	FALLS
DECREASE IN π^e	*LM* SHIFTS LEFT	FALLS	RISES
INCREASE IN M	*LM* SHIFTS RIGHT	RISES	FALLS
DECREASE IN M	*LM* SHIFTS LEFT	FALLS	RISES
INCREASE IN P	*LM* SHIFTS LEFT	FALLS	RISES
DECREASE IN P	*LM* SHIFTS RIGHT	RISES	FALLS
INCREASE IN L_0	*LM* SHIFTS LEFT	FALLS	RISES
DECREASE IN L_0	*LM* SHIFTS RIGHT	RISES	FALLS
INCREASE IN C_0, D_0, N_0	*IS* SHIFTS RIGHT	RISES	RISES
DECREASE IN C_0, D_0, N_0	*IS* SHIFTS LEFT	FALLS	FALLS
INCREASE IN G	*IS* SHIFTS RIGHT	RISES	RISES
DECREASE IN G	*IS* SHIFTS LEFT	FALLS	FALLS
INCREASE IN T	*IS* SHIFTS LEFT	FALLS	FALLS
DECREASE IN T	*IS* SHIFTS RIGHT	RISES	RISES
INCREASE IN E	*IS* SHIFTS RIGHT	RISES	RISES
DECREASE IN E	*IS* SHIFTS LEFT	FALLS	FALLS

economy is initially in equilibrium at point *A,* where *IS* intersects *LM.* At this equilibrium, government policymakers decide to increase aggregate income. To make sure this happens, these policymakers increase government spending *G.* Finally, they try to indirectly increase income by increasing the money supply *M,* hoping to lower interest rates and thereby stimulate investment spending. What will be the net result of these efforts?

The increase in government spending *G* shifts *IS* to the right, and it increases the vertical intercept of *TE* for a given value of *r,* leading to an increase in *Y* and a rightward shift in *IS.* The increase in *M* shifts *LM* to the right (or downward, if you prefer). The increase in *M* lowers the interest rate for a given value of *Y,* leading to this shift in *LM.* We graph these changes in two steps in Figure 5-21.

From the initial equilibrium at point *A,* we first consider the increase in *IS* to *IS'.* If this was all that happened, the new equilibrium would be at point *B,* with a higher interest rate and higher level of income. The horizontal shift in *IS* represents the change in *Y* due to the changes in the vertical intercept of *TE,* given by the multiplier formula in Chapter 4. However, because increases in

FIGURE 5-21
Policy Changes in *IS* and *LM*

If policymakers decide that income level Y_0 is insufficient to produce sufficient jobs and high economic growth, they may try to influence the equilibrium level of income by combinations of new government spending, reduced lump sum taxation, and increases in the money supply.

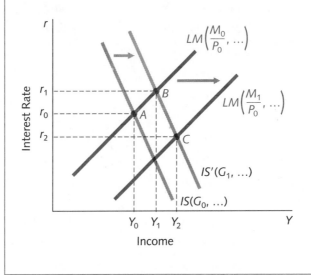

income cause increases in money demand, and hence increases in the real interest rate, there is a reduction in investment spending, and the economy moves to point *B*. The increase in income from point *A* to point *B* is less than what the simple multiplier from Chapter 4 would predict, because the simple multiplier does not consider the effect of the increase in income on the interest rate in the money market, which lowers investment and shifts the vertical intercept of *TE* downward, cancelling a part of the initial increase in the vertical intercept due to the increase in *G* and decrease in *T*. Thus, a multiplier that takes into account these effects of changes in income on money demand and hence on interest rates and investment would be smaller than the simple multiplier that was calculated holding the interest rate constant. This is the contribution of the *IS-LM* model: that the effect of changes in income on the money supply and hence on interest rates and investment is taken into account in determining equilibrium income. The simple total expenditure model of Chapter 4—the "Keynesian cross" model—did not take these effects into account and thus overstated the impact of exogenous factors on real income. At the same time, the Keynesian cross model did not include a role for money market variables such as the money supply, because these variables affect output through changing the interest rate and investment, and again the simple model of Chapter 4 held the interest rate constant.

By continuing with our example, we can see how money has a role in the equilibrium of the economy. Point *B* is not the final equilibrium, because the increase in the money supply *M* shifts *LM* to the right. This shift in *LM* is of an uncertain size, but we have drawn it as a rather large shift in Figure 5-21. Relative to point *B*, the increase in *LM* lowers the interest rate and increases income. The new equilibrium is at point *C*. Relative to point *A*, we know that the shift rightward in both *IS* and *LM* cause *Y* to increase. Relative to point *A*, the shift rightward in *IS* caused *r* to increase, while the shift rightward in *LM* caused *r* to decrease. The net effect is in general uncertain, although in Figure 5-21 we have drawn the net effect as a reduction in *r*. It should be clear that we could have drawn these shifts so that the net effect would be an increase in the real interest rate *r*, or even no change in the real interest rate.

SUMMARY

In this chapter, by using the *IS-LM* model of Sir John Hicks, we relaxed the assumption that the interest rate is exogenous in the goods market and that the level of income is exogenous in the money market. Under a number of assumptions listed in the text, the most important being that the price level is exogenous, the *IS-LM* model allows the joint determination of the interest rate and income. The *IS* curve incorporates the effect of the interest rate on investment spending and hence on income. The *LM* curve incorporates the effect of income on money demand and hence on the interest rate. Utilizing both concepts, we were able to determine the equilibrium interest rate and level of income in the economy, holding the price level constant. Furthermore, we were able to describe the economic forces leading the economy to the equilibrium *r,Y* pair indicated by the *IS-LM* model, and to describe how that equilibrium would change when various forces affecting the economy change.

KEY TERMS

barter

IS Equation

LM Equation

M1

medium of exchange

money

standard of deferred payment

store of wealth

unit of account

QUESTIONS FOR REVIEW AND DISCUSSION

1. Clearly distinguish between the "commodity market" and the "money market."

2. What factor or factors are being held constant in drawing an *IS* curve? What factors change along the *IS* function?

3. What factor or factors are being held constant in drawing an *LM* curve? What factors change along the *LM* function?

4. Why does an *LM* curve (ordinarily) slope upward and to the right?

5. Why is an *IS* curve negatively sloped?

6. Describe *IS-LM* equilibrium; that is, what is the significance of the intersection of *IS* and *LM*?

7. Is it possible for the commodities market to be in equilibrium while the money market is in disequilibrium? How? Would such an equilibrium be stable or unstable? Show graphically!

8. Is it possible for the money market to be in equilibrium while the commodities market is in disequilibrium? How? Would such an equilibrium be stable or unstable? Show graphically!

9. How, specifically, do the *IS* and *LM* functions shift? Analyze the factors causing shifts in both of these functions.

10. How will an increase in the *nominal* stock of money affect *IS* and *LM*? Would changes in the nominal money stock affect the *real* stock of money in the context of the model developed in this chapter? Why or why not?

11. Why do you think the *IS-LM* model is called an "income adjustment model"?

12. Suppose the nominal money stock decreases and autonomous consumption increases simultaneously. Show the effects graphically in terms of the *IS-LM* model. Can the effects on interest rates and/or income be predicted? Why or why not?

13. How will an equal increase in both government spending *G* and lump sum taxes *T* affect *IS* and *LM*? Would this change affect the real interest rate? Is the balanced budget multiplier still positive? Why or why not?

14. The pre-Reagan years have been described as a time of loose monetary policy and tight fiscal policy, and the Reagan years as a time of tight monetary policy and loose fiscal policy. To see how these combinations differ, consider two policies. In the first, you increase the money supply and increase taxes. In the second, you reduce the money supply and reduce taxes. How do the resulting equilibria differ?

15. Holding everything else constant, what is the effect of an increase in the price level on equilibrium income and the interest rate?

PROBLEMS

1. Suppose $c_0 = 30$, $c_1 = .80$, $T_0 = 40$, $d_0 = 15$, $d_1 = 5$, $G_0 = 25$, $n_0 = 12$, $n_1 = 5$, $r = 5$, $E = 7$, and $Y = 75$. Calculate the level of total expenditures given this information.

2. Assume the economy is initially in equilibrium ($IS = LM$) at an interest rate r_0, and national income is Y_0. If government spending is decreased, what happens to the IS and LM curves as well as the equilibrium level of income and the interest rate? Following the decrease in government spending, suppose taxes decrease but not as much as government spending decreased. What is the net effect of this tax cut? Illustrate your answers using an *IS-LM* graph.

3. Explain the process of adjustment to equilibrium in the case where there is a point to the right of the LM and IS curve as well as for the case of a point to the left of the LM curve and to the right of the IS curve.

SUGGESTIONS FOR FURTHER READING

Branson, W. H. *Macroeconomic Theory and Policy.* New York: Harper & Row, 1989, chapters 3–4.

Gali, Jordi. "How Well Does the IS-LM Model Fit Postwar U.S. Data?" *Quarterly Journal of Economics,* vol. 67, May 1992, pp. 709–38.

Hansen, Alvin. *A Guide to Keynes.* New York: McGraw-Hill, 1953.

Hicks, J. R. "Mr. Keynes and the Classics." *Econometrica* 5, April 1937, pp. 147–59.

6 AGGREGATE DEMAND AND SUPPLY

n Chapter 4 we developed a model of aggregate demand in which the interest rate and the price level were held constant. In Chapter 5 we extended this model to the *IS-LM* model by allowing the interest rate to vary while continuing to hold the price level constant. In this chapter we will derive aggregate demand from the *IS-LM* model by allowing the price level to vary and asking how this affects the *IS-LM* equilibrium. We will briefly compare this model of aggregate demand to the Classical aggregate demand curve developed in Chapter 3.

After aggregate demand, we will go on to develop a model of aggregate supply. Recall that we have already developed a Classical model of aggregate supply in Chapter 3. In this chapter we utilize the basic framework developed in Chapter 3, but augmented with the assumption that nominal wages are slow to adjust in a downward direction. This Keynesian model of aggregate supply is upward sloping, indicating that increases in the price level lead to increases in real output. Recall that the Classical aggregate supply curve was vertical or perfectly inelastic, suggesting that in the Classical model increases in the price level did not lead to increases in real output.

By the end of this chapter, you will know

- how to derive aggregate demand from *IS-LM*
- how to identify the determinants of aggregate demand
- how to derive aggregate supply for both the Classical and Keynesian models
- how to identify the determinants of aggregate supply

- how the assumption of nominal wage rigidity is incorporated in Keynesian aggregate supply
- how equilibrium between aggregate demand and aggregate supply determines the equilibrium price level and level of real GDP
- how various concepts of unemployment enter the policy debate.

AGGREGATE DEMAND

AGGREGATE DEMAND (or *AD*) is the set of price level and real output combinations consistent with equilibrium in both the money market and the goods market.

As always, we stress that assumptions are important. In the derivation of **aggregate demand,** it is important to remember which variables are considered endogenous—that is, are explicitly modeled and so vary endogenously with changes in the economy—and which variables are taken to be exogenous—that is, are determined apart from our economic model. The most important variable taken as exogenous in the *IS-LM* model is the price level, and it is the goal of this chapter to treat the price level as endogenous. Variables other than the price level taken as exogenous in the *IS-LM* model, however, are still taken as exogenous in aggregate demand.

DERIVING AGGREGATE DEMAND

To derive aggregate demand *AD* we return to the *IS-LM* model from Chapter 5. Recall that the *IS* and *LM* curves are graphed with the real interest rate on the vertical axis and real income on the horizontal axis. These are the two endogenous variables. The exogenous variables held fixed on the *IS* curve are government spending *G*, taxes *T*, autonomous consumption c_0, autonomous investment d_0, autonomous net exports n_0, and the exchange rate *E*. The exogenous variables held fixed on the *LM* curve are the constant level of money demand L_0, the expected inflation rate π^e, and the level of real money balances *M/P.*

To derive aggregate demand, we ask what effect a change in the price level has on the equilibrium level of real income. That is, we change the price level and find out how this changes the equilibrium level of real income in the *IS-LM* graph. We record the equilibrium level of real income that corresponds to each different price level by plotting these combinations of the price level and equilibrium real income. This relationship between the price level and equilibrium real income is called aggregate demand, and the graph is called the *aggregate demand curve.*

The actual derivation of aggregate demand is illustrated in Figure 6–1. In this figure, graph (a) illustrates the *IS-LM* equilibrium. The real interest rate is on the vertical axis, and real income is on the horizontal axis. In panel (b), the price level is on the vertical axis and real income is on the horizontal axis. Graph (b) will contain our aggregate demand curve.

We begin at a particular equilibrium between *IS* and *LM,* point *A* in panel (a). At point *A,* the *IS* curve intersects the *LM* curve labeled $LM(M_0/P_0,...)$, indicating that this *LM* curve is drawn for given values of real money balances and other variables that determine the position of the *LM* curve, as π^e. The intersection of *IS* and $LM(M_0/P_0,...)$ at point *A* sets the equilibrium real interest rate to r_0 and the equilibrium level of real income to Y_0. However, this equilibrium holds constant all the variables that affect the position of the *IS*

FIGURE 6–1
Deriving the Aggregate
Demand Curve

To derive the aggregate demand curve, we start at point A in graph (a). We trace down from (a) to (b) to find the point where the price level is P_0 and real income is Y_0, which we also label A. To derive another point on aggregate demand, we must raise or lower the price level and see what happens to real income. If the price level decreases from P_0 to P_1, the real money stock increases and the LM curve shifts to the right. We have a new equilibrium between IS and LM at point B in graph (a). We trace down to graph (b) and find the point where the price level is P_1 and real income is Y_1, which we also label point B. Connecting points A and B, we have aggregate demand.

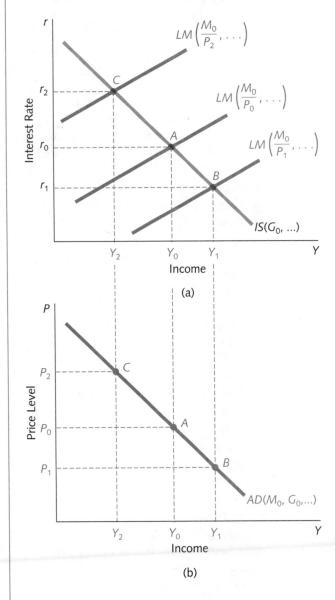

and LM curves, including the price level P_0. We ask how a change in price from P_0 to some other level will alter the level of income. We cannot emphasize too strongly that in deriving aggregate demand we are changing the price level and not changing any other variable that determines IS or LM. Only the equilibrium level of the real interest rate and real income will change.

At point A the price level is P_0 and the resulting level of equilibrium real income is Y_0. This is plotted in panel (b), as point A, where price is P_0 and real income is Y_0. This price level and the resulting level of equilibrium real income give us one point on the aggregate demand curve AD.

To derive another point on the aggregate demand curve we must raise or lower the price level and see what happens to real income. Let's first consider a decrease in the price level to P_1. Thus, when the price level decreases from P_0 to P_1, the real money stock increases from M_0/P_0 to M_0/P_1. (For example, if the money stock were \$100 billion and the initial price level was 100, real money balances would be \$1 billion. If the price level then fell to 50, real money balances would increase to \$2 billion.) This increase in the real money supply requires an offsetting increase in real demand for money. Thus, real income must increase or the real interest rate must fall so that money demand increases. An alternative way to say this is that the LM curve shifts to the right. This rightward shift in LM is illustrated in Figure 6–1(a), by the shift from $LM(M_0/P_0,...)$ to $LM(M_0/P_1,...)$. The intersection of the IS curve, which is unaffected by the change in the price level, and the new LM curve is at point B. At point B, the real interest rate is r_1 and real income is Y_1. We plot the combination P_1, Y_1 as point B in Figure 6–1(b). Point B is a second point on the aggregate demand curve. Finally, going back to the initial IS-LM equilibrium at point A, what happens if the price level rises from P_0 to P_2? Holding everything else constant, the increase in the price level lowers real balances from M_0/P_0 to M_0/P_2. The reduction in real money balances shifts LM to the left, from $LM(M_0/P_0,...)$ to $LM(M_0/P_2,...)$. The intersection of the IS curve with the new LM curve labeled $LM(M_0/P_2,...)$ occurs at point C in the top panel of IS-LM equilibrium. In this case, the equilibrium real interest rate and level of real income are given by r_2, Y_2. The combination of price P_2, real income Y_2 is plotted in panel (b) as point C, a third point on our aggregate demand curve. By increasing or decreasing the price level and always holding constant all other exogenous or fixed variables, we can outline the entire aggregate demand schedule.

Notice that the aggregate demand we derived in Figure 6–1 is downward sloping. This seems reasonable, since the demand curves for apples, oranges, and many other products are downward sloping. *However*, in spite of this similarity, the aggregate demand curve is not downward sloping because a higher price causes consumers to economize on the good purchased. Instead, the aggregate demand curve is downward sloping because a lower price *level* induces an increase in real money supply over real money demand, requiring an increase in income or a reduction in the real interest rate, or both, in order to restore equilibrium between the demand and supply of real money balances. The decrease in the price level sets in motion the forces that lead the economy to a new *IS-LM* equilibrium with a higher level of real income. The aggregate demand curve formalizes this link between the price level and equilibrium real income from *IS-LM* equilibrium.

It bears repeating that to derive the *AD* curve from the *IS-LM* equilibrium we ask what are the effects of a change in the price level. All other exogenous variables are held fixed, including autonomous consumption c_0, autonomous investment d_0, autonomous net exports n_0, tax collection T_0, government spending on goods and services G_0, the exchange rate E_0, autonomous money demand L_0, the nominal money supply M_0, and the expected inflation rate π^e. Changes in these variables will change the *IS-LM* equilibrium even if the price level is held constant, and this has the effect of shifting the AD curve. We now turn to an analysis of some of the variables that shift the *AD* curve.

DETERMINANTS OF AGGREGATE DEMAND

The determinants of *AD* are all of the determinants of *IS* and *LM except* the price level. That is, the determinants of *IS*—c_0, d_0, n_0, T, G, E—and the determinants of *LM* other than the price level—L_0, M, and π^e—are all determinants of aggregate demand.

To bring some organization to the analysis of the determination of *AD*, we will first analyze shifts in aggregate demand that arise from changes in the determinants of the *IS* curve. Then we will turn to an analysis of shifts in aggregate demand that arise from changes in the determinants of the *LM* curve other than the price level itself.

Determinants of IS

Here we consider the effect on aggregate demand of factors that shift *IS*. It turns out that anything causing *IS* to shift to the right will cause *AD* to shift to the right, and anything that causes *IS* to shift to the left will also cause *AD* to shift to the left. We illustrate this idea in Figure 6–2 by considering an increase in government spending. In the *IS-LM* graph at the top of the figure, we show how an increase in government spending from G_0 to G_1 will shift *IS* to the right. Since we are considering only an increase in government spending, we ignore the other determinants of *IS* and just write $IS(G_0)$ to indicate that *IS* depends on the level of government spending. The increase in government spending to G_1 shifts *IS* to the right changing the *IS-LM* equilibrium from point *A* to point *B*, and increasing both the real interest rate and real income. Notice that the price level in graph (b), has remained constant at P_0, and the *LM* curve has remained at $LM(M_0/P_0,...)$ in graph (a).

FIGURE 6–2
Shifts in *IS* and Aggregate
Demand

We start from an equilibrium position, point *A* in graph (a). An increase in government spending shifts the *IS* curve to the right. Holding the price level constant, we see that the aggregate demand curve in graph (b) shifts rightward from point *A* to point *B*. A decrease in government spending will have the opposite results in both (a) and (b).

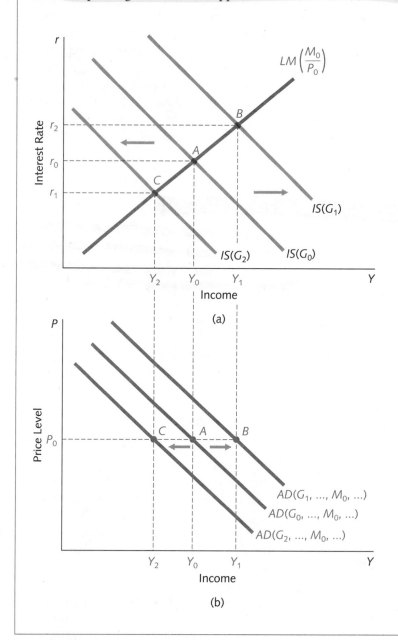

What does this mean for aggregate demand? The initial IS curve for government spending level G_0, $IS(G_0)$, intersects the LM curve with real money balances M_0/P_0 at point A in the IS-LM graph. Point A, with price level P_0 and equilibrium income level Y_0, is one point on the AD curve in (b). This aggregate demand curve is labeled $AD(G_0,...,M_0,...)$ to indicate that the AD curve is valid when government spending is G_0, the nominal money supply is M_0, and other variables affecting IS and LM are held constant. On this AD curve, we also label point A, where the price level is P_0 and real income is Y_0. Point A on the aggregate demand curve in (b) corresponds to point A in the IS-LM graph, (a).

Notice that we could begin at point A in the IS-LM diagram and ask what would be the effect of an increase in the price level on equilibrium real income. This would allow us to trace out the aggregate demand curve AD $(G_0,...,M_0,...)$, just as we derived aggregate demand in Figure 6–1. However, it is not our intent to derive aggregate demand here. Instead, we want to see how changes in government spending will shift aggregate demand. To take an extreme case, during the Korean War federal government purchases nearly tripled between the outbreak of the war in June 1950, and the armistice in July 1953. By studying the effect of government spending on aggregate demand, we could better understand how such a concentrated increase in government purchases would affect the economy.

To see how an increase in government spending shifts aggregate demand, we consider the IS-LM graph in Figure 6–2. The increase in government spending from G_0 to G_1 shifts IS to the right, as we demonstrated in Chapter 5. This is illustrated in panel (a), by the shift from $IS(G_0)$ to $IS(G_1)$. The new equilibrium is at point B. The real interest rate and real income have both increased, and the new equilibrium real income is labeled Y_1. Note that the price level is still P_0, so real money balances and hence LM have not changed.

What has happened in the AD graph? The price level is P_0 and real income is Y_1, labeled as point B in Figure 6–2(b). Notice that income has increased without an increase in the price level, indicating that the aggregate demand curve has shifted to the right. That is, the increase in government spending from G_0 to G_1 has shifted the aggregate demand curve to $AD(G_1,...,M_0,...)$.

Of course, point B is only one point on the new aggregate demand curve labeled $AD(G_0,...,M_0,...)$. We could vary the price level from P_0 and see how equilibrium real income changes, thereby deriving the entire AD curve that passes through point B. This was the exercise conducted in Figure 6–1, and we do not repeat it here. However, we cannot overemphasize the distinction between moving along the aggregate demand curve when the price level changes (a change in the quantity of aggregate goods demanded) and shifts in the aggregate demand curve (a change in aggregate demand). When the price level changes but all exogenous variables are held fixed, we move to another point of the same AD curve. When an exogenous variable changes, such as an increase in government spending from G_0 to G_1, the AD curve shifts at every price level.

In Figure 6–2, we also show the effect of a decrease in government spending. To return again to our earlier example, the 1953–54 recession was brought about by the sharp cutback in government spending associated with the end of the Korean War in 1953. Government spending was reduced even before the final armistice, as defense orders slowed in anticipation of the cessation of hostilities. Federal spending dropped by 20 percent, a drop which exceeded in percentage terms the drop in real income or real GDP during this recession. If any recession can be clearly blamed on reduced government spending, it would be this one. Let us analyze the effects of such a cut in government spending in terms of our IS-LM model.

To begin, we start again at point A, with government spending G_0. We now consider a decrease in government spending to G_2. In the IS-LM graph, the decrease in government spending shifts IS to the left, to $IS(G_2,)$. The real interest rate and level of real income both decline, with real income declining from Y_0 to Y_2. The price level remains at P_0, however, and no other exogenous variables change, so LM is unaffected. The new equilibrium is labeled point C.

In the AD graph, Figure 6.2(b), the initial point was A on AD $(G_0,...,M_0,...)$. After the decrease in government spending, the new position of aggregate demand is indicated by point C, where the price level is P_0 and real income is Y_2. The decrease in government spending has lowered the level of real income at every price level, shifting AD to the left.

There are important reasons to consider the impact of fiscal policy on the economy. Many economists argue that fiscal policy has very strong effects on the economy, and point to the experience of the United States during World War II, when massive increases in government spending seemed to lead the economy out of the Great Depression of the 1930s. Similar experiences during the Korean War and during the Johnson administration's War on Poverty and the war in Vietnam seem to support that argument. Most of these examples are connected with wartime spending, however, and many other economists argue that wartime prosperity is a tricky issue, and that not too much should be made of an economy's wartime performance. See the Insight: "Aggregate Demand and Wartime 'Prosperity': Keynesian Economics or Command Economy?" for a further discussion of this issue.

In conclusion, increases in government spending shift AD to the right, while reductions in government spending shift AD to the left. However, a more general proposition is true here. *Any* change in an exogenous variable that shifts IS to the right will shift AD to the right, and *any* change in an exogenous variable that shifts IS to the left will shift AD to the left. For example, an increase in taxes shifts IS to the left, and will therefore shift AD to the left. Conversely, a decrease in taxes shifts IS to the right, and hence shifts AD to the right. An increase in the exchange rate shifts IS to the right, and will therefore shift AD to the right. A decrease in the exchange rate shifts IS to the left, and hence shifts AD to the left.

INSIGHT

AGGREGATE DEMAND AND WARTIME 'PROSPERITY': KEYNESIAN ECONOMICS OR COMMAND ECONOMY?

Keynesian economics was developed in the midst of the Great Depression of the 1930s. In spite of monetary reforms, massive public works projects such as the WPA (Works Progress Administration), and new government regulations, the U.S. economy continued to falter throughout the 1930s. What appeared to be prosperity began to return as Americans anticipated more direct participation in World War II and as the government began to reorient production to war goods. The increases in government spending that occurred before and after the war are often served up by historians and others as a prime example of Keynesian economics at work, but not according to recent research into the so-called prosperity of the 1940s and into the theoretical explanation for it.

Economist Robert Higgs argues that both the economic measurement of the business cycle (and its related components) and the Keynesian tilt given it for the 1940s are seriously flawed.[a] Higgs argues that the prosperity of the war years was an illusion. While there was no official unemployment, a full two-fifths of the labor force was not being used to produce consumer goods or even goods that would increase U.S. capacity to produce consumer goods after the war was over. The index of real personal consumption per capita rose only two percentage points from 1939 to 1944. Business profits and stock market prices lagged during the war years.

An important point raised by Higgs is that war period data on the macroeconomy are *not* comparable with the data of other periods. The United States, as virtually all economies do in war, became a command economy. This meant that massive reallocations of resources from private production to war goods was accomplished through artificial means such as price controls and quantity restrictions on consumer and other goods. Enormous deficits (for the time at least) were financed through "forced saving" and massive government bond sales. High burdens of search costs, waiting time, queues, coupon use, and so on, were placed on Americans. As Higgs put it, "people were . . . working harder, longer, more inconveniently, and at greater physical risk in order to get the available goods."[b] The command economy performed well at turning out war goods and munitions, but it worked only because authoritarian controls made it work. The same could be said of the noncomparability of macroeconomic performance between the United States and the former U.S.S.R.

Not only do the data not tell the correct story of the so-called wartime prosperity, Higgs argues, but World War II itself did not *cause* the postwar boom in America. In Keynesian terms, the war did not create investments that would later be turned into income and consumption-generative activities through a "multiplier." Rather, expectations were transformed and financial wealth was built up in America during World War II. These laid the groundwork for the genuine spurt of prosperity experienced in the second half of the 1940s and in the decade that followed. World War II did not. One might as well argue that hurricanes and earthquakes create prosperity.   ❏

NOTE: [a]Robert Higgs, "Wartime Prosperity? A Reassessment of the U.S. Economy in the 1940s," *Journal of Economic History* 52 (March 1992), pp. 41–60.
[b]Higgs, "Wartime Prosperity?" p. 53.

PHOTO 6-1
During World War II Women
Entered the U.S. Job Market in
Record Numbers.

Determinants of *LM*

Shifts in the exogenous factors that affect the *LM* curve also shift *AD*. These factors include the nominal money stock *M*, inflation expectations π^e, and exogenous money demand shocks L_0. We could consider any change in a determinant of the *LM* curve that causes *LM* to shift to the right, but for concreteness we will consider an increase in the money supply. At any given price level, an increase in the nominal money supply shifts *LM* to the right, resulting in a higher level of real income in our *IS-LM* model. Thus, at the original price level the higher nominal money supply causes real income to increase, so aggregate demand shifts to the right from its initial position. This is illustrated in Figure 6–3 which includes at the top a graph of *IS-LM* and at the bottom a graph of *AD*. Since we will not shift the *IS* curve, we won't clutter the graph by listing all of the determinants of *IS*. Instead, we just write *IS*, which we will hold constant for this analysis. Likewise, since we are considering only an increase in the nominal money supply, we ignore the other determinants of *LM* and just write $LM(M_0/P_0)$ to indicate that *LM* depends on the level of real money balances M_0/P_0 and other things hold constant.

Starting from an equilibrium position at point A in graph (a), we consider an increase in the nominal money supply. The new intersection of IS and LM is at point B. Holding the price level constant, the aggregate demand curve in graph (b) also shifts to the right, from point A to point B. A decrease in the money supply has the opposite effect in both (a) and (b).

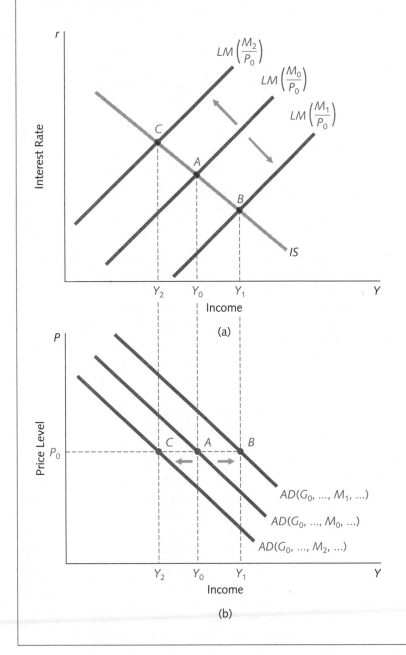

The initial LM curve $LM(M_0/P_0)$ intersects the IS curve at point A in the IS-LM graph. Point A, with price level P_0 and equilibrium income level Y_0, is one point on the AD curve in panel (b). This aggregate demand curve is labeled $AD(G_0,...,M_0,...)$ to indicate that it is the aggregate demand curve when the nominal money supply is M_0. On this aggregate demand curve we label point A, with a price level of P_0 and real income Y_0, to correspond to point A from the IS-LM equilibrium in panel (a).

Now we want to consider an increase in the nominal money supply. The government—the Federal Reserve System—controls the nominal money supply. Why might the nominal money supply increase? One recent example is the recession of 1990–91. In an attempt to counter this recession, the Federal Reserve System increased the rate of growth of the money supply. Why does such a policy action work? Consider an increase in the money supply from M_0 to M_1 in Figure 6–3. In the IS-LM graph, this increases—or shifts rightward—the LM curve, as was demonstrated in Chapter 5. This is illustrated by the shift from $LM(M_0/P_0,...)$ to $LM(M_1/P_0,...)$. The equilibrium shifts to point B, where the real interest rate has declined to r_1 and real income has increased from Y_0 to Y_1.

In the aggregate demand graph, we can illustrate this new IS-LM equilibrium at point B by considering what has happened to the price level and real income. The price level at point B is still P_0, and real income is Y_1. We graph this point on the aggregate demand graph in (b) and also label it point B, to indicate its correspondence to point B on IS-LM. The increase in the nominal money supply has increased equilibrium real income at every price level. That is, aggregate demand has shifted to the right. We label the new aggregate demand curve as $AD(G_0...,M_1,...)$ to indicate that this AD curve is valid when the money supply has increased to M_1. Of course, point B is only one point on this new AD curve, but we could vary the price level from P_0 and see how equilibrium real income changes, thereby deriving the entire AD curve that passes through point B.

In Figure 6–3, we also show the effect of a decrease in the nominal money supply. For instance, prior to the recession of 1990–91, the money supply in the United States had slowed from a rate of 4.8 percent in the fall of 1989 to a rate of 3.7 percent in mid-1990. Could this have been responsible for the recession of 1990–91? What are the effects of a decrease in the money supply?

To answer these questions, we again start at point A in Figure 6–3, where the nominal money supply is M_0, and consider the effect of a decrease in the nominal money supply to M_2. In the IS-LM graph, the decrease in the nominal money supply shifts LM to the left, to $LM(M_2/P_0)$. The new equilibrium is at point C, the equilibrium real interest rate rises, and equilibrium real income declines from Y_0 to Y_2. The price level remains P_0, however, and no other exogenous variables change.

In the aggregate demand graph, the initial position of aggregate demand was at $AD(G_0,...,M_0,...)$. After the decrease in the nominal money supply, the new position of aggregate demand passes through point C, where the price level is P_0 and real income is Y_2. The decrease in the nominal money supply has lowered the level of real income at every price level, shifting aggregate demand to the left. Again, we could vary the price level and derive the entire AD curve that holds when the nominal money supply is M_2, and we label this AD $(G_0,...,M_2,...)$.

In conclusion, increases in the nominal money supply shift aggregate demand to the right, while reductions in the nominal money supply shift aggregate demand to the left. More generally, *any* change in an exogenous variable that shifts LM to the right will shift AD to the right, and *any* change in an exogenous variable that shifts LM to the left will shift AD to the left. For example, an exogenous increase in real money demand L_0 shifts LM to the left, and will therefore shift AD to the left. Conversely, an exogenous decrease in real money demand L_0 shifts LM to the right, and hence shifts AD to the right. An increase in the expected inflation rate π^e shifts LM to the right, and will therefore shift AD to the right, while a decrease in π^e shifts LM to the left, and hence shifts AD to the left.

In Figure 6–4 we draw an aggregate demand curve and indicate all the variables that are held constant along aggregate demand. These include government spending G, taxes T, the exchange rate E, autonomous consumption c_0, autonomous investment d_0, autonomous net exports n_0, the nominal

FIGURE 6–4
The Aggregate Demand Curve and the Constant Variables

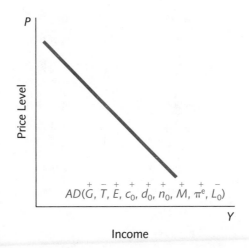

This figure shows all the variables that are held constant along the aggregate demand curve. The + or – sign above the variable indicates the direction of the shift in aggregate demand when the variable increases in value.

money supply M, the expected inflation rate π^e, and autonomous money demand L_0. We summarize the effect of each of these exogenous variables on IS or LM and on AD in Table 6–1. The (+) or (–) above the variables in Figure 6–4 indicates whether an increase in the variable shifts aggregate demand to the right (+) or to the left (–). In Table 6–1 we repeat this information. Variables other than the price level that shift either IS or LM are listed, as are their effects on IS or LM and the resultant effects on AD. For example, the first variable listed is government spending G. An increase in government spending shifts the IS curve to the right and also shifts AD to the right, as demonstrated earlier in Figure 6–2. A decrease in government spending shifts IS to the left and consequently shifts AD to the left. As another example, consider the nominal money stock M. An increase in M increase real money balances and shifts LM to the right. This increases equilibrium real income at every price

TABLE 6–1
Determinants of Aggregate Demand

This table lists the variables that shift aggregate demand, and the effect of an increase or decrease in these variables on aggregate demand, and on either IS or LM.

CHANGE IN VARIABLE	EFFECT ON IS or LM	EFFECT ON AD
INCREASE IN G	IS SHIFTS RIGHT	AD SHIFTS RIGHT
DECREASE IN G	IS SHIFTS LEFT	AD SHIFTS LEFT
INCREASE IN c_o	IS SHIFTS RIGHT	AD SHIFTS RIGHT
DECREASE IN c_o	IS SHIFTS LEFT	AD SHIFTS LEFT
INCREASE IN T	IS SHIFTS LEFT	AD SHIFTS LEFT
DECREASE IN T	IS SHIFTS LEFT	AD SHIFTS LEFT
INCREASE IN d_o	IS SHIFTS RIGHT	AD SHIFTS RIGHT
DECREASE IN d_o	IS SHIFTS LEFT	AD SHIFTS LEFT
INCREASE IN n_o	IS SHIFTS RIGHT	AD SHIFTS RIGHT
DECREASE IN n_o	IS SHIFTS LEFT	AD SHIFTS LEFT
INCREASE IN E	IS SHIFTS RIGHT	AD SHIFTS RIGHT
DECREASE IN E	IS SHIFTS LEFT	AD SHIFTS LEFT
INCREASE IN M	LM SHIFTS RIGHT	AD SHIFTS RIGHT
DECREASE IN M	LM SHIFTS LEFT	AD SHIFTS LEFT
INCREASE IN π^e	LM SHIFTS RIGHT	AD SHIFTS RIGHT
DECREASE IN π^e	LM SHIFTS LEFT	AD SHIFTS LEFT
INCREASE IN L_o	LM SHIFTS LEFT	AD SHIFTS LEFT
DECREASE IN L_o	LM SHIFTS RIGHT	AD SHIFTS RIGHT

level, which means that *AD* shifts to the right. Alternatively, a decrease in *M* shifts *LM* to the left, and hence shifts *AD* leftward.

Up to now, we have concentrated on deriving the aggregate demand curve and detailing which variables shift aggregate demand. We now turn to aggregate supply, the other half of the relations that determine the equilibrium price level and real output.

AGGREGATE SUPPLY

AGGREGATE SUPPLY (or *AS*) is the set of price level and real output combinations consistent with equilibrium in the labor market and with the production function.

Aggregate supply, or *AS,* is the curve giving values for the price level and real GDP that are consistent with equilibrium in the labor market. In essence, we model three macroeconomic markets: the goods market, money market, and labor market. The goods market provides us with the *IS* curve, the money market provides us with the *LM* curve, and the two together provide us with the *AD* curve. The labor market provides us with the *AS* curve. Aggregate supply is the relationship between various price levels and the quantity of goods and services that will be produced at these price levels. As we will see, different views on how the labor market functions will lead to alternative aggregate supply curves, which in turn have very different implications for policy.

THE LABOR MARKET AND AGGREGATE SUPPLY

The production of output requires inputs. The foundation of the supply side of macroeconomic models is found in the markets for inputs. Aggregate supply is determined by the economic behavior of buyers and sellers in these input markets. As a simplification, we will concentrate on the (quantitatively) most important input in our economy—human labor. The principles underlying how and why employing firms hire labor and the conditions under which labor can be induced to work were explored at some length in Chapter 3.[1] In this chapter we see that this view of the labor market provides the foundations for aggregate supply. Future chapters will use the foundations developed here to investigate the importance of different assumptions about the behavior of workers and employers and about the formation of price and wage expectations.

We are now in a position to understand the principles of the labor market as a whole and to show how the supply of and demand for labor interact to

---

[1]The reader may wish to read or re-read those portions of Chapter 3 dealing with the demand and supply of labor.

produce different possible levels of total output. Our model, summarized by equations 6.1 through 6.4, contains the following elements:

$$Y = Y(N, K, Z, \textit{Technology}) \tag{6.1}$$

$$N_D = N_D(W/P, K, Z, \textit{Technology}), \qquad \Delta N_D/\Delta(W/P) < 0 \tag{6.2}$$

$$N_S = N_S(W/P, A), \qquad\qquad \Delta N_S/\Delta(W/P) > 0 \tag{6.3}$$

$$N_D = N_S = N_F, \tag{6.4}$$

where

Y = Real output

N = Aggregate labor input

K = Aggregate amount of capital employed

Z = Aggregate amount of other resources employed

$\textit{Technology}$ = Level of technology or "state of the arts"

N_D = *Demand for labor*

N_S = *Supply of labor*

N_F = Full employment of labor

W = Money or nominal wage

P = Index of the aggregate price level

A = Real wealth of laborers

First, let us consider the production function. The *production function* is a technical relation between inputs and outputs, and the technical relations between inputs and outputs for all firms and industries in the economy are expressed in equation 6.1. We should note at this point that in addition to labor, other inputs affecting production include capital, natural resources (energy, for example), and technology. These factors will be assumed constant. You should recognize, however, that a change in any of these factors would shift the production function upward or downward. We will have occasion to alter some of these factors and to analyze their effects in our discussion of aggregate supply disturbances later in the text. The important point to be made here is that in our model, output is positively related to the input of labor. Moreover, we assume that additions to labor input produce additions to total output, but that these additions get smaller as more and more labor is hired. This condition means that the marginal product of labor, all other factors held constant, is positive but declining. The production function thus displays *diminishing marginal productivity of labor.*[2]

---

[2]Indeed, Neoclassical production theory tells us that no profit-maximizing firm would employ labor (or any other input) where its marginal product is rising or negative. Discussion of this point would take us too far afield, but the interested reader is directed to Michael R. Baye and Richard Beil, *Managerial Economics and Business Strategy,* 1st ed. (Boston: Richard D. Irwin, 1994).

Equation 6.2 describes the demand for labor function, which shows the demand for labor N_D (*equivalent* to the marginal product of labor $\Delta Y/\Delta N$) as a function of the real wage. As the real wage rises, the quantity of labor demanded declines because, it should be remembered, employer-producers will want to hire *less* labor in order to maximize profits. Likewise, as the real wage falls, the quantity of labor demanded will increase, again because producers want to maximize profits.

Notice that a rise in the equilibrium real wage, *ceteris paribus,* indicates a rise in the equilibrium marginal product of labor. A fall in the equilibrium real wage indicates the reverse. The marginal product of labor function (which is just the slope of the production function) *is* the real demand for labor, as shown in Chapter 3. Notice that equation 6.2 also has factors other than the real wage specified in the demand for labor function. Specifically, capital employed, other resources, and technology are assumed to affect the labor demand function—the same factors that affect the production function. This is to be expected since the demand for labor is merely the rate of change in output with respect to labor input, other things constant. Among the other things constant are *K, Z,* and *Technology.* While we will later have occasion to analyze the effects of changing some of these factors, say, a change in technology, it is worth noting that the time period over which most macroeconomic models are assumed to apply is the short run. This means that many of these factors—the stock of capital, technology—may safely be assumed not to change. However, if there is a change in any of these factors, it will affect the production function *and* the demand for labor, and we should always have this fact in mind.

Equation 6.3 gives the supply of labor. The labor supply N_S is expressed as a (positive) function of the real wage W/P, with laborers' real wealth. Changes in the real wealth held by laborers would shift the labor supply rightward or leftward.[3] Institutional factors relating to labor supply are also assumed to be held constant. These include such items as the level of the legally established minimum wage, population growth, the legal status of labor unions, the level of income maintenance programs (unemployment compensation and other transfer payments), the tax structure, and labor force participation. An increase in the number of women in the labor force would affect the labor supply function, for example. We assume that all of these matters are constant.

Equilibrium between labor demand and labor supply is determined by the intersection of labor demand and labor supply, or as stated in equation 6.4, where $N_D = N_S$. This is shown in Figure 6–5, where the model described in equations 6.1 through 6.4 is given a graphic interpretation. The factors or

---

[3]Presumably, an increase in laborers' real wealth would shift the labor supply function leftward, and vice versa. Although we do not explicitly treat these types of "wealth effects" in this book, the interested reader is directed to the excellent treatment of the matter in B. Pesek and T. Saving, *The Foundations of Money and Banking* (New York: Macmillan, 1967), and R. J. Sweeney, *Wealth Effects and Monetary Theory* (New York: Basil Blackwell, 1988).

FIGURE 6-5
The Labor Market and the
Production Function

Equilibrium in the labor market, (b), occurs where the demand for
labor equals the supply of labor, and this determines the equilibrium
level of employment N_F. With employment of N_F, the production
function yields output of Y_F in (a).

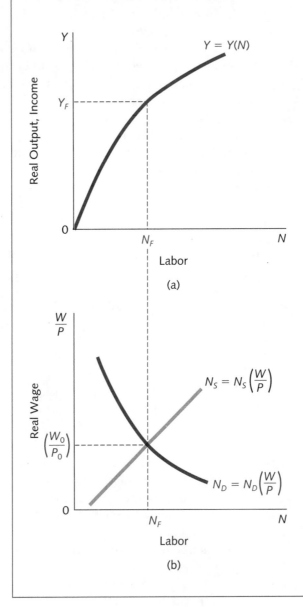

parameters K, Z, and A are all held constant but are not shown in Figure
6–5.

Equilibrium input and output in the economy described by Figure 6–5
occur at input of N_F units of labor, which results—reading up to the
production function—in Y_F units of real output. The equilibrium real wage is

indicated as (W_0/P_0). This is the ratio of the nominal wage rate to the price level that equilibrates the supply of and demand for labor. Of course, the equilibrium real wage (W/P) is a ratio of nominal wages to the price level. Every time the price level changes, there is a proportional increase in the nominal wage rate that will keep the ratio W/P constant.

With this basic structure in mind, we are ready to begin our discussion of aggregate supply, including both the Classical and Keynesian versions of aggregate supply.

ALTERNATIVE CONCEPTS OF AGGREGATE SUPPLY: CLASSICAL AGGREGATE SUPPLY

So far we have merely elaborated on the *Classical* concepts of employment and output first developed in Chapter 3. We emphasize, however, that *any* conception of aggregate supply must include the principles outlined in the simple case discussed above. In other words, there are a number of *different* conceptions of aggregate supply, each with its own use and each resting on changing certain assumptions of the model described earlier. Let us look at several alternative conceptions of aggregate supply along with their accompanying assumptions.

The Classical Aggregate Supply Curve

From a formal point of view, the Classical aggregate supply curve—seen as the relationship between alternative price levels and output produced—is easily derived. If we combine the elements of the labor market and the production function with a simple graphic analysis relating output produced to price levels, Classical aggregate supply may be expressed as in Figure 6–6.

To obtain the Classical aggregate supply curve, consider a reduction in the price level from P_0 to a new level P_1. Assuming that the nominal wage remained at level W_0, the real wage would rise to W_0/P_1, which is *higher* than the equilibrium wage W_0/P_0. At the higher real wage, employers would hire *less* labor since the marginal product of labor (required for profit maximization) would rise. Employment would tend to fall to N_1, which would cause a fall in real output to Y_1.

However, the Classical economists did not view the nominal wage as rigid at W_0. Instead, they viewed nominal wages and prices as perfectly flexible in both upward and downward directions. Furthermore, the adjustment was assumed to occur quickly, so that as soon as prices began to fall from level P_0 (in Figure 6–6), the labor response to unemployment caused by a real wage above equilibrium would be to accept reductions in the nominal wage. Immediate nominal wage and price adjustments meant that economy-wide production would not move from equilibrium at point E in Figure 6–6. Under such assumptions, input remains stable at N_F and the aggregate supply curve is

FIGURE 6–6
Determination of the Classical (Long-Run) Aggregate Supply Curve

Both short-run and long-run concepts of aggregate supply may be developed from the labor market—production function graphs in (a) and (b). This situation produces a vertical Classical or long-run aggregate supply curve, shown in (d).

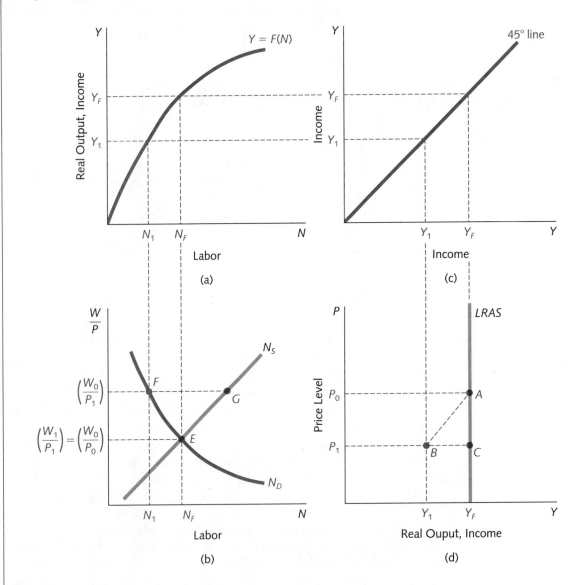

traced out as a vertical line, a portion of which is segment *AC,* which shows income Y_F being produced at both price level P_0 and price level P_1. Thus, given proportionate changes in money wages and prices, aggregate supply remains a vertical line such as that labeled *LRAS* in Figure 6–6. The curve labeled *LRAS* is the Classical supply function, although we label it *LRAS* because it is also designated as the **long-run aggregate supply** curve. This latter designation results from the idea that *LRAS* is the supply curve that would result in the long run, after all labor market adjustments and imperfections worked themselves out.

LONG-RUN AGGREGATE SUPPLY (or *LRAS*) is the vertical or perfectly inelastic aggregate supply curve that corresponds to the Classical model, where prices and wages are flexible, perfect competition holds in both output and labor markets, and the economy is in equilibrium in all markets.

The *LRAS* function will shift rightward or leftward, given a change in any of the factors assumed constant in the production function or in the labor demand and supply functions (see equations 6.1 through 6.3). An increase in technology, for example, will displace the aggregate supply function to the right. An increase in the capital stock or in the use of other inputs such as energy or materials will also lead to a rightward shift in aggregate supply. Decreases in the capital stock, in the amount of other inputs used, or in the state of technology will shift aggregate supply to the left. Thus, the Classical aggregate supply curve is unresponsive to changes in the price level, but is not forever fixed in one place.

The Keynesian Aggregate Supply Curve

An important assumption of the Classical model is that the labor market is always in equilibrium. For this to occur, wages and prices must adjust to changes in supply and demand so that equilibrium is maintained. Keynes questioned this assumption, and argued that the institutional framework of the economy caused prices and nominal wages to be slow to adjust, or rigid. In this case, the economy could not be continually in a Classical equilibrium, since the necessary adjustments in wages and prices could not occur quickly enough. To be specific, Keynes hypothesized that forms of imperfect competition—such as union cartels in labor markets—caused workers to refuse reductions in nominal wages in the face of an excess supply of labor. We turn now to an investigation of the effect of this assumption on our previous derivation of aggregate supply.

Why might wages and prices not fall in the face of reductions in product and labor demand? A possible answer is that the economy needs a period of adjustment. Markets do not appear to function perfectly and instantaneously in the short run. Unemployment and underproduction, in the Classical sense, could occur temporarily. But in the long run, the aggregate supply function would become vertical as wages and prices adjusted. How long would this process take? In clock time, no one knows exactly. Classical writers tend to argue that adjustment either takes place rather quickly or is hindered by government policy interventions.

Keynes agreed with the Classical notion of the demand for labor, that is, that the demand for labor was the marginal product function, but he disagreed with the Classical conception of labor supply. Labor unions caused money wages to be rigid.[4] We will examine two ideas on this rigidity. In the first, the nominal wage is rigid both upwards and downwards, perhaps due to union contracts that fix the nominal wage over a contract period. In the second, the nominal wage is rigid downward, again due to union contracts and other wage setting agreements, but the nominal wage is free to adjust upward in response to excess demand for labor.

Nominal Wage Rigidity

KEYNESIAN AGGREGATE SUPPLY (or *KAS*) is the positively sloped aggregate supply curve derived when the nominal wage is rigid.

The **Keynesian aggregate supply** (or *KAS*) curve for rigid nominal wage is easily derived from the same analysis that allowed derivation of the Classical aggregate supply curve. In Figure 6–7, we ask how the Classical analysis would be modified if the nominal wage was fixed at W_0, the initial value at point E. Recall that in the initial equilibrium, the price level is P_0, the nominal wage is W_0, employment is N_F, and output is Y_F. This equilibrium is labeled point E in the labor market graph, (a), and point A in the aggregate supply graph, (d).

To derive the Keynesian aggregate supply curve *KAS*, consider a reduction in the price level from P_0 to a new level, P_1. The immediate effect is to increase the real wage from W_0/P_0 to W_0/P_1. This causes an excess supply of labor as indicated by line segment FG in (a). Note that this excess supply of labor occurs for two reasons. First, at the higher real wage employers would hire *less* labor. This is indicated by the decline in the quantity of labor demanded from N_F to N_1. Second, the increased real wage increases the quantity of labor supplied, from N_F to N_2. The difference, $N_2 - N_1$ or equivalently line segment FG, indicates the excess supply of labor.

In the Classical model, the response in the labor market to an excess supply of labor is for the nominal wage to decline until equilibrium is restored. However, in the Keynesian analysis the nominal wage cannot decline below W_0 because of wage rigidities. In this case, then, the decrease in the price level has increased the real wage, and the nominal wage will not adjust to restore equilibrium. Employment is determined by labor demand at point F, with employment equal to N_1. Unemployment is determined by the excess supply of labor, or $N_2 - N_1$.

---

[4]Keynes also claimed that laborers reacted to their *money* wage and not their real wage. That is, he claimed that labor supply would not change if the real wage fell via an increase in the price level. In this way, laborers can be "fooled" into taking cuts in real wages because they fail to perceive the connection between an increased price level and their own economic well-being as indicated by the real wage. Just how long they would be fooled is another question. When laborers view an economic variable (such as wages) only in nominal and not in real terms they are said to be under *money illusion*.

FIGURE 6-7

The Keynesian Aggregate Supply Curve with Nominal Wage Rigidity

The short-run Keynesian aggregate supply curve may be developed from the labor market-production function (graphs (a) and (b) of the figure). Equilibrium is point E in (b) and corresponds to point A in (d). With the nominal wage rigid, decrease the price level to P_1. The real wage rises and the quantity of labor demanded falls in (a). Real income falls in (b) and (d). Point B in (d) is where P_1 and Y_1 correspond. Connect points A and B in (d) to obtain KAS, the Keynesian aggregate supply curve.

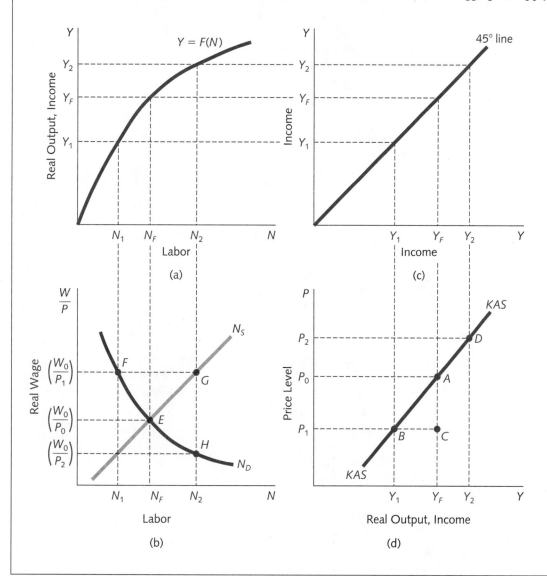

Unemployment *equilibrium* is clearly possible in this system. This is a state in which there is unemployment and no tendency for some force to push the economy toward a lower unemployment rate. The decrease in the price level causes employment to fall, and with a fixed nominal wage there is no equilibrating mechanism that will restore full-employment equilibrium in the labor market. Laborers refuse the cuts in their nominal wages that would restore equilibrium at N_F. Without these, there is no automatic tendency to full employment equilibrium such as exists in the Classical system when workers take cuts in nominal wages.

In Keynes's view, the automatic full-employment mechanisms of the economy were limited. Even if laborers did not take cuts in money wages, according to Keynes, prices would probably fall in the same proportion, leaving the real wage, and thus the unemployment equilibrium at N_1, unaffected. (The Keynesian policy solution to unemployment was to increase aggregate expenditures through fiscal manipulations.) The important implication of Keynes's view for aggregate supply was that the policy-relevant supply curve was positively sloped until full employment. Such a supply curve is useful for examining some short-run static disturbances in the economy.

Notice that the decline in the price level and the resultant decrease in employment to N_1 lead to a decline in output to Y_1, as indicated by the production function. Thus, we have two points on aggregate supply in (d): point *A*, with a price level P_0 and output Y_F, and point *B*, with a price level P_1 and output Y_1. This aggregate supply curve has a positive slope, indicating that increases in the price level will increase output.

What about an increase in the price level above P_0, to P_2? In this case, the immediate effect is to reduce the real wage from W_0/P_0 to W_0/P_2. The result in the labor market is an excess demand for labor. If the nominal wage is also rigid in the face of excess demand for labor, however, then the decline in the real wage does not lead to adjustments in the nominal wage that will restore labor market equilibrium at the full employment level. In this situation it is necessary to specify how employment is determined. A common assumption is that employment is determined by labor demand. The idea is that union labor contracts specify a contractual nominal wage while ceding to employers the decision of how much labor to employ. In this case, the real wage of W_0/P_2 leads to a quantity of labor demanded of N_2, and hence to employment of N_2. Moreover, with employment of N_2 workers, output is Y_2. This point on aggregate supply, with a price level of P_2 and output Y_2, is labeled point D in graph (d).

Notice that the aggregate supply curve so derived, labeled *KAS*, is positively sloped throughout its range. This is due to the assumptions that the nominal wage is fixed *and* that employment is determined by labor demand. Note that the determinants of *KAS* are the capital stock, the quantity of other inputs employed, the state of technology, and the fixed nominal wage W_0. Increases in the capital stock, other input usage, or improvements in the state of technology will all shift *KAS* to the right, while reductions in these factors will all shift *KAS* to the left. In addition, any increase in the fixed nominal wage W_0 will shift KAS to the left, while any reduction in W_0 will shift KAS to the right.

The assumptions underlying KAS are somewhat controversial, especially the assumption that employment is determined by labor demand even when there is an excess demand for labor. Consider again the labor market in Figure 6–7(a). When the real wage falls to W_0/P_2, there is an excess demand for labor. The quantity of labor supplied is N_1, while quantity demanded is N_2. How is it that employment of N_2 is possible? After all, labor supply indicates that only N_1 workers are willing to work. How can the firm induce employment of N_2? It is difficult to answer this question, since labor is a voluntary activity. The alternative is slavery, which is quite illegal. It is possible that labor contracts require the extra employment as a condition of continued employment when the next contract is signed, and that the union job pays sufficiently more than alternative employment opportunities to make working at the reduced real wage attractive during the term of the contract. Still, such an explanation requires a more complex analysis than that undertaken here.

One alternative to this analysis is to consider a situation in which nominal wages are rigid downward due to union contracts, but these same nominal wages are free to rise in the face of excess demand for labor. Such a model is discussed below.

Downward Nominal Wage Rigidity

The Keynesian aggregate supply curve for a downwardly rigid nominal wage is easily derived from the same analysis as above. Consider Figure 6–8. In this figure, we repeat the above analysis, except that the nominal wage is rigid at level W_0 only for positions of less than full employment. In the face of excess demand for labor, the nominal wage is free to increase. Let the initial equilibrium have a price level P_0, nominal wage W_0, employment N_F, and output Y_F. This equilibrium is labeled point E in the labor market graph, (a), and point A in the aggregate supply graph, (d). Now consider a reduction in the price level from P_0 to a new level, P_1. Just as we indicated above, the effect is to increase the nominal wage from W_0/P_0 to W_0/P_1, which causes an excess supply of labor. Because of our Keynesian assumption that the nominal wage cannot decline below W_0, the economy is in a situation of unemployment, with employment of N_1 and output of Y_1. This gives us another point on aggregate supply, point B, with a price level of P_1 and output Y_1. This aggregate supply curve has a positive slope, indicating that increases in the price level will increase output, at least when output is below Y_F.

What about an increase in the price level above P_0, to P_2? In this case, the immediate effect is to reduce the real wage from W_0/P_0 to W_0/P_2. The result in the labor market is an excess demand for labor, and pressure for the nominal wage to rise. Since the nominal wage is only rigid downward, it increases to restore full-employment equilibrium at point E, with a real wage of $W_1/P_2 = W_0/P_0$. Thus, increases in the price level lead to proportional increases in the

FIGURE 6-8
The Keynesian Aggregate Supply Curve with Downward Nominal Wage Rigidity

The short-run Keynesian aggregate supply curve may be developed from the labor market-production function, graphs (a) and (b). In this case, the nominal wage is rigid at level W_0 only for positions of less than full employment. Excess demand for labor causes the nominal wage to increase. The aggregate supply curve is derived as before, although it is positively sloped until full employment, when it becomes vertical. The curve SRAS is valid as long as nominal wages are rigid downward but are allowed to rise upward.

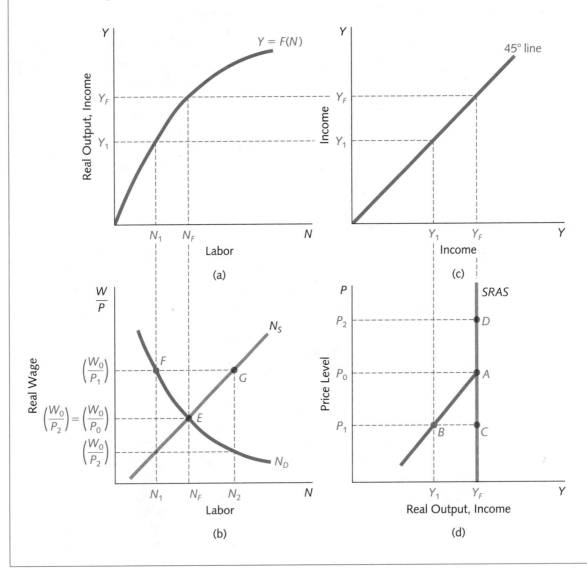

nominal wage, with no change in equilibrium employment or output. The aggregate supply curve is positively sloped up till full employment, and then is vertical. This curve is labeled *SRAS* (short-run aggregate supply curve) in Figure 6–8, to indicate that it is the Keynesian aggregate supply curve, valid as long as nominal wages are rigid downward, and to distinguish it from the aggregate supply curve for a completely rigid nominal wage, *KAS*. Thus, a ***short-run aggregate supply curve*** is a positively sloped portion of the aggregate supply curve resulting from nominal wages being rigid in a downward (but not in an upward) direction.

A SHORT-RUN AGGREGATE SUPPLY CURVE is the upward sloping portion of an aggregate supply curve. It occurs when nominal or money wages are rigid in a downward but not in an upward direction.

Note that the *SRAS* function will shift rightward or leftward, given a change in any of the factors assumed constant in the production function or in the labor demand and supply functions (see equations 6.1 though 6.3). Thus, an increase in the capital stock, in the quantity of other inputs such as energy or materials, or in the state of technology, will all shift *SRAS* to the right, while a decrease in these factors will shift *SRAS* to the left. In addition, *SRAS* will also shift with changes in the fixed nominal wage W_0. Unlike the previous factors, however, an increase in this nominal wage will shift the positively sloped section of *SRAS* upward, while not changing the position of the vertical portion, so that the aggregate supply curve becomes vertical at a higher price level.

AGGREGATE DEMAND AND SUPPLY EQUILIBRIUM

Equilibrium occurs where aggregate demand and aggregate supply intersect, and this equilibrium determines both the price level and the level of real GDP. In Figure 6–9, we use three illustrative aggregate supply curves—AS_0, AS_1, and AS_2—and an aggregate demand curve—*AD*—to demonstrate some features of the *AD-AS* equilibrium. These *AS* curves illustrate the range of possible elasticities for *AS*. For instance, AS_0 is perfectly inelastic; AS_1 has a positive, nonzero elasticity; and AS_2 is perfectly elastic. The curve AS_0 is the supply curve for the Classical model, as derived in Chapter 3 and earlier in this chapter. Moreover, it is the long-run supply curve in many modern macroeconomic models, and is usually associated with a full-employment economy. The important feature of perfectly inelastic aggregate supply is that real GDP is solely determined by *AS*. None of the variables that shift aggregate demand will change GDP if the supply curve is AS_0, although they will change the price level.

An alternative to AS_0 is a supply curve such as AS_1. This supply curve exhibits a nonzero, positive elasticity. It is often associated with a short-run situation, so possible unemployment. The deviation of short-run aggregate supply from long-run aggregate supply is usually taken to be an indication of excess capacity or unemployment in the economy. Notice that the Keynesian aggregate supply curve *KAS* we derived earlier in this chapter is positively sloped as in the case of AS_1. The important feature of supply curves such as

These *AS* curves illustrate the range of possible elasticities for aggregate supply. An increase in aggregate demand from *AD* to *AD'* will have no impact on real income *Y* if the aggregate supply curve is AS_0, which is the Classical case of full employment; will have some impact on real income *Y* if AS_1, which implies there is some excess capacity and unemployment in the economy; and will have large impact on real income if AS_2, which is the depression case with a very large number of unemployed workers.

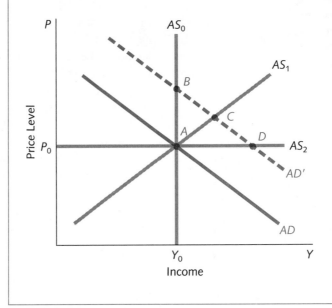

AS_1 is that increases or decreases in *AD* will cause real GDP, as well as the price level, to change.

Finally, consider AS_2. This supply curve is perfectly elastic, which essentially means that absent a change in aggregate supply the price level will remain constant for any level of *AD*. Thus, changes in *AD* result only in changes in real GDP. The price level is completely determined by the position of AS_2. This is the *AS* curve that is implicitly associated with any use of the *IS-LM* model to describe the full effect of exogenous factors on the economy. It is fair to say that modern macroeconomic models do not usually justify use of an aggregate supply curve such as AS_2.

Shifts in Aggregate Demand with Classical Aggregate Supply

The intersection of *AS* and *AD* determines equilibrium real GDP and the equilibrium price level for the economy. There are no endogenous variables held fixed. The *AS-AD* graph thus indicates the equilibrium determination of

FIGURE 6–10
An Increase in Government
Spending with Classical
Aggregate Supply

We start with equilibrium panel at point *A* in (a). With an increase in government spending, as occurred at the height of the Vietnam War, the *AD* curve shifts rightward in (a). In (b), the *IS* curve has shifted rightward. The rise in the price level reduces real money balances causing the *LM* curve to shift leftward. Note that the real interest rate has risen and the level of real income has remained at full employment.

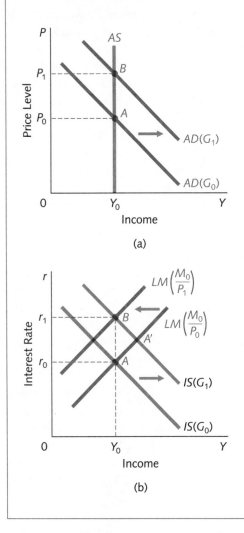

(a)

(b)

both the price level and real output. Then the *IS-LM* diagram can be used to illustrate the determination of the equilibrium real interest rate. For example, consider an increase in government spending such as occurred during the Korean War or during the height of the Vietnam War in 1966–1968, when the economy was already operating near full employment. This is illustrated in Figure 6–10. *AD* and *IS* shift to the right. Since the aggregate supply curve in

Figure 6–10 is perfectly inelastic, the increase in AD results in a new equilibrium between AS and AD, where price has increased from P_0 to P_1 but Y is unchanged at Y_0. What happens to the real interest rate? IS shifts to the right with the increase in G, and in the IS-LM graph it initially appears that both r and Y will increase. However, the increase in P from P_0 to P_1 shifts LM to the left because there has been a reduction in real balances from M_0/P_0 to M_0/P_1. With IS shifting to the right and LM shifting to the left, we can be confident that r increases, but what happens to Y? We cannot tell from the IS-LM graph, *but we don't require the IS-LM graph to give us this information.* We already know from AS-AD that Y is unchanged. Hence, it must be that LM shifts to the left enough to restore real output to the initial level Y_0.

As a second example, consider an increase in the nominal money supply M, as illustrated in Figure 6–11. AD and LM shift to the right. Since the aggregate supply curve in Figure 6–11 is perfectly inelastic, the increase in AD results in a new equilibrium between AS and AD, where price has increased from P_0 to P_1 but Y is unchanged at Y_0. What happens to the real interest rate? LM shifts to the right with the increase in M, and in the IS-LM graph it initially appears that r decreases and Y increases. However, the increase in P from P_0 to P_1 shifts LM to the left, since the rise in the price level reduces real money balances from M_1/P_0 to M_1/P_1. With LM first shifting to the right with the increase in M and then shifting to the left with the increase in P, we cannot tell what happens to either r or Y. However, *we don't require the IS-LM graph to give us this information.* We already know from AS-AD that Y is unchanged. Hence, it must be that LM shifts leftward enough to restore real output to the initial level Y_0. Again, it is the case that the AS-AD graph determines both P and Y, and the IS-LM graph takes the change in P and Y determined from AS-AD and helps us see what happens to r. The IS-LM graph does not itself tell us anything about the final equilibrium level of Y, which is only determined on AS-AD.

In Figures 6–10 and 6–11, we find out that a perfectly inelastic or Classical aggregate supply curve has important implications for the effect of changes in exogenous variables on the economy. With perfectly inelastic AS, an increase in M increases the price level, but has no effect on either Y or r. An increase in G increases P and r, but not Y. These are Classical results, very much like those we saw in Chapter 3, from a Keynesian AD construct.

Shifts in Aggregate Demand with Keynesian Aggregate Supply

As above, the intersection of KAS and AD will determine equilibrium real GDP and the equilibrium price level for the economy. There are no endogenous variables held fixed. The AS-AD graph thus indicates the equilibrium determination of P and Y. Then the IS-LM diagram can be used to illustrate the determination of the equilibrium real interest rate r. For example, consider an increase in government spending such as that proposed by the

FIGURE 6–11
An Increase in the Nominal
Money Supply with Classical
Aggregate Supply

We start with equilibrium at point A in (a). With an increase in the nominal money supply, the aggregate demand curve shifts rightward in (a) and the LM curve shifts rightward in (b). The price level rises in (a) causing the LM curve to shift leftward in (b) since real money balances have returned to their original level. The real interest rate returns to the original rate, and the level of real income remains at full employment. The Classical results hold in this case.

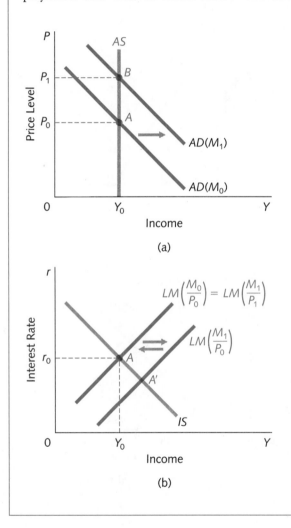

(a)

(b)

Clinton administration on infrastructure. We illustrate this in Figure 6–12. AD and IS both shift to the right. Since the aggregate supply curve in Figure 6–12 is positively sloped, the increase in AD results in a new equilibrium between KAS and AD, where price increases from P_0 to P_1 and output increases from Y_0 to Y_1. What happens to the real interest rate? IS shifts to the right with

FIGURE 6-12
An Increase in Government
Spending with Keynesian
Aggregate Supply

We start with equilibrium, at point A in (a). An increase in government spending by the Clinton Administration on infrastructure such as highways and railroads causes the aggregate demand curve to shift rightward in (a) and the IS curve to shift rightward in (b). The price level rises in (a), which causes the LM curve to shift leftward. The real interest rate rises and the level of real income increases.

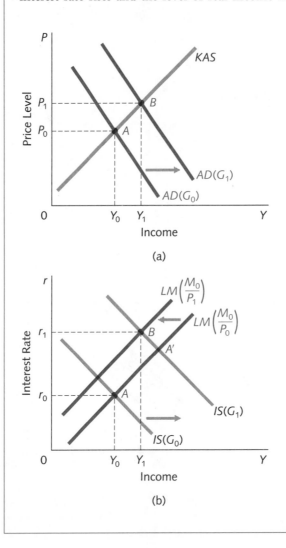

(a)

(b)

the increase in G, and in the IS-LM graph it initially appears that both r and Y will increase, as indicated by point A'. However, this does not take into account the price increase in the aggregate demand and supply graph. Price increases from P_0 to P_1, which reduces real money balances from M_0/P_0 to M_0/P_1 and shifts LM to the left. With IS shifting to the right and LM shifting to the left, we can be confident that r increases, but what happens to Y? We cannot tell from the *IS-LM* graph, *but we don't require the IS-LM graph to give us this information.* We already know from *AS-AD* that Y increases to Y_1. Hence, it must be that *LM* shifts leftward enough so that the new *IS* and *LM* intersect at point *B*, with output at Y_1. This also means that the real interest rate increases further, to A'. Notice again that the *IS-LM* graph does not itself tell us anything about the final equilibrium level of output *Y,* which is determined on *AS-AD.*

Our second example is an increase in the nominal money supply *M,* as illustrated in Figure 6–13. This type of analysis will help us understand the effect of monetary policy on the economy. For example, in October 1982 monetary policy turned more expansionary. At that time, the rate of inflation was falling from the high levels that had prevailed in the late 1970s and early 1980s, and the economy remained in a deep recession. The civilian unemployment rate was almost 10 percent. In the face of these facts, the Federal Reserve System allowed the money supply to grow at double-digit rates in the fourth quarter of 1982 and through the first half of 1983. The strength of the economic recovery in 1983 and early 1984 suggests that the Federal Reserve System's actions may have provided a good deal of monetary stimulus to the economy.[5] In this section, we will see if our theoretical model agrees with this conclusion.

An increase in the money supply will shift *AD* and *LM* to the right. Since the aggregate supply curve in Figure 6–13 is positively sloped, the increase in *AD* results in a new equilibrium, where price has increased from P_0 to P_1 and output has risen from Y_0 to Y_1. What happens to the real interest rate? *LM* shifts to the right with the increase in *M,* and in the *IS-LM* graph it initially appears that r decreases and Y increases. The increase in P from P_0 to P_1, however, shifts *LM* to the left. With *LM* first shifting to the right with the increase in *M* and then shifting to the left with the increase in *P,* we cannot tell what happens to r or *Y. We already know from AS-AD* that Y increases. Hence, it must be that *LM* on net shifts to the right. The initial shift due to the increase in the money supply is greater than the leftward shift due to the increase in the price level. Again we stress that it is the *AS-AD* graph that determines what happens to equilibrium P and *Y.* The *IS-LM* graph takes the change in P and Y from *AS-AD* and helps us see what happens to r. The *IS-LM* graph does not itself tell us anything about the final equilibrium level of *Y,* which is determined only on *AS-AD.*

The above discussion of an increase in the money supply has been at a theoretical level, but issues involving money supply increases are very important in the world economy. See the Global Perspective: "Aggregate Demand and Printing Money" for a discussion of the effect of money supply increases on the Brazilian economy.

---

[5]In this discussion we are treating the increase in the growth rate of the money supply as an increase in the stock of money, and clearly over time an increase in the money growth rate will lead to an increase in the stock of money. However, there are important differences between the money growth rate and the money stock, and we will study these distinctions in Chapter 8.

FIGURE 6-13
An Increase in the Money
Supply with Keynesian
Aggregate Supply

We start with equilibrium at point A in (a). For example, in the fall of
1982 monetary policy turned more expansionary. At that time, inflation was falling, while the economy remained in a recession. An increase in the nominal money supply causes the aggregate demand curve
to shift rightward in (a) and the *LM* curve to shift rightward in (b).
The rise in the price level in (a) causes the *LM* curve to shift leftward.
The real interest rate falls and the level of real income rises.

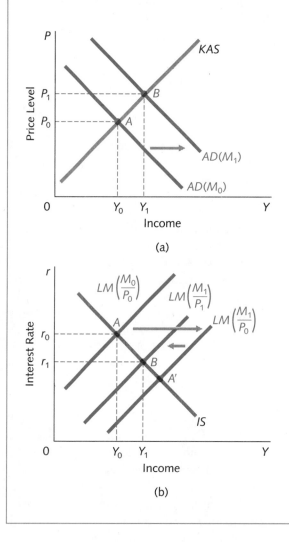

In Figures 6-12 and 6-13, we find that a positively sloped aggregate supply
curve such as *KAS* has important implications for the effect of changes in
exogenous variables on the economy. With a positively sloped aggregate supply,
an increase in *M* increases both the price level and real output. It also reduces
the real interest rate. An increase in *G* increases both the price level and real

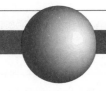

GLOBAL PERSPECTIVE

"AGGREGATE DEMAND AND PRINTING MONEY: THE RECENT CASE IN BRAZIL."

Brazil is a recent example of how printing excessive amounts of new money can lead to hyperinflation, to the undermining of people's confidence in their currency, and to the flight of the Brazilian cruzado into U.S. dollars or into banks in foreign countries. In examining Brazil's inflationary process, one must be careful not to confuse the current stock of money with the printing of new money. The existing stock of money, such as the one in Brazil, supports the existing level of gross domestic product. Brazil created the inflationary problem for itself when its approximately 200 government-run companies had combined losses or deficits amounting to more than $60 billion and the Brazilian government turned to its printing presses to cover the deficits.[a] The *AD-AS* graph we learned in this chapter shows how Brazil created its hyperinflation, which is defined as a rapid rise in the general level of prices of goods and services. (Since World War II, inflation rates of several hundred percent or more for short periods have been common in a number of countries, not just in Brazil.)

In Figure 6–14, an excessive increase in the stock of new money shifts the *AD* curve upward from AD_0 to AD_1, causing the price level to rise from P_0 to P_1. In trying to solve this inflationary problem, some Brazilian economists drew up a plan that could have led to devastation of their economy. Their plan was to reduce the amount of money in the economy by preventing people from withdrawing from their saving and checking accounts for eighteen months. This prohibition also applied to the cash balances of businesses and would have made it impossible for businesses to pay suppliers or to meet their payrolls. The freeze would have affected about 80 percent of the money in circulation. For comparison it would be like closing 80 percent of the U.S. banks because the government had frozen 80 percent of the financial assets of U.S. citizens. This drastic reduction in the money stock can also be shown with the *AD* and *AS* diagram in Figure 6–14. A shrinkage of the money supply as an anti-inflationary policy by Brazil would shift the *AD* curve leftward from AD_1 to AD_2. There would be not only a reduction in the price level from P_1 to P_2 but a substantial decline in real gross domestic product from Y_1 to Y_2. Such a policy could very well have produced a depression in Brazil similar to the Great Depression of the 1930s in the United States, which Milton Friedman says the Federal Reserve caused by reducing the supply of money by 33 percent from 1929 to 1933. Instead of Brazil's plan for a liquidity freeze on assets, an alternative solution would have been to *privatize* the deficit-ridden state-run companies. Then the Brazilian government would no longer have to print new money to cover the losses. People would once again have confidence in their currency and would not try to spend their nominal money balances as fast as they received them. ❑

NOTE [a]Paul Craig Roberts, "Brazil's One-Way Ticket to Disasterville," *Business Week* (May 7, 1990), p. 20.

FIGURE 6-14
Aggregate Demand and Printing
Money: The Recent Case of Brazil

Equilibrium occurs at point E. In Brazil, an excessive increase in the stock of money in the late 1980s causes the aggregate demand curve to shift rightward and prices to rise. A plan to reduce the amount of money by preventing people from withdrawing from their saving and checking accounts for eighteen months would have caused a drastic reduction in the money supply. The aggregate demand curve would shift leftward and the price level and real income would fall to P_2 *and* Y_2.

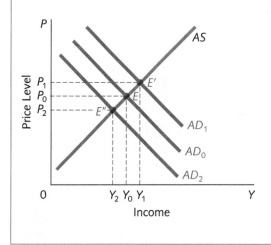

output, as well as the real interest rate. These Keynesian results stand in contrast to the Classical results derived from the perfectly inelastic aggregate supply curve in Figures 6–11 and 6–12, and point out the importance of aggregate supply to policy conclusions.

A Shift in Keynesian Aggregate Supply

Finally, consider a supply shock that reduces Keynesian aggregate supply. Some examples would be the OPEC oil price hikes of 1973 and 1979, or the oil price hike during the summer of 1990 when Iraq invaded Kuwait. Such a shock would shift aggregate supply to the left, as illustrated in Figure 6–15, by the reduction in Keynesian aggregate supply from KAS_0 to KAS_1. What are the macroeconomic effects of this supply shock?

FIGURE 6-15
An Energy Supply Shock with
Keynesian Aggregate Supply

Equilibrium occurs at point A in panel (a). An energy crisis such as the oil price shock that occurred when Iraq invaded Kuwait in August 1990 would cause the Keynesian aggregate supply curve to shift leftward in (a). The price level rises in (a), which causes the LM curve to shift leftward in (b) because of the reduction in real money balances. The real interest rate rises and the level of real income falls.

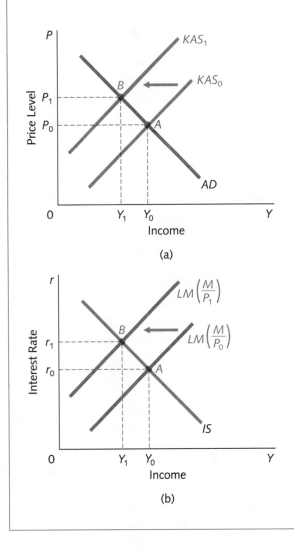

(a)

(b)

Looking first at aggregate demand and supply, we see that the equilibrium changes from point A, with a price level of P_0 and output of Y_0, to point B with a higher price level P_1 and lower output level Y_1. This is an example of the so-called *stagflation*—higher price levels or higher inflation rates, coupled with stagnation in output. What about the real interest rate? There is no change in exogenous determinants of either IS or LM, but the increase in the price level induces a leftward shift in LM from $LM(M/P_0)$ to $LM(M/P_1)$, causing an increase in the real interest rate to r_1. Thus, our model suggests that an adverse supply shock will increase the price level, reduce output, and increase the real interest rate.

FULL EMPLOYMENT: A MEANING RELEVANT FOR POLICY

An important assumption relating to *all* of the aggregate supply functions derived in this chapter (and, implicitly, to all of the macroeconomic models discussed previously in this book), is that a full-employment level of input and output in the economy could be identified. Although we alluded briefly to some of the difficulties related to this concept in Chapter 1, we must come to a far more adequate understanding of the nature of unemployment before tackling the difficult matter of economic policy that constitutes the remainder of this book. Just what does Y_F—a full-employment level of income or output—mean in the context of the macroeconomy? In the Classical model, we concluded that *no* labor would be unemployed. Still, every month we get unemployment figures (usually expressed as a percentage of the labor force) from the BLS and other government agencies. As we recall from Chapter 2, the Bureau of Labor Statistics defines a person as unemployed if, over a survey period, he or she was available for work, had no job, and did some searching for a job. The persistence of an unemployment rate gives us some indication that Y_F does not mean that everyone who is willing to work has a job. Let us look more closely at what we mean by unemployment.

Types of Unemployment

Our implicit conclusion that no unemployment could exist in the economy has rested on certain simplifying assumptions concerning the macroeconomic and microeconomic labor markets. Specifically, we have, except in a few circumstances, assumed that both employers and workers were possessed of perfect information and perfect mobility concerning jobs and job vacancies. This means that the information costs to employers and workers as well as the mobility costs of both groups were assumed to be zero. Given that all workers were perfectly substitutable for one another and that employment adjustments were instantaneous, unemployment was impossible if perfectly flexible wages and prices existed and Say's Law (adequate aggregate demand) applied. In such a world, frictional and structural factors affecting employment as well as insufficient aggregate demand had no place. Let us now look, however, at the real-world impact of these factors on the macro labor market, that is, when our assumptions of perfect (zero-cost) information, perfect mobility, price-wage flexibility, adequate aggregate demand, and so forth, do *not* apply.[6]

FRICTIONAL UNEMPLOYMENT

FRICTIONAL UNEMPLOYMENT is the lack of work that occurs as workers move from one job to another in search of their best allocation in the labor market.

Frictional unemployment will exist even if we assume that workers are homogeneous (or perfectly substitutable) in the eyes of employers and that there is sufficient aggregate demand to employ all workers who are willing to work at given wage and price levels. Frictional unemployment is the result of a lack of information on the part of employers who are seeking workers and of workers who are seeking jobs.

To be more specific, consider the following example. Suppose that there is a change in the *composition* of aggregate demand such that a decline in the demand for workers of a given type in one industry is accompanied by a like increase in demand for the *same* kind of labor in another industry. Clearly, a group of workers will be seeking work and a group of employers will be searching for workers. But information concerning the place and availability of employment is costly to obtain. Economists refer to this feature as *information costs.* A period of job search by temporarily unemployed workers and of recruitment by employers is normally required. The extent of this search will depend on the information costs of getting employers and workers together, on geographic factors, and on the type of worker temporarily unemployed. Meanwhile, the unemployed workers are frictionally unemployed. Frictional unemployment is thus part and parcel of a market system wherein information is imperfect and mobility of labor is costly.

There are, of course, ways to reduce the cost of job search for employers and workers: employment agencies, newspaper advertising, and trade and professional associations all tend to help. Any factor, then, that reduces the time and other resources required for successful job search also reduces the amount of frictional unemployment in the economy. The important point to be made is that the frictionally unemployed are *not* counted in the quantity we have designated N_F (or Y_F) earlier in this chapter.

STRUCTURAL UNEMPLOYMENT

STRUCTURAL UNEMPLOYMENT is the lack of work that occurs because of changes in the basic character of the labor market that leaves some workers with seemingly unsalable skills.

Structural unemployment is a concept that President Lyndon Johnson brought to the attention of Americans in the 1960s. Part of President Johnson's War on Poverty was aimed at curing the unemployment problem in Appalachia, a region peopled by the so-called hard-core unemployed. In economic terms, these individuals were unskilled and untrained for jobs that were in fact available in various sectors of the economy.

---

[6]For an extensive and excellent discussion of the meaning of unemployment, see Don Bellante and Mark Jackson, *Labor Economics: Choice in Labor Markets* (New York: McGraw-Hill, 1983), chapter 16, from which some of the present discussion derives.

In this situation, the composition of demand changes in the economy. Unlike the case of frictional unemployment, structural unemployment exists because the new available jobs require skills other than those possessed by the displaced workers. This means displaced workers will be forced (ultimately) to accept lower wages if they maintain their previous line of work or to invest significant resources in retraining for the skills in demand by new industries. These new industries, moreover, may be in other locales, so that mobility costs may also be an important factor.

Public and private institutions have arisen to reduce the costs of structural unemployment. In addition to the public school systems in the United States, and the various manpower programs of the government administered by the Department of Health and Human Services and other public agencies, many privately operated (for profit) schools teach such marketable skills as computer programming and technology, bartending, hospital management, and so on. The major point is that structural unemployment is typically longer lived, more entrenched, and more costly to reduce than frictional unemployment. As a practical matter, a job search for the structurally unemployed is often greatly prolonged beyond that experienced by the frictionally unemployed. However, neither structurally unemployed nor frictionally unemployed workers, are counted in the quantity designated N_F (or Y_F) earlier in this chapter.

The Natural Rate of Unemployment

The **NATURAL RATE OF UNEMPLOYMENT** is that rate of unemployment that occurs with equilibrium in the labor market. The labor market equilibrium accounts for frictional factors in the economy as well as institutions surrounding labor demand and supply decisions. It consists of both frictional and structural unemployment.

Economists often use the expression **natural rate of unemployment** to describe unemployment that exists for frictional or for some structural reasons. This rate is "natural" in two senses. First, such unemployment is an inevitable outcome of the dynamic character of any economy. The economy is, as experience tells us, ever-changing in the composition of the goods it produces. Frictional and some structural unemployment are necessary by-products of a vibrant and dynamic economic system.

Second, at any moment in time some level of unemployment is consistent with equilibrium in the structure of *real wage* rates. At that natural level of unemployment, as Milton Friedman describes it,

> real wage rates are tending on the average to rise at a "normal" secular rate, i.e., at a rate that can be indefinitely maintained so long as capital formation, technological improvements, etc., remain on their long-run trends. A lower level of unemployment is an indication that there is an excess demand for labor that will produce upward pressure on real wage rates. A higher level of unemployment is an indication that there is an excess supply of labor that will produce downward pressure on real wage rates.[7]

Thus, the concept of a natural rate of unemployment takes account of some structural characteristics of the economy, such as the rate of capital formation

---

[7]Milton Friedman, "The Role of Monetary Policy," *American Economic Review* (March 1968), p. 8.

and technological improvements, as well as the institutional characteristics of the labor and commodity markets. We may therefore identify, as we will in succeeding policy chapters, reasons why the natural rate of unemployment may change over time. For example, altering minimum wage laws or the strength of labor unions or the institution of income maintenance programs may all affect the natural rate.

We are all familiar with the popular concept of "full employment"—which is sometimes reported as an unemployment rate of 4 percent, 6 percent, or 7 percent. Or, alternatively, full employment may be defined as that rate of employment which is consistent with the natural rate of unemployment. We will have the opportunity to use both of these measures in the chapters that follow, but the reader should be aware of the advantages of focusing on the natural rate. It forces us to recognize the dynamic nature of the economy, wherein the unemployment rate is never zero, and it allows us to more easily separate natural unemployment rates from unemployment rates that result from deficiencies of aggregate demand.

In this chapter we point to the problems of separating the factors or parameters affecting the supply side of the economy from those that occur because of aggregate demand shifts. *Changes* in the natural rate of unemployment may well be the result of institutional changes affecting supply. Changing labor market regulations may be an important factor in explaining recent unemployment experience. For example, see Policy Issue: "The Delayed Recovery in Employment After the Recession of 1990–91." Other changes will be analyzed in future chapters and in our discussions of economic policy. The expectations model also equips us to analyze the effects of both demand- and supply-side changes on inflation and unemployment. These matters are complex, as we shall soon discover, but a firm grounding in the alternative concepts of aggregate supply will bring many devilish policy issues into much sharper focus.

SUMMARY

In this chapter we have developed the aggregate demand and supply framework. We began with aggregate demand, which was derived from the *IS-LM* model, by considering the effect of changes in the price level on the *IS-LM* equilibrium. We also found the determinants of aggregate demand from the determinants of *IS* and *LM,* and we saw how changes in these factors would lead to shifts in aggregate demand.

After developing aggregate demand, we turned our attention to aggregate supply. We provided a derivation of the basic model that will serve as our standard of comparison throughout this text, the long-run or Classical aggregate supply curve. We then developed two Keynesian versions of aggregate supply, both built around the assumption of nominal wage rigidity. The first version assumed that nominal wages were rigid in any direction, while the

POLICY ISSUE

THE DELAYED RECOVERY IN EMPLOYMENT AFTER THE RECESSION OF 1990–91

One of the features of the economic recovery that lasted into 1993 is the slow rebound in employment. Joseph A. Ritter of the Federal Reserve Bank of St. Louis has analyzed the average growth in nonfarm payroll employment following seven previous recessions, and compared it to the growth in employment following the most recent recession, which ended in March 1991.[a] He found that, in contrast to previous recessions, employment has barely changed after twenty months of recovery, growing only an anemic 0.3 percent. In other recoveries, employment had grown by an average of 6.8 percent after twenty months, and the previous lowest growth after twenty months was 4.8 percent (in 1961). Recovery after the recession of 1990–91 was clearly different.

What accounted for this phenomenon? One factor is that output itself did not grow as quickly during the recovery, so that labor demand did not grow. Also, productivity growth (output per worker) was strong, so that more output could be obtained from the existing work force without hiring new employees.

There are other factors not mentioned by Ritter. Specifically, there was heightened concern among employers over the cost of hiring an employee. That cost is not simply the wage, a variable cost that the firm can control. The total wage also includes the cost of fringe benefits, which often means providing health insurance. In the political environment of 1992–93, many firms hesitated to hire workers who would bring with them an increased liability in terms of health insurance premiums. This factor applies to those firms that currently do not have a health insurance program since, under President Bill Clinton's health care reform proposal, it appears that firms may be required to provide health insurance to employees. These additional costs increase the fixed cost of hiring additional workers and make firms less likely to hire permanent workers. In such circumstances firms might be more likely to use overtime work to cover any increases in demand for labor. The reasons: Use of overtime or the employment of part-time workers might be less expensive than the additional health care expenditures involved in hiring additional permanent workers. ❑

SOURCE: [a]Joseph A. Ritter, "The Delayed Recovery of Employment," Federal Reserve Bank of St. Louis *National Economic Trends* (February 1993), p. 1.

second assumed downward nominal wage rigidity. We also discussed the determinants of aggregate supply, which includes the effect of changes in the rigid nominal wage on the Keynesian aggregate supply curves.

Finally, we discussed equilibrium between aggregate demand and supply. We demonstrated several analyses of how changes in the determinants of either aggregate demand or aggregate supply would affect that equilibrium. For a Classical aggregate supply curve, we investigated the effect of an increase in government spending and the effect of an increase in the money supply. We found the impact of these changes in exogenous variables on the price level and real output, and then we turned to *IS-LM* to inform us of the impact on the real interest rate. We then adopted a Keynesian aggregate supply curve and repeated this analysis, to demonstrate the importance of the aggregate supply curve to the question of the impact of changes in the determinants of aggregate demand on the macroeconomy. Finally, we investigated the effect of a change in aggregate supply on the price level, real output, and the real interest rate. We used a Keynesian aggregate supply curve to find the impact of an adverse supply shock, described as an exogenous reduction in the use of energy inputs such as occurred during the Iraqi invasion of Kuwait in August 1990.

Our final discussion in this chapter was of alternative concepts of unemployment, and how these ideas relate to the discussion of government policy aimed at achieving less unemployment. In this context it was seen to be important to separate unemployment due to aggregate demand factors from unemployment due to supply-side factors. We noted that changes in the natural rate of unemployment may well be the result of institutional changes affecting supply. We will discuss these issues further as we work through the various models in this text. We note that these matters are complex, as we shall soon discover, but a firm grounding in the alternative concepts of aggregate supply will bring many devilish policy issues into much sharper focus.

KEY TERMS

aggregate demand (AD)

aggregate supply (AS)

frictional unemployment

Keynesian aggregate supply (KAS)

long-run aggregate supply (LRAS)

natural rate of unemployment

short-run aggregate supply curve (SRAS)

structural unemployment

QUESTIONS FOR REVIEW AND DISCUSSION

1. Demonstrate the derivation of aggregate demand from *IS-LM* equilibrium.

2. In the text, the *IS* curve did not shift with changes in the price level. However, there are several reasons why *IS* might be sensitive to the price level. One is that net exports depend on the relative price of U.S. and foreign goods. When the price level in the United States increases, it makes U.S. goods more expensive—lowering exports and raising imports—so that net exports decline. How would a price-level-sensitive *IS* curve alter the derivation of aggregate demand?

3. In the text, the *IS* curve did not shift with changes in the price level. However, there are several reasons why *IS* might be sensitive to the price

level. One is that consumption depends on wealth, and part of wealth is real money balances M/P. Increases in real money balances would increase consumption spending. How would a price-level-sensitive IS curve alter the derivation of aggregate demand?

4. Demonstrate graphically that a decrease in autonomous investment d_0 results in a leftward shift in aggregate demand. Explain this result.

5. Demonstrate graphically that an increase in expected inflation π^e will lead to a rightward shift in aggregate demand. Explain this result.

6. In the great Keynesian-Monetarist debates of the 1960s and 1970s, much was made over the relative slopes of IS and LM. The Monetarists claimed that money demand was interest inelastic, so that changes in the interest rate did not have much of an effect on money demand. Assume that money demand is completely interest inelastic. What does this mean for the LM curve? How does this assumption alter the derivation of aggregate demand? Does an increase in the money supply still increase aggregate demand? What about an increase in government spending? Can you provide a general statement about the effect on aggregate demand of changes in the determinants of IS and of LM for this special case?

7. In the Keynesian-Monetarist debates, the Keynesian claim was that money demand was very sensitive to the interest rate. Assume that money demand is perfectly elastic with respect to changes in the interest rate. What does this mean for the graph of money demand? For the graph of LM? How does this assumption alter the derivation of aggregate demand? Does an increase in the money supply still increase aggregate demand? What about an increase in government spending? Can you provide a general statement about the effect on aggregate demand of changes in the determinants of IS and of LM for this special case?

8. If the aggregate supply curve is perfectly inelastic as in the $LRAS$ curve of this chapter, can fiscal or monetary policy be effective? Why or why not?

9. Some observers of the Keynesian-Monetarist debates have made the comment that these two schools of thought were arguing about aggregate demand when the important issues were those involving aggregate supply. Please comment on this observation.

10. Demonstrate the derivation of the Keynesian aggregate supply curve for a fixed nominal wage.

11. Demonstrate graphically the effect on Keynesian aggregate supply of an increase in the nominal wage. Then do the same for the KAS, derived under the assumption that wages are only rigid downwards.

12. Using aggregate demand and supply analysis with Keynesian aggregate supply, demonstrate the effect on the price level, real output, and the real interest rate of

   (A) an increase in the nominal wage

   (B) an increase in the capital stock

(c) a decrease in autonomous investment

(d) an increase in the expected inflation rate.

PROBLEMS

1. Assume the economy is initially in equilibrium ($IS = LM$). Explain and illustrate the impact of an increase in autonomous consumption and a decrease in expected inflation on the equilibrium interest rate and the level of output as well as on the *IS, LM,* and *AD* curves.

2. Explain the impact of a decrease in government spending on the economy when Classical aggregate supply exists and when Keynesian aggregate supply exists.

SUGGESTIONS FOR FURTHER READING

Barro, Robert J. *Macroeconomics.* New York: John Wiley & Sons, 1993, chapter 20.

Bartlett, Bruce, and Timothy P. Roth, eds. *The Supply-Side Solution.* Chatham, NJ: Chatham House Publishers, 1983.

Fisher, Irving. *The Theory of Interest.* New York: Macmillan, 1930.

Gali, Jordi. "How Well Does the IS-LM Model Fit Postwar U.S. Data?" *Quarterly Journal of Economics* (May 1992), pp. 709–36.

Gallaway, Lowell E., and Richard K. Vedder. *The "Natural" Rate of Unemployment.* Staff Study for Subcommittee on Monetary and Fiscal Policy of the Joint Economic Committee, Congress of the United States. Washington, DC: U.S. Government Printing Office, 1982.

Keynes, John Maynard. *The General Theory of Employment, Interest, and Money.* New York: Harcourt, Brace & World, 1936.

Laidler, David E. W. *The Demand for Money.* New York: Harper-Collins, 1993, chapter 5.

Leijonhufvud, Axel. *On Keynesian Economics and the Economics of Keynes.* New York: Oxford University Press, 1968.

Mankiw, N. Gregory. *Macroeconomics.* New York: Worth Publishers, 1992, chapter 10.

Patinkin, Don. *Money, Interest, and Prices.* 2nd ed., abridged. Cambridge, MA: MIT Press, 1988, chapter 8.

Rukstad, Michael G. *Macroeconomic Decision Making.* Orlando, FL: The Dryden Press, 1992, chapter 8.

Tatom, John A. "The 1990 Oil Price Hike in Perspective." Federal Reserve Bank of St. Louis *Review* (November/December 1991), pp. 3–18.

7 INTERNATIONAL TRADE AND THE MACROECONOMY

n building the various macroeconomic models and in analyzing macroeconomic policies in the earlier chapters, we assumed that the economy was closed to international transactions. This chapter relaxes that assumption and presents the basic framework needed to understand the macroeconomics of an open economy, that is, an economy that trades goods and services and exchanges assets with foreign countries.

We begin by discussing the foreign exchange market. Attention is given to both fixed and flexible exchange rates and to the stability of the foreign exchange market. Next, we discuss recent economic developments that have caused the international system to change its method of solving imbalances in the balance of payments. In the third section, we extend the basic macroeconomic model to the open economy. To clearly explain adjustments to interest rate differentials, changes in exports and imports, and alterations in domestic economic variables, we focus on a small open economy. Here the interrelations between the domestic macroeconomy and its external trade and exchange relations are developed in detail. Finally, we introduce a large open economy, and show how the analysis of the small open economy is modified when the economy is large by international standards.

As we proceed through this chapter, you will learn

- how the foreign exchange market determines the price of foreign currency (also known as the exchange rate)
- how the international system of flexible exchange rates works, and how it compares to a system of fixed exchange rates

- the idea of purchasing power parity, and how it applies to foreign exchange rates
- how to develop and use a model of an open economy to analyze the effects of shifts in various exogenous forces, such as fiscal or monetary policy variables, on an open economy
- the distinction between a closed economy, a small open economy, and a large open economy
- how changes in fiscal policy, and other factors that affect *IS* or *LM,* will impact on the small open economy
- how changes in fiscal policy, and other factors that affect *IS* or *LM,* will impact on the large open economy, and how the effect differs from that of the small open economy.

THE FOREIGN EXCHANGE MARKET

Almost all countries have their own currency. When the citizens of one country want to trade with the citizens of another country, they must convert their currency into the currency of the other country. If U.S. tourists visit Japan, for example, they must convert dollars into yen before they can purchase merchandise from Japanese residents. Because of the need to exchange money from one country for the money of other countries, foreign exchange markets have developed in major cities of the world such as London, New York, Zurich, Paris, and Tokyo. Foreign exchange markets are important because they help facilitate international trade; without them, barter would be the primary method used. Exchange rates for various currencies are determined in foreign exchange markets.

How do we define an exchange rate? An exchange rate is the price of one currency in terms of another currency. The exchange rate links the prices of goods, services, and securities of one country to those of another country. On the basis of the exchange rate or ratio, residents in one country can determine what the prices of foreign goods and services would be in terms of their own country's currency. For example, let us assume that the exchange rate between the U.S. dollar and the British pound is $2 = £1. (*The Wall Street Journal,* TV business shows, and other news sources provide a daily list of the actual New York foreign exchange rates.) This means that the British pound is quoted as $2 per pound (sterling) in the United States. If the price of a wool blanket in Great Britain were £100, the same blanket would cost $200 (£100 × $2 = $200) in U.S. dollars. Suppose we wanted to know how much *one* U.S. dollar ($1) was in terms of British pounds. Dividing £1 by $2, we obtain

$$£1/\$2 = £.5/\$.$$

This tells us that

$$\$1 = £.5.$$

In our example, if we wanted to find the price of the British wool blanket in U.S. dollars, we could also divide

$$£100/(£.5/\$) = \$200.$$

Now suppose that the exchange rate between U.S. dollars and the British pound changes from $2 = £1 to $1 = £1. What does this imply? Will British goods cost more or less to U.S. households? Under the old rate, a U.S. household had to pay $2 to obtain £1. Under the new rate, a U.S. household has to pay only $1 for £1. British pounds are therefore cheaper to buy for U.S. households. Let us use our previous example to understand exactly why. The old price for the British wool blanket in terms of U.S. dollars was $200 (or £100 × ($2/£) = $200); the new price for the British wool blanket in terms

EXCHANGE RATE DEPRECIATION is an exchange rate established by market forces for a domestic country's money wherein less foreign money is obtained in exchange.

of U.S. dollars is $100 (or £100 × ($1/£) = $100). Therefore, for U.S. residents, British goods are now cheaper than they were. We say that the British pound has depreciated, since the price of the British pound in terms of U.S. dollars has declined. This **exchange rate depreciation** means that the price of British goods and services to the United States will be lower, and Great Britain should be able to export more goods to the United States. Further, the increase in quantity demanded for British goods, a result of currency depreciation, puts upward pressure on prices in Great Britain. More generally, depreciation of a currency is a decline, brought about by market forces, in the price of that currency in terms of a foreign currency.[1] If it takes fewer dollars to buy a British pound, then the pound has depreciated relative to the U.S. dollar.

When the British pound is depreciated, what happens to the U.S. dollar? Under the old exchange rate ($2 = £1), $1 equaled £.5. The U.S. dollar has, therefore, appreciated in value to equal £1. The price the British residents will have to pay for one U.S. dollar has risen. More generally, **exchange rate appreciation** of a currency is a rise, brought about by market forces, in the price of that currency in terms of a foreign currency.[2] When it takes more British pounds to purchase a U.S. dollar, the dollar has appreciated relative to the British pound.

EXCHANGE RATE APPRECIATION is an exchange rate established by market forces for a domestic country's money wherein more foreign money is obtained in exchange.

If the U.S. dollar has appreciated in value, a British resident would have to pay more for U.S. goods. For example, a U.S. wool blanket priced at $200 would have cost a British citizen £100 before appreciation of the dollar ($1 = £.5). But after the dollar appreciates to $1 = £1, the same blanket, which is still priced at $200, would cost £200 in Great Britain. Therefore, when the dollar appreciates, the United States becomes a more expensive source of goods and services, and U.S. exports to Great Britain decline.

Flexible Exchange Rates

Under an international system of flexible exchange rates, the exchange rate is determined by the forces of supply and demand for foreign exchange. In pure form, where the exchange rate is allowed to float and to seek its own level, flexible exchange rates follow free market forces. The government *does not* try to influence an exchange rate by buying or selling currency in the foreign exchange market. For an analysis of flexible exchange rates, all that is required is a knowledge of the supply and demand curves. To illustrate the foreign exchange market, assume that the United States and Great Britain are the only countries engaged in international trade and that all of their economic transactions are denominated in pounds. In Figure 7–1, the exchange rate is

[1]Devaluation of the domestic currency is a decline, brought about by government intervention in the official price of a domestic currency in terms of a foreign currency.
[2]Upward revaluation of the domestic currency is a rise, due to government intervention, in the official price of a domestic currency in terms of a foreign currency.

FIGURE 7−1
The Foreign Exchange Market

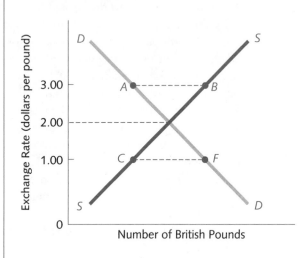

This graph indicates the determination of the equilibrium price (in U.S. dollars) of British pounds, and the equilibrium quantities of British pounds.

expressed in number of dollars per pound and is plotted on the vertical axis; the number of British pounds is plotted on the horizontal axis.

The *DD* curve is the demand for pounds by U.S. residents who use pounds to pay for imports from Britain. The *DD* curve has a negative slope because a decline in the number of dollars per pound makes pounds less expensive to U.S. residents, causing them to import larger quantities of British goods and services. Such goods and services become cheaper in terms of U.S. dollars as the pound depreciates vis-a-vis the dollar. The *SS* curve shows the supply of pounds and is derived on the basis of the demand for U.S. exports in Britain. This *SS* curve has a positive slope because an increase in the number of dollars per pound means that British residents will be willing and able to obtain more dollars per pound. Also, as we learned from our earlier discussion, U.S. goods are less costly with a rise in the exchange rate (*appreciation* of the pound). An increase in the exchange rate, then, induces British residents to purchase more dollars and to import more U.S. goods and services.

Where the *DD* curve intersects the *SS* curve, at point *E,* the market is in equilibrium, and the exchange rate is $2 = £1. To understand this equilibrium position, suppose that the exchange rate was $3 = £1 in Figure 7−1. There would be an excess supply of pounds, shown by the distance *AB.* This excess supply would drive the exchange rate down to the equilibrium position. However, if the exchange rate was $1 = £1, there would be an excess demand for pounds, illustrated by the distance *CF.* This means that U.S. residents bidding for pounds would drive the exchange rate up to the equilibrium position. Once equilibrium is achieved in the foreign exchange market, there is no excess supply of or demand for pounds; the market is cleared.

Fixed Exchange Rates

Under an international system of *fixed exchange rates,* each country chooses a fixed value for its currency and central banks maintain that rate by intervention in the foreign exchange markets.[3] A fixed exchange rate is not always an equilibrium exchange rate. If a government ever happened to choose an exchange rate that coincided with equilibrium in a foreign exchange market, this would be a lucky guess on its part, and with changing international conditions of demand, supply, and technology, the equilibrium condition would not exist very long. Governments really do not know what the exchange rate ought to be.

Therefore, if the British government set the official fixed exchange rate, for example, at $3 = £1 in Figure 7–1, this would be above the equilibrium exchange rate. The horizontal distance *AB* shows an excess supply of pounds at this fixed exchange rate. Since the supply of pounds would be greater than the demand, there would be downward pressure on the exchange rate and it would start to fall toward the equilibrium exchange rate of $2 = £1. To keep the exchange rate at its fixed level of $3 = £1, the British government would have to purchase pounds with dollars obtained from its reserve holdings of dollars. The U.S. government (the Federal Reserve) might also buy pounds with dollars to help stabilize the pound at its fixed level.

On the other hand, suppose the exchange rate was set by the British government at $1 = £1 in Figure 7–1. This rate would be below the equilibrium exchange rate, inducing an excess demand for pounds shown by the horizontal distance *CF.* This would create an upward pressure on the exchange rate, which, if left alone, would move to the equilibrium rate of $2 = £1. In this case, the British government would sell pounds in the foreign exchange market and would buy dollars to hold the exchange rate down at its fixed level. By doing this, it would be adding dollars to its foreign exchange reserves. Thus, under fixed exchange rates the government is continuously in the market buying and selling foreign currencies in an attempt to stabilize (peg) its exchange rate.

FIXED RATES, FLEXIBLE RATES, AND POLICY

In general, the central bank (or monetary authority) loses its independence in controlling the domestic money supply when it embarks on pegging operations. For example, persistent surpluses of foreign currencies in a country under

---

[3]Prior to 1971, the international system was one of fixed exchange rates, established under the Bretton Woods agreement in 1944. Foreign currencies were linked to the U.S. dollar. The exchange rate was allowed to move 1 percent above or below the official fixed exchange rate.

pegging arrangements would force its central bank to purchase foreign currencies, thereby *increasing* the domestic money supply. The central bank loses its independence in setting the domestic money supply, unless a policy of *sterilization* is carried out, that is, the compensation for these increases through central bank sales of securities. Even if sterilization does take place, fixed exchange rates mean that the monetary authority faces instability in its attempt to control interest rates. Thus, the central bank is confronted with the alternative of controlling the exchange rate or controlling the domestic money stock.

Currently the European Community (EC) is moving toward a single currency, and has begun by setting up a system of fixed exchange rates for many of its member countries. This system of exchange rates has been under some pressure, however, and during the latter half of 1992 the English pound was removed from the fixed exchange rate system. Then in 1993 many other currencies were also removed from the fixed exchange rate system. A further analysis of the move toward fixed exchange rates and the final goal of a European central bank is in Global Perspective: "European Monetary Union and the European Central Bank."

Investment, Saving, the Government Deficit, and the Trade Deficit

We have already discussed the national income accounts for the open economy—in particular, the balance of payments—in Chapter 2. Now we want to make use of these ideas to discuss further the relationship between investment, private saving, the government budget deficit, and the current account deficit (net exports). The deficit in net exports and in the government budget are often labeled the *twin deficits,* to indicate that they seem to move together much of the time. Data for these twin deficits are graphed in Figure 7–2. Notice that these deficits increased markedly from 1980 to 1985, after which they began to improve up to 1989. From 1990 through 1992, however, the government budget deficit again increased sharply, while net exports continued to improve.

We begin with the equation describing the relationship between total output and various spending categories. From the national income accounts, we have

$$Y = C + I + G + NX. \tag{7.1}$$

Recall that Y is real GDP, C is real consumption spending, I is real investment spending, G is real government spending, and NX is real net exports of goods and services. Equation 1 describes how we can add up the components of spending on output by different groups—consumers, firms for investment, government, and the net of exports sold abroad over imports—to determine real GDP.

Now consider domestic saving by private individuals and by the government. Private individuals receive income Y, which they can use for consumption spending C, taxes T, or saving S. That is, $Y = C + S + T$, or, after rearranging,

"EUROPEAN MONETARY UNION AND THE EUROPEAN CENTRAL BANK"

One of the most important developments in Western Europe in the post-World War II era is the movement toward establishing a European Monetary Union (EMU) and a common European Central Bank (ECB). In 1989, the DeLors Report set the goal of an EMU that included fixing of the exchange rate among member countries. This would essentially bring about a single currency for Europe and an integration of capital markets.[a] The conduct of monetary policy would no longer be by the central bank in each participating country but would require the establishment of a common European Central Bank. If each country's central bank were allowed to control its own monetary policy, each country would have a different inflation rate, which would lead to different exchange rates, so nominal exchange rates could not be fixed.

Since the policy objective of the ECB is price stability and Germany has been the most successful in achieving low inflation, the ECB is being closely modeled along the lines of the German central bank, the Bundesbank. An Executive Board will conduct policy established by a Central Bank Council, which consists of the six members of the ECB Executive Board plus the central bank governors from the member countries. The ECB is to maintain independence like the Federal Reserve System in the United States, and its statute says it cannot take instructions from member governments or from European Community (EC) institutions.

An accord reached at Maastricht, The Netherlands, in 1991 generally agreed with the strategy suggested by the DeLors Report of a gradual approach to monetary union. Each country that wanted to participate had to put its house in order by achieving price stability and fiscal balance, such as binding limits on budget deficits. The Maastricht Accord established a new European Monetary Institute designed to coordinate the monetary policy of the member countries. It also set a timetable for monetary union

no later than January 1, 1999, and as early as the end of 1996 if seven European countries, a majority, had met the requirements to be a member. Currently, only four countries qualify: Germany, France, Denmark, and Luxembourg. The Netherlands is the only other country likely to meet the test by 1996. Economists speculate that monetary union will be delayed and will include only a minority of the EC countries. The reason for this delay is that the Accord set stringent requirements for countries to enter the union. A country must have an inflation rate close to the average rate of the three EC countries with the lowest rate of inflation. A country's interest rates on long-term government bonds can be only several percentage points above the rates of the three lowest inflation countries. The total government deficit of the country cannot exceed 3 percent of GDP, and the outstanding government debt cannot be more than 60 percent of GDP.

The Accord used exchange rates as a signal of commitment to the EMU. Some economists argue that this strategy was unwise and costly. For example, a number of EC countries were forced to raise their interest rates in line with the increase in German interest rates that occurred when West and East Germany unified, helping to produce a widespread slowdown in economic activity. Then in the summer of 1992, the U.K. pulled out of the targeting system. A number of other countries, including France,

loosened their commitment to the exchange rate targets. Will monetary union still occur? Some economists suggest monetary union can still be achieved if exchange rates remain flexible to allow for adjustments to reflect differences in inflation rates among countries and other economic conditions. In their view, what is important is a movement to-

ward economic and financial integration. Once this integration is achieved, coordination of policies can be enforced, leading to a common currency.   ❑

NOTE [a]See Carl W. Walsh, "EMU and the ECB," Federal Reserve Bank of San Francisco, *FRBSF Weekly Letter,* number 92–93 (June 5, 1992).

PHOTO 7-1
Full Currency Unification is a Major Goal of European Economic Integration.

$$S = Y - C - T. \tag{7.2}$$

Equation 2 defines saving by private individuals, or private saving, as income minus consumption and taxes. Thus, saving is just income not spent on consumption and not paid to the government in taxes. We also want to consider another source of domestic saving, saving by government. To distinguish this from private saving, we will label government saving as S^G.

FIGURE 7-2
Real Net Exports and the
Real Government Budget
Deficit (Federal, State, and
Local), 1976–1992.

In general, real net exports and the real government budget deficit
moved together in the United States during the period 1976–1992.
When the government budget deficit grew in the early 1980s, real net
exports dropped.

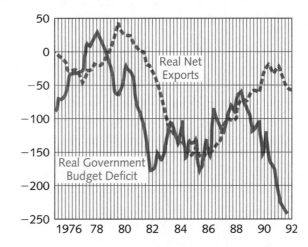

SOURCE: U.S. Department of Commerce, Bureau of Economic Analysis.

Saving by government is defined as government income that is not spent, just
as private saving is income not spent on taxes or consumption. In the case of
government, income is tax receipts net of transfers T and spending is G. Thus,
government saving is

$$S^G = T - G. \tag{7.3}$$

Note that government saving may well be negative. In fact, both government
and private saving may in principle be negative, although only government
saving has been negative in U.S. economic history. Of course, government
saving is simply the opposite of the government budget deficit $G - T$. If the
government is running a government budget deficit, then government saving is
negative, so the government is dissaving. If the government is running a
government budget surplus, government saving is positive.

Now that we have defined saving by individuals and by the government, we
can define total domestic saving, or national saving—saving by all groups in
the country—as the sum of these two components. We do not have a separate
category for saving by firms, because business saving is included in private
saving. If firms save, the saving is either paid out to individuals in dividends or
retained by the firm as retained earnings. In the first case, individuals count the
dividends as income, which can be saved if they so desire. In the second case,
retained earnings increase the value of the firm and increase the wealth of

stockholders, who are also individuals. The increase in wealth can be directly saved by stockholders who continue to hold stock in the company in question, or can be turned into income by selling the stock, and this income can be saved if the individuals so desire. This consideration means that business saving is included in private saving, since businesses are owned by individuals.

Domestic saving thus consists of private plus government saving. We will label domestic saving as national saving S^n and write

$$S^n = S + S^G = (Y - C - T) + (T - G) = Y - C - G. \qquad (7.4)$$

Equation 7.4 points out that national saving is simply national income minus consumption and government spending. Income *not spent* on consumption or on government purchases is saved.

How do we relate saving and investment in the open economy? In the closed economy, national saving was equal to investment, and for the closed economy all investment was domestic investment. In the open economy, national saving is used to fund investment spending, but this can be either domestic or overseas investment. To fund overseas investment, national saving is used to purchase ownership of capital goods in foreign countries. In this case, there is an outflow of U.S. financial assets in the form of U.S. currency, in exchange for an inflow of foreign ownership certificates, such as stock or bond certificates. Of course, the U.S. currency spent abroad to purchase capital does not stay abroad, but returns to the United States as dollars spent by foreigners to purchase U.S. goods, which increases U.S. net exports.

To better see the relationship between overseas investment and net exports, let us return to equation 7.1, which we rewrite by subtracting C and G from both sides to yield

$$Y - C - G = I + NX.$$

Now recall that $Y - C - G$ is national saving, from equation 7.4. This allows us to relate national saving to domestic investment I and net exports NX, as in the following equation:

$$S^n = I + NX, \qquad (7.5)$$

or, making use of the definition of national saving,

$$S^n = S + (T - G) = I + NX. \qquad (7.6)$$

Equations 7.5 and 7.6 are equivalent, but the first stresses the relation between national saving, investment, and net exports, while equation 7.6 stresses the relationship between private saving, government saving, investment, and net exports. We will concentrate on equation 7.6.

Remember that the current account can be thought of as net exports NX, and that the sum of the current account and the capital account is zero. (For simplicity, this discussion ignores any official transactions.) Since the current account and the capital account must sum to zero, we can think of the current account—that is, net exports—as funding the capital account. The capital account can only be positive if the current account is negative, and the capital account is negative if the current account is positive.

How can we make sense of this? Remember, if net exports are positive, the United States is selling more goods overseas than it is buying, and hence it will accumulate foreign currency. But no one in the United States wants to hold foreign currency for its own sake. Instead, foreign currency is traded for goods and services (imports to the United States) and, in the case of positive net exports, for foreign assets. In other words, the United States will use the accumulated foreign currency from positive net exports to pursue investment overseas, so the U.S. capital account is negative. This merely indicates that the purchasing power accumulated by the current account surplus (i.e., $NX > 0$) will be used to purchase capital overseas.

Alternatively put, when goods are sold abroad the selling country gains foreign currency. This currency can be used to purchase either goods or assets from the buying country. Purchases of goods show up as an import in the current account, reducing the current account, and purchases of assets show up as an outflow of capital in the capital account, reducing the capital account. For the accounts to balance, any export must be balanced by *either* an import or a capital purchase. If the export is balanced by an import, then the current account (or net exports) does not change. If the export is balanced by a capital purchase, then the current account—net exports—increases, and the capital account decreases.

In actuality, the United States has a deficit in the current account, so $NX < 0$. In this case, the United States *must have* a surplus in the capital account. What this means is that foreigners are selling U.S. residents many goods and services, thereby accumulating dollars. With these dollars, the same foreigners are choosing to purchase not U.S. goods but U.S. assets. Thus, Honda sells a large quantity of autos in the United States, earning dollars. Instead of buying U.S. goods with these dollars, Honda purchases capital, perhaps by building automobile manufacturing plants in the United States. Similarly, Saudi Arabia sells much oil to the United States, but has chosen to spend many of those dollars on assets, including U.S. government bonds.

What does equation 7.6 indicate about the relationship between saving, investment, the government budget deficit, and the current account deficit? Many economists have used the relationship to argue that the high levels of the U.S. government budget deficit in the 1980s and 1990s are responsible for the high U.S. current account deficit. Consideration of equation 7.6 does indicate that such an argument can be made, but only if both investment and private saving are held constant. If so, the increase in the U.S. government budget deficit is a reduction in government saving, and this must be matched by a reduction in net exports, or an increased deficit position in the current account. Note, however, that the causality in this argument depends on the crucial assumption that private saving and investment are fixed. Other assumptions generate other conclusions. Perhaps it is net exports and investment that are constant, so that an increase in the U.S. government budget deficit causes an increase in private saving. Or perhaps it is net exports and private saving that are constant, so that an increase in the U.S. government budget deficit causes a reduction in investment. The actual effect of the increased U.S. government budget deficit is probably a combination of these possibilities, so that private saving may have increased, net exports increased, and investment declined. Actually sorting through these possibilities turns out to be quite difficult and has occupied the research agendas of many economists.

One explanation for the large current account deficits in the 1980s is that the favorable tax law changes created a very favorable investment climate in the United States, and investment increased. However, private saving S did not increase. The increase in investment with private saving unchanged led to an increase in the current account deficit. This came about because Americans were not willing to fund the increased investment opportunities, but foreigners were. In order to pursue these investment opportunities, foreigners obtained funds, which they did by cutting back on their purchases of U.S. goods while selling increased amounts to the United States. Thus the U.S. current account deficit grew because the U.S. capital account was in surplus, as foreigners funded investments that U.S. savers were not willing to fund.

What is the reality? Probably both the increased investment opportunities and the increased U.S. government budget deficit played roles in the large U.S. current account deficits in the 1980s, especially during the period 1984–1988. Whatever else happened, U.S. private saving has been notoriously low and a fairly constant ratio to GDP. Increases in the government budget deficit and in desired investment, with private saving constant, will probably reinforce each other in driving net exports down as well as leading to increases in the current account deficit.

Purchasing Power Parity

One very important issue in international macroeconomics is the ability to explain exchange rate movements. One approach that has been around for a long time is purchasing power parity. Purchasing power parity is an old and simple idea for exchange rate determination. The idea comes from the economic concept called *the law of one price*. The law of one price says that a good should have only one price in a competitive market, since otherwise all purchasers would buy the good only from the seller posting the lowest price. (The law pertains to a concept of *full* price where all transactions costs are considered.) This simple but very powerful idea should also apply to goods traded internationally. In this case, if we define the market for a particular good that is traded on overseas markets as the world market, then the law of one price says that such a good should have only one price in the market. Thus, if a sweater traded internationally sells for £10 in Britain and $20 in the United States, then this sweater should be the same price in the two countries. That is,

$20 buys a sweater in the United States and £10 buys the same sweater in Britain, so $20 should be the same as £10, or $2 = £1 should be the exchange rate. According to this doctrine, it should make no difference to an American consumer if that person bought the sweater in the United States and paid $20 for it, or first converted that $20 into British pounds (at $2 = £1) and then purchased the sweater in Britain. Of course, this ignores transactions, transportation, and location costs. In the real world, you would have to take these into consideration before making statements about purchasing power parity.

The purchasing power parity idea takes the law of one price one step further, however, and claims that the exchange rate between, say, U.S. dollars and British pounds should not just equate the dollar price of a traded good like a sweater with the pound price of that same good, but that the exchange rate should equate the general U.S. price level with the general British price level. That is, instead of saying that the exchange rate should be such as to make $P^{US}_{sweater} = E \times P^{UK}_{sweater}$, where E is dollars per pound, the purchasing power parity idea is that the exchange rate should be such as to make $CPI^{US} = E \times CPI^{UK}$. This is a very strong claim, and does not in fact stand up to empirical investigation. Still, the law of one price is an idea near and dear to the hearts of economists, and purchasing power parity, as an extension of the law of one price shares in that affection as does the issue of interest rate parity (see the Appendix to this chapter "Interest Rate Parity and Exchange Rates").

The result is that purchasing power parity is an idea that is widely talked about among economists despite its apparent lack of relevance in the real world. Economists and others even calculate purchasing power parity exchange rates—values that the exchange rates would be *if* purchasing power parity held. These calculations can be complex. However, there has recently been a calculation by the editors of *The Economist* magazine of what they call "the Big Mac standard." What they calculate is really the law of one price for Big Macs. They gather data on the price of Big Macs in various cities around the world, and calculate what the exchange rate would have to be so that the prices would all be the same after exchanging currencies. Such an exercise is obviously done with tongue firmly placed in cheek, since Big Macs are not really a traded good. No one could or would fly from the United States to Tokyo just to purchase a Big Mac at a cheaper price than the price quoted in New York. However, the Big Mac index has survived to be calculated again and again because it seems to work. That is, it seems that when exchange rates are not equal to the Big Mac rates, the spot rates adjust over time—a period of months—toward the Big Mac standard rates! Thus, even though purchasing power parity does not hold, it does seem to give useful broad-brush predictions for the future movements of the exchange rates. In particular, when the exchange rates are not equal to the purchasing power parity rates, the prediction is that they have a tendency to move toward the purchasing power parity rates.

As an alternative to the Big Mac index, we calculate another purchasing power parity exchange rate based on an internationally traded good in the Insight: "A Magazine Index of Purchasing Power Parity Exchange Rates."

INSIGHT

A MAGAZINE INDEX OF PURCHASING POWER PARITY EXCHANGE RATES

Rather than give the Big Mac Standard rates, let us consider an application of the idea of the law of one price to another good that is sold in many countries across the globe and priced in local currencies in each of these countries. That good is an excellent news magazine called *The Economist*. *The Economist* lists its worldwide prices on the cover. These prices from the cover for the March 21–27, 1992, issue are listed in Table 7–1. Notice that the

U.S. price is $3.50, the U.K. price is £1.70. An exchange rate of £.4857 = $1 would make these prices the same. In fact, this exchange rate of .4857 pounds per dollar is "*The Economist* Standard." What is the actual spot rate? The spot rate for March 23, 1992, is .587 pounds per dollar (see Table A–1 in the appendix to this chapter), so *The Economist* Standard suggests that the dollar will depreciate relative to the British pound.

We can calculate other exchange rates that make *The Economist* cost the same across countries, and we summarize these calculations in Table 7–2: Column 1 includes a list of countries, column 2 reports the price of *The Economist* in local currency, and column 3 gives

the exchange rates in foreign currency per U.S. dollar that would make *The Economist* cost equivalent amounts in each country. (This is *The Economist* Standard, the exchange rates that would make the law of one price apply to *The Economist*.) Finally, column 4 reports the actual exchange rates on a day in March 1992. For instance, in Australia *The Economist* sells for A$5.50 (five and one-half Australian dollars). Since *The Economist* sells for U.S. $3.50, we calculate *The Economist* Standard exchange rate between Australian dollars and U.S. dollars as 5.50/3.50 = 1.5714 Australian dollars per U.S. dollar. Compare this to a spot exchange rate of 1.3142 Australian dollars per

TABLE 7–1
Single Issue Price of *The Economist*, Week of March 21, 1992.

This table shows the prices charged in various currencies for a single issue of *The Economist*, a news magazine published in Britain.

AUSTRALIA	A$5.50	JAPAN	Y850**825
BRAZIL	CR$12,500	MEXICO	PESO17500
CANADA	C$4.25	NETHERLANDS	FL7.50
CHINA	YUAN 17	RUSSIA	US$3.50
FRANCE	FFr22	SAUDI ARABIA .	RIALS22
GERMANY	DM6.50	SOUTH AFRICA	RAND 9.25
HONG KONG ..	HK$26	SWITZERLAND .	SFr6.50
INDIA	RS45	UK	£1.70
ITALY	LIRE6000	USA	$3.50

U.S. dollar. Clearly, *The Economist* Standard suggests that it should take more Australian dollars to purchase a U.S. dollar, or that the U.S. dollar should appreciate relative to the Australian dollar. In fact, if we compare *The Economist* Standard exchange rates to the actual rates, we see that the U.S. dollar is predicted to depreciate relative to the U.K. pound sterling, the Indian rupee, and the Hong Kong dollar. The U.S. dollar is predicted to appreciate with respect to all other currencies listed. This gives *The Econo-* *mist* Standard's prediction for exchange rate movements. A useful exercise might be to compare *The Economist* Standard to *The Economist*'s Big Mac Standard, but we leave this to the enterprising reader. ❑

TABLE 7–2
The Economist Standard

This table calculates the exchange rates implied by the price list for a single issue of *The Economist,* and compares these to the actual exchange rates that were posted in foreign exchange markets in March 1992.

COUNTRY	LOCAL CURRENCY PRICE	THE ECONOMIST STANDARD	SPOT RATES (3/92)
AUSTRALIA	A$5.50	1.5714	1.3142
BRAZIL	CR$12,500	3571.4286	1857.01
CANADA	C$4.25	1.2143	1.193
FRANCE	FFr22	6.2857	5.6565
GERMANY	DM6.50	1.8571	1.668
HONG KONG	HK$26	7.4286	7.744
INDIA	RS45	12.8571	28.68
ITALY	LIRE6000	1714.2857	1253.84
JAPAN	Y850	242.8571	133.56
MEXICO	PESO17,500	5000.0000	3069
NETHERLANDS	FL7.50	2.1429	1.8779
SAUDI ARABIA	RIALS22	6.2857	3.74
SWITZERLAND	SFr6.50	1.8571	1.5163
U.K.	£1.70	0.4857	0.5819
U.S.	$3.5	1	1

A BRIEF HISTORY OF THE U.S. DOLLAR

Here we briefly review the behavior of the U.S. dollar from the late 1950s, when the United States was part of the Bretton Woods System of fixed exchange rates, to the present, when the U.S. dollar floats relative to the currencies of other industrial countries.

International Change from Fixed to Flexible Exchange Rates

The Bretton Woods System was established by the major trading countries at Bretton Woods, New Hampshire, in 1944. Under Bretton Woods, countries pegged their exchange rates to the U.S. dollar, and the United States maintained the price of gold at $35 per ounce. That is, countries pegged to the dollar, and the U.S. pegged the price of gold. Beginning in 1958, the United States experienced large deficits in its balance of payments, and as the deficit continued, foreign countries began to pile up dollar claims against the United States. Since the United States had agreed to buy and sell gold at $35 per ounce to central banks and foreign treasuries, foreigners had a right to exchange these dollars for gold, and gold flowed out of the United States. The U.S. gold supply fell from $23 billion in 1957 to $10 billion in 1968. In response the United States decided in August 1971 to refuse to exchange gold for U.S. dollars held by foreigners. Because the United States had closed the gold window, major foreign industrial countries, especially West Germany and Japan, held more U.S. dollars than they wanted. These surplus dollars were causing foreign countries to lose control over their domestic money supply. Central banks in these countries were forced to buy U.S. dollars to keep their domestic currency from appreciating but by purchasing dollars, these central banks were expanding their domestic money supply since they were releasing their domestic currency into circulation in order to buy dollars.

The solution to this problem was to move to flexible exchange rates, thereby removing their domestic money supplies from the influence of the United States. As we have seen, under flexible exchange rates basic market forces of supply and demand are allowed to determine the exchange rate.[4]

Recent Developments with the U.S. Dollar

In the 1980s and 1990s, there has been a widespread concern among economists about the volatility of the U.S. dollar. In particular, the concern is about the *real exchange rate,* a measure of the purchasing power of the dollar that takes into account movements in both the exchange rate and the inflation

---

[4]In reality, the international system of flexible exchange rates does have some degree of government intervention to prevent extreme fluctuations in the exchange rate. This is called a managed or "dirty" float.

This figure graphs the effective exchange rate of the U.S. dollar over the period 1978–1992.

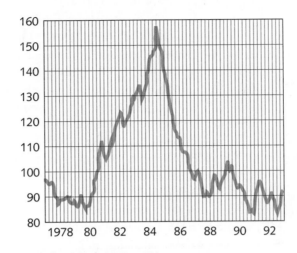

NOTE: Index, March 1973 = 100.
SOURCE: Board of Governors of the Federal Reserve System.

rate in the United States relative to other countries. The real exchange rate between the U.S. dollar and, say, the British pound, can be calculated as

$$e = E \times P_{UK}/P_{US},$$

where E is the exchange rate in U.S. dollars per British pound. A real appreciation in the dollar relative to the pound can occur either because of a decrease in the nominal exchange rate E or because of a decline in the ratio of the U.K. price level to the U.S. price level. In either case, net exports will decline as U.S. exports to Britain decline, because U.S. goods become more expensive in Britain; and U.S. imports from Britain increase, because British goods become less expensive in the United States.[5]

Figure 7–3 shows the effective exchange rate of the U.S. dollar. Effective exchange rate changes are computed as an index, combining the exchange rates between the United States and seventeen other major currencies.[6] The dollar fluctuated by a small amount between 1978 and 1980, reaching one of its

---

[5]The Council of Economic Advisers noted in 1984 that the dollar's sharp rise had made it difficult for U.S. businesses and farmers to compete in world markets, and had resulted in record trade deficits in 1982 and 1983. See Council of Economic Advisers, *Economic Report of the President* (Washington, DC: U.S. Government Printing Office, 1984), p. 5.

[6]For the method of computation of effective exchange rates, see Jacques R. Artus and Rudolf R. Rhomberg, "A Multilateral Exchange Rate Model," *International Monetary Fund Staff Papers*, November 1973, pp. 591–611.

lowest real values in 1980. From July 1980 to its peak in February 1985, the dollar's value increased over 85 percent. From this peak in 1985, the dollar then fell back near its level of 1980, although it exhibited quite a bit of volatility from 1988 through 1992.

Economists have offered a number of reasons for the historic increase in the value of the dollar in the early 1980s. One of the arguments given for the strong rise in the dollar is the large federal budget deficits that began in 1981. The Treasury, by bidding for private funds to finance the increased budget deficit, caused U.S. interest rates to rise relative to foreign rates. These relatively high U.S. interest rates attracted an additional flow of capital funds from foreign countries into the United States (a net capital inflow) and contributed to an appreciation of the dollar. Another argument focused on the role played by the Federal Reserve. Some economists stress that increases in the budget deficit after 1981 could not be the only cause of the strong dollar. They point out that budget deficits are sometimes associated with high currency values and at other times with low currency values. To them, the reason for the initial increase in the real value of the U.S. dollar was U.S. monetary policy. When the Fed changed operating procedures in October 1979 there was a sharp increase in U.S. interest rates relative to foreign rates, creating a strong foreign demand for dollars. Their conclusion is that monetary policy, not fiscal policy, caused the dollar to rise to its high point in 1985.

As the dollar rose in the early 1980s, the U.S. business community began to complain that the strong dollar limited the competitiveness of U.S. products against foreign companies. In the face of mounting concern over the dollar, U.S. policy shifted in the autumn of 1985. A meeting at New York's Plaza Hotel on September 23, 1985, brought together central bankers and finance and treasury officials from the five largest industrial countries, the so-called Group of Five (or G-5): the United States, Japan, Germany, France, and the United Kingdom. As a result of this meeting, the U.S. began to intervene more heavily in the foreign exchange market, selling dollars. U.S. intervention from September to October 1985 was five times the volume of its intervention earlier that year. By early 1987, the dollar had fallen to its lowest level in seven years. In February 1987, at a meeting at the Louvre in Paris, France, of the G-7 (the G-5 plus Italy and Canada), decided to cooperate closely to foster stability of exchange rates around current levels. The Louvre Accord signaled a change in U.S. policy from encouraging the appreciation of foreign currencies to moving toward exchange rate stability. During the rest of 1987, the dollar fell and U.S. intervention in the foreign exchange market consisted largely of dollar purchases. The stock market crash of 1987 and the associated easing by the Federal Reserve of the money supply contributed to a further downward pressure on the dollar. The next major increase in the volume of U.S. intervention came in 1989, and totaled over $20 billion, one of the highest volumes ever. From 1989 to 1993, the dollar fluctuated somewhere near its 1980 level.

THE SMALL OPEN ECONOMY

A SMALL OPEN ECONOMY
is an economy that is so
small it cannot affect the
world real interest rate, but
instead takes that rate as
given.

A LARGE OPEN ECONOMY
is an economy that is so
large that its real interest
rate can vary from the
world real interest rate, and
in effect the large open
economy affects the real
interest rate in the rest of
the world.

When discussing open economy macroeconomics, one must define whether the economy is small or large. There are actually three classifications: closed, small open, and large open. A closed economy is an economy that is closed to the rest of the world. Net exports are zero, so the current account and hence capital account are zero. Because there is no international trade between the closed economy and the rest of the world, there are no financial flows.

A **small open economy** is an economy that is small relative to the rest of the world, so that it takes the world interest rate and world prices of traded goods and services as given. The small open economy cannot affect the world interest rate or world price of traded goods by its actions. It is much like an individual firm in perfect competition: The individual firm takes the market price as given and chooses how much it wants to produce, knowing that its individual production decision has no effect on the market price. Analogously, the small open economy takes the world interest rate and price of traded goods as given, and knows that its individual choices will have no effect on that world interest rate or world prices of traded goods.

Like the small open economy, the **large open economy** trades with the rest of the world. However, the large open economy's actions do affect the world interest rate and the world price of traded goods and services. It is much like a firm with market power. Such a firm knows that its output decision can lead to a change in the market price of its output. Analogously, the large open economy knows that its actions can affect the world interest rate and traded goods prices.

In addition to the issue of the large and small open economies, there is an important distinction between fixed and flexible exchange rates. As we will see, under flexible exchange rates the exchange rate is endogenous, or determined by economic forces in the model, while the domestic money supply is exogenous, or determined outside the model. Under fixed exchange rates, the situation is reversed. The exchange rate is exogenous and the money supply is endogenous.

For now, we will consider a small open economy. The small open economy provides a benchmark for interpreting the behavior of open economies, analogous to the benchmark provided by perfect competition when studying the theory of the firm. The small open economy, like the perfectly competitive firm, cannot alter the market price or market (i.e., world) interest rate. (In reality, nations like the United States are large open economies. That is, actions taken by the United States have an impact on the world interest rate. This adds complications to the model, just as considerations of market power add complications to the theory of the firm. To avoid these complications, we will first consider the case of the small open economy.)

In a small open economy, the domestic interest rate is equal to the world interest rate, and the world interest rate is not affected by changes in government spending in the small open economy. Hence government spending in the small open economy does not affect the interest rate in that economy. What of the large open economy? In this case, the increase in government spending increases the world interest rate and hence the domestic interest rate, but not by as much as if the large economy were closed. Thus, the effect of increasing government spending in the large open economy falls between the effect of increasing government spending in the small open economy and in the closed economy. In this way, the large open economy results can be thought of as an average between the closed economy results and the small open economy results.

The Classical Model of the Small Open Economy

In describing the behavior of the small open economy, we begin with the Classical model, looking only at flexible exchange rates. Moreover, we consider a model where the inputs of both labor and capital are fixed, so that output is also fixed. In the closed economy this would appear at the vertical or perfectly inelastic aggregate supply curve.

As for the demand side, we will consider each of the components of aggregate spending. As before, we will model consumption, investment, government spending and net exports. Moreover, in the small open economy the domestic real interest rate r must be equal to the world real interest rate r^*, with r^* exogenous to the small open economy.

Our goal is to describe net exports. But to do so, we will look at national saving and investment. The national saving equation is written as $S^n = Y - C - G$.

Also recall that we can write our equation for net exports as $NX = S^n - I$, or $NX = S + (T - G) - I$.

To show how net exports are determined, we will need to describe the determination of national saving and investment. For national saving, we have the equation $S^n = Y - C - G$. Since output is fixed, determined by the fixed inputs of capital and labor as Y, consumption is determined by the consumption function as

$$C = c_0 + c_1 (Y - T),$$

where Y is fixed and T is exogenous, so consumption is fixed. Finally, G is exogenous. Hence national saving S^n is determined only by exogenous variables. We graph national saving against the interest rate in Figure 7−4, where we see that it is perfectly inelastic, indicating that national saving does not respond to the interest rate.

What about investment? Investment is given by the investment equation,

$$I = d_0 - d_1 r,$$

and thus it is a function of the interest rate.

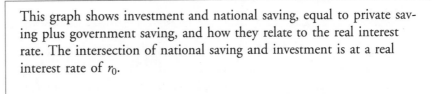

FIGURE 7-4
National Saving and
Investment

This graph shows investment and national saving, equal to private saving plus government saving, and how they relate to the real interest rate. The intersection of national saving and investment is at a real interest rate of r_0.

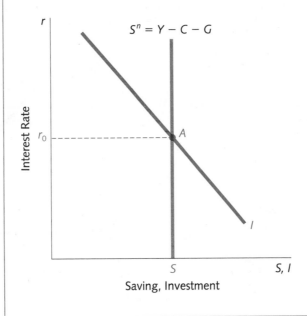

Investment is also graphed in Figure 7–4. Investment is downward sloping, since increases in the real interest rate reduce investment spending. The intersection of the saving and investment curves at point A indicates that an interest rate of r_0 will equate national saving and investment. Indeed, in a closed economy, with net exports of zero, national saving will equal investment and point A will indicate both the equilibrium real interest rate and the equilibrium level of saving and investment. However, in a small open economy, and in this case saving need not equal investment; instead, saving minus investment must equal net exports. In addition, in the small open economy the interest rate is *not* determined by the intersection of the saving and investment curves. Instead, it must equal the given, exogenous world interest rate r^*.

For the small open economy, the world interest rate r^* may be greater than or less than the interest rate that sets national saving equal to investment. These two cases are illustrated in Figure 7–5. In Figure 7–5(a), the world rate is above the rate that equates S^n and I. Because of this, investment declines from $I(r_0)$ to $I(r^*)$. Also, national saving S^n exceeds investment $I(r^*)$. Net exports, the difference between national saving and investment, are positive. The positive net exports indicate that, since national saving exceeds investment,

FIGURE 7−5
The World Interest Rate, National Saving and Investment, and Net Exports

This graph shows how the world interest rate helps determine net exports. In (a), the world interest rate is such that national saving exceeds investment, so net exports are positive. In (b), the world interest rate is such that national saving is less than investment, so net exports are negative.

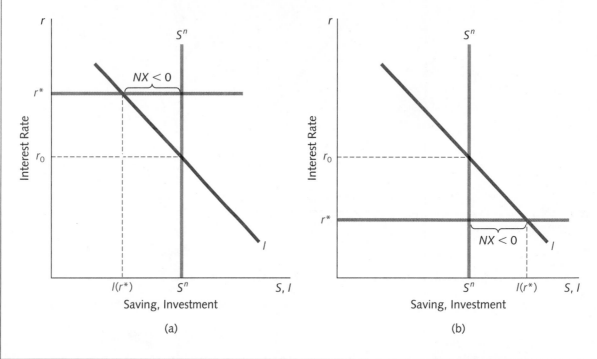

Saving, Investment

(a)   (b)

domestic saving funds investment in foreign countries. That is, the positive net exports indicate a capital outflow (a capital account deficit) which generates net purchases of domestic goods by foreigners, or positive net exports (a current account surplus).

Figure 7−5(b) illustrates the case of r^* below r_0. In this case investment is greater than national saving, so net exports are negative. The high domestic interest rate relative to the world rate leads to an inflow of saving from foreign nations, saving that helps finance U.S. investment. In this case, the negative net exports—the negative current account—are balanced by a capital inflow to the United States, a capital account surplus.

Figure 7−5 demonstrates the determination of net exports. We also want to understand how net exports change when there is a change in one of the underlying components of investment or saving. We will consider two situations: (1) a change in national saving, and (2) a change in investment.

CHANGES IN SAVING

Remember that national saving is the sum of private saving and government saving. Government saving is $T - G$, while private saving is $Y - C - T$, with consumption is determined by the consumption function $C = c_0 + c_1 (Y - T)$. How might national saving change? Clearly, any factor that changes Y, C, or G might change national saving. For example, taxes change consumption and hence national saving. An increase in net taxes T will cause a reduction in consumption spending and hence an increase in private saving and national saving. Government spending directly affects national saving, and a decrease in government spending will increase national saving. Also, autonomous consumption c_0 affects national saving, and a decrease in autonomous consumption will increase national saving. Finally, increases in output Y due to increases in the capital stock or the labor force, or technological change, can increase saving.

What decreases national saving? Decreases in net taxes, increases in government spending, and increases in autonomous consumption will all decrease national saving. We illustrate a decrease in national saving in Figure 7–6. The initial saving schedule is S_0^n. The intersection of the original national saving schedule S_0^n and investment $I(r)$ is at an interest rate r_0, which is above the world interest rate r^*. Thus, at the initial equilibrium the economy has a current account deficit $NX_0 < 0$.

What is the effect of a decrease in national saving to S_1^n? Since the world interest rate is unchanged at r^*, investment stays constant at $I(r^*)$. The decline in national saving, then, increases the gap between saving and investment, which increases the absolute size of net exports, which were already negative, to NX_1. The explanation can again be told in terms of international financial capital flows. There is a constant level of investment and a decline in national saving. Foreign saving flows in to make up for the reduction in national saving. This inflow of foreign saving, a capital account surplus, has a mirror image in a current account deficit, or a decline in net exports. The general conclusion is that anything that reduces national saving without affecting investment will make the current account smaller or, if the current account is already negative, will make the deficit on the current account larger.

In considering factors that affect national saving, notice that two of the factors are policy variables, namely government spending G and net taxes T. Thus, there are important implications of government fiscal policy actions for the current account.

CHANGES IN INVESTMENT

Consider a change in autonomous investment. An increase in autonomous investment will shift the investment schedule to the right, and a reduction in autonomous investment will shift the investment schedule to the left. In

FIGURE 7–6
The Effect of a Change in
Saving on Net Exports

In this graph, there is a shift left in the national saving curve, from S_0^n to S_1^n. In a closed economy this would increase the interest rate from r_0 to r_1. However, in the small open economy the world real interest rate r^* is also the domestic real interest rate. At the original level of national saving, national saving was less than investment, and net exports were negative. The reduction in the national saving curve exacerbates this, and net exports become a larger negative number.

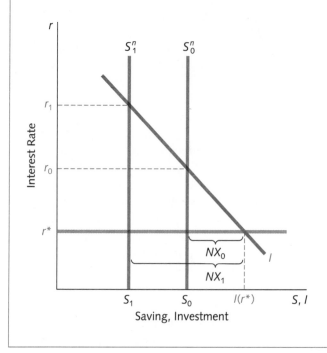

Figure 7–7 we illustrate an increase in autonomous investment. This could occur if the tax treatment of investment became more favorable, or if the expected future returns to investment increase for some other reason. In any event, Figure 7–7 shows the initial investment curve as I_0 and the new investment curve as I_1. The intersection of the initial investment curve and the national saving curve is at r_0, which is greater than the world interest rate r^*. Thus, the economy is initially running a current account deficit, with $I_0(r^*) > S^n$, so that net exports are negative, or $NX_0 < 0$. After the increase in autonomous investment, the intersection of investment and saving curves is at r_1, even further from r^* than r_0. Now investment is even greater than before, so $I_1(r^*) > I_0(r^*) > S^n$, and net exports become a larger negative number NX_1. The increase in autonomous investment has caused an increase in the current account deficit. (If the current account had initially been in surplus, the increase in autonomous investment would reduce this surplus.)

FIGURE 7-7
The Effect of a Change in
Investment on Net Exports

In this graph, there is a shift to the right in the investment curve, from I_0 to I_1. In a closed economy this would increase the interest rate from r_0 to r_1. However, in the small open economy the world real interest rate r^* is also the domestic real interest rate. At the original level of investment, national saving was less than investment, and net exports were negative. The increase in the investment curve exacerbates this, and net exports become a larger negative number.

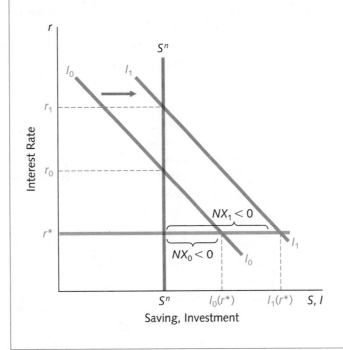

The Mundel-Fleming Model of a Small Open Economy

It is possible to extend our analysis beyond the Classical analysis of the previous section. In fact, the Mundel-Fleming model was designed for just such a purpose. It analyzes a model with the familiar *IS-LM* model developed in Chapter 5. In this section, we present the Mundel-Fleming model for a small open economy.

This model is straightforward. We have the familiar national income identity:

$$Y = C + I + G + NX,$$

and the equations describing consumption, investment, government spending, and net exports, given by

$$C = c_0 + c_1 (Y - T)$$

$$I = d_0 - d_1 r,$$

$$NX = n_0 + n_1 E,$$

with G and T exogenous. These equations can be combined into an IS equation, which will be like the typical IS equation from Chapter 5. An increase in autonomous net exports n_0 causes a rightward shift in IS, and an increase in the exchange rate E (in dollars per unit of foreign currency) also causes a rightward shift in IS.

Along with IS, we have equations for the money market, both real money demand and real money supply, given by

$$(M/P)^d = L_0 + L_1 Y - L_2 (r + \pi^e),$$

$$M^s / P = M / P.$$

We assume the money market is in equilibrium, which allows us to combine these equations and derive an LM equation as we did in Chapter 5. However, there is an additional equation, the equation describing the real interest rate in a small open economy as equal to the world real interest rate, or

$$r = r^*.$$

Thus, we are again analyzing a small open economy, an economy whose domestic real interest rate is always equal to the world real interest rate, an economy which is so small that changes in its capital account have no effect on the world real interest rate.

As we mentioned earlier, the small open economy can have either fixed or flexible exchange rates. We will first analyze the case of flexible exchange rates, and then turn to the case of fixed exchange rates.

FLEXIBLE EXCHANGE RATES

We graph IS, LM, and the relationship $r = r^*$ in Figure 7–8. Notice we explicitly write that IS is a function of the exchange rate by writing $IS(E)$. Remember that increases in E (in dollars per unit of foreign currency) will shift IS to the right. Note too that we graph r^* as a horizontal line, since the world interest rate is exogenous and does not change with domestic real income Y. The intersection of IS and LM will determine the *domestic* real interest rate, but unlike the closed economy or even the large open economy, for the small open economy the intersection of IS and LM must occur at $r = r^*$. In Figure 7–8 we label such an equilibrium point A. At point A, the domestic real interest rate is r^* and the level of real output is Y_0.

What happens if IS and LM do not intersect at a value of the real interest rate equal to r^*? In this case, the intersection will not be an equilibrium in the

FIGURE 7-8
IS, LM, and the World
Interest Rate in the Small
Open Economy

In this graph, *IS* and *LM* intersect at point *A*. Changes in the exchange rate shift *IS* so that *IS* and *LM* intersect at the world real interest rate r^*.

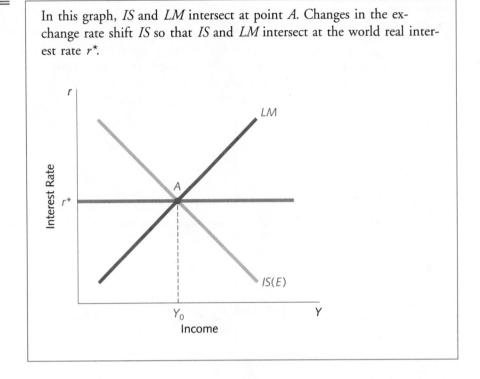

small open economy. Something has to adjust to bring the domestic interest rate equal to the world rate. This also happens after something shifts either *IS* or *LM*, since then the intersection will not be at r^*. We illustrate just this situation in Figure 7–9. In the initial equilibrium the world interest rate is r_0^*, and *IS* intersects *LM* at point *A*, where the domestic interest rate equals r_0^* and output is Y_0. Then the world interest rate increases to r_1^*. At this new world interest rate, *IS* and *LM* are not equal. With interest rate r_1^*, the goods market is in equilibrium at output Y_{IS} and the money market is in equilibrium at output Y_{LM}. Obviously this is not an overall equilibrium, since the income level that equilibrates the money market is above the income level that equilibrates the output market. What adjusts to equilibrate *IS* and *LM*? It is not the interest rate, which is fixed at the world rate, but is instead the exchange rate. The exchange rate must increase (i.e., the dollar must depreciate), shifting *IS* to the right, until at point *B* the economy is again in equilibrium, with *IS* intersecting *LM* at the world interest rate r_1^*.

Why does the exchange rate decline? Immediately after the increase in the world interest rate, the economy is at point *A*, with the domestic rate at r_0^* but the world rate at r_1^*. Domestic investors are encouraged to go abroad where the return to investment is higher. In so doing, the dollar depreciates, since more units of foreign currency are being demanded by U.S. residents on the

The rise in the world interest rate from r^*_0 to r^*_1 causes an outflow of financial capital from the small open economy. This causes a depreciation of the exchange rate for the currency of the small open economy. As the currency depreciates net exports increase, shifting *IS* to the right to point *B*.

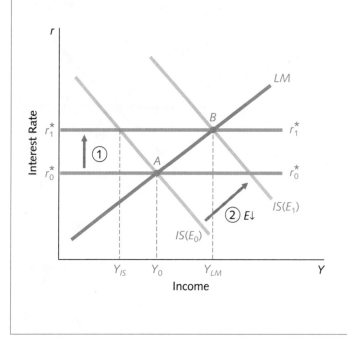

exchange market. This causes net exports to rise. This increase in net exports, or in the current account balance, is equal to the decrease in the capital account when U.S. residents sent their saving abroad in order to receive the higher world interest rate. As the exchange rate increases and net exports rise, *IS* shifts to the right, and this adjustment process continues until the domestic rate and world rate are equal, at point *B* in Figure 7–9. Thus, the increase in the world interest rate leads not only to an increase in the domestic interest rate, but also to an increase in net exports and a depreciation of the dollar.

POLICY ACTIONS WITH FLEXIBLE EXCHANGE RATES

We turn next to an analysis of policy actions and the effect of those actions on the exchange rate and income. In Figure 7–10 we illustrate an increase in government spending. Recall that government spending affects the *IS* curve but not the *LM* curve. The increase in government spending shifts *IS* to the right. The intersection of *IS* and *LM* shifts from point *A* to point *B*. However, at point *B* the domestic interest rate is above the world rate. This results in an

FIGURE 7-10
Fiscal Policy in the Small
Open Economy with Flexible
Exchange Rates

The increase in government spending shifts the *IS* curve to the right. After this shift, *IS* intersects *LM* at point *B*. However, at point *B* the real interest rate is above the world real interest rate. This leads to an inflow of foreign financial capital and an appreciation of the currency, shifting *IS* back to the same position as the original *IS* curve.

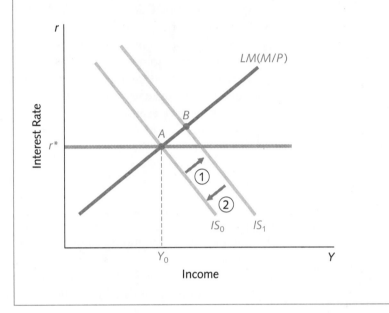

inflow of foreign saving—a capital account surplus—and causes a decline in the exchange rate (an appreciation of the domestic currency) and a decline in net exports—a current account deficit. The result is that *IS* shifts leftward, back to its initial position, to intersect *LM* again at point *A*. Thus, the net effect of an increase in government spending—or indeed of any change that shifts *IS* to the right—is a decline in the exchange rate (an appreciation of the currency) but no change in equilibrium income. This is called crowding out in the small open economy. In the closed economy, an increase in the interest rate crowds out investment spending and at least partially offsets increases in government spending. In the open economy, the interest rate is fixed at the world rate, but the exchange rate appreciates in response to the increase in government spending, and the appreciation is just enough to offset the increase in government spending, so that there is no net increase in equilibrium income or spending.

The analysis in Figure 7–10 is of an increase in government spending, but the same would hold true for an increase in autonomous consumption, investment, or even autonomous net exports. All of these would shift *IS* rightward, with a resultant change in international capital flows that would cause the domestic currency to appreciate, reducing net exports and shifting IS back to its initial location.

Another policy action is an increase in the money supply, illustrated in Figure 7–11. Changes in the money supply will shift the LM curve, and, in particular, increases in the money supply shift LM to the right. In Figure 7–11 the initial LM curve is $LM(M/P)$, and the initial equilibrium is at point A, with an exchange rate of E and income Y_0. An increase in the money supply to M' shifts LM to the right, to $LM(M'/P)$, resulting in an intersection of IS and LM at point B. But at point B, the domestic interest rate is below the world rate. This induces an outflow of saving, as domestic savers take advantage of the more attractive world interest rate. The increased demand for foreign currency bids up the exchange rate, a depreciation of the domestic currency. This causes an increase in net exports, and shifts IS to the right, to $IS(E')$. The new equilibrium is at point C, with an equilibrium income of Y_1. Thus, an increase in the money supply increases the exchange rate, increasing net exports and equilibrium income.

FIGURE 7–11

Monetary Policy in the Small Open Economy with Flexible Exchange Rates

The increase in the money supply from M to M' increases real money balances and shifts the LM curve to the right. After this shift, LM intersects IS at point B. The real interest rate is below the world real interest rate. This leads to an outflow of financial capital and a depreciation of the currency, shifting IS to the right point C. Output has increased from Y_0 to Y_1.

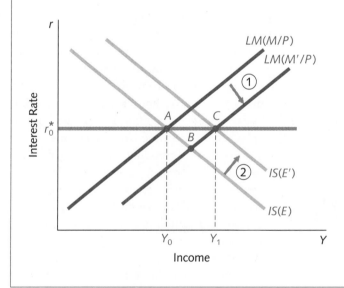

FIXED EXCHANGE RATES

How does the above analysis change if we have fixed exchange rates? In this case, the exchange rate does not adjust to keep the domestic interest rate equal to the world rate. Instead, with a fixed exchange rate, the money supply is endogenous, responding to economic forces in the economy, and it is the money supply that adjusts to keep the domestic and world interest rates equal.

What happens if *IS* and *LM* do not intersect at a value of the real interest rate equal to the world real interest rate r^*? In this case, the money supply will have to adjust to bring the domestic interest rate equal to the world rate. This is also an issue after something shifts either *IS* or *LM*. We illustrate just this situation in Figure 7–12. In the initial equilibrium the world interest rate is r_0^*, and *IS* intersects *LM* at point *A*, where the domestic interest rate equals

FIGURE 7–12

An Increase in the World Real Interest Rate in the Small Open Economy *IS-LM* Model with Fixed Exchange Rates

The rise in the world interest rate from r_0^* to r_1^* causes an outflow of financial capital, as investors move funds to achieve the higher interest rate available overseas. This increased demand for foreign currency causes a depreciation of the exchange rate for the currency of the small open economy. However, with fixed exchange rates the domestic monetary authority supplies additional foreign currency from its foreign currency reserves in order to keep the exchange rate from changing. This reduces the money supply, from *M* to *M'*, in order to shift *LM* to the left, so that *IS* and *LM* intersect at point *B*, at the new world real interest rate. Real income falls from Y_0 to Y_{IS}.

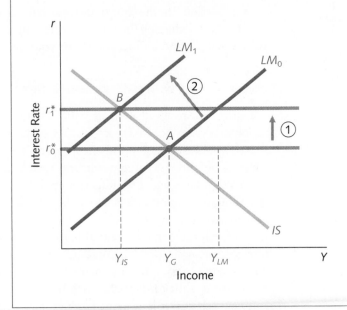

r_0^* and output is Y_0. Then the world interest rate increases to r_1^*. At this new world interest rate, IS and LM are not equal. With interest rate r_1^*, the goods market is in equilibrium at output Y_{IS} and the money market is in equilibrium at output Y_{LM}. With the exchange rate fixed, the money supply must adjust to keep the domestic and world real interest rates equal. In Figure 7–12, this requires a reduction in the money supply to M', shifting LM to the left, to LM_1, in order to have IS and LM intersect at point B. At point B the economy is again in equilibrium, at the world interest rate r_1^*.

Why does the money supply decline? Immediately after the increase in the world interest rate, but before the domestic rate adjusts, the economy is at point A, with the domestic rate at r_0^* but the world rate at r_1^*. Domestic savers are encouraged to send their funds abroad where the return is higher. This increases the demand for the foreign currency, and would tend to bid up the exchange rate and depreciate the domestic currency. However, the exchange rate is fixed. Instead, the increased demand for foreign currency is met by an increase in the supply of foreign currency of sufficient magnitude to keep the exchange rate constant. The foreign central bank trades its currency for the domestic currency, reducing the amount of domestic money in circulation while increasing the foreign money stock. The domestic money supply shrinks and the domestic interest rate rises, since it takes a higher domestic interest rate to make money demand decline to equal the smaller money supply. Eventually the domestic real interest rate rises to equal the world real interest rate, and equilibrium is restored at point B. Thus, the increase in the world interest rate leads not only to an increase in the domestic interest rate, but also to a decrease in the domestic money supply and a decline in real income.

A reduction in the world interest rate would have the opposite effect, leading to a reduction in the domestic real interest rate, an increase in the money supply, and an increase in the equilibrium level of income.

POLICY ACTIONS WITH FIXED EXCHANGE RATES

We turn next to an analysis of policy actions and their effect on the money supply and income. In Figure 7–13 we illustrate an increase in government spending. Recall that government spending affects the IS curve but not the LM curve. The increase in government spending shifts IS to the right. The intersection of IS and LM shifts from point A to point B. However, at point B the domestic interest rate is above the world rate. This results in an inflow of foreign saving, an increase in the supply of foreign currency. Since the exchange rate is fixed, the domestic central bank must purchase this increased supply of foreign currency, supplying domestic currency in the process and increasing the domestic money supply. This increase in the domestic money supply causes the LM curve to shift to the right, to LM_1, so that the intersection of the new IS and new LM curves is at point C, where the domestic real interest rate is again the same as the world rate, but where real income has increased to Y_1. Compare the change in effectiveness of fiscal policy between fixed and flexible

FIGURE 7−13
Fiscal Policy in the Small
Open Economy with Fixed
Exchange Rates

The increase in government spending from G to G' shifts the IS curve to the right. After this shift, IS intersects LM at point B. Since the real interest rate is above the world real interest rate, this leads to an inflow of foreign financial capital and tends to appreciate the currency. However, with fixed exchange rates the monetary authority must respond to this by supplying additional units of the domestic currency. This increases the money supply and shifts the LM curve to point C. Real income has increased from Y_0 to Y_1.

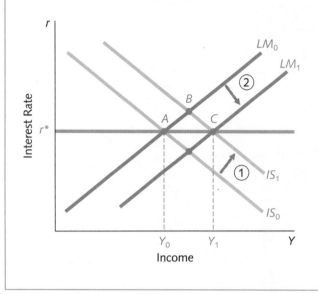

exchange rates: Under flexible exchange rates fiscal policy is ineffective at changing real income, whereas under fixed exchange rates fiscal policy is very effective.

The analysis in Figure 7−13 is for an increase in government spending, but the same would hold true for an increase in autonomous consumption, investment, or even autonomous net exports. All of these would shift IS rightward, with a resultant change in international capital flows that would cause the domestic money supply to increase, and cause equilibrium real income to rise.

Another policy action is an increase in the money supply, illustrated in Figure 7−14. Changes in the money supply will shift the LM curve, and, in particular, increases in the money supply shift LM to the right. In Figure 7−14 the initial LM curve is LM_0, and the initial equilibrium is at point A, with real income Y_0. An increase in the money supply shifts LM to the right, to LM_1, resulting in an intersection of IS and LM at point B. But at point B, the domestic interest rate is below the world rate. This induces an outflow of saving, as domestic savers take advantage of the more attractive world interest

FIGURE 7–14
Monetary Policy in the Small
Open Economy with Fixed
Exchange Rates

The increase in the money supply increases real money balances and shifts the *LM* curve to the right. After this shift, *LM* intersects *IS* at point *B*. The real interest rate is now below the world real interest rate. This leads to an outflow of financial capital and tends to depreciate the currency. To maintain fixed exchange rates the monetary authority must respond by supplying foreign currency out of its foreign currency reserves and letting this shrink the domestic money supply. Thus, the eventual decrease in the money supply, restoring the *LM* curve to its original position at point *A*.

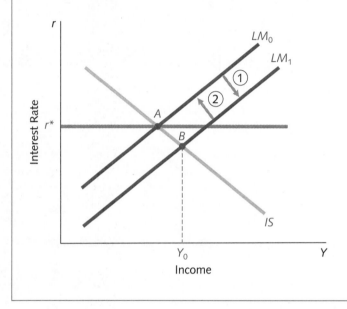

rate. The outflow of financial capital causes an increased demand for foreign currency, a demand that must be met by an increase in the supply of foreign currency in order to maintain the fixed exchange rate. However, this means the foreign central bank buys up the domestic currency, which reduces the domestic money supply and causes the *LM* curve to shift back to the left. In fact, to restore equilibrium between the domestic and world real interest rates, the money supply must decline back to its initial value, and *LM* must therefore shift back to the initial location, at LM_0. Thus, the initial increase in the money supply is completely offset by a reduction in the money supply, keeping equilibrium at point *A*, with no change in equilibrium real income. Again note the change in effectiveness of monetary policy between flexible and fixed exchange rates: Under flexible exchange rates monetary policy is effective at changing real income, whereas under fixed exchange rates monetary policy is ineffective.

The above discussion has been of the small open economy, either with a Classical model or the *IS-LM* model. A second variant is to look at a large open economy model. As mentioned earlier, the large open economy behaves as a cross between a small open economy and a closed economy. For example, an increase in government spending in the large open economy increases the world and domestic interest rates, but not as much as in a closed economy. In a small open economy, the increase in government spending would not change the world or domestic interest rate at all. Thus, the large open economy is something of an average of the behavior of the small open and the closed economy.

THE LARGE OPEN ECONOMY

The main distinction between the small open economy and the large open economy is that in a small open economy the world interest rate and the domestic interest rate must coincide. This is an equilibrium relationship that holds in a small open economy. If it did not hold, there would be capital flows—flows of saving—from domestic nation to foreign nation, or vice versa, until the equilibrium was restored. Thus, if the interest rate in the small open economy were above the world rate, there would be an inflow of foreign financial capital until the domestic interest rate fell to equal the world rate. With flexible exchange rates, this would occur as the demand for the domestic currency caused the exchange rate to appreciate, reducing E and shifting *IS* to the left, and lowering the domestic interest rate. With fixed exchange rates, the increased demand for the domestic currency would induce the monetary authority to increase the supply of the domestic currency, which would cause the *LM* curve to shift to the right and lower the domestic interest rate. In either case, the domestic interest rate in equilibrium would be equal to the world interest rate.

In the large open economy, there is no such equilibrium condition between the domestic and world real interest rates. Instead, in the large open economy there can exist a discrepancy between these two rates as long as the current account balances the capital account. When the domestic interest rate is above the world rate, foreigners have an increased incentive to invest in the domestic economy, causing an inflow of foreign saving—a capital account surplus. This must be balanced by a current account deficit, or $NX < 0$. But this happens because the high domestic interest rate induces a high demand for the domestic currency, leading to an appreciation of the domestic currency (a decrease in E when the exchange rate is in dollars per unit of foreign currency) and thus to a reduction in net exports. Therefore, as the domestic real interest rate rises, the domestic currency must appreciate. However, this relationship between the real interest rate and the real exchange rate does not lead to the balance on the current account or on the capital account being driven to zero, as in the small open economy. Instead, the large open economy can have a persistent situation of a capital account surplus (or deficit), balanced by a current account deficit (or surplus), as long as the domestic real interest rate is above (or below) the world real interest rate.

The level of the real interest rate that equilibrates the current account and the capital account is given by a relationship we call the balance of payments, or BP, line. This line indicates the combinations of the domestic real interest rate and real income that yield a balance of payments between the current account and the capital account. This BP line is an upward sloping line, to indicate that an increase in the domestic real interest rate, which leads to an inflow of foreign saving and hence a current account surplus, is balanced by a current account deficit, caused by an increase in income, which increases imports and hence reduces net exports. As the domestic real rate increases relative to the world rate, there are greater and greater capital flows toward the domestic country. Thus, instead of having a horizontal line at r^* to indicate that the domestic real rate must equal r^*, we have an upward sloping balance of payments line BP. In Figure 7–15, we graph BP. At point B, the world and domestic interest rates are equal, and the balance of payments is such that the capital account and the current account are both zero. At point A, the domestic real interest rate is r_0, which exceeds the world real rate of r^* and results in an inflow of foreign saving. This is a capital account surplus, which will be mirrored in a current account deficit, or $NX < 0$. This current account deficit is induced by an increase in income, which leads to a reduction in net exports. Similarly, at point C the domestic real rate of r_1 is below r^*, causing domestic saving to flow abroad, a capital account deficit but a current account surplus, and $NX > 0$.

Under a flexible exchange rate system, the relationship described above and illustrated in Figure 7–15 requires that a situation of rising domestic real interest rates also be a situation of increased demand for the domestic currency and hence an appreciation of the domestic currency, holding everything else constant. How well does this relationship show up in the data? For the U.S. economy, we graph both the real interest rate and the trade-weighted exchange rate in Figure 7–16. While this graph cannot hold everything else constant, it does give us an idea of whether increases in the domestic interest rate and appreciations of the currency tend to occur together. As the graph indicates, there is a tendency for this relationship to hold. In particular, the large increase in real interest rates during the period 1980–1982 was accompanied by a large appreciation of the dollar from 1981 to 1985. Since 1985, the real interest rate in the U.S. has declined gradually, and the exchange rate has depreciated much more quickly.

How does this affect our analysis of the adjustments to policy actions? In the small open economy, the equilibrium between IS and LM had to occur at the world interest rate r^*. In the large open economy, the equilibrium between IS and LM has to occur on the BP line. To see how this works, consider first the

FIGURE 7-15
The Balance of Payments
Curve

For the large open economy, the domestic real interest rate can be greater or less than the world real interest rate r^*. A domestic rate greater than the world rate induces an inflow of financial capital to the domestic economy—a surplus on the capital account—which must be balanced by net exports. A domestic real interest rate less than the world rate induces an outflow of financial capital from the domestic economy balanced by a positive value for net exports.

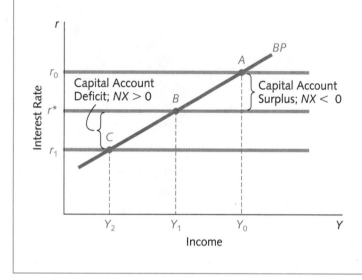

case of flexible exchange rates. A fiscal policy action is illustrated in Figure 7–17. The increase in government spending shifts *IS* to the right, to intersect with *LM* at point *B*. However, the interest rate at point *B* is above the rate that leads to a balance between the current account and the capital account. Instead, the high domestic real rate leads to a capital account surplus that is greater than the current account deficit. Thus, there is a greater demand for dollars, causing the exchange rate to fall—the dollar to appreciate—and net exports to decline. As this occurs, *IS* shifts to the left, eventually returning to point *A*, with an unchanged equilibrium real income. Again, we see a case of crowding out for the large open economy, similar to the case for the small open economy with flexible exchange rates discussed earlier.

The case of monetary policy with flexible exchange rates is also similar to the small open economy, as illustrated in Figure 7–18. Here the increase in the money supply to *M'* shifts *LM* to the right, to intersect with *IS* at point *B*. However, at point *B* the domestic real interest rate is too low for balance between the current account and the capital account. Instead, the low domestic rate leads to a larger capital account deficit than there is a current account surplus. This net increase in demand for foreign currency causes the dollar to depreciate and net exports to increase, shifting *IS* to the right. The final

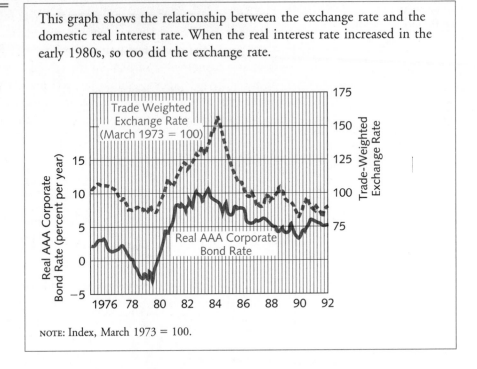

This graph shows the relationship between the exchange rate and the domestic real interest rate. When the real interest rate increased in the early 1980s, so too did the exchange rate.

NOTE: Index, March 1973 = 100.

equilibrium is at point *C,* where the *IS* curve intersects the *LM* curve. Real income has increased to Y_1.

Finally, what about fixed exchange rates? Again, there is a similarity between the large and small open economies. To see this, consider an increase in government spending, such as is illustrated in Figure 7–19. The increase in government spending shifts *IS* to the right, to intersect with *LM* at point *B.* However, the interest rate at point *B* is above the rate that leads to balance between the current account and the capital account. Instead, the high domestic real rate leads to a capital account surplus that is greater than the current account deficit. Thus, there is a greater demand for dollars, causing the domestic monetary authority to supply dollars and increase the money supply. This shifts *LM* to the right, to intersect the new *IS* curve at point *C.* Both the domestic real interest rate and real income have increased. A key point is that fiscal policy in this case of fixed exchange rates is effective at changing real income, just as it was for the small open economy.

The case of monetary policy is also similar to that in the small open economy, as illustrated in Figure 7–20. Here, the increase in the money supply shifts *LM* to the right, to intersect with *IS* at point *B.* However, at point *B* the domestic real interest rate is too low for balance between the current account and the capital account. Instead, the low domestic rate leads to a larger capital account deficit than there is a current account surplus. This net increase in demand for foreign currency must be met by an increase in the supply of the

FIGURE 7−17
Fiscal Policy in the Large
Open Economy with Flexible
Exchange Rates

The increase in government spending shifts the *IS* curve to the right. After this shift, *IS* intersects *LM* at point *B*. The real interest rate is r_1, which is above the level of the real interest rate on the *BP* curve that gives balance between the current account and the capital account r_0. This leads to an inflow of foreign financial capital and an appreciation of the currency, shifting *IS* back to the same position as the original *IS* curve.

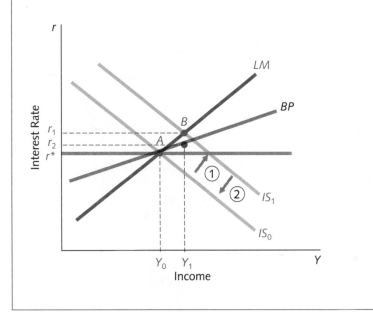

foreign currency. In effect, the dollars that on net are sent overseas to earn a higher interest rate are purchased and held by the foreign central bank, leading to a reduction in the domestic money supply. This shifts *LM* back to the left, to intersect *IS* at the final equilibrium of point *A*. Thus, monetary policy is ineffective with fixed exchange rates.

The key result for both small and large economies is that under flexible exchange rates monetary policy is effective at changing real output and fiscal policy is ineffective, while under fixed exchange rates fiscal policy is effective and monetary policy is ineffective. Thus, we see that the choice of exchange rate regimes is very important to economies and especially to policymakers. It does not make much sense to adopt fixed exchange rates and then expect to stabilize the economy with monetary policy, just as it does not make much sense to adopt flexible exchange rates and then attempt to stabilize the economy with fiscal policy. This is a lesson for both small and large open economies, and a lesson that should be heeded in the United States today. The United States is clearly a large open economy with flexible exchange rates, and

FIGURE 7-18
Monetary Policy in the Large
Open Economy with Flexible
Exchange Rates

The increase in the money supply increases real money balances and shifts the *LM* curve to the right. After this shift, *LM* intersects *IS* at point *B*. The real interest rate is now below the rate that gives a balance of payments. This leads to an outflow of financial capital and a depreciation of the currency, shifting *IS* to the right to point *C*. Equilibrium at point *C* has a higher real interest rate and a higher real income level than at point *A*.

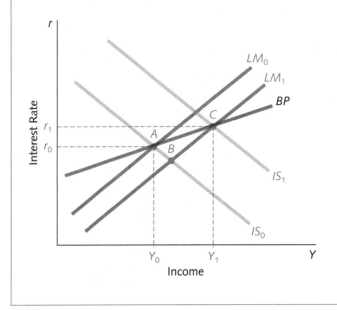

in such a situation monetary policy will be most effective at providing a stabilizing role in the macroeconomy.

To summarize the differences in the effect of monetary and fiscal policy actions on the closed economy, the small open economy, and the large open economy, consider Table 7–3. Here we indicate the predicted effect in the *IS-LM* model of a change in government spending and in the money supply for the closed economy, the small open economy under fixed and flexible exchange rates, and the large open economy under fixed and flexible exchange rates. Notice the comparison of policy effectiveness under these alternatives. For a fiscal policy action—an increase in government spending—the closed economy has an increase in both the real interest rate and real income. In the small open economy, there is no effect on the real interest rate, which is always equal to the world rate. The effect on real income depends on whether exchange rates are fixed or flexible. With fixed exchange rates, the increase in government spending will increase real income, while with flexible exchange

FIGURE 7-19
Fiscal Policy in the Large Open Economy with Fixed Exchange Rates

The increase in government spending shifts the *IS* curve to the right. After this shift, *IS* intersects *LM* at point *B*. The real interest rate is now above the real interest rate consistent with balance of payments, which leads to an inflow of foreign financial capital and tends to appreciate the currency. With fixed exchange rates the monetary authority must respond to this by supplying additional units of the domestic currency, which shifts the *LM* curve to point *C* where the real interest rate has risen to r_1, and real income has increased to Y_1.

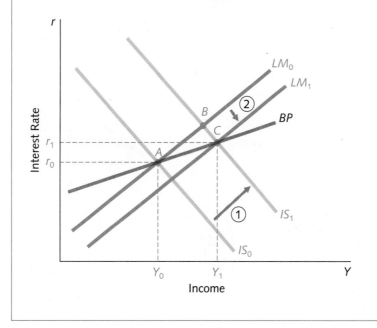

rates the increase in government spending will have no effect on real income. Finally, for the large open economy, the increase in government spending continues to have no effect under flexible exchange rates, but under fixed exchange rates there will be an increase in both the real interest rate and real income, just as in the closed economy.

Table 7–3 also summarizes the effect of monetary policy. An increase in the money supply will decrease the interest rate and increase real income in the closed economy. In the small open economy, there is no effect on the real interest rate, and no effect on real income under fixed exchange rates, but under flexible exchange rates real income will increase. Finally, for the large open economy under fixed exchange rates the monetary policy action is ineffective, but under flexible exchange rates the real interest rate falls and real income increases, similar to the closed economy case. Thus, we see that in

FIGURE 7-20
Monetary Policy in the Large
Open Economy with Fixed
Exchange Rates

The increase in the money supply increases real money balances and shifts the *LM* curve to the right. After this shift, *LM* intersects *IS* at point *B*. The real interest rate is now below the interest rate consistent with balance of payments equilibrium. This leads to an outflow of financial capital and tends to depreciate the currency. To maintain fixed exchange rates the monetary authority must respond by supplying foreign currency out of its foreign currency reserves and letting this shrink the domestic money supply; this restores the *LM* curve to its original position at point *A*.

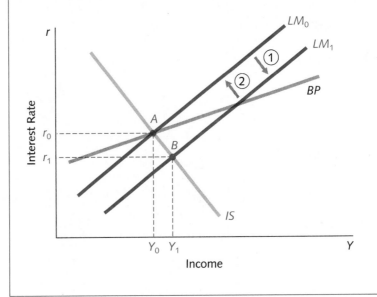

TABLE 7-3
A Comparison of the Effects
of Fiscal and Monetary Policy
in the Closed and Open
Economy

This table summarizes the different responses of the real interest rate and real income to an increase in government spending or an increase in the money supply for the various models discussed in the text.

POLICY ACTION:	ΔG		ΔM	
RESPONSE:	Δr	ΔY	Δr	ΔY
CLOSED ECONOMY	+	+	−	+
SMALL OPEN ECONOMY				
a) FIXED EXCHANGE RATES	o	+	o	o
b) FLEXIBLE EXCHANGE RATES	o	o	o	+
LARGE OPEN ECONOMY				
a) FIXED EXCHANGE RATES	+	+	o	o
b) FLEXIBLE EXCHANGE RATES	o	o	−	+

some ways the large open economy is like the closed economy, and in other ways it is like the small open economy. We also see again the importance of the exchange rate regime to the effectiveness of fiscal and monetary policy in the open economy.

SUMMARY

A model of the demand-side economy incorporating interest rate and income as variables was developed in Chapters 4 through 6. Private spending, public spending, and, in this chapter, a foreign trade and finance sector have now all been accounted for.

We have examined in this chapter the foreign exchange market under flexible and fixed exchange rates, the concepts of government and trade deficits, including recent developments in the U.S. dollar. A foreign trade sector was added to the *IS-LM* model, and this model was used to analyze various fiscal and monetary policy actions.

We need to be aware that our *IS-LM* model relates to income or output determination. We have been studying in this chapter exclusively the principles that determine the aggregate demand for the output of goods and services as if the output and employment associated with various income levels were fixed, or, in the Mundel-Fleming model, reacted passively to demand. The modern role of trade in this macroeconomic process of demand formulation is becoming ever more important.

KEY TERMS

arbitrage possibilities

covered interest arbitrage

covered interest parity

exchange rate appreciation

exchange rate depreciation

forward exchange rate

large open economy

small open economy

spot exchange rate

QUESTIONS FOR REVIEW AND DISCUSSION

1. Define the term *exchange rate*. What is the difference between fixed exchange rates and flexible exchange rates?

2. Suppose the exchange rate between U.S. dollars and the British pound changes from $2 = £1 to $5 = £1. Will British goods cost more or less to U.S. households? Explain why.

3. Is there any difference between depreciation and appreciation of a currency? If so, what is it?

4. If you are going to be visiting France and you read that the dollar is appreciating, does this mean that your hotel in Paris is going to cost you more U.S. dollars or fewer U.S. dollars? Why?

5. Why have economists, in recent years, expressed concern over the decrease in the real value of the dollar relative to other foreign currencies?

6. In a small open economy, an increase in government spending will cause the currency to appreciate. True or false? Explain your answer.

7. In a small open economy, an increase in autonomous saving will cause the currency to appreciate. True or false? Explain your answer.

8. Using the *IS-LM* graph for a small open economy, demonstrate the effect of an increase in the money supply on the exchange rate and on net exports.

9. Using the *IS-LM* graph for a small open economy, explain the effect of an increase in the world interest rate on the exchange rate and on net exports.

10. Using the *IS-LM* graph for a small open economy, explain the effect of an increase in real output on the exchange rate and on net exports. Does the interest rate change?

11. Consider an increase in tariffs in a large open economy. This would reduce imports, and hence increase net exports. We might think of this as an autonomous increase in net exports, an increase in the term n_0 from the net export equation. What effect does this have on the equilibrium quantity of net exports and on the exchange rate?

12. In a large open economy, an increase in government spending will cause the currency to appreciate. True or false? Explain your answer.

13. In a large open economy, an increase in autonomous saving will cause the currency to appreciate. True or false? Explain your answer.

14. Using the *IS-LM* graph for a large open economy, demonstrate the effect of an increase in the money supply on the exchange rate and on net exports.

PROBLEMS

1. Construct a model showing a decrease in the world real interest rate in a small open economy. Use the *IS-LM* model with flexible exchange rates assumed. Do investors move funds to the small open economy with the decrease in world interest rates? Does the currency of the small open economy depreciate or appreciate with respect to the rest of the world? In equilibrium does the interest rate in the small economy rise or fall? Does income rise or fall in equilibrium? Show your results with a graph.

2. Using the *IS-LM* graph for a large open economy, explain the effect of an increase in the world interest rate on the exchange rate and on net exports.

SUGGESTIONS FOR FURTHER READING

Bergstrand, Jeffrey H. "Exchange Rate Variation and Monetary Policy." Federal Reserve Bank of Boston *New England Economic Review* (May/June 1985), pp. 5–18.

————. "Bretton Woods Revisited." Federal Reserve Bank of Boston *New England Economic Review* (September/October 1984), pp. 23–33.

Coughlin, Cletus, and Kees Koedijk. "What Do We Know About the Long Run Exchange Rate?" Federal Reserve Bank of St. Louis *Review* (January/February 1990), pp. 36–48.

Hakkio, Craig. "Is Purchasing Power Parity a Useful Guide to the Dollar?" Federal Reserve Bank of Kansas City *Economic Review* (Third Quarter, 1992), pp. 37–51.

Jacobson, Kristina. "U.S. Foreign Exchange Operations." Federal Reserve Bank of Kansas City *Economic Review* (September/October 1990), pp. 37–50.

McKinnon, Ronald I. *An International Standard for Monetary Stabilization.* Washington, DC: Institute for International Economics, March 1984.

Scarlata, Jodi G. "Institutional Developments in the Globalization of Securities and Futures Markets." Federal Reserve Bank of St. Louis *Review* (January/February 1992), pp. 17-30.

APPENDIX: INTEREST RATE PARITY AND EXCHANGE RATES

The **SPOT EXCHANGE RATE** is the rate at which you can contract today to trade a given amount of one currency for another today.

The foreign exchange market actually consists of two components, a spot market and a forward market. The spot market is the market for trading foreign currencies in which an agreement to exchange currencies is made today at an exchange rate determined today for a trade that will be carried out today. Of course, today means within three days or so, but the idea is that the transaction is carried out right away at a price agreed upon at this time. In contrast, there is a forward market for trading foreign currencies in which an agreement to exchange currencies is made today at an exchange rate determined today for a trade that will be carried out at a specified future date, usually 30 or 90 or 180 days forward. Thus, the spot market is for trades that are not only agreed to, but are carried out today, whereas the forward market is for trades that are agreed to today but that are carried out some time in the future, forward of the date of the contract.

Exchange rates are reported for both the spot and the forward markets, but the forward market is available only in heavily traded currencies. Thus, in Table A-1 we reproduce a table of exchange rate quotes from *The Wall Street*

TABLE A-I
Exchange Rates, Spot and
Forward, March 23, 1992

This table presents a reproduction of the table listing spot and forward exchange rates that appears daily in *The Wall Street Journal.*

EXCHANGE RATES

Monday, March 23, 1992

The New York foreign exchange selling rates below apply to trading among banks in amounts of $1 million and more, as quoted at 3 P.M. Eastern time by Bankers Trust Co., Telerate Systems Inc. and other sources. Retail transactions provide fewer units of foreign currency per dollar.

| | U.S. $ EQUIV. | | CURRENCY PER U.S. $ | |
COUNTRY	MON.	FRI.	MON.	FRI.
ARGENTINA (PESO)	1.01	1.03	.99	.97
AUSTRALIA (DOLLAR)	.7609	.7595	1.3142	1.3167
AUSTRIA (SCHILLING)	.08520	.08510	11.74	11.75
BAHRAIN (DINAR)	2.6532	2.6525	.3769	.3770
BELGIUM (FRANC)	.02913	.02909	34.33	34.37
BRAZIL (CRUZEIRO)	.00054	.00056	1857.01	1784.00
BRITAIN (POUND)	1.7185	1.7140	.5819	.5834
30-DAY FORWARD	1.7086	1.7049	.5853	.5866
90-DAY FORWARD	1.6914	1.6871	.5912	.5927
180-DAY FORWARD	1.6663	1.6620	.6001	.6017
CANADA (DOLLAR)	.8382	.8349	1.1930	1.1978
30-DAY FORWARD	.8362	.8328	1.1959	1.2008
90-DAY FORWARD	.8320	.8284	1.2019	1.2072
180-DAY FORWARD	.8261	.8218	1.2105	1.2168
CZECHOSLOVAKIA (KORUNA)				
COMMERCIAL RATE	.0151617	.0351617	28.4400	28.4400
CHILE (PESO)	.002914	.002952	343.22	338.79
CHINA (RENMINBL)	.182508	.182632	5.4792	5.4755
COLUMBIA (PESO)	.001760	.001689	568.23	592.10
DENMARK (KRONE)	.1545	.1540	6.4710	6.4921
ECUADOR (SUCRE) FLOATING RATE	.000772	.000766	1294.80	1306.01
FINLAND (MARKKA)	.22002	.21939	4.5450	4.5581
FRANCE (FRANC)	.17679	.17646	5.6565	5.6670
30-DAY FORWARD	.17586	.17560	5.6865	5.6948
90-DAY FORWARD	.17423	.17392	5.7397	5.7498
180-DAY FORWARD	.17198	.17172	5.8145	5.8233

TABLE A-1
Exchange Rates, Spot and
Forward, March 23,
1992—*Continued*

COUNTRY	U.S. $ EQUIV.		CURRENCY PER U.S. $	
	MON.	FRI.	MON.	FRI.
GERMANY (MARK)	.5995	.5986	1.6680	1.6705
30-DAY FORWARD	.5966	.5958	1.6763	1.6783
90-DAY FORWARD	.5914	.5905	1.6909	1.6934
180-DAY FORWARD	.5842	.5836	1.7116	1.7134
GREECE (DRACHMA)	.005176	.005171	193.20	193.40
HONG KONG (DOLLAR)	.12913	.12912	7.7440	7.7450
HUNGARY (FORINT)	.0126151	.0126151	79.2700	79.2700
INDIA (RUPEE)	.03487	.03542	28.68	28.23
INDONESIA (RUPIAH)	.0004975	.0004968	2010.01	2013.00
IRELAND (UNT)	1.5993	1.5944	.6253	.6272
ISRAEL (SHEKEL)	.4131	.4248	2.4210	2.3542
ITALY (LIRA)	.0007976	.0007967	1253.84	1255.22
JAPAN (YEN)	.007487	.007477	133.56	133.75
30-DAY FORWARD	.007482	.007472	133.66	133.84
90-DAY FORWARD	.007478	.007468	133.72	133.90
180-DAY FORWARD	.007483	.007473	133.63	133.82
JORDAN (DINAR)	1.4832	1.4874	.6742	.6723
KUWAIT (DINAR)	3.3750	3.3789	.2963	.2960
LEBANON (POUND)	.000844	.000873	1185.00	1145.00
MALAYSIA (RINGGLT)	.3888	.3861	2.5720	2.5900
MALTA (LIRA)	3.0675	3.0722	.3260	.3255
MEXICO (PESO) FLOATING RATE .	.0003258	.0003268	3069.00	3060.00
NETHERLAND (GUILDER)	.5325	.5317	1.8779	1.8809
NEW ZEALAND (DOLLAR)	.5494	.5495	1.8202	1.8198
NORWAY (KRONE)	.1528	.1523	6.5450	6.5674
PAKISTAN (RUPEE)	.0404	.0404	24.77	24.77
PERU (NEW SOL)	1.0686	1.0743	.94	.93
PHILIPPINES (PESO)	.04115	.04016	24.30	24.90
POLAND (ZLOTY)	.00008065	.00008065	12400.01	12400.01
PORTUGAL (ESCUDO)	.006964	.006959	143.60	143.70
SAUDIA ARABIA (RIYAL)	.26738	.26738	3.7400	3.7400
SINGAPORE (DOLLAR)	.6008	.6015	1.6645	1.6625

TABLE A-I
Exchange Rates, Spot and Forward, March 23, 1992—*Continued*

| | U.S. $ EQUIV. | | CURRENCY PER U.S. $ | |
COUNTRY	MON.	FRI.	MON.	FRI.
SOUTH AFRICA (RAND)				
COMMERCIAL RATE	.3461	.3458	2.8890	2.8918
FINANCIAL RATE	.2833	.2801	3.5300	3.5700
SOUTH KOREA (WON)	.0013169	.0012963	759.34	771.41
SPAIN (PESETA)	.009500	.009481	105.27	105.48
SWEDEN (KRONA)	.1654	.1647	6.0475	6.0705
SWITZERLAND (FRANC)	.6595	.6595	1.5163	1.5162
30-DAY FORWARD	.6589	.6570	1.5177	1.5220
90-DAY FORWARD	.6522	.6525	1.5333	1.5325
180-DAY FORWARD	.6467	.6473	1.5463	1.5449
TAIWAN (DOLLAR)	.039565	.039714	25.27	25.18
THAILAND (BAHT)	.03896	.03897	25.67	25.66
TURKEY (LIRA)	.0001630	.0001642	6136.02	6091.00
UNITED ARAB (DIRHAM)	.2723	.2723	3.6725	3.6725
URUGUAY (NEW PESO) FINAN-CIAL	.000354	.000357	2825.00	2800.01
VENEZUELA (BOLIVAR) FLOATING RATE..........................	.01538	.01574	65.00	63.53

SOURCE: *The Wall Street Journal* (March 24, 1992).

The **FORWARD EXCHANGE RATE** is the rate at which you can contract today to trade a given amount of one currency for another at a specified future date.

Journal. Consider the quote for Britain on March 23, 1992. The table lists the exchange rate both in "U.S. $ equivalent," which is the number of dollars it takes to buy one unit of the foreign currency, and in "currency per U.S. $," which is the number of units of the foreign currency that can be bought with one U.S. dollar. For example, on Monday, March 23, it took 1.7185 U.S. dollars to buy 1 British pound, or .587 of a British pound to buy 1 U.S. dollar. These rates are just the inverse of each other, since $1.7185/£ = 1/ (£.587/$). This is the spot rate operative on the date indicated. If you had a sum of dollars (or pounds), you could trade those dollars for pounds at the indicated rate, and the transaction would have to be physically consummated instantly, or at least within a few days of contracting your broker. In contrast, you could also transact at the **forward exchange rates.** For example, the 30-day forward rate between dollars and pounds is $1.7086/£, or £.5853/$. Again, note that these rates are equivalent, with one just the inverse of the other, so that $1.7086/ £ = 1/ (£.5853/$). With a sum of dollars, you could contract to exchange the dollars for pounds at this rate today, but the physical transaction would not take place for 30 days. Further, there are rates quoted for 90 days forward, at $1.6914/£, and 180 days forward, at $1.6663/£.

What determines the spot exchange rates, and what determines the relationship between the spot and forward rates? This entire chapter has been devoted to a discussion of the determination of exchange rates, so we will bypass that question for the time being and return to it later. As for the question of the relationship between the forward and spot exchange rates, it turns out that we know quite a bit about how these are determined, or at least how they are related to each other. An arbitrage condition links the spot and forward exchange rates and foreign and domestic interest rates, and it is to this that our discussion now turns.

In order to understand this arbitrage condition, consider the example of an investor looking for the best possible return. To be concrete, let's assume you are that investor, and you have $10,000 to invest. You might want to invest this money for a period of three months, and you are willing to consider investing it only in safe government bonds or CDs. We have reproduced a table of interest rates in alternative countries in Table A-2. In March 1992 you could earn 4.32 percent annual interest on a three-month investment in the U.S. money market. However, since you only earn this 4.32 percent for three months or one-fourth of a year, after three months you would have earned $10,000 \times (1 + .0432/4) = $10,108. Alternatively, you might want to invest in a three-month equally safe investment in Great Britain (also referred to as

TABLE A-2 International Money and Interest Rates	This table indicates the interest rate on short-term money market instruments for March 17, 1992.

	3 MONTHS
AUSTRALIA	7.42
CANADA	7.42
FRANCE	10.05
GERMANY	11.04
HOLLAND	9.59
ITALY	12.32
JAPAN	4.90
SWITZERLAND	8.57
UK	10.69
USA	4.32

SOURCE: *The Economist* (March 23, 1992) and authors' estimations.

the United Kingdom or U.K.). In this case, you could earn 10.69 percent annual interest on a three-month investment. This seems too good to be true when comparing it to the U.S. rate, and indeed it is. As the astute reader will already have noticed, this 10.69 percent interest rate is the rate of return on placing British pounds in a three-month money market investment in Great Britain. It ignores problems of the exchange rate. Of course, we can take care of those problems in the foreign exchange market.

Remember, you have $10,000 to invest. If you first convert it into pounds at the spot rate of £.587/$, you will have £587 (ignoring brokerage fees for the transactions). You can invest those £587 in a three-month money market account and earn 10.69 percent annual interest. After three months you will have £587 $\times$ (1 + .1069/4) = £5974.51. Of course, now there arises another problem. If you invest in the United States, after three months you have $10,108, whereas with the U.K. investment you have £5974.51. You can then turn the pounds back into dollars at the spot rate available at that time, but there is a risk of exchange rate fluctuations. What is the solution? The solution is to use the forward market. When you trade dollars for pounds and invest at the specified U.K. interest rate, you can calculate that you will have £5974.51 in three months or 90 days. But on the very day that you convert your $10,000 into pounds and invest the pounds in Europe, you can sign a forward contract to sell £5974.51 for dollars. On March 22, 1992, the 90-day forward rate for trading pounds into dollars was 1.6914 dollars per pound, so you would convert your £5974.51 into dollars at this agreed upon price, getting £5974.51 $\times$ $1.6914/£ = $10,105.29. Thus you have two alternative investments, equally risky *as long as the U.S. and U.K. money markets are seen as equally risky.*

From the U.K. investment you can invest $10,000 today, either by converting it into pounds and purchasing a U.K. money market account today, or by signing a contract to convert the pounds you will have in 90 days back into dollars at a set rate. This will give you $10,105.29 in 90 days, with no risk of exchange rate changes. Alternatively, you can just invest the $10,000 in a U.S. 90-day money market account today, and have $10,108 in 90 days. Because these two alternate investments are equally risky, an investor should go with the one that pays the higher return. Of course, this means that the investments should pay the same return; otherwise there would be **arbitrage possibilities**—possibilities for riskless profit by choosing one investment over the other. Such arbitrage guarantees that the market rates of return on these two alternatives stay very close together. Indeed, they should differ only by the transactions cost differences in going to the foreign exchange market twice for the U.K. investment.

In our particular example, the U.S. investment yielded a marginally higher return than the U.K. investment despite the much higher interest rates in Britain. The exchange market thinks the pound will depreciate relative to the dollar over the next 90 days, so that it will take more pounds to buy a dollar 90 days from now. This depreciation of the pound eats up the extra return

ARBITRAGE POSSIBILITIES are possibilities for riskless profit by choosing one investment over another. Arbitrage guarantees that the market rates of return on two alternative investments stay very close together.

COVERED INTEREST ARBITRAGE is the arbitrage that keeps the relative interest rates of two nations related to the difference between the current spot exchange rate and the forward exchange rate.

COVERED INTEREST PARITY is a condition linking the interest rate differential between two nations to the difference between the spot and forward exchange rate.

given by the higher U.K. interest rate, and in fact causes the total return on the U.K. investment to be marginally smaller than the return on the U.S. investment. The U.S. return can be calculated as $(1 + R_{US})$, while the U.K. return is $e_{spot} \times (1 + R_{UK}) \times 1/e_{forward}$ (for an exchange rate in pounds per dollar—the currency per U.S. $ column of Table A-1). For the United States this is $1 + .0432/4 = 1.0108$, and for Britain this is $.587 \times (1 + .1069/4) \times 1/.5912 = 1.0106$. This calculation shows that the U.K. return is slightly lower than the U.S. return, as we already knew.

Consider a U.S.–Canadian example. The U.S. 90-day return will be 1.0108, as we already calculated. In Canada, the 90-day interest rate is 7.42 percent in Table A-2. The spot rate in Canadian dollars per U.S. dollar is 1.730, and the 90-day forward rate is 1.207. The return on investing for 90 days in Canada is $1.730 \times (1 + .0742/4) \times 1/1.207 = 1.0110$, which is slightly higher than the rate of return in the United States. On a $10,000 investment, you would have $10,108 from investing in the United States, and $10,110 from investing in Canada. Of course, this does not take into account brokerage fees, which would tend to be higher for individuals going to the foreign exchange market. The point, however, is that the returns on these two investment opportunities are remarkably similar despite differing nominal interest rates across countries. The arbitrage that keeps these returns equal is called **covered interest arbitrage,** and the condition that these returns are equal is called the **covered interest parity** condition. It holds because the alternative investment choices are equally risky and hence have to pay the same return to keep investors from shifting to another with a higher return.

QUESTIONS

1. What is the interest rate parity condition, and why does it hold? Why might interest rate parity hold when purchasing power parity does not seem to hold?

2. Explain clearly how market forces work to create a tendency to interest rate parity.

8

MONETARISM, INFLATION, AND

UNEMPLOYMENT

Monetarism was a reaction to the Keynesian orthodoxy of the early postwar years. As we have seen, Keynesian economics preached that the economy was unstable due to instabilities in autonomous aggregate demand such as autonomous investment. Because of market imperfections such as nominal wage rigidities, any instabilities in aggregate demand could lead to persistent unemployment, and in such situations the economy had weak or nonexistent forces that would move it back toward full employment. These same rigidities, however, gave policymakers the ability to alter aggregate demand and cause improvements in output and employment. In particular, Keynesians stressed fiscal policy as the appropriate method for stabilizing output and employment.

Monetarism challenged the Keynesian orthodoxy on several fronts. First, the Monetarists, such as Nobel laureate Milton Friedman, considered the economy to be generally stable. Instabilities were blamed on policymakers themselves instead of on autonomous changes in investment or consumption. While in agreement that institutional factors lead to persistent effects of changes in aggregate demand, they disagreed with the Keynesians on the degree of persistence. In fact, they argued that the economy would return to a full employment state more quickly than the Keynesians suggested. The Monetarists downplayed the role of fiscal policy and stressed the ability of monetary policy to affect the economy. More importantly, they believed policymakers did more harm than good when they attempted to manipulate the economy, and unstable policy was blamed for any observed instabilities in the economy. As an alternative to the activist, discretionary Keynesian policy prescriptions, Monetarists argued for stable policy rules, such as Milton Friedman's 3 percent money growth rule, as a way of keeping policy and hence the economy stable.

In this chapter we consider the Monetarist model, and present some of the key differences between the Keynesians and the Monetarists, including their views on inflation and on the policy prescription regarding the Phillips curve trade-off between inflation and unemployment.[1] Monetarists stress that inflation is always and everywhere a monetary phenomenon, and that to cure inflation there must be a reduction in the rate of growth of the money supply.

The important points of this chapter are

- the definition of inflation
- the methods for calculating inflation statistics
- the Monetarist view of inflation as due to money growth
- nonmonetary theories of inflation, such as the wage-push or product monopoly hypothesis
- a Monetarist concept of aggregate supply, including the concept of adaptive expectations and the difference between perceived and actual real wages
- the Phillips curve link between inflation and unemployment and U.S. data on the Phillips curve
- the Monetarist view of an expectations-augmented Phillips curve, and its relation to standard concepts of aggregate demand and supply.

---

[1]A. W. Phillips, "The Relation Between Unemployment and the Rate of Change of Money Wage Rates in the United Kingdom, 1861–1957," *Economica* 25 (November 1958), pp. 283–99.

INFLATION

INFLATION is a persistent increase in the general price level.

The term **inflation** is often misused. Earlier, the "once-and-for-all" increase in the money stock or in the price level was distinguished from the behavior of such variables over time, but these differences must now be drawn into clearer focus. The basic distinction to be made is between the *level* of some variable at some specific time and the *rate of change* in the same variable over time. In the former case, the magnitude of the variable (prices in this case) is of interest (i.e., whether it is high or low). Questions about the *rate of change* concern whether a variable is rising, falling, or remaining the same over time. While this is a somewhat obvious distinction, it must always be kept in mind when dealing with inflation.

Change in a variable may be discussed in several ways, as we noted in Chapter 2. An *absolute* rate of change in prices, for example, may be denoted ΔP, with Δ (delta) meaning "a change in," so $\Delta P = P_t - P_{t-1}$. If the price of a hamburger was \$2 in 1992 and \$3 in 1993, we may say that the simple change in price ($\Delta P_{hamburger}$) was \$1. But there is yet another way of looking at changes in a magnitude such as price, and that is to look at percentage changes. A percentage change in a variable is its absolute change divided by some base level of the variable.

Consider our example. Since the price of hamburgers was \$2 in 1992 and \$3 in 1993, ΔP, the absolute price change, is \$1. But the percentage change is the absolute change divided by the price in the base year, which we will take to be 1992. Thus, the price of hamburgers increases at a rate of $\Delta P/P$, or \$1/\$2 = .50—or 50 percent—over the year.

When we talk about inflation, we will be talking about the annual percentage change in the price level. Even here, however, we must be careful to define exactly what is meant by inflation. Any change in the price level can be reported as an absolute change or converted into a percentage change. What is important is whether the change in the price level is a once-and-for-all change, such as would be caused by a once-and-for-all increase in the money supply, or whether the change in the price level is a recurring phenomenon. In the latter case, the price level is continually rising at some percentage rate over time. Inflation is usually defined as a continually rising price level.

Figure 8-1 illustrates a once-and-for-all change in the money supply. Graph (a) plots the level of the money stock M against time. The money stock is constant until time t_0, at which point it has a once-and-for-all "jump" to a new, higher level. It then remains at this higher level. Graph (b) plots the percentage change in the money stock $\Delta M/M$. Notice that the growth rate of the money stock is zero both before *and* after the once-and-for-all change in the money supply at time t_0. At the time of the once-and-for-all change, the rate of growth of the money supply is very large and is represented by a spike in the graph of the percentage change in the money supply.

FIGURE 8-1

A Once-and-for-all Change in the Money Stock

Graphs (a) and (b) illustrate an increase in the money stock at time t_0. The growth rate of the money stock is zero before and after t_0. Graphs (c) and (d) show a jump in an already increasing money stock. The money stock grows at a steady rate before and after time t_1.

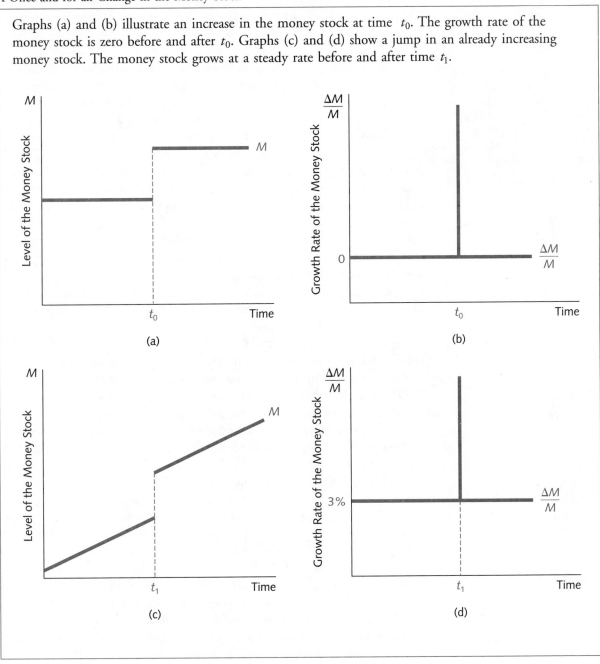

Figure 8-1 (c) and (d) illustrate a once-and-for-all change in the money stock when the money stock is already growing at a 3 percent annual rate. Thus, M grows at a 3 percent annual rate until time t_1. At time t_1, M jumps to a new, higher level, from which it continues to grow at 3 percent a year. Graph (c) illustrates this by a parallel shift in the path of M at time t_1. In Graph (d), the growth rate of M is a constant 3 percent both before *and* after t_1. There is a spike representing a very large growth rate at time t_1 to enable the money supply to jump to its higher level before continuing to grow at 3 percent. Thus, a growing money stock can also experience a once-and-for-all increase.

Figure 8-1 illustrates a way to think about once-and-for-all changes in the *level* of the money stock. This is the type of experiment that is contemplated in both the Classical and Keynesian models when we say that M increases. As an alternative to a once-and-for-all change in the level of M, we can consider a change in the growth rate of M, $\Delta M/M$. This is illustrated in Figure 8-2. In Figure 8-2 (a) and (b) the money stock grows at zero rate until t_0, at which time it grows at a 3 percent rate. In graph (a), the path of M is flat (i.e., constant) until t_0, when it grows at 3 percent, illustrated as an upward sloping path of M. Note that there is no jump in the level of M at time t_0, but only a change in the growth rate. In part (b), we plot the growth rate of M, $\Delta M/M$. Up to time t_0 the growth rate is constant at zero, and at time t_0 the growth rate jumps to 3 percent and is constant thereafter.

Figure 8-2 (c) and (d) illustrate a change in the growth rate of M from 3 percent to 6 percent at time t_1. This gives a change in the slope of the graph of M in (c), and a jump in the growth rate from 3 percent to 6 percent in (d).

Of course, it is possible to have a change in the level and a change in the growth rate at the same time. The key point is that changes in the *level* of M cause a jump in the path of M but no change in the growth rate, while changes in the *growth rate* of M cause a change in the slope of the path for M and a jump in the plot of the growth rate. These alternative changes in the path of M have differing effects on the economy, and shall be a topic of discussion later in this chapter.

Another useful distinction is between **ex ante** (before the fact) and **ex post** (after the fact). This distinction is important in discussing inflation and unemployment problems. For example, suppose you are a banker deciding how to set the nominal rate of interest on loans. Temporarily ignoring your competitors, you will want to consider two factors: (a) the real rate of interest, reflecting fundamental forces of borrowing and lending unrelated to inflation; and (b) your expectation of what will be the inflation rate over the year. (These are the factors that lie behind the famous **Fisher effect** discussed in Chapter 3.) If the real rate of interest is 4 percent and your expected inflation rate is 10 percent, then the nominal interest rate is 14 percent. We say that the *ex ante* real interest rate is 4 percent, meaning that you have set a nominal interest rate of 14 percent expecting 10 percent inflation, and if your expectations are realized then you will earn a 4 percent real return on your loans. However, if

THE EX ANTE real interest rate is the nominal interest rate minus the expected inflation rate.

THE EX POST real interest rate is the nominal interest rate minus the actual inflation rate.

THE FISHER EFFECT is a theory establishing a relationship between the nominal rate of interest (the market rate) and the expected rate of inflation.

FIGURE 8-2
A Change in the Growth Rate of the Money Stock

All four graphs show an increase in the money stock. In (a) and (b), the money stock is constant until t_0, at which time it begins to grow at a rate of 3 percent. In (c) and (d), the money stock is growing at 3 percent until t_1, when it jumps to 6 percent.

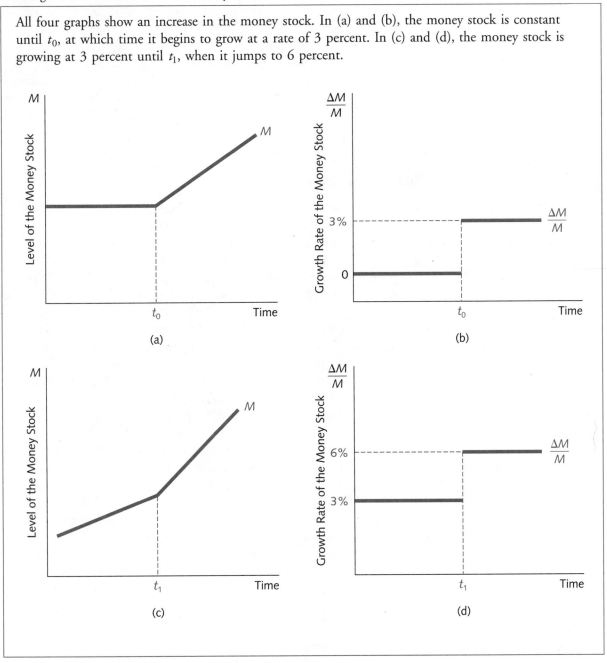

the inflation rate for the year turns out to be 18 percent, the actual real interest rate that you earned will be the nominal interest rate you charged minus the actual inflation rate, 14 percent minus 18 percent or –4 percent. We call this the *ex post* real interest rate, because it can be calculated only after the fact.

Needless to say, you and your boss might be very unhappy with this development, but borrowers will be happy. The point, however, is that *ex ante–ex post* distinctions are often very useful in macro and monetary discussion. Now let us turn to some actual, *ex post* inflation data. A brief review of U.S. experience is useful for tackling a theoretical discussion of how inflation takes place.

Statistics on Inflation

As we indicated in Chapter 2, there are numerous price indices. The Bureau of Labor Statistics (BLS) at the Department of Labor calculates a consumer price index (CPI), shown in Table 8-1 along with the inflation rate, using base year 1982–1984 quantities as weights. There was a 26 percent increase in the CPI during the 1960s, a 98 percent increase during the 1970s, and a 71 percent increase during the 1980s. If we look at presidential terms, the CPI increased by 45 percent during the Carter years, 1977–1980, or almost 10 percent per year. During the Reagan years, 1981–1988, the CPI increased by 44 percent, or about 4.5 percent per year. Finally, during the Bush years, 1989–1992, the CPI increased by about 20 percent, or 4.8 percent per year.

Other patterns are also apparent. Inflation accelerated during the 1960s as the Vietnam War was being fought at the same time the Great Society programs were introduced and President Johnson tried to get by without a tax increase. There was a very slow reduction in the inflation rate in the early 1970s, and then a large increase in 1974–75 due to the OPEC oil price increase, the resulting recession, and the policy response. The inflation rate fell in 1976, but then gradually increased during the next two years and increased dramatically during 1979 and 1980. The 1979 episode coincided with the second large OPEC oil price hike. The 1980s saw a reduction of the inflation rate below double-digit numbers, a reduction accompanied by the very steep recession in the early 1980s. After that reduction, the 1980s and the 1990s to date have been a period of fairly steady inflation. From 1982 to 1992, the inflation rate averaged 3.5 percent.

MONETARISM AND THEORIES OF INFLATION

Monetarism suggests a monetary theory of inflation. The Keynesian theory had been designed around nonmonetary explanations, in fitting with the Keynesian deemphasis of money. We will present both the Monetarist explanation and several nonmonetary explanations in this chapter.

TABLE 8-1
The Consumer Price Index
and Inflation Rate,
1950–1992

In the table, the consumer price index (CPI) for all items is shown, using a base year average of 1982–1984. Since 1950, prices have increased almost six-fold. The yearly inflation rate is shown as the percentage change in the CPI from the previous year.

(1982–1984 = 100)

YEAR	CPI (ALL ITEMS)	INFLATION RATE	YEAR	CPI (ALL ITEMS)	INFLATION RATE
1950	24.1		1971	40.5	4.4%
1951	26.0	7.9%	1972	41.8	3.2%
1952	26.5	1.9%	1973	44.4	8.2%
1953	26.7	0.8%	1974	49.3	11.0%
1954	26.9	0.7%	1975	53.8	9.1%
1955	26.8	0.4%	1976	56.9	5.8%
1956	27.2	1.5%	1977	60.6	6.5%
1957	28.1	3.3%	1978	65.2	7.6%
1958	28.9	2.8%	1979	72.6	11.3%
1959	29.1	0.7%	1980	82.4	13.5%
1960	29.6	1.7%	1981	90.9	10.3%
1961	29.9	1.0%	1982	96.5	6.2%
1962	30.2	1.0%	1983	99.6	3.2%
1963	30.6	1.3%	1984	103.9	4.3%
1964	31.0	1.3%	1985	107.6	3.6%
1965	31.5	1.6%	1986	109.6	1.9%
1966	32.4	2.9%	1987	113.6	3.6%
1967	33.4	3.1%	1988	118.3	4.1%
1968	34.8	4.2%	1989	124.0	4.8%
1969	36.7	5.5%	1990	130.7	5.4%
1970	38.8	5.7%	1991	136.2	4.2%
			1992	142.0	4.1%

SOURCE: Council of Economic Advisors, *Economic Report of the President* (Washington, DC: U.S. Government Printing Office, 1993), p. 411.
NOTE: CPI for November 1992; inflation rate estimated for 1992.

The Monetarist Hypothesis

The Monetarist explanation for inflation—that there is a significant and predictable relation between rates of change in the money stock and rates of change in prices—is of Classical origin. Monetarists such as Nobel laureate Milton Friedman subscribe to this general view, though there is not complete unanimity on all details.[2] The Monetarist view of inflation and unemployment has become so important in contemporary economic discussions that its outline will comprise the remainder of this section.

The Monetarist view has grown out of, and supplements, the simple quantity theory originated by Classical and Neoclassical economists such as Pigou and Fisher (discussed in Chapter 3). Indeed, the conclusions of contemporary Monetarists relating the money stock to the price level are precisely the same as those of the Classical economists. A doubling of the nominal money stock will, in *long-run equilibrium,* result in a doubling of the price level and an unchanged *real* rate of interest. Some of the more enlightening achievements of contemporary Monetarists, however, concern the behavior of macroeconomic variables over the short run, or during the *adjustment period* over which the economy is in disequilibrium. Our discussion of some Monetarist propositions will focus on these matters as well as on long-run considerations. The conception of the quantity theory may be used to discuss the Monetarist conception of inflation. Recall that the equation of exchange identity may be written as

$$MV \equiv PY.$$

As soon as some assumption about money demand and velocity is made, however, this identity becomes the "quantity theory." Monetarists assume that velocity is stable or predictable. We want to consider percentage changes, and the quantity theory tells us that $MV = PY.$ Thus, if M, V, P, and Y are all changed, after the change they must still be related by the quantity equation. Moreover, if M is growing at some rate, say 5 percent, then either V must be falling at 5 percent to keep MV constant, or PY must be growing at 5 percent. For PY to grow at 5 percent, either P must grow at 5 percent with Y constant, or Y must grow at 5 percent with P constant, or P and Y each grow at 2.5 percent, or some such combination. Only in this way will the quantity equation continue to hold while these variables are changing. More generally, we can write the quantity equation in terms of percentage changes as

---

[2]See Milton Friedman, *The Optimal Quantity of Money and Other Essays* (Chicago: Aldine Publishing, 1969); and Milton Friedman and Anna Schwartz, *A Monetary History of the United States, 1867–1960* (Princeton, NJ: Princeton University Press, 1964). For a superb simple introduction to the monetarist position, see J. Houston McCulloch, *Money and Inflation: A Monetarist Approach* (New York: Academic Press, 1975); also see Leonardo Auernheimer and Robert B. Ekelund, Jr., *The Essentials of Money and Banking* (New York: John Wiley & Sons, 1982), Chapters 7 and 8.

$$\Delta M/M + \Delta V/V = \Delta P/P + \Delta Y/Y,$$

or, rearranging the expression, as

$$\Delta P/P = (\Delta M/M + \Delta V/V) - \Delta Y/Y.$$

This equation simply states that the percentage *rate of change* in the price level—that is, the inflation rate, $\Delta P/P$, or π—is equal to the sum of the percentage rates of change in the money supply and actual velocity *minus* the percentage rate of change in real income. If velocity is constant, the percentage rate of change in velocity is zero. Then, if the percentage rate of increase in the money supply ($\Delta M/M$) is 8 percent per year and if real income grows at 3 percent per year, the rate of inflation will be 5 percent per year (i.e., $\Delta P/P = \Delta M/M - \Delta Y/Y = 8\% - 3\% = 5\%$).

Do the conclusions of the long-run static conception of the quantity theory hold here? Clearly they do, since a 5 percentage point increase in the rate of monetary expansion (in our example, from 8 percent to 13 percent) will result in a 5 percentage point increase in the inflation rate (in our example, from 5 percent to 10 percent), with no change in velocity or in the 3 percent growth rate in real income (i.e., $\Delta P/P = 13\% - 3\% = 10\%$.)[3]

THE QUANTITY THEORY WITH VARIABLE VELOCITY

The above discussion assumed that velocity is constant. Note, however, that when using the equation of exchange to develop a theory of real money demand, we would divide both sides by V and by Y to get $(M/P)^d = Y/V$.

Clearly this theory has money demand depending on income. What about the interest rate? We have so far assumed that V is constant, but changes in the interest rate should affect V. Increases in the interest rate make it more costly for individuals to hold their wealth in noninterest bearing or low-interest-bearing money. Thus, increases in the interest rate lead individuals to try to reduce their money holdings, which is accomplished by using the money to purchase other assets or other goods and services. Individuals will not want to hold on to money they receive, but will instead try to quickly exchange it for these alternative assets or goods and services. Money will change hands more often, and velocity increases. Moreover, since velocity is in the denominator, an increase in R will increase V but lower Y/V, which lowers money demand.

---

[3]These long-run conclusions of the quantity theory gave rise to Monetarist Milton Friedman's often quoted policy recommendation that the growth in monetary expansion should follow a growth "rule" of about 3 percent per year since, historically, the growth rate of real income has on average been about 3 percent per year in the United States. If real income is at a no-growth full-employment maximum, the rate of change in monetary expansion is the inflation rate. These and other monetarist (and fiscalist) policy matters will be considered later in this book.

What does it matter if velocity depends on the interest rate instead of being constant? It matters because the nominal interest rate and the inflation rate are linked. Recall that the nominal interest rate consists of two factors: (1) the real rate of interest r, which is the product of the real forces of lending and borrowing in the economy; and (2) the expected inflation rate. Thus, the nominal interest rate may be formally expressed as

$$R = r + \pi^e.$$

The nominal rate is the sum of the real rate and the expected inflation rate. These expressions are simply the Fisher equation, which was discussed at length in Chapter 3. Lenders and borrowers will establish the nominal rate based on *ex ante* expectations of future inflation.

In our earlier analysis with a fixed velocity, an increase in the rate of growth of the money stock led to an equal increase in the rate of growth of inflation. In fact we assume that an increase in that rate of growth in the money supply leads *instantly* to an increased expectation of inflation so that the nominal interest rate immediately increases, causing velocity to rise. Now velocity depends on the interest rate. In this case, an increase in the rate of growth of the money supply still leads to an equal increase in the inflation rate. However, that increase in the rate of growth of the price level now leads, in equilibrium, to an equal increase in the rate of expected inflation and hence to an equal increase in the nominal interest rate. This causes velocity to increase, which reduces the demand for real money balances. Since output growth is not affected by the rate of money creation in this model, the reduction in the demand for real money balances must occur via a reduction in M or an increase in P. Further M is exogenous, or determined outside of the model, so what is required is an increase in P.

What actually happens is that the increase in the interest rate caused by the increased rate of growth of the money stock causes an equal increase in *the rate of growth* of the price level, but it also causes a one-time increase in the *level* of prices. This second effect is due to the increase in velocity, which itself is due to the increase in the interest rate caused by the increased rate of growth of the price level. That is as illustrated in Figure 8-3. In graph (a), the path of the money stock M shows the increase in the growth rate of money at time t_0. Graph (d) shows the time path of real output Y, which is unaffected by what happens at time t_0. Graph (b) shows the path of the price index, which mimics the rate of growth of the money stock, but which also shows a jump in the price level at time t_0. The reason for this jump is shown in graph (c). The increase in velocity at time t_0 is due to the increase in the nominal interest rate, which is caused by the increase in the rate of price growth. Thus, an increase in the rate of growth of the money supply has two effects—the rate of inflation increases by the same amount as the increase in money growth, and the price level also jumps to a higher level when the increase in money growth occurs. This jump in the price level is sufficient to counteract the jump in velocity and allows the quantity equation $MV = PY$ to continue to hold at time t_0.

FIGURE 8-3
A Dynamic Version of the Quantity Theory

An increase in the rate of growth of the money supply at t_0 creates a jump in the price level. As prices and interest rates rise, velocity increases. Income growth is unaffected in (d).

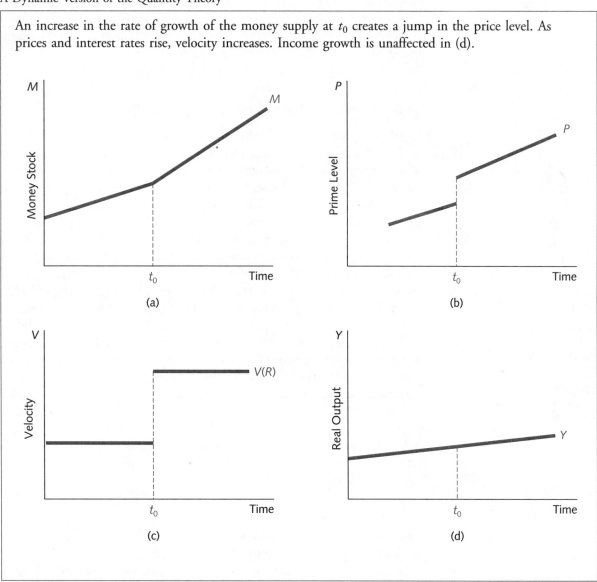

Note well, however, that Figure 8-3 tells us about the long run or steady state results from the increase in the growth rate of the money supply. That is, Figure 8-3 is drawn under the assumption that the increase in the rate of growth of the money supply at time t_0 leads *instantaneously* to an increased *expectation* of inflation, so that the nominal interest rate immediately increases, causing velocity to increase immediately. Thus, the analysis of Figure 8-3 does not hold when expectations of the inflation rate do not adjust immediately to changes in the rate of growth of the money supply. It tells us nothing about how, or how fast, the economy gets to a new "steady-state" inflation equilibrium or how the inflation rate rises in equilibrium. The Monetarist theory of inflation addresses just these points.

Adjustments and Expectations: Anticipated Inflation

In the long-run model of inflation, as outlined in the preceding section, adjustments to equilibrium take place instantaneously. In real-world situations, unfortunately, these neat and convenient conclusions are not generally fulfilled. Adjustments are not automatic, and expectations concerning inflation rates often differ from the actual inflation rates. Expectations concerning inflation rates have a huge impact on the whole economic adjustment process.

There are many theories concerning the formation of expectations. We will cover the important concept of rational expectations in Chapter 9, but for now we will use the approach most often used by the Monetarists. That is, we will use the so-called **adaptive expectations theory,** which states that individuals adapt their expectations about, say, the future course of inflation from their past price experiences. In this theory, most recent experience is given heavier weight than experience of the more distant past. The speed of this adaptation is not necessarily specified, and the theory has been criticized on a number of points (to be discussed in Chapter 9). The adaptive expectations theory is nevertheless sometimes used to explain the phenomenon of short-run inflation.

The basis of the adaptive expectations approach is that it takes *time* for individuals to learn and adapt to actual circumstances. That is, it takes time for individuals to adjust expectations of variables (such as inflation) to match the actual behavior of these variables. As a simple example, adaptive expectations might be written as

$$\pi_t^e = \pi_{t-1},$$

which says that the expectation of the inflation rate that is held at time *t* is just the actual inflation rate at time *t* – 1. Based on this model, then, the expected inflation rate in 1992 would be 4.2 percent because the actual inflation rate in 1991 was 4.2 percent. Obviously this hypothesis suggests that expectations adjust slowly, always responding with a lag to actual experience. Because of this, purely monetary phenomena such as inflation can influence real economic activity. There are two ways that this happens. First, because expectations adjust slowly, it is possible that a better-informed person or government agency may be able to take advantage of the slow way that the rest of us are adjusting our expectations. In effect, a government policymaker may know that our expectations of inflation for 1992 are 4.2 percent and be able to use this fact to manipulate our willingness to supply labor and other commodities. Second, many wages and prices are set either in contracts or, especially for prices, posted

THE ADAPTIVE EXPECTATIONS THEORY proposes that future price expectations are formed over time on the basis of past price experience, with the most recent price experience having the greatest influence.

in catalogs or menus. These wages and prices are determined based on expectations of the inflation rate by the wage earners or firms involved, while the wages or prices will be set by contract or otherwise. If the expectations turn out to be incorrect, they will be revised, but before the revision people will be in situations in which the actual price level is different from what they think it is. This can lead to workers or firms selling their labor or products at prices less than they would in the absence of contracts, catalogs, menus, or other means by which wages and prices are preset for some period of time.

Figure 8-4 shows the path of money prices and output. Up to time period t_0, the monetary authority increases the money supply at 8 percent per year. There is a constant 3 percent growth rate in real income. This produces an actual rate of inflation of 5 percent, as well as an expected inflation rate of 5 percent. The expected inflation rate is equivalent to the actual inflation rate because both are unchanging and sufficient time has passed so that expectations have fully adjusted to the actual inflation rate.

Now suppose that, at time t_0, the Federal Reserve Board suddenly increases the rate of monetary growth to 13 percent. Immediately, real money balances are increased because of the sudden monetary expansion, as are total expenditures on goods and services. But if the growth rate of real income is constant and prices are slow to rise, then interest rates and velocity just decline. Over time, the increased money balances lead to increased expenditures that bid up prices. Actual inflation begins to rise, but price expectations P^e (and hence the interest rate) are slower to adjust. Note that in this process the real money stock rises at first but begins to decline as the actual inflation rate rises *above* the long-run sustainable rate of 10 percent. (This long-run rate is indicated by the solid line in Figure 8-4.) The expected inflation rate (and expected prices P^e) lag behind the actual inflation rate (and actual prices P), and oscillate around the new long-run equilibrium at 10 percent.

Implications of Interest Rate Phenomena

What are the implications of these phenomena for inflation and for inflation policy? There are several. According to Monetarists, the dip in both the nominal and real interest rate that is temporarily observed following an increase in the rate of growth of the money supply has occasionally led politicians, policymakers, and economists astray. Policymakers sometimes use monetary policy in an attempt to lower the nominal and real interest rates, hoping to stimulate aggregate demand (revealing a basic confusion—common among politicians—between real and nominal values). However, the Monetarists warn us that such monetary growth creates only *temporary* reductions in interest rates and causes increases in the inflation rate. Using increases in the money growth rate as a way of keeping interest rates low will require ever-rising rates of growth of the money supply, in order to always keep money growth rate increases ahead of the rising rates of actual and expected inflation. Thus, we see that high inflation rates cause high nominal rates of interest, and that

FIGURE 8-4
Growth in Prices, Money Supply, and Income (Percent)

After an increase in the monetary growth rate (from 8 to 13 percent in the figure), actual inflation rates exceed the rate of inflationary expectations. After the expected rate overshoots and undershoots the actual rate, the expected rate will equal the actual rate. Over the long run, only nominal magnitudes such as the inflation rate and the market interest rate are affected by monetary expansion.

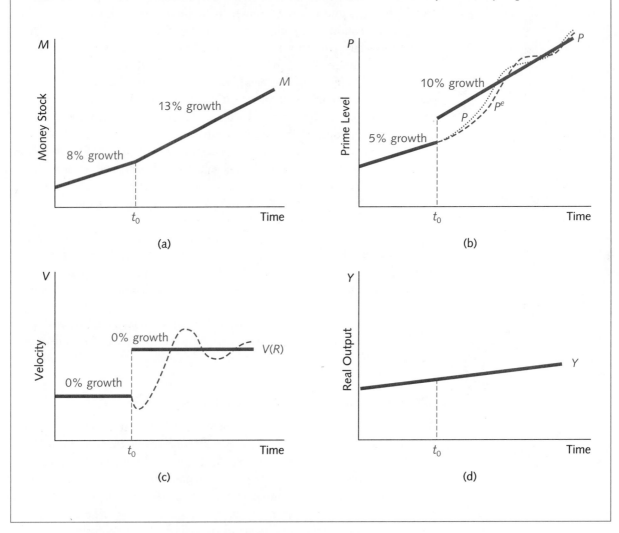

attempts to lower the interest rate by accelerating growth rates of the money supply are temporary expedients that are bound to fail, causing high inflation and high nominal interest rates.

A second implication relating to the Monetarist apparatus of inflation concerns the connection between velocity (the demand for money balances) and the nominal interest rate. Over the short-term adjustment described in

Figure 8-4, for example, as expected inflation rises through time, so does the nominal interest rate. But the nominal interest rate is the opportunity cost of holding money balances. An increase in nominal interest rates means a decrease in holdings of money balances and an increase in velocity. The increase in velocity further intensifies the price level increase, causing measured inflation to be temporarily higher than it would otherwise be. The logic of the Monetarist model of inflation requires velocity to be higher (money balances lower) in equilibrium because of the higher nominal interest rates produced by the higher inflation rate, which itself is due to higher money growth rates.

In the Monetarist view, then, the prime source of inflation is to be found in increases in the rate of monetary expansion, while erratic price behavior is caused by jerky alterations—increases and decreases—in the rate of change in monetary growth, accentuated by price expectations.

One interesting implication of the Monetarist ideas on inflation is that a country can halt inflation by controlling the money supply. This allows small countries a unique way to achieve price stability, by fixing the exchange rate between their currency and that of a large country with a stable currency. Such was the case in Hong Kong, as illustrated in the Global Perspective: "Monetary Lessons of Hong Kong."

Nonmonetary Theories of Inflation

Nonmonetary explanations of inflation have been popular among certain economists and public figures for decades, although the line of reasoning from cause to effect has differed. The common basis for these explanations lies in the presence of monopoly power over some nonhuman resource (such as OPEC's oil), over human resources (such as the case of labor unions), or over the production and sale of final or intermediate goods or services. Wage-push inflation, producers' cost-push inflation, and the wage-price spiral all derive from the existence or supposed existence of monopoly somewhere in the economy.

THE WAGE-PUSH AND PRODUCT MONOPOLY EXPLANATION

Labor unions are the primary culprit in this explanation for inflation. Here the formation of new unions or the increase in union monopoly power permits wage demands higher than labor's productivity. These increased wage demands represent increased costs to businesses. If only parts of an industry (or of industries selling closely related products) were unionized, the union demand, via the competitive system, would be repulsed. But a second part of the wage-push, wage-price spiral argument is that noncompetitive or monopoly conditions exist in the sale of goods. Monopoly on the product side thus permits the increased union wage demands to be passed on—willingly or unwillingly by monopoly producers—to consumers. The result is inflation.

A variation on this story portrays the monopolist as the villain. Here increases in monopoly power permit monopolists to raise prices. Monopoly

"MONETARY LESSONS OF HONG KONG"

Is a central bank really required to control the money supply of a country? While most modern economies have central banks, the historical record shows these banks have had only limited success in smoothing out the fluctuations in the real output of goods and services. Most economists argue that countries must have central banks to prevent excessive increases in the stock of money in order to have stable prices and long-run economic growth. If an economy does not have a central banking system, the creation of money is determined by market forces.

In theory, a small open economy can achieve long-run price stability if it makes the monetary liabilities of its banking sector fully convertible with a stable currency of a major nation at a fixed exchange rate. A recent example of this type of monetary system is the one that existed in Hong Kong from 1983 to 1988.[a] This system had two unique features. First, Hong Kong's currency was issued primarily by the privately owned Hong Kong and Shanghai Banking Corporation (HKSBC). The HKSBC issued currency by purchasing certificates of indebtedness with foreign exchange assets from the government-run Exchange Fund. Then it used the certificates of indebtedness as collateral against which it was authorized to issue Hong Kong dollars. The exchange of foreign exchange assets for these certificates by the HKSBC was at a *fixed exchange rate* set by the government. From 1983 to 1988, the exchange rate was HK 7.80 per U.S. dollar.

The second unique feature of Hong Kong's system was the government did not require bankers to hold reserves to settle claims between banks. Instead, banks held deposits in the HKSBC, which acted as a clearing bank for all interbank transactions in Hong Kong. Hong Kong dollars were exchanged for clearing of bank balances and vice versa. In the

PHOTO 8-1
For Many Years the Internationally Influential Hong Kong Bank Did Not Have a Central Bank.

Hong Kong system, currency and net interbank clearing balances along with the rate of expansion of demand deposits depended on the size of the liabilities of the HKSBC. Thus, this fixed exchange rate system had two implications. First, any Hong Kong dollars that were issued were fully backed by foreign currency, which made them fully convertible at the government's fixed exchange rate. This in turn limited notes and thereby money creation. Second, because there was no central bank, the government had limited control over the money supply. The market determined the equilibrium stock of money at the fixed exchange rate, which was based on the public's preferences between the Hong Kong dollar and foreign currency. This system resembles the textbook version of the gold exchange standard. That is, a purely monetary shock that creates an excess demand or supply of money is restored to monetary equilibrium by the forces of demand and supply. For example, an excess supply of Hong Kong dollars would cause the value of this currency to fall relative to foreign notes. Banks would have the incentive to redeem Hong Kong dollars for foreign currency at the exchange rate offered by the Exchange Fund. Then the banks would make a profit by selling the foreign currency in the market. These actions by the Hong Kong banks resulted in a reduction of currency and the money supply, which in turn limited inflationary pressure and maintained the fixed exchange rate.

Unfortunately, under a fixed exchange rate system like Hong Kong's, shocks to the economy such as changes in aggregate demand or exchange rate misalignments may amplify the effects on real income and inflation. Let us see how an exchange rate misalignment can present problems. While Hong Kong's economy was sound, its currency was pegged to the U.S. dollar. Appreciation and depreciation of the U.S. dollar between 1983 and 1987 were substantial and may have caused volatility in Hong Kong's real rate of growth and inflation. From 1983 to 1985 there was an appreciation in the Hong Kong dollar. Hong Kong's real income grew from 1983 to 1984 then fell sharply to a recession low in 1985. In 1986 the Hong Kong dollar declined sharply. This devaluation of the Hong Kong currency may have produced the temporary boom since real income grew by 14 percent in 1987. Faced with speculative shifts into Hong Kong dollars over the 1985 to 1987 period, the government decided to end the system of passive money creation. Beginning in July 1988, the HKSBC was required to maintain a *noninterest-bearing* Hong Kong dollar account with the Exchange Fund equal to the size of its net clearing balance liability in the interbank market. If the HKSBC's account with the Exchange Fund falls below its net clearing balance, the HKSBC has to pay an interest penalty. This change allows the government to manipulate Hong Kong's money supply by influencing the level of the HKSBC's account with the government Exchange Fund. For example, if the government wants to counter a fall in the Hong Kong dollar, it purchases Hong Kong dollars from the HKSBC, causing a reduction in the value of the HKSBC's account with the Exchange Fund. This means the HKSBC has to reduce the size of the net clearing balance in the interbank market. Once the government started to have the power to control changes in the stock of money, Hong Kong was forced to have the equivalent of a central bank. ❑

NOTE [a]This discussion is drawn from Ramon Moreno, "Monetary Lessons of Hong Kong," Federal Reserve Bank of San Francisco, *FRBSF Weekly Letter* (September 7, 1990).

increases in output prices lead to reductions in real income on the part of wage earners, and union labor market organizations take over. The exercise of union power leads to nominal and (temporarily) real wage increases, which are, via producer monopoly power, passed on to consumers. The process is supposed to continue ad infinitum, producing the wage-price spiral.

Let us examine the argument in some detail. While it is perfectly plausible that unions may alter the natural rate of unemployment and create artificially *high* wage rates and reductions in economy-wide productivity, it is not clear how they can, through *increased* wage demands, create a permanently increasing price level. The point is illustrated in Figure 8-5, which shows static aggregate supply and demand functions with a natural rate of unemployment that corresponds to income level Y_F. Assume now that unions are successful in imposing new wage demands and that monopolists respond by raising prices to consumers. This is represented in Figure 8-5 by a reduction in the supply of output for each level of prices or by the upward shift of the supply curve to short-run $SRAS_1$.

Clearly, the diagram shows a rise in the price level, from P_0 to P_1, a reduction in income to Y_0, and an increase in unemployment from its "natural" level. (We ignore the longer-term effects of union successes on the natural rate of unemployment.)

Market pressures, assuming a constant money stock, make *persistent or ongoing* inflation or a wage-price spiral originating in unions or monopolies

FIGURE 8-5
Cost-Push Inflation

Assuming that unions are able to "push" wages up by labor negotiations and that monopolists respond to the increase by raising prices, the price level will rise to P_1 from P_0 in the figure.

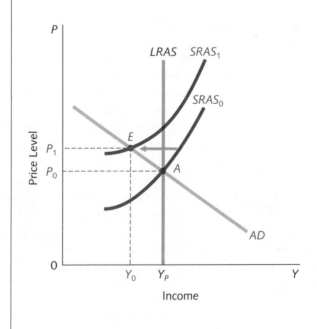

extremely unlikely. With the money stock constant (or growing at a constant rate in a dynamic model), the inflation potential of monopoly pressures is limited. Under such circumstances, a once-and-for-all increase in prices is possible (through reduced productivity and income due to increased union and monopoly activity), but a wage-price spiral, as such, is not likely. Any increases in monopoly power alter "institutions" in the labor market. Aggregate supply shifts leftward in once-and-for-all fashion. The aggregate supply shift to $SRAS_1$ in Figure 8-5 is permanent.

Also, many economists do not believe that the empirical evidence shows that general economic concentration has increased over the last fifty or sixty years in the United States. Union membership, moreover, has declined significantly over the past twenty years. And, further, it is often impossible for monopolies or concentrated industries always to pass on wage increases in the form of higher prices. Whether this is possible depends on the demand elasticity faced by individual monopolists. A number of contemporary economists believe that some of the price level increases (and unemployment) of the post-1950 period may have been generated by monopoly factors but that such factors do not appear to have been responsible for anything like the actual inflationary experience.

NONMONETARY THEORIES OF INFLATION: EVALUATION

If monopoly in labor, commodity, and input markets cannot be used to explain the high inflation rates in the U.S. economy during the 1970s, what explanation can be used? As suggested in the earlier discussion of cost-push phenomena, price increases due to union and monopoly pressures would be limited. Reductions in the demand for *real* money balances and reductions in output, income, and employment would produce some market pressures mitigating the original leftward shift in the aggregate supply curve to $SRAS_1$ (see Figure 8-5). But there is one way in which these price increases resulting from union-monopoly or resource scarcity pressures may be fully validated or accommodated. Consider Figure 8-6, which depicts a wage-price spiral in static terms. With union-monopoly activity increasing in the economy, new supply rigidities are built into the system and the SRAS curve may be thought of as shifting leftward from a full-employment equilibrium at point A, with a price level P_0. If fiscal and monetary restraint is exercised, an (output and unemployment) gap is allowed to persist (with attendant wage-decreasing pressures in the labor market). But if policymakers decide that the unemployment is unacceptable, they may accommodate the situation by increasing budget deficits or by simply increasing the money supply.

The increased money stock shifts the aggregate demand curve rightward. In Figure 8-6, alternative aggregate demand curves are associated with different (increasing) values of the nominal money stock. Thus, one might imagine a wage-price spiral creating a price and income-employment path traced out by a "ratchet" such as *A-B-C-D-E,* and so on, as in Figure 8-6. Here the wage-push argument may serve as an explanation for inflation, but only with some accompanying monetary validation or accommodation.

FIGURE 8-6
The Wage-price Spiral

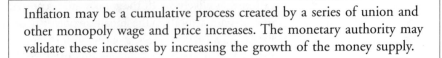

Inflation may be a cumulative process created by a series of union and other monopoly wage and price increases. The monetary authority may validate these increases by increasing the growth of the money supply.

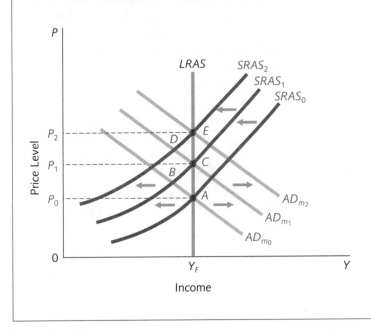

In a similar vein, high energy prices associated with the policies of the Organization of Petroleum Exporting Countries (OPEC) were often held responsible for the high rates of inflation in the 1970s. However, OPEC's emergence can be associated with high inflation rates only by assuming that the monetary authority did not hold fast in the face of rising energy prices or that it did not actively seek to counter the rising price trends. While *short-run* income reductions and price-level increases owing to monopoly or OPEC pressures may have facilitated price *level* increases, the inflation of the 1970s and early 1980s had but one primary cause, at least in the Monetarist view—growth in the money stock.

EMPLOYER AND WORKER EXPECTATIONS: A MODERN CONCEPT OF AGGREGATE SUPPLY

As our Monetarist model of aggregate supply, we will adopt the concept developed by the Monetarist Milton Friedman.[4] Like the Keynesian model of

---

[4]The monetarist model of the present section is contained in Milton Friedman's presidential address to the American Economic Association, "The Role of Monetary Policy," *American Economic Review* (March 1968), pp. 1–17.

aggregate supply, this Monetarist model will be a modification of the Classical model. In the Classical model, the *LRAS* curve was drawn with an (implicit) assumption that the expected price level equaled the actual price level. That is, workers' and firms' expectations of the price level would be correct, equal to the actual price level. Along with instantaneous price and wage adjustments, this assumption resulted in the long-run vertical aggregate supply curve. This Monetarist version of aggregate supply will allow us to examine certain Monetarist propositions concerning inflation and the possibility of an inflation-unemployment trade-off as suggested by the Phillips curve. Let us now look more closely at the expectations of employers and workers.

Expectations of Workers and Employers

The real question facing workers and employers in their decisions to demand and supply labor is not necessarily what the price and wage situation actually is but what they perceive it to be. *Worker and employer expectations are the key in this theory.*

Consider the behavior of employers. To maximize profits, employers will hire labor up to the point where the value of labor's marginal product is equal to the nominal wage, or $P \cdot MP_N = W$. The price P is the price of the firm's output. The wage W is the wage the firm pays to its workers. A firm knows both the price it charges for its product and the wage it pays to its workers. Thus, employers don't have to form predictions of either the price or the wage rate—they know these magnitudes. A rise in prices, with nominal wages constant or rising at a slower rate, always means that employers will hire additional workers. They will increase their input of labor in order to maximize profits.

Now consider workers' perceptions and expectations concerning prices. Workers, by and large, are not paid continuously or daily for labor services; rather, they contract to be paid once or twice a month, or in some cases weekly. This means that when workers decide on how much labor to provide, they are deciding based on an offered nominal wage W and on some expectation of what the price level will be over the future period of work. In addition, they are interested in the prices of the goods they actually purchase, not just the goods that their firms produce. In particular, they care about the prices of bundles of goods that are purchased at different intervals. Because most workers frequently and regularly spend a large portion of their earnings on food, the prices of food items are probably fairly well known to their households. They also spend a large portion of their earnings on housing and on automobiles, but these are items that are purchased relatively infrequently, so there may be years or even decades between purchases. Thus, the prices of housing and of automobiles may not be as well known within their households. Of course, for all of these goods a worker has an idea—that is, an expectation—of the relevant price. The point is that, unlike firms, workers must form an expectation of the price level relevant to their household buying patterns. When workers want to calculate their real wage, they find that the wage W is well known to them, but the price level must be estimated; that is, they form an expectation of the price level P^e. Labor supply decisions are then based on an *expected* real wage W/P^e.

Now suppose that both the price level and the nominal wage are rising, due perhaps to an increase in the money supply. Assume further that the price level is rising at a faster rate than the nominal wage. Thus, the real wage W/P is falling. What will workers do? Although the actual real wage rate is falling, workers will not know the price level P but must form an expectation P^e. The question is how quickly expectations of the price level respond to price level changes. If the expected price level is slow to adjust, then the increase in the nominal wage will lead to an increase in the expected real wage W/P^e, even though the actual real wage W/P is falling. Thus, workers might end up increasing the quantity of labor supplied because the expected real wage is increasing when in fact the real wage is declining. Of course, this is a temporary situation, since eventually price expectations will adjust to the higher actual price level.

Note too that in this situation, since the real wage has actually fallen, employers will demand more labor. Thus, there will be an increase in employment and hence in output during the period when price expectations are not rising as quickly as the actual price level. This is Friedman's explanation for the Phillips curve—when the price level rises faster than expected by workers, there will be a temporary increase in output and employment to levels above the natural rate. When expectations catch up with the actual changes in the price level, output and employment will be restored to the natural rate.

Note that this entire analysis is based on the assumption that the price expectations of workers are slower to adjust than those of employers. However, note too that in the end, workers' expectations do adjust.

The Labor Market and Expectations

We may build the foregoing considerations into the models of aggregate supply previously developed in Chapter 6. In order to reexamine the labor market, we should recall that labor demand and supply are given by

$$N_D = N_D(W/P, K, Z, Technology) \tag{8.1}$$

$$N_S = N_S(W/P, A,). \tag{8.2}$$

Notice that the supply and demand functions were written as functions of the current real wage and other factors or parameters, such as the level of resource and capital use and technology (for demand) and workers' wealth and institutions (for supply). (Notice that there is the possibility that employers may know the price *they* set, but not the *general* price level at all times.)

Although equation 8.1 remains the labor demand equation, the labor supply equation, equation 8.2, must be replaced by Equation 8.3:

$$N_S = N_S(W/P^e, A). \tag{8.3}$$

Equation 8.3 is identical to equation 8.2 except that the real wage term is the expected real wage W/P^e instead of the actual real wage.

How will we analyze equations 8.1 and 8.3? We first require a graphical method for handling the labor market when labor demand depends on the real wage W/P while labor supply depends on the expected real wage W/P^e. Clearly we cannot just put the real wage on the vertical axis and proceed as in earlier chapters, since labor demand and labor supply do not depend on the same real wage term. There are a number of ways to proceed in this situation, and we develop one in the discussion that follows. (This method will also be used in the New Classical model of Chapter 10.)

Consider the Classical labor market equations 8.1 and 8.2. Figure 8-7 demonstrates the relationship between graphs of the Classical labor market with the real wage W/P on the vertical axis and graphs of the labor market with the nominal wage W on the vertical axis. Recall from our discussions of the Classical labor market in Chapter 3 that the labor demand curve is the marginal product of labor, which is the slope of the production function. Profit maximizing firms hire labor until the marginal product of labor is equal to the real wage, and this gives the labor demand curve.

The labor demand and supply curves given in equations 8.1 and 8.2 above are typically drawn with the real wage W/P on the vertical axis and the quantity of labor N on the horizontal axis, as in Figure 8-7(a). All other variables affecting labor demand, such as capital and technology, and labor supply, such as the wealth of workers, determine the equilibrium real wage $(W/P)_0$ and the equilibrium level of employment N_F. As was stressed in discussions of the Classical model, the real wage determined here is the ratio of W to P, but not the levels of W or of P individually. In fact, any W and P will do as long as the ratio of W to P is $(W/P)_0$.

As long as labor demand and labor supply both depend on the real wage, graphs such as Figure 8-7(a) are the preferred method for representing labor market behavior. However, there is an alternative, which is to graph the nominal wage W on the vertical axis against employment N on the horizontal axis. If we do this, both labor demand and labor supply will be functions of the price level, in addition to all the other variables such as K or Z that are held constant. An example of such a graph is given in Figure 8-7(b). Here when the price level is P_0, the intersection of labor demand and supply occurs at a nominal wage of W_0 and an employment level of N_F. The real wage is then calculated to be W_0/P_0, which is the same value as the real wage $(W/P)_0$ from graph (a).

What happens in (a) and (b) if the price level rises from P_0 to P_1? In (a), the initial real wage is $(W/P)_0$, and when the price level is P_0, the nominal wage is $(W/P)_0 \times P_0 = W_0$. An increase in the price level to P_1 will initially lower

FIGURE 8-7
Real and Nominal
Adjustments in the Labor
Market

An increase in the price level initially reduces the real wage in (a) to W_0/P_1. The equilibrium real wage is restored when the nominal wage is bid upward to W_1 in (b).

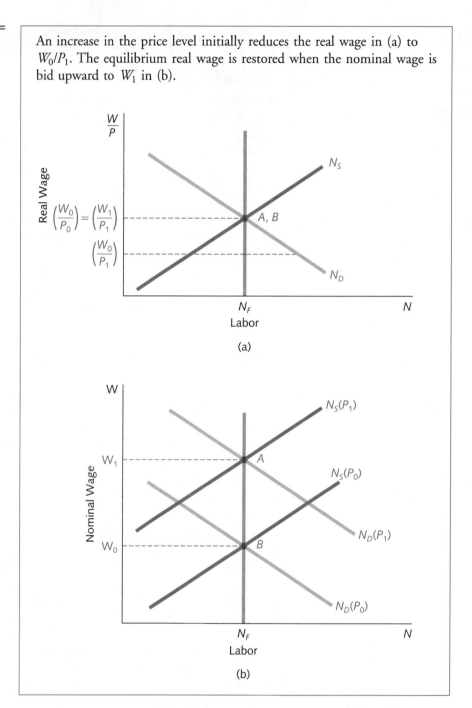

(a)

(b)

the real wage to W_0/P_1, which is less than W_0/P_0. At this lower real wage, the quantity of labor demanded exceeds the quantity supplied, and the real wage is bid up. For a price level of P_1, this requires that the nominal wage rises to a level such that the wage rate divided by P_1 equals W_0/P_0. We might call this wage rate W_1, and say that $W_1/P_1 = W_0/P_0$. Thus, the increase in the price level P results in an increase in the nominal wage W but no change in the real wage W/P or in the employment of labor N_F. The initial equilibrium point A and the final equilibrium point B are at the same position in the graph.

In Figure 8-7(b), the initial price level of P_0 results in an equilibrium nominal wage of W_0 and hence a real wage of W_0/P_0. Employment is at N_F. An increase in the price level to P_1 lowers the real wage as long as the nominal wage is W_0. This lower real wage causes an increase in labor demand from $N_D(P_0)$ to $N_D(P_1)$ and a decrease in labor supply from $N_S(P_0)$ to $N_S(P_1)$. These shifts will be such that the new intersection between labor demand and labor supply is still at an employment level of N_F, and at a wage rate W_1 that is just high enough so that the real wage remains unchanged, or $W_1/P_1 = W_0/P_0$. Thus, the increase in the price level shifts both labor demand and labor supply when only the nominal wage appears on the vertical axis, but shifts them such that the equilibrium quantity of employment and the equilibrium real wage are not affected by the shift. It is in this sense that we can use the graph in Figure 8-7(b) to explain the effect of changes in the price level just as we did in (a).

Of course, in the Classical model there is generally no need to resort to graphs of the type shown in (b). In the Monetarist model, however, we will have occasion to use such graphs. The reason, again, is that the Monetarist model distinguishes actual from expected prices.

The Monetarist model specifies labor demand as in equation 8.1, but modifies labor supply to be equation 8.3. With these labor demand and labor supply curves, it becomes useful to plot these curves on a graph with the nominal wage on the vertical axis. Again, this is so because labor supply is a function of W/P^e while labor demand is a function of W/P. The common element is not W/P but W. In Figure 8-8, labor demand is an explicit function of the price level P, and labor supply is an explicit function of the expected price level P^e. If P and P^e are the same, then the intersection of labor demand and labor supply reproduces the Classical equilibrium as shown in Figure 8-7, with employment at N_F and the real wage equal to $(W/P)_0$. However, if P and P^e diverge, then employment may diverge from N_F and the real wage from $(W/P)_0$.

Let us now review the circumstances discussed earlier in terms of Figure 8-8. Suppose that the growth rate in monetary aggregates increases so that prices and wages begin rising, but with prices rising faster than nominal wages. In this case the actual real wage—the real wage observed by employers—is falling. In their attempt to maximize profits, employers would be willing to hire additional workers so that the marginal product will equal the (lowered) real wage. But would workers be willing to supply more labor at this lower real wage? If they know that the real wage is lower, the answer would be no. In our model, however, workers perceive the real wage to be the expected real wage W/P^e. That is, because price expectations are slow to adjust, workers believe that the higher nominal wages they are receiving mean higher, not lower, real wages.

FIGURE 8-8
The Expectations-Adjusted
Labor Supply Curve

A rise in price expectations has the function of shifting the supply curve to the left. This occurs because a rise in expected prices decreases the expected real wage for every nominal wage. As usual, the demand curve for labor will shift rightward with an increase in the price level.

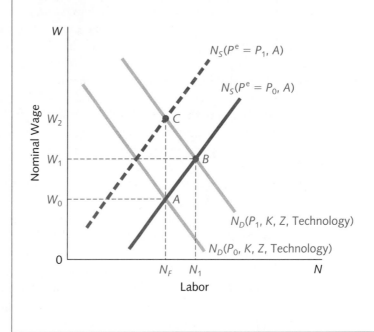

Consider the effect of an increase in the price level in Figure 8-8, beginning from a Classical equilibrium with $P = P^e$ and the initial equilibrium at point A where: $N_D(P_0, K, Z, Technology)$ intersects $N_S(P^e = P_0, A)$ at point A, determining an equilibrium nominal wage rate W_0 and equilibrium employment level N_F. The equilibrium real wage can be calculated as W_0/P_0. What happens if actual prices rise to P_1 while worker perception of the price level stays at $P^e = P_0$? In this case, the increase in the price level increases labor demand, just as it did in Figure 8-7(b). This is illustrated in Figure 8-8 by the rightward shift in labor demand to $N_D(P_1, K, Z, Technology)$. Essentially, the increase in the price level means that firms can receive a higher price for their output, and hence will employ more labor at every nominal wage rate in order to equate the value of marginal product with the nominal wage.

Meanwhile, labor supply does not shift because the expected price level has not changed. Workers are temporarily unaware of the price increase. In this case, the equilibrium is at point B, where the nominal wage is W_1, employment is N_1, and the real wage is W_1/P_1. Is this real wage greater or lesser than the original real wage of W_0/P_0? At first it seems that the answer is ambiguous, since both the nominal wage and the price level have risen. However, it is possible to make a firm conclusion based on additional information. The argument is subtle, so follow closely! We actually know more than just that W and P have increased. We also know that the equilibrium quantity of labor demanded *and* supplied has increased. How could this happen? The increase in the equilibrium quantity of labor supply is easy to explain. At point A, the perceived real wage facing workers was W_0/P_0 because $P^e = P_0$. At point B, the nominal wage has increased while the expected price level has not changed, so the perceived real wage facing workers is W_1/P_0. Workers incorrectly perceive that the increase in the nominal wage from W_0 to W_1 is an increase in the real wage!

How do we explain the increase in the equilibrium quantity of labor demanded? It must be that the real wage has decreased, since otherwise the quantity of labor demanded would not increase. Hence W_1/P_1 is *lower* than W_0/P_0. Otherwise, firms would not be interested in hiring a greater amount of labor. Thus, we know that W_1/P_1 at point B is lower than the initial real wage at point A, W_0/P_0.

The willingness of labor to work at higher perceived real wages and the increased quantity demanded of labor at the realized lowered real wage rate imply that more labor will be hired. In fact, if input level N_F is designated a full-employment level in the sense that N_F corresponds to some natural rate of unemployment, employment level $N_1 - N_F$ may be considered greater than full employment. Note well, however, that full employment in this natural rate context is not the government definition of full employment discussed in Chapter 2.

At point B, the economy is in a state of employment above the natural rate. But this state of affairs cannot last. In the words of Milton Friedman:

> The simultaneous fall ex post in real wages to employers and rise ex ante in real wages to employees is what enabled employment to increase. But the decline ex post in real wages will soon come to affect anticipations. Employees will start to reckon on rising prices of the things they buy and to demand higher nominal wages for the future. "Market" unemployment is below the "natural" level. There is an excess demand for labor so real wages will tend to rise toward their initial level.[5]

That is, workers will eventually "catch on" to what is happening. They see that their actual real wages are falling, and they reevaluate their original price expectations level, increasing P^e. Specifically, expectations will be revised to price level $P^e = P_1$, setting in motion a process that restores the initial level of employment and the real wage.

How do we show this in Figure 8-8? As workers become aware that prices have increased, the expected price level increases to $P^e = P_1$. When this

---

[5]Friedman, "The Role of Monetary Policy," p. 10.

occurs, the labor supply curve shifts to the left, from $N_S(P^e = P_0, A)$ to $N_S(P^e = P_1, A)$. This changes the intersection of labor supply and labor demand from point B to point C. The new equilibrium nominal wage is W_2, equilibrium employment is N_F, and the real wage—both perceived and actual—is W_2/P_1. This real wage is equal to the initial real wage of W_0/P_0, so that the equilibria at points A and C differ only in the levels of W and P, not in the real wage or the level of employment. Note that in moving from the equilibrium at point B to the equilibrium at point C, the perceived real wage declines from W_1/P_0 to W_2/P_1 but the actual real wage increases from W_1/P_1 to W_2/P_1. Thus, workers are initially fooled into working more hours at a lower real wage, but they ultimately catch on and take actions that restore the initial labor market equilibrium.[6] The economy then returns to a full-employment level of input N_F.

A key point to keep in mind is that the equilibrium points labeled A and C in Figure 8-8 correspond to the equilibrium points labeled A and B in Figure 8-9(b). These are points of long-run or Classical equilibrium in the labor market. At these points, both labor demanders and labor suppliers share a common perception of the real wage, and that perception is accurate. The new equilibria allowed by the Monetarist model of the labor market are equilibria such as that illustrated by point B in Figure 8-8, in which labor demanders and suppliers disagree in their perceptions of the real wage. Moreover, in this model labor demanders always have correct perceptions of the real wage, while labor suppliers have faulty perceptions.

Aggregate Supply Curves Based on Price Expectations

We can now develop a notion of the aggregate supply curve based on the kind of price expectation system discussed above. Figure 8-9 develops the notion of aggregate supply, utilizing the labor market principles that we developed in Figure 8-8. The by-now familiar construction used in developing the Classical and Keynesian functions is employed once more in Figure 8-9. Original full-employment equilibrium occurs at point A at the original intersection of the N_D and N_S functions. The input level N_F produces equilibrium output level Y_F, and price level P_0 corresponds to output level Y_F at point A in Figure 8-9(d).

Now assume that an increase in the money supply produces rising prices. Laborers maintain expectations of the price level $P^e = P_0$, but employers adjust labor demand to new price conditions. In the labor market graph, we see that labor supply is unchanged but the higher price level increases the value of marginal product and hence shifts labor demand to the right. The new equilibrium is at point B, with employment of N_1. In the aggregate supply

---

[6]We do not attempt to specify here the actual length of time that this process takes, and it may be the case that the adjustment is more rapid (i.e., workers learn) with each new price increase. We will look at this matter again in connection with the next section on the Phillips curve.

FIGURE 8-9
The Expectations-Adjusted Aggregate Supply Curve

When price expectations rise and labor's expectations lag behind actual increases in the price level, the economy expands output from Y_F to Y_1 in (d). This increase in income is brought about by an increase in labor inputs from N_F to N_1 in (a). When expectations adjust to the new price level, the expectations-adjusted labor supply curve shifts leftward and the economy returns to long-run equilibrium at Y_F and at N_F.

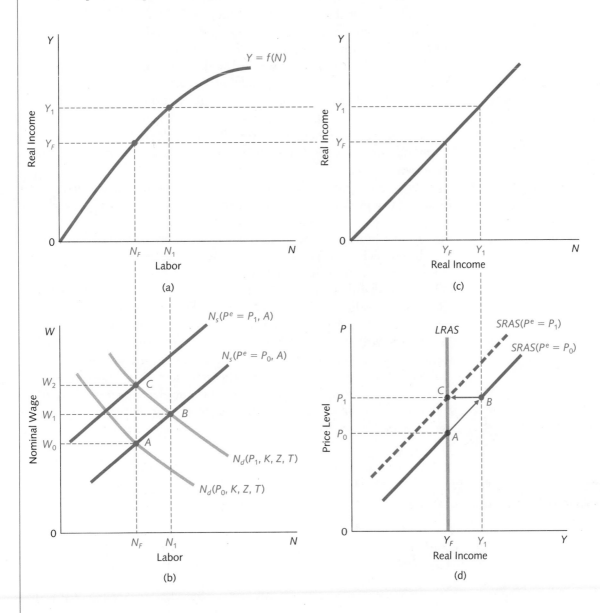

graph, the new higher price level P_1 leads to a new higher level of income Y_1, and this point is labeled B in Figure 8-9(d). Thus, with fixed price expectations $P^e = P_0$ the short-run aggregate supply function is upward sloping between points A and B. Note that this occurs because labor suppliers' expected price level stays constant at $P^e = P_0$, so this short-run supply function is labeled $SRAS(P^e = P_0)$. For the time period over which laborers are "fooled," income exceeds its natural rate by the amount $Y_1 - Y_F$.

Laborers, however, finally "catch on" to the actual erosion in their real wage rates and revise price expectations upward, to $P^e = P_1$. When this happens, labor supply shifts to the left, giving equilibrium at point C in Figure 8-9(a). Employment returns to N_F, causing output to return to Y_F. The short-run aggregate supply curve also shifts leftward, to an intersection at point C corresponding to income level Y_F and a price level P_1. Thus, even though the price level has risen, in the long run, output returns to Y_F, just as in the Classical model. Note, however, that at this point C, there is a new upward-sloping short-run supply curve $SRAS(P^e = P_1)$ drawn through point C, which indicates all levels of possible output when laborers' price expectations are at level $P^e = P_1$.

A short-run expectations-adjusted supply curve is developed assuming that laborers' price expectations lag behind actual increases in the price level. The long-run curve is the result of a series of shifting short-run curves as price expectations catch up. The vertical long-run supply curve (*LRAS* in Figure 8-9(d)) is drawn at the natural rate of output that corresponds to employment at the natural rate of employment, which occurs when actual prices equal the expected prices of both demanders and suppliers of labor. As with the long-run Classical conception of aggregate supply, each higher price level on the vertical supply function corresponds to a higher level of the money stock. As the arrows in Figure 8-9(d) show, there is a short-term adjustment in income, employment, and prices with increases in the price level, but the economy moves back to full-employment equilibrium at a higher price level. Note, however, that we should resist the temptation to describe the price-level increase depicted in Figure 8-9 as inflation. Inflation is a phenomenon of continuous increases in the price level, as we have discussed earlier in this chapter.

INFLATION AND UNEMPLOYMENT

Earlier in this chapter, the discussion of inflation explicitly assumed that employment was at the full-employment level, that is, at the *natural rate of unemployment*. Real output was assumed (in Figure 8-4) to undergo a constant 3 percent growth rate, with which a natural rate of unemployment was associated. We all know, however, that the rate of unemployment has fluctuated widely over the years. The unemployment rate announced each month by the Labor Department is, along with the monthly inflation rate, the biggest economic news discussed by the media. We should note here that persistent unemployment, especially in Europe, has led some to question the idea of a natural rate of unemployment. For more on this, see the Global Perspective: "Is There a Natural Rate of Unemployment in Europe?"

Are there any critical relations between inflation and unemployment? Do the relations between these two essential economic problems vary over the short-run and long-run time horizons? How do expectations about inflation, such as those discussed above, impinge on the economic phenomena of inflation and unemployment? These are the matters we will now consider.

The Phillips Curve: The Empirical Evidence, 1958–1992

British economist A. W. Phillips published a paper in 1958 showing that, for almost a century, an inverse relationship had existed between the *rate* of unemployment and the wage rate changes in England. Since the rate of change of the price level varies closely with the rate of change of nominal wages, a transformation from wage rate–unemployment relations to inflation rate–unemployment relations was made, and the Phillips curve was reborn and rechristened as an *inverse relation between the inflation rate and the unemployment rate*.[7] A typical, though hypothetical, Phillips relation is shown in Figure 8-11, with the inflation rate represented by π on the vertical axis and the unemployment rate by U on the horizontal axis.

The Phillips relation depicted in Figure 8-11 states that high inflation rates are associated with low unemployment rates. For example, a 3 percent unemployment rate is associated with a high 14 percent inflation rate, whereas a 4.5 percent or 5 percent unemployment rate would require a 10 percent or 8 percent inflation rate to be maintained in the economy. While such a relationship appears innocuous, it has several profound implications for macroeconomic policy.

First, there may be some built-in rate of inflation corresponding to a natural rate of unemployment. If the natural rate of unemployment is 5 or 6 percent, the inflation rate supporting it might be 6 or 8 percent, as shown in Figure 8-11. (This is a hypothetical economy, however, and as we shall see the Monetarists strongly questioned this view.) Further, and most important for policy, the Phillips relation suggested to Keynesian economists that there was a trade-off between inflation and unemployment, a trade-off that might be

---

[7]A. W. Phillips, "Relation Between Unemployment and the Rate of Change of Money Wage Rates in the United Kingdom, 1861–1957," *Economica* 25 (November 1958), pp. 283–99. Whether Phillips "invented" the relation is open to question. See Irving Fisher, "A Statistical Relation Between Unemployment and Price Changes," *International Labor Review* (June 1926), pp. 785–92; reprinted as "I Discovered the Phillips Curve," *Journal of Political Economy* (March/April 1973), pp. 496–502. The so-called Phillips curve is thus of Neoclassical origin.

GLOBAL PERSPECTIVE

"IS THERE A NATURAL RATE OF UNEMPLOYMENT IN EUROPE?"

A mainstream theory in macroeconomics for the past twenty years has been the concept that a nation's unemployment rate gravitates toward a "natural" rate, consisting of frictional and structural unemployment. Frictional unemployment includes workers who have just come into the labor force or those who are temporarily between jobs. Structural unemployment occurs when workers do not have the necessary skills to meet the current demands of businesses. According to the natural-rate theory, fiscal and monetary policy can affect how much employment can vary over the business cycle, but it cannot affect the average level of unemployment or the natural rate. During the early 1980s, both the United States and Europe experienced recessions, and their unemployment rates reached the highest levels since the Great Depression.[a] While unemployment rates in the mid-1980s in the United States returned to normal levels, those in Europe kept on rising (see Figure 8-10).

Some economists, especially in Europe, argue that the natural rate theory of unemployment should be replaced by the term "hysteresis," which describes theories in which temporary shifts in aggregate demand cause long-term changes in unemployment. (Some American economists explain an increase in the "unemployment rate" from 3-4 percent to 5-6 per

PHOTO 8-2
Actual Unemployment Rates Have, in General, Been Higher in Europe Than in the United States Over the 1990s.

cent on this basis as well.) If there is hysteresis in the unemployment rate, unemployment remains at high levels. Hysteresis implies that there is no inherent tendency for unemployment to return to its pre-recession level. Almost all theories of hysteresis in unemployment focus on the idea that real wages are not completely flexible even in the long run. A number of economists have developed insider/outsider models to account for this wage rigidity. Insiders are workers in the firm who maintain money wages at high levels even though workers outside the firm are willing to work for less. These insiders prevent firms from hiring the outsiders by raising various costs to the firm. These costs include workers refusing to fully participate in training new outsider workers and by disrupting production through either strikes or slowdowns. Unions enhance insiders' power to act collectively, but power can come even without a union. The key to the insider/outsider model is that once workers lose their jobs, they no longer have the status of insiders. The inside workers are unwilling to reduce wages to get unemployed outsiders rehired. These former workers are viewed by insiders as no longer members of their group and accordingly have no influence. The more exclusive the insider group, the less willing it is to make concessions for wage reductions to increase employment. To explain permanent shifts in unemployment, the notion that aggregate demand fluctuations can cause a reduction in labor's productivity is attached to the insider/outsider model.

A contractionary monetary policy that raises nominal interest rates lowers investment spending on capital goods. This results in reduced capital formation, which in turn lowers the workers' productivity. Without an accompanying fall in the real wage, firms have little incentive to hire outsiders, and the employment rate stays permanently high. Another part of the hysteresis theory focuses on the long-term nature of unemployment itself. When workers are laid off for long periods, their skills may erode. As long as real wages do not decline, firms will be unwilling to hire less-skilled workers. In short, theories of hysteresis propose that the high unemployment rate in Europe is mainly caused by wage rigidity, a reduction in capital formation, and a deterioration in job skills of outside workers. Hysteresis still leaves some unanswered questions. There is little evidence that unions or insider power has increased over the 1980s and even into the 1990s. The power of labor unions has declined in both the United States and Europe. But the U.S. labor market shows some differences compared to Europe. The United States has fewer union members as a percentage of its labor force. Moreover, social welfare programs in the United States are less generous than the ones found in the European Communities. These factors tend to make the U.S. real wages more flexible than Europe's. Thus, the U.S. labor market may be characterized more by the type of Classical labor market envisioned by the natural-rate theory. ❏

NOTE [a]See William W. Long, "Is There a Natural Rate of Unemployment?"Federal Reserve Bank of Philadelphia *Business Review* (March/April 1990), pp. 13–22.

FIGURE 8-10

Unemployment Rates in Europe and the United States, 1968–1992.

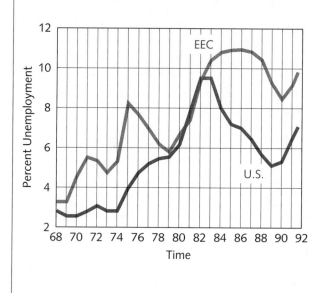

After peaking in 1982, U.S. unemployment returned to more normal levels of between 5 percent and 6 percent—levels thought to represent the natural rate of unemployment. But unemployment in Europe has remained relatively high. It's easy to see why many economists have questioned the natural-rate theory, at least for the European economies.

exploited by policymakers. In order to push unemployment lower and lower, higher and higher inflation rates would be necessary.

It is immediately evident why some economists and politicians have been troubled and others enticed by the prospects offered by the Phillips curve. While Phillips served up the idea as a long-term relation, the apparent relation between short-term inflation and short-term unemployment rates has provoked a great deal of interest. Belief in the relationship (either short term or long term) has also led to some predictable, but injurious, activity among politicians controlling fiscal policy (see Chapter 17). Does the relationship exist, and how might an economic explanation for the link be provided? First, let us look at the actual data.

Figure 8-12 presents annual combinations of the percentage change in the GDP implicit price deflator (the inflation rate) and the unemployment rate as

FIGURE 8-11
A Hypothetical Phillips Curve

The hypothetical Phillips curve of the figure depicts an inverse relationship between the inflation rate and the unemployment rate. For example, a reduction in the inflation rate from 14 to 8 percent is associated with an increase in the unemployment rate from 3 to 5 percent, posing a possible trade-off for policymakers.

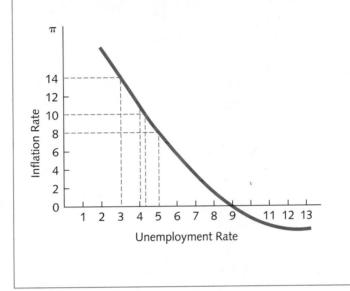

a percentage of the civilian labor force. Between 1959 and 1969, the relationship appears to have been fairly stable and predictable, giving economists and policymakers confidence that the Phillips trade-off did in fact exist. But during the 1970s and 1980s wild and erratic movements of the two rates took over. Inflation rates reached heights not seen in the post-World War II era and the unemployment rates were the highest experienced since the Great Depression of the 1930s. Between 1969 and 1970, 1971 and 1972, 1973 and 1974, 1975 and 1976, 1979 and 1981, 1982 and 1983, 1984 and 1985, 1985 and 1986, 1987 and 1988, and 1989 and 1990 there was a *positive* relationship between the inflation and unemployment rates (see Figure 8-12). There was a negative relationship between inflation and unemployment between 1974 and 1975, 1976 and 1979, and 1981 and 1982; and from 1983 to 1984, 1986 to 1987, 1988 to 1989, 1990 to 1991, and 1991 to 1993. Nevertheless, the post-1969 behavior of the two key rates has caused economists to strongly doubt the validity of the simple Phillips trade-off. Could the Phillips curve itself be shifting outward with higher and higher inflation rates? One very reasonable explanation for these events has been offered—an explanation that features expectations adjustments, splits the Phillips concept into short-run and long-run phenomena, and relates the trade-off to aggregate demand and aggregate supply.

FIGURE 8-12
Inflation and Unemployment,
1958–1993

Actual data on inflation and unemployment suggest that in some relatively short-term periods a trade-off exists between inflation and unemployment. During other periods, however, both unemployment and inflation move in the same direction. This suggests that no long-term Phillips relation exists for the United States.

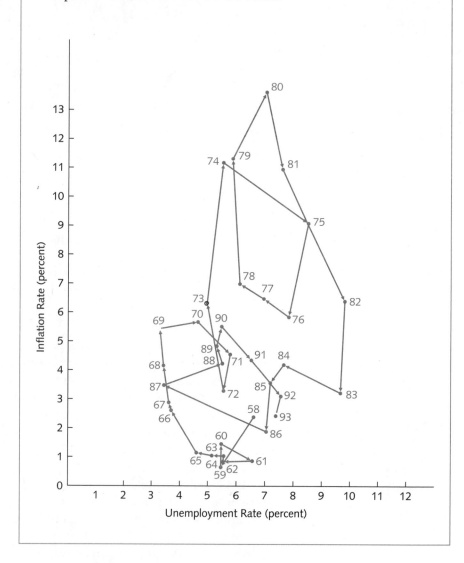

Phillips Curve in a Dynamic AD-AS Setting

In order to make matters more concrete, the Phillips curve discussion may be related to the standard aggregate demand and aggregate supply analysis, but in a dynamic framework, as well as to the Monetarist analysis of inflation theory presented earlier in this chapter. First consider Figure 8-13, which employs the

FIGURE 8-13
Expectations-Augmented
Phillips Phenomena

Short-run Phillips curves are drawn for a given level of price expectations as in the figure. The SRPC will shift rightward if an increase in price expectations occurs and leftward if a decrease occurs.

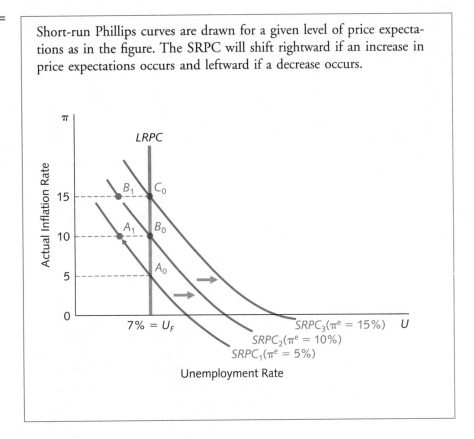

same numbers used in the Monetarist-inflation argument (see Figure 8-4 and accompanying discussion).

THE EXPECTATIONS-AUGMENTED PHILLIPS CURVE

When the actual and expected rates of inflation coincide, the economic perceptions of all market participants—including workers and employers—are in equilibrium in the sense that real forces are determining hiring, employment, and production decisions in the economy. This situation could correspond to a constant rate of monetary expansion and to an equivalence of the actual and expected inflation rates. Over an adjustment period, however, individuals' expectations about prices and the actual prices themselves will differ. Specifically, we will assume that workers' expectations of price increases lag behind employers' expectations. These expectational concepts build a dynamic element into both Phillips phenomena and (as we shall see presently) the aggregate demand-aggregate supply model.

The unemployment rate U and the actual inflation rate are contrasted in Figure 8-13. A series of three short-run Phillips curves ($SRPCs$) is shown along

A LONG-RUN PHILLIPS
CURVE is a vertical line
showing that, after
short-run adjustments in
expectations have taken
place, the aggregate supply
curve in the economy is a
vertical line at the natural
rate of employment (or
unemployment).

with a vertical **long-run Phillips curve** (*LRPC*). We arbitrarily assume that a 7 percent unemployment rate corresponds to the natural rate of unemployment. The *LRPC* is vertical at this natural rate of 7 percent. Assume, as we did earlier in this chapter, that at point A_0, income is growing at a rate of 3 percent per year. Further, assume (as we did in our discussion of inflation theory as summarized in Figure 18.4) that the rate of monetary expansion is 8 percent and that velocity is constant so that the resultant rate of inflation is 5 percent. If expectations of the inflation rate are equal to the actual inflation rate, so that $\pi^e = \pi$, then the economy is undergoing an inflation rate of 5 percent and a natural rate of unemployment of 7 percent.

The economy remains in equilibrium so long as the monetary expansion remains constant at 8 percent and velocity also remains constant. But assume that monetary expansion takes place and that the Federal Reserve begins increasing the money stock at a rate of 13 percent. Inflation begins to rise immediately and, according to the logic of worker-employer expectations adjustments, output will grow and unemployment will fall.

How, exactly, does this happen? According to the expectations-adjusted Phillips curve theory, sometimes called the Friedman-Phelps hypothesis, employers realize very quickly or instantaneously that the inflation rate has increased.[8] Workers' expectations of inflation take longer to adjust, however, and over a short period of time they might be considered to be fixed. Thus, the increase in the inflation rate begins to increase producer prices at a faster rate than it is perceived by workers. Individual employers observe product prices rising and will attempt to hire more labor. Such activity bids up the nominal wage, but not by enough to keep up with the rising price level. Real wages therefore decline and firms will hire more workers. These workers are only willing to work because they see higher nominal wages and do not yet perceive that prices are also higher. *These workers think—incorrectly—that their real wage has risen!* The increased employment leads to more output, which shows up as a temporary increase in the rate of growth of output.

Now return to our numerical example and consider the effects of the new rate of monetary expansion (at 13 percent) in Figure 8-13. Under the circumstances of the model, output grows as unemployment falls. In Figure 8-13, this is shown as a movement up $SRPC_1$ ($\pi^e = 5$ percent) from point A_0 to point A_1. Here the unemployment rate falls temporarily below and income rises temporarily above the natural rate of unemployment. (This latter effect is in contrast to the simplifying assumption of a *constant* rate of income growth in Figure 8-5.)

---

[8]This theory is derived from Milton Friedman. See "The Role of Monetary Policy," *American Economic Review* (March 1968), pp. 1–17; "Wage Determination and Employment," in *Price Theory* (Chicago: Aldine Publishing, 1976); "Nobel Lecture: Inflation and Unemployment," *Journal of Political Economy* (June 1977), pp. 451–72; also see Edmund Phelps, "Money Wage Dynamics and Labor Market Equilibrium," *Journal of Political Economy* 76 (July/August, 1968), pp. 687–711.

But workers will "catch on" to the actual price increases and they will realize that they have experienced lower real wage rates. The expected inflation rate rises to meet the actual inflation rate and the *SRPC* shifts rightward to SRPC (π^e = 10%). The result is a *temporary return* to the *LRPC* (from A_1 to B_0), yielding a temporary fall in income and a rise in the natural rate of unemployment. Still higher rates of monetary expansion will lower the unemployment rate again, but only temporarily and at the cost of higher and higher inflation. Persistent and increasing inflation rates, in this Monetarist theory, are the cost of maintaining unemployment at a rate below the natural rate. Moreover, movements *along* the *SRPC* are due to changes in aggregate demand. As indicated in this example, aggregate demand changes can be initiated by monetary policies. Such policies therefore have, through expectations-adjusted supply curves and the Phillips curve apparatus, critical implications for unemployment and inflation in the economy. For example, the Phillips curve can be used to analyze recent monetary and cycle history. (See Policy Issues: "How Inflation Was Squeezed from the Macroeconomy, 1979–1985".)

SOME IMPLICATIONS OF INFLATION AND UNEMPLOYMENT ANALYSIS

A number of contemporary economists subscribe to the Monetarist view that inflation is everywhere and at all times a monetary phenomenon. While real factors, such as changes in autonomous investment, consumption, and net foreign balances, help to make up real aggregate demand, changes in these factors cannot explain, in the Monetarist view, large and persistent rates of change in prices, income, and employment. Nominal demand changes leading to inflation or **deflation** are thus, in the Monetarist scenario, the results of alterations in monetary expansion. These undesirable changes may spring from Federal Reserve policies or from fiscal policies originating in the U.S. Congress or in the world of politics.

DEFLATION is a persistent decrease in the general price level.

The Monetarist insight into inflation offers yet other implications for policy. As discussed earlier in this chapter, monetary expansion per se has three very desirable initial characteristics: (1) nominal (and real) interest rates are temporarily lowered; (2) the unemployment rate is temporarily forced below the natural level; and (3) the growth rate of income temporarily rises. The desirability of achieving these economic goals in the short run has usually been too attractive for politicians to resist (particularly in election years). Monetary expansion, however, achieves these goals temporarily until inflation expectations catch up, and then at the expense of higher rates of inflation. Policies leading to price stability (monetary contraction) have the opposite, and politically unpopular, short-run effects. It is small wonder that fiscal responsibility and monetary stability are so often talked about but so seldom tried.

HOW INFLATION WAS SQUEEZED FROM THE MACROECONOMY, 1979–1985

Americans experienced rapid inflation in the 1970s, culminating in a 13 percent inflation rate in 1979. Over this period, in the Monetarist view of inflation discussed in this chapter, inflationary expectations gathered force in the late 1970s, contributing to actual inflation experience. High growth rates in the money stock coupled with the once-and-for-all secondary impact of oil price shocks by OPEC, were the ultimate causes of the 1970s inflation in the Monetarist view. Inflationary expectations, however, fanned actual inflation during that period.

In 1979, Federal Reserve Board Chairman Paul Volcker set out to stem the tide of inflation by (partially) instituting a policy of controlling a money aggregate rather than an interest-rate target. There is much dispute among economists over whether the aggregate was faithfully controlled (i.e., whether a variant of "Monetarism" was ever tried—the M1 target was

abandoned off and on over the 1979–1985 period) but there is no denying that inflation was successfully controlled. The Federal Reserve, in the person of Chairman Volcker, managed to convince market participants (workers, buyers, sellers, etc.) that the inflation rate was going to fall. The credit and M1 "crunch" that followed Fed announcements of money curtailment squeezed inflationary expectations out of the economy. It also caused two brief recessions and extremely high unemployment rates, reaching 10.8 percent of the labor force in 1982 and staying above 9 percent in 1983 and 1984.

This situation may be analyzed with tools developed in this chapter, namely with the expectations-augmented Phillips curve apparatus. Consider Figure 8-17, which depicts several short-run Phillips curves for alternative-expected inflation rates along with a vertical long-run Phillips curve at a (rather arbitrarily assumed) 7 percent natural rate of unemployment. We may imagine the economy as operating at point A on $SRPC_0$ in the late 1970s, with high inflationary expectations of 13 percent. At point A in Figure 8-17, expected inflation π^e equals actual inflation π. In 1979 and later, Volcker broke inflationary expectations by announced policy changes

accompanied by sharp decreases in M1. These reductions reduced actual inflation below that expected by workers. These actual reductions caused the amount of labor demanded and supplied to decrease (temporarily) and pushed the unemployment rate higher than the natural rate (to 9.5 percent in 1983 and 1984) along $SRPC_0$ to point B.

Finally, the public recognized that the actual inflation rate was lower and that the Fed was serious about keeping it lower. Expectations of inflation were lowered from 13 percent and again were equal to the natural rate at a 5 percent level. The natural rate of unemployment—assumed to be 7 percent in Figure 8-14—is restored at point C, where inflationary expectations of 5 percent are exactly equal to an actual rate of 5 percent. The abrupt back-breaking of inflationary expectations by the Fed, in the opinion of many economists, not only tamed actual inflation but created a severe unemployment problem as well. Unemployment rates fell by 1985, market interest rates declined, and inflation was controlled. But many at the time believed and some continue to believe that the medicine applied by the Fed in 1979 and later was too strong for the admittedly severe illness of inflation. ❏

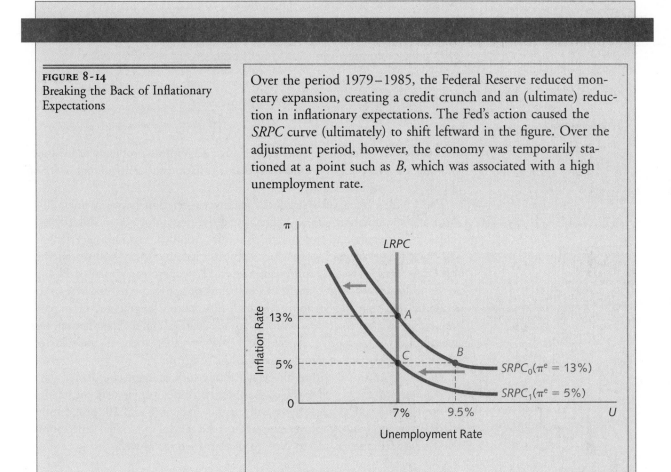

FIGURE 8-14
Breaking the Back of Inflationary Expectations

Over the period 1979–1985, the Federal Reserve reduced monetary expansion, creating a credit crunch and an (ultimate) reduction in inflationary expectations. The Fed's action caused the *SRPC* curve (ultimately) to shift leftward in the figure. Over the adjustment period, however, the economy was temporarily stationed at a point such as *B*, which was associated with a high unemployment rate.

An even more disturbing implication of the Monetarist analysis of inflation and unemployment is that, with high and persistent experience of inflation, individuals may be adjusting expectations at a faster and faster rate. For example, if we contrast the theoretical Phillips curve of Figure 8-17 with the actual U.S. data in Figure 8-14, it appears that there may have been at least two shifts in the short-run Phillips curve since 1969. These data seem to indicate that higher and higher inflationary expectations had been built into the economy with continuous inflationary experience. This meant that the rate of monetary expansion required to temporarily lower interest rates and to raise employment will likewise be higher and higher.

Finally, the Monetarist approach underlines the separate nature of the problems. Inflation, short-run effects notwithstanding, will be tamed *only* by controlling monetary expansion. Permanent redress of unemployment problems or reductions in the natural rate of unemployment require policy alterations in the institutional rigidities surrounding labor supply and an increase in labor productivity. The only way to meet these economic problems, in the Monetarist view, is head-on. Indeed, in the Monetarist view, there are no long-run trade-offs between inflation and unemployment, and no easy monetary policy solution to unemployment problems in the long run.

SUMMARY

This chapter considered the interrelated macroeconomic problems of inflation and unemployment. The Monetarists blame inflation squarely on high rates of growth in the money supply.

The Phillips hypothesis suggested an inverse relation between unemployment and the inflation rate and entertained the uncomfortable possibility of a trade-off between these two macroeconomic variables. Economists Friedman and Phelps developed a theory which demonstrates that the so-called trade-off, if it exists at all, is a short-run phenomenon. Expectations-augmented Phillips curves indicate that employment can be below or above the natural rate in the short run, but that the economy (through expectations augmented of employees and workers) is always tending to the natural rate. The natural rate hypothesis, with adaptive expectations, suggests that there is no trade-off between inflation and unemployment in the long run.

These propositions, within an overall framework of aggregate demand and supply, conform fairly well to the contemporary Monetarist views of the relation between money and prices. As we will see in Chapters 9 and 10, propositions relating to worker and employer expectations are central to rational expectations (New Classical) theory and to Neo-Keynesian theories as well.

KEY TERMS

adaptive expectations theory	Fisher effect
deflation	inflation
ex ante real interest rate	long-run Phillips curve (LRPC)
ex post real interest rate	

QUESTIONS FOR REVIEW AND DISCUSSION

1. Define inflation. Is inflation to be regarded as an absolute change in prices or as a percentage change?

2. How are holdings of real cash balances and expectations of inflation related?

3. Discuss the relationship between expectations of inflation, the nominal interest rate, and the real interest rate. What is the distinction between the *ex ante* and the *ex post* real interest rate? Can the real interest rate ever be negative?

4. Analyze the Monetarist theory of inflation. How is the demand for cash balances related to the Monetarist theory of inflation?

5. What is the adaptive expectations theory?

6. "The inflation rate is high because nominal interest rates are high. Therefore, the Federal Reserve Board should attempt to reduce the nominal interest rate." Discuss.

7. What is the original argument about inflation and unemployment offered by Phillips?

8. How does an adjustment for price expectations alter the original Phillips curve conclusions? Contrast the short-run and long-run versions of the Phillips curve.

9. Does the natural rate of unemployment change along the long-run Phillips curve? Along the short-run Phillips curve? Explain.

10. Combining the extreme Monetarist model of aggregate demand and the Monetarist aggregate supply curve, describe the effect of an increase in the money supply on output, the price level, and the interest rate.

PROBLEMS

1. Combining the extreme Monetarist model of aggregate demand and the Monetarist aggregate supply curve, describe the effect of an increase in government spending on output, the price level, and the interest rate. Develop a graphical argument.

2. Combining the extreme Monetarist model of aggregate demand and the Monetarist aggregate supply curve, describe the effect of an increase in the money growth rate *that leads to an equal increase in the expected and actual inflation rate.* What is the effect on output, the price level, and the interest rate? Is your answer related to the quantity theory of money?

SUGGESTIONS FOR FURTHER READING

Auernheimer, Leonardo, and Robert B. Ekelund, Jr. *The Essentials of Money and Banking.* New York: John Wiley & Sons, 1982.

Baye, Michael R. and Dan A. Black. "The Microeconomic Foundations of Measuring Bracket Creep and Other Tax Changes." *Economic Inquiry* (July 1988), pp. 471–84.

Dwyer, Gerald P., Jr., and R. W. Hafer. "Is Money Irrelevant?" Federal Reserve Bank of St. Louis *Review* (May/June 1988), pp. 3–17.

Friedman, Milton. *The Optimal Quantity of Money and Other Essays.* Chicago: Aldine Publishing, 1969.

Friedman, Milton, and Anna J. Schwartz. *Monetary Trends in the United States and the United Kingdom.* Chicago: University of Chicago Press for the National Bureau of Economic Research, 1982.

Garfinkel, Michelle R. "What is an 'Acceptable' Rate of Inflation?—A Review of the Issues." Federal Reserve Bank of St. Louis *Review* (July/August 1989), pp. 3–15.

Grieder, William. *Secrets of the Temple: How the Federal Reserve Runs the Country.* New York: Simon & Schuster, 1987.

Tatom, John B. "The Welfare Costs of Inflation." Federal Reserve Bank of St. Louis *Review* (December 1983), pp. 9–22.

PART III

MODERN APPROACHES TO MACROECONOMIC MODELING

9

THE NEW CLASSICAL ECONOMICS

AND RATIONAL EXPECTATIONS

THE NEW CLASSICAL
ECONOMICS (NCE) is a
modern approach that
relies on the assumption
that expectations are
formed rationally, and on a
natural rate approach to
modeling aggregate supply.

The **New Classical Economics** (NCE) suggests that the role for monetary policy in the macroeconomy is quite a bit more subtle than the role suggested by the Classical, Keynesian, or even Monetarist models. Some economists have viewed the New Classical Economics as claiming that monetary policy is ineffective, and many New Classical models do prescribe a limited role for monetary policy. Compared to earlier models, the New Classical models have two main distinguishing features, and these features are important for generating some of the novel policy conclusions of the New Classical Economics. The first distinguishing feature is the assumption of rational expectations. Unlike other hypotheses of how expectations are formed, the rational expectations hypothesis theorizes that the predictions formed by individuals in the economy will be consistent with the economic model governing the variable being predicted. That is, expectations should be based on economic theory, and not assumed to be either exogenous or formed by some ad hoc method unrelated to economic theory.

The second distinguishing feature of the New Classical Economics is that the aggregate supply side of economy is based on the natural rate idea espoused by the Monetarists. That is, employment and output are at the natural rate of output unless there is an unexpected change in the economy, and, in particular, in prices.

The New Classical Economics incorporates the hypothesis of rational expectations and the natural rate idea to build a model of the economy that gives Classical results in the long run, but that yields an upward sloping short-run aggregate supply curve for unexpected changes in price. Hence the name New Classical, to indicate that the model is Classical in nature, but can explain short-run deviations from the natural rate of output.

By the end of this chapter, you will know

- the distinction between Classical and New Classical models
- how the hypothesis of rational expectations differs from adaptive expectations
- how rational expectations can be incorporated into a model of the labor market based on asymmetric information to yield a New Classical aggregate supply model
- how changes in aggregate demand and aggregate supply affect the equilibrium price level and output level in a New Classical model
- the criticisms of New Classical models, and the debate over what they have taught us about macroeconomics.

OLD AND NEW CLASSICAL MACROECONOMICS

Before turning to the theory of rational expectations, which is an underpinning of the NCE, it is useful to understand some similarities and distinctions between old and New Classical macroeconomics. The Classicists predicted macroeconomic equilibrium at full employment and full production in the long run. At the root of this prediction was Say's Law, which meant that in the long run *supply created its own demand*. Given the efficiency of markets in the economy, aggregate production would be exactly matched by aggregate spending on goods and services. So long as prices, wages, and interest rates were completely flexible in response to changes in the demand and supply of commodities, labor and other inputs, and financial assets, the economy would tend to function at full employment in the long run.

Another part of Classical thinking—one particularly relevant to modern Monetarist and rational expectations theorizing—is the so-called Classical dichotomy. The ***Classical dichotomy*** is the belief that *in the long run,* value theory (the theory of the formation of relative prices) is independent of monetary theory (the theory of how the price *level* is established). In practical terms, the Classical dichotomy means that the money supply plays a causal role in establishing *nominal* income and prices, and that there is a long-run proportionality between the stock of money and the price level, a feature which itself is based on constant or stable velocity of money (or the demand for money) and the transmission of money injections through cash balances to spending. The conclusion is that real magnitudes (the ones that count) will be left undisturbed by monetary policy changes in the long run. Supporting this conclusion is the Classical assumption of market clearing with flexible wages and prices, an assumption often made in the NCE.

Importantly, the Classical models assumed that all market participants had perfect information about the future. The New Classical Economists drop the assumption about perfect knowledge and argue, instead, that individuals form expectations about the future course of prices and market behavior, and that these expectations may not always turn out to be accurate. People can make mistakes in the NCE. The important point is that Monetarists (see Chapter 8), and in a far more elaborate manner, rational expectationists have developed theories of expectations on the part of input and output market participants that fill in critical gaps in explaining how real output and employment might be affected over the adjustment or short-run period—a period that is extremely relevant to our economic well-being. The modern theory of rational expectations, on which NCE is based, finds its origin in earlier explanations for the short-term trade-off between inflation and unemployment rates.

THE CLASSICAL DICHOTOMY is the belief that in the long run, value theory (the theory of the formation of relative prices) is independent of monetary theory (the theory of how the price *level* is established).

RATIONAL EXPECTATIONS

RATIONAL EXPECTATIONS is a theory that people, on average and through time, will form price expectations consistent with the predictions of the relevant economic theory.

The New Classical Economics based on *rational expectations* is in many ways an extension of the ideas introduced by the Monetarists. The NCE, however, contains a richer view of the manner in which expectations are formed and an even more negative view on the possibility of beneficial activist macroeconomic policy, especially monetary policy. Before turning to the NCE view on the efficacy of policy, consider its view of how expectations of market participants are formed.

Adaptive and Rational Expectations

How might expectations be explained? Why are they the key to the New Classical views of the macroeconomy? Expectations are important because many transactions in our economy are contracts requiring the delivery of commodities, labor, or other inputs at some future date or over some series of future dates; prices for those transactions will be adjusted upward or downward by contract. Business firms, moreover, will post prices for some future period. If these firms expect all other prices to rise at some rate in the future, they can keep the relative price of their own product or service constant only by raising its price at that same rate.

ADAPTIVE EXPECTATIONS is the theory that price expectations formed today are determined by the recent past behavior of prices.

Expectations affect current decisions of all market participants and thus economic activity in the present (and future). The question becomes, how are expectations formed? In the **adaptive expectations** theory, present expectations regarding prices are determined by recent or (some calculation of) past price experience. Such past experience may include a lifetime of price experience or a weighted average of past experience, with more recent experience more heavily counted.

We must note that the Friedman-Phelps interpretation of the expectations-adjusted Phillips curve rests on *asymmetrical* adaptive expectations. Friedman, in particular, argued that all market participants are more familiar with conditions (including prices) surrounding the things they sell than they are with conditions (including prices) surrounding the things they buy. When applied to workers and firms, this principle means that cycles of real output and employment can be generated with fiscal or monetary changes. Suppose, for instance, that the Federal Reserve steps up the rate of growth in M2. This will increase demand for all goods. Firms respond by increasing production, hiring more inputs—including labor—and raising nominal wages in the process. Workers, who process information about their nominal wage more quickly than they process information about the price level, will be willing to supply more labor at the higher *nominal* wage. They perceive the nominal wage increase as a real wage increase, although unbeknownst to them their *real* wage

BUSINESS CYCLES are recurrent fluctuations in business and employment activity due to changes in aggregate demand or aggregate supply.

might actually be falling. Expectations, in other words, have not caught up to actual (inflationary) events, permitting *short-term* increases in employment. ***Business cycles*** *of real output and employment are created in this manner,* although employment and output will return to their natural rates after expectations have adapted to the new actual conditions.

Information and Expectations

A fundamental difference between the Monetarist conception and that of the New Classical Economics relates to the treatment of expectations. It is summed up in the question, do market participants ignore or throw away information or predictions about the future course of the economy and economic activity, or do they rationally anticipate the effects of governmental policies and react in the present in accordance with those rational anticipations? Rational expectationists believe that buyers and sellers of products and resources will react to fiscal, monetary, and other policies by ultimately learning the effects of these policies.

It is important at the outset to distinguish between the effects that the assumption of rational expectations has through monetary policy, on the one hand, and through fiscal policy, on the other. In many New Classical models, monetary policy, if rationally anticipated, will have no *real* effects on the economy. This Classical view is called **policy neutrality.** For example, attempts by the Federal Reserve to improve business conditions may lead it to expand the money stock. If rationally and fully expected, the price level will rise, but there will be no effects on output, real income, or employment.

POLICY NEUTRALITY is the hypothesis which states that changes in the money supply will have no effect on real output and employment, only change nominal variables such as the price level or the nominal wage rate.

According to the NCE, fiscal policy, even if rationally and fully anticipated, can have real effects in the economy. Following the *IS-LM* model of aggregate demand, an increase in government spending or decrease in taxes will increase aggregate demand. Unless there is an effect on aggregate supply, however, it may well be that output is unaffected. It depends in part on the change in taxes. Changes in lump sum taxes might not change aggregate supply, while changes in income taxes and other taxes that alter economic behavior can be expected to shift aggregate supply. Moreover, changes in government spending or lump sum taxes can be expected to change the real interest rate, and this will alter investment even if aggregate supply is unchanged.

To understand the general manner in which rational expectations works, consider an example which, though of a microeconomic nature, will emphasize possible *real* effects. In much of the mid-1980s' discussion of tax reform in Congress, the elimination of deductions was a major part. One hotly debated deduction concerned interest payments on second homes. Suppose the decision is made to eliminate the deduction on second homes but that the policy will not take effect until sometime in the future. Rational expectations theory would tell us that the adjustment in the prices of second homes, now not as desirable without the interest deduction, would begin to take place immediately. Sellers, who rationally expect the price of such dwellings to fall without the former tax benefit, would put such property on the market, and demand for second homes would fall. Such market activity would mean that the effects of the policy would be capitalized in the value of such property long before the policy becomes legally effective. In real terms, the change in relative value created by a change in tax policy will presumably cause fewer beach houses or condos to be built.

According to the rational expectationists, anticipation of how prices, real incomes, and unemployment will be affected by changes in the money supply, in taxes, or in government spending is just as rational, because they are taken into the present calculations of market participants. This, of course, does not mean that *all* market participants are always sophisticated predictors of the effects of contemporary policy enactments. Surprises (i.e., unexpected events) and errors in forecasting remain possible. The rational expectations view is simply that *on average* the prevailing majority of predictions will be correct and that *on average* policy effects will be fully anticipated.

One major criticism of rational expectations has been that it takes time for people to learn. For a discussion of the importance of this issue, see the Policy Issue: "Rational Expectations, Learning, and Macroeconomic Policy."

Anticipated versus Unanticipated Price Changes

The New Classical view that market participants will, correctly on average, anticipate the effects of policy is subject to misinterpretation. Rational expectations theory does not mean, for example, that every market participant will correctly anticipate the effects of policy every time. All market participants do not have to be sophisticated in economic theory nor have the same theory in order for the principles of rational expectations to hold. It is well known that organizations, businesses, and publications hire economists to predict and to rationally anticipate the future effects of policies. Individuals and businesses routinely purchase the expertise of economists and others in making their buying and selling decisions. Those market participants who make consistent errors in predicting the effects of policies would be penalized severely—perhaps to the extent that they would lose an amount of decision-making power in the market.

In the rational expectations theory, surprises are a clear possibility. Formulators of the theory maintain that unfolding economic events such as inflations or unemployment will be partly unanticipated. In formal econometric interpretations of rational expectations, surprises mean that there will be an error term in the equations that describes the macroeconomic system. The existence of rational expectations, however, means that errors in prediction will not be biased, or more in one direction than another. Instead, prediction errors will be

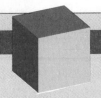

"RATIONAL EXPECTATIONS, LEARNING, AND MACROECONOMIC POLICY"

According to rational expectations, when an economy is in equilibrium, individuals do not make systematic forecasting errors. Most New Classical economists build their models by assuming rational expectations and do not make any explicit statement about the type of learning that takes place in these models. Currently researchers are beginning to focus on the "learning method." They are attempting to answer the question, how are systematic forecasting errors eliminated? In an attempt to analyze individuals with rational expectations, three different approaches have been taken within the rational expectations macroeconomic literature.

The first approach deals with models in which learning is based *only* on the history of the economy.[a] Forecasts are made using historical time series data on a number of variables that people observe. These models exclude any notion of the federal government preference for policymaking or the public's belief about this policy. The second approach to the treatment of expectation formation goes further than the first. These macro models not only use historical time series to forecast expectations but contain the beliefs of other people. That is, individuals in their forecast are concerned with the expectations of one or more players. One of the players may well include the government in its policymaking roles. The policy implications of these models are different from the first in that they may be, for example, extremely sensitive to the public's belief about the government's preferences for monetary policymaking.

The third approach takes into consideration irrelevant information that some people may rationally take into account. This type of information is referred to as a frivolous variable in the model. A good example of this variable is sunspots. When some people think the frivolous variable is important in forming expectations, other people also begin to feel it is rational for them to do likewise. Therefore, the frivolous variable acts as a signaling device to indicate a change in expectation formation. Models of this nature include not only irrelevant historical information, but the expectations of others.

The literature on so-called sunspot equilibria is a distinctly different branch of rational expectations with different policy implications from the first two approaches. The existence of these sunspot models with learning and multiple equilibria suggests a number of possible outcomes including the lack of dynamics converging to equilibrium. In summary, since rational expectations theory provides no learning process, some economists have started to provide their own: Perhaps individuals base their expectations on historical time series, or the expectations of other people, or on sunspots. Unfortunately, there is to date no consensus among economists about which version of rational expectations is correct. ❏

SOURCE: [a]See James B. Bullard, "Learning, Rational Expectations and Policy: A Summary of Recent Research," Federal Reserve Bank of St. Louis *Review* (January/February 1991), pp. 50–58.

DEMAND SHOCKS are surprise changes in the aggregate demand schedule.

SUPPLY SHOCKS are surprise changes in aggregate supply.

randomly distributed (and will average out to zero over time). *Only the unanticipated part of price or other effects will have any impact on the real variables in the economy and, then, only over a short period of time.* Cycles of inflation, unemployment, and real income growth are, therefore, explained solely on the basis of unanticipated **demand** or **supply shocks** that create price surprises in the economy. The source of these shocks can be erratic or unanticipated changes in monetary or fiscal policy; sudden, unexpected changes in technology; changes in resource supply (as from a plague or natural disaster); artificial interferences in markets such as cartel formation; or sudden changes in cartel policy (as experienced under the OPEC regime).

In policy terms, the NCE predicts that the anticipated part of policy effects (specifically price effects) will come to be correctly understood more often over time. Information will be processed more and more efficiently through time so that the effects of policy changes will be more quickly neutralized. Price surprises will still occur, of course, but business cycles will be moderated with consistent governmental policies. While participants in financial markets, such as those for stocks and bonds, are probably better informed (on balance) than their counterparts in output and resource markets, suppliers and demanders of goods and services are as much affected, in theory at least, by policy changes. Our version of the NCE model will stress the labor market and the differences between the information of firms and workers.

THE LABOR MARKET AND THE MACROECONOMY UNDER RATIONAL EXPECTATIONS

We begin our study with the functioning of labor markets, and continue with an explanation of aggregate demand and supply under conditions of rational expectations.

The Labor Market

To begin, consider Figure 9–1, which demonstrates the relationship between graphs of the labor market with the real wage W/P on the vertical axis and graphs of the labor market with the nominal wage W on the vertical axis. Recall from the discussion of the Classical model in Chapters 3 and 8 that labor demand and labor supply can be written as functions of the real wage:

$$N_d = N_d\left(\frac{W}{p}, K\right)$$

and

$$N_s = N_s\left(\frac{W}{P}\right),$$

FIGURE 9–1
The Labor Market Once
More

Graph (a) shows the Classical labor market, with labor demand a function of the marginal product of labor as shown in Chapter 3. Graph (b) shows labor demand and supply as a function of the wage rate, as well as the price level and other arguments. Any change in the price level using these two graphs will result in no change in equilibrium employment, since we do not distinguish between expected and actual prices here. A rise in price will result in an equal change in the nominal wage, leaving real wages unaffected.

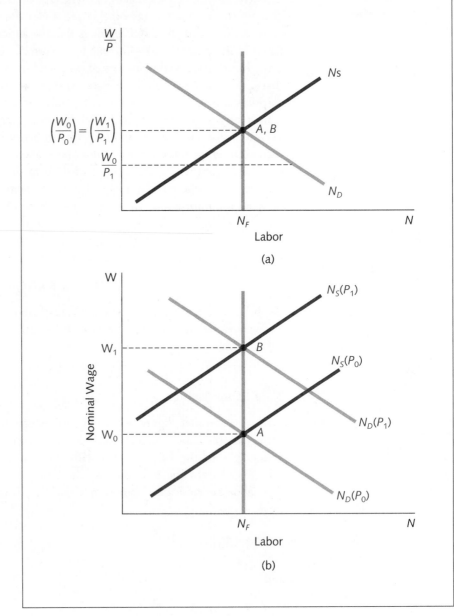

(a)

(b)

where K is the capital stock. Recall too from Chapter 3 that the labor demand curve is the marginal product of labor, which is the slope of the production function. Profit- maximizing firms hire labor until the marginal product of labor is equal to the real wage, and this gives the labor demand curve. The labor demand and supply curves for the Classical model correspond to those in Figure 9–1(a).

To obtain our New Classical model of the labor market, the Classical model is slightly modified. Our version of the New Classical model is a popular one based on asymmetric information between firms and workers. This model specifies labor demand and supply as

$$N_d = N_d\left(\frac{W}{P}, K\right)$$

and

$$N_s = N_s\left(\frac{W}{P^e}\right),$$

where P^e is the expectation of the price level. In this model the question facing workers and firms in their labor supply and labor demand decisions is not necessarily what the price and wage situation actually is but what they expect it to be. Worker and firm expectations of the real wage are the key to this theory. We assume that firms know both the nominal wage and the price of their output, and hence firms know the real wage W/P. Workers, however, do not continuously survey the market prices of all the myriad of goods and services they consume over the course of a month or a year. This means that the expected real wage for workers depends on the nominal wage, which they know, and their rational expectation of the price level. This rational expectation of the price level may differ from the actual price level due to unexpected shocks to the economy, such as unexpected changes in the money supply. Workers, therefore, base their labor supply decision on their expectation of the real wage, given by the known nominal wage W divided by their expectation of the price level P^e.

Using the above labor demand and labor supply curves, it becomes imperative to plot these curves on a graph with the nominal wage on the vertical axis. This is convenient because labor supply is a function of W/P^e while labor demand is a function of W/P. The common element is not W/P but W. To accomplish this, we adapt Figure 9–1(b) to make labor supply a function not of P but of P^e. This is accomplished in Figure 9–2. In this figure, labor demand is an explicit function of the price level P, and labor supply is an explicit function of the expected price level P^e. If P and P^e are the same, then the intersection of labor demand and labor supply reproduces the Classical equilibrium as shown in Figure 9–1, with employment at N_F and the real wage equal to $(W/P)_0$. One example is shown in Figure 9–2 at point A, where $N_D(P_0)$ intersects $N_S(P^e = P_0)$. The equilibrium nominal wage is W_0, the

This diagram is similar to figure 9–1(b), except that labor supply curve N_S depends on the expected price level P^e instead of the actual price level. The labor demand curve N_D continues to depend on the actual price. At the initial equilibrium, the price level equals the expected price level, $P_0 = P^e$, the nominal wage equals W_0, employment is at the natural rate N_F, and labor supply and demand intersect at point A. Now, let there be an unexpected rise in the price level. Since workers' expectations have not changed, the labor supply curve remains at $N_S(P^e = P_0)$, but labor demand increases to $N_D(P_1)$. The wage rises to W_c, and employment rises to N_c. If the price rise had been fully anticipated ($P^e = P_1$), labor supply would shift to $N_S(P^e = P_1)$ and the nominal wage would rise to W_1, with no change in the real wage or employment. The equilibrium points A and B correspond to those in Figure 9–1(b).

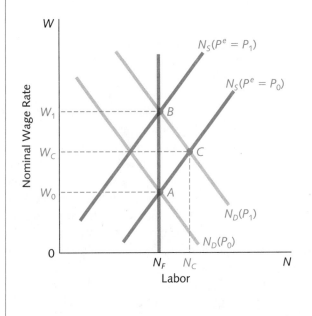

equilibrium employment level is N_F, and the real wage can be calculated as W_0/P_0. At A, notice that workers' expectations of the real wage W/P^e is equal to the actual real wage W_0/P_0, because $P^e = P_0$.

What happens if actual prices rise to P_1, while worker expectations of the price level stay at $P^e = P_0$? In this case, the increase in the price level increases labor demand, just as it did in Figure 9–1(b). This is illustrated in Figure 9–2 by the rightward shift in labor demand to $N_D(P_1)$. Meanwhile, labor supply does not shift because the expected price level has not changed. This is a situation where an unexpected increase in aggregate demand—perhaps an unexpected increase in the money supply—causes an increase in the price level, an increase that workers are temporarily unaware of. In this case, the equilibrium is at point C, where the nominal wage is W_c, employment is N_c, and the real wage is W_c/P_1. This real wage is less than the original real wage of W_0/P_0. How do we know?[1] It must be that the real wage has decreased, since otherwise the quantity of labor demanded would not increase. Hence, W_c/P_1 is *lower* than W_0/P_0.

How does the labor market return to long-run equilibrium in which expected price and actual price coincide? Eventually workers become aware that prices have increased due to the increase in the money supply—over time they get a larger sample of prices of different goods and services from which to form an expectation of the price level—and the expected price level increases to P_1. When this occurs, the labor supply curve shifts to the left, from $N_S(P^e = P_0)$ to $N_S(P^e = P_1)$. The intersection of labor supply and labor demand occurs at point B, determining an equilibrium nominal wage of W_1, an equilibrium quantity of employment of N_F, and a real wage—both perceived and actual—of W_1/P_1. This real wage is equal to the initial real wage of W_0/P_0, so that the equilibria at points A and B differ only in the levels of the nominal wage and price level W and P, not in the real wage or the level of employment. Note that in moving from the equilibrium at point C to the equilibrium at point B, the perceived real wage declines from W_c/P_0 to W_1/P_1 but the actual real wage increases from W_c/P_1 to W_1/P_1.

A key point to keep in mind is that the equilibrium points labeled A and B in Figure 9–2 correspond to the equilibrium points labeled A and B in Figure 9–1(b). These are points of long-run or Classical equilibrium at the natural rate of employment in the labor market. At these points, both labor demanders and labor suppliers share a common expectation of the real wage, and that expectation is accurate. The new equilibria allowed by the modified labor market structure are equilibria such as that illustrated by point C in Figure 9–2, in which labor demanders and suppliers disagree about their expectations of the real wage. Moreover, in our model it is labor demanders whose expectations of the real wage always correspond to the actual real wage, while labor suppliers have mistaken expectations of the price level (and hence of the real wage) because they do not often observe the prices of the goods and services they purchase infrequently.

---

[1]Note that both W and P have increased, and hence we might think that the ratio W/P could increase, decrease, or stay the same. However, we know more than just that W and P have increased. We also know that the equilibrium quantity of labor demanded *and* supplied has increased. How could this happen? The increase in the equilibrium quantity of labor supply is easy to explain. At point A, the perceived real wage facing workers was W_0/P_0 because $P^e = P_0$. At point C, the nominal wage has increased while the expected price level has not changed, so the perceived real wage facing workers is W_c/P_0 because $P^e = P_0$. Workers incorrectly perceive that the increase in the nominal wage from W_0 to W_c is an increase in their real wage!

Aggregate Supply

We can now develop a notion of the aggregate supply curve based on this labor market structure. In this New Classical model, business firms and workers have rational expectations. If there are changes in the price level that are anticipated, these will not affect the level of real output, and aggregate supply will be vertical, just as in the Classical model. If there are changes in the price level that are not anticipated (i.e., that are unexpected by rational agents), then these changes will affect the level of real output, and aggregate supply will be upward sloping. This ability of the New Classical model to exhibit both the Classical vertical aggregate supply curve in the face of expected changes in the price level, and the upward sloping aggregate supply curve characteristic of the Keynesian model in response to unexpected changes in the price level, is why these models are called New Classical.

Figure 9–3 uses the by-now familiar construction of earlier chapters to develop the aggregate supply curve. Here, that construction includes the labor market structure outlined in Figure 9–2. Original full-employment equilibrium occurs at point A in the labor market, at the intersection of $N_D(P_0)$ and $N_S(P^e = P_0)$. The equilibrium quantity of labor input, N_F produces output level Y_F, as indicated by the production function $Y = f(N)$. In the aggregate supply graph, Figure 9–3(d), the initial equilibrium point is represented by point A, with a price of P_0 and an output level of Y_F.

Now assume that the price level increases to P_1. In a Classical or long-run equilibrium, both businesses' and workers' expectations of the price level also increase to $P^e = P_1$. If this occurs, then in the labor market the labor demand curve increases to $N_D(P_1)$ and the labor supply curve decreases to $N_S(P^e = P_1)$. These curves intersect at point C, where the nominal wage is W_1, employment is N_F, and the real wage W_1/P_1 is the same as the initial real wage W_0/P_0. Because employment is unchanged, output is unchanged. This is represented in the aggregate supply graph by point C, where the price is P_1 and output is Y_F. Indeed, any increase in P that is matched by an equal increase in P^e will result in a constant output level of Y_F, and this just yields the standard perfectly inelastic aggregate supply curve of the Classical model, labeled $LRAS$ in Figure 9–3(d).

What happens, however, if the price level increase from P_0 to P_1 and expectations of the price level do not adjust? That is, workers are rational but have not anticipated the increase in the price level, and hence their price expectations remain at $P^e = P_0$. In this case, the labor demand curve increases as before to $N_D(P_1)$, but the labor supply curve remains unchanged at $N_S(P^e = P_0)$. Labor market equilibrium occurs at point B, where the wage is W_B and employment is N_B. The increased employment generates output of Y_B. In the aggregate supply graph, this is represented by point B, where the price level is P_1 and output is Y_B.

Notice that at both points A and B the expected price level of workers has remained constant, at $P^e = P_0$. We say that points A and B lie on a short-run

FIGURE 9−3

Aggregate Supply and Price Expectations

Here we develop an upward sloping short-run aggregate supply curve. In this case a price increase may be unexpected and result in a rise in labor demand with no corresponding rise in labor supply. Income increases to Y_B along the short-run aggregate supply curve $SRAS(P^e = P_0)$. As workers raise their expectations of the price level to P_1, the short-run aggregate supply curve shifts up to $SRAS$ $(P^e = P_1)$. Income falls back to Y_F.

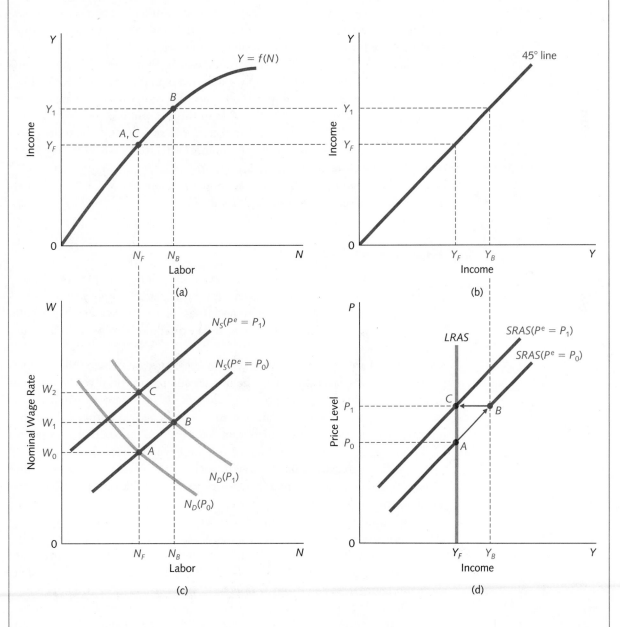

aggregate supply curve that exists when expected prices are equal to P_0, and we label this curve $SRAS(P^e = P_0)$. This supply curve holds whenever the expected price equals P_0, and hence it intersects the long-run aggregate supply curve $LRAS$ at point A, where the price level is P_0. This intersection occurs at point A because at point A the price level is P_0 and the expected price level of workers is P_0. With actual and expected prices equal we have a Classical equilibrium.

How does the short-run aggregate supply curve adjust to changes in the expected price level? For instance, at point B the price level is P_1 but the expected price level is P_0. What happens when workers learn that the price level has increased to P_1? In this case, in the labor market the equilibrium would change from point B, where labor supply was $N_S(P^e = P_0)$, to point C, where labor supply is $N_S(P^e = P_1)$. Employment returns to N_F, and output returns to Y_F. In the aggregate supply graph, the equilibrium is represented by point C, with price P_1 and output Y_F. In terms of short-run aggregate supply, we say that the increase in P^e shifts $SRAS$ to the left, from $SRAS(P^e = P_0)$ to $SRAS(P^e = P_1)$. $SRAS(P^e = P_1)$ intersects $LRAS$ at point C, where the price level is P_1, because this is the only point on $SRAS(P^e = P_1)$ where the expected price is actually correct. Indeed, it is always the case that $SRAS$ intersects $LRAS$ at a price level equal to the expected price level on $SRAS$. Changes in the expected price level always lead to shifts in $SRAS$.

Changes in Aggregate Demand

Suppose that the Federal Reserve increases the money supply and hence increases aggregate demand in a model with the aggregate supply structure that we have just developed. What are the effects of this increase in aggregate demand? The answer depends on the state of expectations, as we will illustrate in Figure 9–4.

Figure 9–4 shows the labor market and the aggregate demand and supply graph for a New Classical model. The initial equilibrium, prior to the increase in the money supply, is the points labeled A. In the aggregate supply and demand diagram, this equilibrium is at a price of P_0 and an output level at the full employment level Y_F. In the labor market, this equilibrium is at a wage rate of W_0 and an employment level at the full employment level N_F.

The initial aggregate demand curve is labeled AD_0. After the increase in the money supply, aggregate demand increases to AD_1. What are the effects on employment and output? As we mentioned above, the answer depends crucially on the state of expectations. Expectations are assumed to be rational, but that doesn't mean that the money supply cannot be increased unexpectedly. If the increase was fully expected and fully anticipated by workers, then the increase in aggregate demand from AD_0 to AD_1 will cause an equal decrease in short-run aggregate supply, from $SRAS(P^e = P_0)$ to $SRAS(P^e = P_3)$. The equilibrium will be at point D, with a price level of P_3 and output of Y_F. In the labor market, this increase in both price and expected price will shift labor demand

FIGURE 9-4
Expectations Adjust to an Increase in Aggregate Demand

As aggregate demand increases to AD_1, perhaps because of an increase in the money supply, the price level is bid up and labor demand increases. What happens next depends upon expectations. Perfectly anticipated increases in the money supply result in an equal increase in prices and wages, with no change in employment or income. The economy moves from point A in each graph to point D. But any time that expectations do not fully perceive the increase in the money supply, income and employment will be above their natural full employment rates. Substantial short-run deviations from these long-run levels can occur.

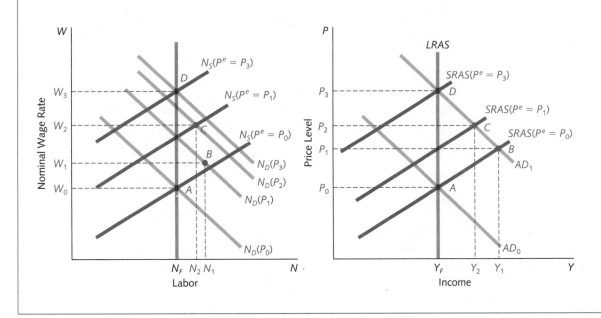

from $N_D(P_0)$ to $N_D(P_3)$ and labor supply from $N_S(P^e = P_0)$ to $N_S(P^e = P_3)$. The new equilibrium will be at point D, with a wage of W_3 and employment of N_F. The real wage will be W_3/P_3, which will be the same as the original real wage W_0/P_0. Thus, the perfectly anticipated increase in the money supply will result only in a higher level of wages and prices, and not in any changes in real variables such as N or Y, which are impervious to anticipated changes in aggregate demand.

These conclusions do not hold if the change in the money supply were *unexpected*. In that case, expected price stays at P_0. Hence, the short-run aggregate supply curve stays at $SRAS(P^e = P_0)$. The intersection of AD_1 with this short-run aggregate supply curve occurs at point B, with a price level of P_1 and output of Y_1. In the labor market, this is represented by a shift in labor demand from $N_D(P_0)$ to $N_D(P_1)$, while labor supply remains at $N_s(P^e = P_0)$. The intersection at point B is the new equilibrium, with a nominal wage of

W_1 and employment of N_1. The real wage is W_1/P_1, which is less than the original real wage of W_0/P_0 for reasons covered in our discussion of Figure 9–2. Meanwhile, because $P^e = P_0$, the perceived real wage has increased to W_1/P_0.

When the economy is in equilibrium at point B, perceived prices are less than actual. Eventually, the expected price level adjusts, and a Classical equilibrium is restored. How might this happen? One example is given in Figure 9–4. At point B, the price level is P_1 while the expected price level is P_0. What happens as workers learn of the change in the price level, and expected prices adjust to equal P_1? In the aggregate demand and supply diagram, when expected prices equal P_1, the short-run aggregate supply curve shifts to the left from $SRAS(P^e = P_0)$ to $SRAS(P^e = P_1)$. Remember that $SRAS(P^e = P_1)$ intersects $LRAS$ where the actual price is P_1. However, after this shift in $SRAS$, the intersection of $SRAS(P^e = P_1)$ and AD_1 occurs at point C, where the price level is P_2 and output is Y_2. Moreover, in the labor market the labor supply curve has shifted from $N_S(P^e = P_0)$ to $N_S(P^e = P_1)$, while labor demand has shifted from $N_D(P_1)$ to $N_D(P_2)$. The equilibrium has changed from point B to point C, where the wage is W_2 and employment is N_2. The actual real wage is still below the initial real wage, and the expected real wage is still above the initial real wage. The very act of adjusting expected prices from P_0 toward P_1 has caused the actual price level to increase above P_1.

There is an end to this, however, because eventually the expected price level will increase to P_3. When the expected price level equals P_3, $SRAS$ intersects $LRAS$ and AD_1 at a price level of P_3, so expected and actual price levels correspond. At this point, the economy is in long-run or Classical equilibrium at output level Y_F. This equilibrium is labeled D. In the labor market, demand is $N_D(P_3)$ and supply is $N_S(P^e = P_3)$, with a wage of W_3 and employment of N_F. The actual real wage and the perceived real wage are both equal to W_3/P_3, which is equal to the initial real wage at point A, W_0/P_0.

It is important to emphasize that the final equilibrium position of the economy is at the point labeled D regardless of whether or not the increase in the money supply was anticipated or unanticipated. However, the path the economy takes in getting from A to D depends crucially on whether or not this change was anticipated. An anticipated change in the money supply under rational expectations will lead to an adjustment directly from A to D, because expectations will correctly foresee and incorporate the necessary adjustment in the price level and expected price level to restore long-run equilibrium. There will be no effects on real output or employment. An *unanticipated* change in the money supply leads to changes in both output and employment because there are price changes that are not met by changes in expectations of the price level. In this case, price expectations of workers will eventually adjust to restore long-run equilibrium, but there may be substantial short-run deviations from the long-run equilibrium.

SUPPLY SHOCKS

So far the discussion has focused on changes in aggregate demand, and the effect of those changes on output and employment. However, there is also the possibility of shocks to aggregate supply, such as the OPEC oil price shocks of 1973 and 1979, the shock of falling oil prices in the 1980s, and the (temporary) increase in oil prices when Iraq invaded Kuwait in 1990. Such events can alter aggregate supply by changing the cost of an important input into production—energy—and thereby affecting output and employment. For more on the OPEC supply shocks see Global Perspective: "OPEC: Was United States Inflation a Product of Arabian Origin?"

The Effect on LRAS and SRAS

To determine the effect of these shocks, we again turn to the four-part diagram that is so useful for deriving aggregate supply curves. In Figure 9–5 we reproduce the diagram we originally used in Figure 9–3 but in this case we also incorporate a change in the production technology. The economy is initially endowed with a production technology $Y = f(N)$, which gives labor demand $N_D(P_0)$. Together with labor supply $N_S(P^e = P_0)$, these imply aggregate supply relationships $LRAS_0$ and $SRAS_0$ $(P^e = P_0)$. The initial equilibrium points are labeled A.

Now consider a technological shock that shifts the production function in the manner indicated in Figure 9–5(a). There are several important features of this shift in the production function. First, it is not due to any change in the price level or in the expected price level. Instead, it is due to a change in the real factors that affect production. The production functions we have looked at have output being produced with labor and capital. If the technology for combining labor and capital gets less efficient, then we may not be able to produce as much output with each quantity of labor input. This could happen if a significant portion of the capital stock becomes useless, either destroyed in a war or natural disaster, or just economically useless because of large increases in the price of other inputs, such as energy, used in conjunction with that capital. We call any such change that reduces the amount of output we can produce from a given amount of labor input a *negative supply shock*. Conversely, *a positive supply shock* would be an increase in the amount of output that we can produce from a given amount of labor input.

A second important feature of the shift in the production function is that it reduces the slope of the production function at every employment level. That is, it reduces the marginal product of labor—and hence labor demand—at every employment level. Thus, not only does the production function shift down to $Y = \bar{f}(N)$, but labor demand declines to $\bar{N}_D(P_0)$. Note too that this shift in labor demand is *not* due to a change in the price level, which has remained P_0.

OPEC: WAS U.S.

INFLATION A PRODUCT

OF ARABIAN ORIGIN?

Important features of the macroeconomic process may originate in supply shocks—such as sudden dislocations in resource availability or price. A variant of the cost-push inflation argument was part of the much-heard complaint of the 1970s that the Organization of Petroleum Exporting Countries (OPEC) cartel was responsible for the high rates of inflation experienced over that decade. First, it is important to understand the nature of a cartel. A *cartel* is a formal association of firms (or nations) acting as a single monopolist under formal or centralized control. Prices and output shares are ordinarily assigned to the various firms (or, in this case, nations) whose behavior is, in some way, monitored or policed. The OPEC cartel (which is still very much in existence) is simply a cartel of the major nations that produce and sell oil and other petroleum products.

The emergence of the OPEC cartel may have shifted (reduced) America's production possibilities frontier, thereby shifting the aggregate supply curve leftward. The resulting reduction in national income could have then accommodated a once-and-for-all increase in prices. National income reductions would have meant a reduction in the quantity of money demanded, facilitating the price increases.

But the same factors operating in the cost-push case would have been operative here also. The initial price increase would have created excess demand for cash balances and excess supply in both commodity and bond markets. Prices in all commodity sectors of the economy would have tended

PHOTO 9-1
Long Gas Lines Accompanied the OPEC Supply Shock of the 1970s.

to fall, at least given a constant nominal money stock. The rise in energy prices would have been accommodated, in large measure, by the fall in the prices of other goods and services. But this, of course, did not happen. Indeed, the United States experienced (between 1979 and 1981) some of its highest inflation rates of this century.

It is most unclear that OPEC had very much to do with this inflation. Many Monetarists suggest that oil price shocks may *temporarily* alter the inflation rate, but this cannot be the entire explanation for the high inflation rates of the late 1970s and early 1980s in the United States. The experience of other developed nations of the world more heavily dependent on OPEC oil than the United States also casts strong doubt on the link between OPEC and the high rates of inflation experienced in America during the late 1970s. Many of these nations experienced significantly lower inflation rates than the United States. Most economists, therefore, are unconvinced that monopoly cost-push or OPEC-type explanations for high inflation rates are satisfactory by themselves. Structural factors related to long-term labor productivity and supply are, of course, elements of the inflation problem, but the best explanation lies elsewhere in the aggregate demand components of macroeconomic equilibrium, especially those related to monetary and fiscal policy.

Inflation has been relatively mild over the 1980s and 1990s, thanks in large part to a controlled monetary policy at the Federal Reserve. Opportunities for individual OPEC members to gain from cheating on cartel arrangements (or outright refusals by some countries—such as Saudi Arabia—to go along with output quotas) have lessened the threat of another severe shock. Should the cartel prove successful in severe output restrictions and should the Federal Reserve decide to accommodate an OPEC shock by increasing the money supply, inflation could well return to the U.S. economic scene.   ❏

What are the effects of these changes in the production function and labor demand? Prices have not changed, but the reduction in labor demand changes the labor market equilibrium from point A to point B, and lowers the equilibrium real wage and equilibrium employment level to (W_1/P_0) and N_{F_1}, respectively. The lower level of employment and the shift in the production function combine to reduce output to Y_{F_1}. In the aggregate supply graph, this is represented by a decline in long-run aggregate supply from $LRAS_0$ to $LRAS_1$. Similarly, short-run aggregate supply declines from $SRAS_0$ $(P^e = P_0)$ to $SRAS_1(P^e = P_0)$. Notice well a few things about these changes in $LRAS$ and $SRAS$. First, the decline in $SRAS$ occurred not due to a change in P^e—P^e is equal to P_0 on both $SRAS_0$ and $SRAS_1$—but due to the change in the production function. Second, $SRAS_1(P^e = P_0)$ intersects $LRAS_1$ where P^e equals the actual price level. That is, these two curves intersect at point B, where the price level is P_0, just as $LRAS_0$ and $SRAS_0(P^e = P_0)$ intersected where the price level was P_0. In other words, $LRAS$ and $SRAS$ shift to the left by equal

FIGURE 9‒5
A Negative Supply Shock

Here, we examine the effects of a negative technological shock. This shock shifts down the production function in (a), which reduces the marginal product of labor and thus shifts the demand for labor leftward. The intersection of labor supply and the new labor demand is at point B. Since the natural rate of unemployment is now lower, the long-run and short-run aggregate supply curves shift leftward from $LRAS_0$ and $SRAS_0$ to $LRAS_1$ and $SRAS_1$. The price level and expected price level do not change, but the real wage declines from W_0/P_0 to W_1/P_0.

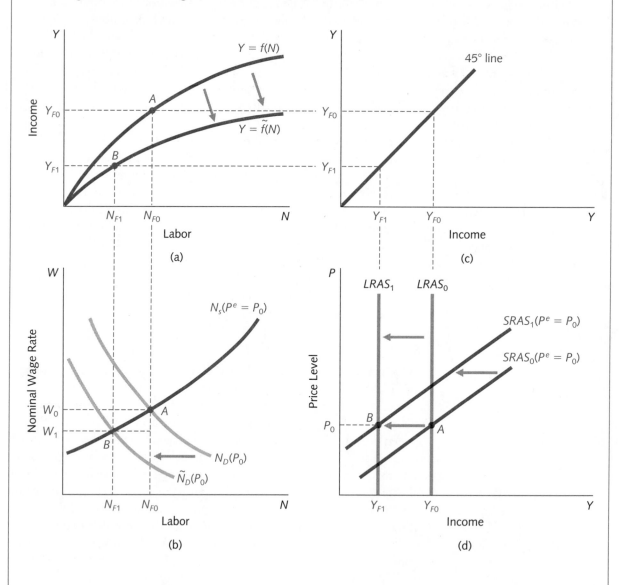

PHOTO 9-2
Natural Disasters, Such as the 7.1 Earthquake That Hit Northern California on October 17, 1989, are Supply Shocks That Have at Least Temporary Impacts on Aggregate Supply.

amounts. Finally, notice that the real wage has declined, from W_0/P_0 to W_1/P_0. This occurs because labor demand has fallen, and again is strictly due to the technological change. There has been no change in the price level or in the expected price level in any of this analysis.

The Effect on Equilibrium Output and Employment

The above discussion was aimed at discovering how a supply shock might shift *LRAS* and *SRAS*. However, this discussion is not sufficient to tell us what happens to the economy when a supply shock occurs. To answer that question we need to consider the changes in *LRAS* and *SRAS* in the context of aggregate demand and aggregate supply. This is especially true in the short run, if the supply shock is *unexpected*. Thus, we now consider the effects of a supply shock on the equilibrium level of output and employment, which we illustrate in Figure 9–6.

In Figure 9–6, the initial equilibrium is at point *A*, where $SRAS_0(P^e = P_0)$ intersects *AD* on $LRAS_0$. The price level is P_0 and output is Y_{F_0}. In the labor market, labor demand is $N_{D_0}(P_0)$ and labor supply is $N_S(P^e = P_0)$, which intersect at point *A*. The wage is W_0 and employment is N_{F_0}.

The supply shock does three things. It shifts *LRAS* to the left, and it shifts *SRAS* to the left by the same amount—*LRAS* becomes $LRAS_1$ and *SRAS* becomes $SRAS_1(P^e = P_0)$. It also shifts labor demand to the left, to $N_{D_1}(P_0)$. If the price level stayed at P_0, then, the economy would be in equilibrium at the points labeled *B* in the labor market and the output market.

Aggregate Demand, Aggregate Supply, and An Unexpected Supply Shock.

In this figure, the price level will change in the face of a negative technology shock. The negative supply shock lowers the marginal product of labor, and shifts long-run aggregate supply and short-run aggregate supply. Aggregate demand and *SRAS* now intersect at *C*. This change in price is unexpected; as soon as workers realize that their real wage has fallen they will adjust their expectations upward. The new equilibrium has labor supply and demand intersecting at point *D*. Income has fallen to Y_{F_1} and labor has fallen to N_{F_1}. The real wage is less than the original level and the price level has increased.

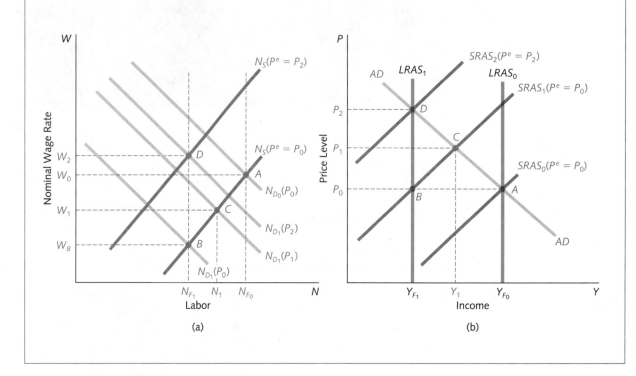

(a)   (b)

The price level will not stay at P_0, however, because aggregate demand is downward sloping. If the supply shock is unanticipated, the short-run equilibrium will be at the intersection of $SRAS_1(P^e = P_0)$ and *AD*, which is at point *C*. The price level will rise to P_1, and output will be at Y_1. For future reference note that while an output of Y_1 is lower than the initial level of output Y_{F_0}, it is above Y_{F_1}. In the labor market, the unanticipated shock does not change the labor supply curve from $N_S(P^e = P_0)$, but the increase in price does change labor demand from $N_{D_1}(P_0)$ at point *B* to $N_{D_1}(P_1)$ at point *C*. Thus, employment is higher than N_{F_1}, but lower than the pre-shock level N_{F_0}.

Eventually, expectations adjust to the increase in price above P_0, however, and in long-run equilibrium $SRAS$ intersects AD on the long-run aggregate supply curve $LRAS_1$. This occurs at point D, where $SRAS_2(P^e = P_2)$ intersects AD and $LRAS_1$ at a price level of P_2. Here the actual and expected prices are the same, and the economy is in long-run equilibrium at output level Y_{F_1}. In the labor market, the increase in price shifts labor demand from $N_{D_1}(P_1)$ to $N_{D_1}(P_2)$, while the increase in expected price shifts labor supply to $N_S(P^e = P_2)$. These intersect at D, a point of long-run equilibrium. The real wage is W_2/P_2, which is less than the pre-shock real wage of W_0/P_0. Employment is N_{F_1}.

What, then, are the effects of a negative supply shock of the type we have analyzed? Employment and output have fallen, as have real wages, and the price level has increased. This supply shock has had a real and deleterious effect on the economy.

There is an interesting feature of the adjustment process of the economy to the shock, however. After the shock occurs but before expectations adjust, output and employment are above their new long-run equilibrium levels. Thus, even though output and employment fall when the shock occurs, in the short run they are above the post-shock long-run or full-employment levels of output and employment. In essence, the short-run effect of an unanticipated supply shock of the type analyzed here will be cushioned somewhat by the fact that expectations don't adjust in the short run. In the long run, of course, or if the shock is anticipated, the full reduction in output and employment will occur. Thus, we will find that the natural rate of employment and output has changed.

Notice too the dilemma a supply shock forces on the policymaker. After the supply shock, output has fallen and the price level has risen, such as the change from equilibrium at point A to equilibrium at point C in Figure 9–6. The policymaker has seen the worst of both worlds—falling output and a rising price level—and now must decide what, if anything, to do. The temptation is often to do something, either to attempt to counteract the fall in output by increasing aggregate demand, or to counter the rise in the price level by reducing aggregate demand. However, increasing aggregate demand will increase output only by further increasing the price level, and decreasing aggregate demand will decrease the price level only by further reducing real output. Neither is an attractive choice. In addition, all of this applies only to the short run. If the supply shock is long lasting or persistent, then the new long-run aggregate supply curve $LRAS_1$ indicates the attainable long-run level of output after the shock, and this is below even the output level at the short-run equilibrium point, C. Thus, attempts by the policymaker to restore real output to its initial position are doomed to fail in the long run if the long-run aggregate supply curve persists in its location at $LRAS_1$. All of these features combine to make negative supply shocks the bane of policymakers. Of course, positive supply shocks work in the opposite way, and confront the policymaker with a choice among favorable elements. We discuss these issues in more detail in Chapter 16.

In Table 9–1, we present a summary of the effects of changes in aggregate demand or aggregate supply on a list of important macroeconomic variables. The first major heading is expected increases in aggregate demand, and the table records the effect of an expected increase in aggregate demand on the nominal wage and the price level, which both increase, and the real wage, employment, and output, which do not change. The entries in the table are derived from Figure 9–4, and describe the movement from long-run equilibrium at point *A* to long-run equilibrium at point *D*.

The second major heading in the table is for an unexpected increase in aggregate demand. Under this heading, we include both the short-run effects,

TABLE 9–1
Response of Economy to Shocks

The table summarizes the short- and long-term effects of expected and unexpected changes in aggregate demand. The impact on important variables such as employment and income from adverse supply shocks is also shown.

I.	EXPECTED INCREASE IN AD	
VARIABLE	EFFECT IN SHORT AND LONG RUN	
W	RISES	
P	RISES	
W/P	NO CHANGE	
N	NO CHANGE	
Y	NO CHANGE	

II.	UNEXPECTED INCREASE IN AD	
VARIABLE	EFFECT IN SHORT RUN	EFFECT IN LONG RUN
W	INCREASES	INCREASES EVEN FURTHER
P	INCREASES	INCREASES EVEN FURTHER
W/P	DECREASES	NO CHANGE
N	INCREASES	NO CHANGE
Y	INCREASES	NO CHANGE

III.	(UNEXPECTED) ADVERSE SUPPLY SHOCK	
VARIABLE	EFFECT IN SHORT RUN	EFFECT IN LONG RUN
W	DECREASES	AMBIGUOUS
P	INCREASES	INCREASES EVEN FURTHER
W/P	DECREASES	DECREASES
N	DECREASES	DECREASES EVEN FURTHER
Y	DECREASES	DECREASES EVEN FURTHER

NOTE: All comparisons are to an initial full employment equilibrium.

for the time period when expected prices are fixed, and the long-run effects, which coincide with the effects of an expected change in aggregate demand. The short-run effects are that the nominal wage and price level increase, but the real wage declines. Employment and output rise. These short-run effects are derived from Figure 9–4, and describe the movement from the initial equilibrium at point A to the short-run equilibrium at point B.

Finally, we include the short-run and long-run effects of an unexpected adverse supply shock. These are derived from Figure 9–6, with the short-run effects being the movement from the initial equilibrium at point A to the short-run equilibrium at point C, and the long-run effects describing the movement from equilibrium at point A to the long-run equilibrium at point D.

Business Cycles and Rational Expectations

The adjustment process to changes in monetary or fiscal policy (or to real shocks as well) may be depicted in the form of cycles around natural paths of real income or employment growth over time. If we assume a monetary or fiscal expansion with partially unanticipated price effects, and if we assume that the anticipations of suppliers and demanders of products and labor are such that outputs and inputs exceed their natural levels when $\pi > \pi^e$ (or $P > P^e$), then cycles of growth in real GDP and in *un*employment through time may be expressed as Figure 9–7 (a) and (b).

The cycles of Figure 9–7 (a) and (b) are suggested in the static analysis discussed previously in this chapter. If we assume that growth in real GDP in the United States follows a natural trend line such as that in Figure 9–7 (a), *unanticipated* or real shocks to aggregate demand will create cycles around the trend line. Under the assumptions of the static models discussed earlier in this chapter, when price exceeds expectations, or $P > P^e$, real output growth exceeds the natural level. Likewise, with reference to Figure 9–7 (b), such higher growth rates than normal create unemployment *below* the natural level. When price expectations exceed the price level, or $P < P^e$, the cycle of growth in real GDP falls below the natural level and the actual rate of unemployment is *above* the natural level, as depicted in Figure 9–7 (a) and (b). The economy would follow a smooth (noncyclical) path only if all policy and real changes leading to price changes were fully anticipated. Cycles, in other words, are the direct result of unanticipated changes resulting from policy or other surprises.

How is it that these cycles persist through time? Why aren't they immediately eliminated once price expectations adjust to equal the actual price level? There are many explanations for the persistence of deviations of output from the natural level. One is that deviations of the actual price level from the expected level cause workers and firms to make decisions concerning capital that cannot be unmade quickly when expectations adjust. For example, workers seeing an increase in their nominal wage and in employment but not perceiving an increase in the price level may decide to make large purchases

FIGURE 9−7

Typical Growth Paths of Income and Employment with Price Surprises under Rational Expectations

Unanticipated movements in economic aggregates can and do influence behavior. This diagram is a summary of expectational effects on income and employment. If the actual and expected price levels were always equal, both unemployment and real GDP growth would always be equal to U_F and Y_F, respectively.

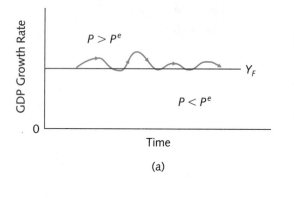

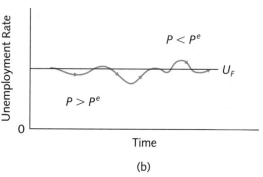

(a)   (b)

such as housing. The increased demand for housing causes builders to start building more housing, and this increased building leads to a persistent increase in output even after the expected price level adjusts. Similarly, other consumer purchases increase when workers think their real wage has increased, and the increased demand may lead to increased investment by firms. Once firms begin building new factories to meet the increased demand, they may decide to continue building them even when the demand returns to its previous levels, leading to an increase in output that is more persistent than the period during which the expected price level is below the actual price level.

Rational Expectations: Some Conclusions

Although the foregoing discussion is a grand simplification of the mechanics of rational expectations theory, it permits us to make some broad observations about this new and important theory on the workings of the macroeconomy. We will first present some ideas on the contribution of New Classical Economics and the idea of rational expectations to our understanding of the macroeconomy. Following this, we will present the main criticisms of the New Classical approach.

RATIONAL EXPECTATIONS THEORY AND THE NEW CLASSICAL ECONOMICS

Even a simplified view of the workings of the rational expectations hypothesis is sufficient to show why it is an important basis for the New Classical Economics. We have seen that the hypothesis suggests that discretionary monetary policy after expectations adjust can have no effects on the *real* variables in the macroeconomic system. This view stems from a micro analytic foundation of behavior in the product and labor markets. The old Classical view of such writers as Adam Smith, John Stuart Mill, and, in this century, A. C. Pigou, emphasized the rationality of market participants, but such rationality was based on an assumption of perfect information. Although there was no explicit modeling of individual markets in Classical economics, their views were punctuated by a belief that participants in individual markets could not be manipulated by government. This stand is made clear in even the earliest Classical literature, as shown in Smith's *Theory of Moral Sentiments*, written in 1759:

> (The economic planner) seems to imagine that he can arrange the different members of society with as much ease as the hand arranges the different pieces upon a chessboard; he does not consider that the different pieces upon the chessboard have no other principle of motion besides that which the hand impresses upon them; but that, in the great chessboard of human society, every single piece has a principle of motion of its own, altogether different from that which the legislator might choose to impress upon it.[2]

Smith's view certainly conforms well to the New Classical belief that the coefficients summarizing the economy are not fixed but themselves change with alterations in government economic planning and discretionary policy. Expectations, in other words, are endogenous to the economic system in both old and new versions of Classical economics.

The New Classical Economics differs from the old school in one crucial respect. Recall from our discussion above that surprises are possible in the form of unanticipated price changes. Market participants in the New Classical Economics do not have perfect information. They are of course rational in the sense that they do not make persistent forecasting errors.

PHOTO 9-3
Adam Smith, the "Father" of Economics, Anticipated the Idea of Rational Expectations as Early as 1759.

CYCLES ARE NOT ELIMINATED UNDER RATIONAL EXPECTATIONS

Another major conclusion of the New Classical Economics is that cycles are not eliminated under rational expectations. Unanticipated policy changes or real changes in the economy—creating supply or demand shocks and unanticipated price changes—can create continuous cycles of real income or unemployment around some trend line. Learning and better prediction on the

---

[2]Adam Smith, *The Theory of Moral Sentiments* (Indianapolis: Liberty Classics, 1976), p. 325; originally published 1759.

part of suppliers and demanders can dampen or amplify the magnitude and duration of cycles created by frequent and similar policy changes, but continuous surprises are a possibility. Economist Robert J. Shiller provides an apt description of the hypothesis as it relates to policy:

> According to the rational expectations approach to econometric policy evaluation, if a policy rule is followed consistently over a long period of time, rational individuals will eventually learn how that policy rule has affected the random character of economic variables, and if these individuals are truly rational, their expectations will not differ substantively from "optimal" forecasts. After a policy rule is adopted it may at first be difficult for individuals to make forecasts of future economic variables and they must rely on crude guesses. . . . The essential assumption that rational expectations theorists then make, however, is that after a transition period, the economy will have reached . . . a "rational expectations equilibrium."[3]

This view holds only for a single policy rule. Continuous policy surprises could create continuous cyclical movement along a steady growth line such as that depicted in Figure 9–2 (a) and (b).

The New Classical Economics shares some important policy conclusions with Monetarism. Since cycles are (ultimately) the product of erratic policy alterations or surprises, stable growth requires both monetary and fiscal rules. Monetarists also urge the Federal Reserve to institute a monetary rule that would create stability under an adaptive expectations system. The New Classical Economics, for equally obvious reasons, supports fiscal stability as well. A balanced budget—long stressed by Monetarists and supply siders—is a frequent policy recommendation of the New Classicals. The stop-and-go character of discretionary monetary and fiscal policy, in other words, is at the heart of exaggerations in the business cycle. While cycles will always likely exist due to natural shocks, such as bad harvests, the capricious nature of international cartels, the erratic nature of investment expectations, and a host of other reasons, discretionary policy cannot help and will likely exacerbate swings in business cycles of real income and employment. In the rational expectations view of the macroeconomy, the best one can hope for is for policy to have no effects. At worst in this new laissez-faire view of the world, discretionary policy is the source, not the solution, of macroeconomic problems.

CRITICISMS OF THE NEW CLASSICAL ECONOMICS

An enormous amount of interest has been generated in the rational expectations approach or more accurately, the nonapproach to policy. Much of the contemporary research has been devoted to the question of whether or not and

[3]Robert J Shiller, "Rational Expectations and the Dynamic Structure of Macroeconomic Models," *Journal of Monetary Economics* 4 (1978), pp. 3–4.

under what conditions the policy-neutral implications of the New Classical Economics hold. A good deal of sophisticated econometric testing has left open the answer to the question, does discretionary policy work?[4] Some of the evidence does not support the major positions of the rational expectationists.[5] Until such testing yields consistent results, the matter of policy neutrality and the *theoretical* foundations of the New Classical Economics will form a lively debate among the rational expectationists and those championing the efficacy of discretionary policy and those with differing theoretical perspectives. In concluding our discussion of the New Classical Economics we briefly highlight two different criticisms of the new macroeconomics. An additional criticism, made by the so called Austrian school, is outlined in the Insight: "An Austrian Perspective on New Classical Economics."

Keynesians, Rational Expectations, and New Classical Economics

While contemporary advocates of discretionary monetary and fiscal policy (some prefer to retain the label Keynesians or New-Keynesians) see value in more sophisticated theories of expectations, they retain a belief in the efficacy of government manipulation of the economy. Policy, to these Keynesians, is nonneutral and necessary in an economy that is inherently and endogenously unstable. The basic dispute is over the form of the expectational assumptions of the rational expectationists and over the related issue of the efficiency of market functioning.

Keynesians (and others) object that the New Classical Economics requires market participants to be more sophisticated than they really are in their abilities to predict. How might we expect buyers of VCRs and sellers of rental properties to utilize intricate and sophisticated theories of economic functioning in order to accurately predict prices, outputs, interest rates, or any othereconomic variable into the future and to quickly and accurately act on the prediction in the present?

Rational expectationists counter with the point that market participants are correct, *but only on average.* If, in other words, policy is itself not random (which would be a peculiar manner of conducting it), those who consistently come up with inaccurate predictions would be severely punished in the market through losses on exchanges. In their own self-interest market participants would attempt to learn the probable effects of policy. Armies of economists in the think-tank or prediction-service business are hired by market participants to help them learn or to give them rational information about the future. It would be strange, indeed, for markets not to react in this manner.

---

[4]For a moderately technical exposition of tests of rational expectations, see the excellent summary by Stephen J. Turnovsky, "Rational Expectations and the Theory of Macroeconomic Policy: An Exposition of Some of the Issues," *Journal of Economic Education* (Winter 1984), pp. 55–69.

[5]Michael C. Lovell, "Tests of the Rational Expectations Hypothesis," *American Economic Review* 76 (March 1986), pp. 110–24.

INSIGHT

AN AUSTRIAN PERSPECTIVE ON NEW CLASSICAL ECONOMICS

A modern Austrian view of the economic process provides the focus for a critique of the rational expectations paradigm. This view emphasizes two major points related to rational expectations:

1. Though professing to provide a micro analytic foundation for understanding macroeconomic phenomena, such as unemployment and GDP growth, the New Classical Economics fails to provide a *sufficiently micro analytic basis* for understanding such phenomena.

2. Though containing important (and well-known) insights, the rational expectations theory completely neglects the informational functions of prices within the market system, a gap that renders it virtually meaningless.

Austrian economists (beginning with Ludwig von Mises in the 1930s) do accept the fundamental tenet of the New Classical Economics—that (at least in the long run) discretionary monetary and fiscal policy will have no beneficial effects on real and important variables within the economic system.[a] However, any *anticipated or unanticipated* policy change will work differently through different markets depending on the informational characteristics of input and output prices in those markets. In the Austrian view of the world, prices are the key elements in providing coordination between buyers and sellers in markets. Endogenous or exogenous (policy) changes will introduce a coordination failure between the plans of buyers and sellers, meaning that both buyers and sellers will adapt their plans to the new information that prices continuously bring to them. Prices are the informational signals in the system.

Any policy change will cause havoc in input and output markets by discoordinating the plans of market participants, but the amount of discoordination will vary in different markets. The speed of the adjustment to a new equilibrium will depend on the institutional and other characteristics of particular markets. Price changes within specific markets will interact, moreover, and the speed of adjustment will depend on how quickly and how well buyers and sellers can process information.

In this view the rational expectationist notion that individuals can immediately pinpoint the impact of policy changes on prices is naive. It robs the economic system of the essential informational characteristics of prices. Although rational expectationists believe only that policy neutrality occurs when the effects of policy changes are fully anticipated, Austrians believe that the view puts the horse before the cart. Market participants cannot possibly know the full price effects of a policy change because the effects of the policy change must be worked through the informational character of price changes in specific markets.

There are, of course, many similarities between the policy positions of Austrians and rational expectationists (as there are between the old Classical school and the Monetarist view), but there are stark contrasts in matters of theory. While it might be premature to ignore the discretionary policy prescriptions of the modern Keynesians, the theory of rational expectations may prove to underlie a more complete understanding of the macroeconomic system. ❑

NOTE: [a]See Roger W. Garrison, "Rational Expectations Offer Nothing That's Both New and True," *The Austrian Economics Newsletter* (Fall 1985), pp. 5–6.

Keynesians also argue that rational expectations theory fails to explain prolonged periods of unemployment and depression. Keynesians, as you might recall from Chapter 6, regard the economy as inherently unstable (especially with regard to investment spending), and characterized by institutionalized sticky prices and wages (from monopolies and other imperfections in both product and labor markets). Also recall that rational expectationists do *not* believe that full production and employment *always* characterized the economic system. Unanticipated policy and price surprises, as we saw earlier in this chapter, caused real variables such as employment and income to diverge from their natural rates. Once market participants discovered the true nature of the policy change, expectations caught up with actual economic magnitudes (such as prices) and the economy returned to the rational expectations equilibrium. An important question is, how long does this take?

Keynesians point to events such as the Great Depression of the 1930s with prolonged periods of unemployment and reduced growth rates in real GDP as proof that market participants do not react in the manner described by the rational expectationists. To restate the question: Even if expectations are rational and even if they eventually return the economy to the natural or full-employment level of output and employment, are the sacrifices acceptable? (Note the modern version of the "all dead in the long run" precept of early Keynesian economics.)

The question is, of course, a good one. The actual situation of the 1930s economy has proved difficult to gauge. Keynesians believe that endogenous factors such as reduced aggregate demand and sticky nominal wages and prices due to effective rigidities in both product and labor markets are the essential explanation for the prolonged depression of the 1930s. Rational expectationists counter by arguing that the depression was prolonged, if not fostered, by wrongheaded government policies. Price changes failed to clear product and labor markets due to the *continuous* and *persistent* policy and institutional changes by the government. Discouragement of business investment and unanticipated policy surprises were the result of the government's increased participation in the private market system. The origins and length of the Great Depression are also placed at the door of the Federal Reserve System, which failed to perceive and correct for the precipitous decline in the real stock of money.

The debate between the Keynesian and the rational expectationist views of the proper role of policy will, of course, continue. Whether discretionary policy or rules give the best results will not be decided by theory or opinion, but by facts, illuminated by econometric testing.

SUMMARY

This chapter has examined the effect of expectations on economic behavior. The contemporary theory of rational expectations, which builds on old Classical economics, Monetarism, and the supply-side perspective, contains a number of implications. One of the most important implications of NCE and rational expectations is policy neutrality. Policy neutrality indicates that, on average and if the effects of policy are fully anticipated, monetary policy will instantly or very quickly affect nominal interest rates and the inflation rate with no impact on real output and employment. Under similar assumptions, activist fiscal policy will either have no effects or the opposite effects intended by policy makers. In this view, market participants perfectly anticipate and immediately react to policy changes, thereby neutralizing them. Demand and supply shock surprises are possible under rational expectations, along with the business cycles they create. Critics claim that the evidence does not support all of the implications of rational expectations and that market participants are somewhat less sophisticated and markets less perfect than is assumed by the defenders of rational expectations. Some argue that rational expectations is not rational at all, since information is too costly to acquire. If information is costly to acquire then economic agents will acquire information up to the point where the marginal benefit just equals the marginal cost of obtaining—and processing—the information. Defenders of rational expectations do not disagree with this statement, but think that rational workers and firms will obtain and utilize the information that is valuable to them, including information on policy actions to the extent that these policy actions have an impact on these workers and firms.

KEY TERMS

adaptive expectations	New Classical Economics (NCE)
business cycles	policy neutrality
Classical dichotomy	rational expectations
demand shocks	supply shocks

QUESTIONS FOR REVIEW AND DISCUSSION

1. Contrast and compare adaptive expectations to rational expectations. What is the essential difference in these two theories of economic behavior?

2. What is the New Classical Economics? How is the theory of rational expectations related to the NCE? To old Classical economics?

3. What is policy neutrality?

4. Suppose that, starting from a balanced budget, the government reduces lump sum taxes and increases borrowing. Under assumptions of rational expectations, will the real effects of this policy change be neutral? Explain.

5. Does the theory of rational expectations hold that the effects of all events are fully anticipated? Explain.

6. What implications does the NCE have for the future of discretionary monetary policy? Discretionary fiscal policy?

7. What is the importance of sticky prices and wages due to monopoly or union power on the policy-neutral implications of the rational expectations hypothesis?

8. Give examples of supply and demand shocks. How do they explain business cycles under the assumption of rational expectations?

9. Suppose that policymakers continuously depend on policy surprises to have real effects on the economy. According to the theory of rational expectations, will these surprises ultimately be fully anticipated?

10. During the last election President Bill Clinton campaigned partly on the idea that government spending should be redirected toward increased investment spending, including investment in physical and human capital (such as education). What would a New Classical Economist say about the macroeconomic effects of this proposal?

11. What will be the impact on real output and the price level of an unanticipated (or unexpected) decrease in autonomous consumer spending? How does this compare to the effect of an anticipated decrease in autonomous consumer spending?

12. What will be the impact on real output and the price level of an unanticipated (or unexpected) increase in net exports? How does this compare to the effect of an anticipated increase in net exports?

13. What is the impact of an (unexpected) earthquake that destroys a large percentage of the capital stock in a country? What happens to output and to the price level? Does the New Classical Economics have any recommendations for a response of monetary or fiscal policy?

14. What is the importance of information in the New Classical Economics? In particular, how does it matter if policymakers know the nature of supply and demand shocks faster and more accurately than the private sector? Does this help make policy effective?

PROBLEMS

1. In 1992 then-President George Bush faced an election year in which the economy was not growing very quickly. Unemployment remained stubbornly higher than it was in the last election in 1988, although it was not all that high by the standards of past recessions (or in comparison with other major industrialized countries of the world at that time). As a New Classical econo-

mist, what advice would you have given the President in setting monetary policy during 1992? Does the New Classical Economics suggest a course of action for a President facing reelection in these circumstances? Show the effects of your advised "course of action" in graphical terms.

2. Suppose that explorers in some small mythical country, Macroland, suddenly discover an entirely new and environmentally safe and clean source of energy to fuel the entire economy. This is, of course, a positive supply shock. Using graphs, trace the effects of this shock through the macroeconomy, reversing the discussion of the negative supply shock discussed in relation to Figures 9–5 and 9–6 in the chapter.

SUGGESTION FOR FURTHER READING

Dotsey, Michael and Robert G. King. "Rational Expectations Business Cycle Models: A Survey." Federal Reserve Bank of Richmond *Economic Review* (March/April 1988), pp. 3-15.

Lucas, Robert E., Jr. "Methods and Problems in Business Cycle Theory." *Journal of Money, Credit, and Banking* (November 1980), pp. 696–715.

Maddock, Rodney, and Michael Carter. "A Child's Guide to Rational Expectations." *Journal of Economic Literature* 20 (March 1982), pp. 139–51.

Muth, John. "Rational Expectations and the Theory of Price Movements." *Econometrica* (July 1961), pp. 315–35.

Sargent, Thomas J. *Rational Expectations and Inflation.* New York: Harper & Row, 1986.

Sheffrin, Steven M. *Rational Expectations.* Cambridge: Cambridge University Press, 1983.

Solow, Robert M. "What to Do (Macroeconomically) When OPEC Comes." In *Rational Expectations and Economic Policy,* ed. Stanley Fischer. Chicago: University of Chicago Press for the National Bureau of Economic Research, 1980, pp. 249–64.

10 NEW KEYNESIAN MODELS

The New Keynesian economics is a response to New Classical Economics. The modeling strategies of the New Classical Economics regarding expectation formation and microeconomic justifications for behavioral assumptions are adopted, but with a central difference: The New Keynesian model suggests that discretionary policy can be effective at altering output and employment.

In this chapter we will provide a fairly broad menu of New Keynesian models. If anything, the New Keynesian economics has provided a wealth of alternatives to the New Classical model. These numerous alternatives are sometimes a distraction from the main point of the New Keynesian approach, which is that models that pay attention to microeconomic foundations and that assume rational expectations do not always lead to full employment, and do not always eliminate a role for policy to influence the behavior of the economy.

In this chapter, we will cover

- the distinction between the (old) Keynesian and the New Keynesian approaches
- the nominal wage contracting model—a prototypical New Keynesian model
- a model built on rigid or sticky output prices, in contrast to the nominal wage contracting model
- issues of coordination failure, an interesting recent line of research in the New Keynesian tradition
- the efficiency wage model as an explanation for rigid wages.

381

OLD AND NEW KEYNESIAN MACROECONOMICS

The New Keynesian macroeconomics has emerged by developing theories of aggregate supply that are different, sometimes in subtle ways, from the theory developed in the New Classical macroeonomics. In this chapter we pursue several diverse New Keynesian ideas. The unifying features of these alternatives are that they all provide a rationale for a model with policy effectiveness. Thus, the New Keynesian approach is very much an answer to the New Classical macroeconomics.

The New Keynesian macroeconomics shares the New Classical emphasis on rational expectations and on the desirability of explicit microeconomic justifications for behavioral assumptions. However, the New Keynesian macroeconomics employs a host of alternatives to the perfectly competitive, market-clearing approach of the New Classical macroeconomic models. Instead, assumptions of sticky (or slowly adjusting) prices or wages, of monopolistic competition, and of newer approaches stressing coordination failures are all used in one way or another to develop the assorted models labeled New Keynesian. These diverse models often vary tremendously in appearance, but share the common feature of the absence of competitive market clearing, and the feature that policy can be effective at changing output and employment. Thus, the New Keynesian models, like the old Keynesian model, give reasons for policymakers to respond to unacceptable levels of output or unemployment.

In this chapter we present the New Keynesian model with sticky nominal wages. This model, developed by Jo Anna Gray and Stanley Fischer, is a typical example of how New Keynesian models build on Keynesian foundations while adapting some of the New Classical ideas presented in Chapter 9. Next, we turn to several more recent approaches to New Keynesian macroeconomics, including a sticky output price model, a model emphasizing coordination failures, and a model of the labor market called the **efficiency wage model.** In all of these approaches, we will point out how policy can be effective in changing output or employment. A discussion of problems with the New Keynesian approach, including an explicit comparison with the New Classical approach, concludes the chapter. Finally, for an introduction to the resurgence of interest among practical policymakers in Keynesian ideas, see the Policy Issue: "Is Keynesianism Making a Comeback?"

EFFICIENCY WAGE MODELS are models in which a firm can lower production costs by paying wages in excess of market-clearing, competitive levels in order to elicit additional effort from workers.

A NEW KEYNESIAN MODEL WITH NOMINAL WAGE CONTRACTS

In the Keynesian model, the nominal wage was assumed to be rigid, at least in the downward direction, so that reductions in aggregate demand (and hence in the price level) would lead to reductions in employment. In Keynes's view, workers would refuse to accept cuts in their nominal wage. In this event

POLICY ISSUE

"IS KEYNESIANISM MAKING A COMEBACK?"

In the mid-1970s countries such as Chile turned to Monetarism and the policy of tight money and free markets to reduce the rate of inflation. But in the 1980s, Bolivia reduced its annual rate of inflation from 50,000 percent to 9 percent based on the Keynesian program of budget and tax revisions suggested by Harvard economist Jeffrey Sachs.

After many years of discredit, Keynes's prescriptions have returned but the expectations are more realistic about how successful his policies will be in stabilizing the economy. The second coming of Keynes is due to a group of young economists such as Lawrence Summers of Harvard, Alan Blinder of Princeton, and Paul Krugman and Rudiger Dornbusch of the Massachusetts Institute of Technology. Robert Litan of the Brookings Institution says that "everybody in policy economics is buying into the New Keynesian mainstream." This includes most Democrats, who are looking to these New Key-

nesians for fresh ideas on the economy. Like Keynes, the New Keynesians view high employment as the top priority of the U.S. government and believe markets require government intervention to produce enough jobs. However, they want to avoid the traditional approach of reducing unemployment by just pumping up government spending. Some of these economists, such as Alan Blinder of Princeton, feel pump priming is "gone forever." They make the case that employment would not fall during a recession if wages were tied to profit sharing. Businesses would think twice about laying off workers when profits fell, since paychecks would decline. Current New Keynesian thinking is to balance the federal budget and raise investment. To some of these economists, this requires increased taxes, including higher income taxes. Others favor raising tax rates on cigarettes, alcohol and gasoline, new taxes on interest earned by foreigners on their U.S. saving deposits, and smaller deductions for advertising expenses businesses can claim on their income taxes.

New Keynesians believe in federal funding aimed at in-

creasing the productivity of the worker. Their programs include government spending on elementary education and technical training. They also feel additional tax money should be spent on bridge and road construction. But some New Keynesians would restore certain tax incentives for businesses such as investment tax credits for new plant and equipment. These credits were lost in the last round of tax reforms in 1986. In addition, they would advocate tax breaks to encourage household savings such as expanding IRAs to include not only retirement but education and housing expenses.

Many New Keynesians believe that their ideas of lower interest rates and reduced federal budgets should be carried over to foreign countries. In other words, they feel the only way to prevent a global recession is for a greater coordination among the industrialized nations of the world on monetary and fiscal policy. These New Keynesians also see a role for the federal government in prodding the world to buy American. That is, foreign governments should use U.S. aid to purchase U.S. goods or for joint ventures with U.S. firms. The New Keynesians point out that this approach was pioneered by the Japanese. While they believe that their proposals are strong, especially for maintaining higher levels of employment, they have plenty of competition in shaping the economy from the Monetarists, supply-siders and New Classicals.

SOURCE: Robert J. Shapiro, "Look Who's Making a Comeback," *U.S. News and World Report* (February 1, 1988), pp. 43–45.

PHOTO 10-1
New Keynesians Emphasize the Necessity of Investments in New Technology Such as Computer Development. Here Macintosh Computers Move Down the Assembly Line at the Apple Factory in California's So-Called "Silicon Valley."

reductions in the price level would not lead to reductions in the nominal wage and an unchanging real wage as predicted by the Classical model. Instead, Keynes argued that reductions in the price level would lead to an *increase* in the real wage (because the nominal wage would not fall) and hence to a reduction in the quantity of labor demanded. Employment would decline, as would output.

In the New Keynesian model of nominal wage contracting, these assumptions are modified. First of all, the nominal wage is assumed to be set for a given period of time in an explicit labor contract or an implicit agreement between employer and employee. The agreement is made *prior* to the period to which it applies. For instance, a new worker and an employer will agree to the terms of employment for the upcoming year before the worker begins a new job. In a union contract, the contract is signed before the three-year period that the contract covers. The important thing is that the nominal wage can increase or decrease between agreements, but during the course of the agreement the nominal wage is fixed. This is the New Keynesian adaptation of the Keynesian downwardly rigid wage.

In addition to a nominal wage that is fixed for the term of the contract, the New Keynesian model makes explicit the information that is in the hands of labor suppliers and demanders when the contract or agreement is negotiated. This is adapted from the New Classical model, which also made explicit assumptions about the available information. In the New Keynesian case, the assumption is that neither workers nor employers know what the price level will be over the course of the nominal wage contract. Instead, they both form rational expectations of this price level based on the information available to them, and they negotiate the nominal wage agreement based on these expectations.

Once the nominal wage is agreed upon, the New Keynesian model assumes that employment is determined by labor demand. The labor agreement is that workers will work at the agreed upon nominal wage for the period of the agreement, *and* that firms will determine the quantity of labor employed. Thus, workers cede to firms the right to determine the quantity of labor employed. This mimics the old Keynesian assumption that, with a fixed nominal wage, employment is determined by labor demand.

Finally, it is assumed that both workers and firms set the level of nominal wages to achieve equality between the expected level of labor supply and the expected level of labor demand over the course of the agreement. In essence, firms and workers form rational expectations of the price level and any other variables that affect labor demand and supply. Each party then predicts the value of labor demand and labor supply based on these expectations. This prediction allows them to calculate the nominal wage that is expected to equate demand and supply. This level of the nominal wage is the level agreed to in the nominal wage contract.

Before going through a graphical explanation of nominal wage determination, it is useful to list the assumptions we have made to this point:

1. The fixed nominal wage that applies to a set period of time is agreed to before the period to which it applies.

2. Workers and firms do not know what the price level will be over the course of the contract. Instead, they both form rational expectations of this price level based on the information available at the time the contract is negotiated.

3. Employment is determined by firms (i.e., by labor demand).

4. Workers and firms negotiate to set the nominal wage at the level that is expected to equate labor supply and labor demand over the contract period.

Nominal Wage Determination

The New Keynesian model incorporates the above assumptions within the model of the labor market that we have used, with modifications, in the chapters on Classical, Keynesian, Monetarist, and New Classical theories. That model as first introduced for the Classical model is reproduced here as

$$N_D = N_D(W/P, K), \tag{10.1}$$

$$N_S = N_S(W/P), \tag{10.2}$$

$$N_D = N_S. \tag{10.3}$$

To reiterate, equation 10.1 is the labor demand equation, specifying the quantity of labor demanded as a function of the real wage W/P, the capital stock K, and other variables not specified, such as the amount of other resources used in production and the state of technology. Equation 10.2 is labor supply, a function of the real wage, and other variables such as the real wealth of workers and other institutional factors. Equation 10.3 specifies that in equilibrium, quantity supplied equals quantity demanded.

The New Keynesian model of nominal wage contracts modifies the Classical model of labor supply as follows. First, workers and firms negotiate a contracted nominal wage W^c that will be constant for the period of the contract. Second, that wage is negotiated at some time prior to the period for which it will hold. Negotiation is based upon expectations of the price level, the capital stock, the state of technology, the wealth of workers, institutional factors, and the amount of other resources available. These expectations are rational expectations, and firms use them to negotiate a nominal wage W^c that is expected to set $N_S = N_D$.

Explicitly, the contracted nominal wage rate in the labor market W^c is determined by the *expected* supply and demand functions. These are given by

$$N_D^e = N_D(W/P^e, K^e), \tag{10.4}$$

$$N_S^e = N_S(W/P^e). \tag{10.5}$$

The contracted nominal wage is that which sets the expected quantities of labor supplied and labor demanded equal, or

$$N_D^e = N_S^e. \tag{10.6}$$

We illustrate this graphically in Figure 10-1. There, the expected labor demand, given by equation 10.4, is graphed along with expected labor supply, given by equation 10.5. The intersection of these curves is at that nominal wage which is expected to bring forth a quantity of labor equal to the quantity demanded. In our New Keynesian model, this wage rate will be chosen as the contracted nominal wage W^c. At the same time, the expected level of employment, from the intersection of the expected supply and demand curves, will be the full-employment level N_F^e. After the wage is set and the actual

FIGURE IO-I
Determination of the
Contract Wage

In the New Keynesian model, the nominal wage agreed upon is that wage expected to equate labor demand and supply over the contract period ($W^c = W^e$). The labor market under these conditions is drawn here. The labor demand and supply depend on expected values. If these expected values differ from their actual values over the contract period, then the contracted nominal wage will stay the same but actual employment will change from N_F^e.

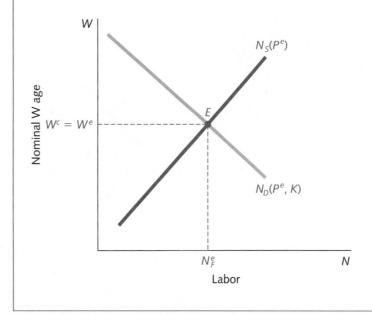

values of prices, the capital stock, and other variables become known, the quantity of labor actually employed will be determined by the labor demand function. Thus, equal quantities of labor supplied and demanded at W^c hold *only in expectation.* Once the contract wage is set, the actual labor demand schedule may differ from what was expected. This difference would occur if the expected values of any of the determinants of labor demand are not realized.

If actual price level, worker wealth, institutional features, the capital stock, other resources, and technology are the same as expected, then the contracted wage will be the market-clearing wage; and actual employment will be at the full-employment level. If any of these determinants differ, then the wage rate will stay at the contracted level W^c, and employment will vary with changes in actual labor demand.

This is illustrated in Figure 10-2. The expected functions for labor demand and supply intersect at point A and determine the nominal wage that is expected to clear the labor market, W^c. The employment level corresponding to point A is the full-employment level N_F. Once the wage is set, it stays at

FIGURE 10-2
Effect of Changes in the Price Level

The contracted nominal wage W^c and equilibrium full-employment level N_F are generated by the intersection of expected labor demand and supply at point A. If the price level is higher than expected, labor demand shifts to the right to $N_D(P_1 > P^e)$. Employment increases to N_1 at point B. If the price level is lower than expected, labor demand shifts to the left to $N_D(P_2 < P^e)$, and employment falls to N_2 at point C.

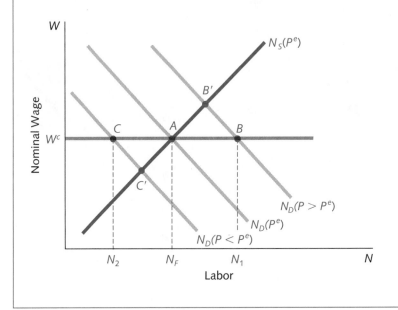

W^c for the course of the contract. If the labor demand curve stays at its expected position, then employment will be at the expected full-employment level N_F. However, if any of the variables affecting labor demand differ from their expected values, then labor demand will differ from expected, and employment will differ from the full-employment level. For example, if the actual price level is greater than the price level expected when the contract was signed, then actual labor demand will exceed the expected labor demand, and the actual labor market position will be at point B, where actual labor demand intersects the contracted nominal wage W^c. At B, the nominal wage is still W^c, but employment is N_1. Thus, just as in the New Classical case, an increase in the price level over its expected level will increase labor demand.

Unlike the New Classical model, however, the increase in labor demand does not lead to a rise in the nominal wage. Instead, the nominal wage is set by contract, and the entire burden of adjusting to the increase in labor demand is on the quantity of employment.

In the New Classical model, the assumption is that labor suppliers may not adjust very quickly to an increase in the actual price level P, while labor demand does adjust quickly. An increase in P would shift labor demand to the right and, labor supply being constant, the intersection of labor demand and supply is now found at point B' in Figure 10-2. The nominal wage and employment would both increase. The real wage would fall, because the increase in the nominal wage in moving from A to B' is not enough to keep up with the increase in the price level. In the long run, of course, the expected price level adjusts; labor supply shifts to the left and intersects labor demand at the full-employment level, but at a higher nominal wage. One key feature of the New Classical analysis is that the economy is in equilibrium at points A and B'. Hence, the New Classical macroeconomics is characterized as an equilibrium approach.

The New Keynesian story is similar in many ways, but is, at its core, a disequilibrium approach. The initial contracted nominal wage W^c is set to clear the labor market if labor demand and supply are at their expected values. If, for example, the price level exceeds the expected price level, however, then labor demand shifts to the right. This occurs because the increase in the price level has lowered the real wage for every nominal wage, so that at every nominal wage business firms will hire more labor. In the New Keynesian model, labor contracts maintain nominal wages at W^c. The contract also states that employment is determined strictly by labor demand. This is illustrated by point B in Figure 10-2. At B, the employment level N_1 exceeds not only N_F but also the employment level that would be generated in a New Classical model at point B'. This is because the New Classical model allows both W and N to adjust to the increase in labor demand. In the New Keynesian model, the adjustment to the increased labor demand is borne solely by employment. It is also the case that the real wage, which is W^c/P at point A, falls in moving to point B as the wage is fixed and prices rise. Of course, in the long run the contract will be renegotiated and the wage will be reset at a level that is expected to clear the labor market in the new contract period. But in the short run, any change in the actual labor demand curve from its expected level will result in departures from point A. These points, such as point B, are all disequilibrium points, where quantity demanded does not equal quantity supplied. Thus, the New Keynesian model is a disequilibrium model.

Note that the New Keynesian model treats increases and decreases in actual labor demand symmetrically, as is illustrated in Figure 10-2. For instance, a decrease in the price level below its expected value P^e will shift the actual labor demand curve below expected labor demand. This leads to another point of disequilibrium C, with the level of employment falling to N_2. Again, note that at point C employment is determined by the quantity of labor demanded at the contracted wage, and not by the intersection of labor demand and supply. Note, too, that this reduction in labor demand results in a greater decrease in employment than would have been generated in the New Classical model. That model would generate an equilibrium at point C', with a reduction in both the nominal wage and in employment. However, this is not as large a reduction in employment as occurs in the New Keynesian model.

Aggregate Supply in the Wage Contracting Model

Using the model of the labor market outlined in Figure 10-2, we use our standard four-part diagram to derive the resulting New Keynesian aggregate supply curve in Figure 10-3. In the diagram, we begin in graph (d) by choosing a price level of P_0. We also assume that the expected price level is P_0. Then, in graph (a), with an actual and expected price level of P_0, we get labor demand and labor supply expected to be $N_D(P^e = P_0)$ and $N_S(P^e = P_0)$, respectively. These intersect at point A and determine the contracted wage W_0^c and the expected employment level N_F. If the actual price stays at P_0 and nothing else changes to shift labor demand, the labor market stays at point A, and employment is N_F. Then the production function, graph (a), tells us that output is Y_F. And, going through graph (c) back to graph (d), we plot point A, where the price is P_0 and output is at the full-employment level Y_F.

Now consider a price increase to P_1, while the wage rate stays at W^c_0. In this case actual labor demand shifts to the right, to $N_D(P_1)$. The nominal wage stays at W_0^c, and employment is determined on the labor demand curve. The labor market is therefore at point B, and employment is N_1. The increase in employment increases output to Y_1, and in graph (d) we plot point B, where the price level is P_1 and output is Y_1. Moreover, any further increase in overall prices above P_1 will shift labor demand further to the right, further increasing employment and output. The result is a point on the aggregate supply curve with a higher price and output level than B. As long as the wage rate is fixed at W_0^c, the supply curve showing the relationship between the price level and output is given by $SRAS(W_0^c)$. It should be noted that the supply curve $SRAS$ (W_0^c) is less steeply sloped than the $SRAS$ curve for the New Classical model.

What happens if the price level stays at P_1 and the wage is renegotiated? When this happens, and if prices are expected to stay at P_1, the new expected level of employment is, again, N_F. This is given by the intersection of N_D (P_1) and $N_S(P^e = P_1)$ at point C. The new contracted nominal wage is W_1^c. If the actual price level stays at P_1, then employment and output are at their full-employment levels, and in (d) this is given by point C, with a price level P_1 and output Y_F. Of course, the short-run aggregate supply curve through point C is drawn for a fixed nominal wage of W_1^c; and if the actual price level rises above the expected level of P_1, the economy will move up the curve labeled $SRAS(W_1^c)$.

Aggregate Demand and Aggregate Supply in the Wage Contracting Model

We now describe equilibrium between the aggregate supply curve developed in Figure 10-3 and aggregate demand. We also describe the adjustment of the economy to changes in aggregate demand, as illustrated in Figure 10-4. The initial equilibrium is at point A in both the labor market and in the overall economy (graphs (a) and (b), respectively). In (d), the short-run aggregate

FIGURE IO-3

The Aggregate Supply Curve

Starting in (d), we assume that the price level is equal to the expected price level P_0. The contracted nominal wage is W_0^c, corresponding to the expected labor demand and supply $N_D(P^e = P_0)$ and N_S $(P^e = P_0)$, respectively. Their intersection at point A generates employment of N_F. and income level Y_F. When price increases to P_1, labor demand increases to $N_D(P_1)$, employment corresponding to point B rises to N_1, output increases to point B on the production function, and income increases to Y_1, corresponding to point B on $SRAS$ (W_0^c).

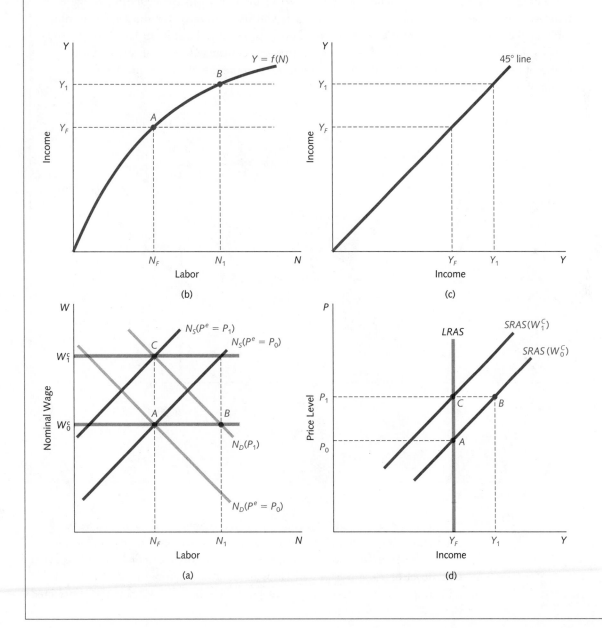

FIGURE 10-4

Response to an Increase in Aggregate Demand

Initially, AD_0, intersects short-run aggregate supply $SRAS(W_0^c)$ at point A, generating a price level of P_0 and income of Y_F. Equilibrium in the labor market is also at point A, where labor demand N_D (P_0) and labor supply $N_S(P_0)$ intersect. The contracted nominal wage, W_0^c, corresponds to the intersection of these labor market curves, and generates an equilibrium employment level of N_F. When aggregate demand increases to AD_1, intersecting the initial $SRAS$ at point B, the price level rises to P_1. In the labor market graph, labor demand increases to $N_D(P_1)$, and employment increases to N_1 at point B. The greater employment generates a higher level of income Y_1 in the economy. If aggregate demand is expected to stay at AD_1, then new contracts will be negotiated for the higher nominal wage of W_1^c at the end of the present contract period. This is shown by the shift in labor supply to $N_S(P_2)$ and labor demand to $N_D(P_2)$, which intersect at the new contracted wage of W_1^c and old equilibrium employment level of N_F. In (b), the new contract is represented by a shift in short-run aggregate supply to $SRAS(W_1^c)$.

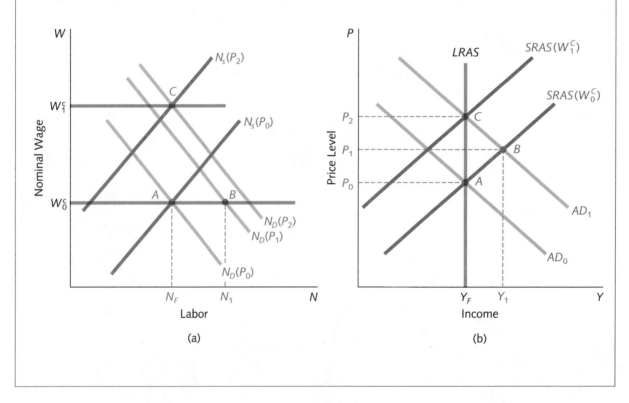

(a)   (b)

supply curve is $SRAS(W_0^c)$ and the initial aggregate demand curve is AD_0. Their intersection at point A determines the price level of P_0 and output of Y_F. In the labor market, the wage W_0^c was negotiated based on an expected price level of P_0 and expected labor demand and supply of $N_D^e(P_0)$ and N_S^e (P_0), respectively. These intersect at point A, where the wage is the contracted value W_0^c and employment is N_F.

Consider now a situation in which, after the wage is set at W_0^c, aggregate demand increases from AD_0 to AD_1. This is illustrated in Figure 10-4 by the rightward shift in aggregate demand, to intersect $SRAS(W_0^c)$ at point B. The price level increases to P_1 and output increases to Y_1. In the labor market, we illustrate the effect of the change in prices above the expected level of P_0 by shifting labor demand to the right, to $N_D(P_1)$. Since the nominal wage is contractually fixed at W_0^c, employment is determined by the quantity demanded, given by point B on the new labor demand curve, increasing the level of employment to N_1. The increased employment is what allows output to increase to Y_1 in the aggregate demand and supply diagram.

Given enough time, contracts are renegotiated. If aggregate demand stays at AD_1, the price level must rise to P_2 for AD_1, $LRAS$, and $SRAS$ to all intersect at the full-employment level of output Y_F. When the *expected* price rises to P_2, expected labor demand increases to $N_D(P^e = P_2)$, expected labor supply decreases to $N_S(P^e = P_2)$, and these intersect at point C, at the full-employment level N_F. The new contractual wage will be W_2^c, which is expected to clear the labor market at the price level P_2. Correspondingly, the aggregate demand and supply curves intersecting at point C are at output level Y_F. Of course, once the new wage contract is agreed to, changes in the price level from P_2 will lead to movements along the new short-run aggregate supply curve $SRAS(W_2^c)$.

In considering changes in aggregate demand, it is important to remember that, once a nominal wage contract is signed, the contractually fixed nominal wage does not adjust *even if changes in the price level are fully recognized by firms and workers*. In the New Classical model there is always the question of whether the change in aggregate demand is anticipated, with anticipated shocks generating Classical effects. In the New Keynesian model described here, the question is whether the change in aggregate demand was anticipated before the wage contract was signed. Once signed, the nominal wage is contractually fixed for the period of the contract. For instance, if a firm and its workers sign an annual contract, only those changes in aggregate demand that are anticipated before the signing of the contract will be incorporated in the expectations that lead to a determination of W^c. Once W^c is set, further changes in aggregate demand will generate employment effects. Even if a change in aggregate demand is recognized by everyone six months into the contract, the nominal wage doesn't adjust in this model. Therefore, changes in aggregate demand that are anticipated or recognized by both workers and firms *after the contract is signed* will have real effects on output and employment until the contract is renegotiated. Even if workers and firms recognize a change in aggregate demand and wish to respond to it, they are locked into a long-term contract. This is quite a different emphasis than in the New Classical model, which predicts no real effects of changes in aggregate demand once both workers and firms recognize that such a change has occurred.

The contractual rigidity of nominal wages also has important implications for the response of the economy to supply shocks. We turn now to analyzing supply shocks with this model.

Supply Shocks

The nominal wage contracting model discussed here can also be used to examine shocks to aggregate supply. As with the New Classical model discussed previously, we will look at an adverse supply shock as a downward shift in the production function. This is illustrated in Figure 10-5(b). The production function rotates clockwise toward the horizontal axis. At every level of employment, the marginal product of labor—the slope of the production function—declines. This shifts labor demand leftward, due not to a change in prices or expected prices, but to a reduction in the marginal product of labor.

To go through the analysis of the supply shock carefully, we start by describing an initial equilibrium and then asking about the effects of the shift in the production function. In the aggregate demand and supply graph in Figure 10-5(d), the initial position is point A, where $LRAS_0$ and $SRAS_0$ (W_0^c) intersect. The initial price level is P_0, and output is Y_{F_0}. In the labor market, labor demand is given by $N_{D_0}(P_0)$, labor supply is $N_{S_0}(P_0)$, and the contractual wage is set at W_0^c.[1] Equilibrium is at point A, at employment level N_{F_0}. On the production function $Y = f_0(N)$, employment of N_{F_0} gives output of Y_{F_0}.

The initial equilibrium at point A is at full employment. We can think of it as occurring after the contract wage is set at W_0^c and before any changes in aggregate demand or supply occur. Now consider the shift in the production function from $Y = f_0(N)$ to $Y = f_1(N)$. As we explained above, this particular change in the production technology reduces the marginal product of labor at every level of output. Thus, labor demand shifts from $N_{D_0}(P_0)$ to $N_{D_1}(P_0)$. Note that the price level has stayed P_0 but the labor demand curve has still shifted. This is due to a change in the marginal product of labor, which is itself due to the shift in the production function.

With the shift in labor demand to $N_{D1}(P_0)$ and the wage fixed at W_0^c, the labor market would initially end up at point C, with employment of N_1 workers. With N_1 workers, output is Y_1 on the new production function $Y = f_1(N)$. Note that this all happens for a price level of P_0, so in the aggregate demand and supply diagram we plot the point C, with price level P_0 and output Y_1.

What happens in the long run? In the long run, the nominal wage will be renegotiated. If the price level stays at P_0, and is expected to remain there through the next contract period, the intersection of labor supply and labor demand will be at point B. The contracted wage will decline to W_1^c, and employment will rise to N_{F_1}. This will be the full-employment level, the point at which labor demand and labor supply intersect when both are based upon a common and correct perception of the price level. With employment of N_{F_1}, output will be Y_{F_1} on the new production function. We plot this as point

---

[1] Labor supply and the initial labor demand curves still refer to expectations. Repeated use of the term "expected," as well as the superscript in notation, is eliminated for simplicity.

FIGURE IO-5
The Effect of a Supply Shock on *SRAS* and *LRAS*

In this figure, we examine the effects of an unexpected supply shock when a nominal wage contract has been signed by workers and firms. The initial equilibrium is given in (d) by the intersection of $LRAS_0$ and $SRAS_0$ at point A, yielding income of Y_{F_0} and price of P_0. This price level leads to a contract wage of W_0^c and employment of N_{F_0} at the intersection of $N_D(P_0)$ and $N_S(P_0)$ at point A in (a). This employment leads to an output level of Y_{F_0} along the production function $Y = f_0(N)$ at point A in (b). When a negative supply shock occurs the production function shifts down to $Y = f_1(N)$, labor demand falls to $N_{D_1}(P_0)$, employment falls to N_1, income falls to Y_1, and the aggregate supply curves shift to $LRAS_1$ and $SRAS_1$. The economic conditions correspond to point C in each of the graphs. Note that the short-run aggregate supply curve has shifted further to the left than *LRAS*. This occurs because of the nominal wage contract. As the price level rises to P_1, labor demand shifts up to $N_D(P_1)$, increasing employment and income to N_{F_1} and Y_{F_1}, respectively. The economy would now be at a point such as D in graphs (a) and (d).

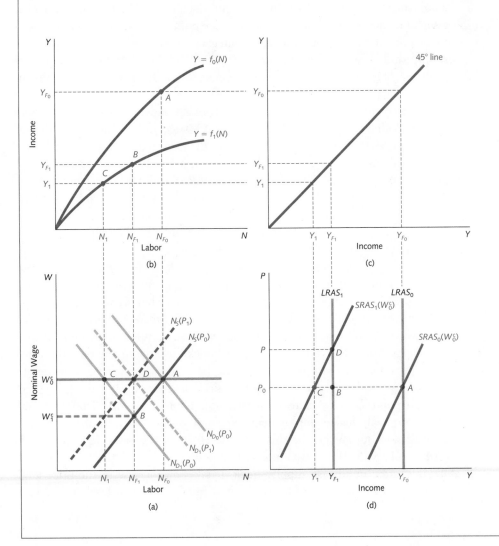

B in the aggregate demand and supply graph, with a price level of P_0 and output of Y_{F_1}.

Note that, for an unchanged price level P_0, we have determined that the leftward shift in output due to the supply shock is to point C in the short run, while wages are fixed at W_0^c, and to point B in the long run, after wage contracts are renegotiated. Point B is but one position on the new long-run aggregate supply curve $LRAS_1$, and indicates the leftward shift in $LRAS$ due to the adverse supply shock. Point C is a point on the short-run aggregate supply curve $SRAS_1(W_0^c)$, the short-run supply curve valid after the supply shock as long as the nominal wage is W_0^c.

Our analysis points out the fact that, for this New Keynesian model, the short-run aggregate supply curve shifts leftward further than the long-run aggregate supply curve in response to an adverse supply shock. This phenomenon is due to the nominal wage contract, which prohibits adjustments in the nominal wage that might aid in the adjustment to the new, lower level of full employment. Such was *not* the case in the New Classical model, which essentially moved to a short-run position like point B in the labor market graph in Figure 10-5, so that short-run aggregate supply and long-run aggregate supply shifted leftward by the same amount. In the New Keynesian model analyzed here, the rigid nominal wage causes a further leftward shift in short-run aggregate supply.

There is a further point to be made in connection with these shifts in $LRAS$ and $SRAS$ after a supply shock. In the New Classical model, the intersection of $LRAS$ and $SRAS$ occurred at a point where the expected price and actual price were equal, so that the economy would be in a Classical equilibrium. In the New Keynesian model, the intersection of $LRAS$ and $SRAS$ does occur at an output level that corresponds to the natural level of output, but the intersection is at a point where the real wage—the contract wage W^c divided by the price level—will clear the labor market at the natural level of employment.

In the New Keynesian model, what price level is consistent with an intersection of short-run aggregate supply and long-run aggregate supply after an adverse supply shock? In Figure 10-5(a), the labor demand curve must intersect the nominal wage level W_0^c at point D, where employment is N_{F_1}. This will give full employment of labor and hence full-employment output (i.e., a point on $LRAS_1$) after the supply shock. To accomplish this, the price level must increase just enough to put labor demand at the appropriate location. We will say that the required price level is P_1, and draw $N_{D_1}(P_1)$ through point D. This increase in the price level in the new labor demand curve N_{D_1} will make employment N_{F_1} and output Y_{F_1}. In the aggregate demand and supply graph, this price level P_1 is the price level at which $LRAS_1$ and $SRAS_1(W^c = W_0^c)$ intersect, at point D.

Thus, after an adverse supply shock, it takes an increase in the price level from P_0 to P_1 to restore output to the new full-employment level at Y_{F_1}. This occurs because the adverse supply shock requires a decrease in the real wage to restore labor market equilibrium. If the price level stays at P_0 and the nominal wage is rigid at W_0^c, there is no variable that can adjust to lower the real wage. This results in a decline in employment, and hence in output, below the new full-employment levels. Only an increase in the price—to P_1 in Figure 10-5—or a renegotiation of the nominal wage—to W_1^c if the price stays at P_0—will restore the labor market to equilibrium. Of course, nothing we have discussed here can counteract the fact that the adverse supply shock has reduced the long-run real wage, employment, and output.

The above analysis has demonstrated just how the *SRAS* and *LRAS* curves shift in response to an adverse supply shock. The case of a positive supply shock is analyzed in a similar way. In fact, the two cases are symmetric. A positive supply shock shifts *LRAS* and *SRAS* to the right, but shifts *SRAS* further to the right than *LRAS*.

AGGREGATE SUPPLY AND DEMAND IN THE CASE OF A SUPPLY SHOCK

We turn now to an analysis of the effect of these shifts in aggregate supply when the price level is determined by the intersection of aggregate supply and demand. In Figure 10-6 we present graphs of both the labor market and of aggregate demand and supply. The initial equilibrium prior to the shock is at point A in both graphs. In the aggregate demand and supply graph, point A is the intersection of aggregate demand $LRAS_0$ and $SRAS_0(W_0^c)$. The initial price level at point A is P_0, and output is at the full-employment level Y_{F_0}.

In the labor market, the initial equilibrium at A was determined by the intersection of expected labor supply and expected labor demand. Expected and actual labor supply is $N_S(P_0)$, and expected and actual labor demand is $N_{D_0}(P_0)$. The contracted nominal wage is W_0^c and employment is N_{F_0}, the full-employment level.

When the supply shock occurs, both *LRAS* and *SRAS* shift leftward, $LRAS_0$ shifts to $LRAS_1$ and $SRAS_0(W_0^c)$ shifts to $SRAS_1(W_0^c)$. As we demonstrated in Figure 10-5, short-run aggregate supply shifts further left than long-run aggregate supply, so that at a price level of P_0 output would be at point C instead of point B.

In the labor market, the adverse supply shock reduces labor demand from $N_{D_0}(P_0)$ to $N_{D_1}(P_0)$. Because the wage is contractually set at W_0^c, employment falls to N_1 at point C on the new labor demand curve, whereas full employment falls to N_{F_1} at point B, where $N_S(P_0)$ intersects $N_{D_1}(P_0)$. Of course, none of this has taken account of the aggregate demand curve. The price level will not stay at P_0 unless aggregate demand were perfectly elastic, a most unlikely occurrence. It turns out that in this model the effect of the adverse supply shock on the economy depends crucially on the slope of

FIGURE 10-6
AS-AD and an Unexpected Supply Shock

The initial equilibrium is at point A in both (a) and (b), with a price level of P_0, wage W^c_0, employment N_{F_0}, income Y_{F_0}, curves $N_{D_0}(P_0)$ and $N_S(P_0)$ in the labor market, and AD_0, $SRAS_0(W^c_0)$, and $LRAS_0$ in the aggregate demand and supply graph. After the negative supply shock, the aggregate supply curves shift back to $LRAS_1$ and $SRAS_1(W^c_0)$, the new full-employment income level being Y_{F_1}. An elastic aggregate demand curve, such as AD_0, will intersect $SRAS$ at point E, causing prices to rise to P_E, labor demand to fall to $N_{D_1}(P^e)$ and income to fall to Y_E. The more inelastic AD_1, will intersect $SRAS_1$ at point F, increase price to P_F, and reduce labor demand to $N_{D_1}(P_F)$. In this case, income will already be at its new full-employment level of Y_{F_1}. If the still more inelastic aggregate demand curve AD_2 is the relevant curve, the intersection between it and $SRAS$ occurs at point D, a price level of P_D, an employment level above the new full-employment level, and income level of Y_D.

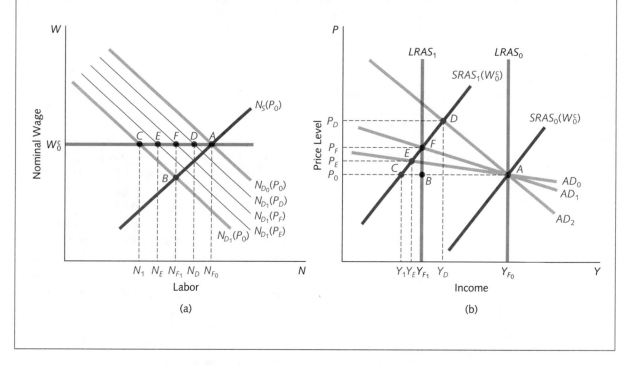

(a)   (b)

aggregate demand. That is why we draw three different aggregate demand curves in Figure 10-6, labeled AD_0, AD_1, and AD_2. AD_0 is the most elastic and AD_2 the least elastic.

Let us first consider the middle case, AD_1. This aggregate demand curve is drawn so that it passes through point A, the initial full-employment equilibrium, and point F, the new full-employment equilibrium for the wage rate W^c_0. Thus, if the economy's aggregate demand curve is AD_1, then after the supply shock the new short-run equilibrium is at the intersection of AD_1 and the new short-run aggregate supply curve $SRAS_1(W^c_0)$ at point F. The price level is P_F, and output is the full-employment level of output Y_{F_1}. Therefore, if the aggregate demand curve is AD_1, the price level will rise just enough to restore output to the full-employment level after the supply shock occurs.

In the labor market, the increase in price from P_0 to P_F will shift labor demand to the right, to $N_{D_1}(P_F)$. This is just the shift needed so that, at wage rate W_0^c, labor demand and hence employment is N_{F_1}. Full employment is restored, albeit at the new, lower level of employment (and output) mandated by the supply shock.

Of course, having an economy in the position analyzed here is serendipitous in the extreme. The aggregate demand curve could just as well be AD_0 or AD_2. If it is AD_0, then the new short-run equilibrium after the shock is at point E, where the price level is P_E and output is Y_E. The increase in price will shift labor demand to $N_{D_1}(P_E)$, which at wage rate W_0^c generates employment of N_E, which is less than full employment, and indeed is the cause for output to be less than full-employment output.

Alternatively, if the aggregate demand curve is AD_2, then the new short-run equilibrium after the shock is at point D, where the price level is P_D and output is Y_D. The increase in price will shift labor demand to $N_{D_1}(P_D)$, which, at wage rate W_0^c, generates employment of N_D, above N_{F_1}. This is more-than-full employment, and indeed is the cause for output to be greater than the full-employment level of output.

Thus, the elasticity of the aggregate demand curve determines whether the economy is operating at more or less than the new full-employment level after a supply shock. Recall that this uncertainty didn't exist in the New Classical model, a result of the fact that SRAS and LRAS both shift to the left by the same amount after an adverse supply shock in that model. In the New Keynesian model, SRAS shifts further left than LRAS, and leads to an ambiguous result as to whether short-run output and employment exceed or fall short of full-employment levels after the supply shock.

Note that no position of aggregate demand—and no prospective shift in aggregate demand—can change the fact that the adverse supply shock has lowered full-employment output. Aggregate demand may have short-run effects on the economy, but it cannot change the fact that the long-run aggregate supply curve has declined. How does the economy get to the long-run equilibrium on LRAS? Basically, it requires renegotiation of the contractual nominal wage. Renegotiating the nominal wage to restore equilibrium in the labor market will shift short-run aggregate supply. The long-run equilibrium will occur when SRAS shifts to intersect aggregate demand on the long-run aggregate supply curve $LRAS_1$. We will further consider this point in our discussions of monetary and fiscal policy in later chapters.

Finally, what about a positive supply shock? Now, SRAS and LRAS shift to the right, with SRAS shifting further right than LRAS. If the price level stays constant, employment and output will exceed the new (and higher) full-employment level. The price level will change, however, because aggregate demand is downward sloping. The rightward shift in SRAS will create a new equilibrium at a lower price level than the original price level. If aggregate demand has just the right slope, then the decline in the price level will be just sufficient to reduce labor demand enough to have employment and output at the full-employment level. If aggregate demand is more elastic than this, price will not fall as much, and both employment and output will exceed the full employment levels. If aggregate demand is less elastic than this, price will fall by more than is required to achieve full employment, and both employment and output will be below the new full-employment level. This analysis is completely symmetric to the case of an adverse supply shock, both in its graphical representation and in its effect on macroeconomic variables.

Summary of New Keynesian Model Based on Nominal Wage Rigidity

This completes our analysis of the New Keynesian model built on nominal wage rigidities. This model is one of the prime alternatives to the New Classical model developed in Chapter 9. To summarize the results of various shocks that can occur to aggregate demand and supply, we present Table 10-1. In this table, we list the effect of changes in aggregate demand, and of supply shocks, on the nominal wage, the price level, the real wage, employment, and output, in both the short run and the long run. For example, for an increase in aggregate demand we summarize the effects as follows. In the short run, an increase in aggregate demand does not change the nominal wage—it is fixed by contract—but does increase the price level and, because *SRAS* is upward sloping, output. The real wage falls because the price level rises and the nominal wage is fixed. Employment increases because labor demand increases with the price level, and because employment is determined on the labor demand curve. In the long run, the nominal wage is renegotiated at a higher level. The price level rises even more than it did in the short run, but real wages are unchanged from the initial full-employment equilibrium. Likewise, employment and output are unchanged from the initial full-employment equilibrium.

All of the results listed here are derived from Figure 10-4 and the accompanying discussion, in which we described the effect on the economy of an increase in aggregate demand.

The cases of adverse and positive supply shocks described in Table 10-1 are similar. The case of adverse supply shocks follows our analysis in Figure 10-6 and the accompanying discussion in the text. For instance, Table 10-1 indicates that in the short run the adverse supply shock leads to no change in the contracted nominal wage, an increase in the price level and hence a reduction in the real wage, and reductions in both employment and output. In the long run, the nominal wage may rise or fall. The price level will have risen relative to the initial equilibrium, but may rise or fall relative to the short-run level. The real wage will decline due to the decrease in the marginal product of labor. Output and employment will both decrease in the long run relative to their initial equilibrium levels, but both may increase or decrease relative to the short-run equilibrium levels. This ambiguity is due to the fact, documented in the text, that the slope of aggregate demand has important implications for

TABLE IO-I

Response of Economy to Shocks

This table is a summary of the impact of shocks in the New Keynesian model. Shocks occur after the wage contract is signed. It encompasses and extends the results found in Figures 10-4 and 10-6, and assumes that the economy is initially at a full-employment equilibrium, with wage contracts signed before the advent of the unexpected demand or supply shocks.

I.   INCREASE IN AD

VARIABLE	EFFECT IN SHORT RUN	EFFECT IN LONG RUN
W	W^c FIXED	W^c INCREASES
P	RISES	RISES FROM SHORT-RUN LEVEL
W/P	DECREASES	NO CHANGE
N	INCREASES	NO CHANGE
Y	INCREASES	NO CHANGE

II.   DECREASE IN AD

VARIABLE	EFFECT IN SHORT RUN	EFFECT IN LONG RUN
W	W^c FIXED	W^c DECREASES
P	DECLINES	FALLS FROM SHORT-RUN LEVEL
W/P	INCREASES	NO CHANGE
N	DECREASES	NO CHANGE
Y	DECREASES	NO CHANGE

III.   ADVERSE SUPPLY SHOCK

VARIABLE	EFFECT IN SHORT RUN	EFFECT IN LONG RUN
W	W^c FIXED	AMBIGUOUS
P	RISES	RISES, BUT AMBIGUOUS CHANGE FROM SHORT-RUN LEVEL
W/P	DECREASES	DECREASES
N	DECREASES	DECREASES, BUT AMBIGUOUS CHANGE FROM SHORT-RUN LEVEL
Y	DECREASES	DECREASES, BUT AMBIGUOUS CHANGE FROM SHORT-RUN LEVEL

IV.   POSITIVE SUPPLY SHOCK

W	W^c FIXED	AMBIGUOUS
P	FALLS	FALLS, BUT AMBIGUOUS CHANGE FROM SHORT-RUN LEVEL

TABLE 10-1
Response of Economy to
Shocks—*Continued*

VARIABLE	EFFECT IN SHORT RUN	EFFECT IN LONG RUN
w/P	INCREASES	INCREASES
N	INCREASES	INCREASES, BUT AMBIGUOUS CHANGE FROM SHORT-RUN LEVEL
Y	INCREASES	INCREASES, BUT AMBIGUOUS CHANGE FROM SHORT-RUN LEVEL

NOTE: All comparisons are to an initial full-employment equilibrium.

whether the short-run employment and output levels are above or below the eventual long-run, full-employment levels of employment and output. Finally, the nominal wage changes, but here the long-run change is ambiguous. For example, consider an adverse supply shock, which will lower the real wage but will increase the price level. The nominal wage may either increase or decrease, depending on the change in the real wage and the price level. If the real wage falls a little but the price level rises a lot, then the nominal wage may rise, even though the nominal wage divided by the price level has to fall.

This summarizes and concludes our present discussion of the New Keynesian model with nominal wage contracts. Certain important features of this model distinguish it from the New Classical model. First, it is basically a disequilibrium model in the short run, with no requirement that employment be determined by the intersection of labor demand and supply. Also, it allows for real effects of changes in aggregate demand in the short run, while wages are contractually fixed, even if these changes are perceived by all participants in the labor market. The only requirement is that the changes in aggregate demand were not perceived at the time the wage contracts were signed. Once locked into a contract, labor suppliers and demanders give up the right to respond to even commonly recognized changes in aggregate demand by adjusting the nominal wage.

Therefore, this New Keynesian model gives a role for policy to affect the economy in the short run, before nominal wages are renegotiated. In the long run, of course, the economy reverts to the Classical equilibrium as determined by the long-run aggregate supply curve. Still, this New Keynesian model has both workers and firms forming rational expectations in the short run. Yet, it generates an effectiveness of policy by the assumption that labor contracts set a nominal wage that is not adjusted during the contract period.

This nominal wage-contracting model is a well-known and popular New Keynesian model. It provides a clear example of a model in which expectations are rational, but in which policy can be effective, due to some type of rigidity in the way the economy responds to shocks. In this model, the rigidity is in the nominal wage, which is set by contract between workers and firms. The model has an intuitive appeal and a cogent explanation for cycles of expansion and contraction based on unexpected shocks to aggregate demand. However, the model is not without its critics.

The main criticism is that, like the New Classical model, the model predicts that in the face of a decrease in aggregate demand, output and employment fall while the real wage increases. That is, the model predicts that we should observe increases in the real wage during recessions, and likewise that during expansions we should see decreases in the real wage. This is at odds with most empirical studies, which find that real wages are constant or perhaps increasing during expansions, and constant or perhaps decreasing during recessions. Thus, the model's predictions of the relationship between employment or output and the real wage do not seem to correspond with the real world as we observe it—perhaps the key failing of this model.

In addition, a number of economists object to models that assume nominal wage contracting, on the grounds that we really don't understand why individuals sign such contracts. We should be careful in making policy recommendations based upon the results of a model that includes behavior we as economists find difficult to explain. It is not, of course, a problem that people sign contracts or make verbal or written agreements to sell their labor services at a preset price. The problem is that we cannot explain why these contracts are written to set a *nominal,* as opposed to a real, wage. New Keynesians typically have little patience with this argument, however, since it is patently clear that individuals *do* sign such agreements. What is unclear is why they do so, and without knowing why, it is difficult to make policy recommendations with any confidence that the recommended policy will increase the well-being of workers and firms in the economy.

The nominal wage-contracting model is not the only New Keynesian explanation for policy effectiveness, however. We will now examine several alternative New Keynesian models. These also attempt to model the economy in a way that allows policy to be effective in influencing employment and output, at least in the short run. These alternatives range from models of rigid output prices to models of coordination failures, as well as what are known as "efficiency wage" models. We turn first to models of output price rigidity.

A NEW KEYNESIAN MODEL WITH STICKY OUTPUT PRICES

We will develop a New Keynesian model with sticky (i.e., slowly adjusting) output prices in two steps. First we explain why sticky prices might exist, and then we develop a model incorporating price rigidities in a macroeconomic framework.

Why Price Rigidity?

Instead of rigid wages, this model looks at output prices and suggests that these prices are not as flexible as the standard New Classical model of perfect competition would imply. In the perfect competition model, individual buyers and sellers are price takers. Sellers simply observe the market price for their product and decide how much to sell. Sellers won't worry about what price to charge—they'll charge the market price. If they attempt to charge a higher price, they will not sell any of their output, and if they attempt to charge a lower price they will merely sacrifice profit without any compensation for the lost profit. Hence, they sell at the market price. Similarly, buyers know they must pay the market price, since offers to buy at less than the market price will be rejected by sellers. Offers to pay more than the market price will be a waste of funds, since buyers can have all they want at the market price. This model of a perfectly competitive market is widely used in New Classical models, but it can be criticized as an unrealistic depiction of the majority of markets in the United States.

Perfect competition requires a large number of well-informed buyers and sellers who act as price takers in the trade of a homogenous product. It also requires free entry and exit of firms and workers. Such assumptions make the perfect competition model seem most valid for industries such as primary agricultural products (at least in the absence of government regulation) and financial markets. In these markets, buyers and sellers can either transact at the market price or not, but they cannot alter the market price by their individual behavior. Such markets often take on the character of an auction market, with continual bid or sell orders on an organized exchange, an activity facilitated by the homogenous nature of the product, be it corn or shares of IBM stock.

In contrast, many products sold in the United States are not sold on auction markets, but are instead sold at prices set by individual firms. Indeed, many goods are sold in a posted-price market—restaurants post prices, newspapers post prices, and catalog companies post prices. In all of these cases, prices do not change very often. Moreover, these prices are posted in nominal terms, and the seller agrees to supply the quantity demanded at the posted price.

How is it that markets exist with posted prices, and prices that change infrequently? New Keynesians explain this behavior by the fact that most firms are in monopolistically competitive markets, and by the fact that it is costly for firms to change prices.

Recall from microeconomics principles class that monopolistic competition occurs when firms have some degree of market power; that is, when firms have some ability to set prices different from those charged by other firms. Monopolistic competition occurs when firms do not sell homogenous products. For example, they may have products that differ in physical characteristics. Or, they may provide a service that differs from that of other firms merely in being closer to some consumers than to others. In such cases, the firm has some latitude in setting a price instead of merely responding to an impersonal market price. This allows it to set prices above marginal cost.

However, the mere existence of monopolistic competition is not sufficient for prices to change infrequently. Instead, there must be an additional reason for firms to hesitate to increase nominal prices. One reason would be the existence of what are called *menu costs*. Menu costs are the costs of changing posted prices, such as menus at a restaurant or the pages of a catalog. More generally, they are any cost that a firm incurs in raising prices and that causes the firm to hesitate to adjust prices continually. Instead, firms stick with the posted prices until conditions change sufficiently to justify paying the costs required to change the prices.

Of course, a natural thought is that these menu costs cannot be very large. New Keynesians respond to this remark in several ways. First of all, these costs are not insignificant. Major mail-order companies, such as Montgomery Ward's catalog sales division, bear a large cost from printing and distributing catalogs, and these costs would be even greater if the catalogs were issued monthly or weekly instead of once or twice a year. Even for restaurants, the cost of printing menus must be taken into account. For grocers, the cost of changing prices is also significant, especially if each item whose price is changed must be individually marked on the shelf. Second, because a monopolistic competitor has a demand curve that is less elastic than that of a competitive firm, it is less sensitive to price changes. Unlike a competitive firm, a monopolistic competitor can charge a price above or below the optimal price and not lose much profit. (Recall that a competitive firm pricing above the optimal price—that is, the market price—will sell no output.) Unless the potential increase in profit from adjusting the price exceeds the menu cost, the monopolistic competitor will not choose to change the price.

A New Keynesian Model with Price Rigidities

To develop a New Keynesian model with price rigidities, we turn first to the graph of aggregate demand and supply, such as is drawn in Figure 10-7. We will assume that the price level at every firm is posted at a level that is expected to clear the output market. In the time period during which the price is posted, the price will not adjust to changes in market conditions. Thus, as in the nominal wage contracting model, the posted price will be rigid until the posting period ends, at which point a new price will be posted.

In Figure 10-7, we capture this feature by drawing the expected level of aggregate supply and demand as $LRAS^e$ and AD^e. (Note that one cannot expect to be off the long-run aggregate supply curve in the typical New Classical or New Keynesian model if expectations are formed rationally, so there is no point in drawing a curve such as $SRAS^e$ in Figure 10-7.) The intersection of $LRAS^e$ and AD^e determines both the expected price level P^e and the expected output level Y_f^e. If expectations are correct, output will be at the

FIGURE 10-7
Determining the Posted Price

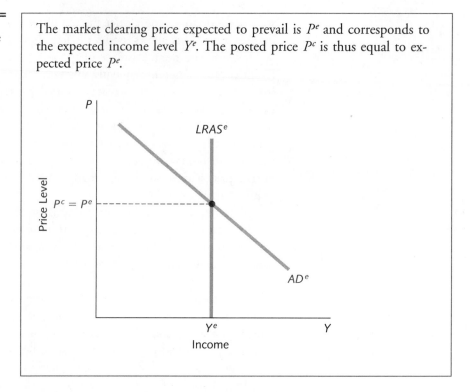

The market clearing price expected to prevail is P^e and corresponds to the expected income level Y^e. The posted price P^c is thus equal to expected price P^e.

full-employment level. The rigid pricing model then assumes that, for the period of time prices are posted and unchanged, the posted price, labeled P^c, will be equal to P^e, as indicated in Figure 10-7. The analogy with how the contracted wage W^c is formed in the labor market in the New Keynesian model of nominal wage contracts should be obvious.

What happens after the price is set at P^c? If aggregate demand stays at its expected value of AD^e and if aggregate supply stays at $LRAS^e$, then output will be at the full-employment level Y_F. What happens if aggregate demand increases or decreases unexpectedly during the period? Such occurrences are illustrated in Figure 10-8. The initial posted price is P_0^c, set at the intersection of $LRAS^e$ and AD_0^e at point A. If aggregate demand increases to AD_1, then at the posted price level P_f^c there will be an excess of aggregate demand over aggregate supply of $Y_1 - Y_F$. The assumption in the posted-price model is that the firms satisfy all demand, so output will be equal to Y_1 at point B. Note that this is clearly a disequilibrium position, since aggregate supply and aggregate demand are not equal at point B.

In the long run, the posted price will be reset. If aggregate demand is expected to be AD_1 and long-run aggregate supply is expected to stay at $LRAS$, then the new posted price will be P_f^c, determined by the intersection of AD_1 and $LRAS^e$ at point C. At this point, output is again expected to be at the full-employment level.

FIGURE IO-8
Changes in *AD* in a
Posted-Price Model

In this figure, the posted price is set at P_0^c, where $LRAS^e$ and AD^e intersect at point *A*. If *AD* increases unexpectedly to AD_1, since prices cannot change, income will increase to Y_1. If prices were allowed to fluctuate freely, the price level would rise to P_1^c and there would be no increase in income. If *AD* falls from AD_0^e to AD_2, income will fall to Y_2. Again, if prices were flexible, the price level would fall to P_2^c.

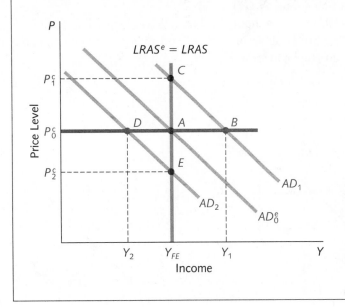

Similarly, starting at point *A* with a posted price of P_0^c, a reduction in aggregate demand to AD_2 will cause a disequilibrium between aggregate supply and demand at the posted price. Again, since firms agree to keep price constant, they will supply the quantity demanded, which is determined at point *D* as Y_2. In the long run, after the price is adjusted and posted at a new level, the price level will fall to P_2^c if aggregate demand is expected to stay at AD_2.

What happens in the labor market when the price is posted and aggregate demand changes? To answer this question, we again refer to our four-part diagram used to develop aggregate supply in previous models. However, now we use it to work backward to the labor market! In Figure 10-9, the posted-price output market is in graph (d). The initial price is P^c, determined by the intersection at point *A* of *LRAS* and AD_0, which are the expected values of aggregate supply and demand. Output is expected to be full-employment output Y_F. If output is Y_F, then the production function tells us that employment must be N_F, as is indicated by point *A* on the production function, graph (b). In the labor market, graph (a), this level of employment

FIGURE 10-9

Changes in *AD* and the Labor Market in the Posted-Price Model

In (d) the posted price equal to P^c and income is Y_{FE}, both determined by the intersection of AD_0 and *LRAS* at point *A*. Suppose *AD* shifts to AD_1. The output level corresponding to the new output point *B* in graph (b) will require the firms to employ N_1 laborers. To obtain this higher employment, firms will have to pay a wage of W_1 and thus are forced off their labor demand curve $N_D(P^c)$. This coincides with point *B* on $N_S(P^c)$ in (a).

Letting *AD* fall to AD_2, output will be at Y_2, corresponding to point *C* on the new aggregate demand curve. The firms will again be forced off their labor demand curve to point *C* on $N_S(P^c)$, which implies an employment level of N_2 and wage W_2.

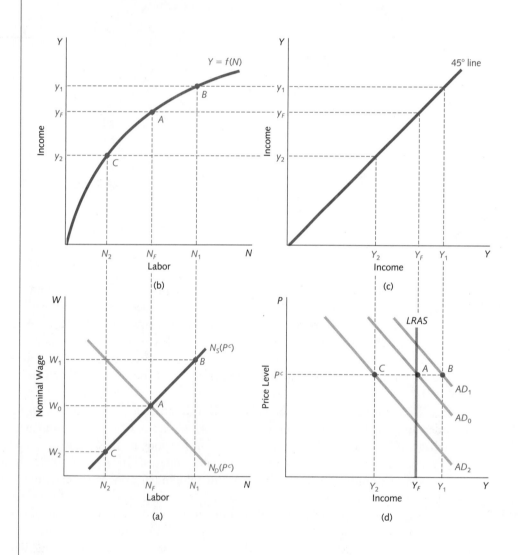

N_F must be the equilibrium that is expected to occur between labor demand and supply. We draw labor demand as $N_D(P^c)$ and labor supply as $N_S(P^c)$, which intersect at point A with an employment level of N_F and a nominal wage of W_0. If expectations are realized, particularly if aggregate demand does not stray from AD_0, then both output and employment will be at full-employment levels.

What happens if aggregate demand increases to AD_1? In this case, we have already seen that firms stand willing to meet the demand at the posted price P^c. In the aggregate demand and supply diagram, this results in production of Y_1, as determined by point B on AD_1. Production of Y_1 requires employment of N_1, as indicated by point B on the production function. Finally, in order to get N_1 workers to work, the labor supply curve indicates that the nominal wage must rise to W_1. This is marked by point B on the labor supply curve, which indicates that a wage of W_1 (and a price level of P^c) is required to induce a quantity of labor of N_1.

Of course, point B is not a point at which labor demand equals labor supply. Since the firm is operating off its supply curve, it is also operating off its demand for labor curve. The assumed willingness of the firm to meet demand at the posted price means that it must be willing to hire the necessary labor, regardless of the state of labor demand. Hence, the disequilibrium in the output market translates into disequilibrium in the labor market.

There are a few things to point out about this analysis of posted prices. First of all, we have seen that this model assumes firms are operating off their supply curve for goods. When aggregate demand increases, firms agree to provide additional goods without increasing prices. Second, if wages are not set by contract, then any increase in employment (in response to an increase in aggregate demand) must be induced by offering workers a higher nominal wage, as illustrated in Figure 10-9. This means that firms are off their labor demand curve and not maximizing profits, at least short-run profits—a situation analogous to the labor market in the nominal wage-contracting model. There, workers were off their labor supply curves, a condition that would also affect their demand for goods and services if the analysis were extended to consider this effect. Thus, the posted-price model, like the nominal wage-contracting model, involves the assumption that economic agents—in this case firms—are not acting to maximize profits, at least in the short run.

How do we explain this failure to maximize? One explanation is that consumers prefer posted prices, and will give more business to firms that post prices. This will allow the firm posting prices to garner a greater market share and greater future profits. However, this explanation will ultimately require a model of imperfect competition, in which firms have some local market power—an explanation we will not pursue further here.

The analysis of a decrease in aggregate demand is similar. Let us return to our initial equilibrium at point A and now consider a reduction in aggregate demand from AD_0 to AD_2. At the posted price of P^c, output will be given by point C on AD_2, or Y_2. However, if the firm produces only Y_2 units of output, it needs only N_2 units of labor, as indicated by point C on the production function. If it needs only N_2 units of labor, however, then the labor supply curve says that it can pay a wage of W_2, as indicated by point C on the labor supply curve. Again, point C is not the intersection of labor supply and labor demand. It is, instead, determined solely by how much the firm must pay to attract the requisite amount of labor to produce the output demanded at a price of P^c.

In the long run, the posted price will adjust to any increase or decrease in aggregate demand, and the change in the price level will alter both labor demand and supply and hence the nominal wage. At the new posted-price equilibrium, the economy will be expected to be in full-employment equilibrium at employment N_F and output Y_F, just as it started out at point A. But the short run, until such price adjustments occur, employment and output will respond directly to changes in aggregate demand.

One key feature of this model of posted prices is the effect of changes in aggregate demand on the real wage. Recall that a telling criticism of the nominal wage-contracting model is the counter-factual prediction that an increase in aggregate demand would lead to an increase in output and a reduction in the real wage. A reduction in aggregate demand would lead to a decrease in output and an increase in the real wage. In other words, real wages are predicted to rise during recessions and fall during expansions—a prediction at odds with the empirical evidence that real wages are pretty much unaffected by the business cycle.

In the model of price rigidities, this prediction is altered. An increase in aggregate demand causes an increase in output, an increase in employment, and an increase in the nominal wage. Since the price level is fixed, this model predicts that the real wage will rise when output is rising, during expansions. Likewise, the model predicts that a reduction in aggregate demand causes nominal and real wages to fall. Thus, real wages fall during recessions. These predictions accord better with empirical findings. Of course, a noncyclical real wage is also in accord with some empirical research, and a model with both nominal wage contracting and posted prices could generate such a prediction. However, we will not pursue this line of reasoning further at this point, since the model would be difficult to analyze.

Finally, before we move on to other New Keynesian models, what are the effects of supply shocks in the model with price rigidities? It turns out the supply shocks have no important effect on the short-run equilibrium in the above model. Consider Figure 10-10, which illustrates a supply shock in this model. The initial equilibrium is at point A, where the initial and the expected long-run aggregate supply curve is $LRAS_0$ and the initial and the expected aggregate demand curve is AD_0. The expected price level is equal to the posted-price level of P^c, and output is expected to be Y_{F_0}.

A supply shock in the posted-price model has no important short-run effects. Assume we start out with the economy in equilibrium at point A at the intersection of AD and $LRAS_0$. The posted price is P^c and output is Y_{F_0}. A negative supply shock moves $LRAS$ left to $LRAS_1$, but does not change AD, or the posted price. The economy stays at point A on AD, but this output level now becomes a point of disequilibrium. Long-run equilibrium requires a rise in the posted price to P_1^c and a lower output of Y_{F_1}, which coincides with point B.

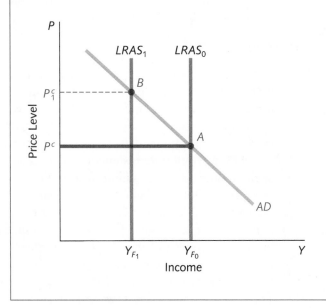

Supply Shocks with Posted Prices

From this equilibrium, what happens if there is an adverse supply shock? This shifts long-run aggregate supply to the left. However, at the posted price of P^c, the aggregate quantity demanded remains Y_{F_0}, even though this is no longer the full-employment output level. Thus, the supply shock merely means that point A, which appeared to be a point of long-run equilibrium, is now a point of disequilibrium. The change in long-run aggregate supply from $LRAS_0$ to $LRAS_1$ does not change output in the short run. What about the labor market? The adverse supply shock will decrease labor demand, but labor supply is unaffected. Since aggregate demand is unchanged, so is output, and the reduction in the production function means that even more workers will be needed to produce the output Y_{F_0}. This increase in employment can occur only by increased nominal wages, inducing a greater quantity of labor supplied. Thus, the nominal—and real—wage increases with an adverse supply shock, at least in the short run. Employment also increases.

In the long run, of course, the price level will adjust as firms change their posted prices in response to the shock. Long-run equilibrium is eventually restored at point *B*, with output falling to Y_{F_1}. The shift in the production function and the decrease in labor demand explain the shift to the left in *LRAS*, and cause the real wage to fall. Thus, the adverse supply shock causes a short-run increase in the real wage in the posted-price model, while in the long run the real wage declines, just like in our other models of aggregate supply.

We now turn to several other New Keynesian ideas.

MODELS OF COORDINATION FAILURE

An issue that comes up recurrently in modern microeconomics is that individuals are often placed in situations requiring strategic interactions between rational economic beings. This has led to the building of macroeconomic models based on the idea of coordination failure in production. The intent is to study models in which the economy might end up at an equilibrium position that is inferior to other possible equilibria merely because of the individual actor's failure to coordinate the optimal set of actions. For example, Keynes talked about underemployment equilibria—a position of rest from which the economy did not tend to move. The unemployment equilibrium would not be exactly like our short-run unemployment equilibrium in the previous models of this chapter, since these are equilibria that last only for the short run—the duration of labor contracts or of posted prices. In our model of coordination failure, the underemployment equilibria are long run. There are no sticky prices or wages that can adjust to make the economy revert to a classical full-employment equilibrium.

To make this point more formally, we will require an introduction to some ideas from game theory. In the following sections, we first use the Prisoners' Dilemma game to introduce the concept of a Nash equilibrium. (The Prisoners' Dilemma game will also prove useful in our discussion of monetary policy as a game between the government and the private sector in Chapter 16.) Next, we discuss the coordination game between two workers to see how their combined work effort can affect production and thereby result in a whole series of Nash equilibria. These alternative Nash equilibria can be ranked as to which is "best" for the two workers, but we will see that there is no reason to think workers will necessarily end up at the best equilibrium. We will interpret an equilibrium other than the best as an underemployment equilibrium of the type Keynes had in mind.

The Prisoners' Dilemma Game

One of the most famous and basic examples for introducing some of the ideas of game theory is called the Prisoners' Dilemma game. In this game, imagine that two prisoners have been arrested for a crime that they jointly committed. The police might charge the prisoners with either of two offenses, one of which is more serious than the other. When the two prisoners are captured they are immediately separated and held incommunicado.

The police first convince each prisoner that there is enough evidence to convict him of the lesser offense, which will cost him one year in prison. Each prisoner is then offered the following deal. If the prisoner confesses to the more serious crime *and* if his confession is vital for convicting his partner of the more serious crime, then the prisoner who confesses will go free. His partner, meanwhile, will be convicted of the serious crime and serve five years in jail. If the prisoner confesses to the more serious crime but his confession turns out to be unnecessary for convicting his partner of that crime, then the prisoner who confesses will be charged with the more serious crime but receive a reduced sentence of three years for his good faith effort. What should each prisoner do?

To address that question, we first present the game in a format that allows us to analyze the situation in Table 10-2.[2] The payoffs, in terms of years in jail, are presented in Table 10-2 for each action that each prisoner might take. For instance, prisoner 1 might confess or not confess, as is indicated across the top of the table. Prisoner 2 might confess or not confess, as is indicated in the left-hand margin of the table. If prisoners 1 and 2 both confess, they will each receive a jail term of three years, since their confessions obviate the need for the other's testimony to convict them of the serious crime. If they both remain silent, then they are both convicted of the minor crime and receive a sentence of one year in jail. Finally, if prisoner 1 remains silent but prisoner 2 confesses, then, in the top right box in the table, we see that prisoner 1 gets five years in jail while prisoner 2 goes free. Conversely, if prisoner 1 confesses while prisoner 2 keeps silent, then in the bottom left box of the table we see that prisoner 2 gets five years in jail while prisoner 1 goes free.

In analyzing games such as the Prisoners' Dilemma, it is useful to remember that the prisoners are kept separate and are unable to communicate with each other. This is a **noncooperative game,** because the prisoners are not allowed to work together to formulate a response to the police. (In a cooperative game such collusion may be allowed.) It is also useful to consider the concepts of a strategy and of a Nash equilibrium. A **strategy** is any action that is feasible, given the information available to a player of the game at the time a decision is to be made. In Table 10-2, the players of the game are the prisoners, and the strategies are confess or don't confess. A **Nash equilibrium** is a set of strategies for the players of the game such that, given the strategies of the other player, no player can improve his payoff by changing his strategy. In Table 10-2, a Nash equilibrium would be the choice of a strategy (i.e., confess, or don't confess) that a prisoner is happy with and doesn't want to change, given the choice of the other prisoner.

A NONCOOPERATIVE GAME is a game in which the players are not allowed to work together to reach an equilibrium, and are not allowed to make binding agreements as to the actions that each will take.

A STRATEGY in a game is any action that is feasible, given the information available to a player of the game at the time a decision is to be made.

A NASH EQUILIBRIUM is a set of strategies for the players of a game such that, given the strategies of the other player, no player can improve his payoff by changing his strategy.

---

[2] A presentation of a game in this format is called the normal form of a game.

A ONE-SHOT GAME is a game that is played only once between the players.

A PURE STRATEGY is a strategy that does not involve a random choice of actions.

A MIXED STRATEGY is a strategy that involves a random device used to choose an action.

Some special features of the game in Table 10-2 should be noted. First of all, this is what is called a **one-shot game.** That is, it will not be repeated. Either the prisoner confesses or he doesn't confess, but he will not again be paired up in the same game with the other prisoner. (At least, not for one or more years. Games in which opponents play against each other time after time are called repeated games.) Second, we will only be considering the **pure strategies** of confess or don't confess. It is possible to devise strategies that are a random mixture of these two pure strategies. For instance, prisoner 1 could have a strategy of flipping a coin and confessing if the coin is heads and not confessing if the coin is tails. This is called a **mixed strategy,** and we will not consider mixed strategies in this example.

Not all games have a Nash equilibrium, especially in pure strategies. Let us see whether the Prisoners' Dilemma has a Nash equilibrium. If player 1 keeps silent, he receives a jail term of one year if player 2 keeps silent, and five years if player 2 confesses. Thus, if player 1 knew that player 2 was going to keep silent, then player 1 is better off to confess. Confessing when player 2 keeps silent reduces player 1's prison term from one year to zero. Moreover, if player 1 knew that player 2 was going to confess, then player 1 would also confess, thereby getting three years in jail instead of the five years he would get if he kept silent. Thus, no matter what player 2 does, player 1 is better off confessing! Again, this is because if player 2 confesses, player 1 is better off

TABLE 10-2
The Prisoners' Dilemma Game

The Prisoners' Dilemma is a game used to show how coordination failures might occur. Here, the two prisoners' inability to coordinate constrains them to accept an inferior situation. Which strategy will be chosen? Note that given all choices, each prisoner is better off confessing, no matter what his partner does. This leads to the result that both players confess and each end up spending three years in jail—despite the fact that both parties would be better off if they did not confess.

	Prisoner 1	
Strategies	Confess	Don't Confess
Confess (Prisoner 2)	3 / 3	5 / 0
Don't Confess (Prisoner 2)	0 / 5	1 / 1

A DOMINANT STRATEGY is a strategy that yields the highest payoff regardless of the actions of your opponents.

confessing (three years in jail instead of five), and if player 2 keeps silent, player 1 is better off confessing (zero years in jail instead of one). We say that player 1 has a **dominant strategy** of confessing. A dominant strategy is a strategy that yields the highest payoff regardless of the actions of your opponents.

Of course, this game is symmetric, and player 2 also has confessing as a dominant strategy. Thus, both player 1 and player 2 want to confess, regardless of the action of the other.

Is this a Nash equilibrium? That is, given that the other prisoner confesses, does either prisoner regret his decision to confess? Let us check prisoner 1 first. Given that prisoner 2 confesses, does prisoner 1 want to change from confess to not confess? Of course not, since by confessing, prisoner 1 gets three years in jail, but by keeping silent prisoner 1 gets five years in jail. Likewise, for prisoner 2; given that prisoner 1 confesses, does prisoner 2 want to change from confess to not confess? Again, the answer is no. Thus, the equilibrium in which both prisoners confess is a Nash equilibrium, in which no player regrets his choice, given the choice of the other player.

A troubling thing about this Nash equilibrium is that the prisoners could obviously do better if they would just both not confess. Perhaps the equilibrium in which they both confess is Nash, but is there another Nash equilibrium in which they both do not confess? (It is important to realize that Nash equilibria are not necessarily unique.) Let us see.

Consider the strategies in which both players do not confess. Is this a Nash equilibrium? Let us look at player 1. Player 1 and player 2 both take the action don't confess. Does player 1 regret this choice, given that player 2 didn't confess? The answer is yes, since player 1 is going to jail for one year by not confessing. Given the action of player 2—to not confess—player 1 will wish he had confessed, and thereby avoided jail. Likewise player 2 will regret not confessing, given that player 1 didn't confess. Thus, the choices of don't confess by both player 1 and player 2 are *not* a Nash equilibrium.

This is an interesting feature of the Prisoners' Dilemma game, that an equilibrium in which both players are better off is not sustainable as a Nash equilibrium. When each plays his dominant strategy both end up in an equilibrium that seems inferior to another possible location in the payoff matrix. This feature is due to the noncooperative nature of this game, in which prisoners cannot communicate and sign binding agreements to play a particular strategy. If players could so collude, then they would both choose not to confess, since this results in a lower prison sentence for each than they get in the Nash equilibrium. However, for such a collusion to work there has to be some way for the prisoners to bind themselves to the strategy of not confessing, since there will still be a temptation to confess and thereby avoid jail altogether if each knows the other will not confess. (Perhaps the purported social custom among criminals of not "ratting" on each other, especially when backed up by threats of violence against someone who violates the custom, is one way for them to collude on the strategy of not confessing.)

We have introduced a number of concepts in game theory and have illustrated their application within the Prisoners' Dilemma game. Now we turn to an example of a coordination game.

A Coordination Game

In our coordination game, production is a function of the minimum of the output of two workers, worker 1 and worker 2. Think of this as a team production process, in which the input of both members of the two-person team is crucial. If worker 1 "goofs off" while worker 2 exerts maximal effort, then output is determined by the effort of the less productive worker. If worker 1 exerts maximal effort while worker 2 goofs off, then again output is determined by the effort of the less productive worker. In particular, hard work by worker 1 cannot make up for lack of effort by worker 2. Thus, the production process may be an assembly line, in which two workers must work with equal effort or speed to attach parts to a car as it moves past. In any case, our production function is given by

$$Y = f(\text{minimum}(N_1, N_2)), \tag{10.7}$$

where N_1 is effort by worker 1, N_2 is effort by worker 2, and minimum (N_1, N_2) indicates that we choose the minimum of N_1 and N_2 to determine the input in our production function.

In our problem, we will consider four gradations of effort: hard work, medium effort, low effort, and no effort. Output is 13 units per worker if the minimal effort is hard work, 9 units per worker if the minimal effort is medium effort, 4 units per worker if the minimal effort is low effort, and 0 units per worker if the minimal effort is no effort. In deciding on what to do, each worker weighs the benefits of effort as measured by per capita output—workers keep their output—with the cost of providing effort. We measure this cost, the disutility of work, in terms of output. We say that hard work costs a worker 3 units of output in lost utility, medium effort costs a worker 2 units of output in lost utility, low effort costs a worker 1 unit of output in lost utility, and no effort costs a worker 0 units of output in lost utility.

Based on the above information, we construct Table 10-3 for our two workers. Across the top of this payoff table are the strategies for worker 1—hard work, medium effort, low effort, and no effort. In the left-hand margin of the payoff table are the strategies of worker 2—hard work, medium effort, low effort, and no effort. In the table are recorded the payoffs to each worker from the various possible combinations. For instance, if both workers work hard, then output per worker is 13 units and the utility cost of hard work is 3 units, giving each worker a net payoff of 10 units of output. If worker 1 exerts a good deal of effort while worker 2 exerts medium effort, then the minimal effort is medium effort and output is 9 units. The payoff to worker 1 is the 9 units of output minus the utility cost of hard work, 3 units of output, for a net payoff of 6 units of output. Meanwhile, worker 2 gets the output of

TABLE 10-3
A Coordination Game

Here we have two workers who must both work together to produce an output. The amount of output produced is determined by the minimum of the effort put in by the two workers. We cannot determine from the game which strategy the workers will choose, but the Nash equilibria all lie on the diagonal from the top left to lower right when each worker selects the same work effort.

		Worker 1			
		Hard Work	Medium Effort	Low Effort	No Effort
Worker 2	Hard Work	10 \ 10	7 \ 6	3 \ 1	0 \ −3
	Medium Effort	6 \ 7	7 \ 7	3 \ 2	0 \ −2
	Low Effort	1 \ 3	2 \ 3	3 \ 3	0 \ −1
	No Effort	−3 \ 0	−2 \ 0	−1 \ 0	0 \ 0

9 units minus the utility cost of medium effort, 2 units of output, for a net payoff of 7 units of output. If worker 1 works hard and worker 2 doesn't work at all, then output is zero because the minimal effort is zero. Worker 2's net payoff is 0 units of output minus a utility cost of 0 units of output, or 0. Worker 1's net payoff is 0 units of output minus a utility cost of hard work of 3 units of output, for a net payoff of −3. The rest of Table 10-3 was constructed in a similar fashion.

What should the workers do in this game? There is no dominant strategy for either player—that is, there is no one level of effort that gives the highest payoff for all possible choices of effort by the other player. What about Nash equilibria? Are there any, and what are they? It turns out that there are four Nash equilibria in this game, and they are where the two workers match effort levels. For instance, one Nash equilibrium is where both players choose hard work. We can check if it is a Nash equilibrium by verifying that neither player wishes to change his choice of effort, given the choice of the other player to choose hard work. For instance, given that worker 2 chooses hard work, would worker 1 wish to choose any other effort level than hard work? The answer is no, because worker 1's net payoff is 10 from choosing hard work, but only 7 from choosing medium effort, only 3 from choosing low effort, and 0 from choosing no effort. Likewise, worker 2 wants to choose hard work if worker 1 has chosen hard work.

What about when both players choose medium effort? If worker 2 chooses medium effort, then worker 1 gets a payoff of 6 by choosing hard work, a payoff of 7 by choosing medium effort, a payoff of 3 by choosing low effort, and a payoff of 0 by choosing no effort. Clearly, worker 1 chooses medium effort. Likewise, given that worker 1 chooses medium effort, worker 2 will be best off by choosing medium effort. Hence, the equilibrium in which both players choose medium effort is Nash.

We can similarly verify that the equilibrium where both players choose low effort is Nash, as is the equilibrium where both players choose no effort. There are four Nash equilibria to this game.

What, then, should a worker do? The answer is to do what the other worker does. However, if this game is played in a noncooperative manner, in which workers must choose a level of effort without communicating with each other, then this answer is not very helpful. In fact, this game is interesting precisely because it presents the workers with four alternative Nash equilibria and no easy way to choose among them. You might observe that these Nash equilibria can be ranked as to which is best for the workers involved, and clearly the equilibrium in which both choose hard work generates the highest payoffs. However, it is also risky in that playing hard work when your opponent plays something less can be very costly in terms of wasted effort. In fact, there have been a number of papers in economics journals in recent years presenting experimental evidence that the noncooperative version of this game does not result in an equilibrium of hard work even in repeated play.[3]

What is the point of this analysis? Coordination problems are not trivial to solve, even in the game presented in Table 10-3 in which there is a set of Nash equilibria that workers agree can be ranked in a particular order in terms of their payoffs. Both workers prefer to be at the equilibrium in which they each choose hard work. However, there is no mechanism in the game presented here that will lead to that equilibrium, and experimental evidence does not make us think that this is the equilibrium that will be achieved. These coordination issues have the potential for explaining persistent shortfalls in output from full employment. Indeed, a Nash equilibrium of no effort is an extreme example of a situation in which workers may coordinate on a "bad" outcome and, since it is a Nash equilibrium, may find it difficult to move from this equilibrium to one of the alternative Nash equilibria. No one worker acting alone could move the economy to another Nash equilibrium, and acting alone could be very costly in terms of wasted effort.

---

[3] These types of coordination problems were discussed by John Bryant in "A Simple Rational Expectations Keynes-Type Model," *Quarterly Journal of Economics* (August 1983), pp. 525–28. Experimental evidence on such games indicates that coordination problems may be an important issue in practice. See John B. Van Huyck, Raymond C. Battalio, and Richard O. Beil, "Strategic Uncertainty, Equilibrium Selection, and Coordination Failure in Average Opinion Games," *Quarterly Journal of Economics* (August 1991), pp. 885–910; and John B. Van Huyck, Raymond C. Battalio, and Richard O. Beil, "Tacit Coordination Games, Strategic Uncertainty, and Coordination Failure," *American Economic Review* (March 1990), pp. 234–48.

The idea of coordination failure can explain an underemployment equilibrium of the type Keynes discussed, in that there is no tendency for the economy to move away from this equilibrium to one that has higher output. Workers become stuck in a situation of underemployment or under-effort, and hence the economy is stuck in an equilibrium with output less than it could be. Note, however, that in this game there is no obvious policy action that will serve to improve this situation. The most obvious need is for some sort of communication between workers, some way to coordinate their efforts so that they both increase their efforts at the same time. The usual macroeconomic tools of fiscal or monetary policy do not seem well suited to this task.

The lessons from the above example are applicable in a number of other cases in addition to the model of production. Perhaps the most relevant for this chapter is that price setting can involve issues of coordination. For instance, two firms may be facing a decision of what price to set. The Nash equilibria will be where both set the same price. If one sets a high price and one a low price, then the firm setting the low price captures a large part of the market and makes a large profit, while the firm setting a high price gets a small share of the market and a lower profit. If both set a low price, then they share the market, and if both set a high price they share the market. Of course, if both set a high price then both earn a higher profit than if both set a low price. This game shares many of the features of the game in Table 10-3, and can be used to explain price stickiness apart from the menu costs explanation given earlier.

Naturally, issues of coordination, competition and "games" are involved in a wide variety of problems, large and small, related to macroeconomic theory and policy. There are, for example, enormous coordination problems attached to the formation of economic unions and to the interrelations between trading blocs. For some insight into one set of "large" coordination problems (to which game theory might apply), see Global Perspective: "The Zollverein, the EC, and the NAFTA: Economic Unions, Competition, and Coordination."

EFFICIENCY WAGE THEORY

Our last excursion into alternative New Keynesian approaches to macroeconomic modeling is to look at the recent development of efficiency wage theory. The basic idea underlying this approach is that production is a function not of the quantity of employment as in $Y = f(N)$, but of the quantity of employment *times* the effort that workers exert. We will use E for effort, (temporarily switching from our use of E for the exchange rate), so the efficiency wage theory postulates that $Y = f(EN)$, so that output is a function of the quantity of efficiency labor EN. In this approach it is not enough merely to hire labor; you also want that labor to work hard. The idea is that labor can to some extent choose how hard, and how efficiently, to work, and that this

GLOBAL PERSPECTIVE

THE ZOLLVEREIN, THE EC, AND THE NAFTA: ECONOMIC UNIONS, COMPETITION, AND COORDINATION

Media news and the 1992 presidential campaigns of George Bush and Bill Clinton were filled with discussions of the economic union between Canada, the United States, and Mexico (the North American Free Trade Agreement or NAFTA). American reaction to policies of the coming union of twelve European countries (the EC or European Community) has also been an important national issue. But economic unions have been common since ancient Greek and Roman times and even before. All unions—for economic betterment and growth, for defense, or for any political purpose—presuppose that mutual gain can be had by enacting policies that *are beneficial to all parties*. However, the *extent* of the union may vary from full political and economic unification, where separate countries may in fact become one, to far less ex-

treme agreements on tariffs and other trade restrictions.

The prototype for a popular form of modern union was the *Zollverein* or customs union of the last century. The name was given by the Prussians to a union established in 1833 to set uniform tariffs among separate German states (initially comprising Hesse Cassel, Hesse Darmstadt, Bavaria, and Wurtemberg) and the rest of the world. Importantly, the agreement specified *no* tariffs or trade restrictions *among* these states. The Zollverein was the nineteenth-century model for many other unions. Many small states, for example, grouped themselves with larger states for customs and free trade purposes. Examples abound: San Marino developed a customs union with Italy in 1862, Monaco with France in 1865, Lichtenstein with Austria in 1875, and Portuguese India with British India in 1878. Some of these nineteenth-century unions survive today.

More critically for the course and direction of twentieth-century trade, the Zollverein is a model for contemporary trade blocs in North America and Western Europe. The most famous economic union in the post-World War II period is the European Economic Commu-

nity or Common Market, which forms the basis for the new European Community of today. By 1994 (if all goes well), the EC will become a unified market of twelve member-nations (the United Kingdom, France, Denmark, Belgium, Greece, Italy, Luxembourg, the Netherlands, Portugal, Ireland, Spain, and a unified Germany). The union will make trade within Europe as regulation-free among the countries of Europe as it is between the states of Massachusetts and New Hampshire. Eventually, all tariff and nontariff barriers will fall to zero and the EC will become the largest and most populous trading area of the world (unless and until the North American experiment in free trade becomes a full reality).

The EC is expected to evolve into a proposed monetary and political union, as well, with common legal rules and a common currency. Different legal systems, dominant religions, and governmental traditions make the extent of fuller union debatable, however. American support for the EC was initially premised upon a common military threat. Now that the states of the former Soviet Union are evolving in the direction of democracies and free markets, the EC may pose a threat to

American interests. This threat takes the form of a giant protectionist monopoly.

Perhaps in reaction to these developments, the North American Free Trade Agreement (NAFTA) was concluded in 1992, which would create an economic customs union among Canada, the United States, and Mexico (such an agreement already existed between the United States and Canada). If the agreement is fully implemented by the Clinton administration, all barriers to trade within these nations may be eliminated within ten years. The economic growth and development that is associated with free trade could create the most potent economic force in the world if the benefits of trade are realized. Then, there is the prospect that all of the Americas (North and South) may someday unite to create a massive customs union.

Many unanswered questions accompany this new world scenario of competing Zollvereins. Not to be minimized is the potential for dissolution of any trade bloc from internal disagreements and dissension. Naturally, interests within the nations composing the EC or the NAFTA will differ. Free trade will promote economic growth *within* these blocs, but a unified front on the part of trading areas with the outside world may in fact encourage new levels of protection and trade wars. Negotiating costs between nations are lowered by such unions. This means that negotiated settlements between blocs of nations may create freer trade. The volume of modern world trade and the economic development of all participating nations may be much increased through the development of these twentieth-century Zollvereins. Unfortunately, it is impossible to predict their exact impact on the welfare of the world's consumers, but economists are in virtual agreement that more trade is preferred to less. ❑

PHOTO 10-2
The Zollverein, a Customs Union of German States in the Early Nineteenth Century, Was an Early Example of Contemporary Attempts at Economic Unification Such as the European Community.

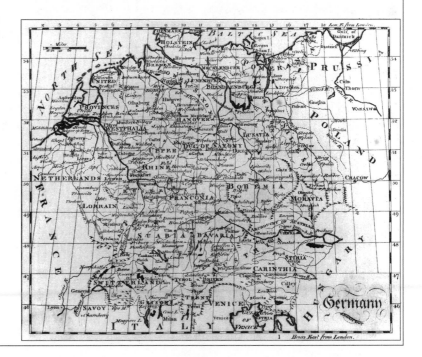

INSIGHT

HENRY FORD AND THE

EFFICIENCY WAGE

Henry Ford, a Michigan farm boy, began to experiment with his first car in 1896. In the fall of 1908 he started to produce the Model T, which was a relatively cheap, standardized vehicle. As sales of the new model increased and the market began to grow, Ford was able to achieve mass assembly-line production on a scale that had never been seen before. The steady reduction in costs and prices was achieved through further integration of manufacturing processes, establishment of branch factories, and an efficient automo-

bile distribution system. In 1913, Ford introduced the Five Dollars a Day plan, doubling the minimum wage of his factory workers. He referred to his five dollars a day for eight hours of work as "profit-sharing and efficiency engineering."[a] Some people hailed him as a Messiah and others called him a lunatic and a threat to the established order. Many different explanations have been given for Ford's dramatic actions, such as he was afraid of unionization, or his wife put the idea into his head for ethical reasons. When the $5 minimum wage for an eight-hour day was announced, there was a "tremendous surge" in output at the Ford factories. The Ford people said it was be-

cause of the increased morale of the workers. But many workers were scared they might lose their jobs, since working at the Ford plant had become one of the most desirable jobs in the world. Some critics suggest that Ford had intended to fire all of his workers and rehire only the best ones. This action would raise the output per person enough for him to profit by the doubling of his minimum wage. Henry Ford appears to be an early pioneer in the efficiency wage. ❑

NOTE: [a]See Jonathan Hughes, *The Vital Few* (New York: Oxford University Press, 1973), pp. 301-303.

choice cannot be completely monitored by the employer. Thus, workers can goof off without getting fired or otherwise punished by their employer. The American automaker Henry Ford might well have pioneered the idea: see Insight: "Henry Ford and the Efficiency Wage."

A crucial issue in efficiency wage theory is how effort is determined. If effort is constant, then there is no difference from standard approaches to the labor market. In the efficiency wage literature, however, effort is assumed to be a function of the real wage, or $E = E(W/P)$. The assumption is that effort increases when the real wage increases, but at a decreasing rate.

The idea for this was originally found in applications to less developed countries, where an increase in the real wage would increase not only the standard of living and health of workers, but also the effort that these workers could sustain. This model has been adapted to fit the economies of developed countries by suggesting that higher real wages reduce the number of workers who quit a firm. A higher real wage makes it more costly for workers to goof off and thereby risk losing their relatively lucrative employment. Finally, firms paying the higher wage will have a greater choice of new job applicants. In all cases, effort or quality of workers increases with the real wage.

What is the effect of making effort a function of the real wage? Firm profits (in real terms) are given by

$$\pi/P = f(E[(W/P)N]) - (W/P)N.$$

Firms must now choose both employment N and the real wage W/P, and they do so to maximize profits. The usual conditions for profit maximization are that the marginal product of labor is set equal to the real wage. However, in the case of efficiency wages the condition is in terms of the marginal product of effort and employment. Employers adjust employment directly, by hiring workers, and they can adjust effort by changing the wage. An example is provided in Table 10-4. Here, Table 10-4(a) gives the production function linking efficiency units of labor EN to output Y. Notice that the marginal product of efficiency units of labor is declining, as indicated in the column labeled $\Delta Y/\Delta(EN)$. Notice too that effort and employment can be perfectly substituted in production. *Any* combination of effort and employment that yields a product EN of 10 will give 35 units of output. Effort may be 10 and employment 1, or effort 2 and employment 5.

Table 10-4(b) gives an example of an effort function linking real wages to the effort put forth by workers. Here an increase in the real wage increases effort, but at a decreasing rate, as indicated by the column labeled $\Delta E/\Delta(W/P)$.

How do firms determine output and employment? The technical details are complex,[4] but we provide an example in Table 10-4(c). The first two columns are the production relationship between efficiency labor and output. The third column gives revenue, PY, assuming that the price P is always $1. Costs are given for three choices of the wage. The first choice is $W = \$4$. When $W = \$4$, effort is 1. Thus, we have a column indicating the employment N that corresponds to every level of efficiency labor EN when effort is 1. We also have a column indicating the cost of hiring workers WN. For example, when $EN = 1$ and effort is 1, we know employment N is 1. Since the wage is $4, the cost of employment is $4. We can compare this to revenue, which is $8, so profits are also $4.

What is the optimal choice of employment when the wage is $4? The optimal choice of employment is $N = 5$. Revenue is $30 and labor costs are $20, so profits are $10. (If employment is 4, profits are also $10.) We indicate this as the profit-maximizing level with ** in the table.

What about other wage rates? We could raise the wage rate to $5, which increases effort to 1.2. With effort of 1.2, each level of efficiency labor EN corresponds to a lower level of employment. For example, when efficiency

---

[4] The conditions are two-fold. The first is that $MP_{EL} \times E = W/P$, and the second that $MP_{EL} \times N \times \partial E/\partial(W/P) = N$. Here MP_{EL} = Marginal Product of Efficiency Labor. If E is a constant, the first condition becomes the familiar $MP_L = W/P$, that is, the marginal product of labor equals the real wage.

TABLE 10-4
Efficiency Wage Model of Employment

The efficiency wage model of employment is based on the idea that firms may be able to increase the effort of their workers, and thus increase output, by raising the real wage paid to existing workers. If this is true, firms must then choose both the level of employment N and the real wage W/P that maximizes profits. This process is explained using a numerical example in the table.

(a) PRODUCTION FUNCTION			(b) EFFORT FUNCTION		
EN	Y	$\Delta Y / \Delta (EN)$	W/P	E	$\Delta E / \Delta (W/P)$
0	0	—	1	.10	—
1	8	8	2	.45	.35
2	15	7	3	.75	.30
3	21	6	4	1.00	.25
4	26	5	5	1.20	.20
5	30	4			
6	33	3			
7	35	2			
8	36	1			
9	36	0			
10	35	−1			

(c) REVENUES AND COSTS FOR DIFFERENT CHOICES OF W/P

EN	Y	PY	W=$4, E=1		W=$5, E=1.2		W=$2, E=.45	
			N	WN	N	WN	N	WN
0	0	$ 0	0	$0	0	$ 0	0	$ 0
1	8	8	1	4	.83	4.17	2.22	4.44
2	15	15	2	8	1.67	8.33	4.44	8.89
3	21	21	3	12	2.50	12.50	6.67	13.34
4	26	26	4	16	3.33	16.67*	8.89	17.78*
5	30	30	5	20**	4.17	20.83	11.11	22.22
6	33	33	6	24	5.00	25.00	13.33	26.67
7	35	35	7	28	5.83	29.17	15.56	31.11
8	36	36	8	32	6.67	33.33	17.78	35.56
9	36	36	9	36	7.5	37.50	20.00	40.00

NOTE: Profit-maximization level is marked with *; profit-maximizing level is marked with **. The price level is assumed to be always $1.

labor is 1, actual employment will be $1/1.2 = .83$. Thus, the higher wage calls forth more effort and hence lowers the level of employment corresponding to each output level. Does this increase profits? It depends on how much additional effort is forthcoming, which lowers employment and employment costs, compared to how much the increase in the wage rate increases employment costs. Again, the table provides an example. For efficiency labor of 2 and effort of 1.2, only $2/1.2 = 1.67$ units of labor need be hired. The cost of that labor is $5 per unit or a total of $8.33, so profits are $15 − $8.33 or $6.67. This is less than the profits earned when the wage was $4 and 2 units of efficiency labor were employed. In fact, after looking at the entire column, we see that the maximum profits when the wage is $5 occur when efficiency labor is 4. Actual employment is $4/1.2 = 3.33$, and labor costs are $16.67. Profits are $26 − $16.67 = $9.33. This is less than the $10 maximum profits that occur when the wage is $4.

What about a lower wage? We also provide an example of a wage of $2. In this case the lower wage tends to lower employment costs, but the lower wage calls forth a lower amount of effort, and this tends to raise employment costs. In fact, with a wage of $2, effort is .45. Thus, when efficiency labor units are 2, this will correspond to $2/.45 = 4.44$ units of actual employment, and labor costs of $8.89. Thus, when the wage is $2, production with 2 units of efficiency labor actually leads to a loss of $8 − $8.89 = −$.89. What is the profit-maximizing output level when the wage is $2? It turns out to be when efficiency labor is 4. Actual employment is $4/.45 = 8.89$, and labor costs are $2 × 8.89 = $17.78. Profits are $26 − $17.78 = $8.22. Again, this is less than the maximum profits that can be earned when the wage rate is $4, so in our example a wage rate of $4 is best. It turns out that in fact the profit-maximizing wage rate is the wage rate that sets the change in effort when there is a change in the wage $\Delta E/\Delta(W/P)$ equal to the ratio of effort to the wage E/W. In our case this occurs where the wage rate is $4, where $\Delta E/\Delta(W/P) = .25$, and where effort is 1, so $E/W = 1/4$. A key feature of this profit-maximization condition is that it does not change with changes in actual employment. That is, the real wage a firm offers will not be related to its level of employment. This is real wage rigidity in its most severe form. Thus, profit-maximizing firms will set a real wage based strictly on the effort function. Employment may vary, but not real wages. Moreover, the existence of an excess supply of labor (i.e., of unemployment) will not affect the real wage set by firms. This explains why real wages are not bid down by the existence of unemployed workers willing to work at a lower wage than existing workers are receiving.

The above analysis gives only a flavor of the efficiency wage theories, but it should allow you to see that this approach can explain the apparent insensitivity of real wages to recessions and expansions. This can clearly explain real wages that are noncyclical, and better matches any mild procyclicality in actual real wages than the nominal wage-contracting model, which predicts a countercyclical real wage. In addition, the efficiency wage model predicts that employment will have to adjust to changes in market conditions, so employment will be procyclical. With the efficiency wage approach, New Keynesian macroeconomists explain these features in a model that allows unemployment.

SUMMARY

In this chapter we have presented two New Keynesian models based on nominal rigidities—the nominal wage contracting model and the model with sticky output prices. Both of these models generate short-run deviations from full employment due to aggregate demand and aggregate supply shocks. These deviations are due to nominal rigidities embedded in the models, either with rigid prices or wages. We examined the effect of both aggregate demand and aggregate supply shocks in these models and briefly discussed some of the implications of these models for aggregate demand management policies.

We then turned to some ideas of game theory, with an example of the Prisoners' Dilemma game, and used these concepts to examine a coordination game between two workers in a team production process. By showing how the model yields a series of possible equilibrium points, we raised the issue of how to choose between these equilibria, and how to get out of a bad equilibrium. These issues provide alternative explanations for sticky price and wage setting, in addition to explaining how a particular team production process can generate a level of less than potential output.

Finally, we briefly reviewed some of the ideas of the efficiency wage approach. We discussed the conclusion that real wages are set apart from labor market conditions, and explained how the efficiency wage approach allows New Keynesian economists to explain some of the observed features of labor markets.

In some sense, the alternative models we present in this chapter are competing explanations for observed characteristics of the macroeconomy. In another sense, they are all models that explain a nominal or real rigidity and show how that rigidity alters the conclusions one would obtain in a Classical or New Classical framework. In this latter sense, these models are all New Keynesian approaches. If anything, the term *New Keynesian* encompasses an embarrassingly large set of alternatives to the Classical tradition. One criticism of the New Keynesian approach, apart from the methodological criticism that many of its models are disequilibrium in nature, is that there needs to be a refinement of this large set of alternative approaches to arrive at a smaller set of empirically justified and theoretically consistent alternatives.

KEY TERMS

dominant strategy	noncooperative game
efficiency wage models	one-shot game
mixed strategy	pure strategy
Nash equilibrium	strategy

QUESTIONS FOR REVIEW AND DISCUSSION

1. How do the New Keynesian models differ from the (old) Keynesian models? How are they similar?

2. How do the New Keynesian models differ from the New Classical models? How are they similar?

3. In the sticky nominal wage model, how does the aggregate supply curve differ from the aggregate supply curve of the New Classical model with imperfect information? In particular, how do the slopes of short-run aggregate supply compare? Also, compare the length of time that it would take to move from an initial position on short-run aggregate supply to the long-run aggregate supply curve in these two models.

4. What are the effects of a decrease in taxes in the New Keynesian model with contracted nominal wages? What is the effect on output, the price level, and the real interest rate in the short run? In the long run?

5. What are the effects of a decrease in the money supply in the New Keynesian model with contracted nominal wages? What is the effect on output, the price level, and the real interest rate in the short run? In the long run?

6. The New Keynesians also use a model in which output prices are rigid. Name some of the goods you purchase, and decide if the prices you pay are flexible, adjusting frequently, or rigid, adjusting infrequently. Do you purchase any goods in which the price is posted, such as from a catalog? How often do such prices change?

7. Consider an increase in the money supply in both the rigid nominal wage model and the rigid output price model. What are the effects on output, the price level, and the interest rate in the short run? In the long run? How do these models agree, and how do they disagree, and why?

8. What criticism of the nominal wage contracting model has led to the development of the rigid output price model? Using an example of an increase in government spending, show how these models differ in an important prediction about the behavior of a macroeconomic variable.

9. Consider a decrease in autonomous investment spending in both the rigid nominal wage model and the rigid output price model. What are the effects on output, the price level, and the interest rate in the short run? In the long run? How do these models agree, and how do they disagree, and why?

10. What is the efficiency wage hypothesis, and how does this theory help explain rigid wages? According to this hypothesis, should real wages decline during an expansion and rise during a contraction? Why or why not?

11. Using the nominal wage contracting model, what policy advice would you give to the President after an adverse supply shock? Should monetary policy be changed, and how? What about fiscal policy?

12. Using the rigid output price model, what policy advice would yougive to the President after an increase in autonomous consumption? Should monetary policy be changed, and how? What about fiscal policy?

13. Using the nominal wage contracting model, what policy advice would you give to the President after an increase in autonomous consumption? Should monetary policy be changed, and how? What about fiscal policy? How do your results compare to those from question 14 above?

PROBLEMS

1. There has been quite a debate over the unemployment situation in Europe, and over the fact that unemployment in Europe declined at a snail's pace during the 1980s, reaching new lows in 1993. Many economists have used the term hysteresis to describe this situation, meaning that the unemployment rate, once low, has risen and moved into a situation of high equilibrium unemployment rates. How does the model of coordination failures help us to understand this problem?

2. Try playing the coordination game with your classmates or friends. Explain the game to them, *but do not discuss choices of effort levels.* Ask them to secretly write down their choice of effort level. Then announce the minimum choice and the hypothetical payoffs that each would receive. *Do not allow them to discuss the choices among each other.* Then play several additional rounds in the same way. What is the result? Do your classmates agree on the high effort equilibrium, or have they ended up at an equilibrium at a lower level of effort?

SUGGESTIONS FOR FURTHER READING

Akerlof, George A., and Janet L. Yellen. *Efficiency Wage Models and the Labor Market.* Cambridge: Cambridge University Press, 1986.

Greenwald, Bruce, and Joseph Stiglitz. "New and Old Keynesians." *The Journal of Economic Perspectives* (Winter 1993), pp. 23–44.

Katz, Lawrence F. "Efficiency Wage Theories: A Partial Evaluation." *NBER Macroeconomics Annual 1986.* Cambridge, MA: MIT Press, 1986.

King, Robert G. "Will the New Keynesian Macroeconomics Resurrect the IS-LM Model?" *The Journal of Economic Perspectives* (Winter 1993), pp. 67–89.

Mankiw, N. Gregory, and David Romer. *New Keynesian Economics,* Volumes 1 and 2. Cambridge, MA: MIT Press, 1991.

Romer, David. "The New Keynesian Synthesis." *The Journal of Economic Perspectives* (Winter 1993), pp. 5–22.

Waller, Christopher J. "Efficiency Wages, Wage Indexation and Macroeconomic Stabilization." *Economic Letters* (1989), pp. 125–28.

THE REAL BUSINESS CYCLE MODEL

The **REAL BUSINESS CYCLE MODEL** is a model that emphasizes intertemporal substitution of labor supply and nonmonetary explanations for business cycles within a market-clearing model of the economy.

The **Real Business Cycle model** is an outgrowth of the New Classical Economics in that it stresses *real factors* in the economy. Developers of the Real Business Cycle idea adopt several of the strategies of the New Classical Economics, especially those regarding expectation formation and the microeconomic justifications for behavioral assumptions. Real Business Cycle models emphasize the real factors that determine output and influence aggregate supply, in contrast to the general emphasis on monetary and demand-side factors in the New Classical and the New Keynesian models.

In this chapter, you will learn

- what the Real Business Cycle model is, and how it is related to the Classical model
- how the Real Business Cycle labor market model differs from other labor market models studied in this text
- how to derive a model of aggregate supply for Real Business Cycle models
- how equilibrium between aggregate supply and demand in Real Business Cycles determines output and the real interest rate
- how the price level is determined in Real Business Cycle models
- the effect of supply shocks in the Real Business Cycle model
- criticisms of Real Business Cycle models

REAL BUSINESS CYCLE THEORY

New Classical and New Keynesian models discussed in Chapters 9 and 10 approach macroeconomics by stressing aggregate demand as a driving force in business cycle fluctuations. Following the Monetarists, both the New Classical and New Keynesian models emphasize the role of money—as well as other elements of aggregate demand—in instigating and perpetuating business cycles. These models differ in that the New Classical approach stresses *equilibrium* modeling, whereas the New Keynesian approach features *disequilibrium* modeling. Both place the responsibility for many business cycles on changes in aggregate demand.

Recently, an offshoot of the New Classical macroeconomics has emerged. Like New Classical macroeconomics, Real Business Cycle theory stresses an equilibrium approach to economic modeling. Unlike New Classical models, however, the Real Business Cycle approach emphasizes the supply side of the model as the initiating and perpetuating force behind business cycles. As we have seen, New Classical (and New Keynesian) macroeconomics devoted considerable effort to developing theories of aggregate supply. But both continued to view aggregate demand as a source of business cycles. For the New Classical model, it was unexpected changes in aggregate demand, while for the New Keynesian model it was changes in aggregate demand occurring after a nominal wage contract was set or a nominal price was posted. The Real Business Cycle theory goes a step further: Within a framework emphasizing equilibrium, it views aggregate supply—or real factors—as the source of business cycles.[1]

What might be the nature of these real factors or "shocks" that influence aggregate supply and hence the business cycle of output and employment? There are many determinants, such as the weather, wars, or a combination of small shocks. For example, in the wake of the Iraqi invasion of Kuwait, the world oil price doubled (between July and October of 1990). As U.S. firms scrambled to economize on energy inputs, U.S. production fell, and along with it, employment fell. While this shock was temporary it had a clear negative impact on the economy. Positive and negative effects on the business cycle may thus be expected from factors that affect aggregate supply. For example, labor productivity may be reduced when capital is destroyed, as in a war or natural disaster. Real Business Cycle theory helps us to understand this.

In many ways, both the New Classical and Real Business Cycle theories are modern attempts to develop a more sophisticated version of the Classical

---

[1]A number of authors contributed to the early development of Real Business Cycle theory, including Finn Kydland and Edward Prescott, "Time to Build and Aggregate Fluctuations," *Econometrica* (November 1982), pp. 1345–70; John Long and Charles Plosser, "Real Business Cycles," *Journal of Political Economy* (February 1983), pp. 39–69; Robert King and Charles Plosser, "Money, Credit, and Prices in a Real Business Cycle," *American Economic Review* (June 1984), pp. 363–80. It seems that Long and Plosser may have first coined the phrase "real business cycles."

model. Both of these modern approaches emphasize careful development of aggregate supply, but they differ in their emphasis on factors causing business cycles. In this chapter, we develop a simplified version of a Real Business Cycle model to convey the main points emphasized in that approach. We begin with a brief review of the Classical and New Classical models, in order to more clearly display the differences between these two models, on the one hand, and the Real Business Cycle approach, on the other.

THE CLASSICAL AND NEW CLASSICAL MODELS

We briefly review the precursors of the Real Business Cycle approach, the Classical and New Classical models. We utilize a representative of these models in which *expected* prices always equal the *actual* price, thereby converting the New Classical model into a Classical model. This latter assumption eliminates the short-run aggregate supply curve generated by worker misperceptions of the price level. (Worker misperceptions would be a needless complication to our analysis without adding anything of importance, since the Real Business Cycle approach does not rely on misperceptions of the price level for its results.) Unlike the simple Classical model of Chapter 3, however, we will consider a model in which the aggregate demand curve is generated by the *IS-LM* model, as in Chapter 7.

Our version of the Classical model is presented in Figure 11–1. There are three graphs: aggregate demand and supply, (a); *IS-LM,* (b); and the labor market, (c). First consider the aggregate demand and supply graph. The aggregate supply curve is perfectly inelastic, which is a central feature of the Classical model that is replicated as the long-run aggregate supply curve in the New Classical Model. Given perfectly inelastic aggregate supply, the role of aggregate demand is merely to determine the price level, which is P_0 in Figure 11–1(a). Only changes in aggregate supply can change output, which is given as Y_0.

Assuming a perfectly inelastic aggregate supply curve, the role of *IS* and *LM* is to determine the interest rate, which is r_0 in Figure 11–1(b). *IS* and *LM* must intersect at output level Y_0, the output level determined by aggregate supply. Moreover, if the *IS* curve shifts due to a change in one of its determinants (such as government spending), then the *LM* curve will also shift so that *IS* and *LM* continue to intersect at output Y_0. The required shift in *LM* is generated by a change in the price level, which will change real money balances and thereby shift *LM*. For example, an increase in government spending will shift *IS* to the right. If *LM* is unchanged, then *IS* and *LM* will intersect at a level of output greater than Y_0. Then the price level increases, lowering real balances and shifting *LM* to the left. The intersection of *IS* and *LM* after *IS* shifts to the right and *LM* shifts to the left will be back at output Y_0, but at a higher real interest rate.

Graph (a) shows the aggregate supply and aggregate demand curves. The aggregate supply curve is perfectly inelastic as Classical theory dictates. In graph (b), IS and LM must intersect at output level Y_0. This, in turn, determines the interest rate r_0. Finally, graph (c) shows the determination of the equilibrium real wage.

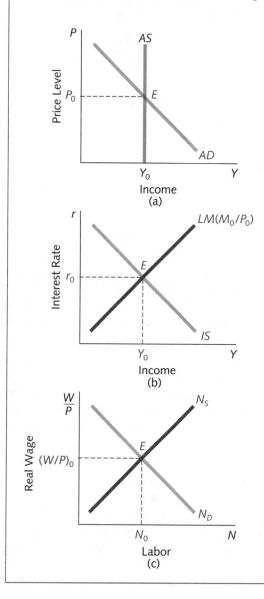

It is also important to recall the effects of changes in the money supply in this model. An increase in the money supply will shift aggregate demand to the right, but with perfectly inelastic aggregate supply the money supply increase will only raise the price level, leaving output unchanged. In the *IS-LM* graph, *LM* shifts down (or to the right) as real money balances increase above M_0 / P_0. *IS* and *LM* intersect at an output level above Y_0. However, the increase in the price level then acts to reduce real money balances. In fact, the increase in the price level must be in *exact* proportion to the increase in the money supply, so that in the end M/P is unchanged. *LM* ends up at its initial position, intersecting *IS* at output level Y_0 and real interest rate r_0. Why such a result? Basically, because output is unchanged. With output unchanged, the increase in money holdings leads to an excess supply of money, which consumers attempt to spend on goods and services. However, with a fixed supply of goods and services, the attempt to spend the additional money balances only drives up the price of these goods and services, so that after the price increase the level of real money balances is restored to its original position. At this level, consumers are satisfied with the real value of their money holdings and do not make any further attempts to reduce these money holdings.

Because we will compare these results to the Real Business Cycle model, we will want to remember the sequence of events in the Classical model in response to the increase in government spending or the money supply. First, there is an increase in government spending, which shifts both *IS* and *AD* to the right, or else there is an increase in the money supply, which shifts both *LM* and *AD* to the right. Second, we look at the aggregate demand and supply graph and find that output is constant and the price level has risen. Third, we look at the *IS-LM* graph to find out what has happened to the interest rate. Thus, the aggregate demand and supply graph determines price P and output Y. The *IS-LM* graph then tells us what has happened to the interest rate, after we know what has happened to P and Y.

Finally, Figure 11–1(c) includes a graph of the labor market, showing the intersection of labor demand and labor supply at a real wage $(W/P)_0$ and an employment level N_0. Recall that in the Classical model the intersection of labor demand and labor supply determines the real wage and employment. Increases in the price level will *not* change the equilibrium real wage, but will instead cause changes only in the nominal wage. Only changes in labor demand or labor supply, such as those caused by supply shocks or changes in the willingness of labor to work, will change the equilibrium real wage or employment level. Changes in factors determining aggregate demand— affecting either *IS* or *LM*—will change only the price level and therefore will not have any impact on the labor market equilibrium.

This brief review sets the stage for the Real Business Cycle model. This model, based upon the Classical model, emphasizes aggregate supply and market clearing. The biggest difference between the two models relates to the labor market.

THE LABOR MARKET IN THE REAL BUSINESS CYCLE MODEL

The Real Business Cycle model builds on the Classical market-clearing model of the labor market. That model is reproduced here as equations 11.1 through 11.3:

$$N_D = N_D(W/P, K), \tag{11.1}$$

$$N_S = N_S(W/P), \tag{11.2}$$

$$N_D = N_S. \tag{11.3}$$

Equation 11.1 is the labor demand equation, specifying labor demand as a function of the real wage W/P and the capital stock K. Other determinants include the amount of other resources used in production, and the state of technology. Equation 11.2 represents labor supply as a function of the real wage. Equation 11.3 specifies that, in equilibrium, labor supply equals labor demand. Holding the determinants of labor demand and supply constant, equations 11.1 and 11.2 are depicted as the labor market in Figure 11–1. The intersection of labor supply and labor demand, as required by equation 11.3, determines the equilibrium real wage and employment level.

Intertemporal Substitution by Laborers

The Real Business Cycle model originates with this basic model of the labor market, but modifies it to stress the intertemporal nature of labor supply decisions. That is, the model stresses the fact that workers will make labor supply decisions based on today's real wage, but *also* on the *expected* level of the real wage tomorrow and on the real interest rate. The basic idea is that workers will decide today whether they want to work today at the real wage currently available, or work tomorrow at the real wage they expect will be available tomorrow. If the real wage is unusually high today, a worker is willing to work extra hard today, while planning to postpone rest and leisure until tomorrow. If the real wage is unusually low today, then a worker will work fewer hours today, preferring to take rest and leisure instead. The worker will plan on working more tomorrow—when the real wage recovers from today's unusually low level—in order to make up for the lost earnings today. The willingness to adjust work schedules over time in response to unusually high or low real wages is called the ***intertemporal substitution of labor.*** Just as consumers substitute in the direction of lower-priced goods when the price of a good increases, workers substitute work hours today for work hours tomorrow when today's work is especially lucrative. Moreover, workers substitute work hours tomorrow instead of work hours today when today's work hours receive a lower reward.

The intertemporal substitution phenomenon may be modeled by specifying that labor supply depends not just on today's real wage, but also on the real wage expected for next period, discounted by the real interest rate. In order to

INTERTEMPORAL
SUBSTITUTION OF LABOR is
the willingness to adjust
work schedules over time
in response to unusually
high or low real wages.

PHOTO II-I
Workers Respond to
Unusually High or Low Wage
Rates by Substituting Labor
Supply over Time.

PRESENT VALUE is a way to
compare the value today of
income or other monetary
values that are received at
different future dates.

proceed, we will need the concept of **present value.** Present value is a way to
compare the value today of income and other monetary values that are received
at different future dates. For example, if you win a lottery you might be offered
the choice of $1,000,000 today, or $100,000 per year for 10 years. Which
should you take? Ignoring all tax considerations, you should take the
$1,000,000 today. Why? The present value of receiving $1,000,000 today is
just $1,000,000. The present value of receiving $100,000 each year for 10
years depends on the interest rate and the exact schedule of payments. Suppose
you receive $100,000 today. That is worth $100,000 in present value. Suppose
your next payment is $100,000 in one year and the interest rate is 5 percent.
The present value of that payment is $100,000/(1.05) = $95,238. Why?
Because if you had $95,238 today, you could save it and earn 5 percent
interest, giving you $100,000 at the end of one year. Hence at 5 percent
interest, $95,238 today is equivalent to $100,000 in one year. We say that
$95,238 is the present value of $100,000 received in one year, when the
interest rate is 5 percent. Note two important features of present value. First, as
long as the interest rate is positive, the present value of future income is less
than the amount you will receive in the future. Second, when the interest rate
changes, present values change. If the interest rate goes up, the present value of
any given future value falls. Thus, $100,000 received in one year has a present
value at 10 percent interest of $100,000/(1.1) = $90,909.

Getting back to our example from the labor market, a worker in 1993 faces
the option of working in 1993 at the real wage $(W/P)_{1993}$, or working in 1994
at the real wage $(W/P)_{1994}$. Of course, in 1993 the present value of the wage
$(W/P)_{1994}$ is $(W/P)_{1994}/(1 + r_{1993})$. A worker compares the 1993 real wage to
the present value in 1993 of the real wage expected for 1994, and decides how
much to work in 1993 and how much to work in 1994. If $(W/P)_{1993}$
increases, labor supply tends to increase in 1993. This is just like the Classical

model. If $(W/P)_{1994}/(1 + r_{1993})$ increases, labor supply tends to decline in 1993. Note that $(W/P)_{1994}/(1 + r_{1993})$ increases if either $(W/P)_{1994}$ increases or if r_{1993} decreases. Consequently, the quantity of labor supplied in 1993 increases if $(W/P)_{1993}$ increases, $(W/P)_{1994}$ decreases, or if r_{1993} increases. The latter two effects are due to intertemporal substitution, and did not appear in our development of the Classical model of the labor market or in adaptations of the Classical model to the Keynesian, Monetarist, New Classical, or New Keynesian models.

The labor market in Real Business Cycle models includes a labor supply curve that incorporates this intertemporal substitution effect. The labor market equations are

$$N_D = N_D[(W/P)_t, K] \tag{11.4}$$

$$N_S = N_S[(W/P)_t, (W/P)_{t+1}/(1 + r_t)] \tag{11.5}$$

$$N_D = N_S. \tag{11.6}$$

Just as in the Classical model, equation 11.4 is the labor demand equation, and labor demand is a function of the current period real wage $(W/P)_t$ and the capital stock K. Equation 11.5 is a labor supply equation that includes the intertemporal substitution effect, which increases with the current period real wage $(W/P)_t$ and decreases with the present value of the expected future real wage $(W/P)_{t+1}/(1 + r_t)$. Equation 11.6 specifies that in equilibrium, labor supply equals labor demand. When the determinants of labor demand and supply including $(W/P)_{t+1}/(1 + r_t)$, are held constant, equations 11.4 and 11.5 may be represented as the labor market, as shown in Figure 11–2. Equilibrium is illustrated by the intersection of labor supply and labor demand at point A, which determines the current period equilibrium real wage $(W/P)_t$ and the employment level.

Employment Changes and Intertemporal Substitution

Figure 11–2 appears to be similar to the graph of the labor market presented in our review of the Classical model in Figure 11–1. The only difference is that labor supply is drawn holding constant the present value of next period's real wage $(W/P)_{t+1}/(1 + r_t)$. Changes in either expectations of next period's real wage or in the real interest rate will shift labor supply. In particular, anything that increases the present value of next period's real wage will reduce labor supply this period. Similarly, anything that reduces the present value of next period's real wage will increase labor supply this period.

Consider, for example, an increase in the real interest rate from r_{t_o} to r_{t_i}. This will reduce the present value of next period's real wage and hence will increase labor supply in the present period. In Figure 11–2 we illustrate such an effect by shifting labor supply to the right. The new intersection of labor supply and labor demand is at point B, with a lower current period real wage and a higher

FIGURE 11−2
Intertemporal Substitution
and the Labor Market

This figure shows what occurs in the labor market when labor supply includes an intertemporal substitution effect. An increase in the interest rate reduces the present value of the real wage in time period t_1. This will increase the labor supply curve in t_1, and thus increase the level of employment from N_0 to N_1.

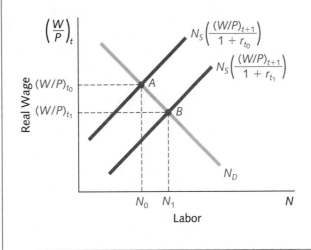

level of employment than before the increase in the real interest rate. An increase in the real interest rate will therefore increase labor supply, lowering the real wage in period t and *increasing* employment. In contrast, a decrease in the real interest rate will decrease labor supply, raising the real wage in period t and *decreasing* employment.

This effect of the real interest rate on labor supply and hence on labor market equilibrium is the feature of Real Business Cycle theory that distinguishes it from the Classical model. In the Classical model, changes in the real interest rate had no effect on labor supply or demand, and no effect on aggregate supply. In the Real Business Cycle model, changes in the real interest rate do affect labor supply and labor market equilibrium. Importantly, alterations in employment end up changing output. In the Real Business Cycle model, aggregate supply is dependent on the real interest rate.

AGGREGATE SUPPLY IN THE REAL BUSINESS CYCLE MODEL

A four-part diagram that includes graphs of the labor market, the production function, and aggregate supply may be used in order to derive aggregate supply in the Real Business Cycle model. This diagram appears as Figure 11−3, with the labor market graph (a) in its familiar position in the lower left-hand

FIGURE 11-3
Deriving Aggregate Supply I

The labor market, represented in (a), determines the equilibrium level of employment. In (b), this level of employment is transformed into levels of output by the production function. The 45-degree line in (c) allows output to be measured on the horizontal axis (d). Finally, (d) contains the perfectly inelastic long-run aggregate supply curve. Increases in the labor supply curve, caused by an increase in the interest rate, result in the *LRAS* curve shifting rightward.

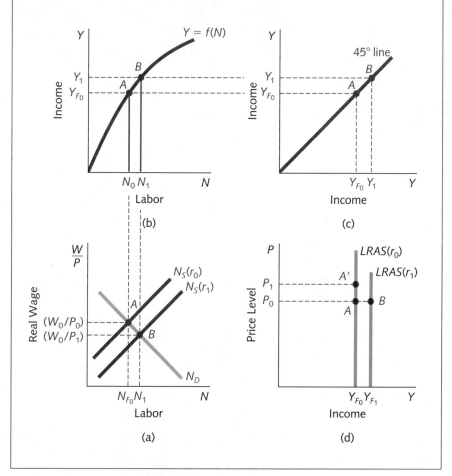

quadrant. The labor market apparatus is taken directly from Figure 11-2 and, like that figure, it displays the real wage on the vertical axis. The only difference from the simple Classical aggregate supply curve derived earlier is that labor supply now depends on the *present value* of the expected real wage for next period, as well as current-period conditions.

In this analysis the expected real wage for next period $(W/P)_{t+1}$ will be held constant, but the real interest rate will vary. The initial level of the real interest rate is assumed to be r_0. We show the initial equilibrium in the labor market as point A, determining a real wage of W_0/P_0 and an employment level of N_{F_0}. With employment of N_{F_0} the production function in Figure 11–3 (b) determines output of Y_{F_0}. Figure 11–3 (c) simply translates output from the vertical axis to the horizontal. In Figure 11–3 (d), aggregate supply is derived. The price level is initially P_0 and output is Y_{F_0}, so point A is one point on aggregate supply.

Aggregate supply may be derived in formal terms. Originating at point A, simply ask what happens if the price level increases to P_1. The increase in the price level will temporarily lower the real wage to W_0/P_1 until the wage rate adjusts in the labor market. This lower real wage leads to an excess demand for labor, and the nominal wage gets bid up until the real wage returns to its equilibrium value of $(W/P)_0$ at point A. Of course, the nominal wage increases, but only by the same percentage as the increase in the price level, so that in equilibrium the real wage does not change. Likewise, equilibrium employment remains at N_{F_0} and the production function indicates that output stays at Y_{F_0}. The return to equilibrium is associated with point A^1 in Figure 11–3 (d), where the price level is P_1 and output is Y_{F_0}.

Notice that this aggregate supply curve, as in the Classical model, is perfectly inelastic. What then makes this a Real Business Cycle model? It is not that aggregate supply is perfectly inelastic, but that aggregate supply *shifts with changes in the real interest rate.* In order to understand this central point, note that labor supply depends on the real interest rate, and that we have held the real interest rate constant at r_0 during our derivation of aggregate supply. We indicate this by labeling the aggregate supply curve $LRAS(r_0)$. Now let the real interest rate increase, say to r_1. Labor supply will shift to the right, as indicated in Figures 11–2 and 11–3. The equilibrium real wage declines, and employment increases. The increased employment will increase output, and there will be a new aggregate supply curve valid for a real interest rate of r_1. The new aggregate supply curve lies to the right of the original aggregate supply curve. Increases in the real interest rate shift the aggregate supply curve to the right, to $LRAS(r_1)$. The aggregate supply curve in the Real Business Cycle model mimics the Classical aggregate supply curve in that it is perfectly inelastic, but the Real Business Cycle aggregate supply curve shifts with changes in the real interest rate.

Real Interest Rates and Labor Market Equilibrium

There is another way to look at this same issue—a method that will make it easier to use the graphical analysis of the Real Business Cycle model. We can develop an alternative version of aggregate supply that has the real interest rate instead of the vertical axis. Consider the four-part diagram in Figure 11–4. At first glance, Figure 11–4 may look like Figure 11–3 and, indeed, it is similar except for the aggregate supply graph in the lower right quadrant. In Figure 11–3, the aggregate supply curve had price on the vertical axis. In Figure 11–4 (d), aggregate supply has the real interest rate on the vertical axis. To distinguish this from our usual aggregate supply curve, we will label this the

FIGURE 11-4
Deriving Aggregate Supply II:
Labor Market Equilibrium

Like Figure 11–3, an increase in the labor supply curve, brought about by an increase in interest rates, leads to higher levels of output. In this figure, the interest rate, as opposed to the price level as in Figure 11–3, is on the vertical axis of aggregate supply. This accounts for the labor market equilibrium curve (the *LE* curve) being upward sloping.

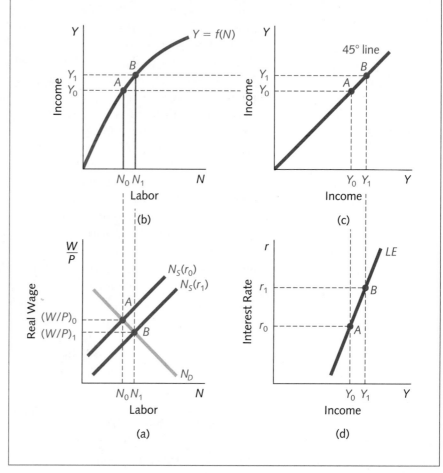

The **LABOR MARKET EQUILIBRIUM CURVE** (*LE*) is the combination of the real interest rate and real output that is consistent with equilibrium in the labor market.

labor market equilibrium curve, or *LE*. Recall that the usual aggregate supply curve is the combination of the price level and real output that is consistent with equilibrium in the labor market. The labor market equilibrium curve is the combination of the real interest rate and real output that is consistent with equilibrium in the labor market.

If a standard aggregate supply curve is constructed for the Real Business Cycle model, the dependence of output on the real interest rate can only be indicated by shifting the vertical aggregate supply curve whenever the real interest rate changes. Our version of aggregate supply, labeled *LE,* avoids this problem by explicitly showing the increase in the quantity of aggregate supply when the real interest rate increases.

For now, however, we want to indicate how the LE curve is derived. Following our earlier discussion we have an initial equilibrium with a price level of P_0 and a real interest rate of r_0 in the four-part diagram in Figure 11–4. To derive LE, start at point A and observe what happens if the real interest rate increases to r_1. In the labor market, the increase in the real interest rate will shift labor supply to the right, resulting in a shift in labor market equilibrium from point A to point B in graph (a). The move from point A to point B leads to a reduction in the equilibrium real wage from $(W/P)_0$ to $(W/P)_1$, and an increase in employment from N_0 to N_1. The increase in employment results, through the production function, graph (b), in an increase in output from Y_0 to Y_1. In the labor market equilibrium curve LE in graph (d), the increase in the real interest rate from r_0 to r_1 results in an increase in output from Y_0 to Y_1. The point r_0-Y_0 is labeled A, the point r_1-Y_1 is labeled B, and both lie on the LE curve. The upward slope of LE indicates that increases in the real interest rate lead, through shifts in labor supply, to an increase in real output.

AGGREGATE SUPPLY AND DEMAND IN A REAL BUSINESS CYCLE MODEL

In the standard approach, aggregate demand is derived from IS-LM analysis, determining a relationship between the price level and real GDP. As for aggregate supply in the Classical model it is perfectly inelastic, indicating that there is *no* effect of the price level on aggregate supply. In other models, the price level does affect output at least along short-run aggregate supply.

Return, for a moment, to the Classical model, and recall that there were three equilibrium relationships to work with. The first is the set of r-Y points consistent with equilibrium in the goods market—the IS curve. The IS curve is not affected by the price level. The second equilibrium relationship is the set of r-Y points consistent with equilibrium in the money market—the LM curve. The LM curve *is* affected by the price level. Finally, the third equilibrium relationship is the aggregate supply curve, which is the set of P-Y points consistent with equilibrium in the labor market. The Classical AS curve is not affected by the interest rate. Of course, in the Classical model AS is not really affected by the price level either, since it is perfectly inelastic. However, other models had upward sloping aggregate supply curves, indicating that output responds to the price level. These three relationships may be combined in certain ways. IS and LM may be used in order to derive AD, a set of P-Y points consistent with equilibrium in both the goods and money markets. AS and AD determine the equilibrium level of both P and Y. Then we use IS and LM to determine the real interest rate.

In the Real Business Cycle model, we encounter a slightly different situation. There are again three equilibrium relationships. The first is the *IS* curve, which is the set of *r*-*Y* points consistent with equilibrium in the goods market. The *IS* curve is not affected by the price level. The second equilibrium relationship is the *LM* curve, the set of *r*-*Y* points consistent with equilibrium in the money market. The *LM* curve *is* affected by the price level. Both the *IS* and the *LM* curves are the same as those used in other models. Finally, the third equilibrium relationship, the *LE* curve, is the set of *r*-*Y* points consistent with equilibrium in the labor market. The *LE* curve does not respond to the price level. How might these three relationships be combined in order to analyze the economy?

If we take the standard approach and combine *IS* and *LM* to derive *AD,* a set of *P*-*Y* points consistent with equilibrium in both the goods and money markets is obtained. For the supply side of the economy, however, we have the *LE* curve, a set of *r*-*Y* points consistent with equilibrium in the labor market. We cannot plot aggregate demand and *LE* on the same graph, since aggregate demand has the price level *P* on the vertical axis, and *LE* has the real interest rate *r* on the vertical axis. However, if we develop *AS* with the price level on the vertical axis, then *AS* will be perfectly inelastic and will shift with changes in the real interest rate. This means that *AS*-*AD* equilibrium cannot be considered as the final determinant of equilibrium *P* and *Y,* since changes in the price level and in real income will change the real interest rate, and changes in this real interest rate will shift *AS,* further changing prices and output. This is a completely unsatisfactory state of affairs.

An alternative to the approach adopted in the text is to combine the two relationships that give equilibrium combinations of *r* and *Y,* which are not affected by *P.* That is, we combine *IS* and *LE. IS* is a set of *r*-*Y* points consistent with equilibrium in the goods market, and, for the Real Business Cycle model, *LE* is a set of *r*-*Y* points consistent with equilibrium in the labor market. Neither *IS* nor *LE* is affected by the price level *P.* Hence, we can combine *AS* and *IS* in order to determine both real output and the real interest rate. The *LM* equation simply determines the price level consistent with the values of the real interest rate and real output determined by *IS*-*AS* equilibrium.

The determination of the real interest rate and real output through *IS*-*LE* equilibrium is illustrated in Figure 11–5. The *IS* curve is negatively sloped, and is a function of government spending *G,* taxes *T,* autonomous consumption c_0, and autonomous investment d_0. The *LE* curve is upward sloping and is taken directly from Figure 11–4. The intersection of *IS* and *LE* at point *A* determines the equilibrium level of the real interest rate as r_0 and the equilibrium level of output as Y_0.

We might ask immediately about the effects of government spending or other variables that affect *IS.* Consider, for example, an increase in government spending. This shifts *IS* to the right, illustrated in Figure 11–5 as a shift in IS_0 to IS_1. The shift in *IS* results in a new equilibrium at point *B* where the equilibrium real interest rate has increased from r_0 to r_1 and real output has

FIGURE II-5
An Increase in Government
Spending.

The *IS* curve is a function of government spending (*G*), taxes (*T*), autonomous consumption (c_0), and autonomous investment (d_0). An increase in the level of government spending (*G*) results in a rightward shift of the *IS* curve (to IS_1). Given the stationary *LE* curve, both interest rates and income rise.

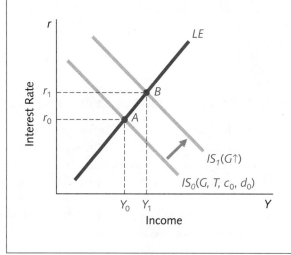

increased from Y_0 to Y_1. This result distinguishes the Real Business Cycle model from the Classical model. In the Classical model aggregate supply is perfectly inelastic, so increases in government spending do not change real output. In the Real Business Cycle model, the quantity of aggregate supply increases with the real interest rate. An increase in government spending increases the real interest rate and calls forth additional effort from labor suppliers, increasing employment and output.

Similar results hold for any factor that shifts *IS* to the right. An increase in government spending, autonomous consumption, or autonomous investment, a decline in taxes, or an increase in net foreign spending will all shift *IS* to the right, increasing equilibrium real interest rates and real output. Likewise, a change in any variable that induces a leftward shift in *IS* will reduce both the real interest rate and output. For changes in factors affecting the *IS* curve the Real Business Cycle model gives results that are very different from the Classical model and that actually correspond to the Keynesian model in many ways.

What happens when there are changes in variables affecting the *LM* curve, such as the money supply? An increase in *M* will change the *LM* relation, but the money supply does not affect either *IS* or *LE*, and hence does not change either the real interest rate or real output. It also does not change any of the underlying labor market features, or the underlying goods market features. In fact, money is neutral in this model, just as in the Classical model: Changes in *M* merely change the price level, without changing real variables.

A final issue concerning Figure 11–5 is the effect of any changes in the price level on the equilibrium. Again, neither *IS* nor *LE* is affected by the price level, so that changes in the price level do not shift either of these curves and hence do not change the equilibrium level of the real interest rate and real output. As in the Classical model, price changes do not affect output. However, it turns out that while the price level does not affect the real interest rate or real output, these two variables do affect the price level, as is demonstrated in the next section.

PRICE ADJUSTMENTS AND THE REAL BUSINESS CYCLE MODEL

Up to this point, the determination of equilibrium output and the real interest rate has been explained. Now it is time to discuss the determination of the price level. In the Real Business Cycle model, the price level is determined from the *LM* equation, which gives a relationship among r, Y, and P for given levels of the exogenous variables M, L_0, and π. Since *IS* and *LE* determine the real interest rate and real output, the *LM* equation determines the price level. To demonstrate how this occurs, we can use the *LE-IS* graph from Figure 11–5, and add to it the standard *LM* curve, which is also graphed with r on the vertical axis and Y on the horizontal. This is shown in Figure 11–6, and we draw the three curves intersecting at point *A*. The equilibrium real interest rate is r_0, the equilibrium level of output is Y_0. The price level is determined by the *LM* curve and adjusts to make the *LM* curve intersect *IS* and *LE* at point *A*. We call this price level P_0. Notice that while *LM* and *LE* are both upward sloping, the *LM* curve is drawn so that it is flatter than the *LE* curve.[2]

Government Spending and Prices

Consider what happens when there is an increase in government spending. Increased government spending shifts *IS* to the right to a new equilibrium at point *B*. At point *B* the interest rate has risen to r_1 and real output has risen to Y_1. The intersection of *LE* and *IS* at point *B* has already been analyzed in Figure 11–5. Our special interest in Figure 11–6 is in the *LM* curve, and what it implies for the price level.

If the price level stays at P_0, then the equilibrium real interest rate and output level at point *B* is not an equilibrium in the money market. The intersection of *LM* and *IS* is at point *C* in Figure 11–6, indicating that money market equilibrium *at a price level P_0* requires a lower interest rate and higher output level than at point *B*. With a constant price level the real money supply

---

[2]The slopes may be reversed, with *LM* steeper than *LE*, but then an increase in the money supply leads to a *decrease* in the price level rather than an increase. We ignore this model as unrealistic.

The *IS* curve shifts rightward as a result of increased levels of government spending, as in Figure 11–5. In addition, increases in the price level lead to decreases in the demand for money. This results in the *LM* curve shifting leftward from $LM(M/P_0)$ to $LM(M/P_1)$.

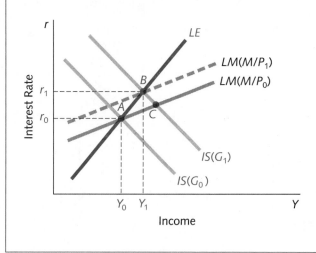

has not changed. As for money demand, the change in equilibrium from *A* to *B* means a simultaneous increase in *r* to r_1, which tends to reduce money demand and in output which tends to increase money demand. With *LM* drawn flatter than *LE* as in Figure 11–6, the net effect is to decrease money demand, resulting in an excess supply of money.

Money demand would equal the fixed money supply if the real interest rate would fall to the level at point *C*, and output would rise to the level at point *C*. As it stands, the excess supply of money cannot be eliminated by a change in *r* or *Y*, since these are set by the intersection of *IS* and *LE* at point *B*. Instead, the price level must adjust in order to decrease the real money supply so that it equals the reduced level of money demand at point *B*. For this to happen the price level rises to some level P_1, reducing real money balances and shifting *LM* upward (or to the left) so that it intersects both *IS* and *LE* at point *B*. The *LM* curve shifts through changes in *P* so as to keep *LM* at the intersection of *IS* and *LE*.

Instead of considering the *LM* curve directly, we can look at the money market that underlies the *LM* curve. In Figure 11–7, the money market tells the same story as the *LM* discussion in Figure 11–6. Remember that the *nominal* interest rate *R* is on the vertical axis, and that the nominal interest rate is equal to the real rate of interest *r* plus the expected rate of inflation π^e. In Figure 11–7, the initial equilibrium is at point *A*, which corresponds to point *A* in Figure 11–6. The initial nominal interest rate is R_0, which is equal to

The money market equilibria shown in the figure correspond with the factors underlying the leftward shift in the *LM* curve in Figure 11−6. Equilibrium is found with a leftward shift in the real money supply and a rightward shift in the demand for money due to increases in income. The final equilibrium is established at interest rate R_1 and point *B*.

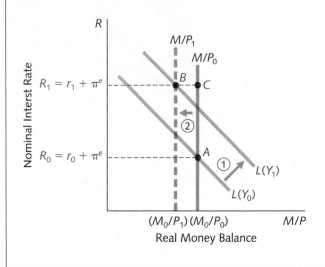

$r_0 + \pi^e$. The initial level of real income is Y_0, which determines the initial level of money demand as $L(Y_0)$. Real money supply is M_0/P_0, and the intersection of real money supply and real money demand is at point *A*.

Now consider the effect of an increase in government spending. This has no direct effect on the money market, but the increase in government spending shifts *IS* to the right, as we illustrated in Figures 11−5 and 11−6, and increases both the interest rate and real output to r_1 and Y_1, respectively. What is the effect in the money market?

First, the increase in output increases money demand to $L(Y_1)$. Second, the real interest rate increases, and with a fixed level of expected inflation, the nominal interest rate increases to $R_1 = r_1 + \pi^e$. The increase in money demand due to the increase in income, and the increase in the interest rate, lead to point *B* on money demand curve $L(Y_1)$. Note, however, that point *B* is not at the intersection of money demand and supply. With an interest rate of R_1, there is an excess supply of real money balances (quantity supplied at point *C*, quantity demanded at point *B*). We would typically think that this excess supply would be eliminated by a reduction in the interest rate, but the interest rate is determined by the intersection of *IS* and *LE*. Instead, the excess supply of money is eliminated by a reduction in the real money supply via an increase in the price level from P_0 to P_1. The money stock is constant at M_0, so this increase in the price level shifts the real money supply to the left to intersect money demand at point B. The money market is brought into equilibrium by price level adjustments.

What is the economic rationale behind this price adjustment? Basically, the excess supply of money is eliminated by the public's attempts to buy goods. Since the quantity of goods is determined by AS and cannot be increased by changes in money holdings, the increased spending results in a rise in the price level. When the price level rises enough, the public will be happy to hold the *real* money stock in existence, and will stop trying to reduce money holdings by purchasing goods. In the Real Business Cycle model, *it is not the interest rate but the price level that adjusts to equilibrate the money market.*

Money Stock Changes and Prices

Finally, what are the effects of changes in the money stock? In Figure 11–8 we analyze an increase in the money stock using our IS-LE-LM graph and our graph of the money market. In the IS-LE-LM graph, the initial equilibrium is at point A, where LE intersects IS at a real interest rate of r_0 and real income Y_0. The LM curve also passes through point A where its position is determined by the real money stock M_0/P_0. Point A on the LM curve is equivalent to point A in the money market graph, where money demand $L(Y_1)$ intersects real money balances M_0/P_0 and where the nominal interest rate is $R_0 = r_0 + \pi^e$.

Consider now what happens when there is an increase in the money supply, from M_0 to M_1. In the IS-LE-LM graph, this would cause—for a constant price level P_0—an increase in real money balances to M_1/P_0 and a consequent shift downward (or to the right) in LM, to $LM(M_1/P_0)$. There would be no change in IS or LE, and hence no change in the equilibrium level of the real interest rate and real output. The downward (or rightward) shift in LM would merely indicate that at point A the money market is not in equilibrium with $r = r_0, Y = Y_0$, and $P = P_0$. Some economic quantity must adjust, and with the real interest rate and real output determined by IS and LE, it is the price level that must change. The price level must increase in order to reduce the real money supply and shift LM up (or leftward). In fact, the price level must just increase enough to restore real money balances to their original level and hence to restore LM to its original level. Thus, we will require $M_1/P_1 = M_0/P_0$. The increase in the nominal money supply is completely offset by an equal percentage increase in the price level. Thus, the Real Business Cycle model produces a Classical prediction that an increase in the money supply of, say, 10 percent will lead to an increase in the price level of 10 percent. Moreover, there is no effect of the increase in the money stock on either real output or the real interest rate.

We can also trace through the increase in the money supply in the money market. Again, the initial equilibrium is at point A, with an initial money supply of M_0/P_0. The increase in the money stock to M_1 increases the real money supply to M_1/P_0, a rightward shift in money supply. At the unchanged

An increase in money from M_0 to M_1 would initially shift the LM curve from LM_0 to LM_1. The increase in real balances is shown in (b). In order to restore equilibrium, price must rise. A price increase reduces the real money supply and restores LM to its original level. In this model, real output remains the same with an increase in money, providing a Classical conclusion.

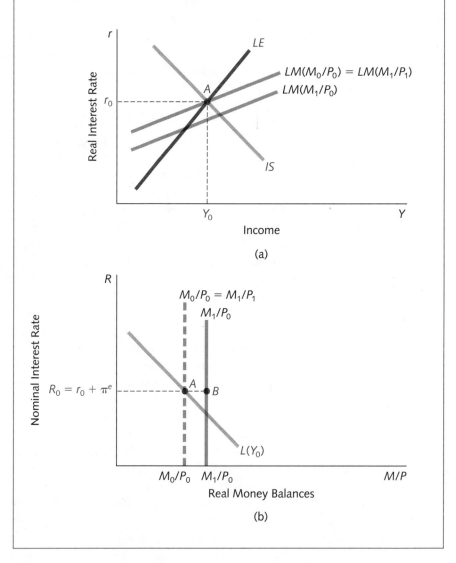

(a)

(b)

real interest rate of r_0 (and with constant π^e) and unchanged real income Y_0, the money demand curve is unchanged, and there is an excess supply of money. As individuals try to dispose of the excess supply of money by buying goods and services, they bid up the price of the fixed supply Y_0, resulting in an increase in the price level. As the price level rises, the real money supply shifts leftward, and when the price level rises to P_1, real money balances are restored to the original level $M_0/P_0 = M_1/P_1$. Thus price adjustments restore equilibrium in the money market.

The above exercises considered changes either in factors that affect the *IS* curve, such as government spending, or in factors that affect the *LM* curve, such as the nominal money stock. These exercises were meant to illustrate the similarities and differences between the Real Business Cycle model and other models we have studied, especially the Classical model.

Like the Classical model, the Real Business Cycle model predicts that money is neutral: Changes in the nominal money stock do *not* change real variables. Unlike the Classical model, the Real Business Cycle model predicts that changes in government spending and in other variables that affect the *IS* curve *will* lead to changes in real output. This may have extremely important implications for policy. Although monetary policy will clearly not be influential in determining output, changes in government spending or taxes might influence the equilibrium level of output.

SUPPLY SHOCKS IN THE REAL BUSINESS CYCLE MODEL

In spite of any impressions given to the contrary in the discussion of changes in the *LM* curve, the primary emphasis in the Real Business Cycle model is on *real shocks* to the supply side of the economy. These shocks are shocks to production—otherwise known as supply shocks. Of course some shocks will affect both demand and supply sides of the system: See, for example, the Global Perspective, "The Effect of a Reduction in Worldwide Defense Spending: Peace as a Macroeconomic Shock."

In this section, we will talk about supply shocks as *shifts in the production function that either increase or decrease the marginal productivity of labor at every level of employment.* There are many possibilities for supply shocks, and in earlier chapters we have adopted the convention of discussing supply shocks as affecting both the production function and the marginal product of labor— that is, the labor demand schedule. Thus, a "good" or positive supply shock will increase the production function. It will allow more output to be produced for a given level of inputs and will increase the marginal product of labor at every level of employment—that is, it will increase labor demand. Likewise, a "bad" or negative supply shock will decrease the production function and will decrease the marginal product of labor at every employment level.

Such a supply shock is illustrated in Figure 11–9, which employs our familiar four-part diagram used to derive *LE*. This diagram may be used to analyze how a supply shock would shift the *LE* curve. The labor market is shown in graph (a). Labor demand is initially given by N_{D_0} and labor supply by $N_S(r_0)$. The intersection of labor supply and demand at point *A* determines both the real wage $(W/P)_0$ and the employment level N_0. Given this level of

GLOBAL PERSPECTIVE

THE EFFECT OF A REDUCTION IN WORLDWIDE DEFENSE SPENDING: PEACE AS A MACROECONOMIC SHOCK

The collapse of the Soviet Union, bringing an end to the Cold War, has affected many national economies and defense industries, producing something akin to a global "supply shock," with demand-side implications as well. From 1972 through 1988 military expenditures consumed about 5 percent of the world's output each year.[a] The share for the less developed countries was slightly higher or 5 1/2 percent, and for some of these countries the relatively large military expenditures helped to undermine economic growth since resources were diverted from important nondefense projects. In 1989 at least 120 countries participated in the arms trade. While all 120 were importers, 47 of them were also exporters. Of those participating in the trade, 93 were less developed countries.

According to geographic region, the Middle East was the leading importer, purchasing $12 billion of foreign-supplied arms. The primary exporting region was the Warsaw Pact countries, exporting around $21 billion.

The size of the arms trade depends on how arms are defined. While any definition is rather arbitrary, the definition used by the U.S. Arms Control and Disarmament Agency (ACDA) is military equipment, "including weapons of war, parts thereof, ammunition, support equipment, and other commodities designed for military use." This ACDA definition includes guided missiles and rockets, military aircraft, armored and nonarmored military vehicles, naval ships, electronic and communications equipment, artillery pieces, infantry weapons, small arms, ammunition and ordnance, uniforms, and parachutes. Dual-use equipment, which can be used for either civilian or military purpose, is included in the arms trade if its primary function is identified as military. However, all foodstuffs, petroleum products, and medical equipment are excluded from the arms list. Also counted in the arms trade is the construction of defense production facilities and licensing fees paid as roy-

alties for the production of military equipment, when they are incorporated in military transfer agreements by countries other than the United States.

Which countries are the chief exporters and importers of arms so defined? The Soviet Union dominates the exporters, but the United States is also prominent, with exports far greater than other countries such as the United Kingdom, France, Mainland China, and Germany. Between them, the United States and the Soviet Union accounted for nearly two-thirds of the world's arms exports over the period 1985–1989 and for slightly more than two-thirds in 1989. One country's arms trade may seem large relative to that of another country, but it still may be small relative to a nation's total economic activity. The country whose arms exports have been largest in relation to its gross output is Israel. The next country, following close behind, is North Korea. However, being an arms seller does not mean prosperity for a nation. For most of the twelve countries that led the world in terms of arms exports as a share of GNP in 1989, their per capita GNP is low by world standards. Absent from the list is the United States, whose arms exports averaged 0.27 percent of GNP in 1985–1989 and 0.22 percent in 1989, and whose 1989 GNP per capita was around $20,910. While the United States and Russia account for the preponderance of arms exports, there is no such dominance among the arms-importing countries. Saudi Arabia was the leading importer over the 1985–1989 period, with only 9 percent of the world's arms imports. Among the leading importers were countries that have been either involved in conflict or threatened by it. Afghanistan, Greece, and Turkey had extraordinary percentage increases in imports between 1985 and 1989.

However, worldwide defense reduction has been under way, especially since 1989.

According to the DRI / McGraw-Hill economic forecasting group, European defense is expected to decline by 52 percent between 1989 and 1997, and U.S. defense spending is forecast to be down 54 percent by 1997. The defense share of U.S. gross domestic product is projected to continue to decline from about 5.2 percent in 1992 to around 3.2 percent by 1997. The sharp drop in defense spending has already had a noticeable impact on the world arms trade. DRI / McGraw-Hill economists calculate that exports of major weapons systems have declined by 53 percent since 1987. While the Persian Gulf nations such as Saudi Arabia and Kuwait have ordered $50 billion in armaments since Iraq invaded Kuwait in 1990, military budgets

in many of the developing nations are either stagnant or declining. Since the economies of Russia and its former allies are too weak to renew another arms race with the Western bloc countries, the DRI / McGraw-Hill economists forecast continued declines in military spending. These declines no doubt will have a worldwide dampening effect on those economies trying to recover from recessions. ❑

NOTE [a]See Norman S. Fieleke, "A Primer on the Arms Trade," Federal Reserve Bank of Boston, *New England Economic Review* (November/December 1991), pp. 47–63, and Gene Koretz, "U.S. Weapons Makers Aren't the Only Ones Taking a Beating," *Business Week* (May 10, 1993), p. 16.

employment, the production function in graph (b), $Y = f_0(N)$, indicates that output will be Y_0. Point A on this production function indicates that employment of N_0 labor will yield output of Y_0.

Figure 11–9 (c) shows the familiar 45-degree line, enabling us to shift output from the vertical axis to the horizontal axis. In (d) we graph the labor market equilibrium curve *LE*. The initial real interest rate is r_0, and output is Y_0, given point A in the figure. If the interest rate is raised or lowered and the resulting changes in the level of output are calculated, the aggregate supply curve that passes through point A, labeled LE_0, may be traced out.

Now consider an *adverse* supply shock. Such a shock has two immediate effects. First, the production function rotates downward from $Y = f_0(N)$ to $Y = f_1(N)$. Notice that this rotation will lower the slope of the production

A negative supply shock involves the lowering of the production function in (b) and an accompanying decrease in the marginal productivity and demand of labor. The effect in (d) is to shift the labor market equilibrium curve from LE_0 to LE_1. This means that at the same interest rate r_0, income is reduced from Y_0 to Y_1.

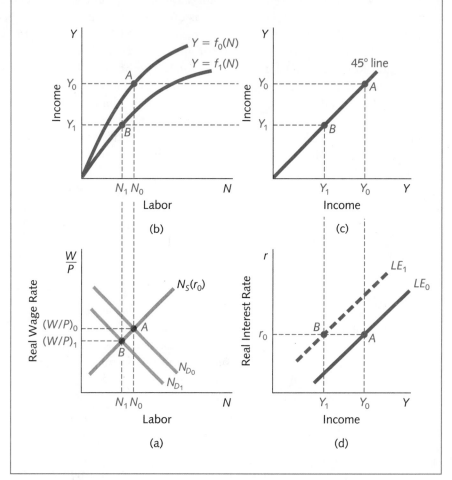

function, which is the marginal product of labor, at each level of employment. This produces the second immediate effect, a leftward shift in labor demand, represented in the labor market by a shift in labor demand from N_{D_0} to N_{D_1}.

These initial impacts of a supply shock produce a whole host of effects that lead to a shift in the labor market equilibrium curve. Consider first the labor market and note that the reduction in labor demand results in a new labor market equilibrium at point B, where the real wage has fallen to $(W/P)_1$ and employment has fallen to N_1. Notice that the real interest rate has remained at r_0, so the labor supply curve has not changed.

The reduction in employment and the downward shift in the production function combine to lower output. With employment at N_1, the new production function $Y = f_1(N)$ indicates that output will be reduced to Y_1. This point on the production function is identified as point B. Output, therefore, declines for two reasons. First, the downward shift in the production function tells us that output would decline for every level of employment due to the supply shock. Second, the decline in the marginal product of labor results in a lower level of employment, which compounds the decline in output.[3]

With output at Y_1, the 45-degree line is used to transfer the output value to the horizontal axis, and the point r_0-Y_1 is shown as point B. Point B is at the same interest rate as point A, indicating that output has fallen at every interest rate. That is, even though the interest rate has stayed r_0 between points A and B, output has fallen from Y_0 to Y_1.

Once we have point B, we can then change the real interest rate and derive the response of output. This would allow us to plot the labor market equilibrium curve labeled LE_1. Actual determination of the effect of a supply shock on the equilibrium real interest rate and real output will require knowledge of how the supply shock affects the intersection of IS and LE, an issue to which we now turn. First, however, we give an example of an adverse supply shock, Hurricane Andrew, which struck Florida, the Gulf of Mexico, and Louisiana in 1992. See the Policy Issue: "Hurricane Andrew: An Exogenous Supply Shock."

Output, Interest Rates, and Supply Shocks

In Figure 11–11, the four-part diagram for deriving LE is combined with the IS curve to further explain adjustment to a supply shock. Figure 11–11 is taken from Figure 11–9, but the IS curve is added in order to show how the equilibrium real interest rate and real income change with supply shocks. In the LE-IS graph (d), initial equilibrium is at point A, where IS intersects LE_0. The equilibrium real interest rate is r_0 and equilibrium real output is Y_0.

In the labor market graph, (a), labor demand is initially N_{D_0} and labor supply is $N_S(r_0)$. These intersect at point A, determining the equilibrium real wage as $(W/P)_0$ and equilibrium employment as N_0. In the production function graph, (b), the production function is $Y = f_0(N)$, so that employment of N_0 generates output of Y_0, as indicated from point A on the production function. This output level corresponds to the initial output level at point A in the IS-LE graph (d).

An adverse supply shock shifts the production function downward to $Y = f_1(N)$ and labor demand shifts left to N_{D_1}. In the labor market, the new

---

[3]In terms of a standard aggregate supply curve, which for the Real Business Cycle model would be a perfectly inelastic or vertical AS curve that shifts with changes in the real interest rate, the adverse supply shock would be represented by a leftward shift in aggregate supply not caused by a change in the real interest rate.

HURRICANE ANDREW: AN EXOGENOUS SUPPLY SHOCK

Supply shocks can be initiated by many causes, including the weather. In 1992, two devastating hurricanes, dubbed Andrew and Iniki, created important short-run supply shocks in the U.S. economy. The worst, Andrew, swept across southern Florida, the Gulf of Mexico, and Louisiana in August 1992 and destroyed or damaged over 100,000 private residences. (Iniki, which hit Hawaii, flattened over 6,500.)

Losses to residential property were more than $9.1 billion; to proprietors' property, $1.2 billion; and to corporate property, $3.5 billion for Andrew alone.[a] While about three-fourths of the total property loss of $14 billion was covered by insurance, Andrew disrupted several major industries—including oil and gas extraction, petroleum refining, and petrochemicals—and reduced industrial production. Losses in personal income, in personal and business property, in crop damage, in insurance company bankruptcies, and in lost profits had a significant effect on the economy.

The impact of Hurricane Andrew may be shown as a supply shock not unlike the one described in Figure 11–9 in the text. The destruction of capital and wealth had the effect of a short-term supply shock as shown in Figure 11–10, disrupting income and production. The labor market equilibrium curve shifts from LE_0 to LE_1, causing an initial shift in income from Y_0 to Y_1. That shift is temporary of course. In the longer run, when the disrupted production and destroyed capital are restored, the LE curve shifts rightward again. (Note that we ignore all effects on aggregate demand here, but the increased expenditures and production required by new building will also shift aggre-

PHOTO 11-2
Hurricane Andrew, One of the Most Devastating Natural Disasters of Recent Decades, Created at Least a Temporary Leftward Shift in Aggregate Supply.

gate demand rightward.) The point is that real supply shocks—related to weather and to a host of other causes—have important impacts on income and production in the economy. ❏

Hurricane Andrew Brings on a Negative Supply Shock

The destruction of resources and capital caused by a disaster such as a hurricane shifts the labor market equilibrium curve to the left from LE_0 to LE_1. While this may be a temporary effect, such supply shocks help create swings in the business cycle of employment and income.

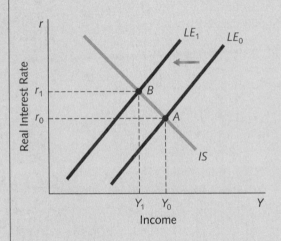

NOTE: [a]Data from *Economic Report of the President* (Washington, DC: U.S. Government Printing Office, 1993), p. 47.

---

equilibrium—for a real interest rate of r_0—is at point *B,* where the real wage has declined to $(W/P)_1$ and employment to N_1. This decline in employment, together with the shift in the production function, provides an output of Y_1 as indicated by point *B* on the production function $Y = f_1(N)$. In the *LE* graph, this is represented by the shift to LE_1.

This is not the end of the story. The real interest rate and real income are *not* determined by *LE* alone, but by the intersection of *LE* and *IS.* This intersection is now at point *C,* where the real interest rate is r_1 and output is Y_1. In the labor market, the increase in the real interest rate to r_1 will shift labor supply

FIGURE II−II
A Supply Shock and *IS* and
LE Equilibrium

When both goods and labor market equilibria are considered, as in
graph (d), a negative supply shock will, in equilibrium, reduce income
and raise real interest rates. In conventional *AD-AS* terms, the aggregate supply curve shifts leftward.

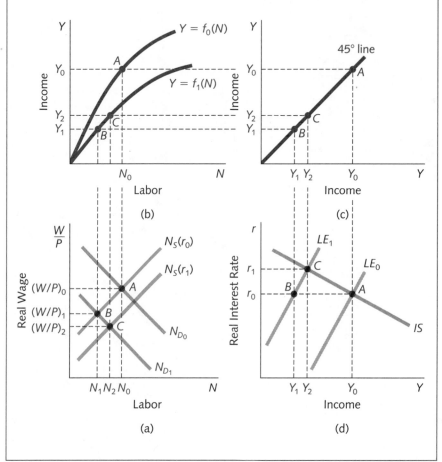

to the right, to $N_S(r_1)$. The intersection of $N_S(r_1)$ and N_{D_1} at point C results
in a further lowering of the real wage to $(W/P)_2$ but an increase in
employment to N_1. The increase in employment increases output to Y_2 as
indicated by point C on production function $Y = f_1(N)$.

One point to keep in mind is that this analysis has considered the effect of
an adverse supply shock when the interest rate changes endogenously, to
preserve *IS-LE* equilibrium after the supply shock induces a shift in *LE.* This
analysis has not considered how another variable can shift *LE,* namely the
expected future real wage $(W/P)^e_{t+1}$. If this wage increases, then labor supply
will shift to the left, as workers will choose to work less today and more
tomorrow, when the real wage is expected to be higher. Changes in the expected
future real wage will shift labor supply and hence the labor market equili-

brium curve *LE,* and in particular increases in the expected future real wage will shift *LE* to the left. This is especially important when considering supply shocks, since the nature of supply shocks can determine how the expected future real wage will change. If a supply shock is temporary, then the expected future real wage should not be affected, and hence the analysis in Figure 11–11 holds true. If the supply shock is permanent, however, an adverse supply shock reduces not only the current real wage but also the expected future real wage. This decline in the expected future real wage would lead to an increase in labor supply, since workers comparing the current real wage to the expected future real wage would now find no difference in the two and hence would be more willing than otherwise to work at the reduced current real wage. This shifts *LE* to the right, partially offsetting the reduction in *LE* shown in Figure 11–11. Thus, an important issue in Real Business Cycle modeling is the permanence of supply shocks. Permanent (or persistent) shocks have less of an impact on output and real interest rates than do temporary shocks.

Adverse Supply Shocks and Business Cycles

Now that we have a nearly complete Real Business Cycle model, let us take stock of the effects on the economy of an adverse supply shock. The real wage is reduced, from $(W/P)_0$ to $(W/P)_2$. Employment declines as does output. Finally, the real interest rate increases. Thus, the adverse supply shock causes a decline in output while the real wage is declining. A positive supply shock would result in an increase in output with the real wage is increasing. Thus, the Real Business Cycle model predicts that the real wage is procyclical. Real Business Cycle enthusiasts argue that this prediction is in better accord with the empirical evidence than the predictions of countercyclical real wages made in the labor-contracting model of the New Keynesians or the worker-misperception model of the New Classicals.

CRITICISMS OF THE REAL BUSINESS CYCLE MODEL

The Real Business Cycle model emphasizes the occurrence of supply shocks as the driving factor in business cycles. Adverse supply shocks cause declines in employment, output, and the real wage, while positive supply shocks cause increases in employment, output, and the real wage. Real changes in spending may also affect employment, output, and the real wage, such as in the analysis of *IS* curve shifts in Figure 11–5, but the emphasis is placed on supply shocks. Monetary changes, or changes in any variables that affect *LM,* will not affect employment, output, the real wage, or the real interest rate. Thus, the Real Business Cycle model retains a strict Classical flavor when analyzing monetary changes.

Table 11–1 points out just how the Real Business Cycle model in the text compares to the New Classical and New Keynesian (wage-contracting) models,

TABLE 11–1 Classical, New Classical, New Keynesian, and Real Business Cycle Models

CHANGE IN EXOGENOUS VARIABLE	CHANGE IN ENDOGENOUS VARIABLE	NEW CLASSICAL AND NEW KEYNESIAN MODELS, SHORT RUN	CLASSICAL MODEL; OR NEW CLASSICAL AND NEW KEYNESIAN MODELS, LONG RUN	REAL BUSINESS CYCLE MODEL
$\Delta G > 0$	ΔY	+	o	+
	ΔP	+	+	$+^a$
	Δr	+	+	+
	$\Delta(W/P)$	−	o	−
	ΔN	+	o	+
$\Delta M > 0$	ΔY	+	o	o
	ΔP	+	+	$+^a$
	Δr	−	o	o
	$\Delta(W/P)$	−	o	o
	ΔN	+	o	o
ADVERSE SUPPLY SHOCK	ΔY	−	−	−
	ΔP	+	+	+
	Δr	+	+	+
	$\Delta(W/P)$	−	−	−
	ΔN	−	−	$-/?^b$

[a]The slope of the *LM* curve must be flatter than the slope of *LE* for these signs to result.
[b]This sign is ambiguous, depending on the nature of the supply shock. For a temporary shock the sign is negative, but for a permanent shock the sign might be negative, zero, or even positive. With a permanent shock, the labor supply curve in Figure 11–11 shifts to the right for two reasons: first, an increase in the real interest rate, as incorporated in the figure, and second, a decrease in the expected future real wage. This second effect will shift labor supply further to the right, increasing employment and possibly restoring employment to its pre-shock level. Output will still have fallen, however, because of the downward shift in the production function.

and also to the Classical model. The short-run effects of the New Classical and New Keynesian models are actually the same for the variables listed in Table 11–1, although the two models would disagree about relative magnitudes, and also about what it takes to get from the short run to the long run. (In the New Classical model, once an unexpected shock becomes widely recognized, we move to the long-run results, while in the New Keynesian model, recognizing the shock is not sufficient. Instead, we have to recognize the shock and then wait until we have the opportunity to renegotiate our wage contracts.) The Classical model is also the long-run version of the New Classical and New Keynesian models.

Notice that our Real Business Cycle model makes the same predictions as the other models for some of the possible shocks. For instance, the predicted response of the economy to an increase in government spending is the same in the Real Business Cycle model as in the short run of the New Classical and New Keynesian models, but differs from the long-run prediction of these two models. For the change in the money supply, the Real Business Cycle model agrees with the long-run or Classical model predictions, but not with the predicted short-run effects in the New Classical and New Keynesian models. It is this result—that money does not affect output or employment, and hence does not "cause" business cycles—that is responsible for the name "Real Business Cycle model." New Classical and New Keynesian models explained business cycles in part as due to unexpected monetary disturbances, or monetary disturbances in conjunction with nominal wage contracts.

Finally, notice that our Real Business Cycle model agrees with the predictions of the other models when there is an adverse supply shock. The only discrepancy is that the Real Business Cycle model is ambiguous about the response of employment to a permanent adverse supply shock, since this also affects the expected future real wage.

Thus, the Real Business Cycle model's central departure from previous explanations of the business cycle is an emphasis on the supply side of the macroeconomy, a deemphasis on monetary explanations of the business cycle, and a reliance on intertemporal substitution to generate changes in labor supply and hence output. Most business cycle models developed after the Classical model emphasized aggregate demand as the primary source of business cycle fluctuations. Even the New Keynesian and New Classical models emphasize aggregate demand as the source of business cycle movements, and these models often (but not always) generate predictions of countercyclical real wages: Real wages rise during recessions and fall during expansions. However, this prediction mainly arose because of the emphasis on demand-side shocks such as changes in the money supply or in autonomous consumption or investment. Even these models will generate procyclical real wages in response to supply shocks, as is indicated in Table 11–1.

One of the main problems with the Real Business Cycle model is that it is difficult to exactly identify supply shocks that can be held responsible for the historical pattern of business cycles. Everyone points to the increase in the real price of imported oil in late 1973 as leading to the recession of 1974–75, and a similar argument can be made about the oil price hike in 1979 and the recession in 1980. But these are only two incidents in business cycle history. Many recessions seem to be caused by demand factors, including monetary factors. The steep recession in 1982 seems to have been due to monetary tightening, and monetary factors may also have been behind the most recent recession of 1990. It is hard to identify real factors responsible for these two recessions, and for numerous other historical cases.

Real Business Cycle enthusiasts have a rejoinder to this argument: Significant supply shocks are not necessarily *large* supply shocks that have a direct impact on the entire economy (such as the oil price shocks of 1973 and 1979). Instead, supply shocks may be specific to one industry or one region. These smaller supply shocks are always occurring, and their cumulative effect can be large. Recessions might occur when there are many small shocks that are predominantly negative due to chance, while expansions might occur when there are many small shocks that are predominantly positive. In addition, these shocks can be perpetuated by a variety of dynamic factors in the economy. This argument cannot be illustrated in the representative Real Business Cycle model developed in this chapter, since our model is an aggregated and stylistic version of a Real Business Cycle model. Real Business Cycle models discussed in the professional journals are far more complicated than the model analyzed in this chapter. In these more complex models it is possible to show that small, randomly occurring shocks that affect only one industry or one region at a time can be magnified into economy-wide movements in real GDP. However, the development and illustration of such effects are beyond the scope of this text. For an example of a supply shock from antiquity, see the Insight: "Supply Shocks Affecting Production: An Example from Ancient Greece."

Controversy over supply shocks remains, however. Numerous small supply shocks are still hard to identify, and in one sense, the critics of Real Business Cycles point out that reliance on numerous small shocks instead of large shocks is merely a way to hide the fact that these shocks are hard to find. Moreover, it is somewhat difficult to conceive of numerous supply shocks constantly having an impact on different industries across the economy. Some supply shocks are easy to identify, such as the oil price shocks mentioned above, or unexpected changes in climate that lead to drought or other weather-related shocks. However, these are all fairly aggregate shocks. The required numerous small shocks are as yet unidentified.

Also, many critics question the intertemporal substitution approach to modeling the labor market. These critics find the idea of intertemporal substitution leading to large changes in labor supply and hence in output very hard to believe. In the view of such critics, the response of labor supply to changes in interest rates is almost zero, as is the response to changes in expected future wages. Thus, this view finds the intertemporal substitution model of the labor market, a foundation of real business cycle modeling, unacceptable.[4] In spite of the continuing controversy, the Real Business Cycle model has raised

---

[4]Intertemporal substitution, which in our model shows up as a dependence of labor supply on the real interest rate, is important to Real Business Cycle models for a number of reasons. For the model in the text, the intertemporal substitution model is what yields the predictions that an increase in government spending, or indeed a change in any variable which shifts *IS* to the right, will lead to an increase in real output and employment, an increase in the real interest rate, and a reduction in the real wage. If labor supply did not depend on the real interest rate, then changes in the real interest rate would not change labor supply or equilibrium employment, and the *LE* equation would be vertical. Then shifts in *IS* would not change output or employment.

INSIGHT

SUPPLY SHOCKS

AFFECTING PRODUCTION:

AN EXAMPLE FROM

ANCIENT GREECE

A "good" supply shock, as noted in the text, is one that increases the production function, allowing more output to be produced for a given level of inputs. Supply shocks have punctuated world history, and the history of Western civilization cannot be understood without appeal to them. In our own time, a shock of relatively short duration was precipitated by the activities of the OPEC oil cartel of the 1970s. The adverse supply shock (in this case) created higher oil and gas prices and a mass movement away from enormous gas-guzzling American cars to smaller, fuel-efficient cars. OPEC lost some of its power to control prices, and Americans witnessed more stable gasoline prices and a return to larger automobiles. But the world will never exactly be the same. New and larger cars were made more efficient, solar and other alternative forms of energy have

found new uses, and production processes have been adjusted permanently to oil shortages and to the possibility of future shortages. Thus, shocks of all kinds—positive and negative—must be analyzed for both short- and long-term effects.

Often, the skeptical and pessimistic observer envisions new and desperate conditions in society from a shock such as the oil crisis. These doomsdayers are in almost all circumstances wrong, as shown by economists S. Charles Maurice and Charles W. Smithson in an interesting book that examines supply shocks over 10,000 years of recorded history.[a] Supply shocks, they argue, never permanently reduce aggregate supply; instead, adjustments to supply shocks produce beneficial effects that, in time, reverse leftward shifts in aggregate supply.

Consider, for example, a supply shock in ancient Greece that marked the transition from the Bronze Age to the Iron Age. Why did our Greek ancestors switch from bronze to iron tools and weapons beginning about 1000 B.C.? The reasons often given—that the Greeks didn't invent iron smelting until 1000 B.C. and

that iron was a much better metal than bronze—are questionable. People in ancient Greece had a knowledge of iron making dating to 3000 B.C. Additionally, hammered bronze tools and weapons are almost as hard and durable as iron ones and will hold an edge almost as well as iron tools. Since neither of these explanations is satisfactory, what other factor may have ushered in the Iron Age?

Consider some conditions existing during the Bronze Age. From trading records, we know that iron was extremely expensive during the Bronze Age: Records from the nineteenth century B.C. indicate that the exchange ratio of iron to silver was 1:40. Bronze is an alloy of about 90 percent copper and 10 percent tin. At the time, copper was abundant—especially relative to iron—and the trading ratio of copper to silver was 200:1. Tin was not so abundant and was probably imported into Greece from Iran, for there is practically no tin in the eastern Mediterranean area. During the Bronze Age, tin exchanged for silver at between 4 and 10 units of tin to 1 unit of silver. Everything considered, the components for a bronze tool cost about 0.05

percent of what an iron tool would have cost. Small wonder the Greeks used bronze.

What happened to alter this situation? We know that around 1000 B.C., tin became extremely scarce in the Aegean. The Greeks experienced a supply shock of enormous severity owing to the wartime disruption of trade caused by the invasion of the Sea Peoples (the Phoenicians) into the eastern Mediterranean.[b] These invasions, lasting from about 1025 to 950 B.C., led to the collapse of the major Bronze Age civilizations— Mycenean Greece, New Kingdom Egypt, and the Hittite Empire.

With tin no longer available, the price of bronze rose precipitously. Old bronze was melted down for its tin content and, because iron now became cheaper relative to bronze, ancient smiths began to forge iron tools and weapons. The response of the Greeks to the "tin crisis" was to usher in the Age of Iron. Even when trade was reestablished and bronze prices fell, iron continued to be used. The crisis had encouraged the smiths to learn to produce iron more cheaply, and iron use was not discontinued even though the Greeks reverted in part to the use of bronze. In short, when resource crises or supply shocks occur, alternatives become cheaper and more attractive. Shocks may mean vastly increased aggregate supply in the future. Each shock must be analyzed, in other words, on the basis of immediate (short-term), long-term, and ultimate effects on productivity, technology, and *new* inventions—those made in response to the initial shock. Viewed in this light, virtually all crises may contain the seeds of economic progress. ❏

NOTE: [a]See S. Charles Maurice and Charles W. Smithson, *Doomsday: 10,000 Years of Economic Crises* (Stanford, CA: Hoover Institution Press, 1985), pp. 95–105, for this and a host of other interesting examples of supply shocks throughout history. [b]The Sea Peoples were themselves users of iron, which probably had a "demonstration effect" on the Greeks.

the consciousness of economists to the role of supply shocks in explaining business cycle behavior and the macroeconomy in general. If supply shocks cannot explain all business cycle behavior, it is also probable that demand shocks cannot explain all business cycle behavior either. Current research, building on the foundations created by Real Business Cycle theory, is combining the best features of all models, and holding demand and supply shocks jointly accountable for business cycle behavior.

SUMMARY

In this chapter, we began with a discussion of the Real Business Cycle model, describing what it is and how it is related to the Classical model. We paid particular attention to distinguishing how the labor market is developed in the

Real Business Cycle model, and how it differs from other labor market models presented in this text. This difference focuses on the intertemporal substitution of labor.

We then turned to a rather detailed discussion of our Real Business Cycle model. We showed how to derive a model of aggregate supply for Real Business Cycle models, which we called the labor market equilibrium curve, or *LE*. We used this curve, along with a traditional *IS* curve, to find the equilibrium determination of real output and the real interest rate. We also discussed price determination and the role of *LM* in determining the price level.

The discussion then turned to supply shocks in the Real Business Cycle model. We analyzed such shocks and their effects on output, the real interest rate, and the price level, and concluded with a discussion of the criticisms of Real Business Cycle models.

KEY TERMS

intertemporal substitution of labor

labor market equilibrium curve

present value

real business cycle model

QUESTIONS FOR REVIEW AND DISCUSSION

1. What is the effect of a decrease in consumption spending in the Real Business Cycle model? Demonstrate your answers graphically.

2. What is the effect of a decrease in the expected rate of inflation in the Real Business Cycle model? Demonstrate your answers graphically.

3. What is the effect of a positive supply shock in the Real Business Cycle model? Demonstrate your answers graphically.

4. Compare and contrast your answers to questions 1–3 above for the Real Business Cycle model with the New Classical model.

5. Compare and contrast your answers to questions 1–3 above for the Real Business Cycle model with the New Keynesian model.

6. What are the main differences between the Real Business Cycle model and the New Classical model? Both are built to be similar to the Classical model, and yet they differ in many key ways. Elaborate on these differences and similarities.

7. Consider a positive supply shock in the Classical, New Classical, and Real Business Cycle models. What is the effect on real wages, employment, output, the price level, and the real interest rate? In what ways do these three models agree? In what ways do they differ?

8. Compare an increase in the money supply in the Classical, New Classical, and Real Business Cycle models. What is the effect on real wages, employment, output, the price level, and the real interest rate? In what ways do these three models agree? In what ways do they differ?

9. Compare an increase in government spending in the Classical, New Classical, and Real Business Cycle models. What is the effect on real wages, employment, output, the price level, and the real interest rate? In what ways do these three models agree? In what ways do they differ?

10. Does the Real Business Cycle model predict a procyclical real wage in all circumstances? That is, in the face of *IS* shocks, *LM* shocks, and *LE* shocks?

11. Can the Real Business Cycle model work without intertemporal substitution of labor? Try to redo the derivations of aggregate supply in the text, but with the assumptions that the real interest rate does not affect labor supply. What is your result?

12. At this stage of the text we have studied the Classical, Keynesian, Monetarist, New Classical, New Keynesian, and Real Business Cycle models. Can you suggest a general strategy for trying to distinguish these models on the basis of the historical evidence?

13. Can you suggest various ways of classifying the six models listed in question 12? One way would be to classify those models in the Classical tradition, as opposed to those in the Keynesian tradition. Can you think of other classifications?

PROBLEMS

1. President Clinton has asked for your advice. He wants to raise taxes and is not sure of the macroeconomic effect. He asks you to tell him as many scenarios as you can. Using the models developed in this text, tell President Clinton the alternative effects of an increase in taxes on the economy. If he asks for a summary that includes your best guess of the likely effect, what will you tell him?

2. You have been appointed as chair of the Board of Governors of the Federal Reserve System and now have the power to set the money supply however you see fit. You are also a believer in the Real Business Cycle model. What are your monetary policy recommendations?

SUGGESTIONS FOR FURTHER READING

Huh, Chan and Bharat Treham. "Real Business Cycles: A Selective Survey." Federal Reserve Bank of San Francisco *Economic Review* (Spring 1991), pp. 3–17.

Mankiw, N. Gregory. "Real Business Cycles: A New Keynesian Perspective." *Economic Perspectives* (Summer 1989), pp. 79–90.

Plosser, Charles I. "Understanding Real Business Cycles." *Economic Perspectives* (Summer 1989), pp. 51–78.

Walsh, Carl E. "New Views of the Business Cycle: Has the Past Emphasis on Money Been Misplaced?" Federal Reserve Bank of Philadelphia *Business Review* (January/February 1986), pp. 3–13.

PART IV

MONEY SUPPLY AND DEMAND

12

THE MONEY SUPPLY PROCESS AND

THE FEDERAL RESERVE SYSTEM

Money is a fundamental element in macroeconomic theory, policy, and practical life. To fully understand the importance of money in a macroeconomic policy discussion we must carefully examine the underlying factors that determine the supply of and demand for money.

While some of the principles regarding the money supply may already be familiar from basic economics courses, a firm understanding of those principles is critical to the foundations of macroeconomics. In this chapter, we examine the role played by the public and commercial banks in the process of money creation in a fractional reserve banking system. We show how changes in the desires of money holders and of bankers can alter the total amount and composition of the money stock.

In the United States the Federal Reserve System has the responsibility of controlling the nation's supply of money and credit. In this chapter we discuss the structure and mechanisms of the Federal Reserve System. We show how the Federal Reserve may bring about changes in the stock of nominal money through its tools (instruments) of monetary policy.

By the end of this chapter, you will know

- the definitions that the Federal Reserve Board uses for money
- the response of the money stock to changes in high-powered money, the desired currency to deposit ratio, and the desired ratio of bank reserves to deposits
- the structure of the Federal Reserve System

- the instruments of monetary policy, or how the Federal Reserve System influences the money supply, including open-market operations, reserve requirements, and discount window policy
- how the money multiplier is influenced by the Federal Reserve System

DEFINITIONS OF MONEY

A **DEMAND DEPOSIT** is a checking account balance that can be obtained on demand from a depository institution.

Money is defined in terms of how it is used. The most important function of money is to serve as a medium of exchange when it passes from hand to hand in trade for goods and services or in paying debts.[1] Money is accepted not for its own sake but for what it will buy. When we think of money in today's society, we usually think in terms of currency and demand deposits. **Demand deposits** are often called checking accounts.

Commercial banks used to be the only institutions able to create money through demand deposits. In the last decade, however, other financial institutions such as savings and loans and credit unions have been allowed to compete with commercial banks through interest-earning checking accounts such as NOW accounts.

In 1980, Congress passed the Depository Institutions Deregulation and Monetary Control Act (known as DIDMCA), which permits all deposit institutions to offer NOW accounts and allows commercial banks to provide automatic transfer services (ATS) from savings to checking accounts. Because of the complex nature of today's banking situation, any reference to commercial banks in this chapter could just as easily mean other depository institutions such as savings and loan associations, credit unions, and savings banks. DIDMCA has extended the control of the Federal Reserve over all deposit institutions.

The money supply can be measured statistically in different ways. The Federal Reserve System's official measures of the monetary aggregates for 1992 are shown in Table 12-1.[2]

The M1 aggregate consists of currency; demand deposits at commercial banks; other checkable deposits such as negotiable orders of withdrawal (NOW and Super NOW); automatic transfer service (ATS) accounts; credit union share draft accounts; and checkable deposits at thrift institutions.

M2 includes all assets in M1 plus savings; small-denomination time deposits (less than $100,000); overnight repurchase agreements (RPs); overnight Eurodollars; and money market deposit accounts (MMDAs).

The M3 aggregate consists of M2 plus large-denomination time deposits and term RP liabilities (in amounts of $100,000 or more) issued by commercial banks and thrift institutions. These assets are not as liquid as those in the narrower measures of the money stock.

The largest monetary aggregate is L, and equals to M3 plus the nonbank public holdings of U.S. savings bonds, short-term Treasury securities, commer-

---

[1]For a discussion of the other functions of money (store of wealth, unit of account, and standard of deferred payment) see Chapter 13. There is also a good discussion by the Council of Economic Advisors in the *Economic Report of the President* (1992), p. 373.

[2]Some minor items are not included in the discussion of the monetary aggregates. For a detailed discussion, see the most recent Federal Reserve *Bulletin*.

TABLE 12-1
Monetary Aggregates,
November 1992 (billions of
dollars)

Each of the monetary aggregates contains items that could be considered "money," providing alternative measures of liquidity for use in analyzing money in the economy.

M1	$1,034.9
M2	3,471.7
M3	4,127.7
L	5,024.8

SOURCE: *Federal Reserve Bulletin* (June 1993).

cial paper, and bankers' acceptances, net of money market mutual fund holdings of these assets. Which of these measures (M1, M2, M3, or L) is most important?[3] Each of these measures has its theoretical and practical strengths and weaknesses as a guide to monetary policy operations. Let us now turn to the conceptual framework of the money creation process and see what role high-powered money and these other factors play in the production of money.

MONEY CREATION: THE CONCEPTUAL FRAMEWORK

In this section, we develop a basic conceptual framework of commercial banking to show how the interaction of the public's and the commercial banks' decision-making processes provides a stable equilibrium of the nominal money stock. Before we can do this, however, we must first explore the various factors affecting the money stock, such as the monetary base or high-powered money, in the desired ratios of currency to demand deposits and reserves to demand deposits.

High-Powered Money and the Money Stock

To understand the basic concept of high-powered money and its relationship to the money stock, we start by assuming there is a single commercial bank, operating in a community where the public desires to hold both currency C and demand deposits D. The money stock is expressed as equation 12.1:

$$M = C + D. \tag{12.1}$$

---

[3]See John R. Walter, "Monetary Aggregates: A User's Guide," Federal Reserve Bank of Richmond *Economic Review* (January/February 1989), pp. 20–28.

In this community the monetary base or high-powered money H consists of the sum of currency held by the public C and currency held by the commercial bank, which are called reserves R. Therefore, the monetary base (high-powered money) is defined as

$$H = C + R. \tag{12.2}$$

The monetary base is called high-powered money because it is used to determine the stock of money. In order to show the variables that affect the stock of money, we present a more specific expression (12.3) for the stock of money M by dividing equation 12.1 by 12.2:

$$\frac{M}{H} = \frac{C + D}{C + R}. \tag{12.3}$$

Equation 12.3 shows the relationship between the total stock of money M and high-powered money H. A given monetary base can result in different-sized monetary stocks depending on the decisions and actions of both the public and the commercial banks.

CURRENCY is coins minted by the U.S. Treasury and paper money such as Federal Reserve notes.

The public has the choice of holding money either as **currency** C or in checkable deposits D. What the public actually does can be seen by looking at the **actual currency-deposit ratio:**

$$c = \frac{C}{D},$$

The ACTUAL CURRENCY-DEPOSIT RATIO is the actual ratio of currency held by the public to demand deposits.

where C is total currency in the hands of the public and D is the checkable deposits owned by the public. The bank may choose to lend out reserves, thus supporting additional deposits, or hold reserves. The extent to which the commercial bank lends out reserves is reflected by the **actual reserve-deposit ratio:**

$$r = \frac{R}{D},$$

The ACTUAL RESERVE-DEPOSIT RATIO is the ratio of commercial bank reserves to deposits.

where R is the total amount of reserves on hand at the commercial bank and D is the bank's deposit liabilities, that is, the deposits made by the public in the commercial bank and held by the bank. If we divide the right-hand side of equation 12.3 by D, where $c = C/D$ and $r = R/D$, we obtain

$$\frac{M}{H} = \frac{C/D + 1}{C/D + R/D} = \frac{(1 + c)}{(c + r)}. \tag{12.4}$$

Equation 12.4 shows that the ratio of the stock of money M to high-powered money H is equal to the ratio $(1 + c)/(c + r)$, which depends on the actual currency-deposit ratio, and the actual reserve-deposit ratio.

The ratio $(1 + c)/(c + r)$ is called the money multiplier, and its value depends on the currency-deposit ratio c and on the reserve ratio r. Smaller values of c, the currency-deposit ratio, mean that the public wants to hold smaller and smaller proportions of currency to demand deposits as money. This implies that banks will hold larger amounts of any given amount of high-powered money, which is the raw material from which they can, by making loans, create deposits and money. Smaller values of c are thus associated with a larger money multiplier. Smaller values of r, the reserve-deposit ratio (or, simply, the reserve ratio), mean that the bank will be able to lend out a larger proportion of any given amount of cash reserves. These loans become deposits (and money) to be held by the public. Smaller r values, other things equal, indicate that the money multiplier is larger. From equation 12.4 we also find that the money multiplier can be expressed as the ratio of the stock of money M to high-powered money H.

To further examine the concept of the money multiplier, we rearrange equation 12.4 as 12.5:

$$M = \frac{1 + c}{c + r} \cdot H = mm \cdot H, \tag{12.5}$$

where mm is the money multiplier, a value larger than 1. The stock of money M is equal to the money multiplier mm multiplied by the stock of high-powered money H. It should be recognized that equation 12.5 is an identity, true by definition. High-powered money H is considered by economists to be an input in the production of money because \$1 of high-powered money will be multiplied by some factor mm that is greater than 1, since r is less than 1.

The Money Multiplier, the Currency to Deposit Ratio, and the Desired Reserve Ratio

In examining the money multiplier, a distinction must be made between the two ways we can view the public's currency-deposit ratio and the commercial bank's reserve-deposit ratio. Given the values for currency C, demand deposits D, and reserves R, we can calculate the actual ratios for c and r. But it must be understood that these actual ratios calculated from the data may not necessarily equal the *desired* ratio of the public and the commercial bank.

To assist in our understanding of why the desired and actual ratios may not be equal, let us first think briefly about the public's desired holdings of currency and demand deposits. The public's **desired currency-deposit ratio,** $c^d = C^d/D^d$, depends on a number of variables such as the bank's service charges, confidence in the bank, and alternative forms of transactions payments. The subterranean—or underground—economy, illegal exchanges, or other activities that people desire to conceal can also have an impact on the public's currency-deposit ratio. For example, the black market activities developed during World War II resulted in the public's holding more cash to deposits. We find, then, that for any given quantity of money the public would like to hold as an asset, there is a desired distribution of money holding between currency and demand deposits.

The **DESIRED CURRENCY-DEPOSIT RATIO** is a certain percentage of demand deposits that money holders want to hold as currency.

Suppose the public's desired currency-deposit ratio is .5. If c^d is .5 then for every $100 of currency held, the public wants to hold $200 in demand deposits. The question is, why does the public desire this particular currency-deposit ratio? Why not some other value?

The public's decision about the desired currency-deposit ratio c^d depends on the benefits and costs of holding money in alternative forms. Some of the benefits of holding demand deposits are safety and the convenience of using commercial banks' accounting services for personal finance. On the other hand, the disadvantages of holding demand deposits are the occasional difficulty in cashing personal checks, especially out-of-town checks; service charges on checking accounts; and the possibility of commercial bank failure. Holding currency, instead of demand deposits, also has its disadvantages. There is always more relative danger in carrying around $10,000 in cash that could be stolen or lost than in holding $5 to buy a movie ticket.

If the public's actual holdings of currency to deposits are not in equilibrium with its desired currency-deposit ratio, it will adjust its actual currency-deposit holdings until both the actual and the desired ratios are in equilibrium. Equilibrium is reached when the desired currency-deposit ratio equals the actual ratio. That is, $c^d = c$.

The DISCOUNT RATE is the interest rate that the Fed charges a deposit institution for a loan.

A CENTRAL BANK is a banker's bank. Commercial banks are regulated by central banks.

LEGAL RESERVES are reserves that depository institutions are allowed by law to claim as reserves, such as deposits held at a Federal Reserve bank.

The commercial bank is similar to the public in that the bank's desired reserve-deposit ratio, r^d, may not equal the bank's actual ratio r. A commercial bank's desired reserve-deposit ratio is also a function of a number of variables such as the return on bonds or on loans; the **discount rate**—the interest rate charged to a commercial bank when it borrows from the **central bank** (Federal Reserve); the federal funds rate—the interest rate a bank must pay for an overnight loan when it borrows from another commercial bank; and overall economic conditions in the United States. When the Federal Reserve imposes a *legal reserve requirement* on the commercial bank, requiring a commercial bank to hold a percentage of its demand deposits on reserve, these **legal reserves** may express only the commercial bank's minimum desired reserve-deposit ratio. A commercial bank may want to hold a reserve-deposit ratio greater than the minimum required by the Fed, a common practice of commercial banks in the Great Depression of the 1930s, especially during the 1937–38 period.

The currency to deposit ratio and reserve-deposit ratio are of theoretical importance, but also of great practical importance, and variations in these ratios can cause painful contractions of the money supply. For a historical example, see the Insight: "The Panic of 1907 and Its Relevance for Monetary Policy Control."

What happens if a commercial bank's actual reserve-deposit ratio is not in line with its desired ratio? The commercial bank will adjust its actual reserve-deposit ratio until the actual reserve-deposit ratio equals the desired ratio. Banks are in equilibrium when $r^d = r = R/D$. In the latter part of the chapter, we also show how changes in both the desired ratios and high-powered money can affect demand deposits and the money stock.

THE PANIC OF 1907 AND ITS RELEVANCE FOR MONETARY CONTROL

An examination of nineteenth- and early twentieth-century history indicates that panics were a continuing feature of the period. Panics are associated with severe reductions in real output, prices, and the money stock. One of the most severe business contractions of the pre-Federal Reserve era was the Panic of 1907. What causes financial panics? The answer provides some essential insights into the causes of monetary instability, today as well as yesterday.

While economic historians have offered a number of reasons for panics, such as too little money circulating in the economy relative to too many goods, simplistic views like these fail to take account of the interrelationships between the monetary base, currency, demand deposits, and the total money stock. These relationships shed light on the Panic of 1907 and on earlier (and later) financial panics.[a]

Over short periods, there was a general inconvertibility between currency and demand deposits. National bank notes, silver certificates, and U.S. notes, which comprised most of the currency in circulation as well as the cash reserves for the banking system, were fairly fixed in supply. The National Banking Act of 1863 had placed limitations on the ability of national banks to create national bank notes. Silver certificates had been issued against a specific amount of silver purchased from silver producers by Congress. While specie (gold) fluctuated, its quantity depended greatly upon the whims of international trade in an era of international bimetallic and gold standards. Since the government's stock of money, therefore, was fairly inelastic over short periods, the monetary base or high-powered money, which commercial banks used as deposit reserves, was also fixed. Any additional currency demand by the public could cause a reduction in reserves held by the commercial banks.

Given that the banking system was on a fractional reserve basis, currency withdrawn from banks meant that bankers had to call (not renew) loans of businesses when they came due. This bank action brought about a reduction in business demand deposits. These currency withdrawals caused further losses of bank cash reserves. Thus, a change in the composition of the public's money holdings (i.e., currency-deposit ratio) produced a change in the total money supply.

Most financial panics can be analyzed in these terms. Either seasonal or unexpected withdrawal of currency from only a few commercial banks could alter the currency-deposit ratio and create problems for the whole banking system. Moreover, if these withdrawals caused a few bank failures, the desired currency-deposit ratio would further increase. Money holders (the public) begin to believe that banks in general are becoming unsafe if just a few banks close their doors. A frightened public withdraws currency from its banks, which in turn creates a fall in the money stock; prices drop and industrial production and employment go down. This is what happened in 1907.

The Bank Panic of 1907 started in mid- to late October of 1907 when the public scrambled for liquidity (cash), forcing runs on the New York clearinghouse banks by correspondent banks. On October 22, the Knickerbocker Trust Company, one of the three largest trust companies in New York, had to suspend payments of cash for demand deposits outstanding. This action by the Knickerbocker Trust Company caused runs on other New York banks. To keep the other New York banks from failing, financier J. P. Morgan organized a money pool of $25 million and clearinghouses made loans from government deposits. These loan measures to New York banks provided only temporary relief because by now country and interior banks were frightened, and they began to demand currency from their New York correspondent banks, which ultimately forced these banks to restrict payments to the public. Some private banks also tried to stem the bank panic by supplying money, which was not legal tender, to the banking system. Clearing-house banks and an emergency association of banks issued bank clearinghouse loan certificates to individual banks in return for the bank's own obligations. These clearinghouse certificates were then issued by the individual banks to their customers and circulated as money. The final result was a nationwide closing of banks and a fall in the money stock by 5 percent, although the private banks had injected 10 percent in high-powered money after its initial decline in 1907.

Unfortunately, this increase in the money stock and demand deposits was not the final result. The public was frightened that banks would fail and the banks, in turn, were afraid they would have to restrict payments to the public. These fears produced an increase in the desired currency-deposit ratio (c^d) and desired reserve-deposit ratio (r^d). Thus, the attempt by the public to change the composition of the money stock along with the bank's desires to hold more cash reserves to meet the public's demand for cash led to a reduction in the stock of money. Even though some private banks helped to reduce currency drains from other private banks by increasing the quantity of high-powered money, the Panic of 1907 reveals a source of instability in all banking systems, both regulated and nonregulated, which is a change in the desires of both the public and the banks to hold more cash relative to deposits. ❑

NOTE: [a]Milton Friedman and Anna J. Schwartz, *A Monetary History of the United States, 1867–1960* (Princeton, NJ: Princeton University Press, 1964), pp. 156–73.

THE STRUCTURE OF THE U.S. CENTRAL BANK

The Federal Reserve System, or the Fed, was established on December 23, 1913, when Woodrow Wilson signed the Federal Reserve Act. The founders of the system were attempting to find a way to counter the periodic financial panics that had occurred in our country. Today, the main purposes of the Fed are to regulate the supply of money to the country; to supervise commercial banks; to provide banking services for the U.S. Treasury; to hold reserves of commercial banks; and to provide for check collection and clearing.

Board of Governors

The Federal Reserve organizational chart is shown in Figure 12-1. At the top of the Federal Reserve System is the Board of Governors, which is composed of seven members appointed by the President of the United States with the approval of the Senate. The chairman of the board plays a dominant role in the formulation of monetary policy.

Federal Open-Market Committee

The Federal Open-Market Committee (FOMC) is an important group within the structure of the system. This committee consists of twelve voting members: the seven members of the Board of Governors plus five presidents from the twelve Federal Reserve banks. All of the presidents of the Federal Reserve banks attend the FOMC meetings, but voting positions are allocated as follows. First, the president of the Federal Reserve Bank of New York is always allocated a voting slot, since the open-market operations are conducted by this bank. The other four voting positions rotate. The presidents of the Chicago and Cleveland banks share one voting position, which they rotate between themselves. The presidents of the other nine banks (Atlanta, Boston, Dallas, Kansas City, Minneapolis, Philadelphia, Richmond, St. Louis, and San

FIGURE 12-1
Federal Reserve
Organizational Chart

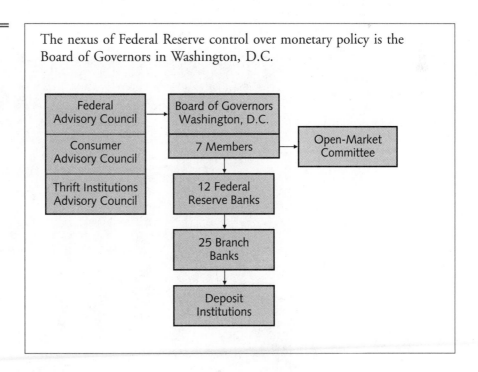

The nexus of Federal Reserve control over monetary policy is the Board of Governors in Washington, D.C.

Francisco) share three voting positions, which are rotated among these nine banks.

The FOMC determines many of the monetary policy actions for the Fed. One method used by the FOMC to control the money supply is the purchase and sale of government securities in the open market, which comprises the dealers in government securities located in New York City. This is the main method used by the Fed for day-to-day monetary control. We will see in a later section how the Fed uses open-market operations to affect the banking system and control the money stock.

The Federal Advisory Council, the Consumer Advisory Council, and the Thrift Institutions Advisory Council

The Federal Advisory Council consists of one member from each Federal Reserve District and meets with the Federal Reserve Board at least four times a year to discuss business and financial conditions and to make advisory recommendations. The Consumer Advisory Council, which includes both consumers and creditor representatives, advises the Board of Governors on its implementation of consumer regulations and other consumer-related matters. The Thrift Institutions Advisory Council, established after the passage of the Monetary Control Act of 1980, provides information and views on the special needs and problems of thrift institutions. This group is made up of represen-

PHOTO 12-1
The Federal Reserve Building in Washington, DC Is the Nexus of Government Control over Money in the United States.

tatives of mutual savings banks, savings and loan associations, and credit unions.

Federal Reserve Banks

There are twelve Federal Reserve banks geographically dispersed among twelve districts (see Figure 12-2). For example, the Federal Reserve Bank of Atlanta serves the sixth district, the outlined area surrounding Atlanta, shown in Figure 12-2. Most of the districts have branches, and there are twenty-five branches altogether. Each of the twelve Federal Reserve banks controls and tends to the needs of the depository institutions in its district. However, the power and control over monetary policy really resides in the Board of Governors in Washington and, most particularly, in the chairman.

FIGURE 12-2

The Federal Reserve System (boundaries of Federal Reserve districts and their branch territories)

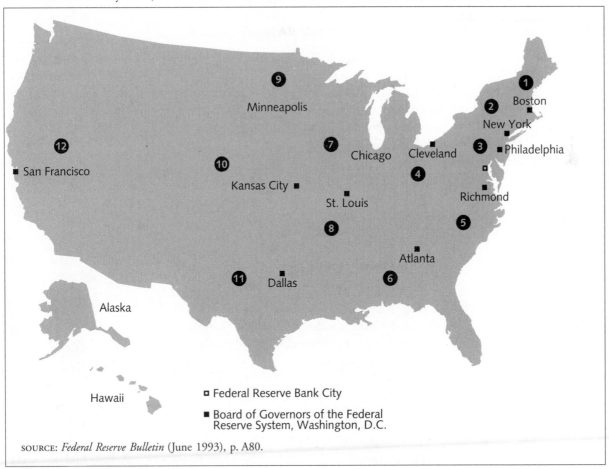

SOURCE: *Federal Reserve Bulletin* (June 1993), p. A80.

Deposit Institutions

The banks and other depository institutions (financial institutions that accept checking and time deposits) comprise our monetary system and consist of approximately 12,000 commercial banks, 2,100 savings and loan associations, 12,000 credit unions, and 500 mutual savings banks. In the past, a distinction was made between commercial banks that were and were not members of the Federal Reserve System. Commercial banks that were not members of the system did not enjoy the same benefits as member commercial banks. For example, nonmember banks could not borrow from the Fed nor use the Fed's check-clearing system. In March 1980, the passage of the DIDMCA changed the distinction between nonmember and member commercial banks. The act requires all deposit institutions to keep a certain percentage of their deposits on reserve with the Federal Reserve district banks, and allows all deposit institutions equal access to the Federal Reserve discount window and to check-clearing services.

THE FEDERAL RESERVE AND THE MONETARY BASE

MONETARY POLICY is decisions by the Fed about the appropriate level of the money stock. It consists of varying the amount of money in the economy to affect spending.

The potential size of the nominal money supply depends primarily on the quantity of reserves held by the commercial banks and other depository institutions. The actions of the Federal Reserve can affect the quantity of commercial bank reserves and thus high-powered money. These actions are called **monetary policy.** The overall picture of monetary policy can be viewed as

A. Monetary policymakers
   1. Fed's Board of Governors
   2. FOMC
B. Major monetary policy tools (instruments)
   1. Legal reserve requirements
   2. Open-market operations
   3. Discount rate policy
C. Monetary targets
   1. Reserves (nonborrowed reserves, etc.)
   2. Monetary aggregates (M1, M2, M3, and L)
   3. Market interest rates, federal funds, etc.
D. Economic goals
   1. Price stability
   2. Full employment
   3. Economic growth
   4. Balance of payments

The monetary policymakers (the Fed's Board of Governors and FOMC) want to achieve certain economic goals such as price stability and full

FIGURE 12-3
The Conduct of Monetary
Policy by the Fed

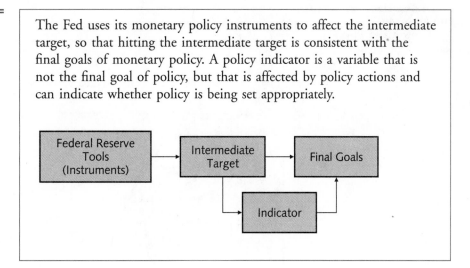

The Fed uses its monetary policy instruments to affect the intermediate target, so that hitting the intermediate target is consistent with the final goals of monetary policy. A policy indicator is a variable that is not the final goal of policy, but that is affected by policy actions and can indicate whether policy is being set appropriately.

employment. However, the Fed cannot directly control these economic goals. It can only work through intermediate steps to obtain them. The Fed can have an impact on commercial bank reserves and on the ability of these reserves to support demand deposits by changing the monetary policy tools (also called instruments) such as discount rates or open-market operations. The Fed does not directly control the intermediate targets (i.e., the money stock), but only the monetary tools that affect the intermediate targets, which in turn have an effect on the economic goals.

Figure 12-3 shows the scheme currently used by the Fed in conducting monetary policy. Under intermediate targeting, the Fed first sets its primary goals for the economy in terms of the rate of growth of final output and the rate of inflation. It then estimates the level or the growth rate for its intermediate target or targets that is most consistent with achieving the final goals. Finally, it sets its policy tools (instruments) at levels commensurate with hitting the intermediate target. Note also that the Fed may use an indicator in the conduct of its monetary policy. An *indicator* is some variable that is influenced by monetary policy and that gives early information on the final possible outcome for the goals. For example, data on retail sales provide one of many possible indicators and are available more quickly than real GDP estimates.

In 1975 Congress began requiring the Fed to formulate monetary policy in terms of monetary growth-rate targets and to report these targets in advance back to Congress.[4] Under the requirements set forth in the Full Employment and Balanced Growth Act of 1978, monetary growth-rate targets have generally been set only once a year. The Fed submits a report to Congress twice

---

[4]The Fed began announcing target ranges following the passage of House Concurrent Resolution 133 in March 1975. See Alfred Broaddus and Marvin Goodfriend, "Base Drift and the Longer Run Growth of M1: Experience from a Decade of Monetary Targeting," Federal Reserve Bank of Richmond *Economic Record* (November/December 1984), pp. 3–14.

FIGURE 12-4
M2 Growth and Target
Ranges

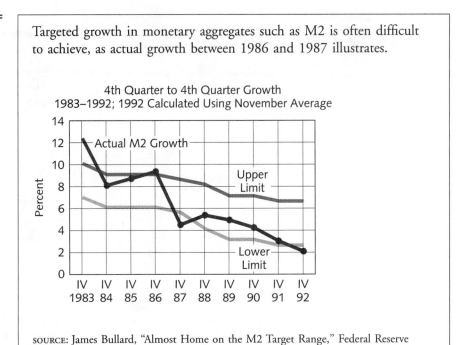

Targeted growth in monetary aggregates such as M2 is often difficult to achieve, as actual growth between 1986 and 1987 illustrates.

4th Quarter to 4th Quarter Growth
1983–1992; 1992 Calculated Using November Average

SOURCE: James Bullard, "Almost Home on the M2 Target Range," Federal Reserve Bank of St. Louis *Monetary Trends,* December 1992, p. 1.

a year, in February and in July. The February report discusses the annual monetary growth-rate targets for the current calendar year, which are expressed as a growth-rate range from the fourth quarter of the previous year to the fourth quarter of the current year. The act provides that the Fed may reconsider the annual ranges at any time. The period to which the annual ranges apply, however, may not be changed. The base period (the fourth quarter of the previous year) would remain the same even if the Fed decided to change the desired growth rates of the monetary aggregates for the year.

At the July meeting and in its midyear report to Congress, the Fed reviews its progress toward achieving its monetary growth targets. At this July meeting it also establishes tentative monetary growth ranges for the following calendar year.[5] Because of a breakdown in the relationship between M1 and nominal GDP in the 1980s, the Fed dropped M1 from its list of intermediate policy targets in 1986 and substituted M2 as its principal monetary aggregate. The Fed determines the monetary growth-rate target for M2 and M3 based on past data and staff forecasts of money demand and of the behavior of the economy for given monetary growth rates. Figure 12-4 illustrates the target ranges for M2 set by the Fed and the actual growth rates of M2 for the period 1983–1992.

[5]See R. W. Hafer, "The FOMC in 1983–84: Setting Policy in an Uncertain World," Federal Reserve Bank of St. Louis *Review* (April 1985), pp. 15–36.

TABLE 12-2
The Monetary Base,
November 1992 (billions of
dollars)

SOURCES		USES	
U.S. GOVERNMENT SECURITIES AND OTHER ASSETS	383.5	CURRENCY IN CIRCULATION	290.0
LOANS TO COMMERCIAL BANKS AND OTHER DEPOSITORY INSTITUTIONS	.1	RESERVES	93.6
MONETARY BASE	383.6		383.6

We find, then, that the Fed's control over the final economic goals is an indirect one and that there are time lags between the implementation of policy tools and their effects on the monetary targets and on the final goals. In the following section, we discuss the Fed's use of monetary policy tools (instruments).

The Legal Reserve Requirement

The reader may recall that the money stock (M1) is composed of both currency in circulation and demand deposits at depository institutions. The Federal Reserve does not actually control the total money stock but only a portion of it called the monetary base or the stock of high-powered money. Table 12-2 shows the monetary base for a simplified balance sheet for the Fed. The assets are the sources of the monetary base and the liabilities are the uses of it. Two of the most important sources of the monetary base are indicated in the left-hand side of the sheet. They are the Fed's holding of government securities and loans to commercial banks. On the right-hand side of the sheet, we find the largest use of the monetary base, which is currency in circulation (i.e., in the hands of the public). The remainder of the base serves as reserves of the commercial banks, consisting of deposits at the Federal Reserve and vault cash held by the commercial banks.

The **monetary base** or high-powered money, therefore, is currency in circulation plus total commercial bank reserves held either as vault cash (currency) or as reserve deposits at the Federal Reserve banks. Notice that this definition of the monetary base now includes commercial bank reserves held by the Fed. Commercial banks are required by the Fed to keep a certain percentage of their demand deposits on reserve (called **required reserves**) either as deposits with the district Federal Reserve bank or as vault cash. The level of the **required reserve ratio,** which is the percentage of deposits that

MONETARY BASE is currency in the hands of the public plus reserves of deposit institutions held either at Federal Reserve banks or as vault cash in deposit institutions.

REQUIRED RESERVES are the minimum amount of legal reserves that a deposit institution is legally required to hold.

The REQUIRED RESERVE RATIO is the ratio of required reserves to deposits.

commercial banks must hold as reserves, is referred to as the Fed's legal reserve requirement.[6]

The Fed controls the demand deposit component of the money stock by setting the legal reserve requirement on demand deposits. If, for example, the public deposited $10,000 of currency in its checking deposit in, say, Alpha Bank, and the level of the required reserve ratio was 20 percent, the Alpha Bank would have to keep $2,000 on reserve with the Fed. The maximum it could lend would be $8,000, which is called **excess reserves.** Excess reserves are reserves held by a commercial bank in excess of required reserves. A change in the required reserve ratio by the Fed to 15 percent would mean that Alpha Bank would have to hold only $1,500 in reserves and could now loan $8,500 (excess reserves), if it so desired.

EXCESS RESERVES are the difference between actual reserves and required reserves.

A change in the reserve requirement by the Fed plays a dual role in the banking and monetary system. Such a change not only produces changes in the stock of a commercial bank's excess reserves but makes high-powered money (the monetary base) either more or less high powered. This result can be verified by using the money multiplier equation from earlier in this chapter. Recall equation 12.5:

$$M = H \cdot mm,$$

where M is the stock of money, H is high-powered money, and

$$mm = \frac{1 + c}{c + r}$$

is the money multiplier, with c the currency-deposit ratio and r the required reserve ratio.[7] The reserve ratio consists of the required reserve ratio, r_r, and the banks excess reserve ratio, r_e. Given the stock of high-powered money H, an increase in the required reserve ratio r would reduce the value of the money multiplier mm. Thus, an increase in the required reserve-deposit ratio reduces the quantity of deposits that can be supported by a given level of reserves, even though total bank reserves have not changed. A smaller money multiplier means a reduction in the stock of money M. Likewise, a reduction in r increases the value of the money multiplier mm and thereby leads to an increase in the stock of money M.

There are some qualifications to the theoretical process described above. The overall impact of a change in the required reserve-deposit ratio depends on the public's demand for loans, on the reserve position of the commercial banks, and on the general economic conditions of the economy.

---

[6]In 1992, the statutory reserve requirements were 10 percent on certain transactions (checkable) deposits and 0 on time deposits.

[7]Before, r^d was the desired reserve-deposit ratio. Now, r_r is the required reserve-deposit ratio. The bank's desired ratio may be greater or equal to the required ratio. However, for simplicity we assume that the desired ratio r^d equals the required reserve-deposit ratio r.

Open-Market Operations

The Fed holds government bonds in its asset portfolio. When it buys or sells these bonds, it can influence high-powered money and hence the stock of money. This discretionary policy is the Fed's most important tool for controlling the money supply. **Open-market operations** are defined as the buying or selling of government bonds in the open market. These affect the reserves of commercial banks and depository institutions, and hence the money supply. The decision to buy or sell government bonds is made by the Fed's Open-Market Committee (FOMC) and these decisions of the FOMC are carried out by the trading desk of the Federal Reserve Bank of New York, which operates directly with certain New York securities dealers.

While the Fed buys and sells through bond dealers, open-market operations can be viewed more easily if we assume that transactions take place directly with the nonbank public and the commercial banks. Let us examine two cases. In the first case, the Fed sells $20 million in securities to the commercial banks.

Simplified balance sheets or "T-accounts" are useful in explaining the operations of commercial banks. T-accounts make use of the "accounting identity," sometimes called the **balance sheet equation,** whereby the sum of all assets must always equal the sum of all liabilities and net worth. T-accounts may also be used to show *changes* in assets and liabilities. Table 12-3 shows only the changes in the relevant T-accounts after an open-market sale. Commercial banks have lost $20 million dollars in reserve assets and gained $20 million in government securities. The Fed loses assets and reserve liabilities in the amount of $20 million. It should be recognized that the excess reserves of the commercial banks, which are the basis for making loans to the nonbank public, have fallen by $20 million. The Fed's open-market sale causes the stock

OPEN-MARKET OPERATIONS are the Fed's purchase and sale in the open private market of various government securities.

The **BALANCE SHEET EQUATION** shows the sum of all assets equal to the sum of all liabilities and capital accounts.

TABLE 12-3   The Fed Sells Securities to Commercial Banks (millions of dollars)

The Fed sells $20 million in securities to a commercial bank. Now the Fed's assets are reduced by the amount of the security sold. The bank receives the security, an increase in its assets, but it also must pay for the security, which it does by giving the Fed $20 million from its reserve account at the Fed. Thus, the bank has now rearranged its assets, reducing reserves by $20 million but increasing securities by $20 million. The Fed has reduced its assets by selling the bond, and reduced its liabilities because the reserve account of the commercial bank has been reduced by $20 million.

COMMERCIAL BANKS		FEDERAL RESERVE	
ASSETS	LIABILITIES	ASSETS	LIABILITIES
(+) SECURITIES $20		(−) SECURITIES $20	(−) RESERVES $20
(−) RESERVES $20			

of high-powered money to decline as indicated by the reduction in reserves (−) in Table 12-3. This reduction in high-powered money leads to a decline in the money stock. If the Fed decides to conduct an open-market purchase and buy $20 million in securities from the commercial banks, then we would have the opposite results. The stock of high-powered money would rise, causing an increase in the stock of money.

What if the Fed sells government securities to the public? In this case there is an immediate decline in the demand deposit component of the stock of money.

Table 12-4 shows the T-account. The public loses demand deposits when it buys government securities and the commercial banks lose reserves at the Fed of $20 million. The quantity of high-powered money has decreased in the banking system. The opposite results are obtained when the Fed buys government securities.

In terms of the model developed in an earlier section, it is a simple matter to describe the result of a change in open-market operations. When the Fed sells (buys) government securities, there is a decline (rise) in the stock of high-powered money.

The theoretical process described in the above model is subject to an important qualification that other things remain constant. When open-market operations are conducted by the Fed and over the period when the effects are working themselves out, loan demand by the public may change; banks may

---

TABLE 12-4   The Fed Sells Securities to the Public (millions of dollars)

The Fed sells $20 million in securities to the public, which pays with a check against its demand deposits. Thus, the public rearranges its assets, holding $20 million less in demand deposits and $20 million more in securities. The Fed has a reduction in its assets of $20 million, but it receives a check for $20 million, which it presents to the commercial bank for payment. When the commercial bank clears the check, it reduces the public's demand deposit account by $20 million and also hands the Fed $20 million from its reserve deposits at the Fed. This lowers the amount the Fed owes the commercial bank, a reduction in Fed liabilities to match the reduction in assets when the security was sold.

PUBLIC		FEDERAL RESERVE		COMMERCIAL BANKS	
ASSETS	LIABILITIES	ASSETS	LIABILITIES	ASSETS	LIABILITIES
(+) SECURITIES $20		(−) SECURITIES $20	(−) RESERVES $20	(−) RESERVES $20	(−) DEMAND DEPOSITS $20
(−) DEMAND DEPOSITS $20					

not be fully loaded up; the public's currency-deposit ratio may be altered; the Treasury may be buying or selling government securities; or a number of other factors may come into play. The conduct of monetary policy is hampered by these real-world difficulties. Nevertheless, day-to-day, week-to-week, and month-to-month changes in high-powered money take place, and the Fed has to be able to account for them in determining policy.

The Discount Rate

Another tool of monetary control deals with a technique by which the Federal Reserve may lend to member banks. This tool is called *discounting*. Commercial banks may borrow from the Fed, just as the public borrows from commercial banks. The interest rate charged to a commercial bank for a temporary loan from the Fed is called the *discount rate*. Under the Monetary Control Act of 1980, any depository institution issuing checking accounts or time deposits has the same discount and borrowing privilege at the Fed as do member banks.

NONBORROWED RESERVES are reserves supplied by the Fed to deposit institutions through open-market operations.

Total reserves supplied by the Fed can be broken down into those supplied at the discount window, called borrowed reserves (*BR*), and those supplied through open-market operations, called **nonborrowed reserves** (*NBR*). The monetary base, therefore, can also be expressed as the sum of *BR, NBR,* and currency held by the nonbank public (*C*). Thus, the money-stock equation can be rewritten as

$$M = mm \cdot (BR + NBR + C).$$

A change in the discount rate affects market interest rates through their impact on borrowing from the Fed.[8] When a commercial bank borrows from the Fed, there is an increase in its reserves. The simple effects can be demonstrated with T-accounts. The commercial bank borrows, let's say, $1 million from the Fed. The T-accounts of Table 12-5 show not only that the commercial bank's reserve assets have increased by $1 million but that its liabilities have risen by the same amount. Turning to the Fed's balance sheet, it indicates a rise in loan asset of $1 million balanced by an increase in commercial bank reserves of $1 million.

The discount rate allows the Fed to restrain or encourage a commercial bank in its borrowing by changing the cost of acquiring reserves through discounting. However, the Fed views borrowing by commercial banks not as a right but as a privilege, which is to be done only in time of need.

While commercial banks may be reluctant to borrow from the Fed, they do watch movements in the discount rate as an indication of Federal Reserve policy. The main influence of changes in the discount rate appears to be its

---

[8]See Daniel L. Thornton, "The Discount Rate and Market Interest Rates: What's the Connection?" Federal Reserve Bank of St. Louis *Review* (June/July 1982), pp. 3–14.

TABLE 12-5
The Fed Lends to a Commercial Bank (millions of dollars)

When the Fed lends $1 to a commercial bank, the Fed's assets increase by $1, and the Fed adds $1 to the bank's reserve account, increasing Fed liabilities by $1. The commercial bank receives an increase in its reserve account, an asset, and also an increase in its liabilities, the $1 it owes the Fed.

COMMERCIAL BANK		FEDERAL RESERVE BANK	
ASSETS	LIABILITIES	ASSETS	LIABILITIES
(+) RESERVES $1	(+) DUE FED $1	(+) LOANS $1	(+) MEMBER BANK RESERVES $1

psychological impact on the expectations of the public and the commercial banks. In other words, changes in the discount rate have "announcement effects" regarding a change in monetary policy. When the Fed lowers the discount rate, the public and the commercial banks visualize an expansion in the money supply and lower interest rates. When the discount rate is raised, commercial banks and the public anticipate that money will be tighter and interest rates will be higher. Consequently, commercial banks restrict credit, consider loan applications more critically, and raise their own rates.

MONETARY CONTROL AND THE FED

CREDIT is a promise of future payment in kind or in money, given in exchange for present money, goods, or services.

From the early years of the Federal Reserve System through the 1920s, the Fed relied on the discount rate as its primary instrument in managing credit conditions in the economy. The Fed simply influenced market interest rates and credit conditions by raising the discount rate to restrain credit and lowering it to encourage credit expansion. Commercial banks could easily borrow from the Fed when they needed reserves since the Fed set the discount rate below market rates. The Fed, therefore, was just accommodating the demand for reserves by the commercial banks. The result was that reserve requirements could not act as an effective constraint in credit expansion. During the 1920s **credit** had a period of rapid growth, reaching a peak in 1929. In the Great Depression of the 1930s, the demand for credit by the public declined. Commercial banks, fearing instability in currency demand, held large amounts of excess reserves. This meant that the legal (required) reserves were again not an important constraint on credit expansion. Beginning during World War II and continuing up through the Treasury-Federal Reserve Accord of 1951, the Fed's policy was to support the price of government bonds by holding interest rates down. Once again legal reserve requirements did not act as a restraint on the expansion of credit. Federal Reserve policy in the 1950s shifted from almost total concern with credit conditions to inclusion of the money stock as a relevant variable for policy. By the late 1970s, M1 became the primary intermediate policy target. This concern by the Fed with the monetary stock was accompanied by a belief that legal reserve requirements were useful for monetary control.[9]

The Fed's belief that reserve requirements are beneficial in controlling the money stock is generally based on the money multiplier. Recall the money stock expansion equation,

$$M = mm \cdot H,$$

where M is the money stock, H is high-powered money, and mm is the money multiplier. If the money multiplier is essentially constant, the Fed can closely control the amount of demand deposits through close control of reserves. In this method of monetary control, reserve requirements are important because they help to stabilize the money multiplier.

But in order to have a stable money multiplier, the Fed has to maintain its control over commercial bank reserves. If the volume of reserves is determined by the demand of the commercial banking system, then reserve requirements cannot constrain the expansion in the money stock. This was the case in the 1920s when demand for reserves was simply accommodated by the Fed.

NET FREE RESERVES are the difference between excess reserves and the borrowing at the Fed.

The FEDERAL FUNDS RATE is the rate charged a commercial bank when it borrows reserves from other commercial banks.

Throughout most of the 1950s and 1960s the Fed executed monetary policy by adjusting discount rates and targeting **net free reserves.** Net free reserves are defined as excess reserves of commercial banks minus their borrowed reserves from the Fed. The Fed achieved restraint on the economy by lowering the target for net free reserves and raising the discount rate. In the early 1970s net free reserves and the discount rate fell into disuse as operating variables. At that time, and throughout the 1970s, the Fed used the **federal funds rate** as the principal operating target of monetary policy. The federal funds rate is the rate of interest that commercial banks pay when they borrow reserves from each other. Since commercial banks are profit oriented and want to make loans, they usually attempt to keep excess reserves as low as possible. But an unexpected drain of reserves can cause a bank's reserves to fall below its required level. This deficiency in reserves can be made up by borrowing from other commercial banks that are temporarily holding excess reserves.[10]

---

[9]See Marvin Goodfriend and Monica Hargraves, "A Historical Assessment of the Rationales and Functions of Reserve Requirements," Federal Reserve Bank of Richmond *Economic Review* (March/April 1983), pp. 3–21. See also Stuart E. Weiner, "The Changing Role of Reserve Requirements in Monetary Policy," Federal Reserve Bank of Kansas City *Economic Review* (Fourth Quarter 1992), pp. 45–64.

[10]A bank can also borrow the excess deposits of nonfinancial corporations. The bank sells a Treasury bill, for example, to the corporation and agrees to buy it back in one or two days. These are referred to as repurchase agreements (RPs) or "repos." For a detailed discussion of repos, see Norman N. Bowsher, "Repurchase Agreements," in *Instruments of the Money Market* (Richmond, VA: Federal Reserve Bank of Richmond, 1981), pp. 52–58.

The federal funds rate reflects the cost of interbank borrowing—in essence, the price of nonborrowed reserves. If the supply of nonborrowed reserves is reduced, the immediate effect is an increase in the federal funds rate. Conversely, an increase in the supply of nonborrowed reserves will bring about a fall in the funds rate. When growth in the money stock was above the desired (target) growth path, the federal funds target was raised through open-market operations. The Fed sold government securities and drained reserves from the commercial banking system. If the Fed desired a more rapid monetary growth, then it would lower the federal funds target by buying government securities in the open market. This type of operation injected reserves into the commercial banking system.

The inflation of the 1970s and the tendency of the Fed to overshoot its intermediate monetary targets raised serious questions about the use of the federal funds rate as an operating target for monetary policy. On October 6, 1979, a major policy shift was announced by Paul Volcker, then chairman of the Federal Reserve Board. He stated that the Fed would begin to pay more attention to nonborrowed reserves as an operating target and less attention to day-to-day fluctuations in the federal funds rate. Thus, the federal funds rate was allowed to adjust to the forces of supply and demand in the federal funds market.

In 1980, with the passage of the Monetary Control Act, Congress extensively reformed the structure of reserve requirements. Prior to this act, reserve requirements for nonmember banks were set by various state banking authorities, whose reserve requirements generally were more lenient than those of the Federal Reserve System.[11] Because of the Fed's noninterest-earning reserve requirements, which put member banks at a competitive disadvantage relative to nonmember banks, commercial banks were leaving the Federal Reserve System to become state-chartered banks. The Fed argued that its ability to control the money stock was weakened as deposits moved outside its reserve requirement jurisdiction. The solution to the problem of Fed membership and deposit attribution was the DIDMCA. Under this act, all depository institutions, whether members of the Federal Reserve System or not, are required to hold reserves in accordance with Fed requirements. Reserve requirements were also made more uniform. Thus, reform in the Monetary Control Act was designed to improve monetary control. However, as we will see in Chapter 13, there were problems in trying to control M1 in the 1980s,

[11] Specifically, thirty of the fifty state banking authorities allowed banks to hold at least a portion of their reserves in interest-earning assets, thirty-six states did not require periodic reporting of reserve and deposit balances, and twenty-two had no monetary penalty for deficient banks. In contrast, members of the Fed had to hold reserves either in their vaults or on deposit at a Fed bank. These reserves earned no interest. Member banks reported their deposit and reserve balances to the Fed on a weekly basis, and a monetary penalty was enforced for deficient banks. For a detailed discussion of the Monetary Control Act, see Thomas F. Cargill and Gillian G. Garcia, *Financial Deregulation and Monetary Control* (Stanford, CA: Hoover Institution Press, Stanford University, 1982).

and even the current switch to M2 as a target is not without its difficulties. Professor Milton Friedman has been critical of the Fed because of its practice of changing targets. He has pointed out that the Fed hits its monetary bull's eye by simply repainting its target. To him, "monetary targets that meant something would contribute to both monetary and economic stability."[12] He notes that monetary targets that are repainted by the Fed due to convenience serve only to confuse the public. In 1982, the Fed abandoned its experiment with nonborrowed reserve targeting, returning to a borrowed reserve target, essentially a disguised federal funds rate target. However, the growth of M2 in the 1990s has been slower than can be explained by the traditional relationship to income and interest rates.[13] In the summer of 1993 the Fed announced a return to federal funds rate targeting and a deemphasis of the intermediate money targets. Policy procedures have come full circle.

The purpose of central bank control in the economy must always be kept firmly in mind. It is to control reserves and the money stock in order to affect economic activity. All countries are faced with the need for a central bank, especially those in the process of evolving towards market forms of production and exchange. See, for example, the Global Perspective, "The Role of a Central Bank in Mainland China's Economic Growth."

REGULATION OF DEPOSIT RATES: THE GARN–ST. GERMAIN ACT OF 1982

In the past, the savings and loan associations (S&Ls), savings banks, and credit unions that make up the thrift industry purchased short-term deposits from the public in order to make larger longer-term fixed loans. The thrift institutions made a profit by charging a higher rate on their loans than they paid on their deposits. They operated under the Fed's Regulation Q, which fixed the rate of interest they were allowed to pay on their time deposits. In time, however, market rates rose above the rates fixed by Regulation Q, and this situation led to *disintermediation*. That is, the public withdrew its funds from the thrift institutions and bought high-yielding assets, such as government securities and money market funds.

As interest rates continued their trend upward, the Fed made several concessions toward permitting market interest rates to be paid to small savers. Experimental permission for negotiable order of withdrawal accounts (NOWs) in the New England states allowed interest (at regulated rates) to be paid on

---

[12]See Milton Friedman, "The Fed Hasn't Changed Its Ways," *The Wall Street Journal* (August 20, 1985), p. 28. Also, for a discussion of instability in the demand for money and monetary targets, see Chapter 13.

[13]For a discussion of recent M2 behavior, see Bryon Higgins, "Policy Implications of Recent M2 Behavior," Federal Reserve Bank of Kansas City *Economic Review* (Third Quarter 1992), pp. 21–36.

THE ROLE OF A CENTRAL BANK IN MAINLAND CHINA'S ECONOMIC GROWTH

Since mainland China's market reform process started in 1978, the Chinese economy has grown at an average rate of almost 9 percent. Many economists predict it will sustain an average growth rate of at least 7 percent per year over the next 10 years. This suggests its gross domestic product, which is unofficially estimated to be as high as $1.2 trillion today, could possibly double by the early part of the twenty-first century, establishing the Republic of China as one of the top five economic powers.[a] Although its per capita income would still be low relative to other developed countries, the size of China's economy would have an impact on global trade, the flow of raw materials, and investment in capital goods. While the Republic of China would be an economic super-power, it would not be like Japan and compete as directly with the United States and European countries. Instead, it would

confine its production activities largely to low-tech industries and light manufacturing. One should recognize that the Republic of China is not really following the Western style of capitalism. Today China's model is a mixed economy where the Chinese leaders want to keep the means of production in the hands of the public sector. Control of the economy, however, is moving away from Beijing and into quasi-public companies operated either by provinces or towns.

The People's Bank in China plays the role of central bank, much as the Federal Reserve System does in the United States. The president of a district Federal Reserve Bank, in a recent speech in Beijing, has suggested that the Fed's experience in working with a rapidly changing, geographically diverse economy may provide a useful guide for the People's Bank of China. He pointed out some basic principles that the People's Bank may want to follow in helping the People's Republic of China continue to move to a market system. First, the People's Bank should not focus on any one policy but rather on the fact that in changing financial markets, a central bank's function is interrelated and must be care-

fully coordinated to maintain a country's financial stability. For example, the Federal Reserve not only conducts monetary policy, but plays an important role within the payments system. It provides many different functions such as check clearing and serving as lender of last resort. It is involved in supervising commercial banks, and it even plays a role in the foreign exchange markets. Coordinating a central bank's involvement in these activities is important to the efficient functioning of an economic and monetary system.

Second, the People's Bank must continue to focus its monetary policy on aggregate price stability. In a market economy, prices play an important role in the efficient allocation of resources, and contribute to economic growth. They play their role best when they function in an environment of aggregate price stability. Market efficiency is essential if an economy is to achieve its maximum potential for growth. Price stability should not be sacrificed for immediate, faster growth. It is shortsighted to adopt policies that temporarily spur the growth of the economy, but soon cause accelerating inflation.

Then the central bank has to move to a tighter monetary policy to prevent further infla tion These erratic policies create distortions leading to a misallocation of resources, and changes in the patterns of consumption and investment, which can cause a reduction in the long-run GDP potential of the economy. Thus, policy actions that may provide short-run benefits may be incompatible with maintaining the maximum rate of economic growth. China's history has indicated that excessive inflation or deflation has created social unrest between borrowers and lenders, between landlords and renters, and between workers and retirees. Price stability minimizes these inherent frictions and helps to maintain the overall long-run standard of living.

Third, the People's Bank needs a degree of independence from other government functions to achieve long-run price stability and long-run financial stability. Independence is important if monetary policy is not to become subservient to fiscal policy. Highly socialized countries have recognized that losses from state-owned businesses increase budget deficits. Therefore, central banks have been forced to monetize government debt— that is, government debt is converted into legal tender. A good example is Russia, where inflation threatens to undermine its reform efforts. Thus, the People's Bank of China needs to be independent if it plans to achieve its financial goals.

The final principle the Federal Reserve Bank president offered is that the People's Bank should pursue a single national monetary policy. Monetary policy cannot do away with regional imbalances in an economy. Financial resources flow inevitably to industries and regions where they can be the most produc-tive. Any attempt by the central bank to allocate credit to a specific region or uses is futile and can be counterproductive. As the People's Republic of China evolves to more fully integrated markets, this principle will increasingly apply. If the People's Bank lends at lower rates in one region of China than it does in other regions, it will not succeed since funds will inevitably flow to regions where the economy and loan demand are stronger. ❑

NOTE [a]Sources for this discussion are Thomas H. Hoenig, "China's Economic Growth with Price Stability: What Role for the Central Bank?" Federal Reserve Bank of Kansas City *Economic Review* (First Quarter 1993), pp. 5–10, and Joyce Barnathan, Pete Engardio, Lynne Curry, and Bruce Einhorn, "China: The Emerging Economic Powerhouse of the 21st Century," *Business Week* (May 17, 1993), p. 56.

money market certificates in June 1978. Automatic transfer service (ATS) accounts followed in November 1978.

The Monetary Control Act of 1980 phased out interest rate ceilings (Regulation Q) by 1986. Nevertheless, even after the passage of the act, the disintermediation problem continued because of the money market mutual fund industry, which offered a small-denomination, no minimum-maturity, market-interest rate deposit to the public. During the summer of 1980 interest rates began to rise rapidly and did not fall significantly until the late summer of 1982. In the meantime, the S&L industry was in a crisis and the actual and potential failure rate of individual institutions was reminiscent of commercial bank failures the 1930s.

The passage of the Garn–St. Germain Act of 1982 was primarily a rescue operation for the S&Ls[14] One of the best-known provisions is that it authorized depository institutions to offer an account "directly equivalent to and competitive with money market mutual funds." This account became widely available in December 14, 1982. Another new account, authorized in January 1983, was the Super NOW account.

The savings and loan crisis has been the center of a large public debate. For one perspective on that debate, see the Policy Issue: "The Savings and Loan Crisis: Causes and Cures."

SUMMARY

In this chapter, we opened with a discussion of how the money stock can be measured statistically; then we explored various factors affecting the stock of money, such as the monetary base or high-powered money. Next, we saw how money holders (the public) participate in the creation of money by their willingness to hold demand deposits in commercial banks and how the commercial banking system creates money when it tries to turn excess currency reserves into loans and demand deposits.

We also presented the institutional structure of the Fed and the scheme currently employed by the Fed in conducting monetary policy. We discussed the Fed's major policy tools, which are reserve requirements, open-market operations and discount rate policy, and its monetary growth-rate targets. We used the money holders–banking systems model to show how monetary policy affects reserves and the ability of those reserves to support demand deposits. The latter part of the chapter concentrated on various elements of the money multiplier and on a brief history of the operating targets the Fed has aimed for in its monetary control. The chapter ended with a discussion of the Garn–St. Germain Depository Institutions Act of 1982 and the continued problems the Fed faces in choosing its monetary targets.

KEY TERMS

actual currency-deposit ratio	credit
actual reserve-deposit ratio	currency
balance sheet equation	demand deposit
central bank	desired currency-deposit ratio (continued on p. 497)

---

[14]See Gillian Garcia et al., "The Garn–St. Germain Depository Institutions Act of 1982," Federal Reserve Bank of Chicago *Economic Perspectives* (March/April 1983), pp. 3–31.

THE SAVINGS AND LOAN CRISIS: CAUSES AND CURES

Much has been written about the savings and loan crisis, and much has been made of this crisis in the popular press and in political campaigns. This crisis has led to the closing of hundreds and even thousands of savings and loan institutions, decimating the industry, and costing taxpayers billions of dollars. What really caused the savings and loan crisis, and how can we make sure that such a problem doesn't occur again? In an insightful analysis, James

Barth, former chief economist at the Federal Home Loan Bank Board, the savings and loan equivalent of the Federal Reserve System's Board of Governors, has provided some answers.[a] Barth identifies eight causes of the crisis:

1. A rigid institutional structure. The structure of S & L institutions, and the regulatory constraints they faced, led them to rely almost totally on savings deposits for funds, and to concentrate their loans almost totally in home mortgages.

2. High and unpredictable interest rates. Interest rates soared in 1979, to unheard of heights, and the S&L industry was caught between rising interest rates on savings accounts—in order to keep

deposits—and low fixed rates on its portfolio of home mortgages. Barth estimates that 85 percent of S&Ls were unprofitable in 1981, and almost all would have been insolvent if forced to value their mortgage portfolios at market prices. Thus, monetary policy actions led to great losses at S&Ls, losses that were difficult to avoid within the institutional structure.

3. Deterioration in asset quality after the decline in oil prices. In Texas and other oil-producing states, the decline in oil prices in the early 1980s triggered regional recessions that were felt by S&Ls in those areas. Real estate values plummeted, many real estate investors became insolvent, and

PHOTO 12-2
Working Class Americans Feared Loss of Their Life Savings as Depositors' "Run" on an S&L in Paterson, New Jersey in 1990.

S&Ls were forced to foreclose on nonperforming loans. This real estate could not be sold by the S&Ls to cover the outstanding loans, further contributing to their insolvency.

4. Federal and state deregulation. Federal deregulation in the early 1980s allowed S&Ls to compete with each other and with banks. While this was a generally a good thing, Barth argues that the timing of this deregulation allowed S&Ls that were already in deep trouble because of the high interest rates of the late 1970s and early 1980s to continue operating with fewer constraints on their behavior. Thus, while deregulation of healthy S&Ls is a good thing, deregulation of S&Ls that were insolvent but still allowed to operate by Federal or state regulators often led to further deterioration of their already bad net asset position.

5. Fraud. Much has been written about fraudulent practices at S&Ls, to the extent that some may believe that fraud is the main reason for the S&L crisis. In fact, Barth reports that fraud seems to have been involved in about half of the failed S&L cases, but he also reports that the contribution of fraud to the cost of closing the failed sav-ings and loans is on average estimated to be from 3 to 10 percent. Thus, fraud and mismanagement did play a role in the S&L crisis, but not the overarching role that the media sometimes want to attribute to it.

6. Increased competition. The handmaiden of deregulation was increased competition, which increased the pressure on marginal S&Ls —which meant most of them. Again, competition is a good thing, encouraging and rewarding efficiency while weeding out weak firms, but in the case of S&Ls most were weak or even insolvent before the deregulation and increased competition occurred.

7. Tax law changes. The Tax Reform Act of 1986 reduced the depreciation allowances on real estate investment, reducing the demand for real estate and thereby reducing real estate values. Again, this led to insolvency of some real estate investors, and hence an increase in foreclosures and non-performing loans at S&Ls.

8. Moral hazard problems of deposit insurance. Federal deposit insurance means that depositors have no incentive to remove their deposits from failing institutions. Usually such actions by depositors, or just the fear of such action, is sufficient to make financial institutions invest in safe and conservative investments. Without such actions by depositors, financial institutions are freer to pursue risky and speculative investments. This is especially a problem for insolvent S&Ls, since they can "go for broke" on speculative investments. If the investments fail, the cost is low, since the institution is insolvent anyhow. If the investment succeeds, the gamble—with taxpayers' money—will have restored solvency to the institution. The only way to prevent such actions is either to close down insolvent institutions or to regulate their behavior. Neither was done very expeditiously in the 1980s.

Thus, Barth argues that a confluence of events led to the S&L crisis. High interest rates in the late 1970s set the stage for the later problems by weakening the balance sheets of S&Ls to the point where most were insolvent in the early 1980s. Then deregulation, which may have been an attempt to allow S&Ls to compete more successfully with banks and better diversify their portfolios, actually caused further problems for already weakened institutions. Added to this was the collapse of real estate prices in Texas and other oil-producing states, which further damaged the balance sheets of S&Ls in these states. Finally, because these insolvent S&Ls were allowed to continue operating, and operating with less regulation than before, and because deposit insurance kept deposits in the hands of these insolvent institutions these, S&Ls actually began to engage in riskier investments, investments that might have paid a high return, but that also had higher chances of not succeeding. These problems, and the additional problem of mismanagement and outright fraud, led to the S&L fiasco, in which billions of dollars of taxpayer money have gone to pay out the required insurance on deposits of failed institutions.

Is there a moral to the story? Barth recommends making sure that financial institutions are adequately capitalized and quickly closing institutions without adequate capital. Allowing insolvent institutions to continue operations invites the worst kind of abuse, since there are then essentially no market forces that act to restrict the behavior of such institutions. ❏

SOURCE: [a]See James R. Barth, *The Great Savings and Loan Debacle* (Washington, DC: The AEI Press, 1991).

Key Terms (cont.)

discount rate	monetary policy
excess reserves	net free reserves
federal funds rate	nonborrowed reserves
legal reserves	open-market operations
monetary base	required reserves
	required reserve ratio

QUESTIONS FOR REVIEW AND DISCUSSION

1. What is the monetary base or high-powered money?

2. What is the money multiplier? What factors determine the size of the money multiplier?

3. Why is the relationship between the monetary base and the money multiplier important?

4. Explain how the money supply M1 is calculated. What is the difference between M1, M2, M3, and L?

5. Explain under what conditions the public's desired currency-deposit ratio may be different from its actual currency-deposit ratio.

6. What effect does an increase in the bank's desired reserve-deposit ratio have on the money stock and demand deposits?

7. Suppose there is a decline in the monetary base in an economy. What effects does this have on the money stock and demand deposits?

8. What would happen to the money stock and demand deposits if we had another banking panic in the United States like the one in 1907?

9. What is the structure of the Federal Reserve System? Where is most of the power centered in the Federal Reserve System?

10. Give some of the changes that have taken place in the monetary system since 1980. Explain why these changes have occurred.

11. What is the difference between the tools, targets, and economic goals of the Fed?

12. What is the scheme used by the Fed in conducting monetary policy?

13. Explain each of the major monetary tools of the Fed and how they affect the monetary base or high-powered money.

14. How does the Fed's buying of government securities in the open market affect the money stock and demand deposits?

15. What if the Fed decided tomorrow to raise the required reserve deposit ratio for deposit institutions in the United States? What impact would this have on the money stock and demand deposits?

PROBLEMS

1. Suppose you are given the following information about some hypothetical economy, Macronesia:
   Reserve/deposit ratio = 0.10
   Currency/deposit ratio = 0.20
   Monetary base = $300 billion
   (a) What is the money multiplier and what is the money supply?
   (b) If the Federal Reserve increases the reserve requirement and, as a result, the reserve/deposit ratio rises to 0.15, then what is the new money multiplier and what is the new money supply?

2. Find c and r for currency = $5 billion, demand deposits = $2 billion, and reserves = $1 billion.

SUGGESTIONS FOR FURTHER READING

Barnett, William A., and Edward K. Offenbacher. "The New Divisia Monetary Aggregates." *Journal of Political Economy* (December 1984), pp. 1049–85.

Barth, James R. *The Great Savings and Loan Debacle*. Washington, DC: The AEI Press, 1991.

Belongia, Michael T., and James A. Chalfant. "Alternative Measures of Money as Indicators of Inflation: A Survey and Some New Evidence." Federal Reserve Bank of St. Louis *Review* (November/December 1990), pp. 20–33.

Bradley, Michael D. and Dennis W. Jansen. "Federal Reserve Operating Procedures in the Eighties: A Dynamic Analysis." *Journal of Money, Credit, and Banking* (August 1986), pp. 478–489.

Brunner, Karl. "The Role of Money and Monetary Policy." Federal Reserve Bank of St. Louis *Review* (September/October 1989), pp. 4–22.

Dueker, Michael D. "Can Nominal GDP Targeting Rules Stabilize the Economy?" Federal Reserve Bank of St. Louis *Review* (May/June 1993), pp. 15–29.

Friedman, Milton. "Lessons from the 1979–82 Monetary Policy Experiment." *AEA Papers and Proceedings* (May 1984), pp. 297–383.

Garcia, Gillian. "The Right Rabbit: Which Intermediate Target Should the Fed Pursue?" Federal Reserve Bank of Chicago *Economic Perspectives* (May/June 1984), pp. 15–31.

Garfinkel, Michelle R. and Daniel L. Thornton. "The Multiplier Approach to the Money Supply Process: A Precautionary Note." Federal Reserve Bank of St. Louis *Review* (July/August 1991), pp. 47–64.

Hakes, David R. "The Objectives and Priorities of Monetary Policy Under Different Federal Reserve Chairmen." *Journal of Money, Credit, and Banking* (August 1990), pp. 327–37.

Hetzel, Robert "How Useful Is M2 Today?" Federal Reserve Bank of Richmond *Economic Review* (September/October 1992), pp. 12–26.

Schwartz, Anna J. "The Misuse of the Fed's Discount Window." Federal Reserve Bank of St. Louis *Review* (September/October 1992), pp. 58–69.

Spindt, Paul A. "Money Is What Money Does: Monetary Aggregates and the Equation of Exchange." *Journal of Political Economy* (February 1985), pp. 175–204.

13 MONEY DEMAND

Theories about money demand are varied, ranging from Classical formulations to more modern treatments. These theories can be broken down into two broad classes: transactions theories and asset or portfolio theories. In the transactions theories the role of money is to serve as an acceptable medium of exchange. The Cambridge cash-balance approach to the demand for money that we studied in Chapter 3 was a transactions theory. Keynes, as we found in Chapter 5, borrowed the treatment of the transactions motive for holding money from the Cambridge quantity theorists. In the modern specification of the demand for money function, the public holds an inventory of money for transaction purposes just as businesses hold inventories of goods. Since there are transactions costs of going between money and other liquid financial assets, the public holds money inventories even though other assets offer higher yields.

Asset or portfolio theories of the demand for money are concerned with the problem of how the public allocates its wealth among a portfolio of assets, which includes money. Each asset in the portfolio yields a flow of explicit income and of implicit (nonmonetary) services. In the case of money, its services include not only the ease of making transactions, but also liquidity and safety, which is a "store of wealth or value" function.

In this chapter, we will take a more detailed look at the transactions theory of money demand developed simultaneously by two economists, William Baumol and James Tobin. Also, we will examine the portfolio theories of money demand of James Tobin and of Milton Friedman.

After reading this chapter, you will know

- how money is defined by the Federal Reserve System
- the Baumol-Tobin inventory approach to the transactions demand for money
- Tobin's portfolio approach, based on household preferences over risk and return
- Friedman's modern quantity theory approach
- why the Federal Reserve system is concerned with identifying a stable money demand function, and how instabilities in money demand can cause problems for monetary policymakers.

THE DEFINITION OF MONEY

MONEY is anything that performs the functions of money: medium of exchange, store of value, unit of account, and standard of deferred payment.

Before we explore the various theories of money demand, let us again briefly examine the definition of money. In Chapter 5, money was defined in terms of how it was used. **Money** was something that served as a medium of exchange, a store of value (wealth), a unit of account, and a standard of deferred payment. Money, as we recall, is an item that is generally acceptable by society and performs the function of medium of exchange when it helps to facilitate exchange in a modern economy. Money serves as a store of value (wealth) since it is fixed in nominal value (i.e., it has a face value), and as a unit of account since it is the measuring rod by which the public's choices can be assessed. Finally, money serves as a standard of deferred payment when it is used to measure the value of repaying a debt over a given period of time.

The above is a brief summary of the economist's conceptual definition of money. In Chapter 12, we found that the Federal Reserve has developed practical statistical definitions of money that it can use in thinking about monetary policy. We will focus on two of these definitions. The first is called M1, and the second M2. M1 is a narrow definition of money designed to correspond most closely to the transactions definition of money, and it includes currency in the hands of the public, traveler's checks, demand deposits, and other checkable deposits.[1] M2 is a somewhat broader definition that includes all of M1 plus money market deposit accounts, money market mutual fund accounts, savings and small time deposits, overnight repurchase agreements, and overnight Eurodollars.

It should be noted that these definitions are not immutable. Because of changes in financial institutions, the Federal Reserve revised its definitions of the monetary aggregates in 1980. The "old" definition of M1 included only currency and demand deposits. The current definition of M1 adds other checkable deposits in response to the public's large use of such deposits—at savings and loans or credit unions, for example—as transactions balances. The idea was to redefine the definitions of money so that they would continue to measure transactions balances. More generally, however, the Federal Reserve and economists in general want to have a measure of money that is useful—in the sense of providing a stable money demand function—both before and after changes in financial institutions, in economic conditions, and in social and political environments.

The question then becomes one of what assets to include in the definition of money that will make the money aggregate—M1, say—bear a stable relationship to a set of determinants of money demand both before and after a period of financial innovation. In principle the idea is straightforward. If we

---

[1]The category "other checkable deposits" comprises negotiable order of withdrawal (NOW) and automatic transfer service (ATS) accounts, credit union share draft accounts, and demand deposits at thrift institutions such as savings and loans.

deal with the transactions demand for money, the money stock should be defined in terms of those assets that serve as an acceptable medium of exchange. This is the idea behind M1. But as we just pointed out, the Federal Reserve today measures M1 (and other monetary aggregates) differently than it did before 1980. That is, the "old" definition of M1 was found unacceptable after a period of financial innovation. We are faced with the concern that the "new" definition may be found similarly wanting after some future period of financial innovation.

The changing definition of M1—or M2, for that matter—also raises the question of whether the redefinition has been successful. That is, does the current definition give a stable money demand relation both before and after the period of financial innovation? As we will see, the answer is that M1 still exhibits an unstable money demand relationship in the later 1970s and early 1980s. The redefinition does not seem to have completely resolved this issue.

To conclude, the practical definition of money is an empirical question, and a question that many economists feel is not completely resolved by the Federal Reserve's current definitions of its monetary aggregates M1 and M2. See the Insight: "Let's Look at the Data on Money Demand" for more information on the behavior of real money balances.

TRANSACTIONS THEORY OF MONEY DEMAND: MODELS BY BAUMOL AND TOBIN

Since the publication of The General Theory in 1936, Keynes's approach to the demand for money has been challenged. Part of the criticism has fallen on his formulation of the transactions demand for money. In Keynes's analysis, the transactions demand for money depended on the paying and spending habits of the community, factors that changed slowly over time. The relationship, then, between holding transactions balances and income was assumed to be constant and linear. Economists who have extended Keynes's theory of the transactions demand for money have used an inventory approach, which is similar to the theory of inventory holding by a business. William Baumol and James Tobin demonstrated that the transactions demand for money was not independent of the interest rate.[2] The basic idea of the Baumol-Tobin approach is that households hold money for transactions to bridge the gap in time between the receipt of income and its expenditure. Total expenditures for a given time period are not all made at the beginning of the period but are spread out over the entire period. Since an opportunity cost is involved in holding money balances-foregone interest-a household may want to hold over

[2]William J. Baumol, "The Transactions Demand for Cash: An Inventory Theoretic Approach," *Quarterly Journal of Economics* (November 1952), pp. 545–56; and James Tobin, "The Interest-Elasticity of Transactions Demand for Cash," *Review of Economics and Statistics* (August 1956), pp. 241–47.

INSIGHT

LET'S LOOK AT THE DATA

ON MONEY DEMAND

In this chapter we discuss the theory of money demand and also some attempts to estimate money demand functions. In order to get a better feel for what the theory is trying to explain, we first look at the data on money demand. We will look at money demand for both narrow money, M1, and a broader money measure, M2.

We first consider M1. We convert the nominal M1 measure provided by the Federal Reserve into a measure of real money balances by dividing M1 by the CPI or consumer price index for this purpose. Further, since money demand theory links real money holdings to both income and an interest rate, we will also look at a measure of real income and a measure of the interest rate, in an attempt to discern any relationship between these variables. Our income measure will be real personal income, and our interest rate measure will be the six-month commercial paper rate.

A graph of real M1 money balances and real personal income is given in Figure 13-1. Real M1 is graphed using the left-hand scale, while real personal income is graphed using the right-hand scale. If we look at real M1, it is immediately obvious that the series has experienced quite a few ups and downs since the early 1970s. In fact, the first big decline in real M1 begins in 1972 or 1973. This decline continues until sometime in 1975, after which there is a slight upward trend until 1977 or 1978, and then another large decline lasting through 1981. Beginning sometime in 1982, real M1 then grows at a fairly steep rate until late 1986 or early 1987, at which point it flattens out for a few years, before falling rather rapidly in 1988 and then flattening out (with a gradual downward trend) in 1989.

FIGURE 13-1
Real Money Demand and Real Personal Income for the United States, 1959–1993

This graph plots real money holdings, defined as M1 divided by the consumer price index, and real personal income.

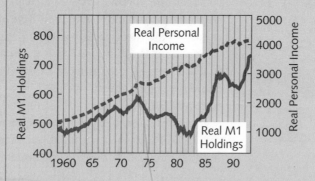

SOURCE: Federal Reserve Bulletin; U.S. Department of Labor, Bureau of Labor Statistics; and U.S. Department of Commerce, Bureau of Economic Analysis.

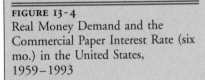

FIGURE 13-4
Real Money Demand and the
Commercial Paper Interest Rate (six
mo.) in the United States,
1959–1993

This graph plots real money holdings, defined as M2 divided by
the consumer price index, and the six-month commercial paper
rate of interest.

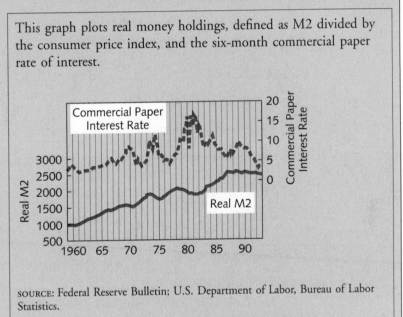

SOURCE: Federal Reserve Bulletin; U.S. Department of Labor, Bureau of Labor
Statistics.

a given time period a portion of its transactions balances in the form of an
interest-earning asset. The higher the interest rate, the more a household would
be willing to switch from holding transactions balances to holding some form
of interest-earning assets.

In the Baumol-Tobin analysis, a household is assumed to receive money
income of Y dollars, which is deposited immediately in an interest-earning
asset such as a savings account. This household is also assumed to have perfect
foresight about its transactions and to spend its income of Y dollars in a steady
stream in the course of a given year. To obtain dollars to carry out its transactions, the household makes withdrawals from its savings account in lots of
M_T dollars spaced evenly throughout the year. To illustrate, if the household's
yearly income, Y, were \$36,000, M_T might be \$36,000 every twelve months,
\$18,000 every six months, \$9,000 every three months, or \$3,000 a month. Over
the course of a year, the number of withdrawals N made by the household is
Y/M_T. For example, if Y were \$36,000 and M_T were \$18,000 every six months,
there would be two withdrawals. To find the **household's average money
holdings** of M_T, we divide the household's money income of Y by the number
of withdrawals N. Figure 13-5 shows the household's money holdings of
$M_T = Y/N = \$18,000$.

FIGURE 13-5
Household's Money Holdings

At the beginning of the year the household's money income is $Y = \$36,000$. If the household makes two even withdrawals during the year, then its money holdings are $M_T = Y/2 = \$18,000$.

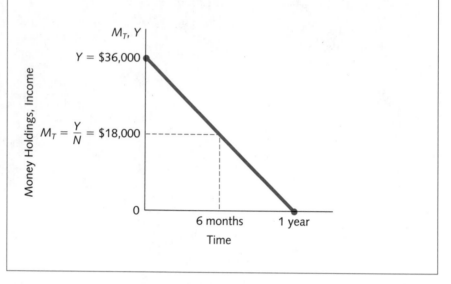

Each time the household makes a withdrawal, it must pay a fixed "broker's fee" of b dollars. The term broker's fee should be interpreted carefully since it covers all the noninterest costs of making a cash withdrawal.[3] In the case of a savings deposit, the broker's fee would include the time and transportation costs in going to the savings and loan to withdraw cash M_T. The total cost in broker's fees for the period is bY/M_T, or the broker's fee b multiplied by the number of withdrawals Y/M_T. Since the household withdraws and spends M_T dollars in a steady stream until it is gone and then withdraws and spends another M_T dollars until it is gone, and so on, the **average money holdings** over the period are $M_T/2$ dollars. For example, suppose M_T is $\$18,000$ every six months out of $\$36,000$ of yearly Y. The average cash balance $M_T/2$ over the six-month period is then $\$18,000/2 = \$9,000$.

Average cash balances held by the household during the six-month period are shown in Figure 13-6. If this average cash holding is held in a savings account, it earns a market rate interest of R. The interest opportunity cost of holding transactions balances for the period is $R \times M_T/2$. The total cost TC that the household must pay for the use of cash to meet transactions needs when it withdraws M_T dollars from its savings account is the sum of the broker's fees and the opportunity cost (foregone interest):

---

[3]The broker's fee could be the cost involved in selling an income-earning asset such as a bond or the time and inconvenience involved in selling an income asset.

FIGURE 13-6

Average Cash Balances of the Household

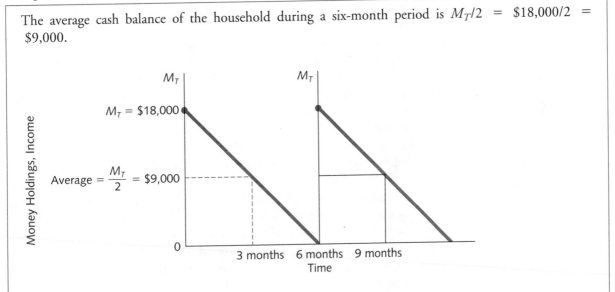

The average cash balance of the household during a six-month period is $M_T/2 = \$18,000/2 = \$9,000$.

$$TC = \frac{bY}{M_T} + R\frac{M_T}{2}. \tag{13.1}$$

The household has to make a decision about the amount of M_T dollars it wants to withdraw from its savings. It selects a value of M_T that minimizes the cost of broker's fees and interest foregone (i.e., opportunity cost).

The Baumol-Tobin equation for the minimizing cost value of M_T is the so-called square root law,[4]

$$M_T = \sqrt{\frac{2bY}{R}}. \tag{13.2}$$

As noted earlier, money holdings over the period have an average value of $M_T/2$. Thus, the real demand for money equation in the Baumol-Tobin analysis is expressed as

$$\frac{M_T}{2P} = \frac{1}{2P}\sqrt{\frac{2bY}{R}}. \tag{13.3}$$

---

[4]The value of M_T is derived mathematically by setting the first derivative of the total cost equation with respect to M_T equal to zero and then solving for M_T, where:

$$\frac{d(TC)}{dM_T} = \frac{-bY}{M_T^2} + \frac{R}{2} = 0.$$

Thus, in the Baumol-Tobin model the real demand for transactions balances is directly proportional to the square root of the value of real income and inversely proportional to the square root of the interest rate. Stated in another way, the value of cash withdrawal M_T is equal to the square root of two times the broker's fees times income Y divided by the interest rate.

The Baumol-Tobin analysis has two important implications. First, the transactions demand for money depends on the interest rate. As the interest rate declines for a given level of income, the demand for real transactions balances increases. Second, equation 13.3 shows that the transactions demand for money rises less than in proportion to any rise in income. This does not support the Classical version of the transactions demand for money, which would predict that money demand does rise in proportion to the level of income. We might say that the Baumol-Tobin transactions model shows that there are economies of scale in using money. People in high-income brackets will hold proportionately less money than people in low-income brackets. Given a fixed brokerage fee, the average cost per dollar of transactions is lower for large transactions since it costs the same amount to transfer $100 as $100,000. Thus, as people move up into higher income brackets their transactions tend to become larger, thereby reducing their average cost per dollar of transactions.

PORTFOLIO THEORIES OF MONEY DEMAND

Portfolio theories of money demand stress that money is held as part of a portfolio of assets, and not just for transactions reasons. We look at Tobin's portfolio approach to liquidity preference, and then at the modern quantity theory.

Tobin's Approach to Liquidity Preference

One difficulty with Keynes's approach to the demand for money was his concept of liquidity preference. Keynes's notion of a speculative demand for money was based on the idea that speculators are uncertain as to the expected direction interest rates will take and therefore choose to hold either bonds or money in their portfolios. In other words, Keynes looked on speculators as holding either idle money balances or bonds, but not both simultaneously. This has been criticized for its lack of realism. Speculators often hold both bonds and money balances. Households may want to diversify their portfolios (hold a mixture of assets).

A solution to this problem was provided by James Tobin[5], who demonstrated why a rational household might want to divide its portfolio between

---

[5]James Tobin, "Liquidity Preference as Behavior Toward Risk," *Review of Economic Studies* (February 1958), pp. 65–87.

bonds and money. Tobin explained the concept of risk by using the household's behavior with regard to portfolio choice.

The key to understanding Tobin's analysis is the proposition about household tastes. Tobin treats the expected return on bonds, which is the total income from the bonds, as providing utility or satisfaction to the household and risk as something that reduces the satisfaction (utility) derived from those earnings. A household with savings has to decide how much it should hold as money balances and how much it should hold in bonds. Assuming that the price level is constant, if the household holds money in its portfolio, there is no risk but there is also no return (i.e., no interest earnings). On the other hand, bonds yield income, which has two components: the interest payment accruing from the bonds, which is a certain value, and the capital gain or loss, which is an uncertain value.

A bond, then, has a non-zero return, but it also has risk attached to it. When a household buys a bond, it expects a certain return—the interest income from the bond. But it also realizes that there is a risk associated with the bond—the possibility of a capital loss. When a household purchases bonds, it is uncertain as to the future course of bond prices. Tobin assumes that the expected value of the yield on holding bonds is equal to the market rate of interest, so that the expected capital gain or loss is zero. If the expected capital loss is zero, the expected return on the bonds is equal to the interest income, given the interest rate. The more bonds the household has in its portfolio, the greater is the expected return (expected interest income), and since this increases household wealth in the next period, it increases utility. If the household's portfolio contains all bonds and no money, the expected return (expected interest income) is maximized; if the portfolio contains only money, the expected return is zero.

Any combination of both bonds and money in the portfolio (i.e., a mixed portfolio) will provide some expected interest income between zero and the maximum. However, the more bonds the household has in its portfolio, the greater is the expected return and the risk of a capital loss due to fluctuation in bond prices. Thus, the risk of a capital loss is maximized if the household possesses all bonds and no money. Of course, a household could avoid risk altogether by holding all of its assets in the form of money balances.

RISK AVERSE people are those who receive diminishing marginal utility of wealth and increasing marginal disutility of risk with each additional bond that they hold in their portfolio.

Tobin assumed that some households are **risk averse.** A household that is risk averse experiences diminishing marginal utility of wealth and increasing marginal disutility of risk when holding bonds. Suppose a household has only money in its portfolio. When it starts to add bonds to its portfolio, two things occur. The first is that the household's total utility of interest income increases. This additional utility occurs each time the household increases its portfolio of bonds, but the additional bonds eventually add less and less to total utility. That is, there is diminishing marginal utility of interest income. The second thing that happens is that the household's total disutility of risk also increases with each additional bond purchased, adding more and more to total disutility (i.e., increasing marginal disutility of risk). The household stops adding bonds to its portfolio when the marginal utility of interest income is equal to the marginal disutility of risk. At this point the household has maximized its total utility. If the household adds one more bond, its marginal disutility of risk will be greater than its marginal utility of interest income.

Tobin's analysis not only explains why a household would want to diversify its portfolio, but it can also be used to derive a relationship between the demand for money and the market rate of interest. The proportions of bonds and money held in the portfolio increase or decrease with changes in the market interest rate. An increase (or decrease) in the interest rate produces both a substitution effect and an income effect (wealth effect). With a rise in the interest rate, the return on bonds increases without an increase in risk. The household will then shift some of its assets from money to bonds, which have become relatively more desirable. This is the substitution effect. It leads to less money being held at a higher market rate of interest. However, a rise in the interest rate also increases the household's income. This means that the household can have not only more return but less risk by holding fewer bonds and more money balances. This is the income effect.[6] If the substitution effect is greater than the income effect, the household will hold more bonds and less money in its portfolio when interest rates rise. Tobin thus clearly has demonstrated that the demand for money can vary inversely with the interest rate.

Friedman's Theory of the Demand for Money

Milton Friedman has developed a modern version of the quantity theory of money that extends the Classical approach.[7] Unlike Keynes, Friedman makes no distinction between the motives for holding money; rather, he takes it for granted that individuals want to hold money. His concern is with the factors that determine how much money households and businesses want to hold in their portfolios under various economic circumstances. Since Friedman views the demand for money as similar to the demand for any other durable good, he applies the general theory of demand in deriving the demand for money. Money, like any other asset, yields utility or a flow of services to its owners. Services arise from money because it is a source of purchasing power. Friedman divides the demanders of money into two groups; wealth holders and businesses. Wealth holders are households that view the money in their

---

[6]The income effect could go in either direction. The household could hold either more or less bonds because of this effect. The outcome really depends on the household's utility function and therefore becomes an empirical matter rather than a theoretical one.

[7]Milton Friedman, "The Quantity Theory of Money: A Restatement," in *Studies in the Quantity Theory of Money* (Chicago: University of Chicago Press, 1956). Also reprinted in Milton Friedman, *The Optimum Quantity of Money* (Chicago: Aldine Publishing, 1969).

portfolios as one of the forms of holding wealth; business firms view money as a factor of production. The three major sets of factors that determine how much money households and business firms will hold at any given time are (1) the total wealth in all forms held by the household or business firm, (2) the opportunity cost of holding money, and (3) the tastes and preferences of the wealth-holding unit.

Let us first discuss the demand for money equation for the individual wealth holder. The equation for the nominal demand for money for the individual can be written as

$$M_d = M_d(Y_P, NH/H, R, \pi^e, P, u), \tag{13.4}$$

where M_d is the nominal demand for money, Y_P is permanent income, NH/H is the percentage ratio of nonhuman wealth to human wealth, R is the rate of interest, π^e is the (expected) percentage rate of change in prices, P is the price level, and u is an index representing taste and preferences.

Friedman argues that the following independent variables should be included in the money demand function:

1. *Total wealth (Y_P).* Permanent income Y_P is used as a surrogate for total wealth.[8] In consumer demand theory, a demand curve is derived on the basis of a **budget constraint.** The budget constraint defines the maximum amount of an asset that can be held by the wealth owner. The constraint is total real wealth since this indicates the maximum money holding by the individual. Wealth holders allocate their total wealth between money and other assets to maximize their utility.

   Friedman's definition of wealth is broader than that of most economists. He includes both nonhuman and human wealth. Nonhuman wealth includes all the conventional assets, such as bonds and equities, but Friedman also includes producer and consumer durable goods. The wealth holder can sell such assets and hold the funds in the form of money balances. Human wealth is the present value of (expected) future labor income. The wealth of many people is primarily of this form. Human wealth is included because an individual can borrow against his or her expected *future* income and then hold the proceeds in the form of money.

   Given an increase in total wealth, there will be a rise in the individual's permanent income Y_P. This will cause the demand for money to increase, assuming, as Friedman does, that money is a normal good and that other things are held constant.

2. *The percentage ratio of nonhuman wealth to human wealth (NH/H).* Various forms of nonhuman wealth can easily be substituted for one another. For example, bonds can be substituted for equities or for money. In the

---

[8]The concept of permanent income is developed at length in Chapter 14.

absence of slavery, however, there is no market for, and therefore no rate of return on, human wealth. Thus, very little substitution between non-human wealth and human wealth can occur. A person could sell bonds and use the amount received to finance an education, thereby improving his or her ability to earn future income; or a person could borrow against future income and use the loan to buy a bond. However, such substitutions between nonhuman and human wealth are small. This limited ability to substitute human wealth for nonhuman wealth such as money balances presents a problem to Friedman. Since Friedman includes total wealth in money demand, he also includes the ratio of nonhuman wealth to human wealth NH/H in money demand. He interprets the variable NH/H as follows: As the ratio of nonhuman wealth to human wealth decreases, there is a greater demand for money to compensate for the limited marketability of human wealth.

3. *The opportunity cost of holding money.* In Friedman's analysis, the opportunity cost of holding money depends on the rate of interest R that could be obtained if an interest-bearing asset such as a bond were held instead of money, and on the expected inflation rate, π^e. Where there is a rise in the market interest rate, the amount of foregone interest income on money holding increases. That is the opportunity cost of holding money increases and money demand decreases.

   The cost of holding money balances also rises with a rise in the expected inflation rate. Holding other things constant, the higher the expected inflation rate, the smaller is the demand for money.

4. *The price level (P).* The demand for money is expressed in nominal terms, not in real terms. For real money balances to remain constant, an increase in the price level requires a proportional increase in the nominal demand for money M_d. The nominal demand for money equation for a wealth holder can be converted into the real demand for money for a wealth holder by dividing both sides of equation 13.4 by P.

5. *Tastes and preferences (u).* This variable stands for all other variables or can affect the wealth holder's preferences for holding money balances. In general Friedman considers tastes as constant over time. Short-run changes in u, therefore, are not to be expected, except under unusual circumstances.

What about the nominal demand for money of businesses? While money is a source of utility to the wealth holder, it is treated as a factor of production by the business firm. By holding money, the firm avoids the inconvenience of barter and has a safe reserve for future emergencies. As a factor of production, money is combined with other factor inputs such as labor and capital, to maximize profits. Friedman argues that instead of permanent income a variable ought to be included in the demand function for money to reflect the size of the business enterprise, such as total transactions, net income or net worth. Also business firms differ from wealth holders in that the only wealth they own is of the nonhuman form. Therefore, the ratio of nonhuman wealth to human wealth is not a factor in the business firm's demand for money function.

Finally, there is a difference between the business firm's and the wealth holder's opportunity cost of holding money. The rates of return on money and other income-earning assets that a business firm considers in its decision making may not be the same ones that confront a wealth holder. For example, a bank rate for a loan may be different to business firms and wealth holders.

INSTABILITY OF MONEY DEMAND AND THE CONDUCT OF MONETARY POLICY

The focus of this section is on the relationship between the demand for money and the Federal Reserve's conduct of monetary policy. The structure of the Federal Reserve and the Fed's economic goals, such as price stability and full employment, was discussed in Chapter 12. As we have seen, the Fed tries to achieve its economic goals through monetary policy instruments, which affect certain intermediate money targets. Of the policy tools or instruments examined in that chapter, open-market operations are the principal instrument of monetary policy. Decisions on open-market operations and on the course of monetary policy are made by the Federal Open-Market Committee (FOMC), which currently meets eight times a year.

In Chapter 12, we also pointed out that in 1975 Congress began to require the Fed to formulate monetary policy in terms of money growth-rate targets, and we reported the target ranges set by the FOMC for M2 in 1992. Here we want to examine how it is that the Fed attempts to hit its targets for the money aggregates. We have seen that the Fed's control of the money stock depends on two factors: its control over high-powered money and the money multiplier. The money multiplier in turn depends in part on the legal reserve ratio and in part on the behavior of the public and the banking system. The M1 money multiplier was very volatile, with a downward trend over the period 1970–1984, but then a sharp upward trend during 1985–86, followed by nearly as sharp a downward trend in the late 1980s. This volatility is attributed to changes in the public's desired currency-deposit ratio and time-deposit ratio. Of particular interest here is the evidence that the public has shifted assets from demand deposits and currency to various other forms of holding money, which contributes to the instability in M1. The implication is that even if the Fed can control high-powered money (i.e., the money base) it still may not have very good control over M1, because the volatility of the money multiplier may cause M1 to overshoot or undershoot the Fed's targets. In fact this is what led the Fed to drop M1 from its list of intermediate policy targets and make M2 its principal monetary aggregate.

How important is this instability in money demand for targeting monetary aggregates such as M1 and M2 and the eventual achievement of the Fed's policy goals? An ideal intermediate monetary policy target should be associated with the goals of monetary policy and readily controlled. The basic *IS-LM* model developed in Chapter 6 provides a convenient framework for analyzing the effects of unpredicted shifts in the public's demand for money on a real income goal. The familiar *IS-LM* schedules are depicted in Figure 13-7.

Remember how the policy process works. The Fed has a goal, and wants to achieve it by manipulating its instruments. First it must make predictions about the nonpolicy components of *IS* and *LM*. We assume that the *IS* schedule's predicted position is IS_0 and that the Fed is using a money stock target (which will be M_0) to achieve a single goal of setting real income at $L_0(Y_0)$.[9] If the Fed's forecast of the public's money demand function as $L_0(Y_0)$ correct and at the same time it hits the money stock target M_0, then the *LM* schedule will be at $LM_0(M_0)$. In this case, the Fed obtains its desired income level of Y_0.

However, unpredicted shifts in money demand for a given level of income and interest rate will cause the *LM* curve to shift even if the Fed hits its money stock target of M_0. In the previous section, we discussed the situation of possible shifts (unpredicted) in the public's demand for money function. Let us examine two real-world situations. In the first case, there was a possible leftward shift in money demand for the 1974–1980 period. Assume the Fed hits its money stock target M_0 but misses its forecast of the public's real money holdings by overpredicting money demand. The Fed predicted money demand of $L_0(Y_0)$ but actual money demand was lower, $L_1(Y_0)$. This means that the *LM* schedule is predicted to be at $LM_0(M_0)$ but it actually is at $LM_1(M_0)$. What happens? Real income is Y_1 instead of Y_0, and the Fed misses its target. Real income is above the desired income goal.

As a second example, consider a situation like that in 1981–1983, when money demand apparently shifted to the right. Again assume the Fed hits the money stock target M_0, but this time it underpredicts the public's money demand as $L_0(Y_0)$ when money demand is actually $L_2(Y_0)$. This means that the predicted position of *LM* is $LM_0(M_0)$, but the actual position of *LM* is at $LM_2(M_0)$. The result is that the level of real income is Y_2 instead of its target value of Y_0. Real income is below the income goal.

In both of the cases analyzed, it was assumed that the Fed was able to hit its money stock target. The problem in both cases is that unpredicted shifts in money demand led the Fed to miss its output target. Instabilities in money demand that are not predictable by the Fed will cause problems for monetary policymakers.

Of course, the analysis presented here was very simple, based only on *IS-LM*. A more realistic analysis would take price level changes into account by introducing the aggregate supply curve into the analysis. Some models, such as the Classical model, would lead one to question just how the Fed could

---

[9]The Fed may not be able to forecast with accuracy the *IS* schedule because aggregate demand factors, such as autonomous investment, government spending, and net foreign expenditures, are changing. An unstable *IS* curve also creates problems for intermediate money targeting.

FIGURE 13-7
The Effect of Instability in the Public's Demand for Money on the Federal Reserve's Real Income Goal

Even if the Fed hits its money target (M_0), an unpredicted change in money demand will cause the LM curve to shift to $LM_1(M_0)$ or $LM_2(M_0)$ and away from the Fed's predicted $LM_0(M_0)$. This is illustrated in graph (a). The shift in money demand is illustrated more directly in graph (b). Note that the resultant equilibrium in graph (a) has real income above or below the desired target level Y_0.

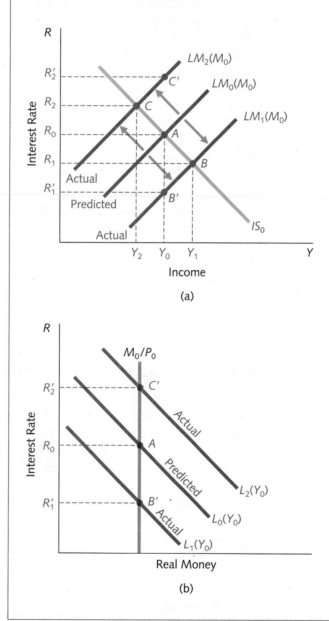

(a)

(b)

reasonably hope to achieve any output target different from that set by long-run aggregate supply. Others would suggest that the Fed can increase aggregate demand and hence output, but only by accepting increases in the price level. In any event, the policy analysis in this section was designed to point out problems with policymaking in an uncertain world, and to point out how instabilities in aggregate demand may make it difficult for the Fed to achieve its final targets, such as for real output, even if it is able to achieve its monetary targets, such as its current M2 targets.

On a practical level, a big problem for monetary targeting and for monetary policy has been the far-reaching effects of both financial innovations and changes in the laws and regulations governing financial institutions. For example, the DIDMC and the Garn-St. Germain Act, authorized money market deposit accounts and Super NOW accounts. The introduction of these new accounts caused problems for M1 targeting because the accounts carried unregulated and highly competitive yields that drew funds away from other financial institutions. These changes caused the Fed to shift its emphasis to broader monetary aggregates. Daniel L. Thornton of the Federal Reserve Bank of St. Louis has shown that the Fed can control M2 only through its control of M1. He outlines changes in the Fed's system of reserve requirements that could enhance its ability to control M2. For the future, changes in the financial and economic environment will continue to influence monetary policymakers' decisions.[10]

Finally, for an international perspective on the relative successes of monetary policy in Japan and the United States, see the Global Perspective: "Monetary Announcements: The Bank of Japan and the Fed."

MONETARISTS VERSUS KEYNESIANS ON THE RECENT INSTABILITY OF MONEY DEMAND AND MONETARY POLICY

The instabilities in money demand, especially those that began in 1979–80 and continue to the present, have created much more concern for Monetarists than for Keynesians. The questions that all economists want to answer is why these instabilities occurred. Both Keynesians and Monetarists agree that the desirability of stabilizing short-run money growth depends on the stability of the public's demand for money function. Many Keynesians believe that money demand is unstable. However, they point out that even though the public's money demand has been subject to unpredictable shifts, short-run money growth volatility has not been a serious problem for the economy.[11] "According to their reasoning, holding the rate of money growth to preestablished targets by the Federal Reserve instead of allowing the Fed to alter money growth in response to changing conditions could create significant costs on the economy.

[10]For a discussion of this view, see Daniel L. Thornton, "Targeting M2: The Issue of Monetary Control," Federal Reserve Bank of St. Louis *Review* (July/August 1992), pp. 23–35.

[11]See Scott E. Hein, "Short-Run Money Growth Volatility: Evidence of Misbehaving Money Demand?" Federal Reserve Bank of St. Louis *Review* 64, no. 6 (June/July 1982), pp. 27–35.

"MONETARY ANNOUNCEMENTS: THE BANK OF JAPAN AND THE FED"

Recessions in Japan tend not to be as severe or as long as the ones in the United States. Why is this the case? Economists have offered various explanations to account for the differences between these countries. One view is that Japan has more wage flexibility and a greater commitment to maintaining long-term employment than the United States. Another explanation is that Japan has a more stable and predictable monetary policy. Economists point out that with a more predictable monetary policy there is less uncertainty about the future course of inflation. Since the rate of inflation is an important part of economic decision making, a reduction in the uncertainty about inflation means fewer business and household decisions have to be revised, which in turn leads to less volatility in economic activity.

Since the late 1970s, the Bank of Japan has made a strong commitment to fighting inflation. Some economists argue that the reason for the Bank of Japan's success is that it announces its monetary targets in advance and then consistently achieves them. The Bank of Japan, therefore, can provide an environment conducive to maintaining a stable real output of goods and services. By containing the amount of its monetary growth, the Bank of Japan lessens the chance that the inflation rate will change and *surprise* the public. In 1975, the U.S. Congress mandated that the Federal Reserve report ranges for the monetary aggregates. The Federal Reserve has established ranges four quarters into the future rather than just one quarter ahead like the Japanese. While the Bank of Japan allows the base of its ranges to drift each quarter, the Fed is usually permitted only one change per year. Some claim that the Federal Reserve cannot consistently hit its monetary target ranges. Moreover, the Federal Reserve's projections are not announced to the public when they are chosen at the Federal Open-

Market Committee meeting. Instead, there is a lag of around six weeks before they are published. Thus, it is argued that the lag in the Federal Reserve's announcement of its forecast and its inability to hit its targets surprises the public about the course of monetary policy actions. The public, faced with these unexpected changes in monetary growth, is uncertain about what the future rates of inflation will be. This uncertainty about the future causes more severe and pronounced fluctuations in U.S. real GDP.

In a study of the inflation value of the Bank of Japan and the Federal Reserve, two economists, Hutchinson and Judd, have taken the critics to task. Using information and other central banks' projections available to the public when the forecasts were undertaken, they have developed a time-series forecasting model of monetary growth for the U.S. and Japan. With their model, they compared the accuracy of their forecasts with the projections made by the Bank of Japan and by the Federal Reserve. Their results suggest the Federal Reserve's projections do make a signifi-

PHOTO 13-1
A Branch of the Prestigious Bank of Japan.

cant contribution to forecasting U.S. monetary growth over and above other information available to the public. Their research also shows the announcement of projections by the Bank of Japan did not play an important role in the bank's successful record in maintaining a low rate of inflation and real output stability. Instead, they conclude that the fundamental reason for the good performances of the Japanese economy was the steadfast commitment by the Bank of Japan to a long-run goal of low inflation despite the changing political and economic environment. ❑

SOURCE Michael Hutchinson and John P. Judd, "Monetary Announcements: The Bank of Japan and the Fed," *FRBSW Weekly Letter,* Federal Reserve Bank of San Francisco, no. 92-15 (April 10, 1992).

For example, if the public desires to hold larger real money balances but is constrained from doing so because of already established and carefully adhered to money targets, the public would have to reduce its demand for goods and services, creating a slowdown in the economy. Then either the fall in income would reduce money demand, or a fall in the price level would increase real balances and restore equality between money demand and supply.

On the other hand, Friedman, a leading Monetarist, argues that money demand *has* been stable during the recent period. He contends that too rapid a money growth can overstimulate an economy, leading to inflation, while too little money growth can precipitate a recession. In his view, Monetarist policy is concerned not only in targeting monetary aggregates but also in achieving a steady and predictable rate of monetary growth in whatever monetary aggregate is targeted. From October 1979 to the summer of 1982, the Fed shifted policy tactics and began a "monetary policy experiment," placing greater emphasis on reducing the growth of money rather than on limiting short-run fluctuations in interest rates. While a Monetarist objective is controlling growth in money aggregates, the extreme volatility of money growth during this period led Friedman to call the 1979–1982 policy experiment anti-Monetarist. Friedman points out that "monetary volatility was higher during the three years of the experiment than in any earlier three-year period since at least the end of World War II."[12] He concludes that the recent evidence from the Fed's monetary policy experiment provides a strong case for a policy of steady predictable monetary growth in M2. For more on this debate over the so-called monetary policy experiment, see the Policy Issue: "Is Monetarism Dead? The U.S. Economy, 1979–1990."

SUMMARY

In this chapter, we opened with a brief review of the definition of money and the possible problems this poses for a stable money demand function. Next, we examined the Baumol-Tobin inventory approach to the transactions demand for money, then the portfolio theories of the demand for money. Here we included Tobin's contribution to liquidity preference as well as Friedman's views on the demand for money. We then examined the relationship between the potential instability of money demand and the problems this can present for the Federal Reserve's conduct of monetary policy. The chapter ended with a discussion of the difference between Monetarists (such as Friedman) and Keynesians on the recent instability of money demand and monetary policy.

KEY TERMS

average money holdings

budget constraint

money

money holdings of household

risk averse people

---

[12]See Milton Friedman, "Lessons from the 1979–82 Monetary Policy Experiment," *American Economic Association Papers and Proceedings* (May 1984), pp. 397–400.

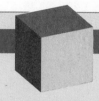

IS MONETARISM DEAD?

THE U.S. ECONOMY,

1979–1992.

A recent focus of the debate over monetary policy is the behavior of the economy over the period 1979–1982, when the Fed was supposedly following a Monetarist strategy, and the post-1982 period. The 1979–1982 period witnessed two sharp recessions (a brief one in 1980 and a longer one in 1981–82). The post-1982 period included a recovery accompanied by the highest growth rate in GNP (6.8 percent in 1984) experienced since the early 1950s. Many believe that economic events over this period do

serious damage to the Monetarist policy position, while Monetarists argue that Monetarism was never tried. The two leading exponents of these positions are Noble laureates James Tobin (advocating the Keynesian position) and Milton Friedman. They have been explicit on their views of fiscal and monetary policy over this period, and especially over the subperiod 1979–1985.

The Monetarist experiment is supposed to have begun in October 1979, when the Fed pledged that it would focus on controlling monetary aggregates.

Keynesians and Monetarists present starkly different interpretations of this period. Tobin's Keynesian position is that the activities of the Fed between 1979 and mid-1982 were an exercise in Monetar-

ism and that events of the period "prove" that the Monetarist principle of "rules not discretion" was an abysmal failure. Monetarists retort that the policies followed by the Fed over the period were hardly an experiment in Monetarism and offer evidence of jerky and unstable monetary growth to back up their claim.

Figure 13-8 presents the evidence on the impact of a volatile velocity over this period. In (a) we graph the percentage change in both M1-velocity and M2-velocity. Note the preponderance of negative values for the percentage change, indicating a decline in velocity. This is even clearer in (b), which graphs both M1-velocity and M2-velocity since 1959. There, the decline in velocity in the early 1980s is especially

PHOTO 13-2
Nobel Prize Winners Milton Friedman (1976) and James Tobin (1981) Take Opposing Positions on the Effectiveness of Discretionary Monetary Policy.

Milton Friedman

James Tobin

clear. This surprising reduction in velocity (an increase in the demand for money) greatly reduced spending and was accompanied by the sharp recession and high unemployment in 1981–82. The attempt to use monetary rules to control the inflation of the late 1970s succeeded, in Tobin's view, but at the costs of high unemployment and sharply reduced output. The results of this "failure of Monetarism," according to Tobin, was the abandonment by the Fed of Monetarism and a return to control of *both* interest rates and monetary aggregates.

Monetarists emphasize the fact that there is a close and predictable relation between M2 growth and nominal GDP with a lag of three to nine months in the effects of M2 on *nominal* GDP. (The effects on other variables may be considerably longer.) They also underline the critical importance of expectations on the stability of velocity or the demand for money so that belief that the Federal Reserve

---

FIGURE 13-8
Percent Change in Velocity and the Level of Velocity

Graph (a) shows the percent change in both M1 and M2 velocity over the period 1979–1992. Graph (b) shows the behavior of M1 velocity and M2 velocity over the period 1959–1992.

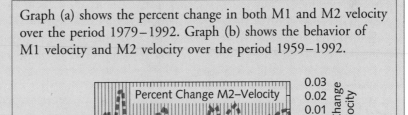

(a)

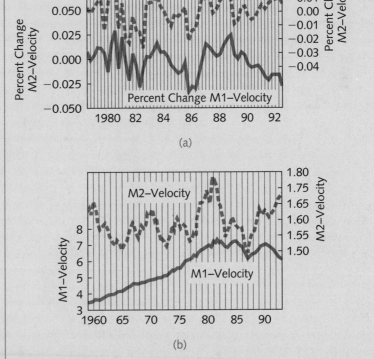

(b)

SOURCE: Federal Reserve Bulletin; U.S. Department of Commerce, Bureau of Economic Analysis.

will follow a predictable and consistent monetary policy will lead to a more stable and predictable velocity. Erratic stop-and-go interest rate policies with money geared to no particular target can only lead to erratic and unpredictable money demand and velocity.

Milton Friedman believes that there is no surer fact than that the Fed did *not* follow Monetarist policies before, during, or after the 1979–1982 period. Indeed, he emphasizes that it was total fail-ure of the Fed to do so that explains the recession of 1981–82 and other events of 1979 onward. As Figure 13-9 seems to show, changes in M2 track changes in nominal GDP with a lag of three to nine months later over the period. A stark and non-Monetarist policy of money growth reductions (especially in M1 growth) in 1979 and again in 1980 set the stage for the observed recessions. Velocity fell, due in large part to the erratic and unpredictable policies of the Fed—hardly a Monetarist-supported event. Friedman remains steadfast in his Monetarist beliefs. Steady monetary growth would have avoided the "roller-coaster" of inflation (in Friedman's view) in the 1960s and 1970s and the unhappy recessions of the early 1980s, caused by miscalculations of the Fed. While the Federal Reserve Board claimed to be aiming at M1 or M2 "targets," it had in fact simply continued its old policies. ❑

FIGURE 13-9
Percent Change Nominal GDP and M1, or Nominal GDP and M2, 1979–1992

Graph (a) shows the percent change in nominal GDP and M1, while graph (b) shows the percent change in nominal GDP and M2.

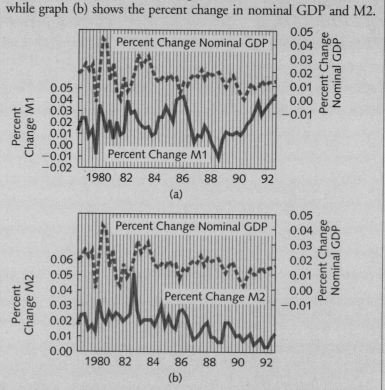

SOURCE: Federal Reserve Bulletin; U.S. Department of Commerce, Bureau of Economic Analysis.

QUESTIONS AND PROBLEMS FOR REVIEW AND DISCUSSION

1. What changes took place in the official definitions of the money aggregates in the early 1980s, and why did these changes occur?

2. Is there a proper definition of money? If there is, what is it?

3. What contribution did William Baumol and James Tobin make to the transactions demand for money?

4. How does the Baumol-Tobin transaction model show there are economies of scale in using money?

5. What impact does an unstable money demand function have on targeting of M1 by the Federal Reserve? Does instability in money demand have any effect on the achievement of the Fed's goals?

6. Is there any real difference between Keynes's approach and Tobin's approach in liquidity preference? If so, what is it?

7. Friedman suggests that a number of independent variables should be included in his theoretical demand for money function. List and briefly explain each of these variables.

8. What is Friedman's view regarding the stability of the demand for money? What implications does this stability have for changes in the level of money income in the economy?

9. What does the empirical evidence show about the relative volatility of real M1 and real M2?

10. Is there any difference between Monetarists and Keynesians on the recent instability of money demand and monetary policy?

11. If the Fed wants to achieve an interest rate target, and this is its only final target, would unpredictable shifts in money demand and hence in *LM* cause the Fed any difficulties? Why or why not?

12. If the Fed wants to achieve an output target and it can predict money demand perfectly but has had troubles predicting the location of the *IS* curve, how would this affect its ability to achieve its output target? Use the *IS-LM* graph to illustrate your answer.

SUGGESTIONS FOR FURTHER READING

Baumol, William J. "The Transactions Demand for Cash: An Inventory Theoretic Approach." *Quarterly Journal of Economics* (November 1952), pp. 545–56.

Cover, James P., and James P. Keeler. "Estimating Money Demand in Log-First-Difference Form." *Southern Economic Journal* (January 1987), pp. 751–67.

Fisher, Douglas, and Myra McCrickard. "Rational Expectations and the Demand for Money: A Nonparametric Test." *Journal of Macroeconomics* (Fall 1992), pp. 573–91.

Friedman, Milton. "The Quantity Theory of Money: A Restatement." In *Studies in the Quantity Theory of Money.* Chicago: University of Chicago Press, 1956.

Hafer, R. W., and Dennis W. Jansen. "The Demand for Money in the United States: Evidence from Cointegration Tests." *Journal of Money, Credit, and Banking* (May 1991), pp. 155–68.

Hoffman, Dennis, and Robert Rasche. "Long-Run Income and Interest Elasticities of Money Demand in the United States." *Review of Economics and Statistics* (November 1991), pp. 665–74.

Laidler, David E. W. *The Demand for Money: Theories, Evidence, & Problems,* 4th ed. New York: Harper Collins, 1993.

Thornton, Daniel L. "Targeting M2: The Issue of Monetary Control." The Federal Reserve Bank of St. Louis *Review* (July/August 1992), pp. 23–35.

Tobin, James. "The Interest-Elasticity of Transactions Demand for Cash." *Review of Economics and Statistics* (August 1956), pp. 241–47.

_____"Liquidity Preference as Behavior Toward Risk." *Review of Economic Studies* (February 1958), pp. 65–87.

PART V

PRIVATE SPENDING DECISIONS

14 CONSUMPTION BEHAVIOR

Private expenditures on consumption are the largest component of total spending in the economy. It should come as no surprise that macroeconomists have paid a tremendous amount of attention to consumption. The purpose of this chapter is to zero in on the major explanations that economists offer for consumption behavior.

We have already introduced a simple theory of consumption, the Keynesian consumption function in linear form as $C = c_0 + c_1 Y_D$. In this chapter we will present the empirical evidence on aggregate consumption and a more detailed account of Keynes's theory, which is now called the absolute income hypothesis. We will also examine the major alternative hypotheses that have been formulated in recent years: (1) the permanent income hypothesis, (2) the life-cycle hypothesis, and (3) permanent income (life-cycle) hypothesis under rational expectations.

After reading this chapter, you will know

- Keynes's absolute income hypothesis
- the difference between a nonproportional and proportional consumption function
- the empirical evidence underlying Keynes's absolute income hypothesis
- Friedman's permanent income hypothesis
- the reconciliation of permanent income with budget study data
- the implications of Friedman's permanent income hypothesis for fiscal policy
- the life-cycle hypothesis of Ando and Modigliani

- the effect of unplanned bequests on household behavior and its implications for aggregate saving in the life-cycle model
- the permanent income (life-cycle) hypothesis under rational expectations.

THE ABSOLUTE INCOME HYPOTHESIS

The absolute income hypothesis is associated with the name of John Maynard Keynes, but even before the publication of the *General Theory* a number of economists had recognized the relationship between consumption expenditures and household income. Keynes was the first, however, to use it as the major building block of macroeconomic analysis. Keynes's ideas about aggregate household consumption expenditures were stated in four principles:

1. *Consumption* C *is a function of disposable income* Y_d. Keynes defined the functional relationship of $C = C(Y_d)$ as the propensity to consume.

2. *The marginal propensity to consume MPC is a value between zero and one.*

3. *As aggregate real disposable income* Y_d *rises, the average propensity to consume APC declines.* Thus, the marginal propensity to consume is less than the average propensity to consume, or *MPC < APC.*

4. *As aggregate real disposable income rises, the marginal propensity to consume declines.* Keynes was, therefore, implying that the consumption function would not be a straight line.

Principles 1 and 2 are essential to building Keynesian models like the IS-LM model we developed in Chapter 4. Not only must consumption be a function of disposable income, $C = C(Y_d)$, but the *MPC* must be positive and less than one ($0 < MPC < 1$). If the *MPC* were equal to or greater than one, this would endanger the stability of the IS-LM model. Keynes's Principles 3 and 4 are *not* essential to Keynesian model construction. The average propensity to consume *APC* can be either greater than or equal to the marginal propensity to consume. Also, as we assumed in Chapter 4, the consumption function can be linear, having a constant slope (*MPC* is constant).

The first three principles have become known as the absolute income hypothesis, which received its name from the early disciples of Keynes. Absolute income means that current income determines the amount of household consumption.

The microeconomics of the absolute income hypothesis were not spelled out by Keynes. But assumptions about household behavior were implied. What were these micro assumptions? First, each household was assumed to be rational and able to maximize utility subject to the household's income constraint. Second, each household possessed complete information about the market. Finally, each household made its choice of goods and services independently of every other household. Let us elaborate on the first three principles of the absolute income hypothesis. As for Principle 1, Keynes stressed that real consumption was a stable function of real disposable income. This means that the intercept and the slope of the linear consumption function $C = c_0 + c_1 Y_d$ do not move about unpredictably. This stability exists because the most important variable or factor affecting consumption expenditures is disposable income. Keynes deemed other variables such as interest rates—a Classical notion—to be of little or no significance in their influence on household consumption.

Keynes's Principle 2, that $0 < MPC < 1$, was based on what he called his "fundamental psychological law." It may be paraphrased as follows: A household will spend more on goods and services as its real disposable income increases, but it will also save part of this increase in disposable income. Thus, Keynes's concept of the marginal propensity to consume is the ratio of the change in consumption to the change in income, or

$$MPC = \frac{\Delta C}{\Delta Y}.$$

A Nonproportional Consumption Function: $APC > MPC$

Keynes's Principle 3 stated that the average propensity to consume declines with rising disposable income. This principle implied that the marginal propensity to consume was less than the average propensity to consume ($MPC < APC$). To understand exactly what this **nonproportional consumption function** is and the relationship between the APC and the MPC is for a nonproportional consumption function, let us use the linear consumption function $C = 40 + .75\,Y$.

In column 1 of Table 14-1, we assume various levels of real income Y, which are then substituted into this linear consumption equation to find the various levels of real consumption in column 2.

The numerical values for the MPC presented in Column 3 were found by dividing the change in consumption ΔC by the change in income ΔY. Notice that the MPC is a constant value of .75. This is the case for any linear consumption function since the slope does not change. The APC in column 4

A NONPROPORTIONAL CONSUMPTION FUNCTION does not have the level of consumption rising in the same proportion as the level of income.

TABLE 14-1
Income, Consumption, *MPC*, and *APC* ($billions)

This table shows a linear and nonproportional consumption function. The *APC* is always greater than the *MPC* in the table.

(1) Y	(2) c = 40 + .75Y	(3) MPC = Δc/Δy	(4) APC = c/Y
100	115		1.15
Δy	Δc	.75	
200	190		.95
Δy	Δc	.75	
300	265		.88
Δy	Δc	.75	
400	340		.85

is found by dividing the level of consumption by the level of income or $APC = C/Y$. We see that the APC does decline from a value of 1.15 when the level of Y is \$100 billion to .85 when the level of Y rises to \$400 billion. Also, the MPC is less than the APC at every level of national income Y. Thus, the linear consumption function $C = 40 + .75Y$ is nonproportional. A linear consumption function is nonproportional if the level of consumption does not rise in the same proportion as the level of income.

A Proportional Consumption Function: APC = MPC

A PROPORTIONAL CONSUMPTION FUNCTION has the level of consumption rising in the same proportion as the level of income.

Having examined the relationship between the APC and the MPC for a nonproportional consumption function, let us now see what this relationship should be for a **proportional consumption function.** To change our earlier linear (nonproportional) consumption function $C = 40 + .75Y$ into a proportional one, assume that the value of the intercept c_0 is now 0 instead of 40. The consumption function becomes $C = .75Y$, a proportional consumption function. Table 14-2 presents the APC and the MPC for this type of consumption function. The value of the MPC equals the value of the APC at all levels of income. As the level of income rises in Table 14-2, the APC does not decline but is constant. A linear consumption function is proportional if it has a zero intercept value.

Empirical Evidence

Keynes's ideas about the consumption function were based on a psychological law rather than on empirical evidence. Immediately following the publication of *The General Theory* in 1936, however, economists began to examine empirically Keynes's consumption hypothesis. But, unlike physical scientists

TABLE 14-2
Income, Consumption, *MPC* and *APC* ($billions)

This table shows a linear and proportional consumption function. The *APC* is equal to the *MPC* in the table.

(1) Y	(2) c = .75Y	(3) MPC = Δc/Δy	(4) APC = c/y
100	75		.75
Δy	Δc	.75	
200	150		.75
Δy	Δc	.75	
300	225		.75
Δy	Δc	.75	
400	300		.75

who could gather their data from experiments conducted in laboratories, economists had to rely on data obtained from the historical records. The historical data available to economists usually come in either of two forms: **cross-sectional data** or **time-series data.** Let us first present the cross-sectional evidence pertaining to Keynes's consumption function.

CROSS-SECTIONAL DATA deal with the economic behavior of different groups, at the same point in time.

TIME-SERIES DATA are concerned with economic behavior over a span of time.

CROSS-SECTIONAL DATA

What exactly are cross-sectional data? Cross-sectional data are recorded for many members of a group at a point in time. If a cross-sectional study is undertaken with respect to the consumption behavior of households, it is called a budget study. Budget studies are usually conducted by government agencies or by various universities. Prior to World War II, budget studies were the main source of the empirical evidence available to analyze Keynes's consumption hypothesis. In budget studies, households are classified by income brackets. These studies aim to reveal how average household consumption differs from one disposable income bracket to another for a particular time period.

For example, Table 14-3 presents budget study data for households for 1987.[1] Note how the *APC* of households declines as we move from the

TABLE 14-3
Income and Consumption, Budget Data for 1987

As households move into higher income brackets, their *APC* remains greater than their *MPC*.

INCOME BRACKET	AVERAGE INCOME	CONSUMPTION	APC	MPC
UNDER $10,000	5,461.50	10,352.00	1.90	0.64
$10,000–19,999	14,537.50	16,151.75	1.11	0.61
20,000–29,999	24,513.50	22,241.50	0.91	0.58
30,000–39,999	34,433.25	28,003.25	0.81	0.51
40,000 AND OVER	63,715.00	42,841.50	0.67	—

SOURCE: Consumer Expenditure Survey Series: Interview Survey, 1984–1987, Report 2332, 1989, pp. 37–40.

[1]The Bureau of Labor Statistics completed its most recent consumer expenditure survey in June 1989. See *Consumer Expenditure Survey Series: Interview Survey,* 1984–1987, U.S. Department of Labor, Report 2332 (Washington, DC: U.S. Government Printing Office, 1989). David W. Wilcox has investigated the sources and methods used to construct the aggregate data on consumer spending in the United States. He is concerned about the implications for the outcome on empirical work. See David W. Wilcox, "The Construction of U.S. Consumption Data: Some Facts and Their Implications for Empirical Work," *American Economic Review* (September 1992), pp. 922–41.

low-income brackets to the high-income brackets. A decline in the *APC* as household disposable income rises indicates a nonproportional consumption function. This is not unique to our example. After examining numerous budget studies, economists have concluded that when each study is examined separately, the cross-sectional evidence suggests that the consumption function is nonproportional. However, the consumption function may not be linear since the *MPC* (slope) does decline as disposable income rises.

Therefore, we find that budget study data like those presented in Table 14-3 provide support to Keynes's consumption hypothesis. Households in the higher income brackets have a higher level of consumption and saving so real consumption increases as real disposable income rises. Also, as households move into higher and higher income brackets, they consume a smaller and smaller proportion of their disposable income. In addition the budget study data show that the *MPC* is positive and less than one and that its value falls below the value of the *APC*. Finally, there is the possibility that the cross-sectional consumption function is nonlinear (i.e., becomes flatter at higher income brackets) since the *MPC* tends to decline as disposable income rises. This result would substantiate Keynes's fourth proposition.

While the early supporters of Keynes found budget studies to be useful in testing his consumption hypothesis, cross-sectional data do have their limitations. One is that budget study data give only the average level of consumption for the households in each disposable income bracket. However, within each disposable income bracket there can be wide variations in consumption expenditures. These variations may be caused by factors other than disposable income. Another limitation of budget study data is that they report differences in household consumption behavior at a point in time. These data give no consideration to how consumption *changes* for all households as their disposable income *changes* over a series of time periods. Economists are interested in such changes. Moreover, in *The General Theory* Keynes was making reference to changes in aggregate consumption associated with changes in aggregate income.[2] One must, therefore, be careful in drawing conclusions from budget (cross-sectional) studies of household income differences and applying them to aggregate household income changes. To examine aggregate consumption behavior of households over time, one must use time-series data, which can show us the change in aggregate income and aggregate consumption from year to year.

TIME-SERIES DATA

During World War II, detailed national income accounts for the United States were developed to assist various war planning agencies. Economists were able to use the data contained in these accounts to estimate aggregate time-series

---

[2]See John Maynard Keynes, *The General Theory of Employment, Interest, and Money* (New York: Harcourt Brace Jovanovich, 1936), pp. 96–97.

consumption functions. An aggregate time-series consumption function traces out the *aggregate* consumption-income relations from one year to another.

From the national income accounts of World War II, time-series consumption functions like the one shown in Figure 14-1 were estimated for the period 1929–1941. The statistical technique used by economists was to fit a regression line that averaged the time-series data for a number of years. Essentially, what we have is a trend line. Like the budget study data, the results of these regressions tended to confirm Keynes's consumption hypothesis. The form of the consumption function, like that of the consumption function presented in Chapter 4, was $C = c_0 + c_1 Y_D$, where $c_0 > 0$ and $0 < c_1 < 1$. That is, the function was nonproportional ($APC > MPC$).

Today, time-series data on consumption expenditures and income are published in the *Survey of Current Business* by the Department of Commerce. Economists have found that when data in which the observation period is a year or a quarter are grouped into short-run periods (i.e., approximately

FIGURE 14-1
An Aggregate Time-Series
Consumption Function

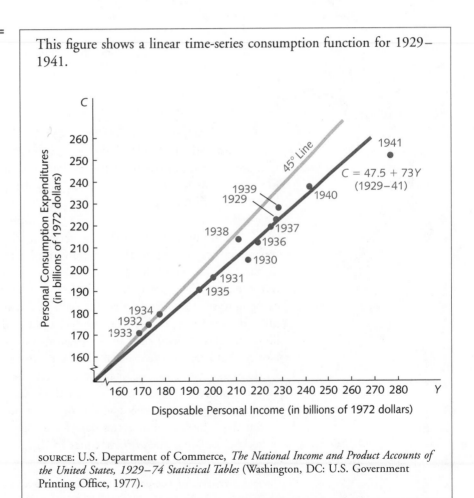

This figure shows a linear time-series consumption function for 1929–1941.

SOURCE: U.S. Department of Commerce, *The National Income and Product Accounts of the United States, 1929–74 Statistical Tables* (Washington, DC: U.S. Government Printing Office, 1977).

FIGURE 14-2
Long-Run and Short-Run
Time-Series Consumption
Functions

For shorter time periods (approximately ten years) time-series data
show a cyclical or short-run consumption function. For longer time
periods (fifty years or more) time-series data indicate a proportional or
long-run consumption function.

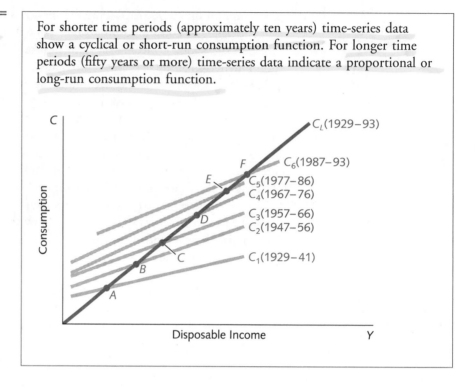

ten-year periods), such as 1929–1941, 1947–1956, 1957–1966, 1967–1976,
1977–1986, and 1987–1993 the regression estimates of a linear consumption
function for each of the short-run periods also indicate that the consumption
function is one of nonproportionality. This also provides support for Keynes's
hypothesis. We should note that a linear consumption function estimated with
time-series data for a short-run period (i.e., approximately ten years) is called a
cyclical consumption function. The term *cyclical* refers to a short-run period
roughly corresponding to the duration of a business cycle.

However, an interesting problem is associated with these cyclical consumption functions. When economists looked at all of these functions displayed on
one graph, they discovered that the cyclical consumption function had shifted
upward over time. To help our understanding of their finding, Figure 14-2
illustrates this upward shift in the cyclical (short-run) consumption function.
Notice that each of the cyclical consumption functions shown, designated as
C_1, C_2, C_3, C_4, C_5, and C_6, is based on a different period of time. Taking each
of these short-run consumption functions separately, the *APC* declines as
income rises and is greater than the *MPC*—a nonproportional function.

But if we look at time-series data for a long period, such as fifty years or
more, we find that the *APC* is equal to the *MPC*.[3] We have a proportional

_____

[3]To measure changes in consumption and income between successive short-run periods, the data
for consumption and income are organized by overlapping decades and then averaged.

consumption function. In other words, if a linear consumption function is estimated using the time-series data for the total period 1929–1993 and the data cover full decades (overlapping), the form of the consumption function would be $C = c_1 Y$. For example, the long-run consumption function might be C_L, the straight line drawn out of the origin of the graph in Figure 14-2 and passing through the points A, B, C, D, E, F on the short-run consumption functions C_1, C_2, C_3, C_4, C_5, and C_6 respectively. A time-series consumption function like C_L, shown in Figure 14-2, is often referred to as a secular consumption function since it may be related to the secular growth of income in the economy. The first major study of the long-run or secular consumption function was published by Simon Kuznets in 1946.[4] Examining the empirical evidence for the 1869–1929 period, Kuznets, using overlapping decade averages of consumption and national income, found that the APC had not declined during the period, but was almost constant. The APC varied between .84 and .89 and averaged about .86. As we recall, this would mean that with a constant APC, the average for the MPC would also be .86. Kuznets's basic results were verified in a later study (1955) by Raymond Goldsmith.[5] Goldsmith estimated a long-run or secular consumption function for the period 1896–1949, and his results showed that the APC out of personal income averaged about .88. Thus, the studies of long-run consumption by Kuznets and Goldsmith did not confirm Keynes's hypothesis that the APC declines with an increase in disposable income.

We may summarize all of these findings by saying that time-series data generate two types of consumption functions. One type is called a short-run or cyclical consumption function, and the other type is referred to as a long-run or secular consumption function. The type of functional relationship obtained with the data depends on the length of the time period chosen and the observation period for the data. For a short time period—approximately ten years of annual or quarterly data—we find a nonproportional relationship between consumption and disposable income. This is the cyclical short-run consumption function. However, for a long period of time—fifty years of data or more (overlapping decades)—we have a proportional relationship between consumption and disposable income, which is the secular or long-run consumption function. The essential question is, what is the fundamental or "true" relationship between consumption and disposable income? Is it nonproportional, with the $APC > MPC$, or is it proportional, with the $APC = MPC$? In the following sections, we will examine modern theories of the consumption function that have attempted to answer this puzzling empirical question.

---

[4]Simon Kuznets, *National Product Since 1869* (Princeton, NJ: Princeton University Press for National Bureau of Economic Research, 1946), p. 119.
[5]Raymond Goldsmith, *A Study of Saving in the United States*, vol. 1 (Princeton, NJ: Princeton University Press, 1955), pp. 398, 400.

THE PERMANENT INCOME HYPOTHESIS

PERMANENT INCOME is income a household anticipates or expects to receive over a number of years in the future, possibly a lifetime.

The **permanent income hypothesis** is associated with the name of Milton Friedman. In *A Theory of the Consumption Function* (1957), Friedman expressed his concern with the proper definition and measurement of income.[6] Keynes's absolute income hypothesis was based on the concept of current income, and, Friedman was critical of consumption as a function of current income.

When a household makes a purchase of a good or service, what type of current income is its decision based on? Is it the household's current weekly, current monthly, or current yearly income? For example, suppose a household knows that it will receive $30,000 in income in the current year, but it also knows that for the month of March and for the first week of October it will receive no income. Would we expect the household not to consume goods and services in March and the first week of October? Probably not. The loss of income for these particular periods would not affect household consumption to any appreciable extent if the household thinks in terms of current yearly income. As we found in earlier sections of this chapter, time-series and cross-sectional studies of the consumption function often use income for the current year as the appropriate time span for measuring income. Moreover, income for the current year is also a concept of income that is measured and recorded by government agencies. Therefore, in our discussion the term *current yearly income* will be the same as *current measured income.*

Friedman rejects the notion that household consumption expenditures are dependent on current income since for him a year is too short a time span in which to make meaningful household spending decisions. Friedman's hypothesis is that household consumption is based on permanent income, or expected income over a number of future years. Friedman breaks measured income into two components: permanent income and transitory income. Measured income can be expressed in the form of a simple equation as

$$Y = Y_P + Y_T,$$

where Y, Y_P, and Y_T represent measured, permanent, and transitory components, respectively. Let us first examine permanent income Y_P. Permanent income results from all those factors that the household regards as determining its wealth.

What exactly makes up the household's wealth? Remember that the household's total wealth is composed of two parts: nonhuman wealth and human wealth. The nonhuman wealth is the real physical and financial assets owned by the household. Real physical assets are items such as real estate and consumer durables (for example, autos, television sets, and washers and dryers). Physical assets generate a flow of income or services to the household. It should

---

[6]See Milton Friedman, *A Theory of the Consumption Function* (Princeton, NJ: Princeton University Press, 1957).

PHOTO 14-1
The Often Observed Consumption Patterns of Medical and Law Students Are Explained by the Fact That They Consume Goods and Services on the Basis of Their Expected Permanent Income, Not on Their Current Incomes.

be noted that the purchase of consumer durables is a form of saving, and consumption of these goods would be the imputed value of the flow of services. Strictly speaking, this flow is a flow of services rendered. Financial assets are items such as stocks and bonds, which also produce a flow of income to the household.

The human wealth part of total wealth, which is called human capital, is the skill and educational training of the household applied in a certain occupation to produce a flow of income. Both human and nonhuman factors, therefore, are involved in household wealth. Wealth is defined as the present value of all future expected income streams. The term *present value* can be explained by an example. If a household deposited $100 in a saving account and the interest rate was 5 percent, it would receive $100(1 + .05), or $105, a year from today. Thus, if a household wanted $105 one year from today with an interest rate of 5 percent, it would have to deposit $100 in its saving account. The $100 would be the present value, and it is obtained by dividing $105 by $(1 + R)$ or $(1 + .05)$. The $5 would be the flow of expected income to the household.

Assuming for simplicity that income continues indefinitely, wealth can be expressed in a formula as

$$A = \frac{Y_P}{r},$$

where A stands for the present value of wealth, Y_P for permanent income, and r for the real rate of interest. Notice that wealth is a stock variable and that permanent income Y_P is a flow variable. If we rewrite the above equation, we have

$$Y_P = Ar,$$

which gives a conceptual picture of permanent income since it is equal to the present value of wealth A times the real rate of interest r. The stock of wealth, except human capital, remains intact and can be passed on to one's heirs. Thus, Ar is the value of the permanent flow of income Y_P that the stock of wealth A will produce.

Transitory income Y_T is not related to permanent income Y_P. We say that the correlation between Y_P and Y_T is zero. Transitory income Y_T results from all those factors that the household considers pure chance, or unexpected. The value for Y_T can be either positive or negative, depending on whether the household has good luck or bad luck. If it has good luck, it experiences a windfall gain, and if it has bad luck, it experiences a loss. Friedman assumes that all *positive transitory income is saved.* This is an important point to remember. For example, if at the end of the year a household received an unexpected bonus, this would be positive transitory income that the household would save. Moreover, the household's measured income for the current year would be greater than its permanent income because of positive transitory income.

On the other hand, *negative transitory income* is dissaving (i.e., negative saving). For example, if a household had an unanticipated illness and therefore was out of work for several months, it would have negative transitory income and thus it would have to dissave. For that year, the measured income of the household would be less than its permanent income. To Friedman, then, the essential problem of using measured income or current yearly income in estimating consumption functions is that measured income can overstate or understate household income because of the transitory component of measured income. In the short run, the positive or negative transitory component is always present in the measurement of household income, but over a long time period positive and negative transitory income will cancel out for the household.

Estimating Permanent Income

Having discussed the meaning of permanent income Y_P and transitory income Y_T we begin to realize that one problem associated with the permanent income hypothesis concerns the empirical measurement of permanent income. While the actual statistical technique of estimating permanent income is rather complex, we can present the basic concept. Although permanent income Y_P is based on the household's expected (or predicted) future income, one way a household can determine the value of its expected income is from past levels of measured income. Suppose a household receives income on the basis of sales commissions. For the past four years, its income has been $12,000, $10,000, $15,000, and $18,000. Taking the average of past income levels would be one way to determine expected income for the next year. Thus, expected income would be $13,750.[7]

---

[7] In Friedman's analysis, permanent income is composed of a trend component plus an exponentially weighted average of past incomes with geometrically declining weights.

($12,000 + $10,000 + $15,000 + $18,000) = $13,750.

Note that the summation of the weights in the example equals 1. However, equal weighing is not a good procedure since households revise their previous estimates of permanent income based on current income experience. Therefore, economists assign lower and lower weights to levels of measured income further and further in the past. Friedman used a seventeen-year weighted average to estimate the fraction of each year's measured income that is permanent and the fraction that is transitory. He assigns a weight of .330 to the current year's measured income, with the weights declining after the current year as follows: .221, .148, .090, .067, .045, .030, .020, . . ., .001.[8] Thus, the current year's permanent income Y_P, is 33 percent of the current year's measured income, plus 22 percent of the preceding year's measured income, and so forth.

Now that we have found how Y_P is estimated, let us turn our attention to consumption. Measured consumption is divided into two components: permanent consumption and transitory consumption. Measured consumption can be written as

$$C = C_P + C_T,$$

where C, C_P, and C_T represent the measured, permanent, and transitory components, respectively. Permanent consumption C_P is the planned consumption of the household. Transitory consumption C_T is the householder's unanticipated consumption. An unexpected purchase of a good because of a bargain price would be positive transitory consumption, and an unexpected delay of a purchase because of the unavailability of the merchandise would be negative transitory consumption. Friedman assumes that transitory consumption C_T is not related to permanent consumption C_P or to transitory income Y_T. Thus, the correlation between C_T and C_P and between C_T and Y_T is zero.

What does the assumption of a zero correlation between transitory consumption C_T and transitory income Y_T mean? For example, if an individual went to Las Vegas and won $1,000 at the dice tables, this winning is unexpected or transitory income. The $1,000 would not affect permanent consumption, and also would not affect transitory consumption. Thus, the individual would tend to save the $1,000. On the other hand, according to the absolute income hypothesis, part of the winning is consumed.

To Friedman, the "true" relationship between consumption and income is proportionality. Permanent consumption is proportional to permanent income. The long-run consumption function is written as

$$C_P = k \cdot Y_P,$$

where permanent consumption C_P is a fraction k of permanent income Y_P. The relationship between permanent consumption C_P and permanent income

---

[8]See Friedman, *Theory of the Consumption Function*, p. 147.

Y_P is shown graphically in Figure 14-3. Notice that the long-run consumption function is drawn out of the origin of the graph.

The fraction k is called the marginal propensity to consume permanent income. It does not depend on the level of permanent income but on the real interest rate r, on the ratio of nonhuman total wealth A, and on a household's taste and preferences and age u; that is, $k = f(r, A, u)$. Before giving Friedman's estimate for k, it should be pointed out that consumption is defined in the physical sense, that is, as the physical consumption of goods and services. As was mentioned earlier, durable goods purchased in the current period are regarded by Friedman as saving to the extent that they are not consumed in the current period. Friedman's estimate of k was .88 based on time-series data for the 1905–1951 period, excluding the war years. That is, he found $C_P = .88\,Y_P$. The k value of .88 is in line with Raymond Goldsmith's estimate of .88 for the 1897–1949 period. Thus, the permanent income hypothesis is consistent with the empirical estimates of the secular (long-run) consumption function.

Reconciliation of Permanent Income with Budget Studies

On the basis of the permanent income hypothesis, Friedman can reconcile his hypothesis with budget studies. Economists have found with budget study data a short-run consumption function $C = c_0 + c_1 Y$, where $c_0 > 0$, because they have based their empirical studies on measured income Y, which contains a transitory component, rather than on permanent income Y_P. To show this, we use Figure 14-4 where measured consumption C and permanent consumption C_P are shown on the vertical axis and measured income Y and permanent income Y_P are on the horizontal axis. For households in the high-income brackets, a larger fraction will have positive transitory income (windfall gains) rather than negative transitory income (temporary losses). Therefore, their

---

FIGURE 14-3
The Consumption Function for the Permanent Income Hypothesis

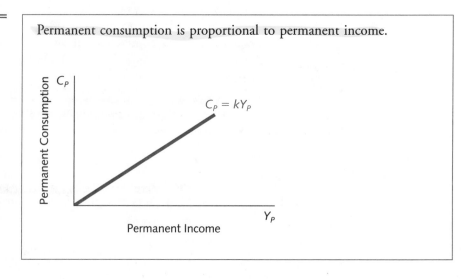

Permanent consumption is proportional to permanent income.

C_P

$C_P = kY_P$

Permanent Consumption

Permanent Income

Y_P

FIGURE 14-4
Reconciliation of Permanent
Income Hypothesis with
Budget Studies

While households in low-income brackets on the average have negative transitory income ($-Y_T'$), households in high-income brackets on the average have positive transitory income ($+Y_T'$). Consumption functions estimated from budget study data fail to consider these transitory components. The basic relationship between permanent consumption (C_P) and permanent income (Y_P) for all households in all income brackets is proportional, as shown in the figure.

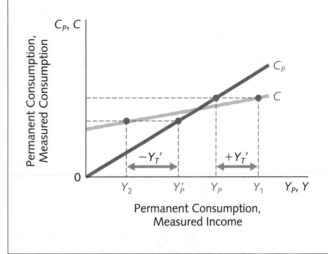

Permanent Consumption,
Measured Income

measured income Y_1 in Figure 14-4 will be greater than their permanent income Y_P. Since households consume on the basis of their permanent income, positive transitory income is saved, which is shown as $+Y_T'$ in the graph. While these high-income households will have a smaller APC out of measured income than will low-income households, their *APC* of permanent income will be constant and equal to the *MPC* out of permanent income. Households in the middle-income brackets have about the same amount of both positive and negative transitory income. Thus, their measured income and the permanent income are the same since the average of transitory income is zero.

A larger fraction of households in the lower-income brackets will have negative transitory income—losses. Low-income families have more misfortune. In this case, measured income Y_2 is less than permanent income Y_P', in Figure 14-4. The difference between Y_2 and Y_P' is negative transitory income $-Y_T'$. Thus, lower-income households would have a higher *APC* of measured income than would higher-income households, but their *APC* of permanent income will be identical to the *APC* of permanent income of the higher-income households.

This analysis of household consumption behavior in various income brackets explains the findings of the budget studies, which show a nonproportional consumption function. If households in high-income brackets have on the average positive transitory income, households in the middle-income brackets have on the average zero transitory income, and households in the low-income brackets on the average have negative transitory income, the cross-sectional data obtained from budget studies would trace out a consumption function with a positive intercept and an $APC > MPC$. But looking at the basic relationship between consumption C_P and permanent income, all households have the same APC of permanent income. This reconciles the short-run and long-run consumption functions estimated with time-series data. As permanent income rises over time in the economy, the APC of permanent income for all households will stay the same. The consumption function for permanent income then, is proportional—a straight line out of the origin of the graph in Figure 14-3.

Permanent Income and Fiscal Policy

Friedman's hypothesis that the MPC out of transitory income is zero also has interesting implications for fiscal policy. Suppose Congress and the President of the United States decide to bolster disposable income, and thereby consumption, with a temporary tax cut. If households feel that this increase in disposable income is transitory income, then they will save it all. The temporary tax cut has not altered the permanent income of households, and therefore there is no stimulus to consumption and to the level of national income and employment in the economy. What if the tax cut was announced and believed to be permanent? Since every consumer would find permanent income raised by the full amount of the tax cut, the response of spending should be rapid and complete.

It is also useful to remember that a number of economic policies and policy changes might be designed to increase permanent income and consumption. Some leading nations have, for example, employed an "industrial policy" to promote economic growth and sustained consumption. Whether these policies should be imported to the United States is an open question, however. In this regard, see the Global Perspective: "Should the United States Import Industrial Policies from Europe, Japan, and Canada to Increase Consumption?"

THE LIFE-CYCLE HYPOTHESIS

LIFE-CYCLE HYPOTHESIS is the theory that consumption depends on the present value of all future income streams being consumed over the lifetime of the average person.

At the same time Friedman was developing his permanent income hypothesis, Albert Ando and Franco Modigliani were formulating a similar theory called the **life-cycle hypothesis** of consumption.[9] The basic difference between the two theories is that in the life-cycle hypothesis consumption depends on the

[9]Franco Modigliani and R. E. Brumberg, "Utility Analysis and the Consumption Function; An Interpretation of Cross-section Data," in *Post-Keynesian Economics,* ed. K. K. Kurihara (New Brunswick, NJ: Rutgers University Press, 1954); and Albert Ando and Franco Modigliani, "The 'Life-Cycle' Hypothesis of Saving: Aggregate Implications and Tests," *American Economic Review* (March 1963), pp. 55–84.

GLOBAL PERSPECTIVE

SHOULD THE UNITED STATES IMPORT INDUSTRIAL POLICIES FROM EUROPE, JAPAN, AND CANADA TO INCREASE CONSUMPTION?

What is industrial policy? Industrial policy, a concept that has been associated with economists in President Bill Clinton's administration, is actually a post-World War II European and Japanese import. The goal is to encourage a high production–high consumption economy. Essential to the idea is that business, industry, and labor form a "partnership" in order to plan economic growth in particular directions. Thus the government extends incentives that will direct technology in certain industries—for example, computers, computer chips, automobiles, high-speed trains, and so on. Among the ideas comprising industrial policy are massive infrastructure investments, direct subsidies to industries, increased reliance on consumption or value added taxes (VATs), nationalized health care, family leave provisions, worker training programs mandated by government, government jobs and apprenticeship programs, and protection of union workers and union interests.

While the United States has maintained less regulation (on balance) and one of the most open world labor markets among nations, the adoption of industrial policy would render the U.S. economy closer to the "managed" economies of Europe, Japan, and Canada. In spite of the enthusiasm generated for industrial policy and government micro management by President Clinton's economic advisors, it is a fair question to ask how these economies have performed over the past fifteen or so years in comparison to U.S. economic performance. According to statistics

TABLE 14-4
International Comparison: Employment, Inflation, and Per Capita Income, 1980– 1993

Despite the institution of "partnerships" between government, business, and labor, the relative performance of Canada, Europe, and Japan has not been clearly superior to the more "market-driven" economy of the United States.

	UNEMPLOYMENT RATE (PERCENT)	CONSUMER INFLATION (PERCENT)	PER-CAPITA GDP (IN DOLLARS)
CANADA	9.5	5.9	$14,984
EUROPE	8.6	6.6	12,948
JAPAN	1.8	2.6	12,806
U.S.	6.9	5.2	17,200

SOURCE: OECD data from Paul Speery, "Must We Copy Our Competitors?", *Investor's Business Daily* (April 13, 1993), p. 1.

from the Organization of Economic Cooperation and Development (OECD), relative average rates of unemployment, consumer inflation, and per-capita GDP between 1980 and 1993 do not provide persuasive evidence for the success of industrial policy. As Table 14-4 shows, the United States led the world in per capita income and (until 1991) was bested only by Japan in terms of unemployment and inflation rates. Unemployment and inflation rates were considerably higher in Europe than in the United States over the period. Labor costs in both Japan and Europe have risen due to the implementation of industrial policy by government. By contrast, labor cost increases in the U.S. moderated (increasing about 3 percent) since 1985. These factors explain the movement of Japanese, German, and other production facilities to the United States. In 1991, Japan entered its most severe recession in two decades. While U.S. growth in employment and output slowed over the same period, American workers still outpaced all others in the world in terms of real purchasing power.

Other data comparisons belie the so-called successes of industrial policy. In January 1993, France's unemployment rate was 10.5 percent and Britain's was 10.8 percent compared to about 7.2 percent in the United States. In Canada the jobless rate hit 10.8 percent in January 1993. In June 1993, the overall unemployment rate in the European Community was 12 percent, a post-war high. Between 1983 and 1989, U.S. employment rose by 2.4 percent per year, which was twice as fast as Japan and four times as fast as Germany. Between 1985 and 1993, U.S. exports as a percentage of GDP almost doubled to 11.5 percent while the Japanese percentage declined to 10.2 percent. U.S. factory and manufacturing output by no means suffers in comparison with Europe's or Japan's.[a]

Such comparative data may not be conclusive. But critics of the implementation of broadbased industrial policies in the United States—policies to replace less regulated production and labor markets—have strong reasons to question their effectiveness at promoting high growth and employment. Regulations and controls created by industrial policy may be far less advantageous in practice and in contrast to the lower level of controls that the United States has established in the post–World War II period. ❑

NOTE [a]Data for this discussion were derived from Paul Sperry, "Must We Copy Our Competitors?", *Investor's Business Daily* (April 13, 1993), pp. 1–2.

present value of wealth A rather than on the present value of wealth A times the real rate of interest, which is permanent income Y_P. The simplest version of the life-cycle hypothesis has the present value of all future income streams being consumed over the lifetime of the average person.

The assumption is that people will attempt to smooth out the flow of their income over the course of their lives so that when they die, their wealth is zero. Figure 14-5 illustrates the life-cycle hypothesis, with the horizontal axis depicting the age of a person over his or her lifetime from birth to death D and the vertical axis showing the flow of income Y, consumption C, and saving S over the person's lifetime. To the average individual, the flow of income, which is the curve Y, is much lower in early age (t_0 to t_1) or in old age (t_2 to D) than in middle age (t_1 to t_2). The consumption stream of an individual, represented by the straight line C, is constant or slightly rising over time. We see in Figure 14-5 that in the early stages of the individual's life, which is from childhood to young adulthood (or the time period t_0 to t_1), the individual is consuming more than he or she is earning. The individual is therefore a net borrower, or dissaver. When the individual reaches the middle stages of life (or time period t_1 to t_2) he or she is earning more income and consuming a lower fraction of it, obviously an attempt to accumulate assets to repay earlier debt and to support the individual in old age or retirement. In this stage, the individual is a net saver. In the final stage of the life cycle, which is old age (or time period t_2 to D), the individual is again a dissaver, using up the assets accumulated in middle age.

The life-cycle hypothesis can easily explain the nonproportional consumption function obtained from budget study (cross-sectional data). At a given point in time, there will be a large proportion of middle-aged people relative to young and old people who will earn income above the average income for all people. This means that these people will be in the high-income brackets. On the other hand, there will be a large proportion of young and old people relative to middle-aged people whose income will be below the average income for all people. This would thereby place them in the low-income brackets. As

FIGURE 14-5
The Life-Cycle Hypothesis

People consume more than their income in their early age and save more than their income in their middle age to support themselves in their old age. In the final stage of their life cycle, people again are consuming more than they are saving.

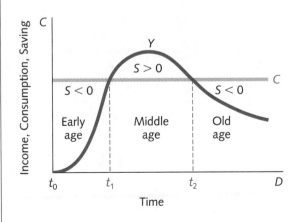

we recall from budget studies, the *APC* is lower for those in the high-income brackets than it is for those in the low-income brackets. Since the *APC* is more than the *MPC*, and therefore not constant in budget studies, the life-cycle hypothesis can provide an explanation for the nonproportional consumption function estimated from this type of cross-sectional data.

On the basis of the life-cycle hypothesis, the basic relationship between consumption and income is the long-run proportional consumption function. Given the assumption that the income distribution and the age distribution of the population remain fairly stable over time, the long-run (secular) consumption function can be written as

$$C = \lambda A,$$

where λ is the marginal propensity to consume and depends, like Friedman's *k,* on the real rate of interest, tastes and preferences, and age, and *A* is the present value of wealth. The present value of wealth *A* can be divided into three parts: (1) the present value of property income such as interest and dividends, (2) the household's current nonproperty or labor income, and (3) the present value of the nonproperty or labor income that the household expects to earn over its lifetime. The aggregate consumption function can be expressed in the form of a linear equation with these various types of wealth specified on the right-hand side of the equation as

$$C_t = \alpha A_t + \alpha Y_t^L + \alpha(T - 1)Y_t^{LE},$$

where C_t is consumption in year *t*, A_t is the present value of property assets at the beginning of year *t*, Y_t^L is current labor income, Y_t^{LE} is the present value of expected future labor income, the T of $(T - 1)$ is the remaining years of life, and each α is an *MPC*.

A major empirical problem with the above equation is how to estimate the present value of expected future labor income Y_t^{LE}. Various alternatives for measuring Y_t^{LE} were tried by Ando and Modigliani. The method that seemed to provide a fairly reasonable estimate was to let expected future labor income be some proportion of current labor income:

$$Y_t^{LE} = \beta Y_t^L \text{ and } 0 < \beta < 1.$$

The consumption equation could then be expressed as

$$C_t = \alpha A_t + \alpha Y_t^L + \alpha\beta(T - 1)Y_t^L$$
$$= \alpha A_1 + \alpha[1 + \beta(T - 1)]Y_t^L.$$

The estimate found by Ando and Modigliani for the consumption function C_t, based on U.S. data was

$$C_t = .06A_t + .7Y_t^L.$$

Using this estimate of C_t, the life-cycle hypothesis can be reconciled with the short-run and long-run consumption functions. In the short run, the amount of property assets is approximately constant. Thus, the term $.06A_t$ would be the intercept of the short-run consumption function and the slope of the function would be $.7$, which is the estimate for $\alpha[1 + \beta(T - 1)]$. With an increase in labor income Y_t^L, the *APC* would decline, which means that the $APC > MPC$. This result of a declining *APC* conforms to estimates of the (nonproportional) short-run consumption function using ten years of time-series data. However, in the long run a steady growth in property assets A_t would shift the short-run consumption function upward, since $.06A_t$—the intercept value—would no longer be a constant but would increase with a positive change in A_t. If there is a steady growth in labor income Y_t^L along with the steady growth in A_t, the only points observed will be on the long-run consumption function drawn out of the origin of the graph.

The *APC* was constant, as we recall, for the (proportional) long-run consumption function estimated by both Kuznets and Goldsmith. To find the *APC* for the consumption function estimated by Ando and Modigliani, we divide both sides of the C_t equation by national income Y_t and obtain

$$\frac{C_t}{Y_t} = .06\frac{A_t}{Y_t} + .7\frac{Y_t^L}{Y_t}.$$

For the *APC*, which is C_t/Y_t, to remain constant, we see that the ratios A_t/Y_t and Y_t^L/Y_t must remain almost constant, or if either goes up, the other has to go down to offset it. The ratios A_t/Y_t and Y_t^L/Y_t have shown secular stability. The asset–national income ratio for households has been around the value of 5 and the labor–national income ratio has been approximately .75. Substituting these values into the equation $C_t/Y_t = .06(5) + .7(.75)$ gives an $APC = .82$ that is close to the values obtained by Kuznets and Goldsmith for the long-run APC. Thus, the Ando-Modigliani life-cycle hypothesis explains the constant APC in the long run and the decline of the APC in the short run.

The life-cycle hypothesis is not without its shortcomings. First, there is a problem associated with the estimate of expected future labor income Y_t^{LE} as some proportion of current labor income, or $Y_t^{LE} = \beta Y_t^L$. What makes the formulation hard to use is that it assumes that changes in current labor income are permanent when, in fact, such changes may be temporary. A change in current labor income may generate a change in future labor income that is in the opposite direction rather than in the same direction. For example, the temporary income tax surcharge imposed in 1968–69 made the change in current income temporary rather than permanent.

A second shortcoming of the life-cycle hypothesis is its assumption that old households are dissavers, when, in fact, they may be savers.[10] This would tend to reduce the ability of the hypothesis to explain the estimated nonproportional consumption function using cross-sectional data from budget studies. Bequests may also have an impact on the analysis. See, for example, the Policy Issue: "Aggregate Saving and Bequests."

THE PERMANENT INCOME (LIFE-CYCLE) HYPOTHESIS UNDER RATIONAL EXPECTATIONS

Studies of the consumption function that employ the permanent income (life-cycle) hypothesis of consumer behavior assume people behave according to an adaptive-expectations mechanism. That is, current and past levels of actual income determine a person's expected future income, possibly over a lifetime. Since permanent income under adaptive expectations is based only on the behavior of current and past income, it does not include all the information that can affect a person's thinking about future income. For example, a major and uncontrollable epidemic could break out in a country and devastate the population. This unfortunate event could cause a reduction in the permanent income of the people but naturally would not be reflected in the past levels of actual income. But it is these past levels of actual income that economists use in estimating permanent income. Thus, when we assume an adaptive-expectations mechanism in estimating permanent income, we are not considering all the information that can affect people's future income.

In recent years, economists such as Marjorie Flavin and Fumio Hayashi have estimated permanent income by employing the theory of rational expectations

[10]See Thad W. Miser, "The Wealth-Age Relation among the Aged," *American Economic Review* (June 1979), pp. 435–43; and "The Dissaving Behavior of the Retired Aging," *Southern Economic Journal* (April 1980), pp. 1197–1205.

rather than the theory of adaptive expectations.[11] According to the theory of rational expectations, people use current available and relevant information in forming their expectations based on a particular model of the economy that they have in mind. All of their past information, together with any current information, is incorporated into their rational expectations of permanent income. However, an estimate of permanent income can be altered by some sudden *unanticipated* change in the current period. If the unanticipated change in real income is substantial, the influence of past period experiences may not swamp it. This unanticipated change in current and real income may lead to a complete revision of expected permanent income. For example, the Persian Gulf War of 1991 implied for the U.S. economy a permanent reduction in real incomes for the foreseeable future. This unanticipated shock could generate a downward revision of the expectation of permanent income and thereby of permanent consumption. Thus, a new piece of information generates a reappraisal of the rational expectations of permanent income.

The Hall Hypothesis

Economist Robert Hall derived a testable implication of the permanent income hypothesis with rational expectations by arguing that consumption evolves according to a random walk with trend. This suggests that the consumption equation could be expressed as:

$$C_t = \lambda + 1.0\ C_{t-1} + u_t \qquad \lambda > 0$$

where λ is trend, C_t is consumption in the current period, C_{t-1} is consumption in the previous period, and u_t is a random error term. This equation allows C_t to be larger or smaller than $\lambda + 1.0\ C_{t-1}$ depending on whether u_t is positive on negative. A random shock will cause u_t to be either positive or negative and thus C_t to be higher or lower. According to the random-walk hypothesis, current consumption should reflect all the information available to the household, and all current consumption changes should be independent of past history. The evidence presented by Hall is thus against an adaptive expectations model. His main empirical finding is that lags of disposable income have no predictive power in explaining consumption behavior. That is, it cannot be used to improve the predictions arising from the random walk with trend. As far as fiscal policy is concerned, Hall concludes that only unex-

---

[11]Life-cycle–permanent income are used together because permanent income can be what a person expects to receive over his or her lifetime, and the life-cycle approach places emphasis on wealth and demographic variables. See Marjorie A. Flavin, "The Adjustment of Consumption to Changing Expectations about Future Income," *Journal of Political Economy* (October 1981), pp. 974–1009; Fumio Hayashi, "The Permanent Income Hypothesis: Estimation and Testing by Instrumental Variables," *Journal of Political Economy* (October 1982), pp. 895–916; and A. A. Haug, "The Random Walk Hypothesis of Consumption and Time Aggregation," *Journal of Macroeconomics* (Fall 1991), pp. 691–700. For a current survey of research on consumption, see also Angus Deaton, *Understanding Consumption* (New York: Oxford University Press, 1992).

POLICY ISSUE

POLICY ISSUE:

AGGREGATE SAVING AND

BEQUESTS

In recent years, empirical research has suggested that the basic life-cycle model cannot account for a realistic level of aggregate saving. However, this research failed to consider the effect that bequests could have on household behavior.

Lars Soderstrom has shown that when unplanned bequests are introduced into the life-cycle model, they account for a large part of *aggregate* saving. Let us see how this saving comes about. In the analysis, Soderstrom attaches importance to uncertainty about the time of death. He argues that as people grow older they will

expect to experience long lives. This, in turn, will make them inclined to revise their consumption plans downward; that is, to save more at each successive age than they originally, say, at age 21, planned to do. Since unplanned bequests are considered in this model, people will die unexpectedly and their net worth will be transferred to surviving heirs. If so, this wealth will to a large extent be saved, at least in the short run, and thus will show up in the amount of aggregate saving.[a] More recently, the work by Andrew Abel supports Soderstrom and demonstrates that accidental bequests by selfish individuals can also account for a potentially sizable fraction of aggregate saving.[b] ❑

SOURCES: [a]Lars Soderstrom, "The Life Cycle Hypothesis and Aggregate Household Saving," *Ameri-

can Economic Review* (June 1982), pp. 590–96. The importance of bequests in aggregate saving has also been established by Lawrence Kotlikoff and Lawrence Summers who report that 80 percent of U.S. household wealth is inherited wealth. See L. J. Kotlikoff and L. Summers, "The Role of Intergenerational Transfers in Aggregate Capital Accumulation," *Journal of Political Economy* (August 1981), pp. 706–32. Also see R. H. Clarida, "Aggregate Stochastic Implications of the Life Cycle Hypothesis," *Quarterly Journal of Economics* (August 1991), pp. 851–67.
[b]Andrew B. Abel, "Precautionary Saving and Accidental Bequests," *American Economic Review* (September 1985), pp. 777–79.

pected changes in policy, such as an unexpected tas reduction, will change consumption. Furthermore, any new information that leads to a revision of expected future income—including announcements of future prices, such as tax law changes or changes in health care provision—can have an immediate effect on consumption, even before the actual policy change occurs.

The Flavin Hypothesis

Marjorie Flavin developed one approach to the theory of rational expectations. Her empirical results indicated sensitivity of consumption to current income; that is, the marginal propensity to consume out of transitory income is not zero, as the permanent income hypothesis suggests, but is instead a positive value. The reason for this finding is that low-income households are faced with liquidity constraints. People who have temporarily low incomes are supposed to maintain their consumption, according to the permanent income hypothesis, by dipping into their savings or by borrowing. However, Flavin finds that this is not the case. People in low-income brackets do not have any savings to maintain their level of consumption, and they cannot borrow because of their lack of physical and financial assets. So, when their income rises these people are no longer liquidity constrained and they increase their consumption by a greater amount than predicted by the permanent-income hypothesis.

The Hayashi Hypothesis

Following in the footsteps of Flavin, Fumio Hayashi examines the consumption function for two types of households: wealth-constrained and liquidity-constrained. The consumption function for the wealth-constrained household depends on real human and nonhuman wealth and the one for the liquidity-constrained household simply depends on real disposable income. For the wealth-constrained households, real human wealth is the present discounted value of the expected future real labor income, and nonhuman wealth is financial assets of households and noncorporate and corporate capital. In testing his consumption function, Hayashi used two different sources for his consumption data series. One data series on consumption was taken from Christensen and Jorgenson and *includes service flows* from consumer durables.[12] The other one was from the National Income and Product Accounts (NIPA), which *excludes service flows* from consumer durables and includes expenditures on consumer durables. He found that the permanent income hypothesis with rational expectations was accepted for the wealth-constrained household but not for the liquidity-constrained household when the consumption measure includes service flows from consumer durables. On the other hand, the hypothesis was rejected for both households on the NIPA consumption measure, but this result did not surprise him because it was not the consumption measure that the permanent income hypothesis tried to explain. Therefore, according to Hayashi, the acceptance or rejection of the permanent income hypothesis seems to depend not only on the assumption of rational expectation behavior on the part of households but also on the choice of the consumption measure used to estimate permanent income (see Insight: "Using Consumption to Forecast Income").

---

[12]L. R. Christensen and D. W. Jorgenson, "Measuring Economic Performance in the Private Sector," in *The Measurement of Economic and Social Performance,* ed. Milton Mass (New York: Columbia University Press for National Bureau of Economic Research, 1973).

"USING CONSUMPTION TO FORECAST INCOME"

While economists usually build very complicated statistical models to forecast the course of the economy, there are much simpler methods of constructing forecasts of real Gross Domestic Product (GDP). One such method relies on the rational expectations version of the permanent income hypothesis that we discussed in this chapter. We recall that according to Milton Friedman's permanent income hypothesis, a person's consumption behavior at a given moment in time depends upon the level of income that individual expects to receive in the future, possibly over a lifetime. If the individual's estimate of permanent income is based on rational expectations, then he or she would use all available information to forecast future income and would not make systematic forecasting errors. That is, while possibly predicting incorrectly from time to time, a person will not systematically over-predict or under-predict income. Thus, the current consumption of a person re-

flects that individual's best forecast of future income.

Since the level of consumption is based on all information known to the person, a change in consumption can take place only when one receives new information about income. Any information from past income does not change current consumption. Past consumption, however, can provide information that can be used to forecast future income. Thus, we will observe the level of real income adjusting to ensure that the consumption-GDP ratio returns to its long-run mean. To help us in our understanding of the forecasting model, consider two examples.

In our first example, there is a decline in real GDP. If people react by reducing their rate of saving to maintain their same level of consumption, it implies that they do not view the fall in their income as permanent. On an empirical basis, one would observe an above-average consumption-GDP ratio and would forecast that real GDP will rise quickly to bring the ratio back to its normal long-run level. In our second example, let us suppose real GDP declines, resulting in a comparable fall in consump-

tion but little change in the rate of saving. This empirical result would suggest that people had interpreted the fall in real GDP as a decline in their permanent income. The consumption-GDP ratio would move very little, so one would not forecast a quick return of real GDP to its long-run level.

Bharat Trehan, economist for the San Francisco Federal Reserve, estimated this permanent income–rational expectations model using time-series data for the period from 1947 to 1991.[a] His results suggested that consumption today does contain important information about future income. But like other forecasting techniques, this approach does not rule out adverse economic developments in the future such as exogenous shocks to the system. This simple model does show how to use available income to forecast the economy without having to specify a highly complex and sophisticated statistical model.   ❏

NOTE: [a]Bharat Trehan, "Using Consumption to Forecast Income," *FRBSF Weekly Letter,* Federal Reserve Bank of San Francisco (June 7, 1991).

SUMMARY

This chapter has shown that the consumption function is a more complex issue than envisioned by Keynes in the *General Theory*. We have examined not only Keynes's absolute income hypothesis and the empirical evidence to support it but also the permanent income hypothesis of Friedman, the life-cycle hypothesis of Ando and Modigliani, and the permanent income (life-cycle) hypothesis under rational expectations.

The reader should keep the underlying principles of the present chapter in mind when interpreting "consumption" in models such as the *IS-LM* model. Nevertheless, despite the number of variables that can affect consumption, there does seem to be a consensus among economists that some form of income, however measured, is the most important variable affecting consumption behavior.

KEY TERMS

cross-sectional data

life-cycle hypothesis

nonproportional consumption function

permanent income hypothesis

proportional consumption function

time-series data

QUESTIONS FOR REVIEW AND DISCUSSION

1. Keynes's ideas about aggregate consumption expenditures were stated in four basic principles. What were those four principles?

2. What exactly are cross-sectional data? How do such data provide support to Keynes's consumption hypothesis?

3. Are there any limitations in using budget study data to test Keynes's consumption hypothesis? If so, what are they?

4. How is an aggregate time-series consumption function defined?

5. Do time-series data generate two different types of consumption function? If so, what are they?

6. How is permanent income defined?

7. To Milton Friedman, is proportionality the "true" relationship between consumption and income? If so, why?

8. How does Friedman reconcile the permanent income hypothesis with budget study data?

9. Suppose there is an unexpected federal income tax cut. If this tax cut is permanent, what impact does it have on permanent income?

10. Is there a basic difference between Ando and Modigliani's life-cycle hypothesis and Friedman's permanent income hypothesis? If so, what is it?

11. Do bequests in the life-cycle model account for a realistic level of aggregate saving for the economy? If so, explain how.

12. How does the theory of rational expectations relate to the permanent income (life-cycle) hypothesis?

13. What empirical contribution did Robert Hall and Marjorie Flavin make to increase our understanding of permanent income with rational expectations?

14. What were Fumio Hayashi's empirical findings about the consumption function with rational expectations?

PROBLEMS

1. Suppose there was a redistribution of income in the United States. What effect would this have on consumption behavior, according to the permanent-income hypothesis?

2. Using the latest *Economic Report of the President* calculate and graph consumption and disposable personal income from 1970 through 1993. (This is a time-series consumption function like the one shown in Figure 14-1.) Is the APC constant in this time-series consumption function? How do you explain the long-term relation of consumption and income for these years?

SUGGESTIONS FOR FURTHER READING

Abel, Andrew B. "Precautionary Saving and Accidental Bequests." *American Economic Review* (September 1985), pp. 777–79.

Ando, Albert, and Franco Modigliani. "The 'Life Cycle' Hypothesis of Saving: Aggregate Implications and Tests." *American Economic Review* (March 1963), pp. 55–84.

Clarida, R. H. "Aggregate Stochastic Implications of Life-Cycle Hypothesis." *Quarterly Journal of Economics* (August 1991), pp. 851–67.

Deaton, Angus. *Understanding Consumption.* New York: Oxford University Press, 1992.

Flavin, Marjorie A. "The Adjustment of Consumption to Changing Expectations about Future Income." *Journal of Political Economy* (October 1981), pp. 974–1009.

Friedman, Milton. *A Theory of the Consumption Function.* Princeton, NJ: Princeton University Press, 1957.

Fuhrer, Jeffrey C. "Do Consumers Behave as the Life-Cycle/Permanent-Income Theory of Consumption Predicts?" Federal Reserve Bank of Boston *New England Economic Review* (September/October 1992), pp. 3–14.

Hall, Robert E. "The Stochastic Implications of the Life-Cycle—Permanent Income Hypothesis." *Journal of Political Economy* (April 1978), pp. 971–987.

Haug, A. A. "The Random Walk Hypothesis of Consumption and Time Aggregation." *Journal of Macroeconomics* (Fall 1991), pp. 691–700.

Mayer, Thomas, ed. *Permanent Income, Wealth, and Consumption.* Berkeley: University of California Press, 1972.

Modigliani, Franco. "Life Cycle, Individual Thrift and Wealth of Nations." *American Economic Review* (June 1986), pp. 297–313.

_____. "The Role of Intergenerational Transfers and Life Cycle Saving in the Accumulation of Wealth." *Journal of Economic Perspectives* (Spring 1988), pp. 15–40.

15

CHANGES IN INVESTMENT

SPENDING

The most volatile component of private spending is investment. Unpredictable flutters in investment spending can send macroeconomic shock waves to income growth, unemployment rates, and inflation. In previous chapters, investment has been treated either as an exogenous variable, or as dependent on the current real interest rate. The focus of this chapter is on various alternative theories of investment, including (1) the Neoclassical approach; (2) the accelerator principle in both the rigid and flexible form; and (3) Tobin's q. We also examine the determinants of residential investment and the factors that affect inventory investment.

Investment is a flow of expenditures on capital goods, which are being used either to replace depreciated capital goods or to add to the economy's capital stock. Investment expenditures can be "disaggregated" into three categories: (1) business fixed investment, which is business spending on plant and equipment; (2) residential construction, which is investment in housing; and (3) inventory investment. Each of these three categories of investment will be examined in this chapter.

After reading this chapter, you will know

- the basic factors businesses examine in determining the profit they expect to accrue from an investment project
- the user costs of capital
- the impact changes in the investment tax credit have on the purchase price of a new capital good
- the Neoclassical approach to investment spending

- the impact that changes in corporate taxes have on investment spending under the Neoclassical approach to investment
- the difference between the rigid accelerator model and the flexible accelerator model
- the Tobin theory of investment behavior and the differences between it and the Neoclassical theory of investment behavior
- how the supply curve for new housing is determined
- the motives for holding inventories
- the new changes in inventory management and how they affect the U.S. economy.

PRIVATE INVESTMENT

While most economists consider consumption expenditures the most stable component of aggregate demand, they also recognize investment expenditures as the most volatile. Look at a recent summary of the evidence. Figure 15–1 depicts the fluctuations of gross private domestic investment and its components from 1982 to 1991. Notice how changes in business inventories fluctuate more than residential and nonresidential investment (plant and equipment). This instability in investment spending can create fluctuations in the level of national income and employment. Thus, most theories of the business cycle have investment playing a central role in the analysis. Yet investment expenditures and capital formation are undertaken by the private sector of the economy, and any attempts to influence such spending can be made only through indirect measures such as a change in tax regulations. It is also the case that foreign investment in the United States affects aggregate investment (see Global Perspective: "Should We Be Concerned About Foreign Direct Investment in the United States?"). Despite this, there is a need to study and to understand the determinants of investment decision making to try to avoid the severe fluctuations that could occur in income, employment, and prices as a result of fluctuations in investment.

FIGURE 15–1
Gross Private Domestic
Investment (seasonally
adjusted annual rates)

The figure shows gross private domestic investment and its subcomponents: nonresidential fixed investment, residential fixed investment, and change in business inventories.

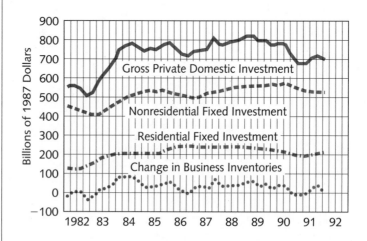

SOURCE: Council of Economic Advisors, *Economic Indicators* June 1992 (Washington DC: U.S. Government Printing Office, 1992) p. 9.

SHOULD WE BE CONCERNED ABOUT FOREIGN DIRECT INVESTMENT IN THE UNITED STATES?

One of the important foreign policy issues facing the United States is foreign investment.[a] *The New York Times* and *The Wall Street Journal* often have articles on foreign investment in the United States. Most of us probably use products of foreign-owned U.S. businesses such as Hamilton Beach appliances, Friskies cat food, Foster Grant sunglasses, a Scripto or Bic pen, or Vaseline Intensive Care hand lotion. Why has foreign investment become so large in the U.S. economy? Because the United States has been spending more on goods and services than it has been producing at home, and it has been importing the difference. Equivalently, the United States has been saving too little compared to its investment, and foreign capital has financed the difference.

Foreigners have been willing to lend largely because U.S. interest rates in the early eighties were higher than foreign rates. However, since the dollar has declined from its peak in 1985, private foreign investment has declined. Foreign investment in the United States can be either direct investment or portfolio investment. Portfolio investment is purely financial assets such as bank deposits, government securities and corporate stocks and bonds. On the other hand, direct investment involves foreign ownership of U.S. property, plant, and equipment and implies an entrepreneurial and managerial role. It generally occurs when a foreign firm finds local production more advantageous than exporting or licensing. These advantages could be in the form of technology, a recognized brand name, size, or favored access to capital or raw material.

Direct investment is the more visible form of foreign investment and stirs the most emotional responses since foreign purchases of major U.S. corporations make front-page news. Yet it accounts for less than a fifth of the foreign assets in the U.S. and grew only about half as fast as private portfolio investment in the 1980s.

What are the benefits of direct foreign investment? The most obvious local benefit is jobs. Larger tax receipts benefit local communities. Often foreign investment brings improvements in technology. For example, Inland Steel and Nippon Steel agreed to establish a U.S. joint venture, which was a state-of-the-art continuous cold mill using technology developed by Nippon. Foreign investors also provide a source of competition in the U.S. economy. A study of the pharmaceutical industry found that because research and development was so expensive, joint ventures with foreign firms were the only way small-to-medium-size U.S. firms could stay competitive.

Another benefit of direct foreign investment is the increase in the variety and quality of goods available to U.S. consumers. While foreign firms could export to the United States, they find they can provide better service, quicker deliveries, customized output, and better technical support if they are located in the United States.

What are the costs to foreign direct investment? People often argue that much foreign investment occurs through takeovers. Because acquisitions are a relatively quick and inexpensive way to gain entry into U.S. markets, they do appear large in foreign direct investment activity. They account for approximately half the number of foreign investments in a given year. But since foreigners tend to acquire U.S. companies whose financial health is below average, they provide managerial talent, technology, and capital to them. They also give U.S. sellers capital funds with which they, in turn, may build new plants.

Some people oppose foreign investment because they feel foreigners are using U.S. firms to gain access to U.S. technology and this could be a threat to national security. For example, Fujitsu wanted to buy Fairchild Semiconductor from Schlumberger, but the Secretaries of Commerce and Defense and most of the U.S. semiconductor industry opposed the sale. National Semiconductor eventually bought Fairchild, and Fujitsu instead built its own semiconductor plant in the United States. Was Fujitsu a major security risk? It is hard to see how since Schlumberger is French and Fairchild had been losing money since 1979. A

lot of opposition to foreign direct investment is the fear that foreigners might use U.S. technology or raw materials against our national interest. These fears have little basis. The U.S. government limits foreign direct investment in areas related to national security such as broadcasting and nuclear and hydroelectric power. Further, foreign-owned U.S. companies are subject to the same tax, securities, antitrust, and labor laws as any U.S.-owned firm.

In an emergency, the United States has the power to impose export controls or to seize foreign assets. The President can also require foreign-owned companies in the United States to give high priority to defense contracts. From the experience of U.S. business in other countries, a multinational is, in a sense, a hostage of the host government and has to cooperate when a country decides to change the rules of the game. Another set of arguments against foreign direct investment is from Americans facing foreign competition who

want to equate the national interest with their own self-interest. They push for restrictions on foreign investment that make themselves better off, but actually make other U.S. citizens worse off. In the case of foreigners buying U.S. companies, usually it is the managers of the acquired firm or its competitors who oppose the transaction and not the stockholders, whose shares can increase if foreign investors want to acquire their company. Just like free trade, unrestricted foreign direct investment promotes economic efficiency, while restrictions on foreign investment reduce it. In summary, foreign direct investment really means a long-term commitment to the U.S. economy. It provides access to other foreign markets, brings technology, and spurs competition. ❑

NOTE [a]The source for this discussion is Jane Sneddon Little, "Foreign Investment in the United States: A Cause for Concern?" Federal Reserve Bank of Boston *New England Economic Review* (July/August 1988), pp. 51–58.

Business Fixed Investment

Why do businesses invest in capital goods? One answer is the profit motive. By investing in additional amounts of plant and equipment, businesses expect to add to their profits. Investment spending, then, depends on *expected* profits. It should be noted that expected profits are not necessarily current profits. The current profit margin of a business may be low, but the business may still invest in capital goods to improve its future profit position. Thus, the decision to invest is based on an estimate by a business of the profits expected to arise from a particular investment project. On what is this profit estimate based?

In determining the profit that is expected to accrue from an investment project, businesses examine two basic factors: (1) the flow of expected net income from the project and (2) the user cost of capital.

EXPECTED NET INCOME

Assume that a business is trying to decide whether to add a new capital good to its existing physical plant, and that the scrap value of this capital good is zero. The capital good is durable, so it can yield a stream of net income for a long period of time. The capital good will be combined with increased amounts of labor, raw materials, and other inputs to produce additional output. Taking the amount of expected additional output and multiplying by an estimated selling price determines the *expected* increase in total revenue that the business will receive from the new machine. For example, suppose the machine is expected to produce 20,000 units each year for ten years—the life of the machine—and the selling price of the output is expected to be $5 per unit. Then the expected increase in total revenue is $100,000 each year, or $5 × 20,000.

However, in employing the new capital good, the business will incur additional operating expenses. It must estimate the expected noncapital costs, such as the additional costs for labor and raw materials. This estimate provides the expected increase in total cost for the business from adding the new capital good. Depreciation of the machine, interest cost, and taxes are treated as the user cost of capital and are excluded from the estimate of added total cost. The user cost is paid out of the expected net income from the new capital good.

The **expected net income** from purchasing the new capital good (machine) is found by subtracting the expected increase in total cost from the expected increase in total revenue. This procedure gives the expected net income. In our example, the expected increase in total revenue was $100,000 annually. If the expected increase in total cost was $75,000, then the expected net income from the new machine would be ($100,000 − $75,000), or $25,000 each year. This may be referred to as the *net annual return* to the capital good.

EXPECTED NET INCOME is the difference between the expected increase in total revenues and the additional operating costs.

The flow of expected net income from the new capital good is a benefit to the business. However, this benefit has to be weighed against the cost of acquiring the capital good. This cost depends on the user cost of capital.

THE (RENTAL) USER COST OF CAPITAL

The USER or RENTAL COST OF CAPITAL is the implicit rental value assigned to all of the costs of using more capital.

The second factor that the business has to examine in its decision to invest is the **user** or **rental cost of capital.** The user costs are (1) the financial cost, (2) depreciation of the capital good, and (3) taxation. The user cost of capital is an implicit rental value assigned to all of the various types of costs imposed on a business that purchases and uses a new capital good.

First let us turn to the financial cost involved in buying a capital good. In purchasing a new capital good, a business has the choice of borrowing the money in the financial market, selling new stock issues, or using its own internal source of funds (i.e., its retained earnings). If the business has to borrow the money, either from a bank or by selling bonds the financial cost is explicitly measured by the current market rate of interest.[1]

The REAL RATE OF INTEREST is equal to the market rate of interest minus the expected rate of inflation.

The business must be careful to distinguish between the real rate of interest and the market or nominal rate of interest when it borrows funds in the capital market. As we recall from Chapter 3, the **real rate of interest** is equal to the nominal rate of interest minus the expected rate of inflation. This relationship can be expressed as

$$r = R - \pi^e,$$

where r is the real rate of interest, R is the nominal rate of interest, and π^e is the expected rate of inflation.

What if a business decides to use its internal funds to finance its investment project? Is a financial cost still involved? The answer is yes. However, in this case it now becomes an implicit cost. When a business uses its own money it forgos the interest it could have earned on those funds if it had placed them in bonds or other earning assets. Since there is this opportunity cost of internal funds, the financial cost is still reflected in the market and real rates of interest.

DEPRECIATION is the decline in the useful value of a fixed asset, such as a building or capital equipment, due to wear and tear, destruction, or obsolescence resulting from better technology.

Another cost a business has to consider in its investment decision is the physical **depreciation** of the capital good. Capital goods deteriorate with use and to maintain their productive efficiency, the business has to allocate funds to cover the cost of this depreciation. Thus, the user cost of capital consists of a financial cost reflected by the real rate of interest and the depreciation cost.[2]

---

[1]We often assume in simplified models of investment decisions that there is only one market rate of interest. In reality, many different market rates of interest exist in the economy. The rate of interest that any given borrower must pay depends on such factors as the size of the loan, the term of the loan, the collateral to secure the loan, and the credit rating of the borrower.

[2]The user cost of capital can be affected by a change in the market price of a newly purchased capital good. If the price of the same type of new capital good rises, this can pull up the price of the used capital good, so then the business registers a capital gain.

Let us now see how taxes can alter the user cost of capital. There are three tax laws that have an impact on the user cost of capital: (1) the corporate income tax, (2) depreciation allowances, and (3) the investment tax credit.

Almost all U.S. corporations are required by law to pay a corporate income tax. To businesses, the decision to invest in capital goods is based on the after-tax profitability of an investment. A decrease (increase) in the corporate tax will raise (lower) the after-tax profits.[3] With a change in corporate taxes, businesses will have more (less) pretax income available to them to cover the financial cost of the investment. This, in turn, lowers (raises) the user cost of capital.

The adverse effect of the corporate income tax on investment is reduced through tax regulations dealing with depreciation allowances. The tax law allows corporations to reduce their corporate tax by deducting the value of depreciation of plant and equipment.

The investment tax credit also influences the user cost of capital. The investment tax credit was enacted in 1962 as part of the Kennedy administration's program to stimulate investment. Under the Economic Recovery Tax Act of 1981, businesses were given a credit against their corporate income tax of up to 10 percent of the amount of new investment. In essence, the investment tax credit reduces the purchase price of a new capital good, and thus reduces the user cost of capital. By raising or lowering the investment tax credit (i.e., the rate), the federal government can restrain or stimulate investment expenditures.[4] The Tax Reform Act of 1986 eliminated the investment tax credit. This tax reform substantially reduced the incentive to invest in business plant and equipment. However, under the Clinton administration there is at the time of this writing a movement to reinstate it.

To assist in our understanding of the user cost of capital, we can summarize our previous discussion of the various components of the user cost as follows:

$$UC = r + d - td. \tag{15.1}$$

That is the user cost UC is equal to the real rate of interest r plus the rate of depreciation d, minus the deduction for depreciation. In addition, a firm might have an investment tax credit tc, which further reduces the user cost of capital. The user cost of capital with the tax credit is

$$UC = (1 - tc)(r + d - td). \tag{15.2}$$

---

[3] Joseph Pechman points out that the higher the corporation tax, the higher the pretax rate of return has to be in order to maintain the after-tax rate of return. See Joseph A. Pechman, *Federal Tax Policy* (New York: W. W. Norton, 1971), p. 117. Also see Martin Feldstein, "Tax Policy for the 1990s: Personal Saving, Business Investment, and Corporate Debt," *The American Economic Review: Papers and Proceedings* (May 1989), pp. 108–112.

[4] To reduce aggregate demand, the federal government suspended the investment tax credit in 1966. The credit was reinstated in 1967 but was suspended again in 1968. It was slightly modified in August 1971 and was increased to a 10 percent maximum in 1975. The Tax Reform Act of 1986 eliminated the investment tax credit. For an interesting discussion on the implications of the Tax Reform Act of 1986, see Joel Slemrod, "Did the Tax Reform Act of 1986 Simplify Tax Matters?" *The Journal of Economic Perspectives* (Winter 1992), pp. 45–58.

Having now examined separately the basic factors involved in investment decision making, we need to see how they are interrelated in the framework of the various investment theories.

The Neoclassical Approach

We begin with the Neoclassical approach to investment. According to the Neoclassical theory of investment behavior, a profit-maximizing firm will employ units of capital until the point at which the expected return on capital, the value of the marginal product of capital, is exactly equal to the user cost of capital. In other words, given the user cost of capital, a perfectly competitive firm determines its desired capital stock by equating the expected rate of return on capital (the value of the marginal product of capital) to the user cost of capital.[5] The value of the marginal product of capital is the increase in total revenue attributable to the addition of one more unit of capital, and is determined by multiplying the marginal product of capital, which is the increase in output resulting from using one more unit of capital, by the price of the final product. The user cost of capital, which we discussed in the previous section, is the cost of adding one more unit of capital in production.

To assist in our understanding of the Neoclassical theory of investment, we present Figure 15–2. This diagram is based on two simplifying assumptions. First, the firm is assumed to be perfectly competitive and to have already made its decision on the number of workers it plans to employ in producing its output. Second, we assume the firm faces no delays in adjusting its use of capital goods. Capital goods can be easily rented, and any amount that is not needed can be returned. The value of the marginal product and the user cost of capital are labeled on the vertical axis, and the stock of capital K on the horizontal axis. Notice that the value of the marginal product curve (VMP_K) is downward-sloping in the diagram.

The user cost of capital is shown as the line UC_0 and is also based on the assumption of perfect competition. Now, the firm must balance the contribution that additional units of capital make to their revenue against the cost of using additional capital. It will rent an additional unit of capital as long as the revenue it receives is greater than the additional cost. The firm will stop renting additional units of capital when the value of the marginal product (VMP_K) is equal to the user cost of capital UC_0. The desired capital stock, K_0, is determined at point A, where the VMP_K line intersects the user cost of capital

---

[5]Henderson and Liebman show how changes in the cost of capital can account for shifts in the composition of business investment in the 1980s. Changes are due primarily to movements in real capital good prices across industries and assets. For example, computer prices fell sharply. See Yolanda K. Henderson and Jeffrey B. Liebman, "Capital Costs, Industrial Mix and the Composition of Business Investment," Federal Reserve Bank of Boston *New England Economic Review* (January/February 1992), pp. 67–92.

FIGURE 15−2
The Neoclassical Approach to
Investment

A firm stops renting additional units of capital when the value of the
marginal product curve (VMP_K) equals the user cost of capital to UC.
A decrease in UC causes an increase in the firm's desired stock of capital to K_1.

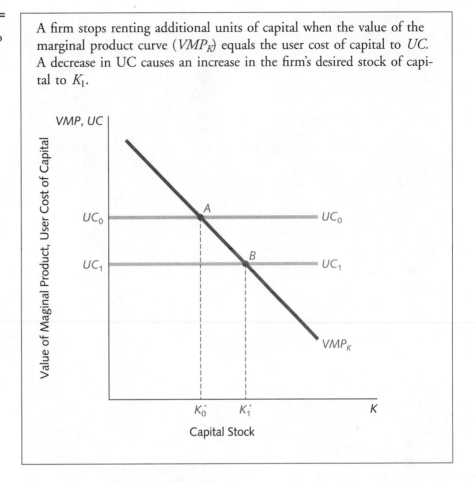

line UC_0. A decrease in the user cost of capital shifts down the line in the
diagram to UC_1 and produces an increase in the desired stock of capital to
K_1, as indicated by the intersection of the VMP_K curve and the UC_1 line at point
B. Thus, according to the Neoclassical theory of investment, as long as the value
of the marginal product is above the user cost of capital, it is profitable for a firm
to continue to add additional units of capital goods until the value of the
marginal product is equal to the user (rental) cost of capital. Once this equilibrium is established ($VMP_K = UC$), it will not pay the firm to continue to invest
in additional capital goods. For a view on U.S. investment in the 1980's, see the
Policy Issue: "Saving and Investment Rates in Japan and America."

The Acceleration Principle

In Keynesian theory, investment may depend on the current level of national
income. An increase in national income induces an increase in investment

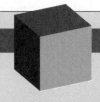

POLICY ISSUE

"SAVING AND INVESTMENT RATES IN JAPAN AND AMERICA"

The conventional wisdom is that the American saving rate is quite low relative to Japan's. In 1991, the saving rate for the United States was 5.3 percent as compared to the Japanese rate of 15 percent. In previous chapters we learned that household saving is an important ingredient to investment in capital goods by businesses. A decline in the saving rate leads to less investment, thereby reducing the economy's ability to produce goods and services. Recent studies suggest that a saving gap between the United States and Japan might not really exist. The gap may be a statistical illusion. One reason for this illusion is that the two countries calculate their national income accounts differently. The American accounting system understates investment while the Japanese system overstates it. The United States values its depreciation of capital goods at the replacement cost of the item rather than at the historical cost as the Japanese do. This means that the American accounting procedure overstates the value of its capital goods used in production, making U.S. investment appear to be lower than that of Japan. You should recall from Chapter 2 that net

PHOTO 15-1
While the Japanese Save at a High Rate, Adjustment for Accounting Factors and Measurement Errors Creates Savings and Investment Rates That Are Comparable for the United States and Japan over the 1980s.

investment is gross investment minus depreciation. If the value of depreciation is higher for the United States, then its net investment is lower.

Another source of the saving-gap illusion is that the United States counts all government expenditures, such as those on bridges, roads, schools, and military hardware, as consumption. The Japanese count such items as investment. If these corrections are made in the U.S. national income accounts, the wide difference we observe in the saving rate between the countries would disappear. Added to the illusion is that some economists measure U.S. investment in nominal net terms rather than in real gross terms. Although no measure is perfect, nominal net terms understates investment because it fails to adjust for differential price changes between capital and other goods. During the 1980s, the U.S. inflation rate rose twice as fast as the price of capital goods so that investment deflated by the price of capital goods exceeded investment deflated by a general price index. Also, even if net investment were zero and gross investment only equaled depreciation, just replacing our old technology with new technology would increase the U.S. productive capability. John A. Tatom, vice president of the St. Louis Federal Reserve Bank, has reported in the bank's publication that over the past twenty-five years net business fixed investment has been falling as a share of GNP. This fall in fixed investment implies a rise in the rate of depreciation that corresponds to a 25 percent increase in the investment share going to equipment. Tatom shows that when the appropriate adjustments are made, the real investment share of GNP in the 1980s was the largest since World War II. One should, therefore, not think of a change in asset mix (i.e., building for equipment) as a decline in investment.

The final statistical illusion is the idea that the United States is the world's largest debtor. A study by William Dewald and Michael Ulan of the U.S. State Department reports that this claim is false, and is based on out-of-date book values, thereby understating U.S. investment abroad by $500 billion. Dewald and Ulan point out that the United States has actually gotten wealthier. ❑

SOURCES: Paul Craig Roberts, "America's 'Saving Crisis' Is a Chimera," *Business Week* (February 12, 1990), p. 20; and "Japan's Growth in Savings Falls," *The New York Times* (March 14, 1992), p. 41.

The ACCELERATION PRINCIPLE is a theory which states that small changes in the demand for consumer goods can generate large changes in the demand for investment (capital) goods.

spending. The **acceleration principle** posits a relationship between the level of investment and the *change* in the level of output of goods.[6] The term *accelerator* refers to this capital-output ratio. For the acceleration principle to apply, all businesses in the economy must be operating at *full capacity*, meaning that all plant and equipment are being fully utilized, with no possibility for increased shifts or additional overtime by workers. To help in our understanding of the accelerator theory, we will use a simple hypothetical example. Let us assume

[6]An early study of the accelerator is by J. M. Clark, "Business Acceleration and the Law of Demand," *Journal of Political Economy* (March 1917), pp. 217–35.

that in the textile business it takes $2 of capital goods (machines) to produce $1 in output (cloth), which would mean that the accelerator or capital-output ratio would be 2/1. Further, let us assume that the businesses in the textile industry have been selling $50 million in cloth each year with an actual capital stock of $100 million, that the machines (capital goods) used to produce the cloth have an average life of ten years, and that each year 1/10 or $10 million worth of the machines (capital stock) wear out and need to be replaced.

Table 15–1 presents the hypothetical example of the acceleration principle for the textile industry. It is assumed that the demand for cloth (output) is an exogenous variable. What we want to explain is the behavior of investment, given the demand for cloth. In year 1, the desired stock of capital is equal to the actual stock, which satisfies the demand for output. Since one machine wears out each year, the annual replacement investment is $10 million. No new machines are added; thus, net investment is zero because gross investment is equal to net investment plus depreciation. Gross investment, therefore, is $10 million. In year 2, the demand for output increases by assumption to $70 million. With an accelerator of 2/1, the desired stock of $140 million, gross investment for this year must increase to $54 million, of which $14 million is for replacement and $40 million is for new machines. Notice that a 40 percent increase in the demand for the output of cloth results in a 440 percent increase in gross investment. In year 3, the demand for the output of cloth increases by 14 percent, to $80 million; gross investment decreases to $36 million, of which $20 million is for new machines and $16 million is for replacement. It is interesting to note that while demand increases from year 2 to year 3, a decline in the absolute rate of increase in the demand for the output of cloth results in a fall in the level of gross investment by $18 million. When the demand for cloth (output) levels off to $80 million in year 4, there is only $16 million in

TABLE 15–1   The Acceleration Principle in the Textile Industry ($ millions)

YEAR	DEMAND FOR OUTPUT (CLOTH)	DESIRED STOCK OF CAPITAL (MACHINES)	ACTUAL STOCK OF CAPITAL (MACHINES)	REPLACEMENT (DEPRECIATION)	NET INVESTMENT (NEW MACHINES)	GROSS INVESTMENT

This table presents a hypothetical example of the acceleration hypothesis for the textile industry.

YEAR	DEMAND FOR OUTPUT (CLOTH)	DESIRED STOCK OF CAPITAL (MACHINES)	ACTUAL STOCK OF CAPITAL (MACHINES)	REPLACEMENT (DEPRECIATION)	NET INVESTMENT (NEW MACHINES)	GROSS INVESTMENT
1	$50	$100	$100	$10	$ 0	$ 10
2	70	140	140	14	40	54
3	80	160	160	16	20	36
4	80	160	160	16	0	16
5	60	120	144	0	-16	-16
6	90	180	180	18	36	54

gross investment, which is for replacement of equipment; net investment is zero. Although the demand for cloth is now 60 percent above the original level of $50 million, gross investment has declined by $20 million in year 4.

Under the acceleration principle in its rigid form, investment falls as soon as the rate of increase in the demand for output slows down—turning points in investment come before turning points in the demand for output. In our example, gross investment reaches its peak of $54 million in year 2, whereas the demand for cloth (output) reaches its peak of $80 million in year 3. In year 5, there is a fall in the demand for cloth (output); however, while the desired stock of capital declines to $120 million, the actual stock of capital can only fall to $144 million. The difference between the desired stock of capital and the actual stock shows "excess capacity" amounting to $24 million. With a reduction in the demand for cloth, the adjustment of the actual stock to the desired stock can come about only by letting $16 million in machinery wear out each year. Thus, Table 15–1 illustrates an important point about the acceleration principle by showing that a fall in the demand for cloth (output) does not produce the same effect on the level of investment as does a rise in the demand for cloth.

Finally, we find in Table 15–1 that in year 6 a substantial rise in the demand for cloth, to $90 million, produces a level of gross investment of $54 million. Businesses replace their worn-out machines and add $36 million worth of new machines to their capital stock. Remember that associated each year with a given level of gross investment is a specific amount of employment that is needed to operate the textile machines. With a change in investment expenditures, there is a resultant change in employment. *From this simple illustration of the acceleration principle in the textile industry, we see how changes in the demand for output can affect investment and lead to cyclical fluctuations in national income and employment.*

The Flexible Accelerator Model

While the rigid accelerator model can be used to explain investment behavior and cyclical fluctuation in national income, it has been subject to criticism. First, the accelerator model in rigid form is mechanical, as we found out in our example of the textile industry. A capital-output ratio was assumed fixed and the industry responded to assumed exogenous changes in the demand for output (cloth). The accelerator model, therefore, required a full adjustment of the capital stock to maintain the required capital-output ratio. In actuality, however, the capital-output ratio may not be fixed by technical requirements.

Another criticism of the acceleration principle is that the assumption of full capacity is necessary for the principle to operate. If the economy experienced excess capacity, businesses would not want to expand their capital stock. They could either have their employees work overtime or expand the number of shifts. Thus, some economists suggest that the acceleration principle may be valid for an economy which is expanding at or near full capacity but that, because of excess capacity, may not be valid for an economy which is below full capacity. Moreover, there is a problem with the definition of excess capacity and full capacity. When a business is faced with an increased demand for its product, at what point does it decide to increase its investment in new capital goods?

Faced with the various criticisms of the rigidity of the acceleration principle, economists have modified its form in order to empirically test and establish its validity. Modifications in the accelerator model have focused primarily on the time structure of the investment process. Lags have been introduced into the accelerator model in order to relate the actual level of capital to past desired levels of capital. This type of model with lagged adjustments is called the flexible accelerator model.[7]

Tobin Q Theory of Investment

The **TOBIN Q THEORY** states that investment spending varies directly with the ratio of the market value of business capital assets to the replacement value of those assets.

Another modern theory of investment, the **Tobin q Theory,** has been advanced by James Tobin.[8] Tobin's q is defined as the ratio of the market value of additional capital goods to the replacement cost of that capital good. According to the q theory, the rate of investment is a function of q.

The description of investment demand behind the Tobin q model is as old as investment theory itself. Investment should be undertaken by the firm if new capital is valued more highly than the costs of replacing it. The value of capital is reflected in the market value of the firm's stock.[9] Businesses, therefore, determine the price they are willing to pay for an investment project after assessing its prospective returns. This price is the demand price for capital assets. The cost of producing new capital goods determines the supply price. A firm that wants to maximize the welfare of its shareholders should invest, as

---

[7]The flexible accelerator model of investment was originated by H. B. Chenery and L. M. Koyck. See H. B. Chenery, "Overcapacity and the Acceleration Principle," *Econometrica* (January 1952), pp. 1–28; and L. M. Koyck, *Distributed Lags and Investment Analysis* (Amsterdam: North-Holland, 1954). The basic flexible accelerator equation used in empirical work is

$$I = K_t - K_{t-1} = \lambda(K_t^* - K_{t-1}),$$

where $0 < \lambda < 1$. The actual change in the capital stock, net investment, is $K_t^* - K_{t-1}^*$, and K_t^* is the desired capital stock. The desired capital stock, K_t^*, depends on the interest rate, the price of the capital good, and the price of the product. Net investment, $K_t^* - K_{t-1}$ is a fraction of the gap between the desired capital stock in the current period K_t^* and the existing stock of capital from the preceding period, K_{t-1}. The λ, called the partial adjustment coefficient, shows how fast the gap between K_t^* and K_{t-1} will be closed. The larger the λ, the faster will be the closing of the gap between the desired stock of capital, K_t^* and K_t^* and the actual stock K_{t-1}.

[8]See James Tobin and William Brainard, "Asset Markets and the Cost of Capital," in *Economic Progress, Private Values and Public Policies: Essays in Honor of William Fellner,* ed. B. Belassa and R. Nelson, (Amsterdam: North-Holland, 1977).

[9]Lindenberg and Ross use common stock, preferred stock, and debt in computing q. See Eric Lindenberg and Stephen Ross, "Tobin's q Ratio and Industrial Organization," *Journal of Business* (January 1981), pp. 1–32.

long as the change in the market value of the stock or its demand price exceeds the cost of the new capital, or its supply price. When this happens the Tobin's q exceeds 1, making investment desirable.

Two points about Tobin q deserve further attention. The first is that the hypothesized relationship between the q ratio and investment suggests that the capital market is in disequilibrium. If capital markets were always in equilibrium, q would equal 1. The relationship between q and investment results from slow movement toward equilibrium. It would not exist if equilibrium was instantaneous.

Some economists have noted that the q theory is nothing more than the Neoclassical theory of investment behavior. For example, Robert Hall has argued that the q theory is basically Jorgenson's Neoclassical theory of investment and that only incomplete information and delivery lags can account for "disequilibrium" values of q. Otherwise investment would keep q equal to one.[10]

Another economist, Yoshikawa, disagrees with Hall and argues that the q theory is a theory that explains how investment is motivated by the short-run disequilibrium that results from the divergence between the value of capital evaluated in the financial market and the price of capital goods. He points out that Jorgenson's Neoclassical theory is basically concerned with the long-run demand for capital. Recently, Sensenbrenner has revisited the conflict between the Jorgenson Neoclassical theory and the q theory. His results for six OECD countries show that a new dynamic q equation is as satisfactory as Jorgenson's equation from an empirical standpoint.[11]

The second point about the q theory is that the theory is not operational as long as q is not observable. The q, which we called marginal q and which is based on new additions to the capital stock, is theoretically appropriate for most purposes. However, empirical work based on the q theory has to utilize average q as a proxy for marginal q.[12] The variables used in calculating average q are observable but may not adequately proxy marginal q.

Residential Investment

In this section, we focus on the determinants of residential investment. The expenditure by households on new homes and apartments is called **residential investment.** Since World War II, new home construction or residential

RESIDENTIAL INVESTMENT is the construction of single and multifamily housing.

[10]Robert E. Hall, "Investment, Interest Rates, and the Effects of Stabilization Policies," *Brookings Papers on Economic Activity* 1 (Washington, DC: The Brookings Institution, 1977), pp. 61–103.
[11]See Hiroshi Yoshikawa, "On the 'q' Theory of Investment," *American Economic Review* 70 (1980). Also see G. Sensenbrenner, "Aggregate Investment, the Stock Market, and the Q Model: Robust Results for Six OECD Countries," *European Economic Review* (May 1991), pp. 769–825.
[12]See Fumio Hayashi, "Tobin's Marginal q and Average q: A Neoclassical Interpretation," *Econometrica* 50:1 (January 1982) pp. 213–24. For a brief literature review of Tobin's q see Henry W. Chappell, Jr., and David C. Ching, "Firms' Acquisition Decisions and Tobin's q Ratio," *Journal of Economics and Business* 36:1 (February 1984), pp. 29–42.

investment has fluctuated with the ups and downs of the business cycle. A marked decline in residential investment was registered in the recessions of 1953–54, 1957–58, 1960–61, 1974–76 and 1990–92.[13] Moreover, new home construction dropped in the mini-recession of 1966, a period in which monetary policy was very tight, and in 1981.

Because of certain theoretical differences, a distinction is made between residential investment and business investment. Theoretical models of residential construction begin with the market for existing houses, while models of business fixed investment start with the determinants of the desired stock of capital.

The existing housing market can be measured directly through the buying and selling of the actual physical units (i.e., houses). The demand and supply curves for the existing stock of houses are shown in Figure 15–3(a). The supply curve for new home construction is depicted in (b). The demand for existing housing stock depends on the following variables: (1) the price of

FIGURE 15–3
Residential Construction

A decrease in the interest rate shifts the demand for houses from DH to DH_1 driving up the price of existing houses from PH_E to PH_1. A rise in the price of existing houses induces an increase in new home construction from RH_0 to RH_1. The supply curve for new homes is shown as S_N in the figure.

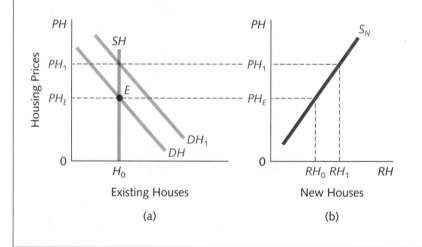

[13]Economists differ about the outlook for real housing prices in the 1990s. Some argue real housing prices may drop because the "baby boom" generation is being followed by a smaller "baby bust" generation. The resulting weaker growth in demand for housing puts downward pressure on prices. Other economists argue that economic factors such as real income growth and reduced housing supply will offset the adverse demographic factors. See C. Alan Garner, "Will the Real Price of Housing Drop Sharply in the 1990s?" Federal Reserve Bank of Kansas City *Economic Review* (Fall Quarter 1992), pp. 55–68.

housing *PH;* (2) the net real return on home ownership; (3) wealth; (4) the real return on other assets; and (5) population.

The first determinant of the demand for housing is the price of housing. The downward-sloping demand curve *DH* indicates that the lower the price of existing housing (*PH*), the greater is the quantity demanded.

A second determinant of housing demand is the net real return on housing. The interest rate and the rental price of housing are major factors in determining the demand for housing. These factors are reflected in the net return variable. Let us see how. The net return on housing is determined by the difference between the gross return or benefits derived from home ownership and the cost of owning a home. The gross return can be measured either by the rent a homeowner receives from renting a house or by an imputed rent. The imputed rent is an estimate of the value of the services an individual receives from actually living in a home. In addition, if the house is expected to increase in value, a capital gain is included in the gross return. The cost of home ownership is largely influenced by the interest rate (e.g., the mortgage rate), although other costs to be considered include property taxes and home depreciation. The net real return from home ownership is found by subtracting the cost of home ownership from the gross return. What happens to the demand for housing when the net return on houses changes? For example, suppose interest rates rise due to tight monetary policy. The net real return on housing would decrease. A decline in the net real return means that houses are not as attractive assets to buyers as they were before, and the *DH* curve in Figure 15–3 shifts to the left.

A third determinant of existing housing demand is wealth. An increase in the wealth of homeowners stimulates demand for housing, and *DH* shifts to the right. The real return on other assets is a fourth determinant of existing housing demand. Because houses are one form of holding wealth, individuals have to consider the real rates of return on other assets, such as stocks and bonds. If the real return on other assets is high, then housing may not be an attractive asset.[14] Under these circumstances, a decrease in the demand for housing would result, producing a leftward shift in the *DH* curve.

The final determinant of housing is population. In the long run, the demand for existing housing increases with population growth. However, it should be emphasized that population growth is a long-run phenomenon as compared to the other determinants we have discussed.

In Figure 15–3(a), the existing supply of housing is shown by the vertical line *SH* and is fixed at any moment in time. The equilibrium price of the existing stock of housing is PH_E and is determined by the intersection of the demand and supply curves for housing, at point *E*.

---

[14]Kopcke, Munnell, and Cook argue that the decline in the personal saving rate during the 1980s may be attributed largely to the national income and product accounts (NIPA) accounting for homeowners' implicit investment in their residences. See Richard W. Kopcke, Alicia H. Munnell, and Leah M. Cook, "The Influence of Housing and Durables on Personal Saving," Federal Reserve Bank of Boston *New England Economic Review* (November/December 1991), pp. 3–28.

The supply curve for new housing is shown as S_N in Figure 15–3(b). The S_N curve takes the normal shape of a supply curve and reflects the rising construction costs as the quantity produced rises. Any change in the cost of producing houses will cause a shift in the S_N curve, which represents the *flow* of new houses for a given time period. The rate at which new homes are constructed is determined by the price of existing houses relative to the factor costs of the construction business.

To see how new residential construction can come about, suppose the interest rate decreased, increasing the net return on housing. The demand for houses shifts to the right, to DH_1, driving up the price of existing houses from PH_E to PH_1. This rise in the price of existing houses induces an increase in residential construction of new homes, from RH_0 to RH_1.

Residential construction takes place each period and adds to the already existing stock of housing. In the long run, the existing supply of housing, curve *SH*, shifts to the right in graph (a), causing a reduction in the price of existing housing. (For simplicity, we have ignored the depreciation in the housing stock.) When the price of existing housing has fallen far enough to make new home construction an unprofitable venture for construction businesses, such construction will stop and the housing stock will remain constant.

INVENTORY INVESTMENT

Since World War II, inventory investment has fluctuated more than any other component of aggregate demand. In each of the postwar recessions, inventory investment has accounted, on the average, for three-fourths of the decline in GDP. For this reason, the postwar recessions have often been referred to as *inventory recessions.*

Table 15–2 shows this decline in constant dollar change in business inventories, providing for much of the business cycle peak-to-trough decline in real GDP. In the recent 1990–91 recession, the decline in real inventory investment of 54.6 percent of the production decline exceeded that in four of the previous eight recessions.

In this section, we examine the factors that could affect the size of inventories (i.e., inventory investment). A number of motives for holding inventories have been suggested: (1) transactions demand, (2) speculative demand, (3) buffer stocks, and (4) backlog of demand. Let us briefly examine each of these.

Transactions Demand

The transactions demand for inventories is similar to the transactions demand for money in Chapter 5 or 13. Businesses need to hold a certain amount of

TABLE 15-2
The Decline in Inventory
Investment in U.S. Recessions

RECESSION PEAK-TROUGH	CHANGE IN REAL INVENTORY INVESTMENT[1]	CHANGE IN REAL GDP[1]	COLUMN I AS A PERCENT OF COLUMN 2
IV/1948–IV/1949	$−28.3 BILLION	$−20.9 BILLION	135.4%
III/1953–II/1954	−11.1 (−18.4)	−37.4 (−43.3)	29.7 (42.5)
III/1957–II/1958	−20.1 (−22.5)	−44.9 (−53.1)	44.8 (42.4)
II/1960–I/1961	−15.7 (−45.5)	5.7 (−15.8)	−275.4 (288.0)
IV/1969–IV/1970	−22.5 (−19.8)	−1.8 (−25.0)	1250.0 (79.2)
IV/1973–I/1975	−84.7	−135.1	62.7
I/1980–III/1980	−44.3 (−10.7)	−97.3 (−98.2)	45.5 (10.9)
III/1981–IV/1982	−80.6 (−35.0)	−104.9 (−110.1)	76.8 (31.8)
III/1990–II/1991	−31.6 (−57.9)	−65.5 (−106.0)	48.2 (54.6)

[1]Prior to 1960, data are expressed in 1982 dollars. From 1960 to the present, data are in 1987 dollars. Numbers in parentheses correspond to the data for the respective peak-to-trough periods for real GDP: II/53–II/54, III/57–I/58, I/60–IV/60, III/69–II/70, I/80–II-80, III/81–III/82 and II/90–I/91.
SOURCE: Kevin L. Kliesen and John A. Tatom, "The Recent Credit Crunch: The Neglected Dimensions." The Federal Reserve Bank of St. Louis *Review* (September/October 1992), pp. 18–36.

inventory to carry out their day-to-day business activities. They realize, however, that costs are involved in holding inventories. These costs consist of interest costs (i.e., financial carrying costs) and brokers' costs. Businesses have to consider interest costs since they have capital funds tied up in inventories. These capital funds have either been borrowed at interest or could have been lent at a market rate of interest. Businesses also have to think about brokers' costs because they will have to replace their stock of inventories. They have to consider, then, the costs of holding or not holding inventories. Thus, they must seek some optimal inventory-sales ratio that minimizes these costs.[15]

Speculative Demand

The speculative demand for inventories is a concept similar to the speculative demand for money. There are two reasons why businesses might want to hold more inventory than they need for transactions purposes: (1) expected shortages of inventories and (2) expected price changes of inventories. As for the first reason, businesses may expect future shortages—for example, in certain raw materials—that would lead to either an increase in their production costs

---

[15]This inventory model is similar to the Baumol-Tobin model for the transactions demand for money, which we studied in Chapter 12. The reader is referred to the Baumol-Tobin model.

or a depletion in their inventory stocks. Therefore, they will purchase and hold more inventory today. For example, if the Bonzo Battery Company expects a shortage of lead for its car batteries next year, then it may hedge against the future and buy and store lead now.

As for the second reason for holding speculative inventories, businesses may expect inventory prices to rise. Thus, they hold inventories in anticipation of making a capital gain. Some economists believe that expected shortages are more important than expected price changes in determining speculative inventory holdings.

Buffer Stocks

Businesses make forecasts of their expected sales, but often they make forecasting errors. If their forecasts of expected sales are wrong, they will find either an unplanned accumulation or an unplanned depletion of finished goods inventories. To prevent a complete depletion of inventories, businesses hold a buffer stock of finished goods inventories to smooth out their filling of orders.

Backlog of Demand

In manufacturing businesses, orders come in for goods and shipments go out. Given an established demand for goods, businesses ship goods at a certain rate. If new orders come in faster than shipments are going out, a backlog of orders occurs. Businesses respond to this increase in established demand by stocking more inventory. On the other hand, if new orders come in more slowly than shipments are going out, businesses reduce their inventory stocks. Businesses, therefore, hold finished goods inventories to smooth out the time flow of goods.

Inventory Management

During the 1980s many firms changed their approach to inventory management because they were pushed by increased foreign competition and reduced profit margins. Some firms focused on inventory reduction directly; others made efforts to implement a quality of time management program or a move toward lean production. See the Insight: "Let's Look at Lean Production" for more information on new inventory management.

Some economists suggest that the current transition to lean inventory systems may exert a drag on the U.S. economy. The drag takes two forms. First, when there is a permanent reduction in the desired inventory-to-sales ratio, goods are absorbed from existing stocks, which means a one-time cut in the pipeline length. With a reduction in the length of the pipeline, current demand for existing stocks is satisfied without replacing them. These inventory

INSIGHT

"LET'S LOOK AT LEAN PRODUCTION"

In the 1950s the lean approach to manufacturing was developed by Toyota. At that time, Japanese auto makers had little capital and a small market. In addition, American occupation forces restricted Japanese management from laying off workers. A Japanese engineer, Taiichi Okno, faced with the capital budget problem of having cars stamped from just a few press lines, developed a simple die-change technique that allowed production workers to change dies every two or three hours in a process that took only three minutes. In contrast, the processes in the United States were plentiful and dedicated to specific tasks. Die changes were made only every few months or years, and die-change specialists usually took a full day to switch the dies. Since Okno had to rely on only a few presses, he found that producing small batches of stamping could save the company money. By making only small batches, the company eliminated the cost of carrying large inventories, and since only a few parts were made before they were assembled into cars, stamping mistakes could be seen and rejected. Quality of parts was kept high.

Lean production also includes asking teams of workers to be responsible not only for spotting and correcting quality but for making suggestions to improve the production process. Another key ingredient of lean production is lean supply, where assemblers and suppliers work together to lower costs and improve quality. First-tier suppliers even help to design the new products. In addition, since there is coordination between the parts suppliers and the assembler, supplies arrive "just in time." The container that transports the parts is viewed by the company as the signaling device. As the parts are used up in the production process, the container is returned to the parts supplier, signaling a demand for more parts. ❑

SOURCE: Jane S. Little, "Changes in Inventory Management: Implication for the U.S. Recovery," Federal Reserve Bank of Boston *New England Economic Review* (November/December, 1992), pp. 37–65.

PHOTO 15-2
Inventory Reductions or Build-Ups and the Reasons for Them Are Major Factors in Explaining Modern U.S. Business Cycles.

changes eliminate about a week's worth of sales in manufacturing or two weeks' worth of production. Second, the new inventory control saves in space and workers. This suggests that over the next few years there may be an excess supply of warehouse space. Manufacturers will need fewer people to move, track, and order materials and inventories of finished goods. Firms involved in retailing have found they can reduce staff for handling inventory as well as clerks for running cash registers and marking and unmarking merchandise. This new approach to inventory management suggests that in the long run, lean inventories will save resources and improve the U.S. economy. On the other hand, in the short run the transition to the new inventory approach will tend to slow the rate of growth of the U.S. economy.

SUMMARY

We have been concerned with investment spending, which many economists regard as the most unstable component of aggregate demand in an economy. Because of investment instability (and unpredictability), fluctuations in national income and employment can and do occur. Various theories of investment, as we have seen, explain the fundamental relationship between certain important economic variables and investment spending. The economic variables important in affecting investment spending are the expected rate of return on capital, the user cost of capital, and changes in the level of output. Fiscal and monetary policy can affect these economic variables, especially the user cost of capital, and subsequently investment behavior.

In this chapter, we presented the Neoclassical theory of fixed investment and the acceleration model in both rigid and flexible form. According to Neoclassical investment theory, a profit-maximizing firm determines its desired capital stock to own by equating the expected rate of return on capital to the user cost of capital. While the rigid accelerator model shows a basic relationship between the level of investment and the change in the level of output of consumer goods, the flexible form of this model allows for a time structure of the investment process. We also looked at the Tobin q theory of investment, which suggests that investment spending varies directly with the ratio of the market value of new capital assets to the replacement value of those assets. The latter part of the chapter focused on the determinants of residential investment, the factors that can affect the size of inventory investment, and current changes in inventory management. Both the refinement of investment categories and such theories as the acceleration hypothesis have provided a good deal of insight for economists in constructing a usable macro theory. Having said this, however, we must remind the reader that, given the obvious complexity of these ideas, a relatively simple concept of investment will be utilized in the remainder of this book.

KEY TERMS

acceleration principle   residential investment

depreciation   Tobin q theory

expected net income   user or rental cost of capital

real rate of interest

QUESTIONS FOR REVIEW AND DISCUSSION

1. What basic factors does a business examine in determining the profit that it expects to accrue from an investment project?

2. How is the user cost of capital defined? What costs does a business have to consider in using a newly purchased capital good?

3. Do depreciation allowances have an impact on the user cost of capital? If so, explain how.

4. How can changes in the investment tax credit reduce the purchase price of a new capital good? Does this have any impact on investment spending? How?

5. Why must a business be careful to distinguish between the real rate of interest and the market rate of interest when it borrows funds from a commercial bank?

6. What is the Neoclassical approach to investment spending?

7. Is there any difference between the rigid accelerator model and the flexible accelerator model? If so, what is it?

8. Explain the Tobin q theory of investment behavior. Is there any difference between this theory and the Neoclassical theory of investment behavior?

9. How is the supply curve for new housing determined?

10. Why do businesses want to hold inventories?

11. What recent changes have been made in inventory management?

PROBLEMS

1. Develop, with graphical and written explanation, the Neoclassical theory of business investment. Explain how the firm's desired stock of capital changes in response to an increase in the user cost of capital.

2. Suppose there is an increase in corporate taxes; what impact would this have on investment spending according to the Neoclassical approach to investment? (Hint: Use the Neoclassical investment model in your analysis.)

SUGGESTIONS FOR FURTHER READING

Auerbach, Alan J. "Taxation, Corporate Financial Policy and the Cost of Capital." *Journal of Economic Literature* (September 1983), pp. 905–40.

Boskin, Michael J. "Tax Policy and Economic Growth: Lessons from the 1980s." *Journal of Economic Perspectives* (Fall 1988), pp. 71–98.

Dixit, Avinash. "Investment and Hysteresis." *Journal of Economic Perspectives* (Winter 1992), pp. 107–32.

Henderson, Yolanda K., and Jeffrey B. Liebman. "Capital Costs, Industrial Mix and the Composition of Business Investment." Federal Reserve Bank of Boston *New England Economic Review* (January/February 1992), pp. 67–92.

Jorgenson, Dale W. "Econometric Studies of Investment Behavior: A Survey." *Journal of Economic Literature* (December 1971), pp. 1111–47.

Kopcke, Richard W. "The Determinants of Business Investment: Has Capital Spending Been Surprisingly Low?" Federal Reserve Bank of Boston *New England Economic Review* (January/February 1993), pp. 3–31.

Kopcke, Richard W., Alicia H. Munnell, and Leah M. Cook. "The Influence of Housing and Durables on Personal Saving." Federal Reserve Bank of Boston *New England Economic Review* (November/December 1991), pp. 3–16.

Lindenberg, Eric, and Stephen Ross. "Tobin's q Ratio and Industrial Organization." *Journal of Business* (January 1981), pp. 1–32.

Pindyck, Robert S. "Irreversibility, Uncertainty, and Investment." *Journal of Economic Literature* (September 1991), pp. 1110–48.

Summers, Lawrence H. "Investment Incentives and the Discounting of Depreciation Allowances." In *The Effects of Taxation on Capital Accumulation,* ed. Martin Feldstein. Chicago: University of Chicago Press, 1987.

Tobin, James, and William Brainard. "Asset Markets and the Cost of Capital." In *Economic Progress, Private Values and Public Policies: Essays in Honor of William Fellner,* ed. B. Belassa and R. Nelson. Amsterdam: North-Holland, 1977.

PART VI

MACROECONOMIC POLICY AND GROWTH

16

MACROECONOMIC POLICY

Exciting and interesting questions in macroeconomics deal with the nation's economic policy. What should be the goals for economic growth, unemployment, or inflation, and how should these goals be achieved? Macroeconomic theory, the subject of previous chapters, has prepared us to answer these policy questions.

Our tactic will be to discuss possible aggregate demand and aggregate supply disturbances affecting output and unemployment and the price level. Predicting the direction of these changes is the role of the macroeconomist.

By the end of this chapter, you will know

- how the ability of policymakers to achieve their goals is influenced by the number of goals relative to the number of policy instruments
- why intermediate targeting of either money aggregates or interest rates is not necessarily the optimal policy for achieving a final output target
- how long-run aggregate supply limits the ability of policymakers to achieve output targets
- the ability of monetary and fiscal policy to stabilize the economy in the face of aggregate demand and aggregate supply disturbances
- the arguments over rules versus discretion in policymaking
- how modern game theory analysis of monetary policy suggests that discretion may be inferior to policy rules
- the concept of an automatic stabilizer
- how nominal income targeting might help stabilize the economy, and the case for and against such a policy rule.

TARGETS AND INSTRUMENTS OF POLICY

An **INSTRUMENT OF POLICY** is a variable that the policymaker can control and can vary to have an impact on the economy.

A **TARGET** for policy is a goal of policy, usually a specific value for an economic variable that the policymaker is trying to achieve.

One of the most important things to learn about policymaking is the relationship between **instruments** or tools of policy, and the targets or goals of policy. Quite some time ago Jan Tinbergen pointed out that a policymaker needs as many independent tools as there are targets. A simple example illustrates this point. Consider the supply and demand graph in Figure 16-1. Equilibrium is at point A, with a price of P_0 and quantity of Q_0. The **targets** of policy are arbitrarily chosen to be point T, with a price of P^T and a quantity Q^T. Thus, there are *two* targets or goals of policy. One is P^T, and the other is Q^T. The precise location of these targets is irrelevant, as long as it is not on the initial supply or demand curves. The question we consider is whether a policymaker can move the equilibrium from point A to the target at point T. Clearly a policymaker able to move both demand and supply could shift demand and supply, so that these curves intersect at point T. An example is given by the dotted line supply and demand curves D' and S'. In this case the policymaker has two independent instruments, one that shifts demand and one that shifts supply.

FIGURE 16-1
Targets in a Demand and Supply Graph

In this figure, the target is to achieve equilibrium at point T, and achieving that target requires shifting demand from D to D' and shifting supply from S to S'.

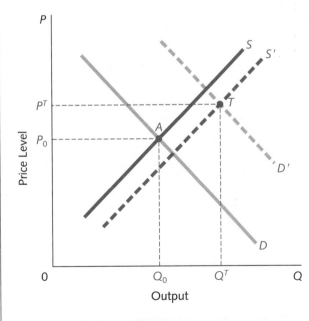

What if the policymaker has only one instrument and can shift only demand? This situation is illustrated in Figure 16-2. Now the policymaker has several choices, but none move the economy to point T. The policymaker can achieve the price target, P^T, by shifting demand to D', giving equilibrium at point B. However, at this equilibrium the output target is missed. The policymaker can achieve the output target Q^T by shifting demand to D''', giving equilibrium at point D. At this equilibrium, the price target is missed. Or the policymaker can compromise, perhaps setting demand at D'', which passes through point T but which gives equilibrium at point C. Here the policymaker misses both targets by a smaller amount. In any event, the policymaker has only one independent instrument, which affects demand, and shifting demand cannot achieve point T. With one instrument, only one target can be achieved. The best the policymaker can achieve is some point on the line segment between points B and D in Figure 16-2. The actual choice will depend on how strongly the policymaker wants to achieve each target, and will likely involve a compromise in which neither target is achieved. However, the

FIGURE 16-2
Targets and Indicators When Only Demand Can Be Changed

In this figure, the target is to achieve equilibrium at point T, but only demand can be shifted by the policymaker. From the initial equilibrium at point A, demand can shift to D' or D'' or D''', setting equilibrium at points B, C, and D, respectively.

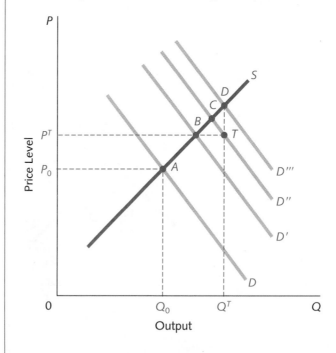

point remains that the policymaker can achieve only one target, by varying one instrument of policy.

The same point would hold if the policymaker can manipulate supply but not demand. We leave this point to the interested reader.

The need for an equal number of instruments and targets is a very general result that has important policy implications. For example, we have discussed policy in a variety of macroeconomic models in this text, as well as the tools that policymakers have at their disposal. The tools of monetary policy are mainly open-market operations, discount window policies, and the required reserve ratio. Changes in any of these instruments of policy will change the money supply, and hence change the *LM* curve and aggregate demand. The tools of fiscal policy are basically government purchases of goods and services, and net tax collections. These policy tools have been analyzed mostly in terms of their ability to shift the *IS* curve and hence aggregate demand. Thus, it seems as if the fiscal and monetary policymakers can exert independent control over *IS* and *LM,* and thereby influence the interest rate and perhaps output. But both sets of policies affect only aggregate demand, not aggregate supply, so that it is not generally possible to achieve both an output target and a price level target. Even though there are many policy instruments, they all exert their main influence on aggregate demand, and hence give policymakers only one *independent* instrument for achieving targets involving output and the price level.

Of course, fiscal policy includes income taxes and other taxes that can have effects on both aggregate demand and aggregate supply. Increases in tax rates can reduce labor supply and thus cause a reduction in aggregate supply. There are also potential supply-side effects of government spending, as emphasized recently in the campaign of President Clinton. Government spending on capital goods, such as roads and other infrastructure, may increase productivity and hence increase aggregate supply. The actual effect of such spending is a point of some controversy in the economics literature, but on a theoretical level it is possible for government spending to exert an effect on both aggregate demand and aggregate supply.

An Example: Money Aggregates versus Interest Rates as Intermediate Targets

An important application of these ideas on instruments and targets is to the issue of **intermediate monetary targets.** An intermediate monetary target is a target that the Fed tries to achieve in the short run, in order to achieve its long-run goal. Intermediate monetary targets are usually stated as targets for a monetary aggregate such as M1 or M2, or as an interest rate target. In any case, these intermediate targets are targets that the Fed sets at levels consistent with its final goals and then tries its best to achieve in the short run.

The debate over intermediate targets is twofold: One debate concerns whether the Fed should use an intermediate targeting procedure. The second debate concerns whether the interest rate or a monetary aggregate should be the intermediate target.

Consider the first question first. Should the Fed use intermediate targets? If the underlying goal is to achieve a final target, the answer would seem to be no. Consider the situation illustrated in Figure 16-3. In graph (a), we illustrate the situation of an intermediate monetary target. The final target is an output target Y^T. The Fed chooses an intermediate money target M^T, which will make *IS* and *LM* intersect at the target level of output as long as there are no further shifts in either *IS* or *LM*. What happens if *IS* shifts to *IS'* or to *IS''*? The equilibrium shifts, changing output, and the target is missed. *LM* does not respond to counteract these changes because the Fed is committed to hitting the intermediate target M^T, which means keeping *LM* at its initial level.

A similar story can be told for the interest rate as an intermediate target, as we illustrate in graph (b) of Figure 16-3. *IS* and *LM* are expected to intersect where the interest rate is r^T and output is Y^T. The intermediate target is r^T, and the Fed commits to changing *LM* in order to keep the interest rate at r^T. To do this, the Fed will counteract any shift in *LM,* and this keeps output at Y^T. But what about a shift in *IS*? If *IS* shifts to *IS'*, then *LM* must shift to LM (M_1/P) in order to keep the interest rate at target. But this causes an increase in output above the target level.

Thus, we see that neither an intermediate monetary target nor interest rate target is optimal if the final goal is to keep output at some target. Instead, the monetary authority should adjust the money supply to respond to deviations in *IS* or *LM* in order to keep output at target. In general this will involve changing both the interest rate and the money supply in response to shifts in the *IS* curve.

Why does the Fed continue to adopt intermediate targets? In part this continues because such targets are easily monitored, and in part because

FIGURE 16-3
Intermediate Money and
Interest Rate Targets and
Shifts in the *IS* Curve

This figure illustrates the effect of a shift in the *IS* curve when the Fed
has adopted an intermediate money target, in graph (a), and an intermediate interest rate target, in graph (b). In (a), the Fed doesn't respond to shifts in the *IS* curve. In (b), the Fed responds by increasing
the money supply, shifting *LM* to the right.

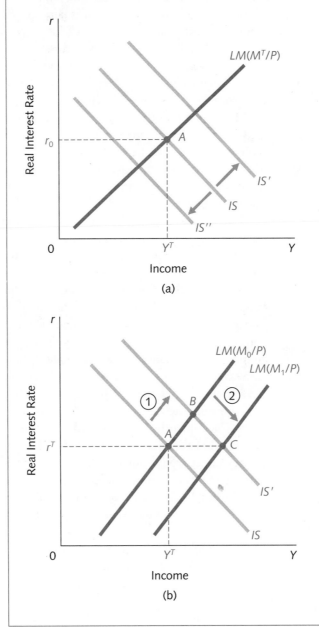

information on the intermediate targets is available relatively frequently. Interest rate data are available daily, or even more frequently if desired and money supply data are available weekly. In contrast, the consumer price index and unemployment rates are available monthly; and the GDP deflator and real GDP are available quarterly. Intermediate targets tend to be variables that can be observed fairly frequently, both for the benefit of the policymaker and of those trying to monitor policy. It is fairly certain that the Fed can exert a strong control over the money supply, at least if given several months to do so, while it is less clear how easily the Fed can act to achieve a price level target or an output target. If nothing else, the lags involved make monitoring the Fed's actions toward achieving a final goal very difficult. It is much easier to see if a monetary aggregate or an interest rate is staying in the Fed's target range.

The second part of the debate is over the choice of intermediate targets. The Fed once targeted interest rates but has shifted to announcing monetary aggregate targets in the last two decades. We should acknowledge, however, that announcing such targets and actually attempting to achieve them are very different things, and many argue that the Fed does not pursue its announced money targets with much determination.

A main reason some economists, and in particular the Monetarists, prefer a monetary aggregate target to an interest rate target is the chance of procyclical errors when the interest rate is the intermediate target. To see this, consider graphs (a) and (b) of Figure 16-4, which illustrate a disturbance originating in the money market and the goods market, respectively. Assuming that r^T is the target interest rate, let us consider the money market disturbance. This disturbance could be a change in the demand for money. In this case, the interest rate target will lead the Fed to an appropriately countercyclical response. For example, if the demand for money balances increases, a leftward shift in the LM curve results, from LM_0 to LM_2. Interest rates rise, and income and employment tend to decline. The Fed responds by attempting to restore the interest rate to r^T. Increasing the money supply will tend to shift LM back to the original level LM_0. Consequently, Fed action to restore interest rates is appropriately countercyclical in the event of a shift in the LM curve. In contrast an intermediate money target would not lead to a policy response to the shift in LM, so the interest rate and output would change away from r^T and Y^T.

Consider, however, a goods market disturbance as the initiating cause of fluctuations. In Figure 16-4(b), an increase in private autonomous expenditures shifts IS from IS_0 to IS_1. Proper countercyclical policy by the Federal Reserve would be to *reduce* the money supply, but this would put further pressure on interest rates. The policy of maintaining interest rates at some level such as r^T would reinforce the initial change in IS with a rightward shift in LM from LM_0 to LM_1. Such a policy would be *procyclical* in nature, stimulating the economy when output is already increasing, and contracting the economy when output is already declining. Note that an intermediate money target would keep the money supply fixed, and hence keep LM at LM_0, leading to less of a procyclical movement in output.

FIGURE 16-4

IS and *LM* Shocks and Intermediate Interest Rate Targets

This figure illustrates the effect of both *LM* shocks, in graph (a), and *IS* shocks, in graph (b), when the Fed has an intermediate interest rate target. In (a), any shift in *LM* the Fed responds by changing the money supply and hence shifting *LM* to counter this change in the interest rate. In (b), the *IS* curve shifts from IS_0 to IS_1, and the Fed responds by increasing the money supply, shifting *LM* from LM_0 to LM_1.

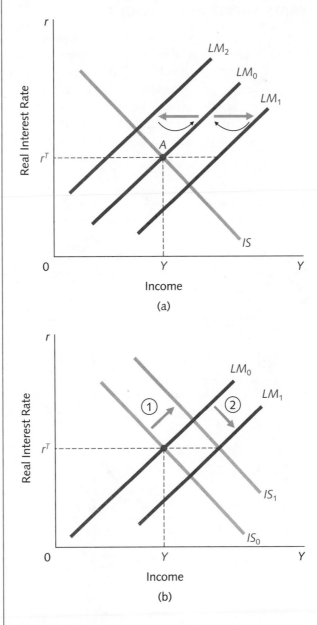

(a)

(b)

The general conclusion is that an intermediate interest rate target is better than an intermediate money target when shocks to the *LM* curve dominate shocks to the *IS* curve, while an intermediate money target is better when shocks to the *IS* curve dominate shocks to the *LM* curve.

LONG-RUN AGGREGATE SUPPLY AND POLICY GOALS

The above points out one constraint on policymakers, and the need to have as many independently acting instruments as policy goals if the goals are to be realized. A second constraint on policy is a long-run constraint imposed by the nature of aggregate supply. In our models, long run aggregate supply is perfectly inelastic. This in itself is a large constraint on policymaking.

Consider, for example, Figure 16-5. The initial equilibrium is at point *A,* where aggregate demand AD_0 intersects both short-run aggregate supply *SRAS*

FIGURE 16-5
Output Targets and Long-Run Equilibrium

In this figure, the output goal is Y^T. The economy is initially in equilibrium at point *A*. Attempts to achieve the target output level by increasing aggregate demand to AD_1 may work in the short run, as illustrated by point *B,* but in the long run, equilibrium is on *LRAS,* such as point *C.*

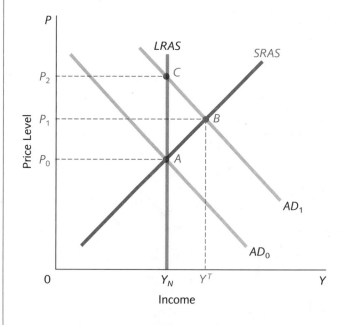

and long-run aggregate supply *LRAS*. At the initial equilibrium, output is at the natural rate Y_N and the price level is P_0.

Suppose, however, that the policymaker has an output goal of Y^T, and can control aggregate demand. In this case there is one goal Y^T and one instrument, which can shift aggregate demand. It would seem that the policymaker could achieve this output goal with the appropriate change in aggregate demand, and indeed in Figure 16-5 a shift of aggregate demand to AD_1 will set the short-run equilibrium at point *B*, achieving the output target. But this is only a short-run equilibrium, and the equilibrium will eventually shift to the long-run equilibrium at point *C*, where output is back at the natural rate as determined by long-run aggregate supply. Thus, the output target can be achieved in the short run by appropriate changes in aggregate demand, but not in the long run. Even with one instrument and one target, the nature of long-run aggregate supply precludes achievement of an arbitrary long-run output goal. The best that can be done is to influence output in the short run. Moreover, in the New Classical model, only an unanticipated shift in aggregate demand to AD_1 would work, since any anticipated shift would lead an instantaneous adjustment of short-run aggregate supply, so that the economy would adjust instantaneously to the long-run equilibrium at point *C*.

To conclude, counting instruments and targets is important, but is not everything. The basic structure of the model is also important, and in modern models the perfectly inelastic long-run aggregate supply curve precludes achieving any long-run output target other than the natural rate of output. This constraint on policymakers is particularly binding in the case of supply shocks, as we will see later in this chapter. But first we turn our attention to an overview of stabilization policy.

We have seen the importance of the number of independent policy instruments relative to the number of targets, as well as the constraint that long-run aggregate supply places on the ability of policymakers to achieve arbitrary levels of output. The shape of long-run aggregate supply provides an answer to the question of why policymakers don't just make output ever larger: The power of government to expand the economy is limited.

This does not preclude a role for macroeconomic policy, however. Even if policy cannot arbitrarily expand output, it may still be able to provide a stabilizing influence on the economy, keeping the economy in the vicinity of some measure of full employment or the natural rate of employment. This is called *stabilization policy*, and is the topic of this section. The basic idea can be explained as follows: The long-run aggregate supply curve both constrains equilibrium output in the long run and indicates the natural rate of output and employment. However, there are disturbances called aggregate **demand disturbances** and aggregate **supply disturbances** that might move the economy away from this natural rate. Policy can perhaps stabilize the equilibrium at the natural rate of output, thereby counteracting the impact of these disturbances.

A DEMAND DISTURBANCE is any aggregate demand shift created by changes in real autonomous factors such as business investment and consumption or by changes in monetary variables such as the money stock.

A SUPPLY DISTURBANCE is an aggregate supply shift caused by changes in any factor affecting the demand or supply of any productive input such as labor.

AGGREGATE DEMAND DISTURBANCES AND STABILIZATION POLICY

The reader should by now be familiar with demand disturbances since they have been considered throughout this book. At this point, we can simply organize what we already know in order to reach an understanding about the basic determinants of aggregate demand. Once this is in hand, it is a short trip to understanding the various policy principles that have been proposed to counteract undesirable changes in aggregate demand.

We may think of two broad sets of variables as determining prices, employment, and output. First, the variables that exert their influence through aggregate supply are *supply-side variables.* Second, variables that exert their influence through aggregate demand are *demand-side variables.* We can further divide both sets of variables into *autonomous factors* and the **policy variables.** Autonomous factors include such things as autonomous consumption or investment spending, or the autonomous level of money demand, or even the position of the production function. Policy variables include government spending, taxes, and at this level of generality, the money supply.[1] We list these factors in Table 16–1.

POLICY VARIABLES are those used in demand or supply management such as fiscal, monetary, or tax policies designed to affect work and input decisions.

TABLE 16-1
Variables that Affect Aggregate Demand and Aggregate Supply

DEMAND-SIDE VARIABLES	
AUTONOMOUS FACTORS	POLICY VARIABLES
AUTONOMOUS CONSUMPTION	MONEY SUPPLY
AUTONOMOUS INVESTMENT	GOVERNMENT SPENDING
AUTONOMOUS NET EXPORTS	TAXES NET OF TRANSFERS
AUTONOMOUS MONEY DEMAND	
EXPECTED INFLATION RATE	
SUPPLY-SIDE VARIABLES	
AUTONOMOUS FACTORS	POLICY VARIABLES
AUTONOMOUS LABOR SUPPLY	GOVERNMENT INFRASTRUCTURE SPENDING
STATE OF TECHNOLOGY	
AUTONOMOUS LABOR DEMAND	TAX RATES ON LABOR INCOME

---

[1]Of course, we have seen in Chapter 12 that the Fed cannot directly control the money supply, but instead must utilize the instruments that it can control—open-market operations, discount window procedures, and reserve requirements—to influence the money supply. For purposes of this chapter, we will assume that the Fed can use these instruments to control the money supply in any way it sees fit.

The policy problem is to see if policymakers are able to offset the autonomous factors, so as to hit their targets as closely as possible.

Demand Disturbances Originating in the Goods Market

Consider a demand disturbance that shifts the *IS* curve. This could be a reduction in autonomous consumption spending, a reduction in autonomous investment spending, or a reduction in autonomous net exports. It could also occur due to an increase in the value of the U.S. dollar, which makes exports more expensive and imports less expensive, reducing net exports. In all these cases, we can analyze the effect of this change using an *IS-LM* graph, and an aggregate demand and supply graph. These are shown in Figure 16-6. The initial intersection of *IS* and *LM* is at point *A*, with an interest rate of r_0 and output of Y_N. In the aggregate demand and supply graph, the equilibrium is at point *A*, where the long-run aggregate supply curve intersects both short-run aggregate supply and aggregate demand. Long-run aggregate supply determines the natural rate level of output as Y_N, and we assume we start in equilibrium at this output level. The initial equilibrium price level is P_0.

What is the effect of the reduction in autonomous spending? Both *IS* and *AD* shift to the left. In the *IS-LM* graph, *IS* shifts from IS_0 to IS_1. The intersection of IS_1 and LM_0 is at point *B*, where the interest rate is r_1 and output Y_1. But this is not even the short-run equilibrium, because it doesn't take into account the changes in aggregate demand and supply. (*Remember:* As we have stressed many times in this text, the *IS* and *LM* curves are drawn holding prices constant. In order to consider the short-run equilibrium we must allow changes in the price level, and for this we must consider aggregate demand and supply.)

In the aggregate demand and supply graph, the reduction in autonomous spending shifts aggregate demand to the left, from AD_0 to AD_1. This shift would result in output of Y_1, as indicated in the *IS-LM* graph, *if prices did not adjust*. Such a point is shown as point *B* in the aggregate demand and supply graph, the amount of output demanded on AD_1 at price level P_0. But this is not an equilibrium point between AD_1 and aggregate supply. Instead, AD_1 and *SRAS* intersect at point *C*, setting the short-run equilibrium output level at Y_2 and the price level at P_2. In the *IS-LM* graph, the analogous point is reached after considering the impact of the fall in the price level. The decrease in the price level will increase real money balances and shift *LM* to the right, to LM_1. The intersection of LM_1 and IS_1 occurs at point *C*, where output is Y_2, as indicated by aggregate demand and supply, and the interest rate is r_2.

This analysis gives the short-run effect of a negative demand shock that originates in the goods market, or with the *IS* curve. Of course, this is only the short-run effect. In the long run, short-run aggregate supply will adjust to the decline in the price level. In the New Classical model expectations will adjust,

This figure shows a shock originating in the goods market, shifting *IS*
and hence *AD* to the left. The shift leftward in *IS* is illustrated in
graph (a), and results in an equilibrium at point *B* if the price level
stays constant. However, in graph (b) we see that the leftward shift in
AD results in an equilibrium at point *C*, where the price level has
fallen. This fall in the price level causes the *LM* curve to shift to the
right in graph (a). The final equilibrium is point *C.*

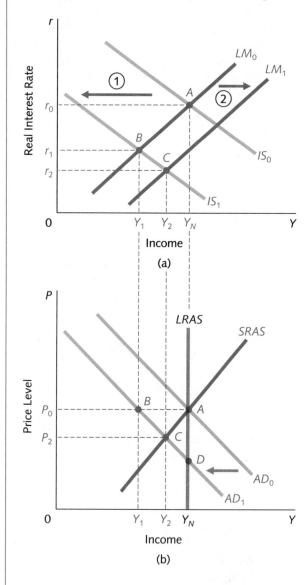

or in the New Keynesian model the contracted wage will adjust, so that the long-run equilibrium is at point D, with output back at the natural rate level Y_N.

For policy purposes, we will be concerned with short-run equilibrium. The idea behind stabilization policy is to counteract adverse shocks to the economy in the short run. The alternative to stabilization policy is to leave the economy alone to adjust to adverse shocks, since it will eventually return to long-run equilibrium. Indeed, the Monetarist view and especially the New Classical view are essentially this one, that the economy's equilibrating mechanisms are strong enough, and act quickly enough, that stabilization policy is neither necessary nor desirable.

How would stabilization policy proceed in the situation described in Figure 16-6? Notice what has happened. The reduction in spending has reduced real output below the natural rate, and this will cause a corresponding reduction in employment, so unemployment will increase. The price level will decline, as will real interest rates.[2] These are some of the traditional indicators of a recession. The appropriate policy response is to "stimulate the economy" by increasing aggregate demand. Policymakers have a wealth of instruments at their disposal to accomplish this task. Fiscal policymakers can increase government spending or reduce taxes. Both will shift IS and aggregate demand to the right. Monetary policymakers can increase the money supply, which will shift LM and aggregate demand to the right.

We look first at fiscal policy, illustrated in Figure 16-7. After the shock, the economy is in equilibrium at the points labeled C in both the IS-LM and the aggregate demand and supply graphs. An increase in government spending or reduction in taxes will shift aggregate demand to the right, to AD_0, and shift IS to the right, to IS_0. Notice that the increase in aggregate demand is just enough to counteract the initial reduction in aggregate demand, so equilibrium is restored at point A, with a price level P_0 and output Y_N. In the IS-LM graph the story is a bit more complicated. The fiscal policy actions cause a rightward shift in IS, to IS_0. If the price level stayed at P_2, this would be the new equilibrium, with output of Y_3. However, the price level rises from P_2 to P_0, and this reduces real money balances, shifting LM leftward from LM_1 to LM_0. The final equilibrium is at point A, with output of Y_N and an interest rate of r_0. The initial equilibrium is restored. Not only output and the price level, but also the real interest rate, are restored to their initial levels. The reduction in private spending has been replaced with either increased government spending or increased consumption (due to the reduction in taxes).

---

[2]Note that this decline in the price level is a once-and-for-all decrease in the price level. On a theoretical level, this is *not* tantamount to inflation, which is defined as the *rate* of increase in prices (e.g., from 15 percent to 20 percent per year). From a pragmatic viewpoint, however, this one-time reduction in the price level is likely to take place in an economy with continually rising prices. Thus, this one-time reduction in the price level may show up in price data such as the CPI as a temporary slowing in the inflation rate.

FIGURE 16-7

A Fiscal Policy Response to a
Shock Originating in the
Goods Market

In response to the goods market shock illustrated in Figure 16-7, the
economy is in the short run at point C. Fiscal policy can respond by
restoring the IS curve to its original position at IS_0, as illustrated in
graph (a), and this also restores aggregate demand to AD_0, as illustrated
in graph (b). The final equilibrium is at point A in both (a) and (b).

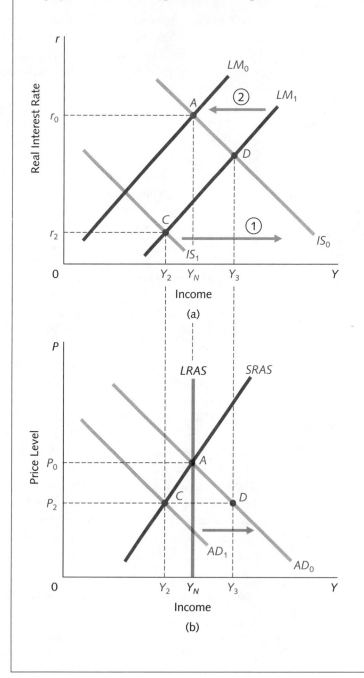

As an alternative, the monetary policymaker could respond to the events shown in Figure 16-6. The effects of counteracting the recession with monetary policy are shown in Figure 16-8. After the adverse *IS* shock, the economy was in equilibrium at the points labeled *C* in both the *IS-LM* and the aggregate demand and supply graphs. An increase in the money supply will shift both aggregate demand and *LM* to the right. Aggregate demand shifts from AD_1 to AD_0, and *LM* shifts from LM_1 to LM_2. In the aggregate demand and supply graph, the increase in aggregate demand is just enough to counteract the initial reduction in aggregate demand, so equilibrium is restored at point *A*, with a price level P_0 and output Y_N. Again, however, the *IS-LM* graph is again more complicated. The increase in the money supply caused *LM* to shift to LM_2. At a price level P_2, the new equilibrium would be at point *D*, with output at Y_3. However, the price level rises from P_2 to P_0, and this reduces real money balances, shifting *LM* leftward from LM_2 to LM_3. The final equilibrium is at point *E*, with output of Y_N and an interest rate of r_4. In this case, the initial equilibrium price level and output level have been restored, but the real interest rate has declined even further, from r_2 to r_4. Thus, monetary policy cannot restore the real interest rate to the initial level.

In the above analysis, it is clear that although the *source* of the unwanted demand disturbance is in the goods market, *either* fiscal or monetary policy may be used to return the economy to the natural rate of unemployment. In general, both fiscal and monetary policies will cause upward pressure on the price level, but will have different effects on the real interest rate. These differences are not unimportant, however, since investment and hence economic growth are in part functions of the real interest rate. Policies that keep the real interest rate low encourage more economic growth.

Disturbances to Demand Originating in the Money Market

A monetary disturbance in the macroeconomy is one that originates from changes in the demand or supply of money. Note that a reduction in the nominal money supply or an increase in autonomous money demand would cause both *LM* and aggregate demand to shift to the left, an adverse disturbance to aggregate demand. Ordinarily, however, the money supply is regarded as a control variable, so we will consider an increase in the demand for money as creating the disturbance. However, it is certainly possible for changes in the money supply to create such a disturbance, and this could come about because of unsuccessful control of the money supply by the Fed.

The effects of this autonomous increase in money demand are illustrated in Figure 16-9, where the initial equilibrium is at the points labeled *A* in both the *IS-LM* and the aggregate demand and aggregate supply graphs. *LM* shifts to the left, from LM_0 to LM_1. With no change in the price level, the new intersection of *IS* and *LM* is at point B, with an increase in the real interest rate from r_0 to r_1 and a reduction in output from Y_N to Y_1. In the aggregate

In response to the goods market shock illustrated in Figure 16-6, the
economy is in the short run at point C. Monetary policy can respond
by shifting LM to LM_2, as illustrated in graph (a). This increase in the
money supply also increases aggregate demand to AD_0, in graph (b).
The final equilibrium is labeled as point E in graph (a) and point A in
graph (b).

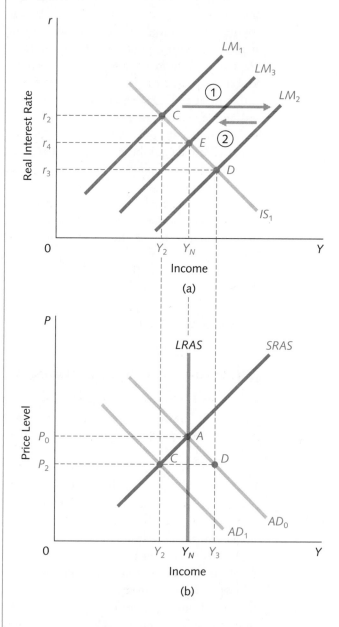

FIGURE 16-9
A Shock Originating in the
Money Market

This figure shows a shock originating in the money market, shifting *LM* and hence *AD* to the left. The initial shift leftward in *LM* from LM_0 to LM_1 is illustrated in (a), and results in an equilibrium at point *B* if the price level stays constant. However, in (b) we see that the leftward shift in *AD* results in an equilibrium at point *C*, where the price level has fallen.

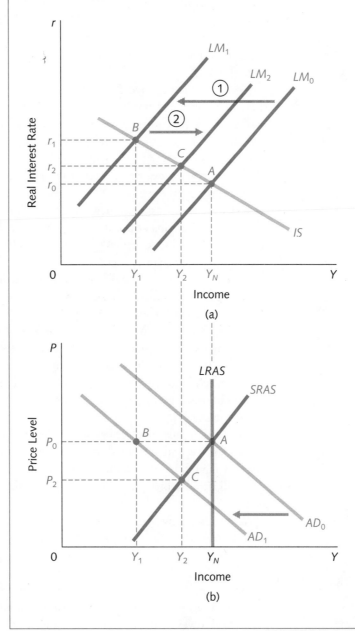

demand and supply graph, this is shown by the leftward shift in aggregate demand, from AD_0 to AD_1. With unchanged prices, the level of output consistent with AD_1 and a price level of P_0 are found at point B as Y_1.

Of course, the price level will change, and short-run equilibrium is found at the intersection of AD_1 and $SRAS$ at point C. The price level falls to P_2, and output falls from Y_N to Y_2.

In the IS-LM graph, the fall in the price level increases real money balances, which shifts LM to the right, from LM_1 to LM_2. The short-run equilibrium after the price adjustment is at point C, where LM_2 intersects IS. Notice that the interest rate has still risen, but from r_0 to r_2, and output has still fallen, but from Y_N to Y_2.

Note that the negative demand shock illustrated in Figure 16-9 comes from the money market, but it has effects similar to those of the adverse goods market shock in Figure 16-6. In terms of aggregate demand and supply, the two shocks are identical. They reduce aggregate demand, resulting in a lower price level and lower level of output. In the IS-LM graph, the goods market shock results in a lower real interest rate, while the money market shock raises the real interest rate.

What are the possible policy responses? Consider first a fiscal policy action. The economy begins at point C in both the IS-LM and the aggregate demand and supply graphs, as shown in Figure 16-10. Either government spending increases, or taxes are reduced, increasing spending and shifting both IS and aggregate demand to the right. This is illustrated in Figure 16-10. The increase in aggregate demand, from AD_1 to AD_0, restores the initial equilibrium at point A. The price level rises from P_2 to P_0, and output rises from Y_2 to Y_N.

In the IS-LM graph, the fiscal stimulus shifts IS to the right, from IS_0 to IS_1. All by itself, this changes the equilibrium from point C to point D, raising both the real interest rate and output. However, the price level rises to P_0, reducing real money balances and shifting LM to the left, from LM_2 to LM_3. The final equilibrium is at point E, with output at Y_N and the real interest rate at r_4.

Notice that this fiscal policy action has restored the pre-shock equilibrium levels of price and output, but the interest rate is now above the pre-shock level. In Figure 16-9, the interest rate increased from r_0 to r_2, and the policy action illustrated in Figure 16-10 increased the real interest rate further, from r_2 to r_4.

As an alternative to this fiscal policy action, there could be a monetary policy response to the recession. The monetary policymaker could increase the money supply, stimulating aggregate demand. This would shift both aggregate demand and the LM curve to the right, as illustrated in Figure 16-11. LM shifts from LM_2 to LM_3, and aggregate demand from AD_1 to AD_0. With prices constant, the increase in the money supply changes the IS-LM equilibrium to point D. However, the increase in aggregate demand increases the price level from P_2 to P_0, reducing real money balances and shifting LM leftward, from

FIGURE 16-10
A Fiscal Policy Response to a
Shock Originating in the
Money Market

In response to the money market shock illustrated in Figure 16-10, the economy is in the short run at point C. Fiscal policy can respond by shifting the IS curve to the right, to IS_1, as illustrated in (a), and this also restores aggregate demand to AD_0, as illustrated in (b).

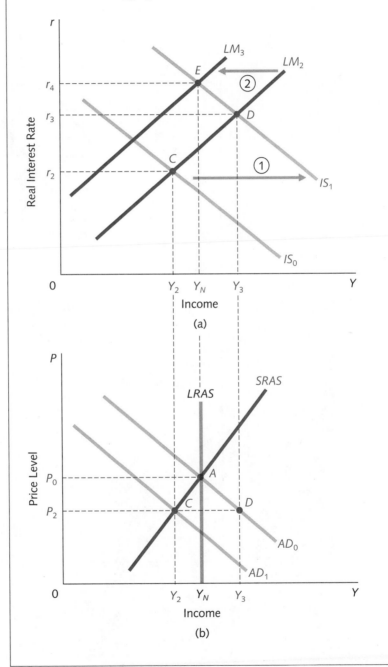

(a)

(b)

FIGURE 16-11
A Monetary Policy Response
to a Shock Originating in the
Money Market

In response to the money market shock illustrated in Figure 16-9, the economy is in the short run at point *C*. Monetary policy can respond by attempting to restore output to the natural rate by increasing the money supply, shifting *LM* to *LM₃*, as illustrated in graph (a). This also increases aggregate demand to *AD₀*, as illustrated in graph (b).

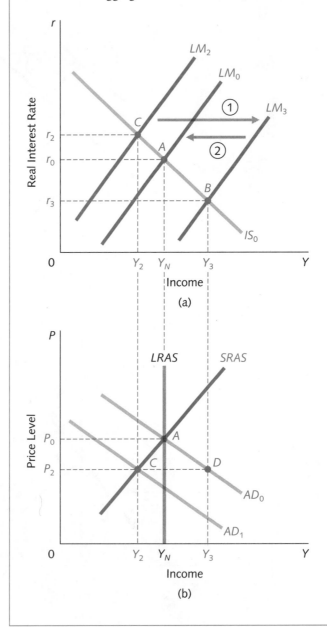

(a)

(b)

LM_3 to LM_0. The final equilibrium is labeled point A in both the IS-LM and the aggregate demand and supply graphs, and is identical in both graphs to the initial equilibrium in Figure 16-9, before the money demand shock. The monetary policy action restores the initial level of income, prices, and the interest rate.

Demand Disturbances as a Source of Price-Level Increases

We have just analyzed a situation when an adverse demand shock leads to a decline in output and an increase in unemployment. In these cases, there would also be decreases in the price level. The static equilibrium model used to discuss this situation may also be used to develop some notion of the source of price increases and of their relation to inflation. As emphasized in many places in this text, inflation is defined as an ongoing increase in the price level. One-time increases in the price level are not (strictly speaking) inflation.

How would inflation occur? Consider Figure 16-12, in which a rightward shift in aggregate demand has caused an increase in the price level. Like a decrease in aggregate demand, the source of the aggregate demand increases may be in the money market or the goods market. The short-run increase in the price level, from P_0 to P_0', is magnified in the long run, when the economy returns to the long-run aggregate supply curve and the price level rises further, to P_1. Theoretically, monetary restraint or contractionary fiscal policy would alleviate the problem. With an appropriate policy, the AD curve of Figure 16-12 could be shifted from AD_1 back to AD_0 by either of these policies.

Is the increase in the price level from P_0 to P_1 inflation? Once the price level has increased to P_1, it does not keep increasing. Thus, it is a one-time change in the price level, due to a one-time change in aggregate demand. Of course, if we are calculating inflation from a series of price levels, we would certainly calculate the change in the price level from P_0 to P_1 as a positive percentage change—inflation—but this would not continue next period.

To have inflation, we need aggregate demand to increase steadily over time, from AD_0 to AD_1 and then on to AD_2 and AD_3. In this way the price level will be continually increasing. How can this happen? Can autonomous spending continue to increase in this way? While theoretically possible, the reality is that autonomous consumption or autonomous investment does not behave in this way. Instead, it turns out that policy variables are the most likely candidates for generating such sustained, ongoing increases in aggregate demand. If the money supply is growing at a fixed rate every year, say 10 percent, then aggregate demand is subject to ongoing increases, and there will be ongoing increases in the price level. This is why money growth is considered to be the prime suspect in any ongoing inflation.

Can fiscal policy cause an ongoing inflation? The answer is a qualified yes. In Chapter 17 we will learn that the government budget constraint links monetary and fiscal policy, so that ongoing deficits might be financed by

This graph illustrates an ongoing inflation. Beginning at point A, aggregate demand increases to AD_1. If aggregate demand is increased again, to AD_2, the price level will rise again. Continued pursuit of policies that shift aggregate demand to the right in hopes of increasing output above the natural rate results in ever-increasing price levels, or an ongoing inflation.

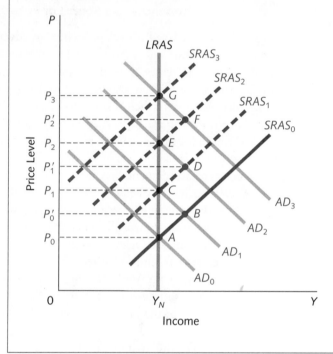

money growth, and money growth can cause inflation. But fiscal policy can directly cause inflation by causing ongoing increases in aggregate demand. Unlike monetary policy, however, there are limits to fiscal policy growth. Government purchases and government transfers cannot grow without bound, so there is a limit to the ability of fiscal policy to cause large inflations.

SUPPLY DISTURBANCES AND STABILIZATION POLICY

Aggregate supply shifts are another source of changes in prices and employment. Supply-side economics has become an important topic in discussions of macroeconomic policy, and modern approaches to macroeconomic modeling place a strong emphasis on modeling the supply side of the economy. Indeed, Real Business Cycle theory places the emphasis squarely on production disturbances, but New Classical and New Keynesian models also stress the importance of aggregate supply.

In this section, we will first analyze the effect of a supply shock on output and the price level. Then we will discuss the options facing the policymaker, and show why supply shocks force the policymaker into a particularly difficult situation.

The Effect of a Supply Disturbance

An adverse supply disturbance is illustrated in Figure 16-13. The economy is initially in equilibrium with aggregate demand curve AD_0, long-run aggregate supply $LRAS_0$, and short-run aggregate supply $SRAS_0$. These all intersect at the

FIGURE 16-13
An Adverse Supply Shock

This figure illustrates an adverse supply shock. The initial short-run and long-run aggregate supply curves, $SRAS_0$ and $LRAS_0$, both shift to the left, to $SRAS_1$ and $LRAS_1$. The pre-shock equilibrium at point A is altered to point B in the short run and point C in the long run. Possible policy responses could be to increase aggregate demand to AD_1, giving short-run equilibrium at point D but long-run equilibrium at point E, or decrease aggregate demand to AD_2, giving short-run (and long-run) equilibrium at point F.

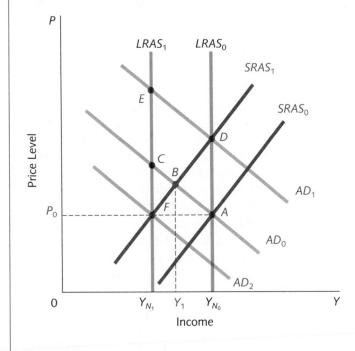

initial equilibrium point, A, determining the price level as P_0 and output as Y_{N_0}. *An adverse supply shock shifts both long-run and short-run aggregate supply to the left.* This is a common feature of supply shocks, and was demonstrated in analyzing supply shocks for all the models in this text. Thus, we illustrate this supply shock as a shift to $LRAS_1$ and $SRAS_1$. One special feature is that these curves continue to intersect at price level P_0 after the supply shock. This is a feature of aggregate supply models built up from the asymmetric information models of the labor market, as used in our New Classical models.[3]

What is the effect of the supply shock? In the short run, the equilibrium is at point B, where $SRAS_1$ intersects AD_0. The price level rises, and output falls to Y_1. In the long run, short-run aggregate supply shifts further to the left, as expectations adjust to take account of the change in the actual price level.[4] The long-run equilibrium is at the intersection of $LRAS_1$ and AD_0, at point C, with an even higher price level and lower output level of Y_{N_1}. Notice the very interesting but also very troubling feature of a supply shock: after a supply shock, output in short-run equilibrium is actually *above* the new natural rate. This is the source of great trouble for policymakers. In particular, they are faced with the difficult choice between attempting to restore output to the original output level, the usual countercyclical policy idea, and helping the economy adjust to the new natural rate of output. The first course of action requires an increase in aggregate demand, to AD_1 in Figure 16-14, so short-run output is at point D, where AD_1 intersects $SRAS_1$. Here the price level is even higher than at point B, but output is restored to Y_{N_0}. However, in the long run the equilibrium will now be at point E, where AD_1 intersects $LRAS_1$, and the eventual increase in the price level will be even greater than it would have been at point C.

An alternative policy is to decide to restore the economy to the *new* natural rate of output as quickly as possible. This requires an actual *reduction* in aggregate demand, from AD_0 to AD_2, in order to restore short-run—and long-run—equilibrium to the natural rate of output. This would lead to short-run equilibrium at point F, where AD_2 intersects $SRAS_1$ and $LRAS_1$. The price level would be P_0, and output would fall to Y_{N_1}. Arguments favoring this policy are that output is going to fall to this level in the long run anyway, since long-run aggregate supply has declined, and this policy does result in a constant price level. However, as a political matter, this is a very difficult policy to pursue, since it involves further reducing output in the face of the supply shock.

The policymaker can also choose a combination of a short-run equilibrium somewhere between points D and F on $SRAS_1$. However, we stress that in the long run output will decline to Y_{N_1} because of the supply shock. Thus, we see that adverse supply shocks face the policymaker with difficult decisions. The

---

[3]In the case of the New Keynesian model with wage contracts, the short-run aggregate supply curve actually shifts further to the left than the long-run aggregate supply curve. The conclusions of this section are basically unaffected by the choice of model of aggregate supply.

[4]Remember that the shift to $SRAS_1$ is due strictly to the supply disturbance. The expected price level on $SRAS_1$ is the same as that on $SRAS_0$, and is equal to P_0.

FIGURE 16-14
The Laffer Curve

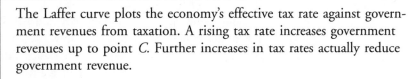

The Laffer curve plots the economy's effective tax rate against government revenues from taxation. A rising tax rate increases government revenues up to point *C*. Further increases in tax rates actually reduce government revenue.

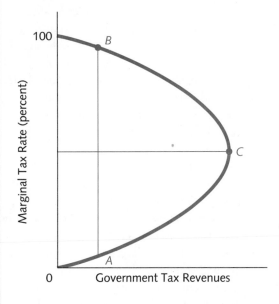

converse is of course that positive supply shocks face the policymaker with easy choices among improvements in the economy, but this is little consolation to a policymaker who must act after an adverse supply shock.

FACTORS AFFECTING LABOR SUPPLY

The previous discussion concerned stabilization policy and aggregate supply shocks. However, some policy actions themselves impact aggregate supply and can alter long-run aggregate supply. In this section we consider some of these, focusing particularly on labor supply, an important feature in all of our models.

Taxes on Work Effort or Wealth: The Laffer Curve

Tax rates have not appeared in our labor supply equation, but a moment's reflection reveals that a change in income tax rates may alter labor supply. A fall in tax rates (an increase in take-home pay for every wage rate) may stimulate work effort, shifting labor supply and hence *SRAS* and *LRAS* rightward, increasing aggregate output and employment, and lowering prices. However a fall in tax rates may lead laborers to supply less labor if workers have a strong desire for leisure. The increased after-tax wage allows them to earn more for every hour worked, so they don't feel that they have to work as many hours as previously. This would shift both *SRAS* and *LRAS* leftward, reducing real GDP and raising prices. Thus, tax rate reductions may increase or decrease aggregate supply.

Let us look at an example. Although there is little empirical evidence on the matter, Arthur B. Laffer argued that in the 1970s marginal tax rates were so high as to create disincentives and that tax rate cuts could cause tax revenue increases. Laffer curve logic was enshrined in President Reagan's stated domestic economic policy, although it was later criticized as a failure. Consider Figure 16-14. Laffer argued that the same government tax revenues could be obtained either at the high marginal tax rate and low production rate represented at point B or at the low tax rate and high production income rate represented at point A.[5] The only way to maximize government tax receipts would be to institute tax rate C. Determination of the exact situation of the U.S. in Figure 16-14 is the major problem, however. If, as Laffer and others believed, the U.S. population will supply more labor, produce higher output and income, and pay larger tax amounts with a tax rate reduction, aggregate supply will *increase*. This will mean a decrease in the natural rate of unemployment and a lessened pressure on the price level, creating a once-and-for-all price-level decrease. In terms of Figure 16-14, Laffer argued that the United States was at the combination of output, tax rates, and government tax receipts that is upward and to the left of point C. A reduction from that marginal tax rate will thus shift *AS* rightward, *possibly* reducing the natural rate of unemployment.

SUPPLY-SIDE ECONOMICS is a term used to describe policies, such as lowering income tax rates or deregulation of markets, which will have the effect of shifting the aggregate supply curve rightward and increasing the natural rate of employment.

Critics of the Laffer version of **supply-side economics** also argue that the plan did not achieve its stated goals. The tax cuts, for example, did not create sufficient additional revenues to cover government expenditures. Indeed, President Clinton campaigned on the theme that trickle-down economics and the whole supply-side idea was a failure. One populist theme from the election campaign was that the rich got rich during the 1980s, and the rest of the country stood still. This theme is examined in more detail in the Policy Issue: "Did Tax Rate Cuts in 1981 and 1986 Give the Rich a Break?"

Another issue during the campaign was the continual slow growth in productivity in the late 1980s and early 1990s. There was a host of proposals from both the Bush and Clinton campaigns for capital gains tax cuts, investment tax credits, increased government spending on infrastructure, and other programs to spur private saving and investment. Bush campaigned as the candidate with a conservative plan for addressing the productivity issue, with plans for tax cuts and slow spending, while Clinton was seen as the candidate espousing increased

---

[5]Jude Wanniski, "Taxes, Revenues, and the 'Laffer Curve,'" *Public Interest* (Winter 1978), pp. 3–16.

DID TAX RATE CUTS IN 1981 AND 1986 GIVE THE RICH A BREAK?

It is often argued that the rich got big breaks during the Reagan-Bush years. Part of the "supply-side" philosophy of these administrations was that reduced taxes would increase work effort and investment in new businesses. Supply-side economics—which inspired these tax cuts—did not achieve the successes that were hoped for and became a negative aspect for President Bush in his unsuccessful bid for

re-election. Tax breaks, it was argued, were a gift to the rich. To what extent is this true?

Economists James D. Gwartney and Richard L. Stroup challenge this view.[a] The top 5 percent of families by income paid *more* in taxes after the tax rate cuts of 1981 and 1986 both as a percentage of total federal taxes paid and in actual amounts. In 1989, the top 5 percent paid 43.7 percent of all federal individual *income taxes,* compared to 37.7 percent in 1977 (see Table 16-2). Over the same period, the rich paid a rising percentage of *total* federal taxation (including income plus other federal taxes) as well—27.7 percent

in 1977 and 30.8 percent in 1989. Simultaneously, those families in the lowest quintile of the income distribution saw their relative share of federal taxes fall. Why did high-income families pay more taxes after their rates were cut? Lower tax rates lured money out of tax shelters and reduced the attractiveness of tax-deductible, business-related expenses. Moreover, lower tax rates encouraged secondary workers (often spouses) in high-income families to work and earn more.

Lower shares of the federal income tax burden for families in the second, middle, and even the fourth quintiles (see table) is somewhat misleading.

PHOTO 16-2
Much Debate Surrounds the So-Called "Greedy 1980s." Junk Bond King Michael Milken Typifies the Era for Many Observers but the Size of the Benefit to the Rich is Unclear.

Payroll deductions (social security and Medicaid contributions) rose dramatically for the middle class over the period. This means that the overall burden on middle-class families may have exceeded those in higher quintile groups. ❑

SOURCES: [a]James D. Gwartney and Richard L. Stroup, "Welfare for the Affluent?" *Washington Times* (May 26, 1992), and Committee on Ways and Means, U.S. House of Representatives, *1992 Green Book* (Washington, DC: U.S. Government Printing Office, 1992).

TABLE 16-2
Shares of the Burden of the Federal Income Tax, for Families, Selected Years 1977 to 1989

	QUINTILES			
	1977	1980	1985	1989
LOWEST	−0.3	−0.2	−0.1	−0.6
SECOND	3.2	3.8	3.4	2.7
MIDDLE	9.8	10.0	9.3	8.5
FOURTH	19.5	20.0	19.1	17.3
FIFTH	67.8	66.4	68.2	72.0
TOP 5%	37.7	36.3	39.1	43.7

SOURCES: James D. Gwartney and Richard L. Stroup, "Welfare for the Affluent?" *Washington Times* (May 26, 1992); and Committee on Ways and Means, U.S. House of Representatives, *1992 Green Book* (Washington, DC: U.S. Government Printing Office, 1992).

government spending, perhaps relabeled "investment." Whether this view of Clinton is accurate will remain to be seen, but Bush's campaign may have suffered from perceived differences between the claims of the candidate and the actual large increases in government spending during the Bush presidency.

PRACTICAL ISSUES IN POLICY IMPLEMENTATION

Although a number of practical problems are important in assessing the usefulness of monetary and fiscal policy, we will first consider the question of *lags* in identifying problems and instituting policy correctives. One such lag is called the *recognition lag*—the time between when a problem begins and the recognition by the policymaker that there is a problem. Recognition of an impending economic problem such as recession is difficult business. Economic indicators and tools of prediction are imperfect. Many forecasts exist, and some give conflicting signals. Which projections are to be used? Those of the Council of Economic Advisers? The Treasury? The Federal Reserve Board?

Another matter is the so-called *administrative lag;* that is, the length of time that elapses between recognition of the business cycle change and, the actual implementation of policy. For example, the Keynesian-inspired 1964 tax cut was proposed over a year before it was actually enacted. The Clinton tax hike of 1993 was proposed during the campaign in 1992 and debated in Congress from early 1993 until its passage in August. Administrative lags mean that the conditions a policy is designed to correct may have passed by the time the policy is enacted. Policy may end up being *procyclical* rather than countercyclical in its effects. For example, during the 1992 presidential campaign President Clinton proposed a fiscal policy action—increased government spending—to boost the sagging economy, which, for most of 1992, had experienced a slow recovery from the recession of 1990–91. However, by the time of his inauguration in January 1993 the economic statistics for the last quarter of 1992 showed the economic recovery to be picking up speed, with real GDP growth well above a 3 percent annual rate. The campaign promise of increased spending would now be a procyclical policy, a stimulus to an economy already exhibiting substantial growth.[6] For monetary policy, in contrast, the Federal Open Market Committee merely meets and debates the issue, and at the conclusion of the meeting any monetary policy action decided upon at the meeting can be immediately carried out.

Finally, there are lags between the time when the policy action is implemented and the actual impact of policy. These are called *effectiveness lags.* A general view is that fiscal policies have shorter effectiveness lags than monetary policy. We should point out that there is an alternative terminology for these lags. In this alternative terminology, *inside lags* are composed of recognition and administrative lags, lags which are inside the policymaking institution. It is widely held that inside lags are a much bigger problem for fiscal policy than for monetary policy. *Outside lags* are the effectiveness lags, and it is widely held that these lags are longer with monetary policy than with fiscal policy.

SHOULD POLICY BE BASED ON RULES OR ON DISCRETION?

A **POLICY RULE** is a rule by which the policymaker sets policy variables.

DISCRETION in policymaking is the ability to set policy each period without regard for past commitments.

Should monetary and fiscal policy be made on a discretionary basis, or should the policymakers adopt and follow a rule for conducting monetary and fiscal policy? This debate on **policy rules** versus **discretion** has a long history in the academic literature. The case for rules has been made most forcefully by Milton Friedman, who argues strongly for a simple, nondiscretionary, and passive rule

---

[6]Indeed, this was the argument made by opponents in the Senate, who successfully filibustered to prevent passage of the original stimulus bill in the Spring of 1993.

for setting monetary policy. The best-known example of a monetary rule is probably his famous 3 percent money growth rule, by which the money supply will grow at 3 percent per year regardless of the state of the economy.

Passive policy rules, such as Friedman's 3 percent growth rule, do not specify that the growth rate of the money supply will change when there is a change in the state of the economy, such as a recession or expansion. There are also *active* monetary policy rules, however. An activist policy rule would specify that money growth will change with changes in economic conditions. For instance, the rule might say that money growth is 3 percent plus an additional 2 percent for every 1 percent increase in the unemployment rate over 7 percent. This is a monetary policy rule which, once adopted, limits the Fed's freedom of action, but it is not a passive rule. Instead, it requires that the money supply growth rate respond to changes in the state of the economy.

Should policy be set by rules or should the policymaker be able to set policy each period without being constrained by a policy rule? As it now stands, the Federal Reserve has a relatively free hand to pursue the monetary policy, subject only to dictates that it report periodically to Congress. There is no rule, such as Friedman's 3 percent money growth rule, that would tie the hands of the Federal Reserve in setting policy.

In the debate over rules versus discretion, it once seemed that the arguments favoring discretion were stronger. Discretion would give the Federal Reserve the ability to change from following a particular rule if it seemed beneficial, while a nondiscretionary rule would lock the Federal Reserve into a plan that might not be the best policy in some future period. Thus, it appeared that discretion would allow the Fed to mimic a policy rule if it seemed the right thing to do, but discretion also preserved the ability of the Federal Reserve to change the rule at low cost. Moreover, there did not seem to be any cost to discretion *per se,* so the argument was basically one of "Why not adopt discretion?" Such a decision would preserve the ability to change policy each period if that proved desirable, but also would allow the Fed to choose—at its own discretion—to follow whatever rule appeared appropriate at any particular time.

Recent research has identified situations in which discretion is *not* costless, however, so that the benefits of being able to change policies have to be weighed against the costs of pursuing discretion. We illustrate the issue of rules versus discretion with two examples. The first is an interpretation of the rules versus discretion question using a game not too different from the Prisoners' Dilemma game discussed in Chapter 10. The second is an interpretation using a graphical model of aggregate demand and supply.

First, consider the following situation facing the Federal Reserve System and the private sector. The Fed faces a choice of setting money growth high or low, and this will set inflation high or low.

What about the private sector? In the private sector, firms and workers negotiate wage contracts based on the expected inflation rate. If they expect the inflation rate to be high, they negotiate a high nominal wage, so that the real wage is at their desired level. If they expect the inflation rate to be low, they negotiate a low nominal wage, so that the real wage is at their desired level.

What if the inflation rate is high but workers negotiate a low nominal wage? In this case workers see their real wage fall. Understandably, they don't like this to occur, especially if they have signed a contract committing to work at the nominal wage. Firms, however, will see the lower real wage and expand employment and output.

What about a high nominal wage but low inflation rate? In this situation, the real wage is higher than desired by firms and workers in negotiations. Firms cut back on output and employment. Workers as a whole are not happy with this situation either, because employment has fallen, although those still working will enjoy a higher real wage.

To complete the picture we need to know the objectives of the Fed. We assume that the Fed has two goals: It prefers a low inflation rate to a high inflation rate. And it prefers a high output level to a low output level.

We make this more concrete in Table 16-3. We assume that the initial price level is 5. This gives us a link between the price levels in the table and a measured inflation rate. By comparing the price level in the table to the initial price level, 5, we can calculate the percentage change in the price level. Part (a) lists the four possible combinations of nominal wages and price levels. Wages can be either low, 5, or high, 10, and the price level can be either high, 10, or low, 5. These alternative price levels determine whether the inflation rate is high or low. Note that a high price level generates a high inflation rate, since a price level of 10 corresponds to an inflation rate of $(10 - 5)/5 = 100$ percent. Similarly, a low price level generates a low inflation rate, since a price level of 5 corresponds to an inflation rate of $(5 - 5)/5 = 0$ percent.

The real wage can be either 1, ½, or 2, depending on the wage rate and the price. Output is determined by the formula $Q = 15 - 5(W/P)$, and varies from 5 to 12.5 units. The important parts of this table are the preferences of the Fed and of the workers. Workers like high real wages, but also like to be employed. When real wages are at the expected level of 1, output will be 10 units—the amount of output and employment desired by workers. When output is above 10 units, employment increases, and workers' utility increases. When output is below 10 units, employment falls, and workers' utility declines. We specify that worker utility is given by the equation $5 \times (W/P) + 2 \times (Q - 10)$. Thus, when the real wage is at the expected level of 1, output is 10 and worker utility is 5. When the real wage is unexpectedly high, this alone tends to increase worker utility, but the decline in output to 5 units reduces employment and worker utility, so that the net effect is to make utility equal to 0. Alternatively, an unexpectedly low real wage tends to decrease worker utility, but the resulting increase in output and employment tends to raise worker utility. The net effect in this case is to reduce utility below zero, to -2.5.

TABLE 16-3　An Illustration of a Monetary Policy Game

Table (a) shows the various combinations of the wage rate and price level, and what they mean for the real wage, output, and the utility of workers and of the Fed. Table (b) then summarizes how the choice of the wage rate and the price level generates different utility for workers and the Fed.

(a)

PRIVATE SECTOR	FED	REAL WAGE	OUTPUT $Q = 15 - 5(w/P)$	WORKER UTILITY $5 \times (w/P) + 2 \times (Q-10)$	FED UTILITY $Q - P/5$
w = 10	P = 10	1	10	5	8
w = 10	P = 5	2	5	0	4
w = 5	P = 10	½	12.5	−2.5	10.5
w = 5	P = 5	1	10	5	9

(b)　FED'S CHOICES

	P = 10	P = 5
w = 10	8 / 5	4 / 0
w = 5	10.5 / -2.5	9 / 5

WORKER'S CHOICES

What about the Fed? The Fed wants a low price level and high output. We write its utility function as $Q - P/5$. We tabulate Fed utility and worker utility for the four combinations of wages and prices given in Table 16-3.

In Table 16-3, part (b), we present this situation in the form of a game, in which the Fed chooses the price level and workers choose the wage rate. The entries in the middle of the table indicate the resulting utility of the Fed and the workers for each combination of wage rate and price. For instance, if the Fed chooses a price level of 10 and workers choose a wage of 10, then the Fed will receive 8 units of utility while workers will receive 5 units of utility. If the Fed had chosen a price level of 5 and workers a wage of 10, then the Fed would receive 4 units of utility and workers 0 units of utility. Thus, both workers and the Fed are happier in the first situation, with a wage rate and price level of 10.

How do we solve this game? That is, how do we decide what the Fed and the workers will do? We look at all four combinations and see if there is one that, once chosen, will not lead either party to desire to change unilaterally its choice. We have already seen that the combination of a price level of 5 and a wage rate of 10 is not satisfactory, and both workers and the Fed would prefer the position with a wage rate and price level of 10. Let us consider a few other points. What about a wage rate and a price level of 5, the lower right combination? In this case, the Fed gets 9 units of utility and workers get 5 units of utility. Would workers want to change? They could increase the wage rate to 10, but if the price level stays at 5 then worker utility will decline, so workers have no incentive to unilaterally change the wage rate. Would the Fed want to change? The Fed could increase the price level to 10, and with a wage of 5 this would increase the Fed's utility to 10.5 units, so the Fed would want to increase the price level.

What about a combination with a price of 10 and a wage of 5? Would workers be happy with this combination? Or would they like to unilaterally adjust the wage? If they raised the wage to 10, then their utility would increase from −2.5 to 5, so workers would raise the real wage. This leads us back to our position with a real wage and a price level of 10. Would either the Fed or workers want to change their choices? The Fed would not, since lowering the price level would reduce Fed utility to 4. Workers would not, since lowering the wage would reduce worker utility to −2.5. Thus, this combination of a high wage and a high price level is what we call a Nash equilibrium. That is, it is a set of choices which neither party to the game has an incentive to alter unilaterally.

The monetary policy game illustrated in Table 16-3 is similar in many respects but not identical to the Prisoners' Dilemma game we discussed in Chapter 10. In this game, the equilibrium is for both parties to set their respective nominal variable as high as possible. The paradoxical conclusion is that workers and the Fed end up in an equilibrium that could be improved upon without either party being hurt. That is, the Nash equilibrium to this game—and to the Prisoners' Dilemma—is inferior to another position in which both players are no worse off than at the Nash equilibrium, but this combination is not itself a Nash equilibrium. To be specific, the combination with a price and wage rate both equal to 5 will yield just as much utility to workers, and more utility to the Fed, than the combination of a high wage and price level. The problem is that this low wage, low price combination is not an equilibrium because the Fed would have an incentive to raise the price level.[7]

This policy game illustrates the problem with discretion. Discretion gives the Fed a choice of choosing a high price or a low price, and given this discretion, the Fed will always choose a high price, since this will always

[7]In fact, the Fed has a dominant strategy of raising the price level, because raising the price level results in higher utility for the Fed regardless of the choice of the workers.

increase the Fed's utility for a given choice by workers. Workers realize this, and find it in their best interest also to choose a high wage. The cost of discretion is that the preferred low price, low wage combination is not achievable as an equilibrium. The Fed can only achieve this preferred combination by credibly committing not to set the price level high. How can this be done? Mere words will not suffice. The expression *talk is cheap* applies here. That is why we use the phrase *credibly commit*. The Fed must somehow tie its hands in a believable way, so that everyone trusts that it will not succumb to the temptation of reneging choosing the high price once workers have contracted a low wage.

How can the Fed credibly commit? Perhaps by some constitutional amendment or other legal mandate from Congress, although then the question might be taken one step backward, and we ask how Congress can credibly commit. Another way is for the Fed to build a reputation as foregoing the temptation to renege. The Fed and workers actually play this game repeatedly, and in a repeated game situation the Fed must compare the benefits to cheating with the benefits of the low wage, low price combination. For example, in a repeated game workers could announce that they would set a low wage this period, and would continue to do so as long as the Fed cooperated and set a low price level. However, workers would also announce that they would respond to any high price level with a high wage in all future periods. In this case, consider the Fed's decision. Workers have already set a low wage. The Fed can cooperate and set a low price, earning 9 units of utility. Or it can renege, setting a high price and earning 10.5 units of utility. However, in the first case the Fed can also earn 9 units of utility in the second period, and in future periods, because workers will keep setting the wage low as long as the Fed sets the price low. In the second case, the Fed reneges, and in the second period and all future periods workers set the wage high, so Fed utility is 8 units. Thus, the Fed can always cooperate and earn utility of $9 + 9 + 9 + \ldots$ over time, or the Fed can cheat and earn utility of $10.5 + 8 + 8 + \ldots$ over time. Which is preferred? If the game is repeated many times and with no known endpoint, such as the game between the Fed and workers, then the Fed may choose to cooperate today in order to "preserve its reputation" and its ability to earn the extra utility in the future. In effect, the Fed gives up a one-time gain from reneging in exchange for the chance to earn a bit more utility for each period the game is played.

What is the conclusion of this analysis? Basically, it is that discretion is not automatically superior to rules. Rules, especially credible rules, allow the Fed to achieve an outcome that it could not otherwise achieve as an equilibrium. Also, discussions of reputation and credibility by the Fed are not pointless, but instead indicate that the Fed is concerned with how its current decisions will affect its long-run utility. The Fed—and other policymakers—may choose to give up some utility today in order to increase its total utility earned over the long run.

The above analysis was a simple example to make the point that monetary policy decisions can be considered as a game between the Fed and the private sector. We can make this more realistic at the expense of making the policy game aspects less clear by using a graphical model—a new Keynesian model with nominal wage contracting. Such a model is drawn in Figure 16-15. In Figure 16-15 the initial equilibrium is at point A, where output is Y_0, the price level is P_0, and the contract wage is W_0^c. Now consider the behavior of the monetary authority. The monetary authority has both an output target and an inflation target. The inflation target might be zero or some other number determined by the need for revenue from money creation. What about the output target? We have typically assumed that the monetary authority wants to achieve the natural rate of output given by *LRAS*, but perhaps the monetary authority actually desires a level of output greater than Y_0, say Y_1. The

FIGURE 16-15
Discretion and Commitment
in Monetary Policy

Beginning in equilibrium at point *A* with output at Y_0, the monetary authority wishes to increase output to Y_1. There are three cases to consider. (1) The monetary authority promises to keep aggregate demand at AD_0. Wage setters sign a wage contract for wage W_0^c, so short-run aggregate supply is $SRAS(W_0^c)$. Then the Fed reneges, increasing aggregate demand to AD_1. This is "cheating" by the Fed. (2) Workers suspect the Fed will cheat, and hence sign a higher nominal wage contract W_1^c, which shifts short-run aggregate supply to $SRAS(W_1^c)$. Now the Fed increases aggregate demand to AD_1, just to get output Y_0. This is the noncooperative solution. (3) The cooperative solution has the Fed announce and stick with keeping aggregate demand at AD_0.

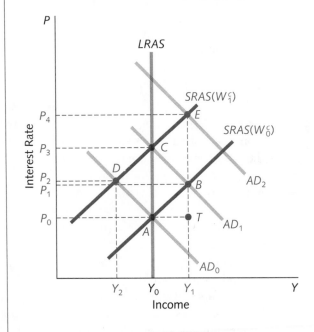

monetary authority acting with discretion might think that it would keep aggregate demand at AD_0 until after wage contracts were signed for W_0^c. This locks in the supply curve at $SRAS(W_0^c)$, and with AD_0 gives output at Y_0 and a price level of P_0. However, once the wage is set, the monetary authority knows that it can increase the money supply, increase AD to AD_1, and achieve its output goal of Y_1 at point B. Doing so means that there will be inflation since $P_1 > P_0$, but this might be acceptable to the monetary authority if it can get output of Y_1. Thus, a monetary authority acting with discretion can have an incentive to announce a policy, say of aggregate demand at AD_0, and then renege on that policy once wages are set, generating a higher level of aggregate demand, say AD_1, and a higher level of output and prices. In the terms of game theory, we would say that the monetary authority had announced its intention to cooperate, and then had cheated on the announcement.

In such a situation, what should wage earners do? When deciding on the wage, wage earners want to predict what the price level will be. If wage earners know that the monetary authority harbors a desire for output level Y_1, then they should not sign a contract for W_0^c. Instead, they should settle for a greater nominal wage, say W_1^c. This makes short-run aggregate supply $SRAS(W_1^c)$, and if the monetary authority keeps aggregate demand at AD_0, equilibrium is at point D, prices will rise to P_2 and output will fall to Y_2. Notice that movements from point A to point D involve inflation *and* a decrease in output, both distasteful to the monetary authority. What will the monetary authority do? It controls aggregate demand, so it can reduce aggregate demand, lowering output further but reducing the inflation rate. Or it can increase aggregate demand, increasing output but paying for it with even higher price levels and inflation.

How will the Fed react? If it has a strong desire not to be too far from Y_1, it will increase aggregate demand to move output from Y_2 toward Y_1. If it moves all the way to output of Y_1, aggregate demand will increase to AD_2, output will be Y_1, and the price level will be P_4, as given by point E. However, each step of the way from Y_2 to Y_1 the increase in output leads to a greater inflation rate. If the monetary authority dislikes inflation, it will decide to compromise, accepting output somewhere between Y_2 and Y_1 and inflation less than that caused by moving to P_4. Moreover, if the wage setters have chosen the wage correctly, the monetary authority will choose point C, where output is at the natural rate Y_0 and prices have increased from P_0 to P_3. Wage setters must set the wage first, but if they set it high enough, the monetary authority must increase aggregate demand just to return output to Y_0, and this generates so much inflation that the monetary authority is unwilling to generate any more in attempts to further increase output. In this way the wage setters can constrain the monetary authority to generate just enough additional aggregate demand to keep output at the natural rate Y_0.

Of course, if the monetary authority announces aggregate demand of AD_0 *and sticks with its pledge,* and if workers believe the pledge, then equilibrium is at point A, output is Y_0, and the price level is P_0. What does the monetary authority think of this? It doesn't like output of Y_0, preferring a higher output level Y_1, but it likes zero inflation. Thus, it achieves its inflation goal but not its output goal. The equilibrium is called the cooperative equilibrium because workers and the monetary authority are cooperating, the monetary authority by keeping aggregate demand at AD_0 and workers by keeping wages at W_0^c.

Consider the alternative, noncooperation.

This is the solution described above, in which starting at point A workers and firms sign nominal wage contracts at a wage W_1^c, a level so high that after the monetary authority increases demand to AD_1 it has experienced so much inflation, from P_0 to P_3, that it does not want to raise aggregate demand further, and is happy to have output of Y_0 at point C. Thus, in the noncooperative equilibrium, output is Y_0, and inflation is the rate of change in prices from P_0 to P_3.

Compare the noncooperative and cooperative equilibria. In both, output is Y_0, below the monetary authority's target value. In the cooperative equilibrium, inflation is zero, which equals the monetary authority's target, but in the noncooperative equilibrium, the inflation rate is greater than zero. Thus, the monetary authority is *better off in the cooperative equilibrium*. But the cooperative equilibrium is one in which the monetary authority follows a rule, the rule being to keep aggregate demand at AD_0. This might be a rule of keeping money growth at 3 percent, or keeping nominal GDP growth at 3 percent. In contrast, discretion allows the monetary policymaker to set the money supply and aggregate demand at any level it desires. Thus, policymaking by rules actually makes the monetary authority better off, if it can commit to obeying the rules. We say *if* because any time the cooperative equilibrium is in force the monetary authority has an incentive to cheat, increasing aggregate demand above the level specified in the rule in order to get output higher than Y_0. Thus, the rule must be believed by wage setters.

Much work has gone into designing rules that are believable, such as constitutional provisions and the like, but it turns out that in situations or games that are repeated over and over, it is the reputation of the participants themselves that allows the rule to be believable. In the above game, if the monetary authority were to cheat, it would get a one-time gain of utility from output being Y_1 instead of Y_0. However, if workers respond by playing noncooperatively from then on, the monetary authority would be faced with inflation of $P_3 - P_0$ each period forever. Hence the monetary authority would face the tradeoff of more output for one period versus more inflation "forever," and could well decide that forever is a long time and forego the opportunity to cheat. This is called a reputational equilibrium in game theory, and it can enforce cooperative equilibria, which would otherwise seem to be unenforceable.

For our purposes, the above analysis illustrates that discretion can result in worse policy outcomes than rules. The commitment to the cooperative rule makes the Fed better off than discretion and destroys the presumption that discretion is obviously better than rules. In fact, such analysis has convinced many economists that monetary policy should be made by rules rather than discretion.

There is a further argument for rules. This argument claims that past mistakes by the Fed should lead us to doubt the judgment of the Federal Reserve. For instance, Milton Friedman accuses the Federal Reserve of allowing the money supply to collapse during the Great Depression, causing it to be both longer and more severe than it otherwise would have been. (See the Insight: "What the Federal Reserve's Board of Governors Did Not Do: 1929–1933"). This leads Friedman to argue that the Federal Reserve System should be required to pursue a strict money growth target. As Friedman wrote:

> Any system which gives so much power and so much discretion to a few men that mistakes . . . can have such far reaching effects is a bad system. It is a bad system to believers in freedom just because it gives a few men such power without any effective check by the body politic—this is the key argument against an "independent" central bank. But it is a bad system even to those who set security (of the banking system) higher than freedom. Mistakes . . . cannot be avoided in a system which disperses responsibility yet gives a few men great power, and which thereby makes important policy actions highly dependent on accidents of personality. This is the key technical argument against an "independent" central bank.[8]

Fiscal Policy

Our discussion has been largely in terms of monetary policy, but fiscal policymakers also face the problem of credible commitment, and fiscal policy can also be analyzed as a game between the fiscal policymaker and the private sector. Consider, for example, the idea of tax amnesty. A tax amnesty is an announcement by the government that it will grant amnesty to any tax cheats who come forth and pay the taxes due. This amnesty is usually freedom from criminal prosecution and from penalties on underpayment of taxes. Usually such an announcement would also be accompanied by an announcement that there will be renewed prosecution of tax cheats who do not claim amnesty as soon as the amnesty period ends. Announcements of a tax amnesty raise revenue for the government, since tax cheats do come forward as a way of avoiding penalties and prosecution. However, a tax amnesty also imposes a cost, because taxpayers who expect periodic tax amnesties will not hesitate as much about cheating on their taxes. They would expect to be able to claim amnesty during some future tax amnesty. Thus, announcements of a tax amnesty are also often accompanied by a promise that the amnesty will not be repeated.

---

[8]Milton Friedman, *Capitalism and Freedom,* (Chicago: University of Chicago Press, 1962), p. 50.

WHAT THE FEDERAL RESERVE'S BOARD OF GOVERNORS DID NOT DO: 1929–1933

A number of theories or explanations about the Great Depression of the 1930s have been offered by economists. While some economists such as Peter Temin argue that the Depression was a result of a sharp decline in autonomous expenditures, particularly consumption expenditures, Milton Friedman and Anna Schwartz place the blame squarely on the Federal Reserve's Board of Governors in Washington.[a] They maintain that it was the passive stance of this group and their later mismanagement that caused the length and severity of the Depression. The question is then, what did the Board of Governors not do?

Prior to the stock market crash in October 1929, there was a dispute between the Federal Reserve Bank of New York and the board over the excessive speculation in the stock market. Early in 1929, the

New York Fed had tried to increase the discount rate but was thwarted by the board.

Moreover, while the members of the board seemed to realize that a serious problem was arising in the stock market, they never asked Congress for control over margin requirements, the down payment required when borrowing to finance a stock purchase. Instead, the board gave some gentle admonitions to commercial banks about not borrowing from the discount window if they were planning to make or maintain speculative loans. On Black Thursday, October 24, 1929, 12,894,650 shares of stock changed hands and stock prices collapsed. As more and more people tried to sell stock, others who could not make their margin calls were sold out. Fear and panic swept the market, and although there were private attempts to stop the decline in stock prices, they were unsuccessful.

The conflict between the New York Fed and the Board of Governors extended into the post-1929 era as well. The New York Fed attempted to act as a central bank by purchasing large amounts of securities in the open market. In

this instance, the board acted to stop these open-market purchases. And so it went. Time after time in the early 1930s the Federal Reserve banks tried to take positive action, but were prevented from doing so by the Board of Governors. The board failed to allow the Federal Reserve banks to do what they were created to do and that was to *act as a lender of the last resort.*

The failure of the Fed to act as a lender of last resort accounts for the large number of bank failures from 1930 through 1933. Furthermore, there was the classic effect of bank panics on the currency-deposit and reserve-deposit ratio. An increase in both ratios occurred after the first banking crises in April 1930 and led to a reduction in high-powered money, which contributed to the decline in the money stock. The board did practically nothing to compensate for the reduction in the money stock; in fact in early 1933, it voted to reduce the quantity of high-powered money.

Faced with panic-inspired currency drains from commercial banks, President Roosevelt, on March 6, 1933, ordered all banks closed including the Federal Reserve banks. In three days Congress passed the Emergency Banking Act, which reopened the banks under the Comptroller of the Currency. In that same year, Congress established the Federal Deposit Insurance Corporation to protect depositors against loss in case an insured bank failed. Later, the Banking Act of 1935 shifted power such as the conduct over open-market operations from the individual Federal Reserve banks to the Board of Governors where such power and final responsibility still resides today.   ❑

NOTE: [a]See Peter Temin, *Did Monetary Forces Cause the Great Depression?* (New York: W. W. Norton, 1976), and also Milton Friedman and Anna J. Schwartz, *A Monetary History of the United States, 1867–1960* (Princeton, NJ: Princeton University Press, 1964), pp. 158–59.

What is the problem with this? The problem is that the promise that the amnesty will not be repeated is not credible. The very fact that the government has announced a tax amnesty will make taxpayers think that another tax amnesty will occur at some future date. In addition, it is very difficult for the government to credibly commit to no future tax amnesties. How would it do so? It could pass a law, but it would take a law to allow a tax amnesty anyway, and a future tax amnesty law could easily contain a provision overturning any past law prohibiting such a thing.

It is actually quite difficult to think of a credible solution to this problem, unless the solution is to destroy the government's reputation for ever holding a tax amnesty. For example, in the *Wall Street Journal* two economists, Robert Barro and Allan Stockman, proposed the following solution: The government should announce the amnesty and then renege, prosecuting those who come forward! If this were done, the tax amnesty would raise revenue, and then the government's reneging would mean that no one would ever again think a tax amnesty announcement were credible. Thus, the government could destroy its own credibility to credibly commit to a "no future amnesties" policy. It would of course be interesting to see how this issue would be treated in the courts.

Automatic Stabilizers

One important class of policy rules is the so-called automatic stabilizers. This term is usually applied to fiscal policy, especially income taxes and transfer programs such as unemployment compensation schemes. These taxes and transfers are "automatically" countercyclical. That is, income taxes decline and transfers increase—so taxes net of transfers decline—when output and employment decline. This decline in taxes net of transfers stimulates aggregate demand, partially (but not totally) offsetting the initial decline in output and employment. In the same way, any increase in output and employment will cause taxes net of transfers to rise and partially offset the initial increase in output and employment.

The key to automatic stabilizers is that they act without any further attention from Congress or the President. Thus, they avoid the recognition and administrative lags that bedevil fiscal policymaking. In fact, Friedman argues that his constant money growth rule would be an automatic stabilizer. Suppose money growth was set at 3 percent. When output was growing faster than 3 percent, the money growth rate of 3 percent would cause prices to fall (if velocity was constant), thus tending to restrain the economy. If output was growing slower than 3 percent, the money growth rate of 3 percent would cause prices to increase, tending to stimulate the economy.

SUMMARY

This chapter introduced some of the elements of macroeconomic policy. Apart from the question of whether or not discretionary policy works, aggregate demand and aggregate supply shocks will produce business cycles in our economy. Advocates of discretionary policy argue that fiscal or monetary policy are effective in compensating for these swings in production, employment, and prices. In this view, shortfalls in employment and output may be eliminated or reduced through discretionary fiscal or monetary expansion.

Aggregate supply disturbances will also destabilize the economy and, in the view of advocates of discretionary policy, such cycles may be moderated by fiscal or monetary means. Supply disturbances include shocks such as the emergence or dissolution of OPEC's power over world oil prices. Advocates of discretion argue that policy and institutional changes might be used effectively to mitigate adverse shocks originating on the supply side of the economy.

KEY TERMS

demand deficiency unemployment
demand disturbance
discretion
intermediate monetary target
policy instrument

policy rule
policy target
policy variables
supply disturbance
supply-side economics

QUESTIONS FOR REVIEW AND DISCUSSION

1. Clearly distinguish between supply and demand disturbances. What are the sources of supply disturbances? Demand disturbances?

2. What is a goods market disturbance? Consider an autonomous increase in consumption spending caused by a change in household preference for present versus future goods. Work through the effects of such a change of P, Y, and r. Does the shape of the aggregate supply curve affect your answer?

3. What is a money market disturbance? Consider an autonomous increase in money demand. Work through the effects of such a change of P, Y, and r. Does the shape of the aggregate supply curve affect your answer?

4. What are the possible policy prescriptions for dealing with an autonomous aggregate demand increase that creates higher price levels? How do these discretionary policy manipulations work?

5. Assume a decrease in money demand for transactions. What are the possible effects on P, Y, and N, assuming a short-run supply curve? What are the possible policy responses to counteract these effects?

6. What is supply-side economics? What, specifically, causes shifts in the aggregate supply function? Can the government influence aggregate supply?

7. How does a change (improvement) in technology affect aggregate supply, the price level, output, and employment? Is there a recommended fiscal or monetary policy action to help with the adjustment process?

8. Suppose that workers' wealth increases. Explain how this change might affect the supply of labor, aggregate supply, and—ultimately—the price level and income.

9. Explain how the natural rate of unemployment is related to aggregate supply. Further, explain how (theoretically) the natural rate of unemployment might change in the context of the simple macro model developed in this chapter.

10. In a Keynesian model, can the government achieve an arbitrary target level for output? What about in the New Classical or New Keynesian models? Does it matter if we are discussing the long run or the short run? Why?

11. Recently there has been an interest by Representative Neil of North Carolina to have the Fed pursue price level stability. If the Fed adopts a price level target, are we fairly sure it can actually achieve such a target in the Classical model? In the Keynesian model? In the New Classical or New Keynesian models? What might be the advantages and disadvantages of a price level target?

12. Explain why the Fed might want to be concerned with maintaining its credibility. Is there a benefit to the Fed from being perceived as anti-inflationary? Why?

13. Discuss the existence and implications of lags for both fiscal and monetary policy. How might such lags produce a procyclical impact on the economy?

14. How do Monetarists, such as Milton Friedman, assess discretionary fiscal and monetary policy? Do Monetarists view the economy as being inherently unstable?

15. What is the conceptual difference between discretionary economic policies and a "rule"? Aren't rules themselves "discretionary"? Why can't discretion do as well as rules in all cases?

16. "A discussion of the effects of discretionary economics (both fiscal and monetary) is unnecessary if rational expectations are assumed to hold at every point in time." Comment.

PROBLEMS

1. In Table 16-3 we developed a monetary policy game between the Fed and workers. Workers had to first sign a nominal wage contract, and then the Fed could choose the price level (or inflation rate).
(a) What if the Fed had to first announce and deliver an inflation rate? What would be the Nash equilibrium in that case? Why?
(b) What if workers could sign cost of living agreements (COLAs) so that their nominal wage would automatically adjust to keep the real wage constant? How would that change the payoff table to the various actions of the Fed and workers?

2. How will the Clinton tax increase of 1993 affect aggregate demand and aggregate supply? What impact will there be on the price level and real output?

SUGGESTIONS FOR FURTHER READING

Bradley, Michael D., and Dennis W. Jansen. "Understanding Nominal Income Targeting," Federal Reserve Bank of St. Louis *Review* (November/December 1989), pp. 31–40.

Ekelund, Robert B., and Mark Thornton. "Schumpeterian Analysis, Supply-Side Economics, and Macroeconomic Policy in the 1920s." *Review of Social Economy* (December 1986), pp. 221–237.

Englander, A. Steven. "Optimal Monetary Policy Design: Rules vs. Discretion Again." In *Intermediate Targets and Indicators for Monetary Policy.* New York: Federal Reserve Bank of New York, 1990, pp. 421–51.

Friedman, Milton. *A Program for Monetary Stability.* Bronx, NY: Fordham University Press, 1959.

Kahn, George A. "Nominal GDP: An Anchor for Monetary Policy?" Federal Reserve Bank of Kansas City *Economic Review* (November 1988), pp. 18–35.

McCallum, Bennett T. "The Case for Rules in the Conduct of Monetary Policy: A Concrete Example." Federal Reserve Bank of Richmond *Economic Review* (September/October, 1987), pp. 10–18.

McNees, Stephen K. "Prospective Nominal GDP Targeting: An Alternative Framework for Monetary Policy." Federal Reserve Bank of Boston *New England Economic Review* (September/October 1987), pp. 3–9.

Steindel, Charles. "Interest Rates as Targets and Indicators for Monetary Policy." In *Intermediate Targets and Indicators for Monetary Policy.* Federal Reserve Bank of New York, 1990, pp. 274–304.

Wenninger, John. "Monetary Aggregates as Intermediate Targets." In *Intermediate Targets and Indicators for Monetary Policy.* Federal Reserve Bank of New York, 1990, pp. 67–108.

17

MACROECONOMIC POLICIES AND

THE POLITICS OF MACROECONOMICS

We have discussed many aspects of macroeconomic policy, both fiscal and monetary. We begin this chapter with an extended discussion of the government budget constraint, which links monetary and fiscal policy in the long run. We then turn to a consideration of monetary and fiscal policy as it is formulated and conducted within the political arena, and in particular we discuss the possibilities of a political business cycle. We also discuss briefly some of the political issues in the independence of the Federal Reserve System from the executive branch of government, and we conclude with a discussion of the actual record of the economy with regard to employment, inflation, and growth in recent years.

By the end of this chapter, you will know

- what the government budget constraint is, and how it limits the choices of monetary and fiscal policy
- how the government budget constraint can indicate whether various methods of financing government budget deficits are sustainable over time
- how the U.S. situation looks with regard to the ongoing budget deficits and the government budget constraint, and in particular whether the U.S. fiscal policy appears to be sustainable over time
- how the idea of Ricardian equivalence challenges conventional notions of the impact of fiscal policy, and how this changes the analysis of the aggregate demand effects of fiscal policy

629

- how considerations of politics and political influence on policy allow insights into the so-called "political business cycles"
- a brief history of the state of the economy and the political and economic policy actions from 1960 to the present.

THE GOVERNMENT BUDGET CONSTRAINT

Perhaps the most important aspect of contemporary fiscal policy, as it relates to economic stability and growth, is the federal budget. A dominating policy aspect has been the high and growing deficit in the federal accounts. Further, macroeconomic policy may be strongly influenced by the *method* of financing growing shortfalls in the federal accounts. To understand this, we must understand the notion of a government budget constraint.

The government budget constraint is, in its simplest form, a requirement that the government cannot spend more than it receives. Government spending on goods and services occurs at time t, in the amount G_t. In nominal terms, this spending is $P_t G_t$. Government also pays the interest and principal on outstanding government bonds. Where does the government obtain the revenue to fund this spending? Government revenue comes from three sources: (1) taxes net of transfers T_t, or in nominal terms $P_t T_t$; (2) government bond sales; and (3) printing money.

What, then, is the government budget constraint? If we put uses of government funds on the left-hand side of an equation, and sources of government funds on the right, the government budget constraint merely indicates that the use of funds equals sources of funds. The use of funds is for government spending $P_t G_t$ and for paying the interest on government bonds outstanding, $R_t B_{t-1}$. This last term is the interest on the debt, which makes up a large part of any discussion of the current U.S. budget problems. *Sources* of funds include taxes $P_t T_t$, money creation or the change in the money supply ΔM_t, and net sales of newly issued bonds (or the change in outstanding bonds), ΔB_t. The last term, ΔB_t, is the increase in the stock of bonds over the stock last period, and thus indicates net new borrowing by the government. We say net new borrowing because the government is constantly redeeming bonds as they come due and often paying for these by selling new bonds. It is the *net* increase (or, perhaps someday, decrease) in the stock of government bonds that concerns us.

We write the government budget constraint as

$$P_t G_t + R_t B_{t-1} = P_t T_t + \Delta M_t + \Delta B_t. \qquad (17.1)$$

As written, the government budget constraint is in nominal terms. This is why we multiply government spending and taxes by the price level. The stock of money is obviously in nominal terms, and so is the stock of bonds. The government budget constraint can be written in real terms by dividing both sides by the price level P_t to get

$$G_t + R_t(B_{t-1}/P_{t-1})(P_{t-1}/P_t) = T_t + \Delta M_t/P_t + (B_t - B_{t-1})/P_t.$$

If we then add B_{t-1}/P_t to both the left and right side, we get

$$G_t + (1 + R_t)(B_{t-1}/P_{t-1})(P_{t-1}/P_t) = T_t + \Delta M_t/P_t + B_t/P_t,$$

or, after some manipulation, as[1]

$$G_t + (1 + r_t)B_{t-1}/P_{t-1} = T_t + \mu_t(M_{t-1}/P_t) + B_t/P_t,$$

where μ_t is the growth rate of the money supply at time t, calculated as $\Delta M_t/M_{t-1}$. Thus, the term μ is the percentage change in the money supply, analogous to π, the inflation rate, which is the percentage change in the price level.

What can be done with the government budget constraint? Basically, it provides information on the government's alternatives in financing its spending decisions. If government purchases G and taxes T are set exogenously—say by the legislative branch of government—then the executive branch has a choice of responding to any deficit or surplus by changing the growth rate of the nominal money supply or by issuing new bonds. That is, it can increase the rate at which it prints money, or it can sell more bonds to finance spending. Notice too that the existing stock of bonds B_{t-1} cannot be changed at time t, but is instead determined from the past period. That is, the government does not have the option of not paying the interest on the debt, represented by $(1 + R_t)B_{t-1}$, unless it actually defaults on its obligations. Instead, the interest on the debt must be paid, and the government budget constraint in effect gives the government a set of possible methods of paying, from reducing spending to raising taxes or selling more bonds or increasing the growth rate of the money supply.

We use the government budget constraint to see just what the government can do to finance its deficits. Let us look at two situations. In the first, the government has a budget deficit at an instant in time, a deficit that it finances by borrowing. We want to discover the limits of this approach to dealing with a deficit. Then, in the second, the government has an ongoing deficit that it wants to finance by borrowing. Again, we consider just how the government is constrained in this situation.

Before proceeding, we again stress that G is government spending on goods and services, that T is taxes minus transfers, and that the government also has to pay interest on the outstanding government debt RB_{t-1}. A government deficit occurs when $G + RB_{t-1}$ is greater than T. This is the deficit commonly reported in the press. However, we will find it useful to speak of a *primary deficit* as an excess of G over T. This concept of the budget deficit does not include interest payments.

---

[1]To derive this equation, first notice that $P_t/P_{t-1} = 1 + \pi_t$, or one plus the inflation rate. The second term on the left-hand side, then, has $1 + R_t$ times (B_{t-1}/P_{t-1}), divided by $1 + \pi_t$, and $(1 + R_t)/(1 + \pi_t) = 1 + r_t$. Another issue concerns the second and third terms on the right-hand side, which we can rewrite as $(\Delta M_t/M_{t-1})(M_{t-1}/P_t)$. Thus, we can use these relationships to further rewrite the government budget constraint as

$$G_t + (1 + r_t)B_{t-1}/P_{t-1} = T_t + (\Delta M_t/M_{t-1})(M_{t-1}/P_t) + B_t/P_t.$$

Finally, $\Delta M_t/M_{t-1}$ is the growth rate of the nominal money supply, which we label μ_t.

A Single Deficit

How can the government finance a one-time deficit? Perhaps it has run a large deficit to finance an extraordinary one-time expenditure. The best example of this is when there is a war. Expenditures soar, and while taxes rise and rationing may occur, these are not enough to pay for wartime expenditures. The classic response is to run a deficit and finance it by borrowing, or selling bonds. This pattern was repeated in the United States during the Civil War, World War I, and World War II, and can also be seen in Britain and other European countries.

To make this issue concrete, consider the following example. A country has usual government purchases of $100, and taxes net of transfers of $100. It has no outstanding government debt, and keeps money growth at zero. This country satisfies the budget constraint given in nominal form in equation 17.1,

$$P_t G_t + R_t B_{t-1} = P_t T_t + \Delta M_t + \Delta B_t,$$

or for our example,

$$\$100 + 0 = \$100 + 0 + 0.$$

Now a large wartime expenditure occurs. In what we will call year 1, or $t = 1$, government purchases are of $150, while taxes net of transfers stay at $100. Now the government has a deficit to finance, and it does so by selling bonds, which promise to pay 10 percent interest. Money growth is kept at zero. The government budget constraint is now satisfied because

$$\$150 + 0 = \$100 + 0 + \$50.$$

That is, the $50 in new bonds ΔB garnered an amount of revenues necessary to fund the additional government purchases.

What happens in year 2? Government purchases return to normal, $100. However, the government now has an outstanding debt of $50. It has several choices on how to deal with this wartime debt. First, it can always raise taxes (or cut spending) by $50 and pay off this debt immediately. These are rather drastic actions, however, and require either a 50 percent reduction in government spending or a 50 percent increase in taxes, an increase the government didn't want to impose even during the war.[2] Second, it can raise taxes or cut transfers, so that taxes net of transfers are $105, or it can cut government purchases to $95, just enough to cover the interest on the debt, which is $5 (10 percent of $50). If it does this every year, then the debt will stay $50 forever. Finally, the government might choose not to do any of the above, but instead just borrow every year to pay the interest on the debt.

---

[2]The government could also cut government spending by a smaller amount, say to $90, and keep spending at $90 for a period of years until the debt is paid off.

Of these three policies, the first and second are fairly straightforward. In the first, the government just raises taxes or cuts spending by enough to pay off the debt. This is both fairly drastic and rather unrealistic. In the second case, the government just raises taxes or cuts spending enough to pay the interest on the debt. This keeps the debt constant at $50 and eventually in a growing economy this will look like a small amount. For example, if GDP is $500, then this debt is initially 10 percent of GDP. However, if GDP grows at 10 percent per year, then in ten years GDP will be $1,179, and the debt will be less than 5 percent of GDP.

What about the third possibility? Is it possible for a government to not pay off the debt, and not pay the interest accruing on the debt? Can the government just continually borrow to pay the interest on its previous borrowings? The answer, perhaps surprisingly, is "it depends."

To see this, we will continue with our example, only now in year 2 government spending is $100, taxes net of transfers are $100, and interest on the debt is .10 × $50 or $5. The government has a primary deficit balance, since $G = T$, but interest payments of $5 are financed by government borrowing. Thus, $\Delta B = \$5$ in year 2, so the outstanding stock of government bonds at the end of year 2 is $55.

What happens in year 3? The primary budget is balanced, with $G = T$. However, the outstanding debt is now $55, on which interest due is .10 × $55 = $5.50. The government now borrows $5.50 to pay this interest, making the outstanding debt at the end of year 3 equal to $60.50.

We summarize this example for years 1 to 10, 15, and 20 in Table 17-1. In this table, the column headings are the categories of the government budget constraint. The rows represent years. In year 1, we see that government spending was $150, interest on the debt was 0 (because there was no debt in year 0), taxes net of transfers were $100, so bonds were sold, making the change in bonds $50. The money supply never changes in this example, so ΔM is always 0. The last column keeps track of the size of the outstanding government debt, calculated as the amount brought forth from last year B_{t-1} plus the new issue from this year ΔB_t. In year 1, this is $0 + $50 = $50.

As the table indicates, the economy in our example has a primary budget balance in every year after year 1. At the same time, this continual financing of interest payments on the debt by new borrowing has the obvious effect of increasing the outstanding debt each period. At first the effect is small—the debt grows by $5 in year 2 and by another $5.50 in year 3—but eventually the debt becomes large, and annual increases in the debt become large. By year 10 the debt is almost $118, and it takes $11.80 of new borrowing (10 percent of $118) just to pay the interest on this debt. By year 20, the debt is $306, and interest payments take $30.60 of new borrowing (10 percent of $306).

The debt is growing inexorably larger, but we want to know if this is a sustainable situation. The answer depends in part on what it means to be sustainable. We will look at a ratio of debt to GDP, and ask how large this ratio

TABLE 17-1 Financing a One-Time Budget Deficit by Continually Rolling Over the Debt

This table begins with a single budget deficit in year 1, and shows how the outstanding government debt grows over time if the government pays the interest on the debt by continually issuing new bonds.

BUDGET CONSTRAINT: $P_t G_t + R_t B_{t-1} = P_t T_t + \Delta M_t + \Delta B_t$

ASSUMING: $R_t = .10$, $\Delta M_t = 0$

YEAR t	G_t	$R_t B_{t-1}$	T_t	ΔB_t	ΔM_t	$B_t = B_{t-1} + \Delta B_t$
1	150	0	100	50	0	$50 = 0 + 50$
2	100	$5 = .10 \times 50$	100	5	0	$55 = 50 + 5$
3	100	$5.5 = .10 \times 55$	100	5.5	0	$60.5 = 55 + 5.5$
4	100	$6.05 = .10 \times 60.5$	100	6.05	0	$66.55 = 60.5 + 6.05$
5	100	$6.655 = .10 \times 66.55$	100	6.655	0	$73.205 = 66.55 + 6.655$
6	100	$7.3205 = .10 \times 73.205$	100	7.3205	0	$80.5255 = 73.205 + 7.3205$
7	100	$8.0526 = .10 \times 80.5255$	100	8.0526	0	$88.5781 = 80.5255 + 8.0526$
8	100	$8.8578 = .10 \times 88.5781$	100	8.8578	0	$97.4359 = 88.5781 + 8.8578$
9	100	$9.7436 = .10 \times 97.4359$	100	9.7436	0	$107.1795 = 97.4359 + 9.7436$
10	100	$10.7180 = .10 \times 107.1795$	100	10.7180	0	$117.8975 = 107.1795 + 10.7180$
15	100	$17.2614 = .10 \times 172.6137$	100	17.2614	0	$189.8751 = 172.6137 + 17.2614$
20	100	$27.7996 = .10 \times 277.9961$	100	27.7996	0	$305.7957 = 277.9961 + 27.7996$

grows over time. Looking at this ratio is similar to what banks do when they look at loan applications. The income of a loan applicant is an indication of ability to pay, and the bank will usually make loans for housing so that the payments don't exceed 30 percent of income. In a similar way, the government's "income" is the net taxes it can collect, and these net taxes are some portion of GDP, currently about 20 percent or so. The government can of course decide to raise this percentage, but clearly it cannot raise it to 100 percent, since then there will be little incentive for taxpayers to work. In general, there is some tax rate less than 100 percent that will garner the most revenue for the government, and this is the most that the government can possibly devote to paying interest on the debt. In addition, the government may have certain purchases and transfer programs that it considers crucial, so the actual amount of taxes available for paying interest will be even lower. The key point is that we don't know exactly how much the government could collect in taxes if that were its only goal, and how much of these taxes could be allocated to interest payments, but all of this will be related to the output of the economy, GDP. Thus, the ratio of government debt to GDP is an indicator of how easily the interest burden of the debt can be managed. When this ratio grows, the interest burden is growing, and when this ratio shrinks, the interest burden is shrinking.

Of course, you will probably wonder if the interest rate isn't important here, since a low interest rate results in lower interest payments, and a high interest rate results in higher interest payments. As it turns out, the interest rate is *very* important, and it is the interest rate relative to the growth rate of the economy that determines the long-run sustainability of the policy we are considering, in which the government continually issues new debt to make interest payments on the existing debt.

We provide an example in Table 17-2. In the first column is the year, and in the second column is the primary deficit $G-T$, which is zero except in year 1. The third column is the stock of outstanding government bonds at the end of the year. In year 1 this is $50, in year 2, $55, and so on. Remember that these numbers were arrived at by assuming an interest rate of 10 percent. These numbers are all copied from Table 17-1.

The remaining columns in Table 17-2 present GDP and the ratio of government debt to GDP, for various assumptions about the growth rate of

TABLE 17-2   A One-Time Budget Deficit and the Debt As a Ratio to GDP

This table calculates the ratio of the outstanding debt to GDP for various growth rates of GDP, using the debt calculations from Table 17-1. The interest rate is 10 percent.

YEAR	$G-T$	B_t	GDP 5% GROWTH		GDP 10% GROWTH		GDP 15% GROWTH	
			GDP	B/GDP	GDP	B/GDP	GDP	B/GDP
1	50	50	500	.10	500	.10	500	.10
2	0	55	525	.1048	550	.10	575	.0957
3	0	60.5	551.25	.1098	605	.10	661.25	.0915
4	0	66.55	578.81	.1150	665.5	.10	760.44	.0875
5	0	73.21	607.75	.1205	732.05	.10	874.50	.0837
6	0	80.53	638.14	.1262	805.26	.10	1005.68	.0801
7	0	88.58	670.05	.1321	885.78	.10	1156.53	.0766
8	0	97.44	703.55	.1385	974.39	.10	1330.01	.0733
9	0	107.18	738.73	.1451	1071.79	.10	1529.51	.0701
10	0	117.90	775.66	.1520	1178.97	.10	1758.94	.0670
15	0	189.80	989.97	.1918	1898.75	.10	3537.85	.0537
20	0	305.80	1263.48	.2420	3057.95	.10	7115.89	.0430

GDP. We look at GDP growth rates of 5 percent, 10 percent, and 15 percent. In all cases, GDP is $500 in year 1. When GDP grows at 5%, it is $500 $\times$ 1.05 = $525 in year 2, $525 $\times$ 1.05 = $551.25 in year 3, and so on. Similar calculations apply when GDP is growing at 10 percent or 15 percent per year.

Look at the ratio of debt to GDP for these three cases. For 5 percent GDP growth, the debt to GDP ratio begins at 10 percent, but steadily increases through time. Each year the denominator, GDP, grows 5 percent, while the numerator, debt, grows 10 percent. By year 10 this ratio has grown to 15 percent. By year 20 it is 24 percent, and there is no end in sight. Unless something changes, the ratio of debt to GDP will grow without bound. Of course, eventually there will be a day when the interest on the debt is greater than the government can possibly pay, and this will force some change in the government's behavior. Either taxes will increase or government purchases or transfer payments will be cut, or the government will start printing money to pay for its spending. Or it will default on its debt.

How does this change if GDP grows more quickly? If GDP grows at 10 percent per year, then both the numerator and the denominator in the debt to GDP ratio grow at 10 percent, and the ratio stays at 10 percent for all time. Thus, with the interest rate equal to the rate of growth of GDP, there is no change over time in the debt to GDP ratio.

Finally, what happens if GDP grows more quickly than the interest rate? In Table 17-2, we have an example with GDP growth at 15 percent. In this case, the ratio of debt to GDP declines through time, so that after ten years it is under 7 percent, and after twenty years it is about 4 percent. The decline will continue as long as GDP growth exceeds the interest rate, so the ratio gets smaller and smaller each year.

Thus, we again ask the question: Can the government finance a one-time deficit by bond finance, and then continually finance the interest on those bonds with new issues of bonds? The answer is yes, if the growth rate of GDP is equal to or greater than the interest rate on those bonds. Otherwise, the answer is no.

This analysis is limited to a one-time deficit, although not necessarily a one-year deficit. For example, a war could be financed by a string of deficits that are bond financed. After the war, the government returns to a balanced primary budget, with $G = T$, but wonders whether it has to actually raise net taxes or cut spending to pay off the debt, or whether it can get by with just selling new bonds to cover the interest payments it owes on the wartime debt. The answer we have found is that such a policy can be used if the growth rate of GDP is equal to or greater than the interest rate on the debt.

There is another case to consider, however, and that is the case of a continual ongoing deficit in the primary budget, financed along with interest payments by new bond issues. We now turn to an analysis of this case.

Ongoing Deficits

Is it possible for the government to finance an ongoing government budget deficit and the associated interest payments by bond issues alone? The answer, as is often the case in economics, is "it depends." It depends on how big the deficit is, what the interest rate is, and on how fast the economy is growing. We again analyze this question with an example.

As in our example above, we begin with a primary budget deficit of $50, with government purchases of $150 and taxes net of transfers of $100. This primary budget deficit occurs every year, however, and is financed by new bonds. In addition, interest payments on the debt are financed by new bond issues.

We illustrate our example in Table 17-3. In year 1, the budget deficit requires a bond issue of $50. In year 2, the primary budget deficit is $50, and the government also owes 10 percent interest on the debt issued in year 1, or $5 (= .10 × $50). The total new bonds issued in year 2 are $55. In year 3, the primary budget deficit is $50, and the interest on the outstanding debt is

TABLE 17-3   Financing an Ongoing Budget Deficit by Continually Rolling Over the Debt

This table begins with an ongoing budget deficit that started in year 1, and shows how the outstanding government debt grows over time if the government finances the ongoing deficits and the interest on the outstanding debt by continually issuing new bonds.

BUDGET CONSTRAINT: $P_tG_t + R_tB_{t-1} = P_tT_t + \Delta M_t + \Delta B_t$

ASSUMING: $R_t = .10, \Delta M_t = 0$

YEAR, t	G_t	R_tB_{t-1}	T_t	ΔB_t	ΔM_t	$B_t = B_{t-1} + \Delta B_t$
1	150	0	100	50	0	50 = 0 + 50
2	150	5 = .10 × 50	100	55	0	105 = 50 + 55
3	150	10.5 = .10 × 105	100	60.5	0	165.5 = 105 + 60.5
4	150	16.55 = .10 × 165.5	100	66.55	0	232.05 = 165.5 + 66.55
5	150	23.21 = .10 × 232.05	100	73.21	0	305.26 = 232.05 + 73.21
6	150	30.53 = .10 × 305.26	100	80.53	0	385.79 = 305.26 + 80.53
7	150	38.58 = .10 × 385.79	100	88.58	0	474.37 = 385.79 + 88.58
8	150	47.44 = .10 × 474.37	100	97.44	0	571.81 = 474.37 + 97.44
9	150	57.18 = .10 × 571.81	100	107.18	0	678.99 = 571.81 + 107.18
10	150	67.90 = .10 × 678.99	100	117.90	0	796.89 = 678.99 + 117.90
15	150	139.88 = .10 × 1398.75	100	189.80	0	1588.55 = 1398.75 + 189.80
20	150	255.80 = .10 × 2557.95	100	305.80	0	2863.75 = 2557.95 + 305.80

.10 × \$105 = \$10.50, so there will be \$60.50 in bonds issued. This is tabulated through year 10, and then for years 15 and 20. As you can see, this policy results in a large growth in the outstanding debt, to \$797 by year 10, \$1,589 by year 15, and \$2,864 by year 20. This growth in the stock of government debt is much greater than that for the one-time deficit in Table 17-1. Is this policy sustainable?

To answer this, we again consider the ratio of debt to GDP for several different growth rates of GDP, as presented in Table 17-4. We consider GDP growth of 5, 10, and 15 percent, and calculate the debt to GDP ratio for years 1 through 10, 15, and 20. Consider first the case of 5 percent GDP growth. The debt to GDP ratio grows rapidly, from 10 percent in year 1 to over 100 percent in year 10. That is, ten year's debt is equal to GDP. After fifteen years, the ratio is 1.6 and after twenty years debt is more than twice the size of GDP. Furthermore, this ratio keeps growing, so that eventually the debt will be many multiples of GDP. Thus the policy is unsustainable. At some point, the policy will have to change. The government cannot keep operating in this manner, and either taxes will have to rise or government purchases and transfer payments fall, or the government will have to resort to money creation to finance its spending. There is no other alternative except default. If sanity does

TABLE 17-4 An Ongoing Budget Deficit and the Debt As a Ratio to GDP

This table calculates the ratio of the outstanding debt to GDP for various growth rates of GDP, using the debt calculations from Table 17-3. The interest rate is 10 percent.

YEAR	$G-T$	B_t	5% GDP GROWTH		10% GDP GROWTH		15% GDP GROWTH	
			GDP	B/GDP	GDP	B/GDP	GDP	B/GDP
1	50	50	500	.10	500	.10	500	.10
2	50	105	525	.20	550	.19	575	.18
3	50	165.5	551.25	.30	605	.27	661.25	.25
4	50	232.05	578.81	.40	665.5	.35	760.44	.31
5	50	305.26	607.75	.50	732.05	.42	874.50	.35
6	50	385.79	638.14	.60	805.26	.48	1005.68	.38
7	50	474.37	670.05	.71	885.78	.54	1156.53	.41
8	50	571.81	703.55	.81	974.39	.59	1330.01	.43
9	50	678.99	738.73	.92	1071.79	.63	1529.51	.44
10	50	796.89	775.66	1.03	1178.97	.68	1758.94	.45
15	50	1588.55	989.97	1.60	1898.75	.84	3537.85	.45
20	50	2863.75	1263.48	2.27	3057.95	.94	7115.89	.40

not intervene, the debt could in theory grow so large that the entire GDP could not even make the interest payment on this debt. Of course, that would never happen in practice, since long before such a point the public would start refusing to lend to the government, and the government would then have to change its behavior.

What about GDP growth of 10 percent? In this case, the policy results in a fairly rapid rise in the debt to GDP ratio, from the initial 10 percent to almost 70 percent by year 10. Eventually the rapid rise in this ratio slows. By year 15, the ratio has grown to 84 percent, and by year 20 to 94 percent. It will keep rising every year, but by smaller and smaller amounts, and will actually end up growing no larger than 110 percent as time goes on forever. This policy causes the long-run debt to GDP ratio to increase markedly, from the initial 10 percent to 110 percent, but it is not an explosive policy; that is, the debt to GDP ratio does not grow without bound. In that respect, it is somewhat similar to the case in Table 17-2 for a one-time budget deficit, in which the debt to GDP ratio also does not grow without bound. It is different from that case, however, because in Table 17-2 the debt to GDP ratio stayed at 10 percent always, whereas in Table 17-4 the continual budget deficits cause the debt to GDP ratio to grow over time, and eventually to grow to be over 100 percent before finally converging to 110 percent.

Finally, what if GDP grows at 15 percent per year? In this case, we get a very interesting phenomenon. Initially the debt to GDP ratio grows, from 10 percent to 45 percent in year 10. Thus, the budget policy causes debt to rise faster than GDP, at least initially. Eventually, however, the growth rate of the debt slows down, while GDP continually grows at 15 percent, so that in year 15 the debt to GDP ratio is 45 percent, the same as in year 10, and by year 20 the ratio is 40 percent. This decline continues through time, so that after a very long time the ratio will approach zero.

What is the conclusion from this example? If GDP growth is less than the interest rate, then this policy of a continual primary budget deficit financed by bond sales is unsustainable. Eventually this policy will have to be changed, or the government will be forced to default. If GDP growth is equal to the interest rate on government debt, then this policy will result in a large increase in the debt to GDP ratio, but this increase will eventually level off, and until it is hardly growing at all. Finally, if the GDP growth rate is greater than the interest rate on the debt, then the debt to GDP ratio first increases but then decreases, gradually declining toward zero.

Our basic result is that the case of a one-time deficit and the case of ongoing deficits are similar in that the relative sizes of the GDP growth rate and the interest rate on the debt determine the ability of government to finance such deficits and the interest payments on the resulting debt with new bond issues. If the GDP growth rate is greater than this interest rate, then debt can be outgrown, as can a constant primary budget deficit. If the GDP growth rate is smaller than the interest rate, then even a one-time budget deficit cannot be financed forever by issuing bonds to cover the deficit and any resulting interest

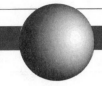

CENTRAL BANK INDEPENDENCE AND INFLATION: INTERNATIONAL EVIDENCE

One argument favoring an independent central bank is that it will be a bulwark against inflation. The argument is that the government (either the majority in a parliamentary democracy, or the executive or legislative branches in the United States) is charged with funding government spending, and has at its disposal taxes and fees, bond sales (or deficit finance), and, potentially, money creation. When the central bank is under the control of the government, the temptation to print money to finance at least a part of government spending is overwhelming. Thus, central banks under the control of the government tend to create more money and hence create more inflation than do central banks that can fend off government pressure to finance spending with money creation.

To test this idea, Alberto Alesina looked at average inflation rates in seventeen industrialized nations over the period 1973–1986, and also at the degree of independence of their central banks. To judge the degree of independence, he used information on institutional arrangements, including whether government officials serve on the governing board, whether the government appoints the head of the central bank, whether there are formal arrangements for the central bank to finance part of any deficit with money creation, and so forth. From this information Alesina constructed an index ranging from a score of 1 for least independent (Italy, Spain, New Zealand, Australia) to a score of 4 for most independent (Switzerland, West Germany). The United States and Japan were the only members in the second most independent group, with a score of 3.

The remaining countries were in the group scored 2, and included Britain, Finland, France, Denmark, Sweden, Norway, Canada, Belgium, and the Netherlands.

The results of this study are summarized in Figure 17-1. Countries with more independent central banks had lower average inflation rates than countries with less independent central banks. For Switzerland and Germany, the average inflation rate was about 4 percent, while for the four countries with the least independent central bank, the average inflation rate was over 12 percent. Thus, the international evidence seems to favor the argument that an independent central bank will be less prone to inflation. ❏

SOURCES: Alberto Alesina, "Politics and Business Cycles in Industrial Democracies," *Economic Policy* 8 (April 1989); and W. Michael Cox, "Two Types of Paper: The Case for Federal Reserve Independence," Federal Reserve Bank of Dallas *The Southwest Economy* (November/December 1992), pp. 4–8.

payments. One concern with unsustainable fiscal policy is that it may cause pressure on the Fed to monetize the debt. This is especially possible when the central bank is not independent of the fiscal policy marker. See the Global Perspective: "Central Bank Independence and Inflation: International Evidence."

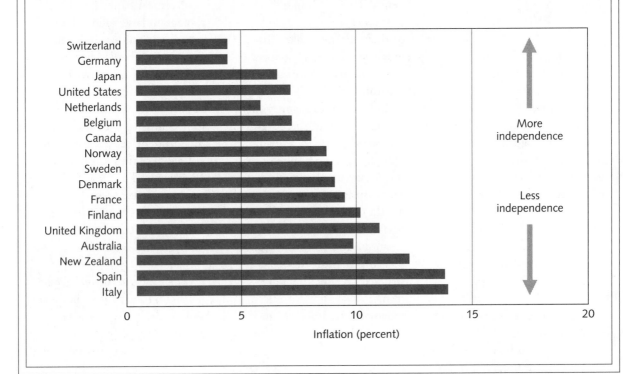

FIGURE 17-1
Average Inflation and Central Bank Independence in Selected Countries

Independence of the central bank from the executive branch of government is classified into four categories, from most independent (Category 1) to least independent (Category IV): Category 1—Switzerland and Germany; Category II—Japan and the United States; Category III—the Netherlands, Belgium, Canada, Norway, Sweden, Denmark, France, Finland and the United Kingdom; and Category IV—Australia, New Zealand, Spain and Italy. See also, "Wise Men from the South," *The Economist* (Feb. 2, 1991), p. 77.

The Current Situation in the United States

The United States has been running large budget deficits in recent years. These deficits became sizable by historical standards in 1975, and then became even larger about 1982. Figure 17-2 shows both the budget surplus or deficit (including interest payments) and the primary budget surplus or deficit (government purchases minus taxes net of transfers), graphed as percentages of GDP. There are several things to notice in this graph. First, the budget had surpluses in the period 1947–1958, and was basically in balance, with some small deficits, throughout the 1960s and early 1970s. In 1975 we see a large deficit spike of nearly 5 percent of GDP, associated with a severe recession and the OPEC oil embargo. The budget moved slowly toward balance, almost getting there briefly in 1979, before falling again at a somewhat slower pace to a deficit of about 5 percent of GDP in 1982 and continuing through 1984 before slowly crawling to a deficit of about 2.5 percent of GDP by the early 1990s. Another thing to note is the spread between the budget deficit and the primary budget deficit. This spread measures the interest payments on the debt, and was fairly constant through the 1970s and even 1980 and 1981. By 1982, however, the spread expanded, and it has maintained this higher level from then on. Indeed, the primary budget was actually in surplus from 1986 to 1990, but the large interest payments on the outstanding debt caused the budget to be in substantial deficit during these years.

Further insight is found in the bottom of Figure 17-2, where we graph interest payments on the debt relative to GDP. Here the relative constancy of

FIGURE 17-2
Plot of Interest Payments on the Debt (Left Scale) and Two Measures of the Deficit, One Including Interest on the Debt and One Not (Right Scale)

This graph shows how interest payments on the debt have grown steeply from the late 1970s to the middle 1980s. The graph also shows the deficit and the primary deficit (excluding interest payments). Note that the primary deficit was in balance from 1987 through the beginning of the 1990s, even though the deficit inclusive of interest payments was in deficit.

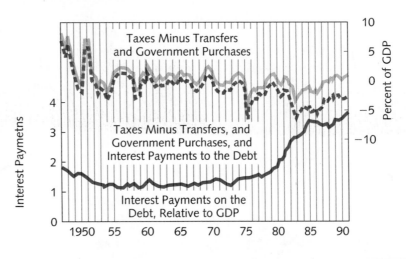

interest payments to GDP from 1947 through 1977 or 1978 is readily apparent, as is the rise in this ratio in the first half of the 1980s and its steadiness thereafter.

To see how this looks relative to our analysis above, we have calculated the average interest rate and the average growth rate of GDP for five-year intervals beginning in 1947. This is presented in Table 17-5. From looking at this, we see that the average growth rate of GDP exceeded the average interest rate by a good margin for every five-year period until 1977–1982. Then the average interest rate of 9.7 percent was almost equal to the 10 percent growth rate of GDP, and in 1982–1987 the average interest rate of 8.4 percent exceeded the 6.8 percent growth rate of GDP. For 1987–1990, the average interest rate of 6.9 percent is basically the same as the rate of GDP growth. Thus, beginning in 1977 the United States embarked on an extended period in which the

---

TABLE 17-5   U.S. Data on the Debt, Deficit, and GDP Growth

The average growth rate of GDP has exceeded the nominal interest rate in the United States over the indicated periods with the exception of 1982–1987, the period in which the U.S. debt to personal income ratio began growing. Notice that government purchases have been on a generally downward path from the early 1950s, reaching a steady 8 or 9 percent of GDP from the early 1970s onward. Taxes as a ratio of GDP have been on an upward trend from the early 1960s through the late 1970s, at which point they have been a fairly steady 20 percent of GDP. Transfer payments have shown a much more pronounced upward trend from the late 1950s through the early 1980s, at which point they stabilized at 12 or 13 percent of GDP. Finally, interest on the debt has increased from 1 percent of GDP in the middle 1970s to 3 percent of GDP at the beginning of the 1990s.

TIME PERIOD	AVERAGE GROWTH RATE GDP	AVERAGE INTEREST RATE	RATIO OF DEBT HELD BY PUBLIC TO PERSONAL INCOME	RATIO OF GOVERNMENT PURCHASES TO GDP	RATIO OF TAXES TO GDP	RATIO OF TRANSFERS TO GDP	RATIO OF INTEREST ON DEBT TO GDP
1947–52	8.5%	1.1%	1.03	.08	.18	.06	.02
1952–57	5.2%	1.8%	.77	.13	.18	.05	.01
1957–62	4.9%	2.8%	.61	.11	.18	.06	.01
1962–67	7.2%	3.7%	.51	.11	.19	.07	.01
1967–72	7.4%	5.4%	.39	.10	.20	.09	.01
1972–77	10.0%	5.9%	.33	.08	.19	.12	.01
1977–82	10.0%	9.7%	.32	.08	.20	.13	.02
1982–87	6.8%	8.4%	.41	.09	.20	.13	.03
1987–90	6.9%	6.7%	.50	.08	.20	.12	.03

average interest rate equaled or exceeded the average growth rate of GDP, and this coincided with a period from 1982 to 1986 of large primary budget deficits. Since then the primary budget was in balance until the recession that began in 1990, but the large deficits and high interest rates of these years had combined to drive the outstanding debt to large heights, reversing a general downward trend in the U.S. debt to GDP ratio that had extended since World War II.

To see the behavior of the outstanding federal debt, we graph both the debt held by the public and the ratio of this debt to personal income in Figure 17-3. This ratio of debt to personal income will proxy for the debt to GDP ratio, since the ratio of personal income to GDP is fairly constant over time. It is apparent that the magnitude of the debt was fairly constant from 1947 through 1975, and hence the growth in GDP made the debt to personal income (and hence the debt to GDP ratio) fall from 1.25 to .32. After 1975, the debt began to grow in magnitude, and this growth continued at a steady pace until about 1981. From 1975 to 1981 the debt to personal income (and by implication the debt to GDP) ratio stayed roughly constant at about .33, as the rising debt kept pace with aggregate income. In about 1982, the growth of the debt increased again, and now the debt was growing faster than aggregate income, because from this point onward the debt to personal income ratio expanded, reaching about 50 percent by 1990.

FIGURE 17-3

Plot of U.S. Government Debt Held by the Public (Right Scale) and the Ratio of Debt Held by the Public To Personal Income (Left Scale)

This graph shows how federal debt held by the public began increasing in the middle 1970s, and then accelerated again in the early 1980s. It also shows how the ratio of this debt to personal income fell from the end of World War II until about 1975, and did not start increasing again until about 1982.

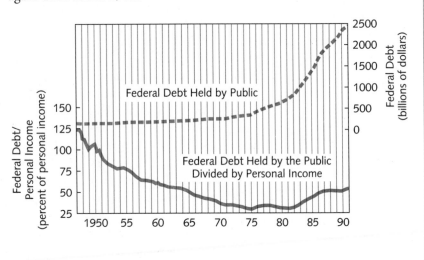

FIGURE 17-4

Plot of Government Spending on Goods and Services, Taxes, Transfer Payments, and Interest on the Debt, All Relative to GDP

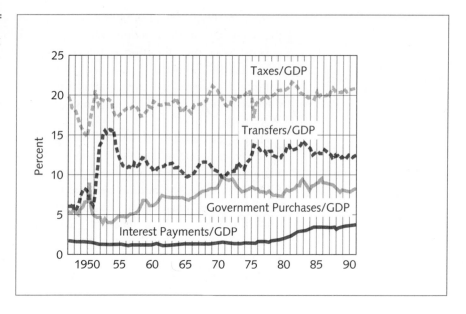

What are the components of the government budget constraint that explain the behavior of the deficit and the primary deficit? Table 17-5 also provides information on the ratio to GDP of government purchases, taxes, transfer payments, and interest payments, information also presented in Figure 17-4. We can see several patterns in these data. First, taxes have risen only slightly since the early 1950s, from 18 percent to 20 percent of GDP. Second, government purchases were a fairly steady 10 or 11 percent of GDP from the late 1950s through the 1960s, but then declined to about 8 percent of GDP from the middle 1970s onward. Third, transfer payments grew as a percent of GDP from 5 or 6 percent in the early 1950s to 12 percent in the middle 1970s, and have remained at about 12 percent from then onward. Finally, interest payments on the debt were about 1 percent of GDP until the late 1970s, at which time they started growing, reaching 3 percent by the middle 1980s and staying roughly constant since then. Thus, all three of the traditional suspects in budget deficits have remained fairly flat over the 1980s. Taxes did take a dip in the early 1980s, but only about 1 percent, and this was made up by the middle 1980s. Transfers may have declined about 1 percent, and government purchases rose about 1 percent in the early and middle 1980s but declined back to 8 percent of GDP by the end of the 1980s. It is interest payments on the debt that have grown substantially as a budget category over this time, from 1 percent to 3 percent of GDP and holding.

What does all this tell us? Is current U.S. fiscal policy sustainable in the long run? The answer is not clear. The U.S. has entered a period in which the interest rate and the rate of GDP growth are comparable, making continual bond finance possible for one-time budget deficits. If 1982 to 1986 was a period of primary budget deficits that are now over, then we should be able to sustain a constant debt to GDP ratio at roughly the level that we had in 1986. However, if primary budget deficits continue, then the United States is likely to find the debt to GDP ratio growing to a new level that will be multiples of the levels in 1986, as we saw in our middle example in Table 17-4. In this case, the debt to GDP ratio may grow substantially, and this in itself could cause trouble if the public decides that the ratio is so high that the government cannot or will not collect enough taxes to pay the interest on the debt. This would lead to a refusal to hold the debt and the need for a change in policy. However, we are not trying to be alarmist. This is only one possible interpretation of the U.S. situation. It is also possible that the era of primary budget deficits is over, except for deficits during recessions, as in 1991. If so, then with current interest rates and rates of GDP growth the U.S. fiscal policy of selling bonds to cover interest due on the debt is a sustainable policy that should result in a fairly constant debt to GDP ratio.

The necessity of paying out large amounts in interest on the debt has already spawned some changes in government behavior, however. There are of course many possibilities for deficit reduction, including traditional approaches such as raising taxes. One recent idea is that of privatization, as described in the enclosed Policy Issue: "Macroeconomics, Deficits, and Urban Privatization."

RICARDIAN EQUIVALENCE

The traditional approach to financing government expenditures holds that bond financing is more expansionary than tax financing. Thus, starting from a balanced budget, an increase in government purchases would be more expansionary if taxes were held constant and the deficit was financed by issuing government bonds. The alternative, increasing taxes, would not increase *IS* or *AD* by as much as the bond-financed increase in government spending.

The idea behind the traditional approach is easy enough to describe. We can begin with the *IS* curve, which has its beginnings in the national income accounting identity:

$$Y = C + I + G + NX.$$

Further, we model consumption as

$$C = c_0 + c_1(Y - T).$$

An increase in government purchases has a direct effect on spending because government purchases *G* directly enter the national income identity. What about the financing of these government purchases? If we finance government purchases with taxes, then we increase taxes net of transfers *T* by the same amount as the increase in *G*. This reduces disposable income and hence consumption spending by the marginal propensity to consume c_1 multiplied by the increase in taxes. Thus, a \$1 increase in government purchases tends to

MACROECONOMICS, DEFICITS, AND URBAN PRIVATIZATION

Rising federal deficits in the 1980s and the unwillingness of the Congress to raise taxes to pay for them led to an important restructuring of responsibilities between federal, state, and local governments. Much of this restructuring has been a cut-off of federal assistance to fund state and local projects, such as roads and road repair, welfare assistance payments, social services, library management, and so on. Left with increasing obligations, constitutional requirements to balance their budgets, and a population unwilling to pay higher local and state taxes, these governmental entities have been forced to experiment with new policies.

In the area of welfare, for example, the state of Michigan placed limits on the number of children per mother that will be supported by welfare subsidies. Many states, in budget binds, have returned functions and reduced payments to local governments.

Urban governments across the nation are faced with the critical problem of cutting services or raising taxes, and a number have responded by implementing innovative proposals called *privatization*.

Privatization may be complete, as when property rights to supply some good or service are returned to the private sector. This happens when local government gives up the right to supply or regulate some good, such as ambulance or garbage collection to private firms. More often privatization is incomplete, as when governments retain rights to supply all or part of the market for some goods and services but let private firms compete to supply the goods and services.

Privatization has its critics, chief among them labor unions, but cities across the country are adopting the scheme to get more "bang for the buck." For example, in Newark, New Jersey, more than twenty city functions are franchised out through private competition, although public departments keep a share of the provision in order to encourage "private-public" competition; in Chicago, Mayor Richard M. Daley has farmed out more than a dozen ser-

vices (including alcohol treatment, tree-stump removal, and custodial and library management services), minimizing city layoffs by encouraging private firms to hire displaced city workers; in San Francisco, social services, garbage re- moval, data processing and engineering design work is "let out" for competitive bid. According to a recent report, the management of the zoo is next.[a]

The incentive to privatize is clear: Cost reductions of 20 to 30 percent may be realized by replacing rigid union work rules and high pay and bureaucracy with competitive provision. The incentive to privatize also explains the opposition to such plans: City worker pay in Philadelphia, for example, averages $50,000 per worker, a budget-busting rate. There is, of course, the danger of privatization becoming a patronage system. Collusion on the part of bidders must be avoided and there must be sufficient competition to ensure that bids approach competitive costs of production. Carefully written contracts with specific performance standards and conditions for renewals can help minimize these difficulties, as can more complete privatization.

The move to privatization is more a response to macroeconomic problems at the federal levels and to budget difficulties at state and local levels than to philosophy. Just as the citizens in the former Soviet Union belatedly realized the value of competition in providing economic efficiency, American cities are now forced to seek out ways for tax dollars to go farther. The appeal to contracting is an admission that the private sector can sometimes produce so-called public goods and services more efficiently than the public sector. Given the deficit problem and the reluctance of populations to pay for inefficiency, governments may have few other choices. ❑

NOTE [a]Jonathan Marshall, "Behind the Move to Privatization," *San Francisco Chronicle* (July 22, 1992), pp. A1, A9.

PHOTO 17-1
Privatization has Resulted from the Shift of Responsibility for Governmentally Produced Goods from the Federal to the State and Local Levels of Government.

increase spending by \$1, while a \$1 increase in taxes tends to lower consumption and hence national spending by the marginal propensity to consume times \$1. The net effect is to increase spending by $(1 - c_1) \times \$1$. This increase in spending shows up as a rightward shift in *IS* and in *AD*. (The effect on equilibrium *real* spending may still be zero, however, if *AS* is perfectly inelastic.)

What about an increase in government purchases financed by issuing bonds? A \$1 increase in *G* will still increase spending by \$1, but now there is no tax effect. Moreover, bonds do not themselves exert an effect, so that the net effect of the increase in government purchases (before any multiplier effect) is to increase national spending dollar for dollar. This shows up as a rightward shift in both *IS* and *AD,* just as in the case of tax financing, *but* the rightward shift here is of a larger magnitude.

In this traditional view, then, deficit financing is more expansionary than is tax financing. But this view assumes taxpayers do not consider that borrowing increases the size of the government debt and hence increases the size of future taxes, or else it assumes taxpayers do not care about future tax liabilities when making current consumption decisions.

The Ricardian view, in contrast, assumes that individuals do take into account the tax liability associated with government borrowing. In fact, the Ricardian view is that individuals treat future tax liabilities that accrue to deficit financing just as they treat current tax liabilities. In this case, there will be no difference in the effect on national spending of tax financing or bond financing of government spending.

The Argument

How does the Ricardian argument proceed? An example clarifies the issues involved. Consider a government that wants to spend $100 this year, 1993, and is trying to decide how to finance this spending. The government leaves the decision up to the taxpayer. The choices are the following: First, the taxpayer can pay a tax bill of $100 this year, 1993. Second, the taxpayer can ask the government to issue a $100 bond, which will be sold in 1993 and the proceeds will be used to finance the government spending. This bond will have to pay the market interest rate if it is to be sold for $100. If the market interest rate is 10 percent, then the bond will have to pay $10 per year in order for it to sell for $100. If the government plans on paying off the bond at the end of one year, then in 1994 it must come up with tax revenue of $110—$100 to pay off the principal and $10 for interest. Thus, the taxpayer will have to pay extra taxes of $110 in 1994.

Does the taxpayer prefer to pay $100 in 1993 or $110 in 1994? When comparing sums of money received (or paid) in different years, it is convenient to turn them into equivalent sums by using the idea of present value. The present value in 1993 of $110 in 1994 is the sum you would have to invest at the market rate of interest in 1993 to equal $110 in 1994. Since every dollar invested in 1993 earns 10 percent interest, $1 in 1993 is "equal" to $1.10 in 1994. Alternatively, $1 in 1993 is the present value of $1.10 in 1994. Similarly, $100 in 1993 is the present value of $110 in 1994. Hence, the taxpayer is faced with paying $100 in 1993 or $110 in 1994, but the present value of both payments is $100. The taxpayer is indifferent, and would say that she did not care which the government decided, taxing $100 in 1993 or borrowing $100 in 1993 and taxing $110 in 1994.

Debt Rollover

You might argue, of course, that the government does not ever pay off the debt, so the prior example is unrealistic. Consider a case, then, in which the government never pays off the debt, but instead just keeps "rolling it over" by refinancing the outstanding debt each year. In 1994 the government pays $10 in interest and rolls over the principal of $100 by issuing a new bond. This new bond will promise to pay $110 in 1995, and will sell for $100 in 1994, giving the government just enough to pay off the bondholder who purchased a bond in 1993. This second bond will mature in 1995, at which time the government will pay $10 in interest and pay off the principal of $100 by issuing a new bond that sells for $100. This can continue ad infinitum, and the only cost to the government is the $10 interest payment it must make each year—to pay the interest on the outstanding principal. The principal can always be refinanced in this manner. But what is the present value to the taxpayers of paying $10 per year forever? It can be calculated as[4]

$$\$10 + \$10/(1.1) + \$10/(1.1^2) + \$10/(1.1^3) + \dots = \$10/(.1) = \$100.$$

Thus, the present value of the third method of financing the deficit is also $100. The taxpayers have the choice of paying $100 today, $110 next year, or $10 every year forever, and as long as the interest rate is 10 percent, the present value of all of these alternatives is $100. Given these considerations, the Ricardian idea is that the taxpayer is indifferent, and the effect on consumption (and thus aggregate spending) is the same for each alternative.

The Ricardian Equivalence Theorem, IS-LM, and AD-AS

The Ricardian Equivalence Theorem postulates that taxpayers regard tax financing and bond financing as equivalent because bond financing merely postpones the payment of taxes but does not change the present value of taxes owed. Thus consumption based on disposable income depends not just on current taxes but on the present value of current and future taxes. An increase in government spending will require either an increase in taxes today or an equivalent increase in the present value of taxes tomorrow, so that is just equal to the increase in government spending. If we reinterpret taxes net of transfers T to be the present value of net taxes, then changes in government purchases G are equal to changes in T. The Ricardian idea is to replace current taxes with the present value of current and future taxes in the consumption function. Moreover, this present value of taxes is equal to G_T, so the consumption function is

$$C = c_0 + c_1 (Y - T_{pv})$$

where

$$T_{pv} = G,$$

---

[4]The formula to use to calculate this sum is $\sum_{i=1}^{\text{infinity}} (1/(1 + r)^i \times \$10) = (1/r) \times \$10 = (1/.1) \times \$10 = \$100$.

so

$$C = c_0 + c_1 (Y - G).$$

It is not that disposable income is directly $Y - G$, but that disposable income is equivalent to $Y - G$.

What difference does this make to our economic models? This change in the consumption function means that the Keynesian cross diagram is altered so that present and future taxes T reduce disposable income and consumption. This means that IS is a function not of current taxes T but of the present value of current plus future taxes G. The net effect of G on total expenditures would be given by $(1 - c_1)$, and the net effect on IS would be given by the new government spending multiplier, $(1 - c_1)/(1 - c_1) = 1$.

Similarly, the Ricardian AD curve would then respond to government spending, but the increase in AD when government purchases increased would not be as great as in the traditional model. Why? Because the tax consequences of increasing government purchases are known to the taxpayer and taken into account when making consumption decisions in the Ricardian view.

It is useful to make this distinction graphically. In Figure 17-5, parts (a) and (b) depict the IS-LM graph and AD graph for the traditional view of government financing, while parts (c) and (d) give the IS-LM and AD graphs for the Ricardian view. In the top graphs, consider an economy starting at point A, where $IS(G_0, T_0)$ intersects $LM(M/P_0)$. Point A is also represented by point A on $AD(G_0, T_0)$. At either point, output is Y_A and the price level is P_0. Now consider an increase in government spending to G_1. If there is an equivalent increase in taxes to T_1, IS shifts to $IS(G_1, T_1)$ and, for a fixed price P_0, the IS-LM equilibrium shifts to point B. This is also represented by point B on $AD(G_1, T_1)$. At point B, output is Y_B and the price level remains at P_0. The movement from point A to point B in the IS-LM graph, or equivalently the shift in AD from $AD(G_0, T_0)$ to $AD(G_1, T_1)$, is known in the traditional literature as the balanced budget change in government spending. It is an increase in government spending that is financed by tax increases.

Alternatively, we can consider an increase in government spending that is bond financed. Again in the traditional approach, this would be represented by an increase in government spending to G_1 but with taxes remaining at T_0. In this case, IS shifts even further to the right, to $IS(G_1, T_0)$, since there is no increase in taxes to partially counteract the change in government spending. For a fixed price P_0, the IS-LM equilibrium shifts to point C. This is also represented by point C on $AD(G_1, T_0)$. Note that AD shifts further to the right with an increase in government spending that is not financed with a tax increase. At point C, output is Y_c and the price level stays at P_0.

Thus, we have presented the traditional analysis of government spending and finance. What is the Ricardian analysis? In the IS-LM framework, we represent the Ricardian approach as recognizing that any increase in government spending is accompanied by an increase in the present value of taxes,

FIGURE 17-5
The Traditional and Ricardian View of Government Spending and Taxes

Graphs (a) and (b) illustrate the traditional view of government spending and taxation. Deficit finance is more expansionary than tax finance.

The Ricardian view is illustrated in graphs (c) and (d). There is no difference between the effect of the increase in government spending if that spending is financed with current taxes, or if it is deficit financed and hence financed with future taxes. The effect of either financing scheme is the same.

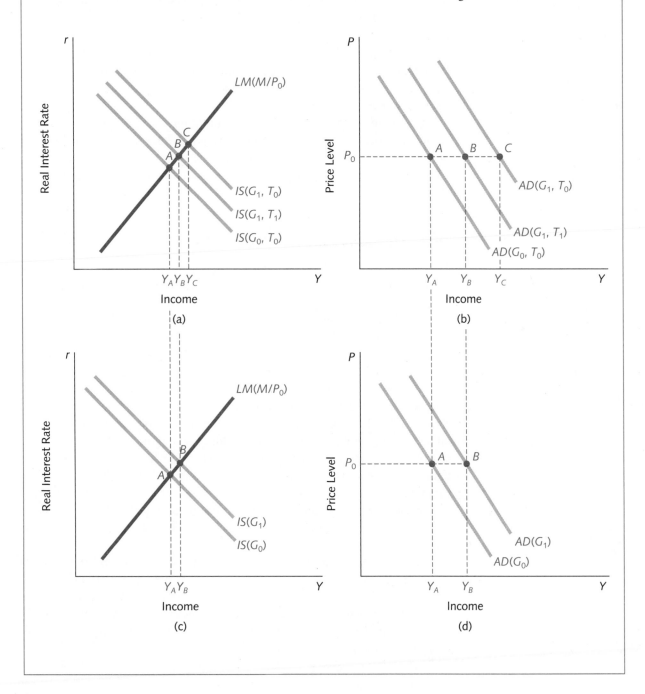

even if current taxes do not change. Moreover, taxpayers care about the present value of taxes instead of simply current taxes. We represent this approach in the bottom two graphs of Figure 17-5. Note that both *IS* and *AD* are functions only of *G*, which represents both government spending and the present value of taxes that pays for that spending. The economy originates at point *A*, where $IS(G_0)$ intersects $LM(M/P_0)$. Point *A* is also represented by point *A* on $AD(G_0)$. At either point, output is Y_A and the price level is P_0. Now consider an increase in government spending to G_1. Since there is an equivalent increase in the present value of taxes, *IS* shifts to $IS(G_1)$ and, for a fixed price P_0, the *IS-LM* equilibrium shifts to point *B*. This is also represented by point *B* on $AD(G_1)$. At point *B*, output is Y_B and the price level stays at P_0.

Note that this movement from point *A* to point *B* in the Ricardian analysis is similar to the movement from point *A* to point *B* for the traditional analysis of a balanced budget increase in government spending. In other words, the Ricardian analysis looks at every increase in government spending as if it were tax financed.

Is the Ricardian Equivalence Theorem Correct?

The validity of the Ricardian Equivalence Theorem seems to require almost unbelievable amounts of foresight and rationality on the part of taxpayers. Taxpayers have to worry about tax bills far into the future, perhaps even beyond their expected lifetime. However, economist Robert Barro, who popularized the modern version of Ricardian Equivalence in the 1970s, has pointed out that this may not be quite the problem it seems, since taxpayers' interest in economic affairs extends beyond their lifetimes to the extent that they are concerned with the well-being of their children. He points out that running up a big debt and leaving it to the next generation may not be consistent with maximizing utility if the utility of today's taxpayers is influenced by the well-being of their children and grandchildren.

Is the Ricardian Equivalence Theorem "valid"? It has theoretical appeal for those who appreciate theories that rely on market forces, perfect competition, complete markets, and consumer rationality. It is not appealing to many economists who worry about market failure and incomplete markets. However, the debate over this hypothesis is more likely to be settled by examining the empirical literature.

There have been many studies of Ricardian Equivalence, and these studies report conflicting results. Some report that various predictions of the Ricardian view are upheld, while others reach the opposite conclusion. For instance, the Ricardian view is that deficits due to tax cuts should not affect market interest rates. (Careful, though! Government spending might affect interest rates.) This Ricardian prediction is surprisingly difficult to falsify in the data, particularly given the strong "intuitive" beliefs on both sides of the issue. The Ricardian proposition has gained followers in the economics profession because of the (surprising?) lack of empirical results that falsify the proposition even in its strongest forms.

POLITICS AND POLICY: THE MOTIVES OF POLITICIANS

PUBLIC CHOICE is a subfield of economic theory which studies the results of imputing economic (i.e., self-interested) behavior to politicians.

A **POLITICAL BUSINESS CYCLE** or PBC implies that actual business cycles may be related to the attempts of politicians to get reelected at periodic intervals.

Although we have studied models with different policy results, our analysis has made one important assumption: Policymakers, fallible though they may be, enact policy changes reflecting their own perceptions of what is "best" for society. That is, policymakers are characterized in traditional macroeconomic literature as being exogenous, or outside the system they are supposed to control. In the traditional conception, politicians (including the President and Congress) act in the public welfare or for the public good.

A modern and rapidly developing area of political and economic thought has provided a very different explanation for the behavior of policymakers. In the past twenty years or so, political scientists and economists have been developing the area of **public choice,** which is concerned with showing that politicians will use the government's economic apparatus (fiscal and monetary policy) to promote their *own* political interests. Macroeconomics, in the view of those who have been developing the notion of a **political business cycle** (PBC), is incomplete if it analyzes only the effects of macroeconomic policy. In this view, a crucial matter to consider is the context within which policies are formulated. In this view, macroeconomic policymaking is the result of the interplay of competitive and self-interested political pressures among incumbent politicians who are up for reelection. Thus, politicians are endogenous, or inside the macroeconomic system. They can manipulate the economy in order to keep themselves in office. Such politically inspired manipulations may be destabilizing, however, and create cyclical phenomena that are not in the public interest. (See the Insight: "The Political Business Cycle and Macroeconomic Variables.")

THE POLITICAL BUSINESS CYCLE: THE NEO-AUSTRIAN VIEW

The above view of the chain of events or the apparatus linking political action to economic consequences requires some clarifications and modifications. In the first place, the model requires shortsightedness on the part of voters with respect to both political voting decisions and the effects of policy changes. Thus, in line with the rational expectations hypothesis, voters would correctly

"THE POLITICAL BUSINESS CYCLE AND MACROECONOMIC VARIABLES"

Can the President of the United States, to improve his popularity and chance of re-election, manipulate policy instruments to affect macro-economic variables? Explanations by economists about this type of incumbent behavior are known as political business cycle (PBC) theories.[a] Models of the PBC are concerned with the relationship between politicians and voters. Politicians, either Republican or Democratic incumbents, are viewed as opportunistic, caring only about staying in power. They try to increase their popularity by engineering an economic expansion just before the eve of an election.

The interaction between the voter and the government is formalized in terms of a voter utility function and a policy reaction function. The President of the United States maximizes his probability of reelection when voter utility is maximized, which occurs when the voter is satisfied with the President's performance. A crucial feature of the PBC is the effect of economic conditions on the voter. While a number of studies by economists have assumed different variables as measures of economic conditions in the voter utility functions, the most common arguments are inflation and unemployment.

The voter utility function is similar to the traditional utility function except voters consider inflation and unemployment as "bads," not "goods." Voter utility is increased with a reduction in both inflation and unemployment. The PBC depends on the existence of an exploitable tradeoff between inflation and unemployment, called the short-run Phillips curve. Since expectations of price increases are assumed to lag behind actual price behavior, the President can use policymaking to reduce unemployment now at the expense of more inflation later on. Once inflationary expectations catch up with actual inflation, the short-run Phillips curve shifts upward, increasing the unemployment rate back to the natural rate of unemployment. In the long run, the Phillips curve is vertical and there is no trade-off between inflation and unemployment.

One recent study has tested the hypothesis that presidential behavior in determination of aggregate economic policy is not opportunistic but rather ideologically motivated. Transfer spending, such as Aid to Families with Dependent Children, food stamps, or social security payments, was used as a type of fiscal policy that typically divided Democrats and Republicans. In the opportunistic model, one would expect the same behavior regardless of party affiliation. If popularity was rising just before the election, either incumbent President would reduce transfer spending since there would be less of a reason to "bribe" voters to ensure reelection. In the ideological model, a rise in popularity would induce opposing effects on transfer spending from a Democratic and a Republican incumbent. Republicans would reduce transfer payments while Democrats would increase them. The results of the test of the opportunistic versus the ideological model indicated that a rise in presidential popularity led to a reduction in transfer payments by both Democratic and Republican administrations.

Some economists have argued that voter preferences should not be based on the unemployment-inflation trade-off—a Phillips curve—but on other effects such as budget financing. In the budget cycle theory, the government can finance its budget by a combination of raising taxes and printing money, assuming it can control the monetary authority. Research has focused on budget cycles that result from deliberate attempts by incumbent presidents to influence the economy in their favor. Near election time the incumbent President tries to impress voters by lowering taxes and increasing government spending. The voter, in turn, views the government's actions as evidence of an effectively operating government.

The economists who argue for the new budget theory feel their approach is more plausible than early PBC theories because it is based on policy instruments that are under the direct control of the government. Other economists counter the budget cycle theorists by suggesting that they have not established a firm link to fluctuations in broad economic activities. Thus, the debate goes on over causes of economic fluctuations in the economy, and the factors central to the PBC theories still remain unsettled. ❏

SOURCES: [a]Sources for this discussion are Phillip A. Cartwright and Charles D. DeLorme, Jr., "The Unemployment-Inflation-Voter Utility Relationship in the Political Business Cycle: Some Evidence," *Southern Economic Journal* 51 (January 1985), pp. 898–905; Chan Guk Huh, "Political Business Cycles," *FRBSF Weekly Letter,* Federal Reserve Bank of San Francisco (December 14, 1990); and Carl E. Walsh and Judy Liles Newman, "Presidential Popularity, Presidential Policies," *FRBSF Weekly Letter,* Federal Reserve Bank of San Francisco (January 31, 1992).

PHOTO 17-2
Federal Reserve Chairman Alan Greenspan Addresses Congress on the State of the Macroeconomy and Monetary Policy.

perceive the intentions of politicians and the effects of the actions on economic variables, thereby neutralizing the political business cycle. Politicians, however, might aim for "surprises," that is, stop-and-go policies designed to confuse the electorate. Some evidence suggests, moreover, that the electorate may indeed be fooled.

An even more telling evaluation of the foregoing model is that termed "neo-Austrian." The neo-Austrian view of the political business cycle stems from the seminal writing of Nobel Prize winner Friedrich A. Hayek.[5] Basically, the neo-Austrian perspective (typified in the previously cited writings of Richard E. Wagner) stresses two very important and related points: (1) that microeconomic influences in specific markets and not aggregate economic variables are the important stuff of political manipulations and (2) that real economic distortions and reductions in income are the result of politically inspired monetary expansions and contractions. Collectively, this may be called a monetary overinvestment theory of the business cycle.

Neo-Austrians characterize the economy as consisting of a set of coordinated and interrelated plans. With a given set of *relative prices,* including an interest rate reflecting a *real* demand for and supply of loanable funds, the efficient distribution of resources in the economy (allowing for uncertainty) is assured by the interconnecting plans of market participants—suppliers and demanders. One aspect of this coordination is that the production of consumer and capital goods optimizes both present and future consumption. At a rate of interest reflecting only the forces of real saving and investment, optimal amounts of resources are devoted to the production of both capital goods (for the future production of consumption goods) and consumer goods (for present consumption).

The important problem raised by neo-Austrian economists with regard to the politically inspired business cycle is that monetary expansions and contractions, through their effects on the nominal rate of interest, upset plans between production for the present and production for the future. Specifically, an artificial lowering of the interest rate through monetary expansion causes overinvestment in capital goods relative to consumer goods. The lower interest rate provides false signals to capital goods producers—signals that are incompatible with the underlying plans of savers-consumers in the economy. The reaction to this overinvestment in capital goods results in a reduction in national income and employment, or a recession in the economy, that will not be relieved until investment and consumption plans are again coordinated. (Depreciation of excess capital equipment and economic losses accompany the bottoming out of the cycle.)

In this conception, the essential problem of political manipulation is that the monetary expansion alters relative prices, creating resource distortions within the economy. Aggregate price changes or inflation rates are incidental to

[5]See Friedrich A. Hayek, *Monetary Theory and the Trade Cycle* (New York: Harcourt Brace Jovanovich, 1932); *Prices and Production,* 2nd ed. (London: Routledge & Kegan Paul, 1935).

the process of political manipulation. Further, in the neo-Austrian concept attention is focused on groups of voters rather than on voters as a whole. While voters as a whole may be influenced to some extent by aggregate inflation and unemployment rates, common sense would tell us that incumbents will attempt, whenever possible, to influence "neutral" or marginal voters in their quest for reelection. For example, social security recipients may be courted by incumbents, but the burden of increased social security contributions may come from the public at large rather than the recipients themselves. The neo-Austrian emphasis on political manipulation therefore focuses attention on the microeconomic incentives and activities of both politicians and voters in the process of politico-economic activities.

MACROECONOMIC BEHAVIOR: 1960–1991

To understand some of the possible impact of macroeconomic policies, we can examine the recent record of macroeconomic variables briefly. Unfortunately, the recent history of the economy is complex and a number of indicators must be explored. For convenience, these are divided into two *sets* of indicators: (1) those related to inflation, unemployment, and income growth and (2) those pertaining to monetary aggregates, the money stock, the monetary base, and interest rates.

Prices, Unemployment, Income, and Monetary Data

Table 17-6 summarizes nominal and real GDP growth, inflation (two measures), and the unemployment rate between 1960 and 1991. Table 17-7 presents the monetary statistics for the period. The M1 statistic, developed by the Federal Reserve System, represents growth in the sum of currency, demand deposits, and other "checkable deposits" at financial institutions, whereas the *monetary base* represents the growth in the sum of currency and bank reserves adjusted for changes in the percentage reserve requirement.[6] The monetary base, or the *stock of high-powered money*, is the raw material from which demand deposits and the aggregate money stock may be expanded or contracted. The prime rate, the interest rate at which commercial banks lend to their best (least risky) customers, and the federal funds rate, the interest rate at which commercial banks and others borrow and lend, are also presented in Table 17-7.

---

[6]An adjustment for reserve requirement changes is necessary in calculating the monetary base since a change in the reserve requirement changes the capacity of any given amount of bank reserves to support demand deposits. That is, the "power" of a given stock of high-powered money is changed by altering the required reserve ratio. This was demonstrated in Chapter 12.

This table gives data for use in interpreting U.S. macroeconomic history since 1960.

YEAR	CPI	GDP DEFLATOR	GDP	REAL GDP	UNEMPLOYMENT RATE
1960	26.01	26.34	511.82	1942.7	5.5
1961	26.27	26.60	529.97	1992.2	6.6
1962	26.59	27.15	570.17	2099.7	5.5
1963	26.93	27.58	602.00	2182.7	5.6
1964	27.27	28.00	644.37	2300.8	5.1
1965	27.72	28.72	699.27	2433.9	4.5
1966	28.57	29.77	766.32	2573.9	3.7
1967	29.34	30.60	810.42	2648.2	3.8
1968	30.59	32.13	885.87	2756.7	3.5
1969	32.25	33.85	957.10	2826.7	3.4
1970	34.15	35.77	1008.2	2818.2	4.9
1971	35.59	37.77	1093.3	2894.5	5.9
1972	36.75	39.56	1201.6	3037.2	5.6
1973	39.06	42.15	1343.1	3185.9	4.8
1974	43.36	45.96	1453.3	3161.7	5.6
1975	47.32	50.47	1580.8	3131.7	8.4
1976	50.05	53.64	1761.7	3283.7	7.7
1977	53.29	57.26	1965.0	3431.3	7.0
1978	57.36	61.45	2219.1	3610.6	6.0
1979	63.81	66.88	2464.3	3684.4	5.8
1980	72.43	72.95	2684.3	3679.6	7.1
1981	79.95	79.95	3000.5	3752.8	7.6
1982	84.87	85.14	3114.8	3658.2	9.7
1983	87.55	88.40	3355.8	3796.1	9.6
1984	91.38	91.72	3724.8	4060.9	7.5
1985	94.65	94.44	3974.1	4207.8	7.1
1986	96.46	96.89	4197.2	4331.8	7.0
1987	100.00	100.00	4486.6	4486.6	6.1
1988	104.05	103.82	4899.0	4718.5	5.4
1989	109.04	108.55	5251.7	4838.0	5.2
1990	114.95	113.20	5521.3	4877.4	5.5
1991	NA	117.77	5677.9	4821.0	7.4

SOURCES: Federal Reserve Bulletin; U.S. Department of Labor, Bureau of Labor Statistics; and U.S. Department of Commerce, Bureau of Economic Analysis.

TABLE 17-7 U.S. M1, M2, Monetary Base, Prime Rate, and Federal Funds Rate

The table gives data on interest rates and money aggregates, helpful for interpreting U.S. monetary history and monetary policy actions since 1960.

YEAR	MI	M2	MONETARY BASE	PRIME RATE	FEDERAL FUNDS RATE
1960	140.31	304.32	44.3	4.8	3.2
1961	143.07	324.86	44.6	4.5	1.9
1962	146.52	350.14	46.0	4.5	2.6
1963	150.99	379.65	47.7	4.5	3.1
1964	156.81	409.36	50.1	4.5	3.4
1965	163.49	442.50	52.6	4.5	4.0
1966	171.01	471.40	55.3	5.6	5.1
1967	177.75	503.69	57.9	5.6	4.2
1968	190.17	545.38	61.7	6.2	5.6
1969	201.46	579.12	65.2	7.9	8.2
1970	209.18	603.19	68.8	7.9	7.1
1971	223.23	676.36	73.9	5.7	4.6
1972	239.09	760.92	79.1	5.2	4.4
1973	256.38	836.29	86.1	8.0	8.7
1974	269.27	887.29	93.4	10.7	10.5
1975	281.47	970.17	99.5	7.8	5.8
1976	297.25	1095.7	106.5	6.8	5.0
1977	320.06	1234.55	114.9	6.8	5.5
1978	346.40	1339.9	125.4	9.0	7.9
1979	372.85	1450.63	135.3	12.6	11.1
1980	395.95	1567.12	147.1	15.2	13.3
1981	425.10	1714.90	156.8	18.8	16.3
1982	453.16	1875.30	166.8	14.8	12.2
1983	503.34	2110.15	182.0	10.7	9.0
1984	538.67	2279.69	196.0	12.0	10.2
1985	587.15	2484.80	210.9	9.9	8.1
1986	666.82	2691.60	229.8	8.3	6.8
1987	744.36	2869.95	250.5	8.2	6.6
1988	776.10	3017.55	268.5	9.3	7.5
1989	783.72	3129.73	280.1	10.8	9.2
1990	811.53	3287.84	298.3	10.0	8.0
1991	860.40	3402.33	338.2	8.2	5.5

SOURCES: Federal Reserve Bulletin; U.S. Department of Labor, Bureau of Labor Statistics; and U.S. Department of Commerce, Bureau of Economic Analysis.

These data tell an interesting story and one that may be interpreted in several ways, as we shall see. First, consider the years 1960–1968, which coincide with the Keynesian administrations of John F. Kennedy and Lyndon B. Johnson. After a relatively stable price level but reasonably high unemployment rates in the late 1950s, the Democrats followed expansionary fiscal policies over the years 1960–1968. Regarded as the most successful Keynesian policy of recent times, the tax cut of 1964 (preceded by the investment tax credit of 1962) appears to have had a fairly dramatic impact on unemployment rates, which fell from 5.2 percent in 1964 to 4.5 percent and 3.8 percent in 1965 and 1966 (the unemployment rate fell throughout the latter 1960s, in fact).

Inflation, however, was not nearly so well-behaved. Deficits created by the tax cut and by our increasing involvement in Vietnam meant that monetary policy was called upon to accommodate fiscal policy; that is, deficits were facilitated by monetary means, and the economy began to experience pressures on prices. Despite the fiscal measure of a (temporary) surcharge in 1968 and a new Republican administration's promise to control inflation, the rate of inflation climbed from 4.7 percent in 1968 to 6.1 percent in 1969 and to about 5.5 percent in 1970. Unemployment, by contrast, hit an unbelievable low (overfull employment?) of 3.5 percent in 1969, a low that has not been reached since. But unemployment rose to almost 4.9 percent in 1970 and to almost 5.9 percent in 1971.

To deal with these twin problems, the Nixon administration embarked on a two-pronged assault. To deal with inflation, price and wage controls were invoked between August 1971 and (effectively) mid-1973. To deal with the growing unemployment problem, an increased rate of monetary expansion was undertaken. These policies appear to have had, temporarily at least, the desired effects. The growth rate in the consumer price level fell from 5.5 percent in 1970 to 3 percent in 1972, and unemployment fell from almost 5.9 percent in 1971 to 4.9 percent in 1973.

The temporary gain on both fronts was short-lived, however. After the cessation of controls in mid-1973, the inflation rate jumped to 8.8 percent for the year, then to an incredible 12.2 percent in 1974. This jump caused the Fed, in the opinion of most Monetarists at least, to overadjust by (too) sharply cutting back the rate of monetary expansion. Between April 1974 and April 1975 currency and demand deposits grew by only 4.4 percent per year, whereas in the previous year they had grown by a full 6 percent per year. Inflation was brought down to a still-high rate of 7 percent, but unemployment increased from 5.6 percent in 1974 to 8.5 percent in 1975. The latter rate was the highest unemployment rate in the United States since the Great Depression of the 1930s. Recession, in other words, took hold of the U.S. economy. While inflation fell to about 5 percent in 1976, unemployment remained at the fairly high level of 7.7 percent.

In 1977, the Democrats under Jimmy Carter again took control of the fiscal apparatus. Political promises to balance the budget, to control inflation, and to reduce unemployment were made, as always, at campaign time (see below for more on these cyclical political effects). However, the facts are clear. During the period 1975–1977, the money stock grew by almost 4 percent; then between 1977 and 1980, the growth *rate* in currency and demand deposits remained fairly *constant,* though it rose in early 1981. Inflation during the Carter term (1977–1981) rose precipitously, from 6.8 percent in 1977 to an incredible 13.3 percent in 1979. Unemployment, though down from deep recession level of 8.5 percent in 1975 to 6 percent in 1978 and 5.8 in 1979, appeared to be fairly resistant to significant reductions below the latter levels, reaching double-digit proportions in 1982.[7]

A combination of these economic factors was probably a large element in the sweeping Reagan victory. The supply-side policies of the Reagan administration also carried a Monetarist flavor, especially regarding monetary stability. Tax reductions, spending reductions, increased incentives to invest, work, and save, and reduced regulation—all of which were intended to accomplish a reduction in overall government growth—were central to the Reagan economic program. These supply-side policies were aimed at creating business expansion and increasing employment. Although a great deal of controversy surrounded these economic policy developments, stable monetary growth as the primary (shorter-term) means of controlling inflation was a feature of Reaganomics.

The results of Reagan's policy of tighter monetary growth in 1981 and in the first half of 1982 created a severe credit crunch leading to a short-run rise in interest rates. The overall unemployment rate jumped from 7.6 percent in 1981 to 9.7 percent in 1982, remaining at that level in 1983 (see Table 17-6). Inflation, however, fell to steady and "acceptable" levels between 1982 and 1988, and just as importantly, inflationary expectations were reduced, thereby bolstering business confidence and the atmosphere of market activity. By 1984 and 1985, the unemployment rate fell from its 1982–83 high level, the real GDP growth rate (in 1984) reached a 25-year high, and interest rates began to decline by mid-1985. Significantly, the Reagan recovery was sufficient to catapult Reagan back into office in a 1984 landslide victory. Huge deficits were a persistent problem throughout Reagan's administration, and major initiatives such as the 1985 Gramm-Rudman-Hollings Act were eventual failures at restraining the deficit. Reagan's second term was marked by continual growth (real GDP grew 3.8 percent during his second term) and continued low inflation (the inflation rate averaged 3.2 percent during his second term). By the end of his second term, the high unemployment rates reached during the recession of the early 1980s were eliminated, and unemployment in 1988 had fallen to 5.5 percent of the labor force.

---

[7]See Philip Cagan, "The Reduction of Inflation and the Magnitude of Unemployment," in *Contemporary Economic Problems,* William Fellner, ed. (Washington, DC: American Enterprise Institute, 1977). It is worth noting that Cagan estimated the *natural* rate of unemployment to be on the order of 6 percent *or more* and not the 4.5–5 percent levels of official measures of full employment. Other economists place the rate at 7 percent.

George Bush was elected in 1989 on a platform of continuing the Reagan policies. His term was marred by a recession late in the term, in 1990–91, and by a slow recovery from that recession. Because of the recession and slow recovery, output growth over the first three years of his term averaged a paltry .7 percent per year, and unemployment rose from 5.3 percent in 1989 to over 7.4 percent in 1991 and 1992. The inflation rate stayed low by pre-Reagan standards, but averaged 4.3 percent for 1989–1991, about 1 percent higher than in Reagan's second term. Finally, the budget deficits continued despite an accord with Congress to raise taxes (violating the "read my lips" promise of no tax hikes) and constrain spending. In part this was due to the recession and slow recovery, but nonetheless the public responded by voting Bush out of office in favor of Bill Clinton. Bill Clinton campaigned on a platform of increased investment spending, in particular government investment spending in infrastructure and education, and on a platform of stimulating the economy to speed recovery from the recession of 1990–91. He also promised higher taxes, especially on the "rich," but with no taxes or even a tax cut for the middle class, and he promised health care reform. While his health care reform package is controversial, it should lead to an expansion in the U.S. health care industry—see the Insight on "Growth of Health Care Services." The coming years will see how well he deals with these issues. As he took office in early 1993, the last quarter statistics for 1992 indicate that the economic recovery has gained steam, with real GDP growing at well over 3 percent per year, with unemployment rates falling, and with sales increasing over previous years. Moreover, the inflation rate remains at low levels. The biggest problem on the horizon is the budget deficit, and three previous presidents have had difficulties meeting promises of a balanced budget. Like President Reagan, President Clinton wants to balance the budget in part by faster growth. Reagan achieved growth via lower tax rates, stimulating aggregate supply and generating the longest peacetime expansion in U.S. history. Clinton wants to do the same, but with government investment spending on infrastructure to stimulate growth. Only time will tell if President Clinton's plan will be carried out successfully, and if he can deliver on his version of that promise.

SUMMARY

A wise philosopher once noted that "it is pointless to beat an elephant because it cannot fly." Likewise, one should not fault politicians for acting optimally under the constraints set out for them under the Constitution and laws of the land. Politicians may try to manipulate macroeconomic and microeconomic variables and events to enhance election or reelection probabilities. This should surprise no one, but Keynesians, and Monetarists and Austrians nevertheless interpret the situation differently. Keynesians retain a belief that the macro-

GROWTH OF HEALTH CARE SERVICES

While the fate and ultimate shape of President Clinton's health care reform package, developed under Hillary Rodham Clinton, remain unknown, the overall outlook for the health services industry under likely reforms remains excellent. The driving force behind expansion of the U.S. health care industry is growing demand for services. The Clinton plan requires all employers to pay for health coverage for their workers. Every American would be eligible for a standard package of benefits, which could be purchased through state-run health alliances. These alliances would try to use their clout to hold down medical costs through "managed competition." Because many of the forces powering expansion of the health care industry are basic demographic and lifestyle trends, government's ability to curb spending for health care probably is very limited. Moreover, President Clinton's pledge to provide basic health care to every American will reinforce demand growth. Among general factors favoring the demand increase for health services are the rapidly expanding elderly population with its relatively higher per capita consumption of medical services; middle-aged baby boomers' increased health care demands; the escalating need for health care services for AIDS patients; medical and scientific advances that save and/or prolong life, thereby creating demand for additional services; the rising popularity of lifestyle choices which increase reliance on professional health caretakers (e.g. single adults

PHOTO 17-3
Hillary Rodham Clinton Speaks to a Meeting of the American Medical Association in Chicago June 13, 1993.

living alone and dual-income households); greater need for health and rehabilitative services to mainstream the handicapped and mentally retarded; the rising demand for elective procedures such as cosmetic surgery; and a litigious atmosphere that spurs defensive medical practices.

Though the short-term effect of health care reform legislation probably is faster growth of industry-wide revenues, prospects for some healthcare providers may diminish. There probably will be a greater emphasis on primary and preventive care. Also, the role of family and general physicians as gatekeepers that control access to specialty physicians probably will expand. Generally, the losers will be hospitals and specialist physicians. The likely winners include health maintenance organizations, outpatient facilities, and family doctors. Nurses and other technically trained health care professionals should also enjoy expanding employment opportunities, but jobs for less skilled hospital and medical office workers may decline.

One shortcoming of the various health reform proposals is that they generally do not fully explore supply-side solutions. For example, there has not been a major push to augment tight supplies of physicians and other highly trained health care professionals. Physicians can command high levels of compensation partly because they face limited direct competition. One solution might be to expand U.S. medical schools while accelerating entry of foreign-trained physicians. The final health care bill may be close to the Clintons' package of managed-care networks and purchasing alliances, but the fear by business of regulation and political control of the health care system may lead to substantial changes in the final product.

SOURCES: Sara Collins, "The Visible Hand," *U.S. News and World Report,* October 4, 1993, pp. 80-86. Mike McNamee and Susan B. Garland, "Business Can't Hide Its Doubts," *Business Week,* September 20, 1993, pp. 30-33.

economy is inherently unstable and therefore must be regulated by fiscal and monetary policies. Most Monetarists and developers of the political business cycle argue the reverse and charge that endogenous politicians and manipulators are the prime source of macroeconomic problems. Sources of real instability, such as those described throughout this book, do exist, but they may be exaggerated by discretionary actions. According to some contemporary economists, politicians and discretionary manipulators must be made to face new rules. In their view, legislative restrictions or a constitutional amendment constraining or eliminating deficits together with the institution of a monetary expansion "rule" would be two most obvious steps toward providing macroeconomic stability in the United States. In spite of this view, and that of the New Classicals, a belief in the effectiveness of discretionary fiscal and monetary policy persists.

KEY TERMS

budget constraint

debt rollover

endogenous politician

neo-Austrian view of the PBC

ongoing budget deficit

one-time budget deficit

public choice

political business cycle

Ricardian equivalence

urban privatization

QUESTIONS FOR REVIEW AND DISCUSSION

1. What are some crucial economic variables that must be studied in an assessment of economic policy? Can you think of others not mentioned in this chapter? What of, say, population statistics?

2. What is an *endogenous* politician? Why do you believe that some economists assume politicians to be self-interested?

3. What are the implications of endogenous politicians for control of the business cycle in the short run? In the long run? Does a two-, four-, or six-year election constraint have any impact on macroeconomic activity?

4. Describe a political business cycle (PBC) in detail.

5. Do you think that the advocates of the political business cycle believe all politicians to be "crooked"? Discuss in detail.

6. If a PBC actually does exist, what constraints could society impose on political behavior to obtain macroeconomic stability? Under these circumstances, which would be more appealing, discretionary policies or fixed-rule policies?

7. What is the government budget constraint? How does it constrain the government?

8. Comment on the following notation: "The government budget constraint is a worthless idea. If the government wants to spend more than it has, it just borrows or prints money. There is no constraint."

9. If the government runs a budget deficit each year, and if the rate of growth of GDP is less than the interest rate on the debt, will the government budget constraint eventually force a change of behavior? Why?

10. As far as the government budget constraint is concerned, does it matter if the government is running a deficit because of a cut in taxes or because of an increase in spending?

11. If the Fed were going to monetize the deficit, how would it do so?

12. Does the Ricardian Equivalence idea suggest that taxes and borrowing to finance government spending have identical effects? Why or why not?

13. Some economists claim that the Ricardian Equivalence idea is that government spending has no effect on the economy. Comment.

PROBLEMS

1. In 1991, the monetary base—the supply of high-powered money, reserves plus currency—was $338 billion. The U.S. deficit was about $150 billion. Comment on the following: "The deficit is really no big deal. All we have to do is get the Federal Reserve System to print enough extra money to cover the deficit, and we won't have to keep increasing the debt." What would be the effects on P, Y, and r of such a policy?

2. Some economists claim that the government budget deficits of the 1980s and early 1990s were due to tax cuts in 1982. Others claim that they are due to increases in government spending. Still others claim they began with high interest rates of the 1980s as the Fed worked to lower the inflation rate. Using Figures 17-2 and 17-3 of this chapter, present a case for or against each of these claims.

SUGGESTIONS FOR FURTHER READING

Alesina, Alberto and Jeffrey Sachs. "Political Parties and the Business Cycle in the United States, 1948-1984." *Journal of Money, Credit, and Banking* (February 1988), pp. 63-82.

Barro, J. Robert "The Ricardian Approach to Budget Deficits." *Journal of Economic Perspectives* (Spring 1989), pp. 37-54.

Cebula, Richard J. *The Deficit Problem in Perspectives.* Lexington, Massachusetts: D.C. Heath and Company, 1987.

Eisner, Robert. "Budget Deficits: Rhetoric and Reality." *Journal of Economic Perspectives* (Spring 1989), pp. 73-93.

Schultze, Charles L. "Is There a Bias Toward Excess in U.S. Government Budgets or Deficits?" *Journal of Economic Perspectives* (Spring 1992), pp. 25-43.

Willett, T. D., ed. *Political Business Cycles: The Political Economy of Money, Inflation and Unemployment.* Durham: Duke University Press, 1988.

18 ECONOMIC GROWTH

In previous chapters, our macroeconomic analysis and policy discussion was chiefly confined to the "short-run" period of time when the capital stock was held constant. This chapter takes a longer-run view. Over long periods, short-term business cycle movements in real GDP are swamped by the growth of real GDP over time. In fact, a case can be made that economic growth is far more important than stabilization policy. The reason that income per person is higher today in the United States than in 1960 is due to economic growth. Sometimes the short-run emphasis on unemployment or on dealing with business cycle fluctuations makes us forget that over the long haul it is the growth rate of the economy that matters most to the well-being of the average citizen.

Not only is growth important, but so is the rate of growth. There is an approximation called the "rule of 72" that illustrates the importance of even small changes in growth rates on the growth of such things as personal income, or per capita personal income. The rule of 72 says that 72 divided by the growth rate will approximately give the number of years it takes for the economy to double in size. For instance, an economy growing at 3 percent per year will double in size in approximately 24 years (72/3 = 24). If the growth rate rises to 4 percent per year, the economy will double in size in 18 years (72/4 = 18). To bring this closer to home, U.S. real GDP grew at a rate of 3.7 percent per year from 1947 to 1973, or U.S. real GDP doubled about every 19.5 years (72/3.7 = 19.5). Thus, the soldiers returning from World War II saw the U.S. economy double in size between 1947 and 1967, just about in time for the first of their children—the first of the baby boom generation—to have finished college. However, from 1974 to 1992, U.S. real GDP grew at a rate of 2.2 percent per year, a rate that would double real GDP in 32.7 years (72/2.2 = 32.7). This slowing of economic growth has important consequences for how well the U.S. economy can keep up with the expectations of its populace. In 1947 a household could expect a fairly rapid rise in standard of living over time. In 1974—or today, 1994—a household can expect a considerably slower rise in standard of living over time.

By the end of this chapter, you will know

- how the Solow growth model is based on a Neoclassical production function
- why constant returns to scale are assumed to be a property of the production function
- how the steady-state ratio of capital to labor is determined
- what economic forces tend to move the economy to the steady state
- how changes in depreciation, labor force growth, technological change, or changes in the saving rate will alter the steady state
- what we mean by the golden rule
- how modern approaches to economic growth bring in different points of view on the Solow growth model.

PRODUCTIVE CAPACITY OF THE ECONOMY

What exactly do we mean by the productive capacity of the economy? The productive capacity of an economy is defined as the real output that the economy could produce if all of its resources were efficiently and fully employed. This does not mean that the unemployment rate of labor is zero, but that the unemployment rate is equal to the natural rate. In previous chapters, various policies were studied, including monetary and fiscal policies whose implementation might solve the problem of unemployment. In this chapter, problems relating to capital formation and productivity in the "long run" are considered. The term *long run* is used here, as in traditional microeconomic analysis, to refer to a period of time when all of the factor inputs (i.e., labor, capital, land, and entrepreneurial ability) and the state of technology are variable. This is to be contrasted with the use of long run in earlier chapters, when it was used to signify only adjustment of expected price to the actual price level. Then we derived long-run aggregate supply as the supply curve relevant when expected and actual price levels were the same, but still the capital stock was taken as fixed.

FIGURE 18−1
Actual and Potential Real GDP, 1947–1992
Solid Line Is Potential Real GDP (Billions of 1987 Dollars)

This graph shows the behavior of real GDP (the solid line) relative to potential real GDP (the dotted line) over the period 1947 to 1992. The trend line is actually a proxy for potential GDP, estimated as the trend rate of growth in GDP over time, with a break in trend at the end of 1973.

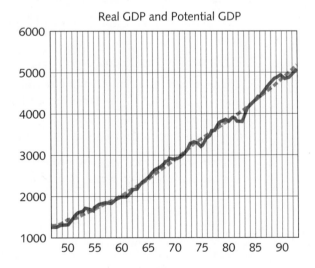

Real GDP and Potential GDP

SOURCES: U.S. Department of Commerce, Bureau of Economic Analysis; and authors' calculations.

ECONOMIC GROWTH is the rate of increase in an economy's full-employment real output or real income over time.

This chapter deals with **economic growth**—an increase in the productive capacity of an economy. The productive capacity of an economy—sometimes called potential output, or potential real GDP—can be expanded by increasing the equilibrium quantity of labor inputs, by increasing the capital stock, and by making technological progress.

The relationship between real output (measured as real GDP) and potential real GDP is shown in Figure 18–1 (p. 671). Potential real GDP lies on a path that is fairly smoothly upward sloping, while actual real GDP moves above and below that path. During the latter part of the 1960s, actual real GDP exceeded potential real GDP. This occurred because spending required for the Vietnam War had reduced the unemployment rate to less than 3.5 percent. After 1973, however, the economy slipped into a recession and actual real GDP moved substantially below potential real GDP. Following the 1974–75 recession, actual real GDP again started moving toward its potential level. By the late 1970s, real GDP again exceeded potential real GDP, until the recessions of 1980 and 1981 forced real GDP below potential. By the middle 1980s, real GDP was again nearly equal to potential real GDP, and this continued again until the recession of 1990–91, which again saw real GDP fall below potential.

THE NEOCLASSICAL GROWTH MODEL

In the mid-1950s, Robert Solow introduced the Neoclassical production function into the study of economic growth.[1] The Neoclassical production function used by Solow has three important properties:

1. The factors of production (labor and capital) can be substituted for each other.
2. Each factor of production experiences diminishing marginal productivity.
3. There are constant returns to scale, which means that when all factor inputs are expanded in the same proportion, real output is expanded in that same proportion. More simply put, if inputs are all doubled (including the capital stock), then output will double.

We will look at each of these properties in turn. Substitutability of inputs such as capital and labor means that a firm can decide to use more capital and less labor, or less capital and more labor, in order to produce the same amount

---

[1]Robert M. Solow, "A Contribution to the Theory of Economic Growth," *Quarterly Journal of Economics* 70 (1956), pp. 65–94. Growth models built on the basis of the Neoclassical production function are referred to as Neoclassical growth models. Other economists whose names are closely associated with these types of models are Swan, Meade, Uzawa, and Tobin.

of output.[2] Why is substitutability between capital and labor important? In explaining economic growth, an important factor is the increase in capital per worker. A distinguishing characteristic of developed nations over nations still developing is that developed nations have a high ratio of capital to labor. Thus, developed nations produce additional output by augmenting labor inputs with capital inputs. If this were not possible, then developed nations would be strictly limited by the size of their populations, and not able to substitute larger capital stocks to increase output.

Another important feature of Neoclassical production functions is diminishing marginal physical product. Recall that an increase in the labor supply, with the capital stock held constant, will produce an increase in real output, but that this increase in output diminishes as the labor supply increases. This feature is responsible for the downward sloping labor demand curves that we derived for the Classical model in Chapter 3 and used throughout this text. There are also diminishing returns to adding capital to a fixed labor stock.

Why is this feature of diminishing returns important? First of all, without it we would not have downward sloping labor demand—or capital demand. More to the point, diminishing returns means that even though factors are substitutes, it becomes ever more costly to get more output by just increasing the quantity of one input. Diminishing returns explains why economic growth is not usually based strictly on an increased employment of one input.

Finally, we will assume that the Neoclassical production function exhibits constant returns to scale. This means that if we double all inputs, capital and labor both, we will double output. Solow used this form of the production function for three reasons. First, there was empirical support for such a specification. Second, it simplified his modeling task. Third, the idea that doubling all inputs leads to a doubling of output is intuitively plausible.

In addition to our assumptions on the production function, we also assume that the economy is perfectly competitive. Each factor of production is paid according to its marginal product, and the economy is at full employment. We will look at a particular Neoclassical production function called the Cobb-Douglas production function, given by

$$Y = A(t)\, K^a\, N^{1-a}, \tag{18.1}$$

where Y is real output, $A(t)$ is an index of technological know-how at time t, K is the stock of capital, and N is the supply of labor. For the sake of simplicity, we will begin by assuming that technological change does not take place, so $A(t)$ is constant over time, and always just equal to A.

---

[2]This stands in contrast to production functions with fixed proportions between inputs, such as the so-called Leontieff production functions. These production functions require exact proportions between capital and labor. With such a production function, if one input is held constant, no amount of increase in the other input will lead to any change in output.

PUBLIC CAPITAL AND

PRIVATE OUTPUT

An issue that has been hotly debated in the economics profession in the past few years, and which came to the forefront of the political debates during the presidential election of 1992, is government spending on capital. In the political arena, this is often called government spending on infrastructure, but the meaning is similar.

In the economics literature, this issue was brought to the fore in a series of articles by David Aschauer, who includes the government capital stock in the production function as

$$Y = A\, K^a\, N^{1-a-b}\, KG^b,$$

where KG is the supply of government-owned capital.[a] If we divide both sides by employment, we can write this in per capita terms as

$$(Y/N) = A\,(K/N)^a\,(KG/N)^b.$$

In his own estimates of this equation, John Tatom reports $a = .22$ and $b = .28$, indicating that an increase in the ratio of public capital to employment has a larger effect on output than the same percentage increase in the ratio of private capital to employment![b] This result has led Aschauer and others to call for increased government investment, a call that has been echoed in the presidential campaign.

In his work, Tatom also criticizes the above estimates on a number of grounds. First, these estimates ignore

the effect of energy prices on output. Tatom has found that higher energy prices have a substantial negative effect on output, and that these higher energy prices during the middle 1970s to very early 1980s occurred at exactly the time that the ratio of public capital to employment was falling. The stock of highways, streets, and educational facilities per capita began declining in 1975, just when energy prices rose. The decline in the stock of highways and streets per capita occurred because the interstate highway system was nearing completion. The decline in educational facilities per capita began in 1975 because the percentage of the population of school age, between 5 and 24 years of age, began to decline from 38 percent of the population in

---

PHOTO 18-1
A Major Thrust of Bill Clinton's Recommendations for Change During His Campaign for the Presidency Was to Increase Public Investments in Deteriorating Infrastructure.

1975 to 29 percent in 1990. This led to a reduction in the number of buildings for education. Thus, two main components of government capital began to decline (on a per capita basis) in 1975, just when energy prices were rising. Omitting consideration of energy prices from the production function can therefore result in biased results. After including the price of energy, Tatom finds that the effect of public capital falls to .13.

Another question raised about Aschauer's results is whether there is a reverse causation between income and the demand for public capital goods. It may be that rising income at the state or national level leads to an increased demand for public capital spending, and this is what generates Aschauer's results. In other words, the relationship may be that spending on public capital goods rises because of higher income levels, and not that higher income levels are the result of more spending on public capital goods.

The conclusion that Tatom draws from these arguments is that, when account is taken of all these factors, there is no statistically significant evidence that spending on public capital goods leads to increased output. According to Tatom, initial claims to the contrary were based on spurious statistical estimates. ❑

SOURCES: [a]See David Alan Aschauer, "Fiscal Policy and Aggregate Demand," *American Economic Review* (March 1985), pp. 117–127; "Is Public Expenditure Productive?" *Journal of Monetary Economics* (March 1989), pp. 177–200; and Randall W. Eberts, "Public Infrastructure and Regional Economic Developments," Federal Reserve Bank of Cleveland *Economic Review* (Quarter 1, 1990), pp. 15–27.
[b]See John A. Tatom, "Should Government Spending on Capital Goods Be Raised?" Federal Reserve Bank of St. Louis *Review* (March/April 1991), pp. 3–16; and "Public Capital and Private Sector Performance," Federal Reserve Bank of St. Louis *Review* (May/June 1991), pp. 3–16.

There are other production functions besides that given above. Recently there has been a large debate over the importance and role of publicly provided capital in the production process. For an overview of this debate, see the Policy Issue: "Public Capital and Private Output."

Long-Run Properties of the Production Function

In earlier chapters we emphasized the law of diminishing returns. The law of diminishing returns says that the marginal product of a variable factor diminishes as the use of that factor increases, holding all other inputs fixed. One example of this property occurs in farming, where a farmer adds fertilizer, a variable factor, to land, a fixed factor. As long as land is fixed, adding more and more pounds of fertilizer will eventually add fewer and fewer additional bushels of output. In fact, the marginal product of fertilizer will eventually be negative, because too much fertilizer will actually destroy a crop.

We consider a specific Cobb-Douglas production function of the form:

$$Y = K^{.3} N^{.7}.$$

Here we have assumed values for the exponents on capital and labor, and we have set the index of technical change A to be one. For this production function, we can calculate the amount of output that is produced with various amounts of capital and labor.

The law of diminishing returns is a short run concept, and holds when a variable input is increased while holding another input fixed. The law of diminishing returns also holds if we assume that the employment of labor is fixed and the use of capital varies. It will be useful to explicitly review the marginal product of capital for a given level of labor. This will drive home the idea that diminishing returns is a concept that applies any time one input increases while one or more are held constant, and not just to labor.

In Table 18–1 we provide two examples of a production function with the employment of labor held fixed at 4 units ($N = 4$) and 8 units ($N = 8$). The capital stock is allowed to vary from 0 to 12 units of capital. We continue to use the production function $Y = K^{.3} N^{.7}$, and we compute the resulting output for the various levels of capital inputs. Figure 18–1 also plots the

TABLE 18–1

Production Function and Marginal Product of Capital $Y = K^{.3} N^{.7}$. Two Cases with Capital Fixed, $N = 4$ and $N = 8$

The analysis here fixes the level of labor and varies capital inputs. Zero to 12 units of capital (in column 1) are combined with 4 units of labor (column 2) to generate output (column 3). Column 4 shows that the law of diminishing marginal returns occurs for capital, as additional units of capital lead to smaller increases in output. Columns 5 through 7 demonstrate the same experiment with labor fixed at 8 units.

K	N	Y	$\Delta Y/\Delta K$	N	Y	$\Delta Y/\Delta K$
0	4	0	—	8	0	—
1	4	2.63	2.63	8	4.28	4.28
2	4	3.24	0.61	8	5.27	0.99
3	4	3.66	0.42	8	5.96	0.69
4	4	4	0.34	8	6.49	0.53
5	4	4.27	0.27	8	6.94	0.45
6	4	4.51	0.24	8	7.33	0.39
7	4	4.73	0.22	8	7.68	0.35
8	4	4.92	0.19	8	8.00	0.32
9	4	5.10	0.18	8	8.28	0.28
10	4	5.26	0.16	8	8.55	0.27
11	4	5.41	0.15	8	8.80	0.25
12	4	5.56	0.15	8	9.03	0.23

FIGURE 18–2
Production Function
$N = 4$ and $N = 8$.

Here, the production function is graphed by holding labor fixed and varying the units of capital. This figure summarizes the data from Table 18–1. Note that each additional unit of capital brings smaller increases in output, and that an increase in the labor units from 4 to 8 shifts the whole production function upward.

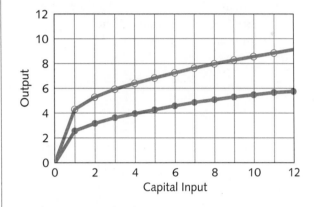

NOTE: $Y = K^3 N^7$.

amount of output that we obtain as the amount of capital varies from 0 to 12 units for our two levels of employment. Notice that the production functions graphed in this figure also exhibit the usual Neoclassical shape, in which the production function is always upward sloping, but with a slope that flattens as more and more units of capital are added to the fixed level of employment. We also report the marginal product of capital in Table 18–1, $\Delta Y / \Delta K$, for the cases in which labor inputs are fixed at 4 and at 8. Notice that the marginal product of labor does indeed diminish as the firm employs more and more capital with a fixed level of employment of labor.

The key feature in the above analysis is that we are discussing a property of the production function that holds when one or more of the factors of production are held constant. Thus, in our fertilizer example the factor *land* was held fixed. Our farmer could adjust the amount of fertilizer used, but not the amount of land, and hence the concept of diminishing returns was sufficient. However, for our study of growth, capital is a variable input, so we will have to make use of another concept, the idea of *constant returns to scale*. Constant returns to scale is a property of our production function when *all* factors of production change by the same proportion. Thus, instead of merely increasing fertilizer usage on the same amount of land, we will ask what happens to output if we double *both* fertilizer usage and land. That is, we are envisioning doubling the size of a farm and doubling the amount of fertilizer used. We want to know what will happen to output. In this case, most people

TABLE 18-2
Production Function: Output
Per Worker.
$Y/N=(K^{.3}N^{.7})/N = (K/N)^{.3}$
Case of Capital and Labor
Varying in Proportion of
$K = 2N$.

The production functions used in this chapter have the property of constant returns to scale: a proportional increase in both factors of production increases output by the same proportion. This fact is demonstrated here. The capital labor ratio (column 4) stays at 2, but each unit is increased by 50 percent as we move down the column. Output (column 3) also increases by 50 percent each time, showing the property of constant returns. The average product of labor is given in column 5, and is constant.

K	N	Y	K/N	Y/N
1	.5	.61	2	1.23
1.5	.75	.92	2	1.23
2	1	1.23	2	1.23
3	1.5	1.84	2	1.23
4	2	2.46	2	1.23
6	3	3.69	2	1.23
8	4	4.92	2	1.23
12	6	7.38	2	1.23
16	8	9.84	2	1.23
24	12	14.77	2	1.23
32	16	19.69	2	1.23
48	24	29.54	2	1.23
64	32	39.39	2	1.23

would suggest that output would also double, and in fact this is exactly what we mean by constant returns to scale.[3]

Consider our Cobb-Douglas production function:

$$Y = A K^a N^{1-a}. \tag{18.2}$$

---

[3]Mathematically, we say that a production function exhibits constant returns to scale if the following holds for all numbers z:

$$zY = F(zK, zN).$$

For example, if $z = 2$, then a doubling of inputs leads to a doubling of output.

Many production functions have the property of constant returns to scale, and many others do not. We are concerned only with those that do. One example of such a production function is $Y = aK + bN$. For instance, let $a = 1$ and $b = 2$, so $Y = K + 2N$. Further, suppose we employ 10 units of capital and 5 units of labor, so $K = 10$ and $N = 5$. Output is $Y = 10 + 2 \times 5 = 20$. Now we double both K and N, to 20 units of capital and 10 units of labor. Output will then be $Y = 20 + 2 \times 10 = 40$, and will also have doubled.

FIGURE 18-3
Production Function:
Labor and Capital Both Vary;
$K = 2N$

This figure is based upon Table 18–3. With constant returns to scale technology, and with both inputs changing by equal amounts, output also changes in the same proportion. The production function is only drawn against capital, for simplicity, but both labor and capital are being increased along the straight-line production function.

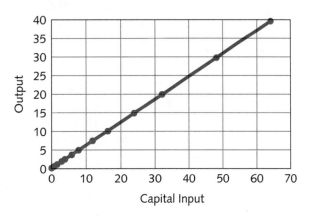

As long as the exponents on capital and labor sum to one, this production function will have constant returns to scale.[4] In Table 18–2 we provide an example of constant returns to scale, using our previous production function $Y = K^{.3} N^{.7}$. We begin with capital of 1 unit and labor of .5 units, so $Y = 1^{.3} .5^{.7} = .6156$. Then we increase both capital and labor by 50 percent, so that the capital stock is 1.5 units and labor input is .75 units. Output is $Y = 1.5^{.3} .75^{.7} = .9234$, which, as we can check to see, is also a 50 percent increase in output, since $.6156 \times 1.5 = .9234$. Table 18–2 provides many examples of proportional increases in both inputs, and the corresponding equal proportional increase in output. However, a graphical presentation makes constant returns to scale very easy to detect, as shown in Figure 18–3. There we graph output against one of the inputs, in this case the capital stock. However, it is very important to remember that *both inputs are changing in the same proportion as the capital stock increases.* Thus, on the graph an increase in the capital stock from 10 units to 20 units is accompanied by an increase in the quantity of labor from 5 units to 10 units. The striking feature of Figure 18–3 is that the production function is a straight line. This is the graphical feature of a constant

---

[4]A general form of the Cobb-Douglas production function can be written as $Y = AK^a N^b$, and the exponents a and b need not sum to one. If they do sum to one, or $a + b = 1$, then the production function will exhibit constant returns to scale. However, if $a + b < 1$, then output will not double, and the Cobb-Douglas production function will exhibit diminishing returns to scale. If $a + b > 1$, output will more than double, and the Cobb-Douglas production function will exhibit increasing returns to scale.

TABLE 18-3
Production Function: Output
per Worker and Marginal
Product per Worker of
Capital Y/N = (K/N).3

This table shows how changes in the inputs lead to changes in output. The constant returns to scale production function has been changed into per worker terms by dividing by N. Note that capital is the variable input, while labor is fixed at 4 units. The marginal product of capital is shown in column 4, the capital labor ratio in column 5, output per worker in column 6, and the marginal product of capital per unit of labor in terms of output per unit of labor in column 7. Note that columns 4 and 7 are the same.

K	N	Y	$\Delta Y/\Delta K$	K/N	Y/N	$\Delta(Y/N)/\Delta(K/N)$
0	4	0	—	0	0	—
1	4	2.63	2.63	.25	.65	2.63
2	4	3.24	0.61	.5	.81	0.61
3	4	3.66	0.42	.75	.91	0.42
4	4	4.00	0.33	1	1.00	0.33
5	4	4.27	0.27	1.25	1.06	0.27
6	4	4.51	0.24	1.5	1.12	0.24
7	4	4.73	0.21	1.75	1.18	0.21
8	4	4.92	0.19	2	1.23	0.19
9	4	5.10	0.17	2.25	1.27	0.17
10	4	5.26	0.16	2.5	1.31	0.16
11	4	5.41	0.15	2.75	1.35	0.15
12	4	5.56	0.14	3	1.39	0.14

returns to scale production function *when one allows all inputs to change proportionally.* If we triple all the inputs, we triple the output, and so on. Always remember, though, that if one input is held fixed then we have diminishing returns, which occur even for a constant returns to scale production function, as can be seen in Figures 18–1 and 18–2.

In addition to the intuitive attractiveness of constant returns to scale, a useful feature of these production functions is that we can rewrite them in terms of output per worker or output per capita, and when we do so we find that output per worker is a function of capital input per worker. For the Cobb-Douglas case, we can write output per worker as[5]

---

[5]In the Cobb-Douglas production function we have $Y = AK^aN^b$. Dividing both sides by N, we get $Y/N = (AK^aN^b)/N = AK^aN^{b-1} = A(K/N)^aN^{a+b-1}$. If there are constant returns to scale, then $a + b = 1$, and $Y/N = A(K/N)^a$, and output per capita is a function of the capital stock per capita. Note, however, that without constant returns to scale, per worker output cannot be written as a function of only capital per worker K/N. Finally, note that we could transform everything into output per unit of capital instead of output per unit of labor.

FIGURE 18–4
Production Function, Output
Per Worker

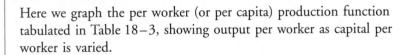

Here we graph the per worker (or per capita) production function tabulated in Table 18–3, showing output per worker as capital per worker is varied.

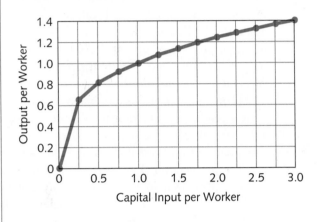

$Y/N = A(K/N)^a$.

As an example of writing a constant returns to scale production function in per capita terms, we can reconsider our earlier example from Table 18–1, in which labor was fixed at 4 units and capital varies from 0 to 12 units. Output is determined by the production function,

$Y = K^{.3} N^{.7}$,

or, in terms of output per worker:

$Y/N = (K/N)^{.3}$.

In Table 18–3, we not only show the inputs of capital and labor and the resulting output, but we also calculate the capital to labor ratio K/N and output per worker Y/N. Thus, we have an initial level of capital of 0, and labor is 4, so the capital-labor ratio is 0. Output is also 0 (since $Y = 0^{.3} 4^{.7} = 0$), as is output per worker.

What happens when capital rises to 1 unit? Now output is 2.63 units ($Y = 1^{.3} 4^{.7} = 2.63$). The capital-labor ratio is 1/4 or .25, and output per worker is 2.63/4 = .65. Notice that we could have calculated per worker output directly, as $Y/N = (1/4)^{.3}$, and this would also give us output per worker as .6598.

We graph output per worker against capital per worker in Figure 18–4. Notice that the production function has the usual Neoclassical shape, even though it is in terms of output per worker and capital input per worker. As the capital stock increases while labor inputs stay constant, capital per worker rises, and so does output per worker. However, increases in capital per worker bring forth increases in output per worker, but at an ever-declining rate. This is the law of diminishing returns at work, just as we saw in Table 18–2 and Figure 18–4. In fact, it turns out that the marginal product of capital per worker for the output per worker production function is the same as the marginal product of capital calculated for the production function from Table 18–1. This can be seen in Table 18–3, where we calculate both the marginal product of capital $\Delta Y/\Delta K$ and the marginal product of capital per unit of labor in terms of output per unit of labor, or $\Delta(Y/N)/\Delta(K/N)$. These two columns are identical.

The main point of this discussion of constant returns to scale is that we can write a production function with constant returns to scale in per capita terms, a property that will be put to good use in our future discussion. In fact, from this point forward we will consider that we have already transformed our production function $Y = A K^a N^{1-a}$ into per capita terms as $Y/N = A (K/N)^a$. Moreover, in order to simplify notation we will define output per worker as y, so $y = Y/N$, and capital per worker as k, so $k = K/N$. Our production function in per capita terms is

$$y = A k^a.$$

With $A = 1$ and $a = .3$, this is the production function graphed in Figure 18–4 and tabulated in Table 18–3. This example is representative of all such production functions, however, and Figure 18–5 provides a graph of such a production function.

This production function looks typical of the usual Neoclassical production function, even those not written in per capita terms. For instance, if k is zero, output is zero. That is, some capital is essential to production. Labor alone cannot produce output. As k increases, output increases, but at a diminishing rate. This is due to diminishing returns. If we hold labor fixed, then increases in capital just increase k, and the law of diminishing returns dictates that this will increase output at a decreasing rate. For the case we show in Figure 18–5, increases in k eventually cause almost no change in output per capita y, but we do not have decreases in y. That is, this is not an example of the production relationship between land and fertilizer. In that case, eventually there would be actual decreases in output per acre as fertilizer per acre increased.

Finally, remember that the slope of the production function in Figure 18–5 is the marginal product of capital—the increase in per capita output from an increase in the per capita capital stock. We show this at point A, where the slope of the production function—at a per capita capital stock of k_A—tells us the marginal product of capital per worker. Increases in k lead to a lower slope of the production function, indicating a lower marginal product of capital.

This, then, provides the essential supply side of the Solow growth model. We have left for later discussion the issues of the growth rate of the labor force, and issues of the rate at which capital wears out—the depreciation rate. The astute reader will also have noticed that this model makes no distinction between the labor force and population. In essence, we have assumed that the

FIGURE 18-5
The Typical Shape of the
Per-Worker Production
Function.

A typical per capita production function is shown in this graph. Output per capita $y = Y/N$ is a function of capital per capita $k = K/N$. As capital increases with labor fixed k increases, which increases output along the production function $f(k)$. Note that the decreasing slope of the production function indicates the presence of decreasing returns to capital, with further increases in the capital-labor ratio bringing almost no increase in output per capita.

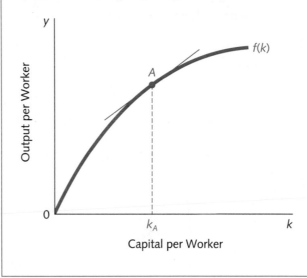

labor force is some fixed fraction of the population, so that there is no operative labor force participation decision. We might as well say that the labor force is equivalent to the population, since the analysis is unaltered. Issues of changing labor force participation rates are not addressed in the Solow growth model.

Demand in Solow's Neoclassical Growth Model

The demand side of the Solow growth model is fairly simple. There is no government sector and no foreign sector. All output is divided up between consumption and investment spending, so we have that

$$Y = C + I.$$

We can write this in per capita terms by dividing both sides by employment, to obtain

$$y = Y/N = C/N + I/N. \qquad (18.3)$$

Thus, output per worker is divided into consumption spending per worker and investment spending per worker.

The above looks at the division of total output into two categories of spending, consumption and investment. An alternative is to look at how households dispose of this income. There are no taxes and no imports, so consumers can either use their income to consume, or use it to save. Thus, we have the relationship for households that

$$Y = C + S.$$

In the Solow growth model, consumption and saving are modeled as fixed fractions of output, so that

$$C = cY$$

and

$$S = sY,$$

where c is the marginal propensity to consume out of income, s is the marginal propensity to save out of income, and $c + s = 1$.

On a per worker basis, saving can be written as

$$S/N = s(Y/N) = sy. \tag{18.4}$$

Similarly, per capita consumption can be written as

$$C/N = (1 - s)(Y/N) = (1 - s)y.$$

In Table 18–4 we provide an example of per capita output and how it is divided among consumption and saving. We have used the production function presented earlier in Figure 18–2. We calculate output per worker, and then we calculate saving per worker and consumption per worker by assuming that saving is 20 percent of income ($s = .2$), and consumption is 80 percent of income, ($c = .8$). We also graph output per worker, consumption per worker, and saving per worker as functions of the capital-labor ratio in Figure 18–6. Notice, for example, that when the capital-labor ratio is 1, output per worker is also 1, which gets divided into consumption of .8 units of output per worker and saving of .2 units of output per worker.

So far we have found that output gets divided between consumption and investment spending, $Y = C + I$ and that households divide up income into consumption and saving. In equilibrium, these two alternative ways of looking at income must be the same, which means that $C + S = C + I$, or that saving equals investment. In per capita terms, this equilibrium condition is written as $I/N = S/N$. Further, we will regard investment and saving as always in equilibrium. Thus, our graphs of output and saving are equivalently graphs of output and investment. In fact, because consumption is just output minus saving (which is also output minus investment) we will just plot output and investment. Consumption is then given by the distance between output and investment. This is illustrated in Figure 18–7. At a given value of the capital-labor ratio, such as k_0, output per worker is y_0, which is divided into

TABLE 18 – 4

Output, Consumption, and Saving Per Worker $Y/N = (K^{.3}N^{.7})/N = (K/N)^{.3}$ $S/N = .2\ Y/N.\ C/N = .8\ Y/N$ Case of Labor Is Fixed at $N = 4$

In the Solow model, output per worker (Y/N) is divided into consumption per worker (C/N) and saving per worker (S/N). Using the production function with labor fixed at 4 units, this table shows output per worker, saving per worker, and consumption per worker, as the capital stock is increased from 0 to 20 units. We have assumed that workers save a constant proportion of income, 0.20, and consume a constant proportion of income, 0.80. This can be seen by looking at row 5 of the table across each column. Capital and labor both equal 4 units, the capital-labor ratio is 1 unit, and output is also 1 unit. Workers save .2 units of this output and consume .8 units. Note that consumption is simply output minus saving.

K	N	k = K/N	y = Y/N	s/N = s y/N	c/N = c y/N
0	4	0	0	0	0
1	4	.25	.65	.13	.52
2	4	.5	.81	.16	.64
3	4	.75	.91	.18	.73
4	4	1.00	1.00	.20	.80
5	4	1.25	1.06	.21	.85
6	4	1.5	1.12	.22	.90
7	4	1.75	1.18	.23	.94
8	4	2.00	1.23	.24	.98
9	4	2.25	1.27	.25	1.02
10	4	2.5	1.31	.26	1.05
11	4	2.75	1.35	.27	1.08
12	4	3.00	1.39	.27	1.11
13	4	3.25	1.42	.28	1.13
14	4	3.5	1.45	.29	1.16
15	4	3.75	1.48	.29	1.18
16	4	4	1.51	.30	1.21
17	4	4.25	1.54	.30	1.23
18	4	4.5	1.57	.31	1.25
19	4	4.75	1.59	.31	1.27
20	4	5.00	1.62	.32	1.29

FIGURE 18-6
Per Worker Output,
Consumption, and Saving

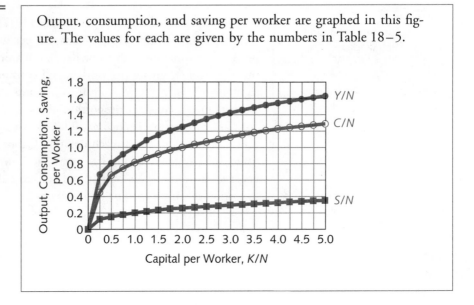

Output, consumption, and saving per worker are graphed in this figure. The values for each are given by the numbers in Table 18-5.

saving (or investment) and consumption. To calculate consumption, we just take the difference between output and investment. This is marked as $(C/N)_0$ in Figure 18-7, and is the vertical distance between the per capita production function and the per capita saving and investment function.

We have now described how the capital-labor ratio determines output and investment. However, we have not said how the capital-labor ratio is determined. For this, we need to consider two additional features, the depreciation of the capital stock and the growth of the labor force.

Changes in the Capital Stock and Depreciation

The final element in our discussion of the Solow growth model is to discuss *elements other than investment* that tend to change the capital-labor ratio over time. For this, we have to talk both about forces that lead to increases in the capital stock relative to the level of employment and forces that tend to reduce the capital stock relative to employment.

We first look at *depreciation*. Each year some of the capital stock in an economy is used up or wears out in the process of producing goods and services. This is depreciation, and it is a technological factor that reduces the capital stock over time. Unless offset by purchases of additional capital, depreciation will tend to reduce the capital stock and hence the capital-labor ratio.

We also look at growth in the labor force. So far we have been assuming that the labor force was constant, and that variations in the capital-labor ratio were caused by changes in the capital stock. However, it is also useful to consider labor force growth. Labor force growth, for a given capital stock, will reduce the ratio of capital to labor.

FIGURE 18-7
Output, Consumption, and
Saving Per Worker

The fact that consumption per worker is simply output per worker minus saving per worker is illustrated in this graph. We have left out the consumption per worker curve. At the capital-labor ratio of k_0, investment and saving per worker are equal to $(S/N)_0$ or, equivalently $(I/N)_0$, while consumption per worker is equal to output per worker $(Y/N)_0$ minus saving per worker $(C/N)_0$.

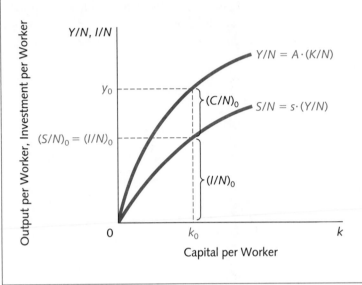

DEPRECIATION

For the depreciation effect, we simply assume that capital wears out at a constant rate, which we call the depreciation rate δ. For instance, if $\delta = 5$ percent, then each year 5 percent of the capital stock wears out. That is, the capital stock declines in size by δK each year. What does this mean for the capital-labor ratio? For a fixed labor force, depreciation reduces not just the capital stock but also the capital-labor ratio. The decline in the capital-labor ratio due to depreciation is $\delta K/L$, or just δk. This is graphed in Figure 18-8 as the straight line through the origin with slope δ. When $k = 0$, there is no capital to wear out, so depreciation is zero. As the capital-labor ratio increases, the amount of depreciation rises linearly.

GROWTH IN THE LABOR FORCE

The second factor leading to a reduction in the capital-labor ratio is labor force growth, or, if the participation rate is constant, just population growth. As the labor force grows, a given capital stock provides less and less capital per worker. In fact, the capital-labor ratio declines by the percentage growth rate of the labor force times the capital-labor ratio itself. If the labor force is growing at n

FIGURE 18–8
Depreciation and Labor Force
Growth

Depreciation of the capital stock lowers the capital-labor ratio, meaning that a certain amount of capital must be replaced each period to keep the capital-labor ratio at any given level. We have a single line, $(\delta + n)k$, which demonstrates the total fall in the capital-labor ratio due to increases in the labor force and depreciation of the capital stock by adding these two effects together. This line is called the investment line, since it shows how much investment is necessary to keep the capital-labor ratio constant, after accounting for reductions in the ratio due to depreciation and growth in labor.

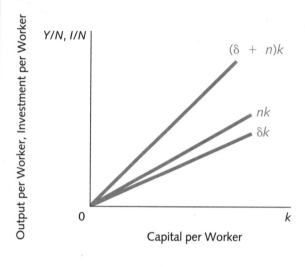

FIGURE 18–8
Depreciation and Labor Force Growth

percent per year, then the capital-labor ratio is falling by $n(K/N) = nk$, where n is the labor force growth rate.

Figure 18–8 indicates this decline in the capital-labor ratio due to labor force growth by the line nk. If the capital-labor ratio is zero, then with zero capital the capital-labor ratio is zero regardless of labor growth. If the growth rate of the labor force were zero, or $n = 0$, then the capital-labor ratio would not diminish due to labor force growth. The higher the growth rate of the labor force, the faster the capital-labor ratio declines due to this factor.

Figure 18–8 also sums these two forces that cause a tendency for the capital-labor ratio to decline. Thus, we can consider both depreciation and labor force growth together as the line $(\delta + n)k$. This is the total reduction in the capital-labor ratio k that will occur due to depreciation and labor force growth. We should make clear in passing that while Figure 18–8 shows the labor growth rate n to be greater than the depreciation rate δ, there is no necessity that this be so. In fact, we would have a perfectly good model if $n = 0$.

INVESTMENT AND GROWTH IN THE CAPITAL-LABOR RATIO

The actual change in the capital-labor ratio depends on the strength of the force tending to increase the capital-labor ratio, I/N, and the strength of the forces tending to reduce the capital-labor ratio, $(\delta + n)k$. If investment is greater than the effect of depreciation and labor force growth, so $I/N > (\delta + n)k$, then the capital-labor ratio will grow. If investment is less than the effect of depreciation and labor force growth, so $I/N < (\delta + n)k$, then the capital-labor ratio will shrink. Finally, if investment just offsets the forces of depreciation and labor force growth, so $I/N = (\delta + n)k$, then the capital-labor ratio doesn't change. In this last case, investment adds just enough new capital to supply capital to the new workers who are hired due to labor force growth, and to make up for capital wearing out due to depreciation. Such a situation is called the **steady state,** since it occurs when the capital-labor ratio is steady, or unchanging. The steady state will be our long-run equilibrium.

> The **STEADY STATE** occurs when the economy reaches a capital-labor ratio that is stable, given the depreciation rate, the state of technology, the rate of growth of the labor force, and the saving rate.

Steady-State Equilibrium

As we indicated above, the steady state in the Solow growth model occurs when the capital-labor ratio is constant, and this occurs when investment per capita I/N equals the $(\delta + n)k$. We illustrate this graphically by combining Figures 18–7 and 18–8, as in Figure 18–9. On the horizontal axis of this figure we have the capital-labor ratio k and on the vertical axis we plot functions of k, including output $y = k^a$, investment $I/N = sk^a$, and the decline in k due to depreciation and labor force growth $(\delta + n)k$. Remember that the capital stock is constant when $sy = (\delta + n)k$, and this occurs at point A, at a capital-labor ratio of k^*. The capital-labor ratio k^* is the steady state capital-labor ratio, the level of k at which there is no net change in k due to investment, depreciation, or labor force growth. The steady-state value of output per capita is at point A', where we see that a capital-labor ratio of k^* brings forth output of y^*. Likewise, the steady-state level of investment (and saving) per capita is given by point A, or $(I/N)^*$. Finally, steady-state consumption is just the difference between steady-state output and steady state saving (or, equivalently, investment), so $(C/N)^* = y^* - (I/N)^*$, the distance between points A and A'.

We have argued that k^* is a steady-state equilibrium. What forces will tend to bring the economy to this steady-state equilibrium? What forces drive k to k^*? We illustrate these in Figure 18–10. For instance, consider k_L, a value of the capital-labor ratio lower than the steady-state value k^*. At k_L, the forces of depreciation and labor force growth tend to reduce k by $(\delta + n)k_L$, as shown by point B. Meanwhile, the force of investment tends to increase k by $(I/N)_L$, as given by point C. On net, the additional capital due to investment is larger than capital required just to counter depreciation and labor force growth, so the capital-labor ratio grows. This can be seen by looking at the

FIGURE 18–9
Determination of Steady-State
Equilibrium

This diagram combines the investment per worker line, the output per worker line, and the saving per worker line. Where the capital-labor ratio is equal to k^*, output per worker y^* is given by point A' on the production per worker line, while investment per worker $(I/N)^*$ for k^* is given by point A on the saving per worker line. The difference between points A' and A, is equal to consumption per worker $(C/N)^*$.

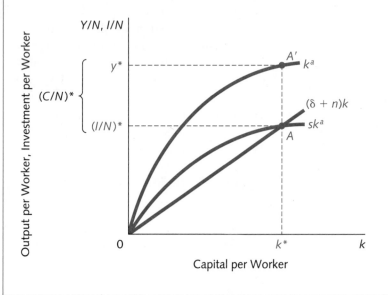

difference between investment and the sum of depreciation and labor force growth $(I/N)_L - (\delta + n)k_L$, which is positive. With a capital-labor ratio of k_L, investment in new capital adds to the capital-labor ratio faster than depreciation and labor force growth reduces the capital-labor ratio, and thus the capital-labor ratio tends to increase. This increase will continue as long as $(I/N) > (\delta + n)k$, which holds for all k between zero and k^*. Of course, when the capital-labor ratio is equal to the steady-state value k^* then the capital-labor ratio does not change.

What about levels of the capital-labor ratio above k^*? The example given in Figure 18–10 is k_U. At k_U, the forces tending to reduce the capital-labor ratio are given by $(\delta + n)k_U$, as shown by point D. The forces tending to increase the capital-labor ratio are given by $(I/N)_U$, as shown by point E. Here $(I/N)_U < (\delta + n)k_U$, so the forces tending to reduce the capital-labor ratio are stronger than the force of investment, and the capital-labor ratio will decline. Moreover, the capital-labor ratio will decline for all values of the capital-labor ratio greater than the steady-state value k^*.

We have found that when the capital-labor ratio is below or above the steady-state level, economic forces will lead to a change in the capital-labor ratio

FIGURE 18–10
Adjustment to the Steady-
State

The steady state level of the capital-labor ratio is k^*, denoted by point A. At points to the right of k^*, saving per worker will be less than the combination of labor force growth and capital depreciation and the capital-labor ratio will fall toward k^*. At points to the left of k^*, saving per worker is greater than that needed to replace capital because of depreciation and labor force growth, so the capital-labor ratio rises toward k^*.

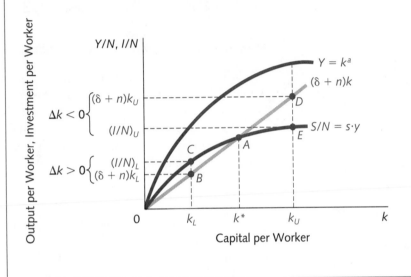

toward the steady-state level. We have also described the steady-state equilibrium. One important feature is that, in the absence of technical change, an economy in the steady state will not experience any change in either the capital-labor ratio k^* or in per capita output $A(k^*)^a$. Thus, the Neoclassical growth model cannot explain growing per capita output except by technical change, represented by changes in the parameter A. We will say more about this later in this chapter.

Determinants of the Steady-State Equilibrium

In any analysis of equilibrium, we are interested not only in a description of the equilibrium and the economic forces leading to that equilibrium, but also in factors that can cause the equilibrium to change. In supply and demand analysis, we describe the equilibrium as the intersection of supply and demand, and we explain how excess supply or demand will lead to price adjustments that lead to the equilibrium. Then we turn to an explanation of the determinants of supply and demand, to see how changes in these determinants will lead to shifts in supply or demand and hence to a change in the equilibrium. Similarly, in our growth model we want to know what factors will lead to a shift from one steady-state equilibrium to another, and how this will change the steady-state capital-labor ratio and the level of output per worker.

Three sets of factors can lead to a change in the steady-state equilibrium in our growth model: The first is an increase in either the depreciation rate δ or the rate of labor force growth n. These factors both tend to reduce the capital-labor ratio. The second is a change in the marginal propensity to save s. The third is technological change, which we model with the parameter A in the production function. We will consider each of these in turn.

CHANGES IN DEPRECIATION OR LABOR FORCE GROWTH

Both δ and n, depreciation and the labor force growth rate, tend to cause the capital-labor ratio to decline, so an increase in either will cause the capital-labor ratio to tend to decline at a faster rate. We illustrate the effects of an increase in these factors in Figure 18–11. The initial level of depreciation and labor force growth is $(\delta + n)_0$, which gives the line indicating this effect for different levels of the capital-labor ratio as $(\delta + n)_0 k$. The initial steady state is at point

FIGURE 18–11
An Increase in the
Depreciation Rate

What happens if either the labor force growth rate or the depreciation rate of capital increases? An increase in either n or δ shifts up the investment line from $(\delta + n)_0 k$ to $(\delta + n)_1 k$. If the economy is originally at the steady-state, with a capital-labor ratio of k_0^*, the increase in $(\delta + n)k$ will mean that the saving per worker will no longer support this capital-labor ratio. The capital-labor ratio will begin to decline until it reaches the new steady-state capital-labor ratio of k_1^*.

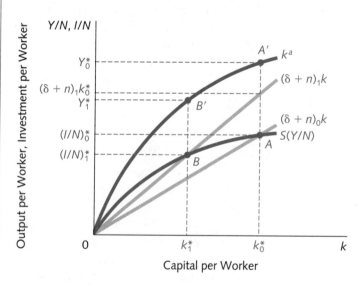

A, where this line intersects the investment curve. The steady-state capital-labor ratio is k_0^*. Initial steady-state per capita output is y_0^*, given by point A', and the steady state level of investment is $(I/N)_0^*$.

The increase in the depreciation rate and the rate of labor force growth will shift the line indicating the effect on the capital-labor ratio to $(\delta + n)_1 k$. The new steady state is then where this line intersects the investment curve, at point *B*, where the steady-state capital-labor ratio is k_1^*. The new steady state output is given at point B′ as y_1^*, and steady-state investment is given at point *B* as $(I/N)_1^*$.

To summarize, an increase in either the depreciation rate or the growth rate of the labor force will lower the steady-state capital-labor ratio, lower per capita output, and lower per capita investment (and saving). Thus, anyone interested in increasing per capita output would advocate taking steps to reduce depreciation of capital or to reduce labor force growth rates. In particular, there is an implication that reducing the labor force growth rate, or the population growth rate, can increase the steady state capital-labor ratio and the steady state level of output per capita.

CHANGES IN THE SAVING RATE

The saving rate *s* determines the proportion of output saved, which is also the proportion invested. This is the proportion of output used to create new capital. Saving and investment tend to increase the capital stock and hence cause the capital-labor ratio to rise. An increase in *s*, the proportion of output saved and turned into new capital, will cause the capital-labor ratio to increase at a faster rate.

We illustrate the effect of an increase in the saving rate *s* in Figure 18–12. The saving rate is initially s_0, and the initial steady state is determined by the intersection of the saving curve $s_0 k^a$ and the line representing depreciation and labor force growth $(\delta + n)k$. This occurs at point *A*, and determines both the initial steady-state capital-labor ratio k_0^* and the steady-state per capita output level y_0^*. The corresponding level of investment per capita is $(I/N)_0^*$.

What happens when the saving rate increases to s_1? The saving curve shifts up, to $s_1 k^a$. At the original capital-labor ratio k_0^* saving and investment is now given by point A'', which is above the amount of capital needed to replace depreciation and supply capital for new workers. This increase in investment leads to an increase in the capital-labor ratio. The new steady-state is determined at point *B*, where the new saving curve intersects the line indicating depreciation and labor force growth. The new steady state capital-labor ratio is k_1^*, and steady-state output is found at point B′ as y_1^*. Steady-state investment is then given at point B as $(I/N)_1^*$. The increase in the saving rate has increased the steady-state capital-labor ratio, increased per capita output, and increased per capita investment and saving. Thus, anyone interested in increasing per capita output should want to do something to increase the rate of saving in the economy. In closed economies, this can occur

FIGURE 18–12
An Increase in the Saving
Rate

What happens to the steady-state capital-labor ratio if the saving rate increases? An increase in the saving rate from s_0 to s_1 shifts up the saving per worker function from $s_0(Y/K)$ to $s_1(Y/K)$. With the original steady state at k_0^*, this increase in saving per worker implies that the economy can now support a higher capital-labor ratio k_1^*, where the new saving function intersects the $(\delta + n)k$ line at point B. Since the saving per worker at k_0^* is denoted by A'', it is greater than the amount necessary to keep the capital-labor ratio constant. Therefore, the capital-labor ratio increases toward its new steady state, k_1^*.

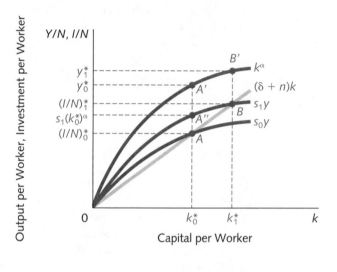

by increasing either private saving or public saving (e.g., by reducing the government budget deficit), although we don't explicitly model public saving here. Policies might also be enacted to encourage private saving, such as taxing consumption more than saving, or reducing taxes on interest and dividend earnings on accumulated savings.

CHANGES IN TECHNOLOGY

The production function determines how much output and for a given saving rate, how much saving and investment the economy generates at each capital-labor ratio. Increases in the production function that generate more output for each capital-labor ratio will also generate more saving and investment, and hence tend to cause the steady-state capital-labor ratio to increase. For pedagogical reasons we will analyze only what is called neutral

FIGURE 18–13
An Increase in Technology

Suppose the economy is initially at steady state A, with the capital-labor ratio of k_0^*. The initial production function is $y = A_0 k^a$, and the corresponding saving function is $I/N = s A_0 k^a$. A positive change in technology shifts the production function up to $y = A_1 k^a$, and the saving function up to $I/N = s A_1 k^a$. The new steady state is given by the intersection of the new saving function and the $(\delta + n)k$ line at point B. The new steady-state capital-labor ratio is k_1^*. Output, saving, and consumption per worker are all higher after the technological change.

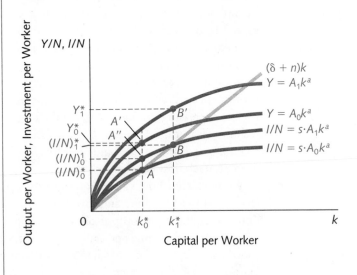

technological change, change that does not tend to change the capital-labor ratio *at a given level of output*.[6]

We illustrate a change in technology in Figure 18–13. The production function changes from $y = A_0 k^a$ to $y = A_1 k^a$, where A_1 is greater than A_0. The increase in A is an increase in technology that leads to more output per capita at every level of the capital-labor ratio—making this form of technical change neutral. (That is, if the capital-labor ratio is fixed, output will rise but will not lead to a change in the capital-labor ratio.)

---

[6]There are many types of changes in the production function that can be considered, and technological change can take many forms. Three of interest are technological change that is neutral (that does not affect the capital-labor ratio at a given level of output); technological change that is labor saving (that tends to increase the capital-labor ratio at a given level of output); and technological change that is labor using (that tends to lower the capital-labor ratio at a given level of output).

The initial steady state is at point A, where the saving schedule sA_0k^a intersects the line $(\delta + n)k$. The initial steady-state capital-labor ratio is k_0^*, and output is y_0^* as indicated by point A'. Finally, the initial steady-state level of investment is $(I/N)_0^*$.

Now consider the increase in technology, so that A_0 increases to A_1. This is shown in Figure 18–13 as the upward shift in the production function to $y = A_1k^a$, and the accompanying upward shift in the saving curve. At the initial steady state, the increase in the saving curve means that saving and investment are given by $(I/N)_0'$, as indicated by point A'', while depreciation and labor force growth are given by $(\delta + n)k_0^*$ at point A. This increase in investment over the sum of depreciation and labor force growth means that the capital-labor ratio will rise. Indeed, it will rise until the new steady-state is reached, at point B, where the capital-labor ratio is k_1^*, output is y_1^*, and investment is $(I/N)^*_1$. The increase in technology has increased the steady-state capital-labor ratio, increased per capita output, and increased per capita investment and saving. Thus, anyone interested in increasing per capita output (i.e., in increasing productivity) should advocate policies that tend to speed up technological improvements. Such policies as encouraging investment in new technology, exploration, and research and development are all ways to promote technical change.

We have seen how various occurrences can alter the long-run equilibrium level of output per capita and investment per capita. Moreover, since consumption per capita is just output per capita minus investment per capita (because investment and saving per capita are always equal), we could return to the above analysis and ask what happens to consumption per capita in each case. Unfortunately, the answer is not so straightforward. We can say with confidence that an increase in the saving rate will increase per capita output, but it is not always true that this will also lead to an increase in per capita consumption. Since it is maximum consumption per capita, and not maximum output per capita, that is most often seen as an economic goal to be analyzed in the Solow growth model, it behooves us to analyze what conditions would lead to the attainment of this goal. In particular, what is the optimal level of the capital-labor ratio that will yield the largest steady-state value of consumption per capita? To answer this question, we turn to the next section and a discussion of the **golden rule.**

The GOLDEN RULE is the dictum to choose the capital-labor ratio such that consumption per worker in the steady state is maximized.

The Golden Rule of Capital Growth

The golden rule level of capital per worker is the level that yields the highest per capita consumption, given the depreciation rate, the state of technology, and the rate of labor force growth. We want to change the saving rate s in such a way as to maximize per capita consumption. Finally, we will show that maximizing per capita consumption is *not* the same as maximizing per capita income. We will demonstrate the folly of maximizing income per capita, in that the maximum per capita income is achieved with per capita consumption of zero.

In order to find the golden rule level of the capital-labor ratio, consider Figure 18–14. We graph the per capita production function $y = Ak^a$, and alternate saving functions of saving rate s_1 and saving rate s_2, The depreciation and labor force growth line is $(\delta + n)\,k$. Different values for the saving rate will determine different steady-state levels of the capital-labor ratio. These different steady-state capital-labor ratios will yield different per capita output and per capita saving, and hence different levels of per capita consumption, which is $C/N = y - S/N$.

First consider a savings rate of zero, or $s = 0$. In this case, the saving function is a horizontal line coincident with the horizontal axis. Households save none of their income. Because of this, investment—which is equal to saving—is also zero. The economy is not building any new capital. The capital-labor ratio shrinks toward zero. In fact, the steady-state capital-labor ratio is in this case exactly zero, as determined by the intersection of the saving function and the line $(\delta + n)k$. Further, output is zero, as is consumption. This is illustrated by point A in Figure 18–14, which is just the origin of the graph.

Next we consider a saving rate of s_1, which is greater than zero but less than s_2. For example, we could set $s_1 = .1$. So households would save 10 percent of income. Now the steady-state capital-labor ratio is k_1^*. Steady-state output per

FIGURE 18–14
The Saving Rate and
Consumption Per Worker

Different saving rates imply different steady-state levels of capital per worker and thus different levels of output and consumption per worker. Assume that the saving rate is equal to 1. In this case, everything that is produced is saved, consumption equals 0, and the economy has the greatest capital-labor ratio it can achieve k^*_{max}. Income per worker is maximized by k^*_{max}, but obviously this is not a very attractive situation, since consumption per worker is 0.

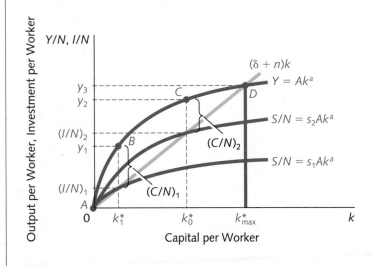

capita is $y_1 = A(k_1{}^*)^a$, and is marked by point B in Figure 18–16. Steady-state consumption is $(C/N)_1 = y_1 - (I/N)_1$. Note that the increase in the saving rate has actually increased both steady-state income and steady-state consumption, which were both zero at point A.

Our third case is a saving rate s_2, a number greater than s_1 but less than one. Perhaps $s_2 = .2$, so households save 20 percent of their income. Now the steady-state capital-labor ratio rises to $k_2{}^*$. Steady-state output per capita is $y_2 = A(k_2{}^*)^a$, marked by point C in Figure 18–14. Steady-state consumption is $(C/N)_2 = y_2 - (I/N)_2$. Note that the increase in the saving rate has increased both the steady-state capital-labor ratio and the steady-state level of per capita income. Has per capita consumption also increased? We have seen that per capita income has increased, but so has per capita saving, so we cannot tell if consumption per capita has increased or decreased. It depends which has increased more, income or saving. At low levels of the capital-labor ratio k, increases in k cause income to increase faster than saving. However, at high levels of the capital-labor ratio, increases in k can cause income to increase at a slower rate than saving. Consumption is maximized when additions to the capital-labor ratio change income by the same amount as saving. However, before we get to this point we want to consider one more saving rate.

The final saving rate we consider is $s = 1$. That is, consumers save all of their income. In this case, the saving schedule coincides with the production function. The steady-state capital-labor ratio is determined by the intersection of the saving schedule—the production function—with the line representing $(\delta + n)k$. We call this capital-labor ratio k_{max}, because it is the maximum possible capital-labor ratio for this economy. At k_{max}, output is $y_{max} = A(k_{max})^a$, as is saving. Consumption is zero, since all output is saved. Thus, the increase in the saving rate from s_2 to 1 increases both the steady-state capital-labor ratio and per capita income, but it reduces per capita consumption to zero. That is why we said that maximizing per capita income is not the same as maximizing per capita consumption. A saving rate of one maximizes per capita income, but makes consumption zero.

How, then, do we determine the actual level of the saving rate to maximize per capita consumption? To answer this question, we will want to consider how changes in the saving rate s impact per capita consumption and output. In Figure 18–14, notice that for our four saving rates, 0, s_1, s_2, and 1, we can find the steady-state level of saving along the line $(\delta + n)k$. For example, as the saving rate rose from s_1 to s_2, steady-state saving and investment rose from $(I/N)_1$ to $(I/N)_2$ on the line $(\delta + n)k$. Then consumption per capita is just the distance between this line and the production function.

Now consider Figure 18–15, where we graph the production function and the line $(\delta + n)k$. Our discussion of saving rates has already demonstrated that any capital-labor ratio between zero and $k^*{}_{max}$ can be achieved by varying the saving rate from zero to one. Which saving rate will maximize consumption per capita? We illustrate several alternative levels of the steady-state capital-labor ratio in Figure 18–15, and each will correspond to a different saving rate.

FIGURE 18-15
The Golden Rule

A saving rate of s_1 corresponds to a steady-state capital per worker of k_1^*, and a consumption per capita of c_1. A saving rate of s_2 yields a slightly higher level of steady-state capital per worker k_2^*, and greater consumption per capita of c_2. An even higher saving rate generates a steady-state capital per worker level of k^{**}, and the golden rule consumption per capita of c_{max}. This is the golden rule capital-labor ratio because a higher or lower capital-labor ratio leads to lower consumption. At k_3^* too much is being saved, reducing steady-state consumption per worker.

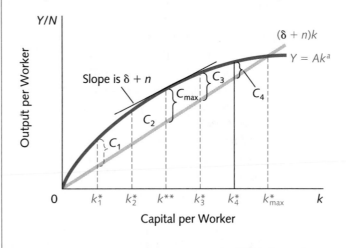

These capital-labor ratios vary from zero to k^*_{max}. Beginning with a saving rate of zero, $s = 0$, we have a steady-state capital-labor ratio of zero. As we increase the saving rate, the steady-state capital-labor ratio rises above zero. For example, we assume that the saving rate is s_1. This implies a steady-state capital-labor ratio of k_1^*. Then consumption per capita is $(C/N)_1$. If we increase the saving rate more, to s_2, the steady-state capital-labor ratio is k_2^*, and consumption per capita is $(C/N)_2$. As we keep increasing the saving rate, eventually we increase the saving rate to a value we call s^{**}, which gives a steady-state capital-labor ratio of k^{**}, and consumption per capita of $(C/N)_{max}$. This will be the maximum amount of consumption per capita, and it occurs where the slope of the per capita production function is just equal to the slope of the line $(\delta + n)k$, which is $(\delta + n)$. Since the slope of the per capita production function is just the marginal product of capital, this condition for the largest amount of consumption per capita is that the marginal product of capital is equal to the rate of depreciation plus the rate of labor force growth.

At k^{**}, the marginal product of capital is equal to $(\delta + n)$. This is a steady state, so that saving per capita (i.e., investment per capita) is just sufficient to offset the effects of depreciation and labor force growth and therefore keep the capital-labor ratio constant. But it is a special steady state, called the golden rule, because the marginal product of capital is equal to $(\delta + n)$. This condition means that the additional output from increasing the capital-labor ratio, the marginal product of capital, is just equal to the additional investment required to maintain the steady state, which is $(\delta + n)$, the sum of depreciation plus labor force growth. When this happens, consumption, the difference between output and investment, stays constant.

As the saving rate is increased beyond s^{**}, say to s_3, the steady-state capital-labor ratio rises above k^{**}, to k_3^*. Output per capita also increases, to y_3, but saving increases more, so that consumption per capita falls to $(C/N)_3$, which is less than $(C/N)_{\max}$. The increase in the saving rate above s^{**} has increased income per capita, but reduced consumption per capita.

If we increase the saving rate further, to s_4 or so $s = 1$, the steady-state capital-labor ratio increases further, to k_4^* or to $k^*_{\max}$, respectively. Again, output per capita increases as the capital-labor ratio increases, but saving per capita increases more, so that consumption per capita falls to $(C/N)_4$ or to 0, respectively.

What is the conclusion? First, maximizing consumption per capita and maximizing income per capita are not at all the same goal. Second, consumption per capita is maximized by choosing a capital-labor ratio so that the slope of the production function—the marginal product of capital—is just equal to the rate of depreciation plus labor force growth $(\delta + n)$. In this way, the additional gain in output from adding a unit of capital, the marginal product of capital, is just equal to the additional saving and investment required to maintain the capital-labor ratio constant. In other words, at k^{**}, very small increases or decreases in the capital-labor ratio will change both output and the saving required to keep the capital labor ratio at k^{**} by the same amount, keeping steady-state consumption constant. However, for any move away from k^{**}, changes in the capital-labor ratio will cause output and the required amount of saving to change by different amounts.

The value of the capital-labor ratio, which maximizes the steady-state level of consumption per capita, and which we have labeled k^{**}, is known as the golden rule. This golden rule capital-labor ratio can be achieved by choosing the appropriate saving rate, which we have labeled s^{**}, so that the saving schedule sy equals $(\delta + n)k$ at a capital-labor ratio of k^{**}. For the Solow growth model with given values for the depreciation rate, labor force growth rate, and level of technology, there is a single golden rule level of the capital-labor ratio, and there is a saving rate that will allow the economy to achieve this golden rule. Once the golden rule is achieved, the economy reaches the maximum possible level of consumption per capita, and no further increases in steady-state consumption per capita are possible without a change in depreciation, labor force growth, or a change in technology.

We have spent a large part of this chapter developing the theory of the Solow growth model. One thing that the theory has made clear is that an economy, once it gets to the steady state of its choice—and, in particular, once it gets to the golden rule level of the capital-labor ratio—will not experience any further growth in per capita income or consumption without technological changes or a change in the depreciation rate or rate of labor force growth. This is a strong prediction. Since the depreciation rate and labor force growth rate are taken as exogenous, and are not seen as changing very much or very often, the Solow growth model requires technological change for economic growth. Without technological change, the economy in the steady state will have a constant per capita income level.

To be concrete, consider the U.S. economy, which experiences growth in per capita income on the order of 1 or 2 percent per year. How does the Solow growth model explain this ongoing increase in per capita income? It may be that the United States is continually growing toward an unchanging golden rule value and hasn't quite gotten there yet after a mere 200 years of existence, but this strains credibility. In addition, the Solow growth model would predict that growth would slow as we get closer and closer to the steady state. Instead, the Solow growth model explains continued growth in per capita income in countries like the United States by ongoing improvements in technology. These improvements result in continual shifts in the production function and continual moves to higher and higher levels of both the capital-labor ratio and output per capita, with concurrent increases in per capita consumption. Thus, the Solow growth model relies on exogenous, unfamiliar, but intuitively plausible improvements in technology to explain continuing economic growth in developed nations such as the United States. How reasonable is this assumption? We turn to empirical evidence on this issue in the next section.

LABOR PRODUCTIVITY: THE 1970s, 1980s and 1990s

Over most of the 1970s and into the 1980s a "labor productivity problem" and its relationship to U.S. economic development occupied the attention of economists. Before concluding this chapter, let us turn briefly to the problem.

There are numerous measures of productivity, each depending on how employment and output are measured, but a popular one is real GDP per worker.[7] Labor productivity grew steadily from 1947 to 1969 on average, with high rates of increases in labor productivity in the early 1950s and again in the

---

[7]The analysis of productivity growth—that is, pinpointing the theoretical and actual causes of the growth in labor productivity—is somewhat complicated. Several excellent papers by John Tatom are accessible to readers of this book. See John A. Tatom, "Energy Prices and Capital Formation: 1972–77," Federal Reserve Bank of St. Louis *Review* 61 (May 1979), pp. 2–9; "The 'Problem' of Procyclical Real Wages and Productivity," *Journal of Political Economy* 88 (February 1980), pp. 385–94; and "The Productivity Problem," Federal Reserve Bank of St. Louis *Review* 61 (September 1979), pp. 3–16.

middle 1960s. From 1948 through 1969 the growth trend in real GDP per worker was about 2.4 percent per year, but from 1970 to 1980 the growth trend in this statistic approximated *zero*! From 1981 through 1990, growth in real GDP per worker was again positive, and averaged 1.2 percent, somewhat less than the 1947–1969 period, but greater than the 1970–1980 period. The behavior of real GDP per worker can be seen in Figure 18–16. It is apparent that there have been times of rapid increases in this measure of labor productivity, and other times, such as the middle to late 1950s, and again in the 1970s, when this measure did not change much at all.

The behavior of this measure of productivity in the 1970s is particularly difficult to explain. Economists have believed that labor productivity is related to fluctuations in the business cycle. Growth in labor productivity slows down during recessions and speeds up during expansions. (There are various explanations for this phenomenon.) Unfortunately, the cyclical explanation does not fit well with the data for the 1970s. There was a severe recession in the period 1973–1975, but productivity was essentially constant from well before that recession until well after it was over, or from about 1969 to 1981. Adding to the intrigue is that this productivity slowdown was a worldwide phenomenon in the industrialized countries, although the magnitude of the slowdown did vary from country to country.

There are several possible and plausible explanations for the lack of growth in labor productivity in the 1970s, and some of these can help explain the

FIGURE 18–16
Labor Productivity, 1947–1990 (Real GDP per Worker, in 1987 Dollars)

This figure demonstrates the growth in labor productivity from 1947 to the present. Note that real GDP per worker in constant dollars rose rapidly during the 1950s and 1960s but slowed down during the late 1960s to the early 1980s. Economists have had difficulty explaining the slowdown of labor productivity during the early 1970s.

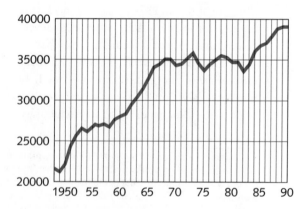

SOURCES: U.S. Department of Commerce, Bureau of Economic Analysis, and U.S. Department of Labor, Bureau of Labor Analysis.

slower growth during the 1980s than during the period 1947–1969. One explanation is the rate of capital formation. There was a slowdown in the rate of growth in the capital stock per worker during the 1970s. During the 1970s the rate of capital formation per worker was .6 percent, compared with an average of 2.9 percent during the 1950s and 1960s. Estimates of the impact of capital formation on labor productivity may *understate* that impact for two reasons: (1) the measures of capital stock may not account for that part of the stock which has been rendered obsolete through the sharp relative increase in the price of energy resources, and (2) pollution-abatement investments, though figured as part of new capital formation, do not produce "measured" output and do not tend to enhance labor productivity.

Explanations for reduced capital formation in the 1970s and the first few years of the 1980s are extremely varied and controversial. Among the favorite candidates were larger federal government deficits, inflation, the U.S. tax system, and the sharp rise in the price of energy due to the OPEC cartel. One of the complaints about the tax system is that the capital gains tax is not indexed to the inflation rate, so taxes are paid on nominal gains even when there are no real gains.

While other factors undoubtedly affected productivity, it is important to note that since capital formation is a major determinant of productivity growth, these (possible) factors—energy, government policies, and so on—may also have been the source of an explanation for reduced productivity growth in the U.S. economy. Some even argue that capital formation in the 1980s was also low and contributed to the relatively slow growth in productivity compared to the 1950s and 1960s and to other developed nations of the world over the 1980s. However, this view is not universally shared—see the Global Perspective on "U.S. Investment in the 1980s."

During the 1980s productivity grew much more than it did over the 1970s, but still it was slower than during the 1950s and 1960s. However, as the 1990s opened, productivity growth accelerated, and was well over 2 percent during 1992. It may be that the dismal growth in productivity in the 1970s is well behind us, and that future productivity growth may be nearer to the postwar average rate of 1.5 percent, or even the average rate of 2.4 percent that prevailed before the 1970s.

PROS AND CONS OF THE SOLOW GROWTH MODEL

The Solow growth model seems to work well in explaining the behavior of the U.S. economy and that of other well-developed countries, although some economists find the reliance on exogenous technological change to explain continuing growth in per capita income and consumption somewhat troubling. A bigger problem for the theory in terms of predictive ability is how it does in explaining the behavior of the underdeveloped or "poor" countries of

U.S. INVESTMENT

IN THE 1980s

There is quite a controversy over how to analyze U.S. investment in the 1980s. On one side of the controversy stand many economists who claim that the large budget deficits of this period crowded out domestic investment, so that the capital stock was not growing fast enough to sustain productivity growth at historical levels. Evidence of this crowding out is the high real interest rates of this period. According to this view, the decline in investment in the 1980s bodes ill for future U.S. economic growth. This is especially so, according to critics, when U.S. growth over the period is compared to other developed nations such as Japan or Germany.

An alternative view has been espoused by other economists, who argue that the tax reductions of the 1980s substantially boosted incentives to invest. Evidence of these large incentives to invest is the strong demand by foreigners to invest in the United States, which showed up as an appreciation of the dollar, and the high interest rates caused by the worldwide desire to invest in the United States.

Recently economist John Tatom at the Federal Reserve Bank of St. Louis has attempted to reconcile these views.[a] He argues that investment did *not* fall in the 1980s. In fact, there was an increase in investment in part because of the decline in the relative price of capital goods. Consider Figure 18–17, which plots both the GDP deflator and the deflator for investment expenditures. Dur-

FIGURE 18-17
Graph of GDP Deflator and the Implicit Price Deflator for Gross Investment

Economist John Tatom has argued that investment actually increased during the 1980s because of a fall in the relative price of capital goods. This figure indicates that the price of capital goods (measured by the implicit price deflator for investment) after 1981 did in fact fall, relative to the price of all other final goods and services (measured by the GDP deflator).

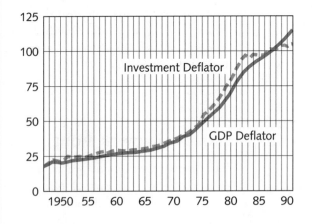

SOURCE: Department of Commerce, Bureau of Economic Analysis

ing the period 1975–1981, capital goods rose in price relative to the average price level in the economy, as indicated by the rise in the investment deflator relative to the GDP deflator. During the period after 1981, however, the deflator for capital goods increased very slowly relative to the GDP deflator, so the relative price of capital goods has fallen during this period, encouraging investment.

What about the level of investment itself? This can be seen in Figure 18–18, where we plot both nominal Gross Private Domestic Investment as a ratio of nominal GDP, and real Gross Private Domestic Investment as a ratio of real GDP. We expect these measures to be the same, but the big differences in the behavior of the price indices for GDP and for GPDI mean that the ratio of real GPDI to real GDP will give a truer indication of the relative size of investment. As can be seen in this graph, investment as a percent of GDP in real terms did not decline in the 1980s relative to earlier periods, with the exception of the large declines during the recessions of 1980 and 1981–82. (There is also a large decline during the recession of 1974–75.) In fact, we calculate the ratio of investment to GDP over presidential terms in Table 18–5, where we can see that the ratio of investment to GDP was not lower during the 1980s than over the period 1961–1990. In fact, it

FIGURE 18–18

Gross Private Domestic Investment as a Share of GDP Calculated as Nominal GPDI Divided by Nominal GDP, and Real GPDI Divided by Real GDP

If gross private investment actually did increase during the 1980s, then we should see its percentage of GDP, in real terms, increase relative to its nominal percentage of GDP during this time period. This is in fact indicated by the data in this graph. The ratio of investment to GDP in real terms is given by the dashed line, while the same ratio in nominal terms is indicated by the solid line. Because of the fall in the price of investment relative to other components of GDP, gross private domestic investment actually increased as a percent of GDP during the 1980s.

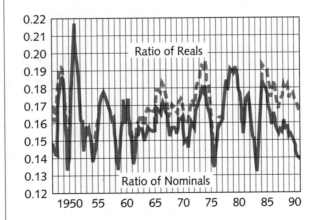

SOURCE: Department of Commerce, Bureau of Economic Analysis

was slightly higher, especially considering the fact that the early 1980s saw a severe recession that diminished investment relative to GDP, as do all recessions.

How can we explain the claims that investment fell during the 1980s? These claims are based on net investment, not gross investment. Table 18–5 also shows the ratio of net investment to real GDP, which did decline markedly in the 1980s. This is also apparent in Figure 18–19,

which plots gross private domestic investment and net private domestic investment as fractions of GDP. This graph show no obvious decline in gross investment as a percent of GDP, but does show a decline in net investment as a percent of GDP.

What can explain this disparity between gross and net investment? The difference between these two measures of investment is depreciation, and the fall in net investment is telling us that depreciation

increased during the 1980s. We might ask how this could happen. One reason could be that the capital stock suddenly began depreciating faster in the 1980s. Another reason could be that the mix of investment shifted toward purchases of capital that has a shorter life than it once did. For example, investment in equipment depreciates more quickly than investment in structures (e.g., factory buildings). One oft-cited example is the large investment in per-

TABLE 18–5
Gross and Net Private Domestic Investment as a Fraction of GDP

This table indicates that the claims that investment fell during the 1980s were based on net investment, which takes into account depreciation of capital, rather than gross investment. Net investment as a percentage of GDP, as indicated in the third column, did actually fall during this time period. But gross investment as a percentage of GDP rose, as indicated in the second column. This difference between gross and net investment during the 1980s may be attributed to investment in capital equipment, which depreciates more quickly.

YEARS	REAL GPDI/REAL GDP	REAL NPDI/REAL GDP
1961–1964	16.1%	7.0%
1965–1968	17.2%	8.4%
1969–1972	17.0%	7.5%
1973–1976	16.9%	6.7%
1977–1980	17.8%	7.1%
1981–1984	16.5%	4.5%
1985–1988	17.5%	5.4%
1989–1990	17.1%	4.4%
1961–1990	17.0%	5.6%

SOURCE: Department of Commerce, Bureau of Economic Analysis

sonal computers in the 1980s, an investment in a capital good that did not even exist in prior decades. Personal computers are assigned a high depreciation rate, and hence investment in these goods will be subject to a high depreciation rate. Of course, this should not be taken to mean that investment in a structure would have been preferable just because it has a lower depreciation rate. In addition, there is an interesting and unaddressed question of the way to measure investment in goods such as computers, which are innovating quickly. Those who purchased the original IBM PC for $5,000 or more in the early 1980s purchased a piece of equipment that depreciated quickly, especially compared to the frontier of computing power. It is highly likely that this PC is still usable, but also likely that few would want to use it, since 486 PC machines are now available for a fraction of the price of the original IBM PC. This rapid technological advance in the personal computer field means that measuring investment is a very interesting undertaking. How do you compare a $5,000 investment in an IBM PC in 1985 versus a $3,000 investment in a 486 PC today? Clearly the price has dropped even in nominal terms, but clearly the quality-adjusted price has dropped even more, by orders of magnitude if we use computing speed as our measure of quality.

The main point is that if investment shifted toward equipment in the 1980s, this would cause the capital stock to depreciate more quickly. Tatom shows that there has

FIGURE 18-19
Ratio of Gross Private Domestic Investment and Net Private Domestic Investment to GDP

This figure indicates that gross private domestic investment and net private domestic investment, both as a percentage of GDP, did behave differently during the 1980s. There is no obvious decline in gross investment as a percent of GDP, but there is a decline in net investment over this period.

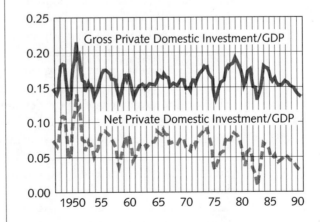

SOURCE: Department of Commerce, Bureau of Economic Analysis

been some move toward increased purchases of equipment relative to structures from 1963 through 1978, but there was a fall in this ratio through 1983, before it again began rising. Thus, equipment investment has generally been rising as a share of total investment and might explain some of the increase in depreciation. However, this does not appear to be the whole story. Another explanation is likely to be that the method of computing net investment is flawed. According to Tatom, the method of estimating depreciation in the national income and product accounts has not been adjusted since the 1940s. Denison and other students of investment have

stated preferences for working with the gross investment numbers just because of this.

Finally, what might this mean for productivity and for the capital-labor ratio? Has the capital-labor ratio declined? Tatom writes that the growth of the labor force slowed in the 1980s, from 2.7 percent per year during the period 1974–1979 to 1.7 percent from 1979 to 1988. This slowing in labor force growth means that some slowing in capital growth is possible while still maintaining the capital-labor ratio. Indeed, Tatom points out that the net nonresidential fixed capital stock grew at 3.2 percent from 1974 to 1979 and 2.9 percent from 1979 to 1988.

Coupled with the labor force growth numbers, this means that the capital labor ratio grew at .5 percent (3.2 percent − 2.7 percent) per year during the period 1974–1979, and 1.2 percent (2.9 percent − 1.7 percent) per year from 1979 to 1988. Thus, Tatom concludes that investment did not decline in the 1980s, and that if anything the growth in the capital labor ratio accelerated during this period. ❑

NOTE [a] John A. Tatom, "U.S. Investment in the 1980s: The Real Story," Federal Reserve Bank of St. Louis *Review* (March/April 1989), pp. 3–16.

the world. These nations have a production technology available to them that depends on the level of capital accumulation relative to the labor force, and on the state of technology. Obviously, poor nations have less capital and a lower state of technology than developed nations. The problem is not explaining why the poor nations are poor, but explaining why they *remain* poor. Presumably, they should be able to hasten their advancement by using the technological achievements already made by the developed nations. That is, poor nations do not have to develop the technology themselves, but can instead imitate the developments of the industrialized nations. Moreover, with a low capital-labor ratio, the marginal product of capital is very high in poor nations. This will cause high returns to capital in poor nations relative to developed nations, and should attract capital to the poor nations, further hastening their advance. In fact, without ongoing technological change in the developed nations, we should see the poor nations converging very quickly to the levels of per capita income that are achieved in the developed nations. Even with ongoing technological change, the poor nations should grow faster than the developed nations. The developed nations grow only with technological advance, while the poor nations grow with increases in the capital-labor ratio encouraged by higher returns to capital than in developed nations, and due to quicker technological advances fueled by the public availability at relatively low cost of the technological prowess originating from the developed nations. Thus, the Solow growth model predicts that the per capita income levels of developed and poor nations should be converging over time.

Unfortunately, this is at odds with the historical record. The difference in per capita output between the richest and poorest nations is larger now than it was a hundred years ago, and shows no sign of diminishing. Moreover, countries in relatively similar situations a hundred years ago now find themselves with vastly different levels of per capita income. Some countries such as Korea and Taiwan, two of the so-called Asian tigers, have experienced remarkable growth in per capita income over the last three decades. Other countries such as India have shown little change in per capita income relative to the growth rate of per capita income in the developed countries. The Solow growth model does little to explain these discrepancies. As Robert Lucas says, "The standard model is too egalitarian to fit the observed world."[8] The standard model predicts that poor nations will catch up with rich nations, that per capita incomes will converge over time, and that poor nations will experience faster growth than rich nations. These predictions are at odds with the real world.

MODERN GROWTH THEORY

To address the concerns expressed by Lucas and others about the standard growth models built around the Solow growth model, it is necessary to consider the basic underpinnings of the model in more detail. Basically, the Solow growth model begins with a standard production technology built around diminishing returns. That is, holding all inputs constant but one, an increase in the variable input will cause output to increase, but at a diminishing rate. Alternatively put, the marginal product of any one resource diminishes as use of that resource increases. In the Solow growth model, this shows up as a diminishing marginal product of capital. Growth in Solow's model is due to one of two factors: capital accumulation or technological change. Capital accumulation means accumulation of capital relative to labor, or increasing the ratio of capital to labor. But this increase in capital relative to labor is analogous to any increase in capital with labor constant. The production function exhibits

---

[8]"On the Mechanics of Economic Development," 1987 Nancy L. Schwartz Memorial Lecture, J. L. Kellogg Graduate School of Management, Northwestern University, p. 11.

diminishing returns, so increases in the capital-labor ratio will eventually produce less and less additions to output. Diminishing returns puts a natural barrier in the place of economic growth, a natural tendency for rich countries to grow more slowly than poor countries, since rich countries get less additional output per capita out of each unit of capital accumulation per worker.

Modern growth theory tries to get around this barrier to growth caused by diminishing returns. One way it does so is by stressing human capital as an input into production, in addition to physical capital and labor. Human capital can be an investment in ideas, ideas designed to increase future productivity. Attending school and learning new skills can be actions that improve human capital. They are investments not in physical capital but in the productivity of the person who gains these skills. Like investment in physical capital, current output is given up in exchange for greater future output. For example, attending college sacrifices the current income that could have been earned from working in the hopes that the skills and knowledge gained in college will increase future earnings. College training is investment in the productivity of a human being, and hence labeled human capital investment, but it shares several features with investment in physical capital. However, one difference is that the returns to human capital may not fall when human capital accumulates. With physical capital, adding more and more capital to a fixed quantity of labor inputs will result in smaller and smaller additions to output. Physical capital is subject to diminishing returns. Human capital, however, may not be so constrained. Adding more and more knowledge to a production process will cause output to rise, and the increase in output may not decrease as more and more human capital is applied to the production process. This approach is promising in several ways. First, it holds forth the promise of explaining at least in part the technological process that appears as an exogenous feature in the Solow growth model. Individuals have an incentive to invest in human capital, which can be thought of as increasing technology, represented by A in our production function $y = Ak^a$. Notice that holding capital and labor constant, and hence k constant, increases in A always yield the same marginal increase in output. Technology is not subject to diminishing returns. If human capital can be thought of as investing in technological improvement, it too may not be subject to diminishing returns.

A second issue is that, with different levels of investment in human capital across nations, there may well be different levels of long-run per capita income. There may be no tendency for per capita income levels to converge. This would explain real-world observations on the lack of convergence of growth rates across countries.

A third issue is the appropriate model of the nature of human capital. Human capital can be thought of as having characteristics of both a private good and a public good. As a private good, human capital accrues benefits only to the person possessing the human capital. The person owning the human capital can use the human capital, but he or she can exclude anyone else from using it, and his or her use would mean that no one else could use it. This feature makes human capital similar to private goods, such as a hamburger you are about to consume. You can exclude me from consuming it, and your consumption of it means that I cannot consume it. However, human capital also seems to have a special characteristic: even though one person uses it, it will still be available for others to use or enjoy. That is, your use of human capital does not preclude me from using it, giving human capital a characteristic in common with public goods. For example, consider national defense, perhaps the most frequently cited example of a public good. If it is provided, I get the benefit of it whether you want me to have it or not—it is not exclusive—and your enjoyment of it does not at all preclude me from getting the benefit of it—it is nonrival. Human capital shares one of these characteristics—it is exclusive, but nonrival.

The issue of human capital as a public or private good raises important issues for social policy, since public goods are supplied at inefficiently low levels by a competitive market. Social policy prescriptions for public goods are for the government to act to somehow encourage the provision of the public goods. Such encouragement often takes the forms of subsidies to producers of the public good. Thus, there is a case for subsidizing the attainment of human capital, such as education or other job training.

These issues are very much in a state of flux, but the debate over the so-called modern growth theory promises to add much to our understanding of economic growth and development. The economics profession can hope to gain a better understanding of economic growth and a better understanding of the persistent inequalities in per capita incomes among countries by the research being done in this area today. Issues under current scrutiny include increasing returns to scale due not just to human capital but to public capital (or infrastructure), health and education, and research and development efforts. Also important is the issue of property rights, and more importantly, intellectual property rights. These ongoing topics of research promise important and exciting ongoing developments in the study of growth theory.

SUMMARY

In this chapter, we first examined the growth performance of the U.S. economy from the 1960s to the mid-1980s. Next, we presented Neoclassical growth models with and without technological progress. We provided some empirical estimates of U.S. technological progress and of the sources of growth of potential real national income. We then focused on the labor productivity problem of the 1970s and the 1980s and discussed some of the possible causes for the lack of growth of labor productivity. Finally, we concluded with a review of modern growth theory, an approach to growth theory that stresses increasing returns to scale as the means of explaining several anomalies in the predictions of the Solow growth model.

KEY TERMS

disembodied technological change   golden rule

economic growth   steady state

embodied technical change

QUESTIONS FOR REVIEW AND DISCUSSION

1. Explain the expression "productive capacity of an economy." Does productive capacity have any bearing on economic growth?

2. Is there any difference between the potential level of GDP and the actual level of GDP?

3. What position has the Council of Economic Advisers under the Reagan, Bush and Clinton administrations taken toward economic growth in the 1980s and 1990s?

4. In the Neoclassical growth model, what must occur in an economy if labor productivity is to increase in the absence of technological progress?

5. Why might economists be more interested in the rate of growth of real output per worker than in the rate of growth of real output?

6. In the Neoclassical growth model, does an increase in the marginal propensity to save have any impact on the economy?

7. Give some possible explanations for the decline in labor productivity in the United States in the 1970s and 1980s.

8. What are some of the pros and cons of the Solow growth model?

PROBLEMS

1. Suppose that you are in charge of briefing President Clinton on the factors that would contribute to economic growth in the 1990s. Outline a set of factors. How would changes in labor productivity relate to your set of factors? Are there unforeseen factors—such as supply shocks—that could interfere with your projections? What are some of them?

2. Did supply-side economics contribute to a slight upturn in productivity in the 1990s?

SUGGESTIONS FOR FURTHER READING

Federal Reserve Bank of Kansas City. *Policies for Long-Run Economic Growth* Symposium, Jackson Hole, Wyoming, August 27-29, 1992.

Kahn, George A. "Sluggish Job Growth: Is Rising Productivity or an Anemic Recovery to Blame?" Federal Reserve Bank of Kansas City *Economic Review* (Third Quarter 1993), pp. 5-42.

Kennedy, Paul. *The Rise and Fall of the Great Powers: Economic Change and Military Conflict from 1500 to 2000.* New York: Random House, 1987.

Lucas, Robert E., Jr. "On the Mechanics of Economic Development," *Journal of Monetary Economics* 23 (1988), pp. 3–42.

Mankiw, N. Gregory, et al. "A Contribution to the Empirics of Economic Growth." *Quarterly Journal of Economics* (1992), pp. 407–37.

Romer, Paul. "Crazy Explanations for the Productivity Slowdown." *NBER Macroeconomics Annual* (1987), pp. 163–210.

Solow, Robert M. "A Contribution to the Theory of Economic Growth." *Quarterly Journal of Economics* 70 (February 1956), pp. 65–94.

Tatom, John A. "The 'Problem' of Procyclical Real Wages and Productivity." *Journal of Political Economy* 8 (February 1980), pp. 385–94.

_____. "U.S. Investment in the 1980s: The Real Story." Federal Reserve Bank of St. Louis *Review* (March/April 1989), pp. 3–16.

_____. "Should Government Spending on Capital Goods Be Raised?" Federal Reserve Bank of St. Louis *Review* (March/April 1991), pp. 3–16.

_____. "Public Capital and Private Sector Performance." Federal Reserve Bank of St. Louis *Review* (May/June 1991), pp. 3–16.

GLOSSARY

The *acceleration principle* is a theory which states that small changes in the demand for consumer goods can generate large changes in the demand for investment (capital) goods needed for their production.

The *actual currency-deposit ratio* is a certain percentage of demand deposits that moneyholders actually hold at a given point in time, which may not correspond to their wants or desired holdings.

The *actual reserve-deposit ratio* is a certain percentage of demand deposits that a financial institution such as a commercial bank holds in reserve at a given point in time.

Adaptive expectations is the theory that price expectations formed today are determined by the recent past behavior of prices.

The *adaptive expectations theory* plays a central role in the Monetarist explanation of inflation. It proposes that future price expectations are formed over time on the basis of past price experience, with the most recent price experience having the greatest influence.

An *administrative lag* is the time between the recognition of an economic problem by Congress or by the Federal Reserve and the institution of attempted policy correctives.

Aggregate production function is a relationship between maximum physical output and a set of inputs, given the existing technology.

Aggregate demand includes everyone's—consumers, businesses, government, and importers—willingness and ability to spend on all goods and services at alternative price *levels*. The aggregate demand curve is inversely related to the price level.

Aggregate supply is the willingness and ability of all producers of the millions of goods and services produced in the economy to supply these goods at alternative price levels. Aggregate supply is positively related to the price level.

Aggregates or *aggregate variables* are variables that equal the sum of individual values for a variable. For example, aggregate consumption equals the sum of all consumption by individuals.

An *appreciation of the dollar* occurs when it takes fewer dollars to buy a single unit of a foreign currency. If the exchange rate is in dollars per unit of a foreign currency, then an appreciation occurs when the exchange rate decreases.

Arbitrage possibilities are possibilities for riskless profit by choosing one investment over another. Arbitrage guarantees that the market rates of return on two alternative investments stay very close together.

Average money holdings is money holdings (M_T) divided by 2.

Balance of payments is a statement of the money value of all transactions between a country and the rest of the world during a given period of time.

The *balance sheet equation* shows the sum of all assets equal to the sum of all liabilities and capital accounts.

The *balanced budget multiplier* is a number by which an exogenous change in both government spending and taxes such that the government budget balance does not change, is multiplied to get a change in equilibrium national income. For *lump sum taxes,* the balanced budget multiplier is one.

In *barter,* goods must be exchanged for other goods.

Barter economy is an economy in which there is no money, so that goods are exchanged directly for other goods.

Base year is the year against which comparisons of relative changes are made.

The *budget constraint* is the total real wealth of the wealth holder.

Budget deficits occur when government expenditures are greater than tax revenues.

Budget policies are fiscal policies dealing with the government budget, such as congressional taxation and expenditure policies.

Budget surpluses occur when tax revenues are greater than government expenditures.

Business cycles are recurrent fluctuations in business and employment activity due to changes in aggregate demand or aggregate supply.

The *capital market* is the market where saving or the supply of capital funds adjusts to investment or the demand for capital funds.

A *central bank* is a banker's bank. Commercial banks are regulated by central banks.

Ceteris paribus is economic jargon (borrowed from Latin) meaning "all other variables are held constant."

The *civilian labor force* is those persons who are employed and those who are unemployed among nonmilitary persons.

Classical macroeconomists emphasize the automatic equilibrating features of the economy, stressing that full employment will occur in a competitive system by market adjustments in prices, wages, and interest rates.

The *classical dichotomy* is the belief that in the long run, value theory (the theory of the formation of relative prices) is independent of monetary theory (the theory of how the price *level* is established).

The *consumption function* is the relationship between planned consumption expenditures of households and their current disposable income.

Covered interest arbitrage is the arbitrage that keeps the relative interest rates of two nations related to the difference between the current spot exchange rate and the forward exchange rate.

Covered interest parity is a condition linking the interest rate differential between two nations to the difference between the spot and forward exchange rate.

Credit is a promise of future payment in kind or in money given in exchange for present money, goods, or services.

Cross-sectional data deal with the economic behavior of different groups, at the same point in time.

The *crowding-out effect* is a reduction in consumption and investment spending as a result of higher interest rates brought about by budget deficits that are financed by federal government borrowing in the capital market.

Currency is coins minted by the U.S. Treasury and paper currency, which consists of Federal Reserve notes issued by the Federal Reserve banks.

A *debit* is any transaction that results in a money outflow or payment to a foreign country.

Deflation is a persistent decrease in the general price level.

Demand deficiency unemployment exists when aggregate demand is insufficient to create a full or natural rate of employment at stable prices.

A *demand deposit* is a checking account balance that can be obtained on demand from a deposit institution.

A *demand disturbance* is any aggregate demand shift created by changes in real autonomous factors such as business investment and consumption or by changes in monetary variables such as the money stock.

Demand shocks are surprise changes in the aggregate demand schedule due to changes in the demand for components of demand from the private sector or from fiscal or monetary policy.

Depreciation is the decline in the useful value of a fixed asset, such as a building or capital equipment, due to wear and tear, destruction, or obsolescence resulting from better technology.

A *depreciation of the dollar* occurs when it takes more dollars to buy a single unit of a foreign currency. If the exchange rate is in dollars per unit of a foreign currency, then a depreciation occurs when the exchange rate increases.

The *desired currency-deposit ratio* is a certain percentage of demand deposits that moneyholders want to hold as currency.

The *discount rate* is the interest rate that the Fed charges a deposit institution for a loan.

Discretion in policymaking is the ability to set policy each period without regard for past commitments.

Discretionary policies are policies that require decisions on the part of Congress, the President, or the Federal Reserve System before they can be enacted.

Disembodied technological change does not depend on changes in the inputs of capital or labor.

Disposable personal income is what people have left to spend out of their personal income after they pay their taxes.

A *dominant strategy* is a strategy that yields the highest payoff regardless of the actions of your opponents.

Economic growth is the rate of increase in an economy's full-employment real output or real income over time.

Efficiency wage models are models in which a firm can lower production costs by paying wages in excess of market clearing, competitive levels in order to elicit additional effort from workers. Such models can explain wage rigidity and unemployment.

Embodied technological change depends on changes in the inputs of capital or labor.

Endogenous variables in economic models are variables that are determined within a model. Variables determined within the model are affected by changes in other variables, including exogenous variables. Further, endogenous variables are modeled by stating some behavioral or functional characteristic.

The *equation of exchange* relates the stock of money and the velocity of circulation of money to the price level and the level of real output, and is written as $MV_y \equiv PY$.

The *ex ante* real interest rate is the nominal interest rate minus the expected inflation rate.

Excess reserves are the difference between legal reserves and required reserves.

The *exchange rate* is the number of dollars required to purchase one unit of a foreign currency.

Exchange rate appreciation is an exchange rate established by market forces for a domestic country's money wherein more foreign money is obtained in exchange.

Exchange rate depreciation is an exchange rate established by market forces for a domestic country's money wherein less foreign money is obtained in exchange.

Exogenous variables in economic models are variables that are determined outside a model, but that have an effect on the model and in particular on the endogenous variables. There is no attempt to explain why an exogenous variable takes any particular value, but there is an attempt to explain how the exogenous variables affect the endogenous variables.

Expected net income is the difference between the expected increase in total revenues and the additional operating costs.

The *ex post* real interest rate is the nominal interest rate minus the actual inflation rate.

The *federal funds rate* is the rate charged a commercial bank when it borrows reserve funds from other commercial banks temporarily holding excess reserves.

Fiscalism is a term used to describe a post-Keynesian or neo-Keynesian policy position that features demand management as the primary tool of economic stabilization. Further, the preferred tools for such a demand policy are fiscal rather than monetary.

Fiscal policy is the utilization of government spending and/or taxing policies to affect aggregate economic behavior.

Fisher effect is the concept that shows that the market (nominal) rate of interest is equal to the real rate of interest plus the anticipated rate of change of prices.

Flow variable is a variable that may be described as changing (growing or declining) at some rate per unit of time. The price level growth i.e. the inflation rate is a flow, telling the change in the price level per unit of time.

The *forward exchange rate* is the rate at which you can contract today to trade a given amount of one currency for another at a specified future date.

Frictional unemployment is the lack of work that occurs as workers move from one job to another in search of their best allocation in the labor market.

Full employment is the level of employment at which there may exist some amount of "frictional" or "transitional" unemployment but at which resources are otherwise fully utilized in the production of output.

The *golden rule* is the dictum to choose the capital-labor ratio such that consumption per worker in the steady state is maximized. The golden rule is reached when the saving rate is at a level so that the marginal product of capital at the implied steady-state capital-labor ratio is equal to the depreciation rate plus the rate of growth of the labor force.

Gross domestic product is the total value of all the final goods and services produced by factors located in a nation during a specific period of time, usually a year.

Gross national product is the total value of all the final goods and services produced by factors owned by residents of a nation during a specific period of time, usually a year.

Hoarding is storing money that is neither saved nor spent.

A *household's money holdings* (M_T) is the household's money income (Y) divided by the number of withdrawals (N).

An *identity* is a statement that is true by definition.

Inflation is a persistent increase in the general price level.

An *injection* into the income stream is any autonomous increase in total expenditures that adds potential spending to the income-expenditure stream.

An *instrument of policy* is a variable that the policymaker can control and can vary in order to have an impact on the economy.

An *intermediate monetary target* is a target the policymaker tries to achieve not because of an interest in the intermediate target itself, but because it helps the policymaker achieve a final target.

Intertemporal substitution of labor is the willingness to adjust work schedules over time in response to unusually high or low real wages.

Investment is business spending for capital assets such as plant, equipment, and inventory.

The *IS equation* is the various combinations of the real interest rate r and output Y that are consistent with equilibrium in the goods market.

Keynesian macroeconomists emphasize institutional rigidities such as unions and firms with market power, and the existence of nominal contracting, that prevent or slow the automatic equilibrating forces stressed by the classical economists. Keynesians stress the long adjustment periods required for automatic forces to work, and argue instead in favor of government action to speed the adjustment to equilibrium. Moreover, they argue that there is no guarantee that equilibrium will entail full employment.

Keynesian aggregate supply (or *KAS*) is the positively sloped aggregate supply curve derived when the nominal wage is rigid.

The *labor market equilibrium curve* (*LME*) is the combination of the real interest rate and real output that is consistent with equilibrium in the labor market.

A *large open economy* is an economy that is so large that its real interest rate can vary from the world real interest rate, and in effect the large open economy has an effect on the real interest rate in the rest of the world.

A *leakage* from the income stream is any autonomous decrease in total expenditures that withdraws potential spending from the income-expenditure stream.

Legal reserve requirements are the legally mandated reserve ratios set by the Fed and applied to commercial banks and other financial institutions. Such requirements force these financial institutions to hold a percentage of checking, savings, and other types of deposits as cash reserves.

Legal reserves are reserves that depository institutions are allowed by law to claim as reserves, such as deposits held at a Federal Reserve bank.

Life-cycle hypothesis is the theory that consumption depends on the present value of all future income streams being consumed over the lifetime of the average person.

The *LM equation* is the various combinations of the real interest rate r and output Y that are consistent with equilibrium in the money market.

Long-run aggregate supply (or *LRAS*) is the vertical or perfectly inelastic aggregate supply curve that corresponds to the Classical model, where prices and wages are flexible, perfect competition holds in both output and labor markets, and the economy is in equilibrium in all markets.

A *long-run Phillips curve* is a vertical line showing that, after short-run adjustments in expectations have taken place, the aggregate supply curve in the economy is a vertical line at the natural rate of employment (or unemployment).

Lump sum taxes are taxes levied on households that are unrelated to endogenous variables, most specifically income.

M1 is a definition of money widely used by the Federal Reserve. It is the sum of the following: currency, including coins and paper money outside banks; demand deposits (checking accounts) at commercial banks; NOW accounts (interest-earning accounts upon which owners may write a check); travelers checks and ATS accounts (automatic transfer savings accounts, which are automatically transferred to an individual's checking account when the checking account falls to a minimum level).

Macroeconomic policy includes a broad spectrum of related tools—both monetary and fiscal—to promote the macroeconomic goals of price stability, full employment, and high sustained economic growth.

Macroeconomic theory studies the causes of and interrelationships among aggregate economic phenomena (phenomena concerning the economy as a whole) such as inflation, the growth rate of income, and the rate of unemployment.

The *marginal product of labor* is a ratio expressing the change in total product ($\triangle Y$) to an incremental change in the utilization of the labor input ($\triangle N$), all other inputs being held constant in quantity. In other words, it is the addition to total production attributable to the addition of one unit of labor to the production process, the stock of capital remaining unchanged.

The *marginal propensity to consume* (or *MPC*) is the change in planned consumption expenditures divided by the change in disposable income.

The *marginal propensity to save* (or *MPS*) is the change in planned saving divided by the change in disposable income.

The *medium of exchange* is an item that is accepted in exchange for other goods.

Microeconomics investigates how individuals in society (as opposed to the economy as a whole) choose to allocate scarce income or resources among competing wants or production objectives.

A *mixed strategy* is a strategy that involves a random device used to choose an action. For example, in a mixed strategy a player may choose an action based on the outcome of a coin toss, or of a roll of the dice.

The *monetarist policy position* on economic stabilization emphasizes aggregate demand control through monetary stability. Monetarists support rules of monetary growth rather than discretionary policy due to the unpredictability of lags and effects.

Monetarists are macroeconomists who dispute some of the Keynesian positions, especially the extreme claims of the ineffectiveness of monetary policy. Monetarists tend to support Classical positions, but do agree that the economy can be disrupted from equilibrium for long periods of time, especially by inappropriate policy actions. They tend to favor policy rules instead of discretionary policies.

Monetary base is currency in the hands of the public plus reserves of deposit institutions held either at Federal Reserve banks or as vault cash in deposit institutions.

Monetary policy is conducted by the Federal Reserve and consists of the manipulation of bank reserves through alterations in the discount rate, open market sales and purchases of securities, and changes in reserve requirements. Financial system reserve changes affect the money stock and interest rates, which can change private consumption and investment expenditures (aggregate demand) and thus employment, output, and prices.

Money is anything that performs the functions of money: medium of exchange, store of value, unit of account, and standard of deferred payment.

Money wage is the money value (or face value) of what workers are paid for the use of their labor.

The *multiplier* is a number by which a change in an exogenous variable is multiplied to get a change in equilibrium national income.

A *Nash equilibrium* is a set of strategies for the players of a game such that, given the strategies of the other player, no player can improve his payoff by changing his strategy.

National income is the total income earned by factors in an economy as they produce goods and services.

The *natural rate of unemployment* is that rate of unemployment that occurs with equilibrium in the labor market. The labor market equilibrium accounts for frictional factors in the economy as well as institutions surrounding labor demand and supply decisions. It consists of both frictional and structural unemployment.

Net free reserves are the difference between excess reserves and the borrowing at the Fed.

Net national product is the value of all production that occurs in an economy in excess of the products needed to replace the capital used up during the production period.

The *New Classical Economics (NCE)* is a modern approach that has developed from the Classical and Monetarist traditions. The NCE views the macroeconomy as self-adjusting, which guarantees full employment in the long run. In the short run, output and employment may differ from full-employment levels due to misperceptions of the price level. Two distinguishing features of the NCE are the reliance on the assumption that expectations are formed rationally, and the reliance on a natural rate approach to modeling aggregate supply.

New Keynesian economists incorporate some of the strategies of the New Classical ideas, especially rational expectations, into the traditional Keynesian view that institutional and nominal rigidities slow or negate the automatic equilibrating forces that the Classical economists rely upon.

A *noncooperative game* is a game in which the players are not allowed to work together to reach an equilibrium, and, in fact, are not allowed to make binding agreements as to the actions that each will take.

Nominal income (or *money income*) is simply the actual dollar amount of one's income.

Nonborrowed reserves are reserves supplied by the Fed to deposit institutions through open-market operations.

A *nonproportional consumption function* does not have the level of consumption rising in the same proportion as the level of income.

A *one-shot game* is a game that is only played once. Play will not be repeated between the players.

Open-market operations are the selling and buying of government securities by the Fed on the private bond market.

An *outside lag* in either fiscal or monetary policy is the time between the implementation of policy correctives and the actual effects of the policy.

Pegging is the practice by the Federal Reserve Board of targeting interest rates (or the federal funds rate) at some specific level.

The *permanent income hypothesis* is income a household anticipates or expects to receive over a number of years in the future, possibly a lifetime.

Personal income is the total amount of income people in an economy earn or are given from all sources, including earnings and transfers.

Personal saving is the difference between a person's income and his or her consumption expenditures.

Policy neutrality is the hypothesis which states that changes in the money supply will have no effect on real output and employment. Instead, changes in the money supply will only change nominal variables such as the price level or the nominal wage rate.

A *policy rule* is a rule by which the policymaker sets policy variables. Policy rules constrain the behavior of policymakers, so that they cannot act with complete discretion.

Policy variables are those used in demand or supply management such as fiscal, monetary, or tax policies designed to affect work and input decisions.

A *political business cycle* or *PBC* implies that actual business cycles of inflation or deflation and swings in the unemployment rate may be related to the attempts of politicians to get reelected at periodic intervals.

Present value is a way to compare the value today of income or other monetary values that are received at different future dates. The present value of a future payment is that payment divided by the term (one plus the interest rate), raised to the power of the number of years until the payment is received. For example, in 1994 the present value of a promised $100,000 to be paid in the year 2000 is $\$100,000/(1+r_{1994,2000})^6$, where $r_{1994,2000}$ is the annual interest rate between 1994 and the year 2000 and 6 is the number of years until the payment is received.

A *production function* is the technical relationship between labor resource input and aggregate output, assuming that technology, other resources, and institutions are held constant.

A *proportional consumption function* has the level of consumption rising in the same proportion as the level of income.

Public choice is a subfield of general economic theory which studies the results of imputing economic (i.e., self-interested) behavior to politicians.

A *pure strategy* is a strategy that does not involve a random choice of actions, such as flipping a coin to decide who goes first.

Quantity theory of money is a theory that hypothesizes that a change in the money stock causes a proportional change in the price level because velocity and physical output are unaffected by the quantity of money.

Rational expectations is a theory that people, on average and through time, will form price expectations consistent with the predictions of the relevant economic theory.

The *rational expectations policy-neutral position* emphasizes the ability of market participants to adjust to policy change. Over time and in the extreme, individual behavior is perfectly adjusted so that macroeconomic policies are perfectly circumvented.

The *Real Business Cycle model* is a model that emphasizes intertemporal substitution of labor supply and nonmonetary explanations for business cycles within a market-clearing model of the economy.

The *real exchange rate* is the exchange rate multiplied by the ratio of the foreign price level to the domestic price level. It tells us how much a unit of foreign currency can buy in the United States relative to how much a unit of foreign currency can buy in its own economy.

Real income is the actual amount of goods and services that you may purchase with your money income.

The *real rate of interest* is equal to the market rate of interest minus the expected rate of inflation. It is also a rate that reflects the true incentive of households to save and businesses to invest.

Real wage is the amount of goods and services that workers can obtain with money wages.

Residential investment is the construction of single and multifamily housing.

The *required reserve ratio* is the amount of money that a deposit institution must keep available as specified by the Fed in the form of a percentage of a deposit institution's deposits.

Required reserves are the minimum amount of legal reserves (cash) plus deposits at the Fed that a deposit institution is required to hold by the Fed to back its deposits.

Risk averse people are those who receive diminishing marginal utility of wealth and increasing marginal disutility of risk with each additional bond that they hold in their portfolio.

Say's Law is an assumption of Classical economists that the act of supplying goods creates a corresponding demand for those goods.

A *small open economy* is an economy that is so small it cannot affect the world real interest rate, but instead takes that rate as given.

The *spot exchange rate* is the rate at which you can contract today to trade a given amount of one currency for another today.

A *standard of deferred payment* is an item that serves as a measure of value over time.

The *steady state* occurs when the economy reaches a capital-labor ratio that is stable, given the depreciation rate, the state of technology, the rate of growth of the labor force, and the saving rate. In the steady state, the flow of new capital from investment just equals the draw on capital due to depreciation and the need to supply new workers with capital.

Stock variable is the level of a variable at some point in time. The price level is a stock, giving a measure of the level of prices at a point in time.

A *store of wealth* is a good or other item (such as a financial asset) that individuals hold in order to maintain a claim over present and future goods and services.

A *strategy* in a game is any action that is feasible, given the information available to a player of the game at the time a decision is to be made.

Structural unemployment is the lack of work that occurs because of changes in the basic character of the labor market that leaves some workers with seemingly unsalable skills.

A *supply disturbance* is an aggregate supply shift caused by changes in any factor affecting the demand or supply of any productive input such as labor.

Supply shocks are surprise changes in aggregate supply that result from changes in technology, resource availability, natural disasters, and other factors influencing aggregate supply.

Supply-side economics is a term used to describe policies, such as lowering income tax rates or deregulation of markets, which will have the effect of shifting the aggregate supply curve rightward and increasing the natural rate of employment.

A *target* for policy is a goal of policy, usually a specific value for an economic variable that the policymaker is trying to achieve.

Time preference is the preference of individuals or households for consuming present goods rather than future goods. It indicates that individuals prefer current satisfaction to future satisfaction, everything else being constant.

Time-series data are concerned with economic behavior over a span of time.

The *Tobin q theory* states that investment spending varies directly with the ratio of the market value of business capital assets to the replacement value of those assets.

The *total labor force* is those persons who are employed and those who are unemployed among nonmilitary persons, plus those persons employed by the military.

Transfer payments are nominal payments made by governments and businesses to people for whom no goods or services are concurrently rendered.

The *unemployment rate* is the percentage of the total labor force that is unemployed.

A *unit of account* is an item that serves as a measuring rod for the values of all economic goods. Prices are usually stated in terms of the unit of account.

The *user* or *rental cost of capital* is the implicit rental value assigned to all of the costs of using more capital.

The *value-added approach* is the dollar value of a firm's sales minus the value of intermediate goods purchased for use in production.

INDEX

PHOTO CREDITS